The Best of

PARIS

REVISED EDITION

Publisher and Editor-in-Chief
Christian Millau

Editor
Colleen Dunn Bates

Contributing Editors/Translators
Alice Brinton, Timothy Carlson,
François Dupuigrenet Desroussilles, David Downie,
Sheila Mooney, Jennifer Rylaarsdam, Margery L. Schwartz

Coordination
Sophie Gayot

Prentice Hall Travel Editor
Amit Shah

Operations
Alain Gayot

Directed by
André Gayot
◆

Editorial Staff, French-language edition

Editor
Loly Clerc

Assistant Editors
Danielle Girard, Agnès Marillier, Marie Louison

Contributing Editors
Jean-Marie Baron, Pierre Crisol, Alyette de Crozet,Christine Drouard,
Martine Fourreau, Les Gourmands Associés, Catherine Guérif, Barbara Guignebert,
Annette Knapen, Pierre Léonforte, Philippe Manez, Anne-Marie Olry,
Patrick Saletta, Véronique Sothias, Jean-Luc Toula-Breysse,
Isabelle Valentin, Dominique Vayr

PRENTICE HALL
New York ■ London ■ Toronto ■ Sydney ■ Tokyo ■ Singapore

FLIP

*Other Gault Millau Guides Available
from Prentice Hall Trade Division*

The Best of Chicago
The Best of France
The Best of Hong Kong
The Best of Italy
The Best of London
The Best of Los Angeles
The Best of New England
The Best of New York
The Best of San Francisco
The Best of Washington, D.C.

Copyright © 1990
by Gault Millau, Inc.

Published by Prentice Hall Trade Division
A Division of Simon & Schuster Inc.
15 Columbus Circle
New York, New York 10023

Please address all comments regarding *The Best of Paris* to:
Gault Millau, Inc.
P.O. Box 361144
Los Angeles, CA 90036

Library of Congress Cataloging-in-Publication Data
The Best of Paris. Rev. ed. of: The Best of Paris / Gault Millau;
translation of: Le guide de Paris. Rev. ed. /
written by Christian Millau. c1986.
1. Paris (France)—Description—1975—Guide-books. I. Bates,
Colleen Dunn. II. Gault, Henri, 1929– . Guide de Paris. III. Title: Paris.
DC708.B47 1990   914.404'839   89-23240
ISBN 0-13-073123-4

Special thanks to the staff of Prentice Hall Travel for their invaluable aid
in producing these Gault Millau guides.

Printed in the United States of America

CONTENTS

Gault Millau's penchant for observing everything that's good (and bad) about food and the dining experience is what made these guides so popular in the first place. Here you'll find candid, penetrating and often amusing reviews of the very, very best, the undiscovered and the undeserving. Listed by arrondissements of the city, including a section on the suburbs. Includes the Toque Tally and an index of restaurants by cuisine.

A hotel guide to suit every taste. Where to spend a few days treated as royalty. Where to get the most for your money. Where to find the finest service, the most charm, the best location.

Paris's palate may be found in its restaurants, but its heart and soul are found in its many cafés, wine bars, pubs and rendezvous spots. Where to hang out with a coffee and a copy of *Figaro*, where to meet for a kir, where to refresh yourself with a snack or a glass of wine.

A tour of some of the city's most amusing and exciting nightspots, with discerning commentary on what goes on in Paris after dark. Where to go and where to avoid.

PARIS

A CITY ABOIL

City of Light, Stupefying Spectacle or Moveable Feast—call it what you will, *Gai Paris* is as alive in the collective fantasies of the Western world as its streets are crawling with humanity of every imaginable origin, shape, shade, size and social station. From the crêpe-stand-studded rue Saint-André-des-Arts, which snakes through the Latin Quarter, to the silk-wrapped glamour and classic chic of avenue Montaigne, to the Marché d'Aligre, which looks like it was lifted from downtown Algiers, Paris is one of those throbbing capitals that churns out legends—and spawns myths—like they were going out of style. As we dash to press, Paris is aboil: clubs, restaurants and even museums are popping up as fast as others are closing down. More than 11 million inhabitants (2.2 million within the old city walls) are this minute streaking along underground freeways, winging into busy airports and commuting to ultra-modern, futuristic satellite business centers, making Paris shine among the world's most up-to-date cities. Yet nothing *seems* to have changed in decades, perhaps centuries: The familiar face of central Paris changes slowly indeed, almost imperceptibly. The bustling *grands boulevards* are still lined with giant sycamores that spread over crowded cafés. *Bouquinistes* go on hawking their books along the Seine's noisy *quais*. The open-air markets and specialty food shops in practically every *quartier* disgorge their wares on teeming sidewalks. And gardens lifted from Impressionist paintings, like the Luxembourg or Parc Monceau, continue to fill daily with armies of au pairs pushing babies in luxurious carriages down carefully raked gravel lanes. No wonder droves of urban trekkers, travel enthusiasts and pilgrims to the mecca of existentialism spend their days seeking the Paris of yore. Well, Paris is the quintessential Old World city, trussed up by an often boggling—and sometimes debilitating—cultural tradition and groaning under the weight of artistic wonders that are the envy of much of the civilized world. And it is old, old, old.

Since Day One, about 5,000 years ago, Parisian life has flowed along the Seine. Paris's twenty arrondissements spiral outward clockwise from the Ile de la Cité, its geographical and historical hub. The Cité, where Notre-Dame rears its Gothic bell towers, was the fortified capital of the Parisii, a Gallic tribe that Julius Caesar trounced circa 52 B.C. Then came the Gallo-Roman period, which lasted several centuries. Although this period left practically no monuments (except the baths at Cluny and the Arena), the city was laid out once and for all. Fast forward: Clovis makes Paris the capital of the empire in 508. Fast forward again: Hugues Capet, the founding father of the Capetian dynasty, makes Paris (i.e., the Ile de la Cité) his capital. And here we are, 1,000 years later, and the Cité is still an island, detached in every sense from the life of the Left and Right Banks and from the nearby Ile Saint-Louis, famous nowadays as much for its ice cream as its seventeenth-century architecture. Only place Dauphine, with its lovely triangular garden, antiques shops and brasseries, affords a backward glance of old Paris.

Way back in 1208, the cathedral schools of Paris were united into a single university on the Left Bank. As you might expect, students flooded into the neighborhood. And they have remained there ever since. From Jussieu in the fifth arrondissement to Saint-Germain-de-Prés in the sixth—commonly though inaccurately known as the *Quartier Latin*—the narrow, twisting streets are thronged by a decidedly young, casual crowd. So the concentration of late-night cafés, clubs, art galleries and bistros comes as no surprise. To many, the Latin Quarter is synonymous with The Real Paris: Saint-Michel, Saint-Germain, Odéon.

The Latin Quarter's sometimes snooty neighbor—still part of the Left Bank but altogether a different world—is the fashionable seventh arrondissement. The key words here are: Eiffel Tower, Invalides, Ecole Militaire and Palais Bourbon, plus at least a dozen ministries (don't get flustered when cabinet ministers and visiting dignitaries descend with their bullet-proof retinues). Some of Paris's finest restaurants, shops and hotels line the seventh's wide, handsome avenues.

At about the time the Latin Quarter was sprouting around the *civitas philosophorum*, the less-than-humble *Ville* on the Right Bank was lifting its patrician nose. Starting in the Middle Ages, merchants and the middle class settled into the *bourgs* around the villas and palaces of the nobility. Over time, the Louvre, the Tuileries, the Palais-Royal, place Louis-XV (now place de la Concorde), place Vendôme and place des Victoires became the landmarks that set the tone of the Right Bank. In the eighteenth and nineteenth centuries the well-bred and better-heeled built their major theaters there: the Opéra-Comique and Comédie-Française, the Palais Garnier Opéra and many others. They were soon flanked by the Grand Palais and Petit Palais. Napoléon's Arc de Triomphe crowns this upscale ensemble. Now, as then, the Champs-Elysées and surrounding grand avenues and boulevards of the first, eighth and sixteenth arrondisse-ments are the best place to take a mink for a stroll or shop for diamonds before dining at the legendary Maxim's or Lucas-Carton, to name two of the most famous. But tennis shoes are equally at home: The Champs-Elysées—on every tourist itinerary—has also become the haunt of the *Banlieusards*. These youngsters from the outskirts take the RER express subway to Etoile and spend hours at the Virgin mega–music store, or at the dozens of franchise *restos* and multiscreen movie theaters strung along the drag.

But many a Right Bank devotee will steer you off the thoroughfares and into the maze of nineteenth-century *passages*—passage des Panoramas or Galerie Vivienne, for example—scattered around the second, ninth and tenth arrondissements. Chockablock with boutiques, restaurants, food and wine shops and even hotels, these covered emporium-passageways are animated year-round, not just during a rainstorm. The soulful, industrious *faubourgs*—former working-class neighborhoods lying beyond the seventeenth-century city gates, now central Paris—whose higgledy-piggledy buildings snake out from the grand boulevards, are all too often overlooked. Likewise the garment district in the second and third arrondissements. A cross between Bangkok and lower Manhattan, it is a colorful hive of incessant activity and a great place to buy ready-to-wear and casual clothing direct from the factory.

The nearby Marais district, from Centre Pompidou to Musée Picasso and east to place de la Bastille, used to be up and coming. Now it's up, up and away, a Parisian showcase of gentrification with a sky-high boutique-per-block ratio. Such venerable giants as Brasserie Bofinger—the oldest and one of the handsomest in town—stand firm in the ebb and flow of new (and often excellent) restaurants and tea houses. The Musée Carnavalet and Hôtel de Sully have been scrubbed and buttressed. The harmonious place des Vosges (1605) has been trimmed and returfed, its newly plumbed fountains splashing to the great delight of locals and tourists alike. The Marais is also home to France's distinguished and ancient Jewish population. Take a walk down rue des Rosiers and discover any number of delicatessens and kosher food emporiums.

On the other side of place de la Bastille, big bucks and revolutionary zeal—*Vive le Bicentennaire!*—have worked their magic on the neighborhood. The new Théâtre de la Bastille opera house is the turbo-charged motor that is transforming Faubourg Saint-Antoine, rue de la Roquette, rue de Lappe and rue de Charonne into the latest haven for hipsters, artists and restaurateurs with a flair for the profitably offbeat. Expect big changes in this neighborhood when the opera really starts to hum (its first regular season starts in early 1990).

Above all, Paris is a city for walking, and this may be your best way to see Montmartre, although a funicular will carry those with sore feet to the top. In any case, do not linger in the lower depths of Pigalle. The old Moulin Rouge and its can-can dancers' risqué naughtiness have disappeared beneath the sleaze of porno paraphernalia. But just a little farther up the hill, the steep steps and winding byways of Montmartre keep a village atmosphere alive in this most sophisticated of cities. Don't despise the droves of sightseers and would-be Picassos packed onto place du Tertre, a traditional stronghold of artists. Instead, duck into that wedding cake of a church, Sacre Coeur, and most of all admire the stupendous view of Paris laid out at your feet.

For those in search of the ethnic and the offbeat, Paris's thirteenth arrondissement is the equivalent of New York's Chinatown (though lacking entirely in the picturesque). If you can pick your way through the forest of high-rise housing and sprawling supermarkets, you'll find a profusion of culinary treats from Asia.

Guidebooks justly like to refer to unassailable authorities when serving up Paris in introductions like this. We think that's swell, except for one small problem: What does *unassailable* mean? Ernest Hemingway, child of the tipsy twenties and a dubious authority on Paris-beyond-La-Coupole, correctly called this sprawling metropolis "a moveable feast." Food—both spiritual and material—is indeed paramount here, from snails and scallops served with a cool Sancerre white to duck breast in a green-pepper-corn sauce washed down with a brawny Bordeaux. While she doubtless enjoyed the feast, writer Katherine Anne Porter called Hemingway's Paris "shallow, trivial and silly." George Orwell was down and out in Paris, dreaming of a rare *steack frites*, while Henry

Miller was discovering the tropics in brasseries around the ever-dicey place Clichy. A gourmand at heart, Lawrence Durrell loves Paris because here he feels "on a par with a good cheese or a bad one." That's understandable, given the hundreds of varieties of cow, goat and sheep curd available here, and the millennial traditions attached to them.

Since selection is the rod by which guidebooks are measured, we will spare you the wisdom of Henry James, F. Scott Fitzgerald, Victor Hugo and company, ad infinitum. In short, you can find anything here: the great, the mediocre, the mundane, the sublime and the overrated. We hope the pages that follow will inspire you to seek—and help you to find—the best Paris has to offer.

A DISCLAIMER

Readers are advised that prices and conditions change over the course of time. The restaurants, hotels, shops and other establishments reviewed in this book have been reviewed over a period of time, and the reviews reflect the personal experiences of the reviewers. The reviewers and publishers cannot be held responsible for the experiences of the reader related to the establishments reviewed. Readers are invited to write the publisher with ideas, comments and suggestions for future editions.

RESTAURANTS

INTRODUCTION

A MANY-SPLENDORED EXPERIENCE

The lure of Paris's restaurants is powerful indeed. We've heard of an American lady who on impulse purchased a transatlantic plane ticket, so compelling was her craving for Robuchon's homard aux artichauts. And it is not rare for people who have never even set foot in the French capital to know the names of all the fashionable chefs and their specialties. Dining out in Paris is a many-splendored experience. Elegance reigns here to a degree not often attained in the restaurants of other cities; Le Grand Véfour, Maxim's and Lucas-Carton, for instance, are classified historical landmarks, with interiors of unparalleled beauty. These and the city's other most celebrated establishments also offer distinguished service: From the maîtres d'hôtel and the sommeliers to the lowest busboys, the staffs are stylish and professional, a real *corps d'élite*. And the food, on a night when a chef like Alain Senderens is particularly inspired, can be memorable, even thrilling, a joy to the eye and a feast for the palate.

If your tastes or your finances lead you to prefer less exalted places to dine, look through our reviews for Paris's many marvelous bistros, brasseries and home-style restaurants, where prices are (usually) substantially lower than in the *grands restaurants* and where the atmosphere is more relaxed and informal, even if the place is rather elegant. Parisians have a fondness for their neighborhood bistros, where they can be sure of finding familiar, traditional dishes, often with a regional accent (southwestern, Alsatian, Provençal), so if you go in for local color, those are the places to try. Brasseries are perfect for when you want to eat just a single course instead of a full French-style meal (but don't try ordering just a salad at Lipp!), or to have a bite at an odd hour. They tend to stay open quite late and usually do not accept reservations.

RESTAURANT SAVVY

• At Paris's best-known restaurants, you must reserve a table far in advance—at least three weeks, sometimes two or three months for such places as Robuchon and Taillevent. Reservation requests from abroad are taken much more seriously if they are accompanied by a deposit of, say, 300 francs (about $50). Tables at less celebrated spots can be reserved one or two days ahead, or even on the morning of the day you wish to dine. If you cannot honor your reservation, don't forget to call the restaurant and cancel.

• Men should wear a jacket and tie in any Parisian restaurant of some standing. Women are well advised to dress up, wearing pantsuits only if they are the highest in fashion. Luxury restaurants do not take the question of dress lightly, so be forewarned. At the more modest restaurants, of course, more casual wear is perfectly acceptable.

•When you go to a top restaurant, let the headwaiter suggest some possibilities from the menu (you'll find that they quite often speak English, though they always appreciate an attempt on the diner's part to speak French). Likewise, the sommelier's job is to give diners expert advice on the choosing of a good wine—regardless of price. Don't be afraid to seek his opinion, and to tell him your budget.

•Dinner service starts around 8 p.m. in most Paris restaurants. People start appearing in the finer restaurants about 9 p.m. Luncheon is served between 12:30 p.m. and 2 p.m. In addition to the standard *carte*, or à la carte menu, you will frequently be offered a choice of all-inclusive fixed-price meals called *menus*, which are generally a very good value. Also common is the many-course sampling menu, or *menu dégustation*, a good (though not always economical) way to get an overview of a restaurant's specialties. Daily specials, or *plats du jour*, are usually reliable, inexpensive and prepared with fresh ingredients (whatever the chef found at the market that morning).

•French law mandates that the service charge, usually 15 percent, always be included in the menu prices. You are not obliged to leave an additional tip, but it is good form to leave a little more if the service was particularly good.

•The opening and closing times we've quoted are always subject to change, particularly holiday closings, so be sure to call ahead.

•Many chefs have the bad habit of changing restaurants frequently, which means a restaurant can turn mediocre or even bad in just a few days. Chef-owned restaurants tend to be more stable, but even they can decline: A successful owner may be tempted to accept too many diners, which can result in a drop in quality. Should this be your experience, please don't hold us responsible!

ABOUT THE REVIEWS

RANKINGS & TOQUES

Gault Millau ranks restaurants in the same manner than French students are graded: on a scale of zero to twenty, twenty being unattainable perfection. The rankings reflect *only* the quality of the cooking; decor, service, reception and atmosphere do not influence the rating. They are explicitly commented on within the reviews. Restaurants ranked thirteen and above are distinguished with toques (chef's hats), according to the table on the following page:

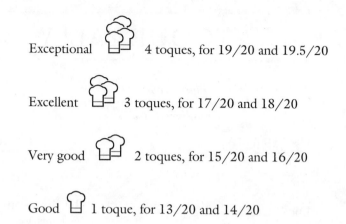

Exceptional   4 toques, for 19/20 and 19.5/20

Excellent   3 toques, for 17/20 and 18/20

Very good   2 toques, for 15/20 and 16/20

Good   1 toque, for 13/20 and 14/20

Toques in red denote restaurants serving modern cuisine; toques in black denote restaurants serving traditional food.

Keep in mind that these ranks are *relative*. One toque for 13/20 is not a very good ranking for a highly reputed (and very expensive) temple of fine dining, but it is quite complimentary for a small place without much pretension.

PRICES

At the end of each restaurant review, prices are given—either à la carte or menus (fixed-price meals) or both. A la carte prices are those of an average meal (an appetizer, main course, dessert and coffee) for one person, including service and a half bottle of a relatively modest wine. Lovers of the great Bordeaux, Burgundies and Champagnes will, of course, face stiffer tabs. The menu prices quoted are for a complete multicourse meal for one person, including service but excluding wine, unless otherwise noted. These fixed-price menus often give diners on a budget a chance to sample the cuisine of an otherwise expensive restaurant.

Prices in red denote restaurants that offer a particularly good value.

SYMBOLS &ABBREVIATIONS

☼ "Les Lauriers du Terroir": an award given to chefs who prepare noteworthy traditional or regional recipes.

M. (or MM. or Mme. or Mlle.): proprietor's, proprietors' or manager's name

Air cond.: Air conditioning

Credit Cards

V: VISA, or Carte Bleue

AE: American Express

DC: Diners Club

MC: MasterCard, or Eurocard

TOQUE TALLY

Red toques: nouvelle or modern cuisine
Black toques: classic cuisine
The numbers following each restaurant refer to its
arrondissement or suburban town.

19.5/20

Lucas-Carton (8th)
Robuchon (16th)

19/20

Taillevent (8th)
Vivarois (16th)
Michel Rostang (17th)
Guy Savoy (17th)

18/20

Carré des Feuillants (1st)
L'Ambroisie (4th)
Jacques Cagna (6th)
Arpège (7th)
La Divellec (7th)
Le Duc (14th)
Faugeron (16th)
La Vieille Fontaine
(Maisons-Laffitte)
Les Trois Marches (Versailles)

La Tour d'Argent (5th)

17/20

Le Bourdonnais (7th)
Jules Verne (7th)
La Marée (8th)
La Maison Blanche (15th)
Olympe (15th)
Patrick Lenôtre (16th)
La Pré Catelan (16th)
Apicius (17th)
Clos Longchamp (17th)
Le Manoir de Paris (17th)
A. Beauvilliers (18th)

Drouant (2nd)
Laurent (8th)

16/20

Gérard Besson (1st)
Miravile (Gilles Epié) (5th)
Bellecour (7th)
Le Dauphin (7th)
Duquesnoy (7th)
Les Ambassadeurs (8th)
Chiberta (8th)
Elysée-Lenôtre (8th)
Au Petit Montmorency (8th)
Alain Rayé (8th)
La Table d'Anvers (9th)

Au Pressoir (12th)
Au Trou Gascon (12th)
Les Célébrités (15th)
Morot-Gaudry (15th)
Le Relais de Sèvres (15th)
Jean-Claude Ferrero (16th)
Michel Pasquet (16th)
Le Toit de Passy (16th)
La Barrière de Clichy (17th)
Maître Corbeau (17th)
La Belle Epoque (Châteaufort)
Duc d'Enghien (Enghien)
Le Tastevin (Maisons-Laffitte)
Jacqueline Fénix (Neuilly-sur-Seine)
A la Grâce de Dieu (Le Vesinet)

Ledoyen (8th)
La Gourmandise (12th)
Pavillon Montsouris (14th)
La Petite Bretonnière (15th)
Conti (16th)
La Braisière (17th)
Guyvonne (17th)
La Toque (17th)
Les Fusains (18th)
Au Pavillon Puebla (19th)
Les Magnolias (Le Perreux)
Le Jardin des Lavandières (Pontoise)
Chez Henri (Romainville)

Espadon (1st)
Pierre Traiteur (1st)
Ambassade d'Auvergne (3rd)
Benoit (4th)
La Bûcherie (5th)
Dodin-Bouffant (5th)
Au Pactole (5th)
Princesse (6th)
Relais Louis XIII (6th)
Le Récamier (7th)
Le Bristol (8th)
Lamazère (8th)
Maxim's (8th)
Chez Michel (10th)
Chez Philippe (11th)
A Sousceyrac (11th)
Lous Landés (14th)
Bistro 121 (15th)
Pierre Vedel (15th)
Chez Augusta (17th)
Michel Comby (17th)
Alain Morel (17th)
Paul et France (17th)
Pétrus (17th)
Au Cochon d'Or (19th)
Relais des Gardes (Meudon)
Jenny Jacquet (Neuilly-sur-Seine)
Gasnier (Puteaux)

Goumard (1st)
Le Grand Véfour (1st)
Lasserre (8th)
La Marée (8th)
La Cagouille (14th)
La Grande Cascade (16th)
Le Petit Bedon (16th)
Le Petit Colombier (17th)
Sormani (17th)
Au Comte de Gascogne
(Boulogne-Billancourt)

15/20

Le Céladon (2nd)
La Corbeille (2nd)
Au Franc Pinot (4th)
Au Quai des Ormes (4th)
Le Chat Grippé (6th)
Paris (6th)
Bistrot de Paris (7th)
La Ferme Saint-Simon (7th)
La Couronne (8th)

THE WORLD'S CUISINES

FRENCH - BOURGEOIS

At the restaurants listed below, you can enjoy such satisfying bourgeois dishes as pot-au-feu, boeuf mode, tête de veau, blanquettes, tripe, lamb sauté and pigs' trotters. See also French - Regional.

Allard (6th)
L'Ami Louis (3rd)
Astier (11th)
Babkine (7th)
Benoit (4th)
Le Bistrot d'à Côté (17th)
Le Bistrot de la Gaîté (14th)
Le Boeuf Bourguignon (9th)
Le Chardenoux (11th)
Aux Charpentiers (6th)
Chez Georges (17th)
Chez Marcel (12th)
Chez Pauline (1st)
Chez René (5th)
La Gauloise (15th)
Au Gourmet de l'Isle (4th)
La Grille (10th)
Joséphine (6th)
Lescure (1st)
Le Manoir Normand (8th)
Le Maquis (18th)
Le Petit Marguery (13th)
Le Petit-Saint-Benoît (6th)
Le Relais 44 (8th)
La Route du Beaujolais (15th)
Le Val d'Or (8th)

FRENCH - BRASSERIES

L'Alsace (8th)
Le Boeuf sur le Toit (8th)
Bofinger (4th)
Brasserie Flo (10th)
Brasserie Löwenbräu (8th)
Brasserie Lutétia (6th)
Brasserie de l'Ile-Saint-Louis (4th)
Brasserie Stella (16th)
Fortune des Mers (13th)
Le Grand Café Capucines (9th)
Julien (10th)
Lipp (6th)
Le Muniche (6th)
Olympe (15th)
Le Pavillon Baltard (1st)
Taverne Kronenbourg (9th)
Terminus Nord (10th)

FRENCH - REGIONAL

• Auvergne: potée au chou, tripoux, chou farci, barbe de sapeur, jambonneau aux lentilles.
• Bordelais and the Southwest: foie gras, confits, cèpes, cassoulet, truffles
• Bourgogne and Lyonnais: navarin, andouillette, escargot, "saladiers," tablier de sapeur
• Jura: escargot, coq au vin jaune
• Provence: aïoli, bouillabaisse, bourride, pieds and paquets

ALSACE - LORRAINE

See also French - Brasseries
L'Alsace (8th)
Chez Jenny (3rd)
La Providence (1st)
Taverne Kronenbourg (9th)

AUVERGNE/CENTRAL FRANCE

Ambassade d'Auvergne (3rd)
L'Artois (8th)
Auberge des Deux Signes (5th)

Le Grenadin (8th)
La Lozère (6th)
Pierre Traiteur (1st)
Savy (8th)

BRITTANY
Les Armes de Bretagne (14th)

BURGUNDY/LYON
Bellecour (7th)
Chez les Anges (7th)
La Foux (6th)
Moissonnier (5th)
Le Petit Mâchon (15th)
Le Récamier (7th)

JURA/FRANCHE-COMTE
Chez Maître Paul (6th)
Saint-Moritz (8th)

NORMANDY
Chez Fernand (11th)
Pharamond (1st)

POITOU/CHARENTE
Taverne des Templiers (3rd)

PROVENCE/CORSICA
Aux Senteurs de Provence (15th)

SOUTHWEST
Auberge de Jarente (4th)
Auberge Landaise (9th)
Carré des Feuillants (1st)
Le Chat Grippé (6th)
Lamazère (8th)
Lous Landés (14th)
Le Petit Zinc (6th)
La Petite Bretonnière (15th)
Le Quercy (9th)
Le Repaire de Cartouche (11th)
A Sourceyrac (11th)
Sud-Ouest (5th)
Thoumieux (7th)

Au Trou Gascon (12th)
La Truffière (5th)
Pierre Vedel (15th)

FRENCH - SEAFOOD

L'Alsace (8th)
Les Armes de Bretagne (14th)
Brasserie Stella (16th)
La Cagouille (14th)
Chez Augusta (17th)
Le Coin du Caviar (4th)
Dessirier (17th)
Le Divellec (7th)
Le Duc (14th)
Fortune des Mers (13th)
Les Glénan (7th)
Goumard (1st)
Le Grand Café Capucines (9th)
La Grille (10th)
Guyvonne (17th)
Aux Iles Marquises (14th)
Lamazère (8th)
Le Louis XIV (10th)
La Marée (8th)
Le Muniche (6th)
Le New Port (10th)
Pétrus (17th)
Au Pied de Cochon (1st)
Le Presbourg (16th)
Villars Palace (5th)

AFRICAN

Paris-Dakar (10th)

AMERICAN/CANADIAN

Le Western (15th)

CENTRAL EUROPEAN

Goldenberg (17th)
Le Paprika (5th)

CHINESE/THAI/ VIETNAMESE

Le Château de Chine (8th)
Chez Vong (8th)
Chez Vong aux Halles (1st)
Chieng-Mai (5th)
Aux Délices de Szechuen (7th)
Erawan (15th)
Au Jardin du Printemps (8th)
Kim-Anh (15th)
Pagoda (9th)
La P'tite Tonkinoise (10th)
Restaurant A (5th)
Thai-Siam (17th)
Tan Dinh (7th)
Tsé Yang (16th)
Vi Foc (16th)
Le Wei-Ya (11th)

GERMAN

Brasserie Löwenbräu (8th)
Au Vieux Berlin (8th)

GREEK/MIDDLE EASTERN

Fakhr el Dine (8th)
Fakhr el Dine (16th)
L'Olivier-Ouzerie (14th)
La Taverne du Nil (2nd)
Ugarit (5th)

INDIAN/INDONESIAN

Indra (8th)

Raajmahal (15th)
Soma (8th)

ITALIAN

Le Carpaccio (8th)
Conti (16th)
La Fontana (8th)
Pizzéria Les Artistes (15th)
Sormani (17th)

JAPANESE/KOREAN

Benkay (15th)
Uri (15th)

NORTH AFRICAN

Charly de Bab-el-Oued (17th)
Martin Alma (8th)
Wally (4th)

RUSSIAN

Le Samovar (1st)

SCANDINAVIAN

Copenhague et Flora Danica (8th)

SPANISH/PORTUGUESE

Saudade (1st)

SWISS

Mövenpick (9th)

FIRST ARRONDISSEMENT

(13) L'Absinthe

24, pl. du Marché-Saint-Honoré
42 60 02 45, 42 61 03 32

M. Malabard. Open until 11:30 p.m. Closed Sat. lunch & Sun. Terrace dining. Pets allowed. Parking. Cards: V, AE, DC.

A new chef and a new manager haven't changed the oh-so-Parisian style of this restaurant, which has been serving discerning diners for the past ten years. M. Malabard, the owner, keeps an attentive eye on his little 1900s-style dining room (a bit labored but highly decorative) and weathers the volatile tastes and times. His patrons—and they are never lacking—are primarily young, lively and appreciative of fine food. The cuisine is contemporary, with a touch of country flavors, and consistently well prepared: roast lotte with paprika, Basque-inspired grilled tuna steak and filet of lamb with eggplant au gratin. The terrace overlooking the Marché-Saint-Honoré is delightful for warm-weather dining.

A la carte: 300F.

(14) Armand au Palais Royal

6, rue de Beaujolais - 42 60 05 11

M. Paillat. Open until 1 a.m. Closed Sat. lunch, Sun. & Dec. 23-27. Air cond. Pets allowed. Cards: V, AE, DC.

One of the few eating places in Paris whose continued success has not triggered a slight contempt for the less-than-affluent customer. And what a godsend, considering its spectacular location facing the arcades of the Palais-Royal. The lighting at night plays stunningly on the ancient stones, the welcome is cordial, and Jean-Pierre Ferron's selectively modern cuisine is just what discriminating theatergoers are clamoring for. The short à la carte menu changes frequently, but you'll always like the crayfish tails in tarragon butter, galantine of rabbit with foie gras, oxtail in red wine and those exquisite warm, thin apple tartelettes. There are some fine wines this side of 100 francs, though they won't help your check much.

A la carte: 350F. Menus: 170F (lunch only), 138F.

(16) Gérard Besson

5, rue Coq-Héron - 42 33 14 74

M. Besson. Open until 10 p.m. Closed Sun., 3 weeks in July & last 2 weeks of Dec. Air cond. Pets allowed. Cards: V, AE.

Gérard Besson is happy in his little Les Halles restaurant, in which the mirrored walls reflect the light-colored furnishings, soft lights, sparkling crystal and white dinnerware. A distinguished chef (a national award winner) and disciple of Garin, Chapel and Jamin, Besson also knows how to make his customers happy—by serving tasty, classic dishes executed with a light, modern touch. Savory home cooking is given a fresh interpretation by a master chef: his "sausage" of foie gras with pistachios, terrine of duck with seasoned vegetables, salmon steak in red-wine aspic with a bell pepper mousse, and his unforgettable scrambled eggs à la Georges Garin with tomatoes, diced truffles, chives and mustard.

Excellent desserts (warm fruit tarts with ice cream, cream puffs with caramel ice cream, tea sorbet) and a sumptuous wine cellar housing some 45,000 bottles will send the check soaring unless you choose from the very reasonable lunch-only menu.

A la carte: 400-600F. Menu: 230F (weekday lunch only).

11/20 Bistro de la Gare

30, rue St-Denis - 42 60 84 92
See Sixth Arrondissement.

(18) Carré des Feuillants 🍴

14, rue de Castiglione - 42 86 82 82

M. Dutournier. Open until 10:30 p.m. Closed Sat. lunch (& Sat. dinner in July & Aug.) & Sun. Air cond. Pets allowed. Cards: V, AE.

After leaving Au Trou Gascon to woo the luxury dining trade and the place Vendôme, chef Alain Dutournier opened this spectacular restaurant on the very site where the Feuillant ("constitutional monarchist") Club fanned the flames of the revolution, and promptly found himself the target of sharp debate. He was accused of rejecting the culinary heritage of his native Gascony and of serving his ambition better than his customers; there were complaints that prices were out of sight. Happily, all that is forgotten now, and the food at Le Carré des Feuillants is better than ever. Dutournier has returned to his roots, and the result is a subtle, sophisticated cuisine based on the best foodstuffs the southwest has to offer.

But first, a word about the decor. It has absolutely nothing in common with the Gascon manor it was originally planned to resemble. Instead, prospective diners walk into what looks like a Roman atrium before turning right into the dining rooms, where Murano chandeliers cast an eerie blue glow on a collection of hyper-realist still lifes hung on golden woodwork. On the whole, the setting is engagingly theatrical and festive, with handsomely laid tables set far enough apart to ensure quiet dining.

Dutournier is a wizard at capturing the authentic flavors of his superb ingredients and delivering them, heightened and enhanced by his deft touch, to your plate. Take, for example, such minor masterpieces as his chestnut bouillon with bits of pheasant breast, his terrine of venison and foie gras with cranberry aspic, or his tender boned partridge enveloped in a cabbage leaf with hazelnuts and foie gras. Noteworthy as well are mackerel filets marinated with yellow, red and green peppers, a mélange of fava beans and asparagus with aged Chalosse ham, delectable morels stuffed with calf's brains, rich and savory eel pâté and his fabulous garbure, a traditional "poor man's" cabbage soup, which he turns into a rich man's dish with the addition of goose confit, country ham and sausages.

Less robust appetites can fall back on succulent roast Pauillac lamb with young garlic, or indescribably flavorful Bazas beef, aged to perfection under Dutournier's supervision. Finish up with an exquisite frozen nougatine topped with a walnut praline, or a sensational berry-strewn feuillantine pastry accompanied by intensely fragrant vanilla ice cream (made to order!), and you will wonder how anyone could maintain that Dutournier has his heart and soul anywhere but in his kitchen, or any interest except his clients' at heart.

The wine cellar under Jean-Guy Loustau's

able stewardship houses an astonishing array of treasures from Bordeaux, the southwest and Burgundy, along with less familiar wines from Chile, Spain and Australia.

A la carte: 400-600F. Menus: 230F (lunch only), 420F, 560F (menu dégustation, wine incl.).

⑬ Le Caveau du Palais
19, pl. Dauphine - 43 26 04 28

M. Dieuleveut. Open until 10:30 p.m. (11 p.m. in summer). Closed Sat. (off-season) & Sun. Air cond. Terrace dining. Pets allowed. Cards: V, AE.

Members of the legal profession—a pretty picky lot—patronize this two-level bistro, whose old stonework and beams are reminiscent of bygone days. The prices are beginning to reflect its charm, and its cuisine is well thought out by head chef Pascal Loué, who wisely limits himself to a simple repertoire of fresh, top-quality products served in generous portions: fisherman's catch (sole, salmon, lotte), a fricassée of kidneys and sweetbreads with honey and good grilled meats. Fine wines are sold by the glass at the bar that divides the rooms.

A la carte: 280-300F.

⑭ Chez Pauline
5, rue Villedo - 42 61 79 01

M. Génin. Open until 10:30 p.m. Closed Sat. dinner, Sun., July 14-Aug. 17 & Dec. 23-Jan. 2. Air cond. Pets allowed. Cards: V.

Even without succumbing to the fresh truffles in puff pastry or the Breton lobster stew with noodles—neither of which is the type of dish you're likely to look for in this old-style bistro—you'll find that Andre Génin's prices have a painful sting. But who complains in the face of such generous portions, such fresh, high-quality ingredients and such good humor? Delicious terrines, wonderful red-mullet filets in a Chinese marinade, young asparagus from the Côte d'Azur under a velvety hollandaise, filet of turbot poached to perfection and served with a simple white-wine sauce, stuffed cabbage and an excellent molded rice dessert—in short, this is classic cooking adapted to modern life and the cost-of-living index. There's also a fine selection of Arabian coffees and an extensive wine cellar.

A la carte: 300F and up.

12/20 Chez Vong aux Halles

10, rue de la Grande-Truanderie
42 96 29 89, 42 86 09 36

M. Vong Vai Lam. Open until 1 a.m. Closed Sun. Air cond. Terrace dining. Pets allowed. Cards: V, AE, DC, MC.

Authentic Oriental antiques decorate both floors of these Gothic cellars turned mandarin palace. Other art objects, such as the cleverly sculptured vegetable displays created by the two chefs in charge of the kitchen, aren't as long-lived. These ornamental creations will appear on any banquet table you order—a day in advance, please. The cuisine seems to have reached a plateau: On our visit the dim sum were too expensive and uneven in quality, and while the glazed Peking duck and the chicken with ginger were in the tradition, a pork stew was dull. Sorry, the toque has gone.

A la carte: 300F.

13 L'Escargot Montorgueil

38, rue Montorgueil - 42 36 83 51

Mme. Saladin-Terrail. Open daily until 11 p.m. Closed Jan. 1, May 1 & week of Aug. 15. Pets allowed. Cards: V, AE, DC, MC.

Despite her best efforts, Kouikette Terrail, the charming sister of Claude (owner of La Tour d'Argent), still can't seem to whip her staff into shape and dispel what appears to be a chronically mild state of confusion in the kitchen—with the exception of certain traditionally fine dishes: escargots, obviously, in a variety of forms, foie gras and pigs' knuckles. In contrast, the sautéed veal kidney flamed in brandy was dried out, and, alas, those succulent strawberry fritters had vanished from the menu. The wine list isn't what it used to be, either. Thank heavens for the still-intact, elegant, attractive Restoration-period interior, with its splendid ceilings, wrought-iron staircase and antique mirrors that even now seem to reflect Sarah Bernhardt's presence.

A la carte: 350F. Menu: 184F.

15 Espadon

(Hôtel Ritz)

15, pl. Vendôme - 42 60 38 30

M. Klein. Open daily until 11 p.m. Air cond. Garden dining. Parking. No pets. Telex 220262. Cards: V, AE, DC, MC.

You have to visit in the winter to taste the char (similar to trout), so rarely found in Paris, that Guy Legay brings in from a crater lake in the Puy-de-Dôme region. Cooked plain in its own juices, it is clearly the king of fish. Legay's talent rests on this very simplicity—a world apart from "the grand Ritz style," or worse, the pretentious elegance of Ledoyen, where he trained for a short while. Though his gift for classic cuisine went astray temporarily, it has now found itself in the geniune everyday cooking we all appreciate: cod cheeks, salt-cured salmon, casserole of sweetbreads and tiny onions, roast chicken with thyme, tenderloin of herbed lamb. It is the type of cooking that thumbs its nose at the international set who pay the dinner bills in solid gold in this opulent Napoléon III–style winter garden. The service is among the finest in the world, and the sommelier, Georges Lepré, is a virtuoso.

A la carte: 600-800F. Menu: 310F.

14 La Fermette du Sud-Ouest

31, rue Coquillière - 42 36 73 55

M. Naulet. Open until 10 p.m. Closed Sun. Pets allowed. Cards: V.

You'd think you were entering an old-fashioned country inn, where the tables are crowded together and the regulars wouldn't give up their seats on any account. Butcher-turned-chef Christian Naulet, who sports a handlebar mustache and has the ruddy face of the Périgord region, lacks his native region's accent but has all the culinary know-how that makes his boudin (sausage) with onions and lard possibly the finest in Paris—not to mention his country sausage, duck and cured shoulder of pork. Naulet provides an hour and a half of honest dining pleasure just steps away from the limp fries and anemic burgers of the former Trou des Halles. You'd best avoid the stuffed quail and the apple tart, however; they're not as good as the gras-double (a Lyonnais tripe dish) with fennel and the Périgord pastry with crème anglaise. The wine list is on the short side.

A la carte: 200F and up.

Goumard

17, rue Duphot - 42 60 36 07

M. Goumard. Open until 10:30 p.m. Closed Sun. & Mon. Air cond. Pets allowed. Cards: V, AE, DC, MC.

Twice or three times a week, Jean-Claude Goumard is one of the few Paris restaurant owners who bids for and obtains the very best food items at the Rungis market. That's the unseen side of his success. Ostensibly, his is one of the top seafood places in town because of the exceptionally high-quality produce that's delivered daily to the kitchens of head chef Georges Landriot. The rest is a matter of strict attention to detail (which results in consistency) wedded to a spark of talent—enough at least to combine crab rémoulade and smoked salmon into a marvelously fresh-tasting, appetizing dish or to turn poached lobster into a light, festive, delicious invention. A few desserts are worth three toques, like the feathery pear tart with caramel sauce. Expect a cordial reception by the owner's son and an attractive decor of blue and yellow Spanish tiles. One more point in this edition.

A la carte: 500-600F.

Le Grand Véfour

17, rue de Beaujolais - 42 96 56 27

M. Ruggieri. Open until 10:15 p.m. Closed Sat. lunch, Sun. & Aug. Parking. Air cond. No pets. Cards: V, AE, DC.

The magic of the Véfour lies in the fact that you could dine among empty tables in perfect contentment, free to admire the exquisite surroundings that Jean Taittinger's good taste and family fortune have restored to their former glory: carved boiserie ceilings, graceful painted allegories under glass, lush carpeting, tables with white linens among black-and-gold Directoire chairs. The place evokes memories of such immortals as Napoléon, Jean Cocteau, Victor Hugo and Colette, who once lounged on these red velvet banquettes in the soft glow of the Palais-Royal gardens. There would even be time to complain about the tasteless imitation-Empire chandelier hanging overhead.

But the Véfour is no place for solitary musings, having become a great crowd-drawer since its revival by the Taittinger group. Now, at the scene of important business luncheons and dinners, guests can rely on prompt and efficient service under the expert guidance of Béatrice Ruggieri. The pleasure of dining at the Véfour has taken a leap forward with the arrival of the 30-year-old chef, Jean-Claude Lhonneur, who had already made a name for himself in the Céladon's kitchens and at Les Célébrités, under the aegis of chef Robuchon. But don't expect the kind of astounding creations turned out by his former boss, for Lhonneur, a native of the Berry region, favors a light, modernized classic cuisine. He strives for simple, uncontrived, delicate flavors expertly assembled and seasoned, as in his terrine of chicken livers; scrambled eggs with salmon roe and chives; firm, chunky filet of peppered sole; poached sea bass with perfectly prepared aromatic vegetables; and veal tenderloin in an herb sauce (served whole in defiance of the current foolish practice of cutting it up). Among all these beauties, we can't conceal one recent disappointment we had with a tired, overcooked daurade (gilt-head), which was about as tasty as a plate full of cotton balls.

Lhonneur also called in his brother Frédéric, an accomplished pastry maker, whose warm apple confections and bittersweet-chocolate-nut crusts with orange sauce are out of this world. If the à la carte bill is also unbelievable, the fixed-price lunch menu, with a wide variety of dishes, is a good buy: With a fine Bordeaux for 100 francs, you'll spend about 400 francs and walk away with an unforgettable memory.

A la carte: 600-800F. Menu: 305F (lunch only).

12/20 Gros Minet

1, rue des Prouvaires - 42 33 02 62

M. Nocchi. Open until midnight. Closed Mon. & Sat. lunch, Sun. Pets allowed. Cards: V, AE, DC, MC.

The decor is a '30s pub with up-to-date wiring and plumbing. Maurice Nocchi makes a splendid host. His bar is a period piece, and his customers, always animated and thirsty, keep the place lively until the wee hours. No-nonsense cooking with a southwestern French touch (cassoulet, roast duck) and a Madiran (red wine from the Hautes-Pyrénées) that you won't forget.

A la carte: 180F. Menus: 60F(lunch only), 98F.

10/20 Hippopotamus

25, rue Berger - 45 08 00 29
See Eighth Arrondissement.

12/20 Lescure

7, rue de Mondovi - 42 60 18 91
M. Lascaud. Open until 10 p.m. Closed Sat. dinner, Sun., July & Dec. 23-Jan. 1. Terrace dining. Pets allowed. Cards: V.

A cheerful family place with a menu that justly proclaims: "Our reputation goes back to 1919." The decor is abundantly rustic, the service instantaneous and expert, the clientele fanatic (the American Embassy practically lives here), and the cooking genuinely home style (pot-au-feu, aïoli, bourguignons and so on).

A la carte: 150F. Menu: 80F(wine incl.).

14) Mercure Galant

15, rue des Petits-Champs
42 96 98 89, 42 97 53 85
M. Caille. Open until 10:30 p.m. Closed Sat. lunch, Sun. & holidays. Pets allowed. Cards: V.

After fifteen years at the helm of this attractive, authentic turn-of-the-century eating establishment, M. Caille can be justly proud of his uninterrupted success. On each of our visits to the elegantly faded restaurant, with its plush wall coverings, beveled mirrors and deep-cushioned banquettes, Caille also proved to be a first-rate host; the service was courteous, near perfect and prompt (business lunches are never allowed to drag on), and no detail was overlooked (appetizers, delicious dark bread and butter brought to the table immediately, excellent fresh petits fours). Chef Ferranti pays equally meticulous attention to his job, providing a choice of dishes that is modest (more so than the prices) and shows great care for the finished product. The vegetable terrine with a liver mousse is slightly overwhelmed by its carrot flavor, but the roast turbot with oysters and the sweetbreads in a light wine sauce with macaroni au gratin are faultless, as are the incredibly feathery millefeuilles. At dinner, ex-

cellent wines complement an inviting menu.

A la carte: 400-500F. Menus: 230F and 345F (dinner only).

13) La Passion

41, rue des Petits-Champs
42 97 53 41
M. Zellenwarger. Open until 10:30 p.m. Closed Sat. lunch & Sun. Air cond. No pets. Cards: V, AE, DC.

Gilles Zellenwarger, a bearded young chef who trained under Guérard and Pangaud, has taken over this rather staid but comfortable (in a pleasantly flowery sort of way) establishment. His à la carte menu may be conventional, but he has all the technical know-how to update a classic cuisine. Our meal included a savory rabbit terrine with a well-seasoned green salad, calf's head accompanied by sautéed sweetbreads and baby vegetables, and a light creamy molded rice dessert. The Beaujolais, on the other hand, was terribly mediocre.

A la carte: 250F. Menu: 180F.

12/20 Le Pavillon Baltard

9, rue Coquillière - 42 36 22 00
M. Tissot. Open daily until 1 a.m. Terrace dining. Pets allowed. Cards: V, AE, DC, MC.

After years of dust, excavation and street barriers, the gardens are actually being laid out in "the hole" (the excavation site of the old Paris markets now at Rungis); Le Pavillon Baltard stares straight out at them. So we'll have to visit there again (before the remodeling does away with Slavik's "farmhouse" decor) to sample the sausages, confits and choucroute (Sauerkraut).

A la carte: 230F. Menu: 138F.

14) Pharamond

24, rue de la Grande-Truanderie
42 33 06 72
M. Hyvonnet. Open until 10 p.m. Closed Mon. lunch, Sun. & July. Terrace dining. Pets allowed. Cards: V, AE, DC.

The extravagant development that replaced the old Paris marketplace, Les Halles, is by no stretch of the imagination any more exotic or attractive than the beloved old open-air market. For instance, one of our favorite Les Halles restaurants is one of the old-timers: the phenomenal Pharamond, the ancient temple dedicated to tripes à la mode de Caen, where you can also worship sausage from Jargeau and grilled pigs' feet. As the "modern" style wears thin, this bistro seems younger and livelier each year—with its wood paneling, flowered tiles, Belle Epoque fixtures and mirrors and intimate dining rooms. The cuisine is up-to-date and welcomes new ideas. Good wines in addition to pear and apple cider.

A la carte: 230-250F.

12/20 Au Pied de Cochon

6, rue Coquillière - 42 36 11 75
MM. Blanc. Open daily 24 hrs. Air cond. Terrace dining. Pets allowed. Cards: V, AE, DC.

Eighty-five thousand pigs' feet annually and one ton of shellfish daily and nightly. The most famous institution in Les Halles never closes its doors. Day and night, 365 days a year, it churns out nonstop pork dishes, seafood platters, onion soup and grilled meats. Run by the Blanc family and an able manager, the machine rattles on, while people in the street stare at the goings-on inside, fascinated by the sight of this venerable house suddenly left standing alone at the edge of "the hole," the site of the long-awaited gardens that are replacing Les Halles, Paris's former marketplace.

A la carte: 230F and up.

(15) Pierre Traiteur

10, rue de Richelieu - 42 96 09 17, 42 96 27 17
M. Dez. Open until 10:15 p.m. Closed Sat., Sun., holidays & Aug. Pets allowed. Cards: V, AE, DC.

Quick, let's restore Pierre Traiteur's two toques! In our last edition of *The Best of France*, Daniel Dez, the new owner of this cozy, prosperous bistro, did not receive the rating of his illustrious predecessor, Claude Nouyrigat, because the restaurant changed hands at press time and the chef had flown the coop. But we are relieved to report that Pierre Traiteur continues to run smoothly. The restaurant's many regulars are as enthusiastic as ever about the fresh mackerel in cider, the chicory with bacon salad, the unctuous duck liver, the blood-sausage-and-onion galette, the salmon with béarnaise and the skate with browned butter; and they continue to wash down this hearty fare with the cellar's captivating little wines (the Chinon is out of this world).

A la carte: 280-400F.

(14) Le Poquelin

17, rue Molière - 42 96 22 19
M. Guillaumin. Open until 10:30 p.m. Closed Sat. lunch, Sun. & Aug. 1-20. Air cond. Pets allowed. Cards: V, AE, DC.

On the brown-and-ivory-striped wallpaper are a host of engravings, some quite old, evoking the plays of Poquelin, alias Molière. And on Michel Guillaumin's menu are numerous reminders of his years at Taillevent and even of his years here when it was called Les Barrières, when Claude Verger ran the kitchens. Hence our impression of having tasted this cooking before: excellent and consistent, with the emphasis on updating traditional recipes and lightening classic dishes. Fine salads (like the chopped bottom round of beef with fresh tomatoes or the slices of veal kidney and crisp cabbage), well-prepared fish, choice wild game in season and delectable desserts (especially the famous flat tart à la Claude Verger). The wine list is still developing.

A la carte: 300F. Menu: 173F.

11/20 La Providence

6, rue de la Sourdière - 42 60 46 13
Mme. Schweitzer. Open until 11:30 p.m. Closed Sat., Sun. & holidays. Air cond. Pets allowed. Cards: V, AE, DC, MC.

An attractive reminder of what bistros used to look like, La Providence is a popular place, especially in the evening, to eat cured beef, Spätzle, Lorraine stew and several Alsatian specialties (the owner comes from there), washed down with Ottrott red wine at a modest price and, after dinner, mouth-watering white brandies.

A la carte: 150F. Menus: 73F (lunch only, wine incl.), 99F.

11/20 Le Samovar

14, rue Sauval - 42 61 77 74
M. Siew. Dinner only. Open until 1 a.m. Closed Sun. Air cond. Pets allowed. Cards: V, AE.

It's party time in the evening, with singers and balalaika players, pickled herring, blinis, shashlik and vatrouchka. With its attractive menus and delicious vodkas from all over served in carafes, Le Samovar is one of the best little Russian places in Paris.

A la carte: 230-300F. Menus: 130F (weekdays only), 170F, 320F (wine incl.).

13 Saudade

34, rue des Bourdonnais - 42 36 30 71
*M. Machado. Open until 11:30 p.m. Closed
Sun., Aug. 1-Sept. 6 & Dec. 23-27. Air cond.
No pets. Cards: V, AE, DC.*

The great Portuguese food you kept looking
for in Lisbon and Porto is found here, in a
setting of rough-plastered walls decorated with
tiles and folk art. The cooking is skillfully from
traditional recipes and is served with vintage
port and surprisingly good Portuguese wines.
There is cod and more cod (in a stew with
cabbage—superb!), marinated roast suckling
pig, an almond tart and a wine-tasting bar.
A la carte: 200F.

12/20 Willi's Wine Bar

13, rue des Petits-Champs
42 61 05 09
*M. Williamson. Open until 11 p.m. Closed Sun.
Pets allowed. Cards: V.*

Mark Williamson is an extremely knowledgeable British wine expert who provides
200 wines to choose from, including an incomparable collection of Côtes-du-Rhône and rare
labels from all over the world. Excellent selection by the glass. These beautiful wines will
accompany a generous and fresh cuisine: roast
duck, clams with herbs. Good fixed-price
menu.
A la carte: 200F. Menu: 138F (wine incl.).

SECOND ARRONDISSEMENT

12/20 L'Amanguier

110, rue de Richelieu - 42 96 37 79
*M. Derderian. Open daily until midnight.
Closed May 1. Air cond. Terrace dining. Pets
allowed. Cards: V, AE, DC.*

This delightful little chain is going strong,
including its latest link in Chicago. The decor
creates the illusion of a flower garden, the
pastries look and taste marvelous (baked by
Framboisier, same company), and the cooking
is all quality and freshness: crab with cucumber,
ravioli à la crème, lamb au gratin. Among the
good choice of wines, none is too expensive.
A la carte: 180F. Menu: 100F.

13 Auberge Perraudin

164, rue Montmartre - 42 36 71 09
*M. Perraudin. Open until 11 p.m. Closed Sat.
lunch (& dinner in July), Sun. & Aug. Air
cond. Pets allowed. Cards: V, AE, DC.*

The new decor, including a paneled ceiling
and wall-to-wall carpeting, is a distinct improvement over the old, even if it does sacrifice
individuality for comfort. Chef Perraudin, a
disciple of Orsi and Bocuse and a true devotee
of his art, appears to have lost a bit of steam,
though his cuisine remains light and meticulously prepared. The à la carte selections are
cautiously modern, but there is just one fixed-
price menu (whose quality-to-price ratio is not
as attractive as it has been in the past): a
pungent terrine of mackerel, cod in puff pastry,

an overripe Brie and a delicious warm apple
tart. It can all be accompanied by a number of
good little wines at ordinary prices.
A la carte: 250-350F. Menus: 150F, 250F,
320F.

11/20 Brasserie Gus

157, rue Montmartre - 42 36 68 40
*M. Prigent. Open for lunch weekdays; open for
dinner Fri. until midnight. Closed Sat. & Sun.
Pets allowed. Cards: V.*

Good everyday cooking with an individual
touch at moderate prices, served with sharp
little wines by the pitcher. The nostalgic decor
is typical of an old-time Alsatian brasserie and
is the oldest in the city (it has been preserved
intact since 1870). Try the filet of hogfish with
eggplant, lobster in the shell (a Brittany specialty) or veal tenderloin with red currants.
A la carte: 200F.

15 Le Céladon

(Hôtel Westminster)
15, rue Daunou - 47 03 40 42
*M. Borri. Open until 10:30 p.m. Closed Sat.,
Sun. & Aug. 2-Sept. 2. Air cond. Pets allowed.
Parking. Telex 680035. Cards: V, AE, DC, MC.*

The spontaneous, inviting, intelligent cuisine of Joël Boilleaut, who recently took over
from Jean-Claude Lhonneur (gone to Le
Grand Véfour), is exactly what one would
prefer to eat in these elegant yet informal

surroundings, where the serpentine-green tile blends well with the willow-green silk and pale-rose chair covers. In short, neither the ambience nor the cooking evokes the ceremonial boredom common to luxury eating places. The new chef, former right-hand man to Michel Kérever at the Duc d'Enghien, creates precise, savory, decorative and thoroughly modern dishes. The crab ravioli with a light basil-flavored cream sauce and the cod steak with potatoes involve more technical expertise than imagination, and let's hope that in the future this young chef will develop more personality—perhaps in the style of his delectable pork filets en crépinette with a curry sauce. For a remarkable dessert, try the chocolate macaroons in a coffee crème anglaise. The lunch menu/carte combination keeps the check under 300 francs, including a Bordeaux.

Menu/carte: 270F.

La Corbeille
154, rue Montmartre - 40 26 30 87
M. Cario. Open until 10:30 p.m. Closed Sat. lunch & Sun. Air cond. Pets allowed. Cards: V, AE.

Chef Jean-Pierre Cario has never been afraid of hard work. In the course of a brilliant career that took him from Lasserre to Denis to Pétrus to, finally, a cramped little bistro on one of Paris's grand boulevards, he never stopped growing, building, creating. As a result, he is now the proud owner of a three-star hotel with a score of pretty rooms, as well as a restaurant endowed with ultra-modern kitchens, cozy private salons and a dining room that boasts well-spaced tables, cushiony banquettes, intimate lighting and even a special nook for nonsmokers. The walls are decorated with fruit-and-flower frescoes in tones of apricot and cinnamon; while not every detail is in the best taste, the overall effect is fresh and attractive, with a garden-like air. Cario's cuisine isn't the most imaginative in town, but he knows how to coax the most out of top-quality ingredients. We urge you to sample his smoked fish and meats, prepared on the premises with Provençal lemon and orange wood. Also delectable are the escalope of duck liver with caramelized turnips, the snails with butter-stewed cabbage, the salmon baked in its skin with an onion compote, the lusty daube of beef and hog's jowls *"comme en Avignon"* and the tangy fricassée of farm-bred chicken in cider

vinegar. Desserts are uniformly excellent. Our only question is why Cario doesn't follow his Provençal leanings a little further and give his menu a more pronounced southern accent.

La Corbeille's fixed-price luncheons give a whole new meaning to the concept of "fast" food: For 185 francs you get a clutch of fat Marennes oysters, a plat du jour and a dessert. At dinner, a tasting menu offers six courses, each accompanied by an appropriate wine, all for a very attractive price.

A la carte: 360-450F. Menus: 185F (lunch only), 285F and 345F (dinner only, wine incl.).

12/20 Coup de Coeur
19, rue St-Augustin - 47 03 45 70
MM. Namura & Oudin. Open until 10:30 p.m. Closed Sat. lunch & Sun. Pets allowed. Cards: V, AE, DC.

The interior is 100 percent gray (it's all the rage) with gorgeous but uncomfortable dining chairs designed by Philippe Starck. And the cuisine is in keeping with the rest: light, entertaining and up-to-date. Try the trout tartare, the brill (like sand dab) with lemon confit and the burnt-almond ice cream with pistachios. Good fixed-price menu, but the wines are too expensive.

A la carte: 230-250F. Menu: 118F.

Drouant
18, rue Gaillon - 42 65 15 16
M. Ody. Open daily until 10:30 p.m. Air cond. Parking. Pets allowed. Cards: V, AE, DC.

This restaurant has the great distinction of hosting the monthly literary luncheons of the ten-member Prix Goncourt jury. Robert Sabatier, head gourmand of that prestigious group, warned his host: "Be careful—my colleagues have classic tastes, so don't upset them." Chef James Baron listened respectfully but went right ahead with his own plans. Being a "modern" chef, he had no intention of inaugurating Drouant by serving the literary lions lobster Thermidor and tournedos Rossini! The Tuesday before the Prix Goncourt (the most famous literary prize in France) was to be awarded, the jury gathered in the oval, magnificently paneled dining room. The members gasped at the menu: oysters poached in their own juices with caviar and a lemon-flavored cream sauce; sole with a creamy watercress garnish; fried onions and tomato pulp; squab with fried celery; assorted cheeses from Authès; and a raspberry tart. Not exactly revolutionary, but a fresh chapter nonetheless in the gastronomic epic of this illustrious body. The verdict was unanimous: Baron deserved the Prix Goncourt *de la cuisine*!

We can confirm this favorable report after tasting some half dozen dishes in the small room adjoining the celebrated Goncourt salon. But Baron's talent came as no surprise to us, since we've long admired this largely self-taught culinary loner from Vendée. He sprinted from Maxim's to Lenôtre and on to Troisgros before settling down in a small hotel opposite the railroad station in Cholet, the former capital of the handkerchief industry and not exactly a hive of gastronomic activity. He came back to Paris, arriving just in time to rescue Drouant, founded as an oyster bar in 1880 and suffering from a decline.

Decorators Zanetti and Slavik completely revamped the restaurant's interior, with its splendid wrought-iron and marble staircase (considered one of Ruhlmann's masterpieces), re-creating the atmosphere of those wild years between the two world wars, using marquetry furniture, etched mirrors and Lalique-inspired sconces like the ones found on board the great transatlantic liners of that era. The cool elegance of the main dining room is warmed by vases of vivid flowers and by the subtle harmonies of carpeting, draperies and chair covers, by ideal lighting and by a series of striking Boldini-esque portraits of society swells. There, for the 40 or so guests divided between the ground floor and the mezzanine, Baron offers his short but appetizing menu, which highlights his individual talent—more classic now than when we first discovered him, but stylish and adroit: poached turbot with hollandaise, John Dory with coarse mustard, grilled salmon with beurre blanc, veal au Grand Marnier and an exquisite fricassée of veal kidneys and sweetbreads spiked with juniper.

Le Café (formerly the Grill), to the left of the entrance, seats 60 under a ceiling whose marine decoration poet Jean Cocteau compared to "the ocean's sky." Dark paneling, mirrors, marble, soft leather banquettes, gray ostrich-skin wallpaper and little yellow lamps on the tables create an appealing effect. Two glamorous hostesses are there to greet diners, and the service is bent on pleasing business lunchers who may enjoy (until 3 in the afternoon) a plate of oysters and grilled salmon or a slice of roast beef served in the grand manner on a marble slab.

A la carte: 500F (Le Café: 300F). Menu: 200F (dinner only at Le Café, wine incl.).

10/20 Hippopotamus

1, bd des Capucines - 47 42 75 70
See Eighth Arrondissement.

12/20 Isse

56, rue Ste-Anne - 42 96 67 76
M. Sudo. Open until 10:30 p.m. Closed Sat. lunch, Sun. & Aug. 1-15. Air cond. Pets allowed.

Fashion designer Kenzo's eating place needs a shot in the arm. The service and prices are as stiff as ever; fish dishes are spectacular in appearance and lunch menus are attractive, but you begin to find a sameness about everything. Try the raw live California-type lobster and the fluffy fritters.

A la carte: 300F. Menu: 110F (lunch only).

12/20 Perry Brothers Restaurant

20, passage des Panoramas
42 33 31 80
MM. Perry & Zelaya. Open until 7 p.m. Closed Sat. & Sun. Pets allowed. Cards: V.

Chef Alan Perry is a sturdy Welshman whose approach to food is anything but insular. Inspiration for his cosmopolitan cooking comes from sources as diverse as northern Europe and Southeast Asia, via the Mediterranean and the U.S. Typical offerings from his menu—which, incidentally, he revises daily—might include delicate scallop ravioli in a creamy basil sauce, a hearty New York deli-style sandwich heaped high with pastrami and corned beef, a spicy chicken saté or a robust dish of poached finnan haddie (smoked haddock) in a smooth Cheddar sauce. Wine journalist Fiona Beeston has put together an equally international wine list, with representatives from Italy, Chile and Australia alongside the French contingent. Good news: Many bottles are priced around 100 francs, and a selection of fine wines is always available by the glass. All this good eating and drinking goes on within the picturesque passage des Panoramas, in sleek silvery-gray and gray-green surroundings created by co-owner Jorge Zelaya, a professional graphic designer.

A la carte: 175F. Menu: 125F.

12/20 Le Petit Coin de la Bourse

16, rue Feydeau - 45 08 00 08
*M. Andron. Open until 10:30 p.m. Closed Sat.
& Sun. Pets allowed. Cards: V, AE, DC.*

An amusing and typical turn-of-the-century Parisian bistro. The Belle Epoque decor is a bit faded though still appealing on the main floor and upstairs. The cooking also attempts to appeal: rabbit terrine with pistachios, beef filet in a wine sauce, thin tarts à la Verger.

A la carte: 280-300F. Menu: 150F (dinner only).

Pile ou Face (Heads or Tails)

52 bis, rue Notre-Dame-des-Victoires
42 33 64 33
MM. Udron, Dumergue & Marquet. Open until 10 p.m. Closed Sat., Sun., Aug., Dec. 24-Jan. 1 & holidays. Air cond. Pets allowed. Cards: V.

The name of this restaurant belies the purposeful attitude of its ruling triumvirate. The cuisine of chef/partner Claude Udron, who, with no grand credentials, leaves nothing to chance, and the last few meals he prepared for us nearly warranted two toques: a sumptuous spinach soup, ravioli filled with herbed escargots, filet of beef with foie gras (pleasant echo of a tournedos Rossini) garnished with a delicious shredded potato pancake, filet of red mullet in olive oil with celery stalks, and a light, crusty apple pastry. Simplicity, freshness, exquisite presentations—all these, plus the homemade bread and petits fours, are points in favor. The wine list has blossomed, and the service is first-rate in an elegant if slightly confining decor.

A la carte: 300F.

12/20 Le Saint-Amour

8, rue de Port-Mahon - 47 42 63 82
Mme. Bouché-Pillon. Open until 10:30 p.m. Closed Sat. lunch (& dinner in July & Aug.), Sun., July 14-Aug. 15 & holidays. Air cond. Pets allowed. Cards: V, AE, DC.

A stone's throw from the main boulevards and their cheap eateries, this is a real restaurant: responsible, reliable and comfortable (the cozy interior is partitioned by banquettes on the second floor). A typical fixed-price menu: eggs poached in red-wine sauce, homemade duck confit, Brie from Meaux and tarte tatin.

A la carte: 250-280F. Menu: 170F.

11/20 La Taverne du Nil

9, rue du Nil - 42 33 51 82
Mlle. Khalil. Open until 8 p.m. Closed Sun. & Aug. 15-30. No pets. Cards: V, AE.

Tablecloths, napkins, a cordial reception (by a former member of the Marist Fathers of Byblos) and belly dancing on weekends can all be yours for a bargain price. You'll dine on mezze (an assortment of seven appetizers), falafel and chiche taouk (marinated chicken).

Menus: 71F, 90F, 120F.

THIRD ARRONDISSEMENT

Ambassade d'Auvergne

22, rue du Grenier-Saint-Lazare
42 72 31 22
M. Petrucci. Open daily until 11 p.m. Air cond. Pets allowed. Cards: V.

Retired from his tripe and his cabbage soup, the delightful paterfamilias, Joseph Petrucci, scarcely ever appears in his "legation" barded with pork cuts and cured hams. But his diplomatic ministers—daughters, sons-in-law and a staff of loyal veterans—are adept at celebrating both the visual and the gastronomic delights of the Auvergne. The restaurant has been refurbished from cellar to roof and looks even more characteristically Auvergnat: more rustic and even older. Gone are the calf's head with kiwis and lobster with currants. The latest culinary fashion in the Auvergne calls for lentil salad, pigs' feet with fourme cheese, daube of duck, boudin sausage with chestnuts, stuffed breast of veal and cured pork. Châteaugay or Saint-Pourçain are wines that go well with all of these dishes, and if you're really in the swing of things, you'll want to visit the table d'hôte, perhaps the last of its breed in Paris, and cut yourself a slice of Auvergnat pork. If you don't come from the Auvergne, a meal at the Ambassade will make you wish you did.

A la carte: 190-280F.

(14) L'Ami Louis
32, rue de Vertbois - 48 87 77 48

M. De la Brosse. Open until 10:30 p.m. Closed Mon., Tues. & July 10-Sept. 31. Pets allowed. Cards: V, AE, DC.

For some, nothing has changed at L'Ami Louis; for others, nothing is as good as it was in the good old days. For our part, let's be frank enough—while taking nothing away from the pleasure of good memories—to acknowledge that if L'Ami Louis is no longer the best bistro in Paris, it has carefully preserved its heritage: both the astonishing bric-a-brac decor and the plates heaped high with hearty fare that makes up in honesty what it lacks in finesse. The boys in the back play the old songs well enough, as they have for twenty years, slicing thick slabs of foie gras, sautéing the mushrooms, roasting joints of beef, chickens, racks of lamb and game, and frying the golden potatoes here. Unquestionably, the soul of this bistro temple has slipped away, along with the perfectionist touch of old Papa Antoine, but the walls are still solid, if flaking, and Louis, the eternal maître d' and sommelier, is still fiddling with his bottles and his rickety dining chairs, God bless him.

A la carte: 550-700F.

11/20 Chez Jenny
39, bd du Temple - 42 74 75 75

M. Siljegovic. Open daily until 1 a.m. Terrace dining. Pets allowed. Cards: V, DC.

The marquetry in the upstairs dining room is truly remarkable, which is more than one can say about the legendary varieties (five) of choucroute that are served here. The excellent Alsatian charcuterie is really what sells the choucroute.

A la carte: 200-230F.

12/20 La Guirlande de Julie
25, pl. des Vosges - 48 87 94 07

M. Grolier. Open until 11 p.m. Closed Mon., Tues. & Dec. 18-Jan. 18. Terrace dining. Pets allowed. Cards: V, AE, MC.

The pleasant new winter-garden decor highlights the superb beams of this historic house on the legendary place des Vosges. The new owner has designed an attractive 125-franc fixed-price menu based on a tasty pot-au-feu. The cuisine (mackerel rillettes, fish chowder, duck confit in cider and a bitter-chocolate cake) is unpretentious and quite popular with the crowds that fill up the dining room and, on fine days, the terrace that overlooks the recently redesigned place des Vosges.

A la carte: 200F. Menus: 80F (weekday lunch only), 125F.

(13) Taverne des Templiers ✪
106, rue Vieille-du-Temple
42 78 74 67

M. Bertrand. Open until 10 p.m. Closed Sat., Sun. & Aug. Pets allowed. Cards: V, DC.

With its intimate setting in a conventional but comfortable Louis XIII style, complete with a splendid beamed ceiling, the Taverne is a great place for a quiet lunch or a romantic dinner. The delightful neighborhood is right next door to the Musée Picasso. The owner's wife is all smiles, the service is unobtrusive, and Guy Bertrand's cooking conveys the bright, delicious country flavors of the Charente region, to which he adds his own personal and seasonal touches. From the short à la carte menu, we suggest the foie gras in wine aspic, warm oysters in a creamy herb sauce, herbed frog soup, fricassée of chevreau (kid) à la saintongeaise, parsleyed eel, lobster soufflé and one of the good regional wines at moderate prices.

A la carte: 250F.

FOURTH ARRONDISSEMENT

(18) L'Ambroisie
9, pl. des Vosges - 42 78 51 45

M. Pacaud. Open until 10:15 p.m. Closed Mon., Sun., 1 week in Feb. & 1st 3 weeks of Aug. Air cond. No pets. Cards: V.

The charming and discreet Pacauds left their cramped quarters on the quai de la Tournelle and moved to the majestic place des Vosges. Unfortunately, there is no view of it, as the dining room, which used to be a goldsmith's workshop, is windowless. But L'Ambroisie is spacious, handsomely proportioned and stylishly elegant, thanks to decorator François-Joseph Graf. Twenty-five guests can eat in the main dining room, fifteen more in a smaller one. To ornament the street level of this historic mansion, known as the Hôtel de Luynes during the tenancy of its seventeenth-century owner, a marvelous inlaid flooring of ancient tiles in various shades of ocher has been installed, as well as wood paneling, carved wood chairs, decorative objects displayed on a sideboard, a rich tapestry stretching the length of the central wall and soft lighting. In short, everything is in place to delight the eye and prepare for a celebration. Chef Pacaud offers a mousse of bell peppers with tomato purée, ravioli filled with crab cooked in shellfish broth, a combination of lobster and sweetbreads, spicy turbot filet, crayfish split and basted with tarragon butter, a feuilleté of fresh truffles, braised oxtail (Bernard Pacaud's trademark and a trademark of his menu) and a fabulous roast rib steak. The elegant but unpretentious meals have warranted one more point in this edition. The few desserts offered are remarkable: a traditional savarin, coffee mousse with melted chocolate, vanilla napoleons. The wine list, also short, is well balanced, including the best Côtes-du-Rhône and a nice selection from Languedoc.

A la carte: 650F and up.

11/20 Auberge de Jarente

7, rue de Jarente - 42 77 49 35
M. Charriton. Open until 10:30 p.m. Closed Sun., Mon. & Aug. 5-Sept. 5. Pets allowed. Cards: V, AE, DC, MC.

A delightful place with Basque customers, a Basque atmosphere and chef and Basque cuisine: pipérade (Basque omelet), Béarn andouille (sausages) and two house specialties: paella on Friday and Saturday and cassoulet the rest of the week.

A la carte: 160F. Menus: 106F (wine incl.), 94F, 145F.

⑮ Benoit

20, rue St-Martin - 42 72 25 76
M. Petit. Open until 10 p.m. Closed Sat., Sun., April 9-16 & July 31-Aug. 20. Air cond. Terrace dining. Pets allowed. No cards.

Even though he's called the pope of Paris bistros, Michel Petit takes his customers quite seriously. The founder's grandson, Petit clearly intends to perpetuate the things that make his admirable restaurant, which opened in 1912, so attractive: the authentic stucco interior, the mirrors and light-oak cabinetry, the cordial service and, of course, the beef pot-au-feu à la parisienne (a mouth-watering cold stew that has been on the menu for 70 years), braised beef, cassoulet maison with plump beans that melt in your mouth, the best pot roast (sharing honors with Pierre Traiteur) and exquisite cod au gratin. In addition to exercising their talent for cuisine bourgeoise, Petit and his chef, Dany Bulot, borrow almost cavalierly from the modern repertoire—for instance, skate with shallots and herbs in a pie crust, a small duck pâté in puff pastry with a memorable pear sauce, and poached salmon with a chiffonnade (minced sorrel, lettuce, parsley and chervil in butter). In short, Petit is a conservative who nevertheless marches steadily forward—along with the prices. Excellent wine cellar, strong on Beaujolais. It's time for another toque.

A la carte: 350-550F.

12/20 Bofinger

3-7, rue de la Bastille - 42 72 87 82
M. Alexandre. Open daily until 1 a.m. Air cond. Terrace dining. Pets allowed. Cards: V, AE, DC, MC.

This brasserie, the oldest in Paris, is a typical one, with brass decorations, glass dome, marquetry, leather banquettes, aproned waiters and the lunch and dinner crowd hunched over choucroute, oysters and the chef's special of the day. The wine list is short but good.

A la carte: 250F. Menu: 149F.

10/20 Brasserie de l'Ile-Saint-Louis

55, quai de Bourbon - 43 54 02 59
M. Guepratte. Open until 1:30 a.m. Closed Thurs. lunch, Wed. & Aug. Pets allowed. No cards.

The chef's name is Wagner, and he will sing, in key, all about Sauerkraut. It's Bayreuth in a cheerier mood, with froth-capped beer mugs and strings of sausages overhead.

A la carte: 180F.

⑬ Coconnas

2 bis, pl. des Vosges - 42 78 58 16
M. Terrail. Open until 10:15 p.m. Closed Mon., Tues. & Dec. 18-Jan. 20. Terrace dining. Pets allowed. Cards: V, AE, DC.

Every day, not just on Sunday, Claude Terrail (also owner of the famous Tour d'Argent) has something special for his guests— either on the short à la carte menu created by chef Denis Dumusois, or in the fixed-price meal "with no surprises," which includes, for instance, petit salé of duck, steamed hen with plenty of vegetables, a chocolate marquise and a half bottle of Côtes-du-Rhône. In warm weather, a few tables are set under the arcades facing the majestic square. It's a marvelous sight (inside, the decor is less inspiring).

A la carte: 300F. Menu: 145F (wine incl.).

12/20 Le Coin du Caviar

2, rue de la Bastille - 48 04 82 93
M. Nebot. Open until midnight. Closed Sun. Air cond. Pets allowed. Cards: V, AE, DC.

Along the Champs-Elysées and at the Madeleine, caviar is a thriving business; near the Bastille, it's a tougher sell. The decor is attractive and the food of good quality, but prices are stiff and accidents can happen (like the salmon overcooked on one side). Good apple strudel.

A la carte: 250-300F. Menu: 132F (lunch only).

Au Franc Pinot

1, quai de Bourbon - 43 29 46 98
M. Meyruey. Open until 11 p.m. Closed Sun. & Mon. Pets allowed. Cards: V, MC.

Get ready: This place has cellars reaching down to the level of the Seine in one of the oldest bistros in Paris, a beaming host, muted lighting (but not so dim that you don't notice the low-grade flatware settings), excellent wines by the glass or carafe (there's a wine bar on the main floor) and a kitchen that retains its two toques despite a few shortcomings. It's a pleasant restaurant for a quiet business lunch (superb warm oysters with zucchini, breast of chicken with baby vegetables, a cheese tray and a nut cake are about 200 francs, with a carafe of Anjou red) or a romantic dinner of exquisitely fresh-tasting squab vinaigrette; Scottish salmon just a shade overcooked with some wonderfully fragrant chanterelles that could stand being less sandy and better seasoned; excellent stuffed saddle of milk-fed lamb; and a delicate coconut flan (preferable to the apple tart or the pear with almond custard, both of which are below par). Patrice Guyader, who trained with Robuchon and has been cooking

at Au Franc Pinot for many years, is a good technician and innovator, but he might do well to develop simpler, not-so-rich dishes.

A la carte: 350-400F. Menus: 150F (lunch only), 180F.

12/20 Au Gourmet de l'Isle

42, rue St-Louis-en-l'Ile - 43 26 79 27
M. Bourdeau. Open until 10:30 p.m. Closed Mon. & Thurs. Cards: V.

It gets elbow-to-elbow with loyal customers who flock here both to admire the 90-year-old owner's magnificent mustache and to eat the sensational andouillette (pork sausage) with kidney beans, the boudin (blood sausage) and the quince tart. Other trademarks include a beamed ceiling on the street floor, a handsome vaulted cellar and a good fixed-price menu.

A la carte: 180F. Menu: 100F.

10/20 Hippopotamus

1, bd Beaumarchais - 42 72 98 37
See Eighth Arrondissement.

Au Quai des Ormes

72, quai de l'Hôtel-de-Ville
42 74 72 22
M. Bourrier. Open until 10:30 p.m. Closed Sat. lunch, Sun. & July 29-Aug. 29. Air cond. Terrace dining. Pets allowed. Cards: V.

Mme. Masraff left to join her husband in New York, and this lovely house on the banks of the Seine, close to city hall, has found a new owner from Lyon: Yves Bourrier, a most likable mustachioed gentleman who recently gave up one of the best restaurants in Neuilly to come here. Bourrier's generous, inventive cuisine is based on the freshest produce. One can only regret that the prices are not as magnetic as they once were. Many of the Masraff's à la carte selections are still served, and the two fixed-price menus (the "bourgeois" at lunch and the low-calorie "to keep the ladies happy") are greatly expanded. Several delicious new dishes, such as the ravioli filled with sweetbreads and suprême of pheasant forestière, have appeared. The delightful view of the Seine and the Ile Saint-Louis from upstairs, above the relentless traffic along the riverside is delightful.

A la carte: 400F and up. Menus: 185F (lunch only), 210F, 350F (dinner only).

13 Wally
16, rue Le Regrattier - 43 25 01 39
M. Chouaqui. Open until 10:30 p.m. Closed Sun., Jan. 15-30 & Sept. 15-30. Air cond. Cards: V, DC.

The masterly couscous of former camel driver Wally Chouaki is different from the ordinary liquid-doused, greasy couscous you find in Paris; here, it is perfectly dry, served without broth or vegetables. You can tell how light and finely ground the semolina is, and how tasty the accompanying merguez and grilled lamb are. This delicious dish is the centerpiece of the copious fixed-price menu (the only one offered), which includes a delectable b'stilla (a savory-sweet chicken and almond pastry) and stuffed sardines. The decor is also special: It resembles a luxurious tent ornamented with valuable rugs, Berber decorations and furniture tastefully inlaid with mother-of-pearl. Prompt service can be expected at the small tables separated by antique Arabian screens.

Menu: 260F.

FIFTH ARRONDISSEMENT

13 Auberge des Deux Signes
46, rue Galande - 43 25 46 56
M. Dhulster. Open until 10:30 p.m. Closed Sun. (July & Aug.). Pets allowed. Cards: V, AE, DC, MC.

The musical feature of this impressive medieval setting, formerly the Chapel of St. Blaise, is unique: Customers select their meal from the "menu" of over 1,000 records of ancient music, some quite rare. It's a humorous touch from the good-humored owner, Georges Dhulster, whose name sounds Flemish but whose accent traces him to the Auvergne. The cooking reflects both influences, which is not surprising, as the new chef comes from Lamazère: savory pounti (a rustic casserole with bacon, onion and Swiss chard), served with a rather uninteresting salad of crisp cabbage; excellent medallions of veal from Cantal; goose confit with cèpes. The rest of the menu is not so exciting, the service snail-paced, and the atmosphere touristy. But in the evening, there is a marvelous view from the upstairs dining room of floodlit Notre-Dame and the church of Saint-Julien-le-Pauvre.

A la carte: 400-500F. Menus: 150F (dinner only), 180F (lunch only, wine incl.), 240F.

15 La Bûcherie
41, rue de la Bûcherie - 43 54 78 06
M. Bosque. Open daily until 12:30 a.m. Air cond. Terrace dining. Pets allowed. Cards: V, AE, DC.

Lately, people have been going to La Bûcherie less for the food than for the pleasant atmosphere, the crackling fire, the friendly host and the fashionable clientele. But Bernard Bosque wants to avoid the reputation of running an "in" restaurant. He is, after all, an excellent cook, successful at adapting classic and bourgeois cuisine to modern tastes. He may have been off the mark in the past, but now he's back in form. We enjoyed two perfect meals worthy of two toques—one on the terrace facing Notre-Dame, the other in the back room, which is less cheerful—fresh foie gras with truffle juice, crayfish-stuffed cabbage, salmon soufflé with crayfish and dried cod, duck confit seasoned with sorrel, a light-as-a-bubble Black Forest cake and a pear tart with almond cream. The service is unusually courteous and attentive, and the table settings are becoming more and more elegant (new linens, attractive dishes). The wine cellar is heavy on Bordeaux and ought to include a few more affordable labels, some regional selections and more whites, which are practically nonexistent.

A la carte: 350F.

12/20 Chez René
14, bd St-Germain - 43 54 30 23
M. Cinquin. Open until 10:15 p.m. Closed Sat., Sun., July 27-Sept. 3 & Dec. 23-Jan. 3. Pets allowed.

The best things about this old, typically Parisian corner bistro are its Swiss chard au gratin, beef rib steak Bercy, country sausage and boeuf bourguignon—and, of course, the comfortable imitation-leather banquettes, genuine polished brass and unfailingly cheerful mood. The Chénas and Juliénas, bottled by the owner, have something to do with it.

A la carte: 180-200F.

12/20 Chez Toutoune

5, rue de Pontoise - 43 26 56 81
Mme. Dejean. Open until 10:45 p.m. Closed Sun., Aug. 15-Sept. 15 & Dec. 20-Jan. 3. Terrace dining. Pets allowed. Cards: V.

The famous fixed-price menu of blond Toutoune (a.k.a. Colette Dejean) is as reliable and substantial as ever, and the prices are steady; only the descriptions change. This year's offerings include a tureen of the soup du jour (as much as you can eat), herring or terrines, cod or the cook's daily special and chocolate soufflé. Wines by the pitcher are served in this whitewashed interior.

Menu: 147F.

12/20 Chieng-Mai

12, rue Frédéric-Sauton - 43 25 45 45
M. Takounseun. Open until 11:30 p.m. Closed Sun., Aug. 1-15 & Dec. 26-Jan. 9. Air cond. Pets allowed. Cards: V, AE.

Be prepared for syrupy music and a lot of bowing and scraping as you enter. The decor, though impersonal and without much character, is admittedly comfortable, and the Thai cuisine for the most part is authentic: grilled mussels with lemon grass, delicious breast of duck flavored with basil and pepper, and an attractive basket of fish wrapped in banana leaves, all of which can be accompanied by unusual rice wines. The inviting fixed-price menus feature an assortment of dishes.

A la carte: 160F. Menus: 129F, 153F, 166F.

⑭ Clavel

65, quai de la Tournelle - 46 33 18 65
M. Piras & Mme. Clavel. Open until 10:30 p.m. Closed Sun. dinner, Mon., 1 week in Feb. & Aug. 8-29. No pets. Cards: V, AE, DC.

The new owners have elected to freshen up the place (this used to be Alain Passard's L'Ambroisie, which is now in the place des Vosges) with beige and black wallpaper and flowers everywhere. The new chef is young Jean-Yves Guichard, who was trained by his pastry-making parents in the Vendée and by François Clerc at La Vieille Fontaine. If you like clever, elegant cooking, you won't be disappointed, though you will pay handsomely

for it: lobster ravioli with chives, roast Bresse pigeon, skate wing with mustard seed and leeks, honey-glazed apple tart.

A la carte: 350-400F. Menus: 160F (weekday lunch only), 200F.

⑬ Diapason

30, rue des Bernardins - 43 54 21 13
M. Olivier. Open until 10:30 p.m. Closed Sat. lunch & Sun. Pets allowed. Cards: V, AE, DC.

The appealing decor remains as it was when chef Duquesnoy presided here not long ago. It's not easy to compete with such a cooking talent, but the young chef, Jean-Claude Olivier (who's making his debut at Diapason), has developed a well-planned, enjoyable menu at reasonable prices. We sampled the smoked frogs' legs in garlic butter (a tasty and unusual dish), veal kidney, Lyon sausage with plump beans and a sample of four chocolate cakes.

A la carte: 260-280F. Menus: 145F (lunch only), 180F (dinner only, wine incl.).

⑮ Dodin-Bouffant

25, rue Frédéric-Sauton - 43 25 25 14
Mme. Cartier. Open until midnight. Closed Sun., Aug. 6-Sept. 7 & 10 days at Christmas. Air cond. Terrace dining. Pets allowed. Cards: V, DC.

Long after the departure of Jacques Manière, the slight misunderstanding that Dodin-Bouffant is the first-class bistro he created lives on. Hence some disappointed patrons, who discover a decor that's not terribly engaging, sometimes disorganized service, a clientele more noisy than elegant—in short, the lively, cordial ambience of a good brasserie instead of that of the stylish restaurant they expected to find. With this in mind, they'll agree with us that Dodin-Bouffant remains one of the most congenial spots on the Left Bank both at lunch and late in the evening. Apart from the short list of market-fresh offerings (primarily fish), the à la carte menu is devoted to a superb collection of shellfish, which may be selected directly from the huge saltwater holding tanks on the premises, and to traditional, lightened country-style cooking: some of the finer samplings include ragoût of mussels and pasta shells, fricassée of cod provençal, daube of oysters and pigs' feet, calf's head fricassée with rosemary and good desserts. The wine list includes many regional selections for less than 100 francs.

A la carte: 330-360F. Menu: 155F (lunch only).

10/20 Hippopotamus

9, rue Lagrange - 43 54 13 99
See Eighth Arrondissement.

Miravile

(Gilles Epié)
25, quai de la Tournelle - 46 34 07 78
M. Epié. Open until 11 p.m. Closed Sat. lunch, Sun. & Jan. 1-17. Air cond. Pets allowed. Cards: V, AE, DC, MC.

Gilles Epié gave up his Café Saint-Honoré for this little restaurant near La Tour d'Argent, whose longtime chef, Arthur Keller, has raised it to the top ranks of Paris bistros. The decor (sand-colored walls, café au lait–lacquered ceiling, excellent lighting) has been tastefully re-done by Epié's charming wife, Muriel. A young chef who worked with François Clerc and for the Café de Paris in Brussels, Gilles's cooking is imaginative, generous and unpretentious: salad of pot-au-feu, daube of beef cheek, salmon with puréed cabbage, French toast with glazed apples. Prices have risen from their modest beginnings, and the wine list includes a number of pleasant lesser-known and affordable labels. One more point in this edition.

A la carte: 280-450F. Menu: 150F (lunch only), 350F.

Moissonnier ۞

28, rue des Fossés-Saint-Bernard
43 29 87 65
M. Moissonnier. Open until 10 p.m. Closed Sun. dinner, Mon. & Aug. 1-Sept. 5. Pets allowed.

An unmistakable wine-country decor on the second floor and a bourgeois one downstairs. For 28 years, André Moissonnier has stuck to his country cooking, the cuisine of Bresse, Burgundy and the specialties of Lyon: gras-double (sautéed tripe) with onions, quenelles, a traveling salad bar from which you can make a meal, and whipped potatoes au gratin. For dessert, try the good wild-raspberry sherbet or oeufs à la neige, and throughout your meal sip a fine Brouilly or Bourgueil (served in the

traditional mug), which the owner has tasted, selected from the grower and drawn for you from a barrel in his cellar.

A la carte: 200F.

Au Pactole

44, bd St-Germain - 46 33 31 31,
43 26 92 28
M. Magne. Open until 10:45 p.m. Closed Sat. lunch & Sun. Air cond. Terrace dining. Pets allowed. Cards: V, AE.

Slavik's new decor has revived the tired old Pactole, which was originally put together by Manière and later patched up by Noelle and Roland Magne. The cuisine had been suffering from a loss of identity; Magne's forte is not inventiveness. But things are looking a little brighter lately. His best efforts are in the classic vein: lobster salad with pasta, duck foie gras from the Landes, salmon with tarragon, roast beef with marrow in a salt crust, minced veal kidney seasoned with basil. All these consistent and savory dishes are well worth two toques.

A la carte: 250-500F. Menus: 180F (weekday lunch only), 280F.

Le Paprika

43, rue Poliveau - 43.31 65 86
M. Csekö. Open until 11:30 p.m. Closed Sun. & July 13-Aug. 31. Air cond. Parking. Pets allowed. Cards: V, AE, DC.

Dominique Csekö, one of the owners, cooks this Hungarian cuisine, which is truly original and unfamiliar. Come some evening when music is playing (remarkable gypsy group) and taste the cinnamon-flavored cherry soup, Puszta crêpes stuffed with veal goulash, mushroom strudel and fresh pork with white beans, marjoram and smoked sausage. Many varieties of excellent sweet strudel, plus the famous layer cake (vanilla, chocolate, almond) and outstanding Tokays and the heavy red wine called "bull's blood."

A la carte: 300-350F. Menu: 85F (lunch only).

Restaurant A

45, rue de Poissy - 46 33 85 54
M. Huynh-Kien. Open until 11 p.m. Closed Mon. Air cond. Cards: AE.

The plain though not inelegant interior is regularly decorated with extraordinary vegetable sculptures. Over the years, the owner has made a specialty of preparing those great Chinese banquet platters that have all but vanished from the Paris scene, including such dishes as imperial shrimp, the casserole of fish and shellfish simmered (for 48 hours) in a thick, fragrant broth, and the pork fritters Kowloon, a Cantonese specialty, with green peppers and pineapple.

A la carte: 200F. Menu: 90F.

⑬ Sud-Ouest ✪
(L'Escarmouche)
40, rue Montagne-Sainte-Geneviève
46 33 30 46

M. Bourgain Open until 10:30 p.m. Closed Sun. & Aug. Pets allowed. Cards: V, AE, DC.

This is the loveliest stone interior you'll find tucked away beneath the Montagne Sainte-Geneviève, an ancient arched crypt that sets off, with stunning elegance, the Louis XIII chairs and flower vases. Classic cuisine of southwest France is served exclusively, the best of which includes garlic-flavored tourin (onion soup), homemade foie gras, cassoulet with breast of duck, warm goat cheese with a nut salad and an array of desserts in addition to the excellent tart. Eating à la carte can be a bit costly, even with a little Gaillac wine for about 70 francs.

A la carte: 300F. Menus: 150F, 190F.

La Tour d'Argent
⑱ 15-17, quai de la Tournelle
43 54 23 31

M. Terrail. Open until 10 p.m. Closed Mon. Parking. Pets allowed. Cards: V, AE, DC.

Claude Terrail wears his age well—mainly because he seems not to age at all. And the same might be said of La Tour d'Argent. After 400 years, the place can only be called ageless. If Terrail would just stay with us for another century or two, you could be sure that in the Paris of the third millennium, while others down "food pills," King Claude would still be up in his tower, numbering ducks, gallantly kissing ladies' hands, napping his fish with sauce Dugléré and transforming callow young busboys into stylish waiters.

Behind the jaunty boutonnière, squirish bearing and sparkling conversation of this eternal *jeune homme* there lurks a demanding professional—and one of the world's most successful restaurateurs. And perhaps the last of his particular breed. For of all the grand Parisian restaurants—Maxim's, Lucas-Carton, Le Grand Véfour, Ledoyen—only La Tour hasn't changed hands, hasn't lost an iota of its mystique. Terrail could easily let his establishment survive on its glorious reputation, or create a factitious glory through publicity and the press. Yet he chooses to run his restaurant with unflagging rigor and the highest standards, thereby putting it in a class by itself. From the fabled wine cellars to the gastronomic museum in the ground-floor salon, from the newly revamped seventh-floor terrace (with its incomparable view of Notre-Dame) to the dining room just below, not an inch escapes the master's gimlet eye. Whether or not one shares Terrail's taste for the grandiose and the ostentatious, it's impossible to resist the magical atmosphere of this singular restaurant, a glass balcony perched high above the Seine. And we would surely succumb to its charm more often, if only the foie gras didn't cost 400 francs and the prawns 450 francs!

But how vulgar to speak of money, with our mouths full of lobster aspic, caviar, poached prawns, sea bass in Noilly, and poussins with truffle juice. Let's just say that chef Manuel Martinez is the ideal choice to head La Tour's kitchens. His tastes and preferences harmonize perfectly with Terrail's conservative bent (hence the black, not red, toques). Yet the classic cuisine Martinez embraces is considerably lighter than one might suspect, and delectable to boot. He gives such dishes as duckling with peaches, veal cutlet and sweetbreads with lobster, and a double veal chop with a tarragon-scented jus a welcome liveliness and lightness (but even he can't improve the heavy, molten pike quenelle André Terrail, which would never be missed were it stricken from the menu). Desserts—chocolatine with tart cherries, warm vanilla millefeuille, soufflé Grand-Marnier—are not exactly revolutionary, but they are competently turned out, and a measurable improvement over past examples encountered here.

No oenophile should leave leave without perusing the tome jocularly referred to as the wine "list." With entries that range from Pomerol to the Côte-de-Nuit, from Sauternes to Alsace, from Lafite '45 at 12,000 francs to Savennières at 110 francs, it makes for fascinating reading.

A la carte: 900F and up. Menu: 330F (weekday lunch only).

La Truffière ♔
4, rue Blainville - 46 33 29 82
MM. Sainsard. Open until 10:30 p.m. Closed Mon. & July 24-Aug. 28. Air cond. Pets allowed. Cards: V, AE, DC, MC.

Like a lovely pike in a vulgar fishbowl, this delightful old bistro clings to its specialties—foie gras, a confit of gizzards and a Périgord cassoulet—in a neighborhood (the Contrescarpe) overrun by more or less greasy Middle Eastern and Oriental eateries. Under the high-beamed ceiling, the brothers Sainsard pursue both the bohemian life and truffles and foie gras. Alain is in the kitchen, trying to fashion all these rich ingredients into a distinctive cuisine. Though it isn't easy, he's often successful—truffle tarte, an assortment of three foies gras, breast of duck with périgourdine sauce, such top-notch desserts as warm feuilletés and bittersweet-chocolate mousse. Good selection of wines and Armagnacs.

A la carte: 300F. Menus:85F (weekday lunch only, wine incl.), 130F, 210F.

12/20 Ugarit
41, rue Censier - 47 07 90 81
M. Doumid. Open until 11 p.m. Closed Sun. Terrace dining. Pets allowed. Cards: V, DC.

The Armenians in Paris consider Ugarit their star restaurant, a notion they share with language professors and all lovers of hummus, lissane (calf's tongue with pistachios), tarator (garlic-sauced chicken) and many more tasty items. The other dishes and kebabs are not terribly exciting.

A la carte: 150F. Menu: 60F (weekday lunch only).

12/20 Le Vieux Chêne
69, rue Mouffetard - 43 37 71 51
M. Tartare. Open until 11:30 p.m. Closed Sun. & Mon. Cards: V, AE, DC.

This former Apache dance hall and meeting place of the 1848 revolutionaries is strictly a dive, albeit a tidied-up one, that offers a colorful slice of Parisian life among all those dismal Greek bistros. You dine "from the blackboard" on breast of duck with kumquats or sweetbreads with crayfish. The food is good, inexpensive and served with a smile.

A la carte: 180F. Menus:55F (weekday lunch only, wine incl.), 125F (dinner only).

Villars Palace
8, rue Descartes - 43 26 39 08
M. Pontoizeau. Open daily until 11 p.m. Air cond. Terrace dining. Parking. Pets allowed. Cards: V, AE, DC.

This modern bistro has a new owner, a new facade by the architect Kenzo and a new chef, Henri Morel. This young man has lots of enthusiasm but hasn't quite found a direction yet, resulting in some weak opening courses and desserts. On the other hand, the pan-fried red mullet filets are excellent, and the fish terrine and fried sole goujonnettes with cucumbers good. Service is nice but uneven; the wines are expensive.

A la carte: 350F and up. Menu: 160F (lunch only).

SIXTH ARRONDISSEMENT

Allard
41, rue St-André-des-Arts
43 26 48 23
M. Bouchard. Open until 10 p.m. Closed Sat., Sun., Aug. & year-end holidays. Air cond. Pets allowed. Cards: V, AE, DC.

The new owner has caught the spirit of this legendary bistro, and Mme. Fernande Allard's departure and the head maître d's retirement have not disrupted the ambience—the reception is still relaxed and friendly, and the decor remains unchanged and pleasantly antiquated.

After several quite disappointing meals these last few years, we have of late rediscovered almost all of the good tastes this place had in its better days. Witness the excellent ham, which this time around had not been left in the refrigerator too long, the not-too-fatty duck terrine and the thick, juicy turbot in beurre blanc, so much better than before. There is still room for improvement, however, particularly in the dessert department.

A la carte: 280-450F.

11/20 L'Assiette au Boeuf

22, rue Guillaume-Apollinaire
42 60 88 44

M. Beaugrand. Open daily until 1 a.m. Terrace dining. Pets allowed. Cards: V.

The outstanding interior decoration by Slavik combines tastefully lit mirrored walls with elaborate woodwork. For years the standard menu of salads, grilled meats and french fries has provided the neighborhood with honest, no-frills fare for those in a hurry. Desserts are always good.

A la carte: 100-110F. Menu: 63F (wine incl.).

⑭ Le Bélier

(L'Hôtel)
13, rue des Beaux-Arts - 43 25 27 22
M. Duboucheron. Open daily until 12:30 a.m. Air cond. Pets allowed. Telex 270870. Cards: V, AE, DC.

A longtime favorite for its atmosphere, pleasant piano bar, delightful fountain, flowers, tree trunk, the gorgeous evanescent creatures it attracts and the memories of Oscar Wilde and Mistinguett, Le Bélier has recently truly come into its own, serving a light, flavorful and authentic cuisine and wines from a small, attractive cellar. Try the saffron-flavored three-fish stew, duckling in lemon and honey, and rice made with milk and pine nuts.

A la carte: 250F. Menus: 150F (lunch only), 160F (dinner only).

11/20 Bistro de la Gare

59, bd du Montparnasse - 45 48 38 01
M. Bissonnet. Open daily until 1 a.m. No cards.

Bistro de la Gare boasts an authentic, well-restored turn-of-the-century pub decor that makes up for the so-so cooking (which, at least, doesn't pretend to be more than it is): shellfish, salads, grilled meats, specials of the day.

There's an endless (37) list of desserts, a few of which are quite good.

A la carte: 130-150F.

12/20 Brasserie Lutétia

(Hôtel Lutétia)
23, rue de Sèvres - 45 44 38 10
M. Scicard. Open daily until midnight. Air cond. Terrace dining. Pets allowed. Telex 270424. Cards: V, AE, DC, MC.

The sparkling, comfortable decor by Slavik and Sonia Rykiel has greatly improved this good brasserie, which serves both modern and rustic dishes (the latter are given a Parisian touch): fondant of rabbit in aspic, satiny and fragrant with tarragon; cervelas (spicy dried sausage) with lentils; fried andouille sausages; sauerkraut; whole calf's head; filet of sander in a Bouzy wine sauce; and exciting desserts. You can also expect impeccable service, the best oysters around and a memorable Côtes-du-Rhône for 68 francs.

A la carte: 250-280F. Menu: 88F.

⚬ Jacques Cagna

18 14, rue des Grands-Augustins
43 26 49 39
M. Cagna & Mme. Logereau. Open until 10:30 p.m. Closed Sat., Sun., Dec. 22-Jan. 2 & Aug. 4-Sept. 3. Air cond. Pets allowed. Cards: V, AE, DC.

Intelligent (he speaks English and Spanish and is studying Japanese), with a scorching sense of humor and a passion for antiques and adventure, young Jacques Cagna, ex-merchant marine, is an appealing mixture of knockabout, Rive Gauche sophisticate and serious culinary professional. By dropping anchor in this old part of Paris and working hard, and with a little help from decorator Daniel Pasgrimaud, Cagna has transformed this fourteenth-century house into a most delightful little kingdom. It has original exposed beams, salmon-colored walls hung with Flemish still lifes, light-oak furnishings, trompe l'oeil paintings and a small salon at the foot of the stairs leading up to the dining room, which has some fine old frescoes set into the wainscoting. All this works marvelously as a preface to a sound, well-balanced cuisine that is modern but not overrefined, light but not insipid, and bold enough to welcome a breath of country air—in the form of potato pancakes, salad of smoked goose and potted gizzards and a marvelous dish of pig's jowls with carrots and puréed potatoes, a recipe Cagna's mother gave him.

Cagna remains a country lad at heart, equally at home in a more sophisticated milieu, whose tastes are focused and whose blends of flavors are rarely off target, whether he's preparing cannelloni stuffed with cream of lobster, brill with oysters in a watercress sauce, veal fricassée with fresh ginger or squab sauced with honey and Sauternes. The menu varies, of course, but try not to miss the scrambled eggs with sea urchin, the scallops sautéed in truffle juice—if only for the delectable dwarf potatoes with chives that come with it. And if you've sworn off beef, have his filet of Scottish beef with truffles: It may restore your appetite for meat. Desserts rarely change on the menu, but we will never tire of the glazed almond mousse and the Queen of Sheba (chocolate-nut cake with a custard sauce).

Cagna's 50,000-bottle cellar, an enormous number for a small restaurant, was assembled with great care and includes famous labels as well as lesser-known Côtes-du-Rhône and Burgundies priced between 100 and 200 francs. All of the above explains the success of this restaurant, modest at lunch but overwhelming in the evening, when Cagna's sister, Anny, his partner for more than twenty years, plays hostess to the Parisian and international regulars who come here for a crash course in French culture.

A la carte: 500-800F. Menu: 245F (lunch only).

Le Calvet
165, bd St-Germain - 45 48 93 51
M. Watelet. Open until 10:30 p.m. Closed Aug. 3-28. Air cond. Pets allowed. Cards: V, AE, DC.

The new management (1985) has replaced the worn red Hungarian decor with pale-rose table linens and velvet curtains that do wonders for the handsome stone walls. Chef Jean-Pierre Bouchereau, who rated a toque at Chez Nous in Montfort-l'Amaury, retains that ranking at Le Calvet, despite his timidity in properly reducing sauces and his lack of conviction with seasonings. It would take ever so little to improve the grilled sole, the rabbit stew, the blanquette of turbot with asparagus and lobster, and the mustard-flavored fricassée of

lotte. The excellent pastries and delicate little tuiles need no improvement. Respectable wine cellar and two inviting fixed-price menus.

A la carte: 300F. Menus: 109F, 175F.

Charly de Bab-el-Oued
9 bis, bd du Montparnasse
47 34 68 63
See Seventeenth Arrondissement.

12/20 Aux Charpentiers
10, rue Mabillon - 43 26 30 05
M. Bardèche. Open until 11:30 p.m. Closed Sun., Dec. 25-Jan. 1 & holidays. Terrace dining. Pets allowed. Cards: V, AE, DC.

The "daily special," an established Parisian tradition, is served in what was once a carpenters' guild hall that dates back to 1856 and retains its warmth and simplicity. The owner is a delightfully theatrical character, the aïoli, stuffed cabbage, petit salé (poached, lightly salted pork loin chop) and veal sauté are delectable, and the blood sausage is unforgettable.

A la carte: 180F.

Le Chat Grippé
87, rue d'Assas - 43 54 70 00
M Prunières. Open until 10:30 p.m. Closed Sat. lunch, Easter & Aug. Air cond. Cards: V, MC.

This little bistro, which opened a few years ago in an old butcher shop, has been run for the last four years by its owner, chef Marc Prunières, a native of Quercy, who has turned it into an attractive, relaxing, unpretentious place. The dark, mirrored interior, handsomely adorned with garnet velvet, is complemented by the friendly reception and efficient service. As for the food, since Prunières hired a young disciple of Senderens and Ferrero, it has improved markedly: a fricassée of fresh chanterelles seasoned with garlic and parsley, beef filet with fresh liver in a pie crust, and a savory saddle of lamb fragrant with rosemary. The expensive wine list is rich in Bordeaux and Cahors.

A la carte: 250F. Menus: 120F (weekday lunch only), 180F (dinner only).

12/20 Chez Maître Paul 🖤

12, rue Monsieur-le-Prince
43 54 74 59

M. Gaugain. Open until 10:30 p.m. Closed Sun., Mon., Dec. 24-Jan. 2 & Aug. Pets allowed. Cards: V, AE, DC.

In this unassuming little corner restaurant, chef Gaugain has been turning out some of the best Savoyard cooking you'll find in Paris: fish stew in Arbois wine, coq au vin (in white wine), sweetbreads simmered in Château-Chalon and so on. Excellent Jura wines.

A la carte: 200F. Menu: 165F (wine incl.).

11/20 Dominique

19, rue Bréa - 43 27 08 80

M. Wiernik-Aronson. Open until 10:15 p.m. Closed Feb. school vacation & July 17-Aug. 16. Air cond. Pets allowed. Cards: V, AE, DC.

Dominique is the oldest, and still the best, Russian attraction in town, at least when you're talking about the combination bar/grocery store at the entrance, which draws discriminating customers from all over Montparnasse. Marvelous smoked salmon, borscht and herring.

A la carte: 200-300F. Menu: 152F (wine incl.).

11/20 Drugstore Saint-Germain

149, bd St-Germain - 42 22 92 50

M. Boutersky. Open daily until 1:30 a.m. Air cond. Pets allowed. Cards: V, AE, DC.

The omnipresent decorating hand of Slavik has done it again, this time transforming an old decor into a spectacle of metal palm trees and gigantic pineapple light fixtures. As for the cuisine, it has remained unchanged: salads, daily specials and ice creams.

A la carte: 160-180F. Menu: 60F.

⑬ La Foux

2, rue Clément - 43 25 77 66

M. Guini. Open until 10:30 p.m. Closed Sun. Air cond. Pets allowed. Cards: V, AE.

Alex Guini, a dear, colorful fellow (growing stouter every year), has spruced up his pleasant modern decor that attracts publishing-industry types. He features the cooking of Nice and Lyon; his gras-double (tripe) is tops. Mme. Guini is there to welcome you. On winter Saturdays, there are choice tidbits (Lyon specialties) to whet your appetite.

A la carte: 300F and up. Menu: 145F (weekdays only).

10/20 Hippopotamus

119, bd Montparnasse - 43 20 37 04

See Eighth Arrondissement.

⑭ Joséphine

(Chez Dumonet)
117, rue du Cherche-Midi
45 48 52 40

M. Dumonet. Open until 10:30 p.m. Closed Sat., Sun. & July. Terrace dining. Pets allowed. Cards: V.

Always smiling and cordial as he caresses a bottle of Armagnac and strokes his beard, owner Jean Dumonet is an avid seafarer, though the menu in his venerable bistro gives no clue to this passion. Of course, you'll find skate (in a cream sauce with capers), sole (with a fondue of leeks) and John Dory (spiced with ginger); but what really draws the customers—who tend to be casual, perhaps socially prominent, sorts—are the leg of lamb (Wednesday lunch), truffled andouillette feuilleté, boeuf bourguignon with fresh noodles, navarin of lamb and duck confit. They also enjoy the elegant simplicity of the oak-paneled and etched-mirror decor. The wine cellar, too, is admirable, with a stock including fine estate Burgundies, Banyuls (a sweet apéritif or dessert wine) bottled by Dr. Parcé, and a dozen or more prestigious 1961 Bordeaux from Le Clos Montmartre that cost a small fortune (920 francs)—plus other vintages that go as high as 9,000 francs a bottle. But never fear, an excellent Chinon can be yours for a mere 80 francs.

A la carte: 250-400F.

11/20 Lapérouse

51, quai des Grands-Augustins
43 26 68 04

M. Alexandre. Open until 11:30 p.m. Closed Sun. dinner & Mon. Air cond. Pets allowed. Cards: V, AE, DC.

The great Lapérouse disappeared ages ago, and it's most unlikely that the owner of the brasserie Bofinger, who performed the rescue operation, will ever resurrect the past. Decorator Pierre Pothier has salvaged the framework of this admirable turn-of-the-century monument, artfully combining genuine and fake elements, and has restored the six small dining rooms on whose mirrors the fortune-hunting ladies of that period inscribed, with their diamond rings, the names of their "protectors." Pothier also enlarged the ground floor and turned the third floor into one large, attractive room overlooking the quays along the Seine. Despite the striking effect of the new decor, the new chef indulges in heaviness and thick sauces, as seen in the fricassée of frogs' legs and escargots with chervil and the lotte-and-lobster navarin.

A la carte: 380-450F. Menu: 180F.

11/20 Lipp

151, bd St-Germain - 45 48 53 91
Mme. Cazes. Open daily until 2 a.m. Closed July 14-Aug. 16. Air cond. Pets allowed. Cards: AE, DC.

Lipp without Roger Cazes is still Lipp, of course, but it isn't really the same. This glossy brasserie still serves some 400 to 500 clients every day, but the clientele is not as choice as once it was—no longer does *le Tout-Paris* line up to beg for a table. After 26 years of faithful service, heir-apparent Michel Cazes was passed over, and the direction of Lipp was entrusted to a certain M. Perrichon, an interior architect. Though the staff is as gracious and efficient as ever, a curious atmosphere of interregnum prevails, intensified by rumors of an imminent sellout. Time will tell. In any case, a sadly stringy dish of boeuf au gros sel recently confirmed our suspicion that the food is not up to its former level (which was never, in any case, very exalted). Since Paris abounds these days in brasseries offering tip-top meals, Lipp is doomed to suffer by comparison. Sic transit gloria. . . .

A la carte: 200-320F.

11/20 La Lozère ✿

4, rue Hautefeuille - 43 54 26 64
Mme. Almeras. Open until 10:30 p.m. Closed Sun., Mon., Dec. 24-31 & Aug. Pets allowed. No cards.

Dedicated to a celebration of the Lozère region—bracing mountain air and the robust cooking smells of tripoux vinaigrette (sheep's tripe and feet), goat cheese and herb sausage—La Lozère has a dignified interior of exposed beams and worn stones.

A la carte: 130F. Menu: 73F (lunch only, wine incl.), 90F, 109F.

13 La Marlotte

55, rue du Cherche-Midi - 45 48 86 79
Mme. Agaud & M. Bouvier. Open until 11 p.m. Closed Sat., Sun. & Aug. Air cond. Terrace dining. Cards: AE, DC.

This is a happy marriage of good home cooking and pretty dinnerware. In the evening you dine by candlelight under a beamed ceiling on regional duck specialties, andouillette in white wine, sausage and veal confit—all first-rate and meticulously prepared. Your fellow diners will be people who want good cooking and know where to find it. The young owners keep an eye on everything, including the fine quality of their house wines and the price of your meal.

A la carte: 200-250F.

13 Le Muniche

27, rue de Buci - 46 33 62 09
MM. Layrac. Open daily until 3 a.m. Air cond. Terrace dining. Pets allowed. Telex 201820. Cards: V, AE, DC, MC.

More power to the Layrac brothers, from the Aveyron country, for ferreting out such good little wines, for supplying the public with fresh oysters year-round, for keeping an honest country-style kitchen and for maintaining over the years one of the liveliest and most popular brasseries in town. If you're lucky enough (and the chances are dim indeed) to obtain a "box," you'll have what might be compared to a compartment on a sightseeing train, along with an evening of noisy fun, and you'll be waited on by an attentive staff that manages to stay alert and smiling into the wee hours. You can dine on all kinds of sauerkraut, rosy, thick-sliced calves' liver au gratin, duck confit, grilled pig's tail and ears, chicken in the pot and more.

A la carte: 220F. Menu: 127F.

15 Paris

(Hôtel Lutétia)
23, rue de Sèvres - 45 48 74 34
M. Scicard. Open until 10 p.m. Closed Sun., Mon., Aug. & 1 wk in Feb. Air cond. Parking. Pets allowed. Cards: V, AE, DC, MC.

In the sternly elegant art deco interior (inspired by Slavik and Sonia Rykiel) that replaced the Lutétia's dreary old tea room, Jacky Fréon has succeeded in impressing us with a cuisine that explains why Joël Robuchon hired him as an assistant. He is a sound technician who has a fine nose for subtle flavors: His fresh salmon in lobster sauce (which won him the Bocuse award), breast of duckling with foie gras, braised pork in cabbage leaves and his exquisite coffee-flavored baba manage to keep the tables filled. At lunch, these and other dishes appear on a fixed-price menu for 260 francs—a bargain in this neighborhood.

A la carte: 350-500F. Menu: 260F (lunch only).

10/20 Le Petit Saint-Benoît

4, rue St-Benoît - 42 60 27 92
M. Gervais. Open until 10 p.m. Closed Sat., Sun. & Aug. Terrace dining. Pets allowed. No cards.

At this most highbrow terrace in Paris, temporarily or permanently broke members of the fashionable set gather to eat shepherd's pie and roast veal.

A la carte: 80-100F.

(13) Le Petit Zinc

25, rue de Buci - 43 33 51 66
MM. Layrac. Open daily until 3 a.m. Air cond. Terrace dining. Pets allowed. Cards: V, AE, DC, MC.

Le Petit Zinc serves the same country cooking as next-door neighbor Muniche, emphasizing southwestern specialties: Corrèze sausage with chestnuts, duck thighs with apples and that famous heaping plate of grilled pork. Also, fresh seafood is served year-round, as is Sauerkraut and excellent calves' liver cut thick for two. Only the customers change: Nowadays they're quiet and better behaved. The decor hasn't budged in 30 years, since the time when its well-worn furniture, lace curtains and 1900s ambience introduced the "bistro" style to Paris.

A la carte: 250F. Menu: 127F.

(15) Princesse

(Castel)
15, rue Princesse - 43 26 90 22
M. Castel. Open until 1 a.m. Dinner only. Closed Sun. & Aug. Air cond. Pets allowed. Telex 203835. Cards: V, AE, DC.

The Castel is like the Bank of France or Fort Knox: impregnable and everlasting. A hundred years from now there will still be a Castel in the corridor to welcome the chosen few and to turn away—from the Princesse club—those who don't belong but would like to. From cellar to attic, this establishment, one of the

great dining spots in Paris, will continue to pack in the worldly set: to the discothèque to dance and drink; to Le Foyer on the main floor for a salad or a meat dish; or to the more formal dining room on the second floor for scrambled eggs with sea urchins, mustard-flavored brill or squab stuffed with morels. Count on spending 200 to 250 francs in Le Foyer and 500 to 600 francs if you eat upstairs.

A la carte: 200-600F.

(15) Relais Louis XIII

8, rue des Grands-Augustins
43 26 75 96
M. Poindessault. Open until 10:15 p.m. Closed Mon. lunch, Sun. & Aug. Air cond. Pets allowed. Cards: V, AE, DC, MC.

This lovingly preserved site of the Grands-Augustins convent, where Louis XIII was proclaimed king on the evening following Henri IV's assassination, is probably one of the finest restaurants of its kind in the city. Sturdy beams, genuine patina and historical paintings (you dine beneath the gazes of Louis XIII, Anne of Austria and Francis I) lend the setting a distinct charm rather than comfort (some tables and banquettes are rather cramped). The kitchens, where Manuel Martinez reigned for the last eight years before leaving for La Tour d'Argent, are now in the hands of giant, debonair Georges Piron, 38, who creates his dishes with daring: red mullet chaud-froid served as an amuse-gueule with vegetables tartare; a delicious cold nage of crustaceans with peppermint; devilish poultry wings stuffed with escargots; and sweetbreads with baby vegetables. For dessert, try the curious but refreshing grapefruit-orange terrine en gelée. You'll pay a king's ransom for this regal meal.

A la carte: 500-600F. Menu: 190F (lunch only).

11/20 La Vigneraie

16, rue du Dragon - 45 48 57 04
M. Sabatier. Open daily until 1 a.m. Air cond. Terrace dining. Pets allowed. Cards: V, AE, DC.

A few solid (and expensive) daily specials (pot-au-feu, salmon filet) and good cold dishes are served with a respectable collection of wines by the glass (Bordeaux only). Good fixed-price menu and fast service at lunch.

A la carte: 250-280F. Menus: 75F (lunch only, wine incl.), 149F (weekdays only).

SEVENTH ARRONDISSEMENT

(13) Antoine et Antoinette

16, av. Rapp - 45 51 75 61

MM. Pernot. Open until 10:30 p.m. Closed Sat. (except dinner in summer), Sun. & Easter school vacation. Terrace dining. Pets allowed. Cards: V, AE, DC.

Film director Jacques Becker and scriptwriter Françoise Giroud used to lunch here with their film crew, and this tranquil restaurant is named after the heroes of their movie. The decor has been freshened up, the terrace overlooking the avenue is delightfully quiet in summer, and Jean-Claude Pernot's cooking relies on the best seasonal products. The composition of his highly professional, non-hyperimaginative menu includes lotte with fresh spinach, good homemade duck foie gras, rack of lamb seasoned with thyme and some pleasant classic desserts (tarte tatin, pear charlotte). Expect a warm reception from co-owner Ghislaine Pernot.

A la carte: 300F.

Arpège

(18) 84, rue de Varenne - 45 51 47 33, 45 51 20 02

M. Passard. Open until 10:30 p.m. Closed Sat., Sun. lunch & July 30-Aug. 18. Air cond. Pets allowed. Cards: V, AE, DC.

Alain Passard quit this address as an underling when it housed L'Archestrate. Having proved himself at Duc d'Enghien, then at Carlton in Brussels, he has returned as owner. The "A" (for Archestrate) inscribed on the elegant Limoges dinnerware and the silverware now applies to Arpège. The threadbare furnishings in the small dining room are gone, and a coat of fresh paint and new fabrics have spruced things up a little. The decor is still unfinished, but instant success has encouraged Passard to make further improvements worthy of his cuisine. You'll agree that he's an extremely talented young chef after tasting his cabbage stuffed with crab in a mustard sauce, squab with lemon-flavored endive, saddle of hare with walnuts and cèpes (the meat is coated with ground nuts—a sensational dish!) and his superb desserts (licorice-flavored millefeuilles,

tomato stuffed with a sweet filling, cocoa squares steeped in citrus fruits, macaroon with raspberry sauce). He's also to be congratulated for an exceptional fixed-price lunch menu at 150 francs (three courses plus cheese and dessert), which is undoubtedly one of the best values in the city. The new young wine steward deserves credit for developing the moderately priced wine list. One more point in this edition.

A la carte: 500-700F. Menus: 150F (lunch only), 400F.

11/20 Babkine

(Chez Germaine)

30, rue Pierre-Leroux - 42 73 28 34

M. Babkine. Open until 9 p.m. Closed Sat. dinner, Sun., Aug. & Dec. 24-Jan. 2. No pets. No cards.

Château dining on oilcloth. At this gold-medal address, the line forms on the sidewalk for the rabbit sauté, the coq au vin, the calf's head and so on.

A la carte: 60-68F.

12/20 Le Balisier

20, rue Rousselet - 47 34 66 29

MM. Lucas. Open until 10 p.m. Closed Sat. lunch, Sun. & Aug. Pets allowed. Cards: V, AE, DC.

This pleasant, simple, two-level little family restaurant recently spruced up its decor, but Mama is still in charge of the dining room and her son the kitchen. There are winners (remarkably cooked fresh salmon) and losers (sole smothered in almonds); it's just going to take a little time to sort things out. Excellent choice of wines.

Menus: 60F (lunch only, wine incl.), 100F (wine incl.), 145F (menu/carte).

12/20 La Belle France & Le Parisien

Eiffel Tower, Champ-de-Mars

45 55 20 04

M. Ody. Open daily until 10 p.m. Air cond. No pets. Telex 205789. Cards: V.

On the second level of the Eiffel Tower, with a panoramic view of the city, Le Parisien is below (snacks and grilled meats) and La Belle France just above it (brasserie-style cooking).

A la carte: 200F. Menus: 85F, 170F.

Bellecour

16

22, rue Surcouf - 45 51 46 93,
45 55 68 38

*M. Goutagny. Open until 10:30 p.m. Closed Sat.
lunch (& Sat. dinner in seas.), Sun. & Aug.
10-Sept. 1. Air cond. Terrace dining. Pets allowed. Cards: V, AE, DC, MC.*

Gérard Goutagny has orchestrated a great
comeback for this veteran bistro, which had
seen better days. Only one or two of the Lyon
specialties are still on the menu (primarily as a
concession to the old regulars); André Plunian,
the chef who took over a year or so ago, has
his own way of doing things. We discovered
Plunian a few years back at Château-du-Loir,
then traced him to Le Mans, where, two years
ago, we awarded him his second toque. This
giant of a man is bursting with talent; he has
ideas and direction, and his mastery of his art
lacks only the aura of authority enjoyed by the
greatest chefs. Anyway, he's on the right track
with such dishes as raw salmon and caviar in a
light cream sauce, crab wrapped in cabbage
leaves, the distinctive, ultra-light wild rabbit
pâté in puff pastry and the cod with white beans
au gratin. For dessert, you can still count on
the handsome creations of M. Goutagny, a
trained pastry maker and former pupil of
Bernachon: His glazed fig tart is delicious but
could stand less sugar. There's a fine choice of
Burgundies and Beaujolais. The service, provided by a competent, attentive young staff in
a fine redecorated interior, is a welcome improvement. Call it a resurrection, or maybe a
second birth.

A la carte: 300F. Menus: 200F (lunch only,
wine incl.), 250F (dinner only).

Bistrot de Paris

15

33, rue de Lille - 42 61 16 83

*M. Oliver. Open until 11 p.m. Closed Sat. lunch
& Sun. Pets allowed. Cards: V.*

As one of our colleagues once remarked,
why would anyone ask when reserving a table,
"Is the boss around?" Michel Oliver only
bends over the stove for the TV cameras and
to put the finishing touches on packaged foods
that delight the customers of self-service food
emporiums. Unlike others, he has the good
sense and the integrity not to exploit his culinary fame, and he long ago turned over the
Bistrot's kitchens to Jean-Pierre Frelet. Frelet
is responsible for the clever dishes on the

"modern" menu, which features eggplant and
fresh cod caviar, marinated sardines, calves'
liver with mashed onions, lemon fricassée of
chicken, braised andouillette on Mondays and
veal blanquette on Tuesdays. This light, bourgeois cooking generally turns out quite well.
Once in a while it takes a tumble; most recently, neither the cassoulet, whose brown
crust someone forgot to add, nor the cherry
aspic on the pork that's all the rage made a
good impression. But the bittersweet-chocolate cake, almond cream and glazed nougat are
all marvelous. Ditto the Bordeaux—greater or
lesser—listed at reasonable prices. The enduring Parisian atmosphere in this 25-year-old
restaurant decorated like a century-old bistro—where business has perked up considerably since the nearby Musée d'Orsay
opened—makes lunch or dinner a truly relaxing, pleasurable experience.

A la carte: 300-500F.

Le Bourdonnais

17

113, av. de La Bourdonnais
47 05 47 96

*Mme. Coat. Open daily until 11 p.m. Air cond.
Pets allowed. Cards: V, AE.*

Micheline Coat has not yet decided whether
to ditch Le Bourdonnais's second name, La
Cantine des Gourmets, which scarcely conveys
the elegant refinement of this small, typically
Parisian restaurant. Yet surely anyone would be
overjoyed to have this kind of mess hall—a
charming decor of mirrored walls hung with
salmon-colored fabric, white woodwork, marvelous flowers everywhere. Coat has a knack
for arranging a room—which is not so easy
when the room is narrow—and for keeping her
faithful customers (government and business
personalities) happy by treating each as an
individual. The chef is 26-year-old Philippe
Bardau, who assisted previous chef Régis Mahé
for four years and who, like Mahé, worked for
a while at Maximin. Bardau has kept pretty
much to the established style and seems to be
quite at home with it. Clients surely will agree
that Le Bourdonnais deserves to keep the three
toques it was first awarded in 1986.

Coat, a superb hostess, and her staff present
the menu and their recommendations to each
table in a most charming manner. Perhaps they
will suggest the tarragon-flavored loin of rabbit
with kidney, sole and smoked salmon in aspic
with a tarragon cream sauce, pan-fried sea bass

with artichokes and rosemary, sea bream garnished with a fennel mousse and saffron-flavored fresh noodles, grilled duck with olive butter and Roquefort, or poached pigeon with a mousse of fresh peas. Desserts include glazed nougat and oranges poached in a raspberry purée with honey butter.

The 200-franc fixed menu at lunch includes wine, coffee and, for example, daube of duck and ham, broiled salmon with potatoes, and orange aspic.

A la carte: 350-500F. Menus: 200F (lunch only, wine incl.), 250F (dinner only, wine incl.), 380F (menu dégustation).

12/20 Le Champ de Mars

17, av. de La Motte-Picquet
47 05 57 99

M. Gellé. Open until 10:15 p.m. Closed Tues. dinner, Mon. & July 15-Aug. 15. Terrace dining. Pets allowed. Cards: V, AE, DC.

The few excellent dishes here are prepared in the traditional fashion and served in a rustic, rather charming provincial decor by a squadron of motherly waitresses: delicious cold cuts, pike sauced with beurre blanc, calf's head, stuffed cabbage and so on. Good choice of regional wines.

A la carte: 230-250F. Menu: 106F.

⑬ Chez les Anges

54, bd de Latour-Maubourg
47 05 89 86, 45 55 69 26

Mme. Delmas. Open until 10:30 p.m. Closed Sun. dinner. Air cond. Pets allowed. Cards: V, AE, DC, MC.

For 30 years this peaceful house in the Invalides district has been serving poached eggs en meurette, excellent parsleyed ham, beef in wine sauce and calves' liver served in thick slices. It's getting a bit stale now and could use a touch of imagination in the cuisine and in the decor, which features wine-colored wood paneling and carpeting. But despite the unoriginality of the Burgundian cuisine of chef Bernard Labrosse, who has worked at Chez les Anges for fifteen years, it is nonetheless honest and classic: fish and shellfish steamed in a fennel-seasoned broth, lamb stew and a dessert of almonds, raisins, hazelnuts and figs covered with candied nougat. There's an impressive colony of government officials on hand at lunchtime; at night, you'll find candlelight, soft music and a more eclectic crowd, despite the steep prices.

A la carte: 400F. Menu: 200F.

⑬ Chez Françoise

Invalides Air Terminal - 47 05 49 03

M. Demessence. Open until 11 p.m. Closed Sun. dinner & Aug. Parking. Pets allowed. Cards: V, AE, DC.

A miniature virgin forest besieges the glass wall, its greenery adding a cheerful note to the vast barn-like terminal. Many business people and government officials come here to park themselves in the comfortable wicker chairs set in the attractive, noisy but not hectic setting. The cooking is valiant, unpretentious bistro fare: roast lamb or rabbit, andouillette, salmon and warm apple tart or île flottante (floating island). Prices are high, except on the "parliamentary" fixed-price lunch menu, which contains just about the best this well-run restaurant has to offer. Good owners' Beaujolais is served in carafes.

A la carte: 250-300F. Menu: 130F.

⑬ Chez Muriel et Isabelle

94, bd de Latour-Maubourg
45 51 37 96

Mlle. Dechaut. Open until 10 p.m. Closed Sat., Sun., Aug. & Dec. 23-Jan. 1. Terrace dining. Pets allowed. Cards: V.

Muriel focuses on what's happening in the tiny dining room, with its daintily draped tables and ever-present flowers. Isabelle produces some inspired home cooking (hare terrine with cooked apples, young rabbit simmered with mustard and prunes) that has a distinct personality and favors the use—and overuse—of spices (she comes from Spain). We've had an interesting marinade of salmon and capitaine (a bony fish caught off the West African coast), except the flavors were dulled by too much herbs and ginger; tasty tuna terrine and broccoli with a mushroom-based sauce; excellent pan-fried calves' liver; and faultless vanilla crème brûlée. Wine is served by the glass, and in warm weather you can eat at one of two tables on the terrace facing the garden and dome of the Invalides.

A la carte: 280F. Menu: 180F (lunch only, wine incl.).

⑬ Chez Ribe
15, av. de Suffren - 45 66 53 79
M. Pérès. Open until 10:30 p.m. Closed Sun., 2 weeks in Aug., Dec. 25 & Jan. 1. Terrace dining. Pets allowed. Cards: V, AE, DC, MC.

Antoine Pérès knows how to run a bistro. He keeps a sharp eye on the quality of what he buys, as well as on the dining atmosphere and the generous portions he serves. The service is friendly, the tables roomy, and on the single fixed-price menu there are several simple, tasty dishes from the grill: fresh salmon, breast of duck or roast squab chicken "à l'américaine," and for dessert, a delicious chocolate cake with a light crème anglaise that's not too sweet. Even with a red Anjou at 42 francs, the bill is remarkably merciful.

Menu: 142F.

⑯ Le Dauphin
(Sofitel Paris Invalides)
32, rue Ste-Dominique - 45 55 91 80
M. Potier. Open daily until 10 p.m. Air cond. Parking. Pets allowed. Telex 250019. Cards: V, AE, DC, MC.

The cuisine of the new chef, Marc Bayon, is about the only thing that unites the right and left wings these days at the nearby National Assembly. This Lyon-born chef comes by way of Marseille, bringing a burst of sunshine to the neighborhod. His "decorative" cuisine is so pretty we'd like to frame it, yet he doesn't rest on appearance alone. There's also plenty of flavor to be found in the stunning cold vegetable omelet (with slivers of smoked salmon); sweetbreads terrine with prawns and an onion-orange compote; Breton lobster cooked to perfection, married with olive oil; little "bundles" of red mullet, salmon and merlu surrounded by fennel roots and exquisite green vegetables; "pascalines" of lamb (noisettes, feet, sweetbreads, brains, tongue) with little Provençal stuffings; glazed nougat with fruit and creamed saffron; and crunchy chocolate with a pistachio mousse. Everything rings of powerful flavors, precise and sharp, that express the charm of Mediteranean cuisine.

A la carte: 350-500F. Menu: 210F (weekday lunch only).

⑬ Aux Délices de Szechuen
40, av. Duquesne - 43 06 22 55
Mme. Lau. Open until 10:30 p.m. Closed Mon., Aug. 1-22 & Dec. 22-26. Air cond. Terrace dining. No pets. Cards: V, AE.

The cooking here is generally Chinese and occasionally Szechwan tailored to Western tastes, the decor is subdued Oriental with a lovely overhanging terrace, the service is excellent, and the clientele is stylish and from the neighborhood. As for the food, it's overwhelmingly civilized (no outrageous exotic items): crab-leg soup, sautéed chicken with walnuts, beef filet with spiced orange peel (it could stand more peel) and lovely coriander-flavored steamed turbot.

A la carte: 220F. Menu: 87F (weekdays only).

⑱ Le Divellec
107, rue de l'Université - 45 51 91 96
M. Le Divellec. Open until 10 p.m. Closed Sun., Mon., Aug., Dec. 24-Jan. 4. Air cond. Pets allowed. Cards: V, AE, DC.

The blue-and-white dining room, with natural-colored fabrics and candles aglow in sparkling chandeliers, looks like an exclusive yacht club. And you should be aware that the maître d' in gray flannel who appears promptly at your table is not just anybody. His name is Antoine Ventura, an articulate, witty and, on occasion, sarcastic man who recently penned an amusing book about his profession, which diners would do well to consult before letting Ventura show them to their seats.

Le Divellec himself is a gentle giant whose affability is as renowned as his love for the briny deep and its denizens. Since his personal tastes lean to simple, straightforward preparations of his cherished fish and crustaceans, we are perplexed by his recent forays into fussy, haute cuisine–style cookery. Take, for example, the wonderfully firm, beautifully cooked red mullet, whose flavor was cancelled out by a vaguely Moroccan garnish based on pickled lemons; or the savory sautéed tuna paired unsuccessfully (in our view) with duck foie gras. Is it to please a certain faction of his clientele that he's gone overboard? It's a pity, for Le Divellec's special genius is preserving and enhancing the delicate, natural flavors of seafood. We'd swim a mile for his briny Breton oysters, expertly seasoned warm crab, meaty prawns steamed on a bed of seaweed, fish soup with garlicky rouille, goujonettes of sole with periwinkle butter, bass cooked in its skin with shallot cream or sublimely simple baked lobster with a coral-based sauce.

We feel we must also mention the complaints that have come our way about niggardly portions and negligent service. The latter problem now seems to be solved, or nearly solved. But the wine service remains well below par for an establishment of this caliber.

A la carte: 650F and up. Menus: 250F and 350F (lunch only).

16 Duquesnoy
6, av. Bosquet - 47 05 96 78
M. Duquesnoy. Open until 10:15 p.m. Closed Sat. lunch, Sun. & Aug. Air cond. Pets allowed. Cards: V, AE.

Jean-Paul Duquesnoy moved in during the summer of 1987 to a decor—willow-green walls framed by antique, well-lit paneling—that celebrated the glories of Burgundy. Although the atmosphere is less beguilingly feminine than in the other Duquesnoy on the rue des Bernardins, it's quite comfortable. Françoise Duquesnoy is there to greet you, and her staff actively looks after you. Chef Duquesnoy operates in spacious kitchens instead of the cramped, smoky quarters he had before, and this alone has lifted his spirits. Not to mention the heady excitement of seeing his tables fill up regularly (his next-door neighbors/customers are TV executives and government officials armed with their legendary expense accounts). His delicate cuisine doesn't vary much, but it would be hard to tire of the red mullet with flaked potatoes, the sweetbreads roasted in celery juice, the andouillette in puff pastry with a sauce Choron (béarnaise sauce with tomatoes) and the fondant of pigs' feet and foie gras en croûte that accompanies salad greens in walnut oil. But why is the salad disparaged by referring to it as "petite"? And why is the salmon in an herb vinaigrette? And while we're listing our complaints, we might as well let on that we can't rave about the terrine of eggplant and anchovies, and that the pasta in lobster ravioli was lumpish. Desserts, on the other hand, are feathery light, particu-

larly the honey-and-nut glazed nougat with caramel sauce, which is superb. Excellent wine list at more or less reasonable prices.

A la carte: 400-600F. Menus: 220F (lunch only).

15 La Ferme Saint-Simon
6, rue St-Simon - 45 48 35 74
M. Vandenhende. Open until 10:15 p.m. Closed Sat. lunch, Sun. & Aug. 1-21. Air cond. Pets allowed. Cards: V.

Government officials pay closer attention to their lunch plates here at the farm (ferme) than to their morning sessions at the nearby Palais-Bourbon. The regulars are fairly prominent people who feel at home in this light interior—a trifle too ornate—extended by another smaller, cozier room opening into the winter garden, with its trellis and clumps of fake greenery hanging from the ceiling. Francis Vandenhende manages his Ferme Saint-Simon and his Manoir de Paris on the rue Pierre Demours (seventeenth arrondissement) down to the last detail. The same cordial reception awaits you, the same prompt service, and though the cuisine here isn't as ambitious as at the Manoir, it is inventive and flavorful: excellent ravioli with warm oysters and essence of seaweed, salmon filet in a butter sauce flavored with leeks, braised pigeon and a first-rate sautéed lamb with basil. The desserts are equally good: delicious apricot tarte soufflé and glazed millefeuilles. Good choice of wines, including twenty or so at about 100 francs. The bill for a meal of this caliber is quite reasonable.

A la carte: 300-350F. Menu: 185F (lunch only, wine incl.).

14 La Flamberge
12, av. Rapp - 47 05 91 37
M. Albistur. Hours & closings vary. Air cond. Pets allowed. Cards: V, AE, DC, MC.

Louis Albistur's new decor is light, cheerful and chic (tall mirrors, flowers at every table and patterned carpeting). For the longest time, he has been feeding TV stars from the rue Cognacq-Jay, and lately he has regained his form. The food is better than ever—well prepared, expensive and attentively served: prawn and artichoke salad, mixed roasted fish (salmon, sole, lotte, red snapper) served with a basil mousseline, good desserts. And let's not forget the poached oysters in Champagne sauce, which are out of this world, as is the Délice de La Flamberge, a yellow plum soup with vanilla ice cream (though it could stand a fraction less sugar).

A la carte: 350F.

14 Les Glénan

54, rue de Bourgogne - 45 51 61 09
M. Brisbois. Open until 10:30 p.m. Closed Sat. lunch, Sun. & Aug. Pets allowed. Cards: V, AE, DC.

At lunchtime, government officials can order a light, refreshing, ideal meal—timbale of smoked salmon with mussels, filet of roast sea bream with zucchini, and a caramelized grapefruit—before heading back to their benches in the Chamber of Deputies. In the evening, however, you'll want to linger in the freshly redecorated dining room, over the fine seafood prepared by the new head chef, Jean-Luc Sanguillon. Though technically sound and curious to try out new combinations and contrasts of flavors, he still seems a trifle unsure of himself: too much raw fish, too many finely minced or shredded preparations and superfluous "exotic" afterthoughts (like those mangoes atop the superb tomato-garnished turbot). Surely he'll work things out—and judging from his delicious garlic-flavored cod soufflé and faultless apple tart, he's already starting to. Well-rounded wine cellar.

A la carte: 300F. Menu: 140F.

12/20 L'Oeillade

10, rue St-Simon - 42 22 01 60
Mmes. Kornicki & Papadopoulos. Open until 9:45 p.m. Closed Sat. lunch, Sun. & holidays. Air cond. Pets allowed. Cards: V, AE, DC.

Inspired by their success, Evelyne and Catherine are adding more fixed-price menus. The food is as good and fresh as ever, and the portions as generous. For example, for 120 francs you can order fig sorbet, melon and mango atop smoked breast of duck, leg of lamb in cumin butter and a delectable apple tart. With a small pitcher of Côtes-du-Rhône or Sauvignon for 10 francs, you won't be ruined.

A la carte: 150F. Menus: 82F (lunch only), 99F, 126F.

15 Le Récamier

4, rue Récamier - 45 48 86 58
M. Cantegrit. Open until 10:30 p.m. Closed Sun. Air cond. Garden dining. Parking. Pets allowed. Cards: V, DC, MC.

Is it because he suspects that the publishers who patronize his restaurant really can't read that Martin Cantegrit has stopped revising his à la carte menu? In any event, this delightful Burgundian has no reason to worry; his Empire dining room and, on sunny days, the terrace—an oasis in this dead-end street that opens onto a minigarden—have been packed for years. So there's no point asking your waiter for the menu. Simply order eggs en meurette, wild mushroom terrine, and boeuf bourguignon or veal kidneys in Santenay wine. All the dishes are good and well presented; the wines, exquisite; the atmosphere, pleasantly subdued. So what's there to complain about? Only the tab, which tops the cooking!

A la carte: 350-450F.

14 Tan Dinh

60, rue de Verneuil - 45 44 04 84
MM. Vifian. Open until 11 p.m. Closed Sun. & Aug. 1-15. Pets allowed. No cards.

Always packed (in the evening, at least), this inviting restaurant is done in light, modern tones and avoids any junky, "exotic" effects. M. Vifian Sr. and his two sons, Robert in the kitchen and Freddy, who manages the dining room and the sumptuous cellar, are men of great taste and refinement. They have absorbed French culture while retaining their Vietnamese heritage, and the outstanding success of their double cuisine is unparalleled in Paris. It's a modern version of traditional Vietnamese cooking—call it an Asian response to French nouvelle cuisine. After looking over the short menu (a relief from the customary telephone directory you have to wade through), you'll want to try the golden triangles stuffed with lobster and ginkgo nuts, scallop fritters with water chestnuts, salad of crab and mango, red mullet with coriander seeds, sea bream rolled in leeks and cumin, tender morsels of lamb simmered with lemon grass, ravioli stuffed with smoked goose, or lamb stew with a pungent oyster sauce. You won't believe your eyes when you see the wine list, which includes a fantastic collection of Pomerols that would impress even a Bordeaux vintner.

A la carte: 225-300F.

10/20 Le Télégraphe

41, rue de Lille - 40 15 06 65
M. Marck. Open daily until 12:45 a.m. Air cond. Garden dining. Pets allowed. Cards: V, AE, DC, MC.

Le Télégraphe represents an outstanding remodeling operation performed on a 1900-vintage building that once housed a branch of the postal, telephone and telegraph services. The spacious dining room is alive with a crew of efficient waitresses and a cuisine that slips down the gullet like a letter down a mailbox (scallops au gros sel, basil-flavored skate, roast meats).

Menu/carte: 175F (wine incl.).

12/20 Thoumieux 🍴

79, rue St-Dominique - 47 05 49 75
M. Bassalert. Open until 11:30 p.m. Closed Mon. Pets allowed. Telex 205635. No cards

This old bistro has been redecorated in the Parisian style, but it didn't lose its Corrèze atmosphere in the process. Prices are kind to the wallet, and the plates are well heaped with serious, solid regional cooking: homemade cassoulet with duck confit, sausage from the Limousin and calf's head, among other entrées. The house red costs 30 francs and is fruity like a Cahors.

A la carte: 160F. Menu: 47F.

Jules Verne

17 Eiffel Tower (2nd level) - 45 55 61 44
M. Ody. Open daily until 10:30 p.m. Air cond. Parking. Telex 205789. Cards: V, AE, DC.

Perched on the knees of a tower that recently celebrated its 100th birthday, Jules Verne is still just a kid: eleven years old in 1990, but what a bundle of health! Once the public's curiosity was satisfied, the success of this steel-and-glass landmark pinned to the Paris skyline could have tumbled faster than spent fireworks on Bastille Day. Yet the reservation book keeps filling up, and Parisians who haven't been back since they wore knee pants long to give it another go. Oddly enough, you see fewer foreigners than in the other great Paris restaurants. Instead of becoming a tourist attraction, Jules Verne has endeared itself to Parisians, who flock to its tables as eagerly as to Robuchon, Savoy and Taillevent.

Award-winning chef Louis Grondard isn't one to rest on his laurels; indeed, success seems to inspire this modest, hard-working cook. His excellent cuisine is classic yet light, with a modern, imaginative touch that comes through in Provençal asparagus napped in a mousseline sauce sparked with blood-orange juice, in red mullet with tomato butter, accompanied by chicken-liver ravioli, in scallops paired with nutmeg-scented Belgian endive, in salmon spiced with star anise, and in a surprising cinnamon sauce that enlivens a darkly delicious bitter-chocolate cake. What's more, this alumnus of Taillevent and Maxim's de Roissy creates these dishes in a cabin-sized kitchen that vibrates with every gust of wind!

A la carte: 600F. Menu: 220F (weekday lunch only).

EIGHTH ARRONDISSEMENT

12/20 L'Alsace

39, av. des Champs-Elysées
43 59 44 24
M. Blanc. Open daily 24 hours. Air cond. Terrace dining. Pets allowed. Telex 280888. Cards: V, AE, DC.

The worst thing about this big corner brasserie that never sleeps used to be its pale pseudo-Alsatian decor. Then Slavik stepped in, bringing trompe l'oeil decorations, beveled mirrors and warm, rosy lighting. The improved decor can only attract more customers to the magnificent oysters and excellent Sauerkraut for which this restaurant is known. Very good Alsatian wines.

A la carte: 250F.

Les Ambassadeurs
(Hôtel de Crillon)
10, pl. de la Concorde - 42 65 24 24
M. Roche. Open daily until 10:30 p.m. Air cond. Terrace dining. Parking. No pets. Telex 290241. Cards: V, AE, DC.

Before he became an international pastry guru, Christian Constant was once the right arm of chef Guy Legay at the Ritz (no less). Nostalgic, perhaps, for the rarefied air of a luxury hotel, he now commands the Crillon's kitchens, replacing André Signoret, who had replaced Jean-Paul Bonin. In short, chefs may come and go, but the grand French culinary tradition remains firmly in place within the marble walls of one of the capital's most spectacular dining rooms. Soon after his arrival, Constant served us a solid three-toque meal. Light and delicious, refined but not precious, it was the work of a thoroughbred pro. Our next visit found us seated under the parasols on a (rather skimpily) flowered patio, wondering why our enthusiasm had waned. Was it because the food's flavors seemed insufficiently defined, the seasonings too timid? The crayfish and purslane salad with an anemic garnish of Greek mushrooms, the andouillette of pigs' trotters, the red mullet sautéed with spices and the pigeon wings with foie gras were not triple-toque material. On the other hand, several other dishes were: casserole-roasted Bresse chicken with tarragon, an old-fashioned blancmange (a kind of pudding) and a craquelin (light, crispy cake) with preserved chestnuts and praline sauce. The cellar, too, is top-notch, tended by Jean-Claude Maître. Tabs are predictably stiff at Les Ambassadeurs, but the fixed-price menu served at lunch is a royal bargain, for such luxury and elegance.
A la carte: 600-800F. Menu: 280F (weekday lunch only).

12/20 L'Artois
13, rue d'Artois - 42 25 01 10
M. Rouzeyrol. Open until 9:30 p.m. Closed Sat., Sun., Easter, July 14-Sept. 1 & Dec. 25. Pets allowed. No cards.

A rustic, casual decor that hasn't changed for 30 years, and service by friendly waitresses under the direction of Isidore Rouzeyrol, the founder's son: Viva l'Auvergne! The cuisine runs to grilled boudin from Corrèze, homemade pork products, coq au vin de Cahors,

apricot tart and good bottles of wine that run about 70 francs.
A la carte: 210F.

11/20 L'Assiette au Boeuf
123, av. des Champs-Elysées
47 20 01 13
See Sixth Arrondissement.

Bacchus Gourmand
21, rue François-Ier - 47 20 15 83
M. Signoret. Open until 10:30 p.m. Closed Sat., Sun. & Aug. Air cond. Terrace dining. Pets allowed. Cards: V, AE, DC.

A fortune went into the creation of this spacious restaurant in the cellars of the Maison de la Vigne et du Vin (House of Vineyards and Wine). The round interior is simple and luxurious, the waiters wear tuxedos and white gloves, and the bill is worth its weight in gold. The wine list has been greatly improved, but with food priced this high, one certainly can't expect to find many "little" wines. The cooking, after having gotten off to a great start, has become mired in needless complexities, costly ingredients and the confusion of form with substance. Why add both raspberry vinegar and juniper butter to smoked salmon? Why combine both capers and red onions with sweetbreads? And why serve magnificent veal ribs en croûte when the pastry arrives soggy? We're not saying that Bacchus Gourmand is unworthy of a toque, but it is unworthy of two. And is it worth the price?
A la carte: 450-600F. Menu: 280F.

Baumann Marbeuf
15, rue Marbeuf - 47 20 11 11
M. Baumann. Open until 1 a.m. Closed Sat. lunch, Sun. & July 10-Aug. 28. Air cond. Terrace dining. Pets allowed. Cards: V, AE, DC, MC.

Guy-Pierre Baumann is the self-appointed ambassador of superlative Bazas beef in Paris. He ages the beef slowly in a cold-storage room before trimming it into loins, standing ribs and spareribs. Meat fanciers will also appreciate his Scottish beef and tartare dishes. The Baumann choucroute (with bacon, duck or fish) is famous, oysters and shellfish are on display in a large bed of ice, and there is a variety of desserts. The upstairs dining room has been remodeled by Slavik to resemble a Belle Epoque Viennese pastry shop. The chef is from

Le Camélia; good wines are listed for less than 100 francs (excellent Riesling and Pinot Noir); and, best of all, the bill in your saucer won't give you a bellyache.

A la carte: 220F.

12/20 Le Boeuf sur le Toit

34, rue du Colisée - 43 59 83 80

M. Bucher. Open daily until 2 a.m. Air cond. Pets allowed. Telex 281396. Cards: V, AE, DC.

They say that everything Jean-Paul Bucher touches turns to gold, and he continues to cash in at this building, declared "historic," where business failures were once the norm. Each night a dinner crowd of well-heeled Parisians besieges the spacious dining room, redecorated in a 1925-era style; and now the siege extends to afternoon tea or cocktails. Also, if you're an overworked mother, the management will organize a special birthday celebration for your darling youngster. The kitchen, which for a while seemed to have run out of steam, has bounced back and is serving such respectable brasserie fare as fresh foie gras, oysters (superb display at the entrance), cassoulet of goose, rib of beef, and pigs' feet.

A la carte: 200-300F. Menu: 350F (wine incl.).

11/20 La Boutique à Sandwichs

12, rue du Colisée - 43 59 56 69

MM. Schick. Open until 1 a.m. Closed Sun. & Aug. Pets allowed. Cards: V.

Come here for delicious sandwiches: They're fresh and tasty, and there's a variety to choose from. A few regional (Valais) items and the famous pickelfleish (beef brisket à l'Alsacienne) are served at crowded tables on two levels in typical deli fashion.

A la carte: 130F.

11/20 Brasserie Löwenbräu

84, av. des Champs-Elysées
45 62 78 63

M. Rath. Open daily until 2 a.m. Air cond. Parking. Cards: V, AE, DC, MC.

Brass fixtures, Tyrolean songs and dirndl skirts on the mezzanine, along with so-so choucroute served in an arena-like setting tucked away behind the shopping arcade. And, of course, draft beer is drawn from kegs shipped directly by the breweries.

A la carte: 250F.

15 Le Bristol

112, rue du Faubourg-Saint-Honoré
42 66 91 45

M. Marcelin. Open daily until 10:30 p.m. Air cond. Parking. No pets. Telex 280961. Cards: V, AE, DC, MC.

While the city's luxury-hotel business is stumbling, Le Bristol marches resolutely forward, secure in its position as one of the finest hotels in town. Le Bristol's restaurant is a sight less successful, though the posh international set maintains a steady presence. And when the warm weather returns, the restaurant moves to its summer quarters around the delightful inner garden, hidden away in the heart of Faubourg-Saint-Honoré, where you can enjoy a preseason country vacation in a wicker armchair. But if you had visions of a picnic on the grass in shirtsleeves, forget it! Summer and winter alike, one eats in style.

Our recent criticism of Le Bristol's wine list apparently touched a nerve, because manager Jean-Paul Lefay has since stocked up on excellent growers' Burgundies, which now keep company with the classed-growth Bordeaux in the cellar. At the stove, award-winning chef Emile Tabourdiau works with a wealth of top-notch ingredients that usually (though not always) yield appetizing results on the plate. After a botched meal, we were obliged to confiscate the Bristol's second toque, which we now gladly restore—permanently, we hope. What convinced us that the kitchen was back in its usual fine form was a tasty poached duck liver, a firm, thick escalope of turbot napped with a delicate Sauternes sauce, a classic suprême of chicken enrobed in an interesting cream of petits pois, a tender and rosy veal kidney sautéed in Pomerol and an honorable array of desserts.

A la carte: 550F and up. Menus: 370F, 450F.

12/20 Café Terminus

(HôtelConcorde-Saint-Lazare)
108, rue St-Lazare - 42 94 22 22

M. Blazy. Open daily until 11 p.m. Air cond. Parking. Pets allowed. Telex 650442. Cards: V, AE, DC, MC.

There's a piano in the entrance of this bistro, in which they serve excellent chef's specials and wine by the glass until late in the evening. In the attractive dining room decorated by Slavik and Sonia Rykiel you can order mérou (grouper) tartare with spinach sprouts and duck with raspberry vinegar. The regional menu changes each month.

A la carte: 250F. Menus: 138F, 182F.

⑬ Le Carpaccio

(Hôtel Royal Monceau)
35-39, av. Hoche - 45 62 76 87
M. Bouhellec. Open daily until 10:30 p.m. Closed Aug. Air cond. Parking. No pets. Telex 650351. Cards: V, AE, DC, MC.

Signor Paracucchi (of La Locanda dell'Angelo, near Pisa, one of the finest restaurants in Italy) drops in once in a while to check on the cuisine that bears his signature. The kitchen crew, after a long struggle to attain some degree of teamwork, has finally got its act together and is turning out a respectable product. The fettuccine with tomatoes and basil, the steamed giant shrimp from the Gulf of Genoa, the artichokes simmered in olive oil and their own juice, and the assorted fish from the grill deserved a toque. A stylish international clientele partially fills the spacious, comfortable dining room, which looks pretentious and lacks warmth. The bill, on the other hand, will singe your fingers.

A la carte: 400-600F. Menus: 250F (lunch only, wine incl.), 300F (dinner only, wine incl.).

⑬ Le Château de Chine

9, rue de La Trémoille - 47 23 80 90
Mme. Ting. Open until 11 p.m. Closed Sat. lunch. Air cond. Pets allowed. Cards: V, AE.

It's so comfortable lounging on the well-cushioned salmon-colored velveteen banquettes, being pampered by the charming Mme. Ting, who comes from Shanghai. The Chinese decor is tasteful, and the relatively short à la carte menu runs the gamut of basic, classic Chinese cuisine, attractively presented and impeccably served: five-fragrance chicken, grilled Oriental-style sole, fried ravioli and duck with pineapple.

A la carte: 200F.

⑭ Chez Edgard

4, rue Marbeuf - 47 20 51 15
M. Benmussa. Open until 12:30 a.m. Closed Sun. Terrace dining. Pets allowed. Cards: V, AE, DC, MC.

Having been patronized by a cluster of ministers and honored with his name paraded on the front page of *The Wall Street Journal*, what's next for Chez Edgard's owner, Paul Benmussa? The Académie Française? Or perhaps the presidential palace (he has fervent support on both the left and the right)? This Tunisian-born Frenchman, who might have made a respectable living running a neighborhood restaurant if he hadn't gotten the bright idea of wooing and winning the media powers-that-be, has enjoyed an amazing career. Articulate yet discreet, ambitious but realistic, he grew chummy with influential journalists (the Europe-1 radio crowd practically camps in his dining room) and incumbent and expectant ministers and secretaries of state—the people who rule and those preparing to do so. Like a magician, Benmussa orchestrates their comings and goings so that rivals never meet. Yet he still finds time to look after everyone personally, the somebodies as well as the nobodies. That's his secret: making his guests believe that each is a singularly important individual. And he does it without an ounce of flattery.

"Monsieur Paul" holds another winning card—his devoted, amiable and highly professional staff. So what about the food, you ask? It's better than ever since Chez Edgard veteran Jean-Pierre Cassagne was put in charge of the kitchen. There's nothing fancy about this solid, bourgeois fare, but the ingredients are of fine quality and their preparation is carefully overseen—witness the tasty grilled tuna with peppers and tomatoes, filet of sole au gratin with fresh noodles, flank steak with shallots and farm-raised capon with cèpes. Good wines (note that the great ones are unbeatably priced) flow in this spacious scarlet dining room, where there's always something going on to catch your eye and witty remarks to catch your ear.

A la carte: 300-400F. Menus: 230F, 285F and 335F (wine incl.).

⑬ Chez Tante Louise

41, rue Boissy-d'Anglas - 42 65 06 85, 42 65 28 19
Mme. Lhiabastres. Open until 10:30 p.m. Closed Sat., Sun., 1 wk .in May & 3 wks. in Aug. Air cond. Pets allowed. Cards: V, AE, DC.

The new owners of this cozy, 60-year-old bistro have found a deserving chef who does his best to justify the stiff tabs: well-prepared rabbit stew, for example (it's not simple), Challans duck in a light orange sauce and a perfect sauté of lamb à la printanière. The pastries (tartes, millefeuilles) are fresh and expertly made, and the everyday wines are good. The new decor is sunnier (yellow with a range of earth tones) than the last and even cozier, with nice carpeting.

A la carte: 300F. Menu: 170F.

12/20 **Chez Vong**

27, rue du Colisée - 43 59 77 12, 45 63 61 65

M. Vong Vai Lam. Open until midnight. Closed Sun. Air cond. Parking. Pets allowed. Cards: V, AE, DC.

The carved wood dividers, the large, flower-decked, attractively set tables, the authentic decorations and the cozy corner dining spots for two make Vong one of the most elegant Chinese restaurants in town. It also used to be one of the best, but has fallen off a bit in spite of such enticing specialties as Cantonese dim sum, Vietnamese ravioli, chicken gros sel and the delicious Cantonese roast duck. Excellent service and parking attendant at the door.

A la carte: 230-250F.

Chiberta

3, rue Arsène-Houssaye - 45 63 77 90, 45 63 72 44

M. Richard. Open until 11 p.m. Closed Sat., Sun., Aug. & 1 wk. end Dec. Air cond. Pets allowed. Cards: V, AE, DC.

Things are looking up for Chiberta now that Philippe Da Silva, formerly second in command, has been given full charge of the kitchen. The restaurant's repertoire of dishes now boasts the clear, well-defined flavors that it sometimes lacked in the past. And since the food is as handsomely presented as ever, a lunch or dinner in this elegant dining room, where silvery mirrors reflect opulent floral arrangements and elegant patrons, is a highly festive occasion.

Chef Da Silva has a gift for choosing herbs and spices, and he is a first-rate saucier as well. A shellfish fumet with a bass note of truffle naps lobster cannelloni like a silken mantle; a curry-and-Sauternes sauce lightly veils thick, beautifully cooked red mullet filets surrounded by fava beans and chanterelles; the fragrances of truffle and walnut oil blend suavely with a salad of baby pigeon and lobster; and meaty pieces of young rabbit escorted by a thick slice of foie gras, despite the fussy garnish of red currants,

are pure succulence. Miniature orange babas (cakes) paired with orange sorbet make a light, bright finish to a splendid repast, washed down with Rousseau's Gevrey-Chambertin '85.

Burgundies and Bordeaux are the cellar's strong suits—other regions get pretty short shrift. But the wines are judiciously selected by owner Louis-Noël Richard and Raphaël, the capable dining room manager. Chiberta has long been one of the most seductive restaurants on the Champs-Elysées, but it is now also one of the very best.

A la carte: 500-700F.

⑭ **Clovis**

(Pullman Windsor)

4, av. Bertie-Albrecht - 45 61 15 32

M. Rameau. Open until 10:30 p.m. Closed Sat., Sun., Aug. & Dec. 26-Jan. 1. Air cond. Parking. Pets allowed. Cards: V, AE, DC, MC.

The Uginox ceiling used to stick in our craw. But it disappeared, along with a tired-out decor, when this Frantel hotel restaurant was transformed into an elegant Pullman car. With its movable partitions, pastel tones, American blinds, well-spaced tables, comfortable chairs and abundant plants and flowers, the Clovis has become gracious, and can expect to attract the dinner crowd that previously snubbed it. Dominique Roué, who replaced chef Pierre Larapidie, is a talented young man who has worked with the best (La Tour d'Argent, Michel Rostang and Robuchon). His cuisine, however, did not strike us as being as good as his predecessor's. A dull oxtail stew, an overcooked scallop of sander with useless truffles, an excellent filet of veal with vegetables and good cheesecake left us thinking that we had just eaten at a one-toque restaurant. And so, for the moment, that's what it is.

Menus: 165F (dinner only), 235F (lunch only), 322F.

⑬ **Copenhague et Flora Danica**

142, av. des Champs-Elysées
43 59 20 41

M. Engstrom. Copenhague: open until 10:30 p.m.; closed Sun., Jan. 1-7 & July 30-Aug. 27. Flora: open daily until 10:30 p.m. Air cond. No pets. Cards: V, AE, DC, MC.

Invented here in 1974 and eagerly adopted throughout the gastronomic world, the recipe for salmon "of purists"—grilled on one side only—remains the chief attraction on the menu. This remarkably pale, moist salmon is also prepared in a number of other ways: in cream sauce, smoked in the Danish fashion, poached in court bouillon or with spinach. Start with an array of extraordinarily tasty herring (fried, smoked, marinated, in sour cream), and don't hesitate to follow it up with reindeer tenderloin flavored with bilberries, Frikadellen (meatballs) with red cabbage, or cured duck. You'll receive excellent service both upstairs in the comfortable, sedate atmosphere of the Copenhague and downstairs in the luxurious snack bar and attractive summer patio of Flora Danica, where you can order just about the same dishes (for just about the same price).

A la carte: 250F (Flora Danica), 350F (Copenhague).

11/20 La Cour Saint-Germain

19, rue Marbeuf - 47 23 84 25
M. Ajalbert. Open daily until midnight. Air cond. Terrace dining. Pets allowed. Cards: V, AE, DC.

This small chain (four branches in Paris) has a single formula: salad sprinkled with nuts and a piece of beef (wine and dessert are extra). Pleasant winter-garden decor.

Menu: 68F.

15 La Couronne

(Hôtel Warwick)
5, rue de Berri - 45 63 14 11,
45 63 78 49
M. Muhle. Open until 10:30 p.m. Closed Sun. & holidays. Air cond. Parking. Pets allowed. Telex 642295. Cards: V, AE, DC, MC.

Let's forget earlier disappointments and crow about the recent faultless performance: pan-fried escargots with mushrooms and beef marrow, ravioli stuffed with sea urchins and creamed scallops, braised turbot with vin jaune (yellow wine) and mashed onions, lamb pot-au-feu, veal kidneys with mushrooms, orange-flavored custard, crème brûlée with brown sugar. All these display Van Gessel at his best, a solid, top-flight chef adept at combining bold flavors and fragrances. His talent permeates the Warwick's dining room, which would otherwise be mighty dull, with its commonplace, uninspired decor. There's a good choice of wines at affordable prices (the Saint-Emilion for 95 francs is a rare find on the Champs-Elysées). The fixed-price menu at 195 francs is

also a good example of the Warwick's efforts to hold prices in check, a policy of savvy hotel managers who want to keep their rooms filled.

A la carte: 350-450F. Menu: 210F, 380F.

11/20 Drugstore des Champs-Elysées

133, av. des Champs-Elysées
47 23 54 34
M. Masetti. Open daily until 1:30 a.m. Air cond. Pets allowed. Cards: V, AE, DC.

The decor is amusing, the grownups are funny to watch, and the children happily slurp butterscotch sundaes and banana splits. There are also grilled dishes, hamburgers and even some country fare that isn't half-bad (andouillette, confits). Fast, friendly service.

A la carte: 160-180F. Menu: 60F.

11/20 Le Drugstorien

(Drugstore Matignon)
21, av. Matignon - 43 59 38 70
M. Anghelovici. Open daily until 12:30 a.m. Air cond. Pets allowed. Cards: V, AE, DC.

The pleasant terrace on the second floor boasts a panoramic view of what's doing over by the carré Marigny, the site of Marcel Proust's immortal foliage and the philatelic trade. The à la carte menu appears to be pretty tacky, but the cooking is quite respectable: good foie gras, sole with chopped chives, broiled tournedos.

A la carte: 280F. Menu: 144F.

16 Elysée-Lenôtre

10, av. des Champs-Elysées
42 65 85 10
M. Lenôtre. Open until 10:30 p.m. Closed Sat. lunch & Sun. Air cond. Terrace dining. Parking. Pets allowed. Cards: V.

The bad news recently was that supposedly well-informed diners did not think much of this turn-of-the-century landmark, once one of the royal tables in the capital. Last spring, however, its good reputation returned with the first swallows, especially with the first swallows of the customers who kept the outdoor terrace full all day during good weather. Manager Gérard Mallet and his staff have done their job well, perhaps spurred on by the recent increase in competition, notably from Ledoyen across the street. Whatever the reason, they have created a delightful oasis in this little countryside corner of central Paris, where even parking is not a problem, and where the service is a model of forethought and consideration, blessedly free of ostentatious display.

At lunch a 300-franc fixed-price menu is offered on the terrace, in the main dining room, under the languid gaze of the goddesses wriggling on the fabulous Belle Epoque wedding-cake ceiling, and upstairs in a restrained, pretty setting that is less dizzying. The choice of dishes offered on this menu is wide enough to avoid boredom: a little haddock pie with lentils, a vegetable galette with thyme flowers, a dodine of whiting and salmon (overcooked) in anchovy butter, a boneless breast of chicken braised with zucchini and graced with a delicious watercress sauce, and a light vegetable stew with a braised veal steak. Cheeses follow, as does a choice from about ten desserts, including the kitchen's latest creation, Le Plaisir, a layering of mousse and coffee sauce that was too treacly to win our admiration.

The à la carte menu obviously harbors bigger ambitions. The offerings are attractive: oysters on a bed of endive; roast prawns and a cauliflower soufflé with paprika; sea trout swimming in Sauternes; wild salmon in puff pastry; old-fashioned chicken in a pot; Norman duck with lentils, pears and cinnamon; and young Bresse pigeon with foie gras and stewed cabbage. In short, excellent ingredients are well matched with each other, and occasionally you even encounter a little creativity. Nothing is exceptional, however, nor is the dining room staff large enough to justify such daunting prices. Twenty years ago, perhaps Elysée-Lenôtre would have been perfect, but today the expectations and the competition are both so high in the luxury hotel business that one demands a little more. But we cannot deny that this is a lovely place.

A la carte: 450-800F. Menu: 300F (lunch only).

⑬ Fakhr el Dine

3, rue Quentin-Bauchart - 47 23 74 24, 47 23 44 42

M. Bou Antoun. Open daily until midnight. Air cond. Pets allowed. Cards: V, AE, DC.

This place serves one of the finest selections of mezze—those cold or hot hors d'oeuvres that you can make a meal out of as the Lebanese do—in town. Try the sanacel (salad of bone marrow), kebe naye (ground raw lamb and semolina), fatayers (meat patties with spinach), sojok (spicy sausage flamed and sprinkled with lemon) and the delectable grilled kafta (ground meat mixed with pine nuts and parsley and grilled over an open fire). This authentic ethnic fare, accompanied by potent Lebanese wines, is served in a friendly enough manner in a cozily exotic little room, all of which earns Fakhr el Dine one toque.

A la carte: 250F. Menus: 136F (lunch only), 130F.

⑭ La Fermette Marbeuf 1900

5, rue Marbeuf - 47 20 63 53, 47 23 31 31

M. Laurent. Open daily until 11:30 p.m. Terrace dining. Pets allowed. Cards: V, AE, DC, MC.

La Fermette's year-round success is no stroke of luck. The Belle Epoque decor is enchanting (it's listed as a historical landmark), the prices are reasonable (the 150-franc fixed-price menu is the best bargain in the neighborhood), there are no fewer than 32 wines for under 100 francs, and the dependable cooking avoids trendiness and concentrates on turning first-class ingredients into light, well-balanced, cleverly prepared dishes. Try the soufflé of snails with garlic butter in puff pastry, sherry-flavored omelet with goose confit, spiced escalope of bass or Bresse guinea-fowl in a cream sauce with chopped chives; then finish with the chocolate cake with a bittersweet-chocolate icing or the glazed nougat with a raspberry purée. In all, it's a cuisine created by a heroic team of culinary acrobats who withstand the daily assault of hundreds of hungry customers.

A la carte: 250-350F. Menu: 150F (dinner and Sunday and holiday lunch only).

12/20 La Fontana

26, av. des Champs-Elysées 42 25 14 72

M. Giordani. Open daily until 12:15 a.m. Air cond. Garden dining. No pets. Cards: V, AE.

The site (remodeled) of the ephemeral Prunier-Elysées is now a new Italian restaurant owned by Signor Giordani (who used to run Il Beato on the rue Malar). The terrace facing the fountain is delightful, the staff is Italian to the hilt, and the calamari fritti, scampi and baked lasagne taste pretty good.

A la carte: 180-220F. Menu: 78F.

⑬ Fouquet's

99, av. des Champs-Elysées
47 23 70 60

M. Casanova. Open daily until 12:30 a.m. Terrace dining. Pets allowed. Telex 648227. Cards: V, AE, DC, MC.

He's been working at the same stove for more than 33 years, but chef Pierre Ducroux is no graybeard, although Fouquet's will soon observe its 100th year in business. There'll be a celebration dinner in honor of the occasion, and it's sure to be a success. When the kitchen crew decides to put on a show, they turn out exceptional dishes, especially if kept to simple, traditional fare. For example, Pauillac lamb with crunchy potatoes sarladaise, juicy and perfectly cooked; or mustard-coated brill with shepherd's pie; and, on Thursdays, an extremely popular pot-au-feu in three separate dishes. A good pastry chef prepares simple but flavorful creamy desserts and light, appetizing babas. It costs 300 francs and then some to lunch, dine or have late supper in this last bastion of Parisian civility on the forlorn Champs-Elysées, whose character, alas, is lost forever.

A la carte: 300-500F. Menu: 195F.

⑭ Le Grenadin

44-46, rue de Naples - 45 63 28 92

M. Cirotte. Open until 10:30 p.m. Closed Sat., Sun., week of July 14, week of Aug. 15 & 1 week at Christmas. Air cond. Pets allowed. Cards: V, AE, DC.

Patrick Cirotte finally bought the porter's lodge next to his restaurant and transformed it into an exceptionally cheerful place, with lovely salmon-toned murals. His wife manages the dining room while he works in his pint-size basement kitchen. We liked the Sancerre ham smoked over grapevine trimmings, the thick-cut, undercooked Norwegian salmon with two sauces and the delectable bittersweet-chocolate marquise, not too sweet, with a pistachio crème anglaise. Good choice of wines, especially from Sancerre, the Cirottes' home turf, and delicious homemade breads.

A la carte: 300F and up. Menus: 180F (lunch only), 280F and 310F (dinner only).

12/20 Hédiard

21, pl. de la Madeleine - 42 66 09 00

Mme. Haug. Open until 10:30 p.m. Closed Sun. Air cond. Pets allowed. Cards: V, AE, DC.

Good, reliable cooking (on the whole) is served to a fashionable clientele at lunchtime (mostly businesswomen or their social-minded sisters) in a decor of wainscoting and pale fabrics above a catering shop. "Vintage" (skinned and boned) sardines in the can, roast Pauillac lamb and breast of duck are accompanied by expensive and wonderful house wines.

A la carte: 350F.

10/20 Hippopotamus

6, av. Franklin-Roosevelt - 42 25 77 96

M. Guignard. Open daily until 1 a.m. Air cond. Pets allowed. Cards: V.

Sometimes you run into a tough piece of beef or a foul-mouthed waitress, but after twenty years in the fast-food business (this Hippo is the granddaddy of the chain), on the whole they deserve credit for serving good grilled meats with matchstick french fries and standard sauces, along with wines by the pitcher. Other branches in the eighth arrondissement: 42, av. des Champs-Elysées (45 53 40 84); 46, av. de Wagram (46 22 13 96); 20, rue Quentin-Bauchart (47 20 30 14).

A la carte: 150F. Menu: 73F.

⑭ Indra

10, rue du Commandant-Rivière
43 59 46 40

M. Gupta. Open until 11 p.m. Closed Sat. lunch & Sun. Air cond. Pets allowed. Telex 670416. Cards: V, AE, DC, MC.

M. Gupta is your jovial host, and you'll probably feel slightly overwhelmed by the dark, hyperdecorative carved woodwork imported from his native India—as well as by the excellent Indian cooking that friendly, silent, incredibly polite waiters bring to your table. You'll enjoy tandoori specialties (from a special charcoal-fed oven); a variety of curries, including shrimp, chicken and lamb; marvelous mulligatawny (lentil) soup; coconut chicken and rice; salted or sugared fritters; and seven kinds of delicious breads. Or try the Indian-style eggplant and the lamb pilaf (shahjahani), with its outstandingly fragrant basmati rice. Several kinds of homemade lassi (fermented milk) are worth tasting.

A la carte: 230F. Menus: 160F (lunch only), 190F, 220F, 240F.

⑬ Au Jardin du Printemps

32, rue de Penthièvre - 43 59 32 91

M. Tan Le-Bieng. Open until 11:30 p.m. Closed Sun. & Aug. Air cond. No pets. Cards: V, AE, DC.

The Tan brothers have a matchless flair for publicity: They love to see photos of themselves with the loyal Parisian celebrities who have been coming here for years. Perhaps the pretty decor has something to do with it, or the friendly atmosphere and consistently good Chinese-Vietnamese cuisine: shrimp flavored with mint or salted and grilled, roast chicken with lemon grass, brochette of beef marinated in sake.

A la carte: 250F.

⑭ Le Jardin du Royal Monceau

(Hôtel Royal Monceau)
35, av. Hoche - 45 62 96 02

M. Bouhellec. Open daily until 10:30 p.m. Air cond. Garden dining. Parking. No pets. Telex 650361. Cards: V, AE, DC, MC.

The Royal Monceau's vast inner courtyard becomes a picture-book flower garden in summer. A harpist plays in the evening, the notes echoed by songbirds; you'd think you were lost in the country, miles from the Champs-Elysées. Chef Gabriel Biscay's cuisine attempts to promote this gentle illusion—not by extravagant means but with light, richly flavored dishes that are elegantly presented: roast filets of red mullet with olive butter and cardamom, pan-fried lotte in red wine and chives, stir-fried lamb with lemon and saffron and delicious desserts. Light, appetizing dishes are served in a leafy setting around the hotel's splendid basement swimming pool.

A la carte: 450-500F. Menu: 260F.

⑮ Lamazère

23, rue de Ponthieu - 43 59 66 66

M. Lamazère. Open until 11 p.m. Closed Sun. & Aug. Air cond. Parking. No pets. Cards: V, AE, DC, MC.

Though he's a talented magician, it is highly unlikely that Roger Lamazère recognized the Gault Millau reviewer who recently came away from two meals at Lamazère with contradic-

tory impressions. The first experience was marred by an insipid prawn soufflé with chervil butter, followed by overcooked turbot braised with criste-marine (a kind of seaweed); yet a second visit yielded a fine traditional repast of fresh foie gras, mellow duck confit with sautéed potatoes and fat Agenais prunes soaked in lusty Cahors wine. It's as if the chef's magic touch deserted him when he abandoned his native Périgord and its robust products. It could also be that Roger Lamazère has too much on his mind of late, what with his new food-processing venture. He has been a favorite of ours for so long, since his early days in a bistro on rue des Martyrs, where he introduced Parisians to southwestern fare back in the '60s, that we feel we can speak frankly to our old friend: Roger, please, use your magic powers to put your restaurant back on track!

A la carte: 500-700F. Menu: 290F (lunch only, wine incl.).

⑯ Lasserre

17, av. Franklin-Roosevelt
43 59 53 43

M. Lasserre. Open until 10:30 p.m. Closed Mon. lunch, Sun. & July 30-Aug. 28. Air cond. Terrace dining. No pets. Parking. No cards.

Where in Paris can you eat lobster Newburg or a truffle in puff pastry made the way they were in 1950? Where else but Lasserre? Few restaurants can duplicate the Lasserre style of cooking even if they try. We say this in all sincerity, convinced as we are that the talent of chef Marc Daniel, a great admirer of Robuchon, is largely responsible for the success of these old-fashioned dishes. We also feel that the grandiloquent menu is properly accented by a staff trained to perform its stately ballet in the "grand manner" and by the intimidating starchiness of the lavish provincial decor, which lies open to the stars when the roof is retracted (the drapes have been cleaned; the carpeting is new). And, frankly, is it fair to insist on labeling Lasserre the repository of ostentation when René Lasserre has tried hard in recent years to evolve toward a less pompous style of cooking? In our last edition we were pleased to note a serious effort to simplify and fine-tune preparations.

Aside from a tenderloin of veal with sugar peas that was nothing to rave about, our latest meal within these venerable walls was nearly worthy of three toques: a light, fragrant feuilleté of golden, crunchy chanterelles; a perfectly poached turbot with the bone in and a faultless hollandaise sauce; followed by a marvelous cake of roasted hazelnuts and chocolate. A single question remains: Is it worth the astronomical price? You be the judge. The outstanding wine cellar is one of Paris's richest in Burgundies and Bordeaux, especially in great Bordeaux vintages. We'd like it better if the wine steward, who insists on serving reds at room temperature on the hottest days, didn't take offense at our request for a slightly chilled bottle.

A la carte: 700-800F.

Laurent

41, av. Gabriel - 47 23 79 18

M. Ehrlich. Open until 11 p.m. Closed Sat. lunch, Sun. & holidays. Air cond. Garden dining. No pets. Parking. Cards: V, AE, DC.

Laurent did well to turn over the kitchens to Bernard Guilhaudin. This 36-year-old chef, who has worked for private households (including six years with art dealer Daniel Wildenstein) and trained under Chapel, has what it takes to do well here: a modified classic approach, free of the constraints of the grand style, with clear, bold flavors and a resourceful technique. His lobster with broad beans in an chilled consommé and his miniature lobster wrapped in a feathery light crust are magnificent dishes. His bass pan-fried in its skin; thick filet of sole garnished only with mushrooms; ravioli filled with foie gras and truffle essence; "American" charcoal-broiled steak; veal cutlet cooked on one side only and garnished with herb butter and a purée of celery stalks and tops; and such clever, elegant desserts as the "two soufflés" (warm chocolate and cold coffee) all mark the advent of a genuinely flavorful cuisine at one of the long-standing greats among Paris restaurants.

We almost forgot the wines! Philippe Bourguignon, one of the friendliest and most knowledgeable sommeliers in town, is certainly not neglecting his cellar, which he lovingly put together. Unfortunately, its prices don't make it any easier to face the final bill; there are two wines for less than 100 francs, but dinner for one can still soar to 800 francs or more.

A la carte: 600F and up. Menus: 350F (lunch only), 720F and 880F (dinner only).

Ledoyen

Carré des Champs-Elysées

47 42 23 23

M. Nessi. Open until 10:30 p.m. (Carré 12:30 a.m.). Closed Sun. Garden dining. No pets. Parking. Telex 642116. Cards: V, AE, DC.

While attending Régine's glittering housewarming for Ledoyen, her latest Parisian venture, we felt a distinct urge to make things more than just warm for decorator François Lamotte. Inspired, it appears, by the sublime sets of Visconti's classic film, *The Leopard*, Lamotte came up with a decor that the Leopard himself, that proud Sicilian aristocrat, would surely find (as we did) full of errors and lapses of taste.

Were the building and gardens not so fine, were the volumes and proportions of the rooms not so remarkable, we wouldn't bother to make an issue of the decor. But it's hard not to imagine—and regret—what might have been made of the place, given the enormous effort and sums of money that went into it. The basic idea is appealing enough, and indeed there is a lot to like about this sumptuous collection of expensive bits and pieces: the woodwork in the main dining room (called Le Guépard), the handsome upholstery, the tubs that hold a lush profusion of plants, and the artful lighting. And how can one resist the drolly kitsch atrium, where stained glass, classical columns and campy torch-bearing bayadères parody the foyer of a high-class nineteenth-century bordello?

But it is precisely because Lamotte so nearly got it right that his slip-ups are all the more noticeable—and irritating. Why on earth did he choose that garnet-hued carpet, which manages to clash with every other color around it? Why are the "cloud-edged" ceilings so ineptly painted, and the bay windows dressed with silly, skimpy *bouillonné* curtains? And in the otherwise attractive blond-wood-paneled bar, why did Lamotte perpetrate that dreadful color scheme of orange on bordeaux? It certainly doesn't induce one to linger over a drink!

As for Le Carré des Champs-Elysées, a separate dining room (with a terrace for sunny days) designed with business lunches and dinners in mind, it is naturally done in a sober, subdued style. Yet Lamotte might have tried a bit harder: The merest touch of charm or whimsy would have given the room a much-needed lift. Is it too late to set things right? Probably not. Régine, never one to walk away from a challenge, may just take it into her head to do it all over again.

Jacques Maximin designed Le Guépard's menu and supervised the kitchen for a short period just after the opening. Now his former associate, Philippe Dorange, has taken over those duties, though Maximin puts in brief appearances when he can tear himself away from his own new venture in Nice. Only prime, costly raw materials pass the portals of the kitchen, where they are transformed into the "neo-Provençal" dishes that are Maximin's trademark. On two visits, we found the hot offerings superior to the cold ones, which evinced a bland, "made ahead and made to last" quality typical of catered food. Not that the hot dishes were problem-free: a crayfish bouillon with chanterelles was lackluster, lasagne with John Dory seemed anemic, and a harsh reduction of lamb juices marred a tian of lamb, spinach and zucchini. These disappointments were redeemed by a brilliant millefeuille of lobster and polenta, shellfish ratatouille with basil butter, and a daube of John Dory in a mushroom fumet with gnocchi (we could have gorged on that last dish till we burst!). And a silken, ethereal gratin of lobster and macaroni was a little masterpiece, truly vintage Maximin. Desserts—frozen mandarin confit, almondy crêpes with Grand Marnier, petits fours and chocolates—are dizzyingly delicious, fashioned by a gifted young pastry chef. Dizzying, too, is the speed with which the check rises to vertiginous heights—particularly since the cellar is rich in great Bordeaux, well stocked with fine Burgundies and utterly deficient in modest regional bottles.

Food at the less-expensive Le Carré des Champs-Elysées is less ambitious and, frankly, much less memorable (our two-toque rating applies only to Le Guépard). But if we overlook the clumsily seasoned salad and quite overcooked fish, Le Carré's chef turns out some perfectly decent bourgeois dishes, such as onion soup gratinée, chicken with mustard and steak with shallots.

Le Guépard: A la carte, 800F; menus, 500F, 600F, 700F. Le Carré des Champs-Elysées: menus, 250F and 350F (wine incl.).

La Ligne
30, rue Jean-Mermoz - 42 25 52 65, 43 59 15 16

M. Speyer. Open until 10:30 p.m. Closed Sat., Sun. & Aug. Air cond. Pets allowed. Cards: V, AE, DC.

Jean Speyer has sold his restaurant to a new owner, who was in the process of rejuvenating the decor at the time of this writing. In contrast to some of our readers' experiences, we found a cheerful reception, efficient service and the good cooking of new chef Roger Pauly, who has a slightly complicated but elegant style: scallops and prawns in saffron, perfectly steamed bass filet in a lovely ginger sauce and a remarkable layered pastry of crêpes with kiwis, apples and oranges.

A la carte: 400F. Menu: 250F (wine incl.).

Le Lord Gourmand
9, rue Lord-Byron - 43 59 07 27, 45 62 66 06

M. Borne. Open until 10:30 p.m. Closed Sat. & Sun. Pets allowed. Cards: V, AE.

Roland Borne, Le Lord Gourmand's new owner/chef, had barely gotten his feet wet when we ate at his restaurant, and still it was worth at least a toque. We expect this rating to be confirmed and even raised, just as soon as this well-trained young chef gains control of his new place, finishes his daytime military service and has a chance to improve the intimate but dog-eared decor. Try the grilled bass and skate in a cold bouillabaisse and the fatted Bresse fowl in a pot-au-feu with truffles. The dessert list needs rounding out and the prices rounding down.

A la carte: 300 and up. Menus: 165F (lunch only), 300F (dinner only).

Lucas-Carton
9, pl. de la Madeleine - 42 65 22 90
M. Senderens. Open until 10:30 p.m. Closed Sat., Sun., July 27-Aug. 20 & Dec. 21-Jan. 2. Air cond. Parking. No pets. Telex 281088. Cards: V.

If Alain Senderens has a pet subject, it's the need for a culinary copyright. Imitators—and there are hordes of them—drive him up the wall, and he can't see why a special dish doesn't warrant the same artistic protection as a song or a couturier's design. The public doesn't care a bit about such futile debates. They don't want to hear who invented salade folle, truffle soup, stuffed zucchini flowers or bay scallop ravioli. They know that each "creation" is derived from a prior or parallel one, and what makes the difference is an element that defies protection: talent.

Everyone must have had the experience of turning out a second-rate copy by botching a recipe, not to mention an entire meal. Lucas-Carton proved this not long ago with a dinner prepared by Senderens, but not Senderens at his best. This type of slip happens to every great chef—his clients also have their off days—and argues less in favor of artistic protection than simple modesty. But let's close the subject and recall the positive things . . . for instance, the marvelous millefeuille of foie gras with celery and apples accompanied by a glass of mellow Jurançon; cod cooked in its skin (all juices thereby kept intact) garnished with herbed potatoes; a fabulous dish of rabbit named for Senderens's grandmother, Isidoria (the loin wrapped in caul fat, brushed with mustard and roasted, then the front legs oven-braised, the thigh meat shredded and mixed with herbs and foie gras, while the kidneys and liver were served separately on the side), escorted by a '76 Chinon from Couly-Dutheil; veal kidney with fava beans paired with Nau's '82 Bourgueil; and chocolate cake perfumed with raspberries, perfectly partnered with a Pineau des Charentes. It's a dazzling performance, a sublime succession of flavors, for which we thank not only the master of the house but his executive chef, Bertrand Gueneron, and his lieutenant, Philippe Peudenier.

Some readers are immune to the "Senderens magic." They complain about the food, the stingy portions (they have a point there) and the offhand service (there, too); they also profess shock at the tabs. But we're not shocked. Luxury, as they say, has its price, and if you feel like spending 20,000 francs at Lucas-Carton for a bottle of Pétrus 1945, don't complain about it afterward to the Office of Consumer Affairs. Moreover, stung by such bad-mouthing, Senderens has come up with a pair of "business" fixed-price menus that give smaller budgets the chance to get in on the fun (as long as they do it at lunchtime).

Upstairs, indiscreet affairs once flourished over Champagne bottles, and on November 10, 1918, Clemenceau, Foch and the Allied command sat around a table and arranged the hour of the Armistice. Nowadays, the private rooms are reserved for business luncheons, while in the gray-and-blue "club room," Paris yuppies and entertainment people rub elbows and eat home-cooking for the price they would pay downstairs for a bottle of Meursault.

A la carte: 700-800F and up. Menus: 350F and 400F (lunch only), 700F, 900F (wine incl.).

⑬ Le Manoir Normand
77, bd de Courcelles - 42 27 38 97
M. Pommerai. Open until 10:30 p.m. Closed Sun. Terrace dining. Pets allowed. Cards: V, AE, DC.

Each day has its special dish: veal tenderloin with crayfish on Monday, chicken with mushrooms on Tuesday, veal kidney on Wednesday, and so it goes. What we like best of all is the succulent chicken that Rémi Pommerai roasts on a spit that you can watch turning in the huge fireplace, which, along with the two lobster tanks, false timbers in the ceiling and other "inventions," ornaments his fanciful manor house. The cooking is always reliable and not as heavy as you might expect, for Pommerai is an able craftsman. The excellent fixed-price menu includes a sausage-and-potato salad made with olive oil, a baron of rabbit with fresh pasta and a homemade tarte.

A la carte: 260-280F. Menu: 125F.

⑭ Le Marcande
52, rue de Miromesnil - 42 65 19 14
M. Pouliquen. Open until 10:30 p.m. Closed Sat., Sun. & Aug. 5-28. Pets allowed. Cards: V, AE, DC.

We tend to expect something a little better from the teamwork of that great chef Michel Lorain (La Côte Saint-Jacques in Joigny), who plans the menu, and bearded Thierry Lemoine, a pupil of Lorain's who carries it out. Still, the poached eggs with wild asparagus, fresh cod and puréed garlic, and filets of red mullet in white sauce that we had at our last meal were not disappointing. And in summer, when you can escape the dreary dining room decor, the pleasure of eating in the delightful garden courtyard is dulled only by the shock of reading the bill. First-class service.

A la carte: 400F. Menus: 210F (lunch only), 380F (dinner only).

La Marée

1, rue Daru - 47 63 52 42

M. Trompier. Open until 10:30 p.m. Closed Sat., Sun. & July 29-Aug. 29. Air cond. Parking. Cards: V, DC.

'Tis a sad thing indeed to sit down to a meal in a spot we've happily frequented for more than 30 years to find nothing—but nothing— to praise on our plates. That's what happened to us recently at La Marée. It all started with an utterly bland fish piccata served with a salad of undercooked cold potatoes. Next came overcooked cod in a pretty good garlic-spiked tomato sauce. Finally, we were presented with a pear feuilleté with a heavy, doughy crust. Now, we don't think such a collection of dishes is worthy of Eric Trompier, a charming young host who loves the business he inherited from his father, Marcel, or of longtime La Marée chef Gérard Rouillard, whose classic repertoire has (until now) never failed to please. Was it the departure of his excellent sous-chef that derailed his culinary train?

To make sure our experience wasn't just a fluke, we sent two of our reviewers (separately, and anonymously, of course) to assess the situation. Alas, their impressions confirmed our own: One spoke of tough pastry, obviously prepared ahead, in a dish of curried langoustines; the other lamented a mushy, overcooked steamed sea bass and a cottony turbot with mustard sauce. Nor did the platter of little pastries, of very uneven quality, elicit much enthusiasm, for while the savarin, the coffee éclair and the praline meringue were delicate and good, the pear and blueberry tarts were so-so at best. In short, the team in the kitchen must pull itself together if La Marée is to remain among Paris's top seafood restaurants. To be sure, loyal patrons from the worlds of politics and business keep the reservation book full. But if the food continues its slide, even they may tire of patronizing the aging, dim dining room, embellished solely by two fine paintings of the Flemish school.

Two trump cards that the restaurant retains are its flawless service and a wine list that numbers more than 500 different labels. Prize-winning sommelier Didier Bordas has moved on, leaving the cellar in the hands of bashful young M. Bertin. Despite these good things, we cannot let La Marée retain its third toque— though we remove it in the fervent hope that we shall soon be able to put it back.

A la carte: 450-700F.

Martin Alma

44, rue Jean-Goujon - 43 59 28 25, 43 59 28 78

M. Casanova. Open until 11:30 p.m. Closed Sun. dinner & Mon. Air cond. Parking. Cards: V.

A favorite hangout of Paris socialites in the 1950s that subsequently fell from grace (for good reasons), Martin Alma was recently taken over by Charles Casanova and redecorated by Jean Dives (of *Maison et Jardin* magazine). Blue and black tiles, natural-wood dividers and comfortable zebra-striped armchairs make for an attractive, sophisticated backdrop for the humble couscous ritual. The cuisine remains North African (plus paella on Wednesdays), with magnificent appetizers (salad of roast peppers), lamb tajine (stew) with lemon, and couscous mechoui served with tasty spit-roasted lamb that you can watch turning. We give it one toque.

A la carte: 250F.

Maxim's

3, rue Royale - 42 65 27 94

M. Cardin. Open daily until 11:30 p.m. (1 a.m. Sat.). Closed Sun. in July & Aug. Parking. No pets. Telex 210311. Cards: V, AE, DC.

Maxim's old habitués will tell you that people don't go to the world's most beautiful restaurant merely to eat. Eat! What a vulgar idea! There is so much to see, to hear and to gossip about at this monument to the high life, where crowned heads and merchant princes once lived it up like there was no tomorrow. Who cares if the salmon koulibiac (pastry-wrapped pie) is about as flaky as a headstone? So what if the lamb stew is spoiled by a strong, gluey stock? What's the difference if you order a pastry and the waiter brings you something resembling heavy artillery?

All kidding aside, chef Michel Menant is a great cook—or could be, in a 50-seat restaurant. But since he is obliged to serve hundreds of meals each day, he can't always guarantee quality. Yet on occasion he does turn out some delicious dishes, like the excellent beef in aspic we enjoyed the other day, along with some succulent Bresse chicken with fresh morels. Another time we greedily gobbled up a dish of poached lobster followed by baby lamb with eggplant gratin. The trouble is, all you can be sure of when you eat at Maxim's is that the check will be staggering (quail eggs with caviar are a steal—or should we say grand larceny?—at 370 francs). Actually, you can also be sure of an urbane welcome from Jean-Pierre Guéval, a model of courtesy, and of service in the grand manner, with wordly maître d's and gangly busboys straight out of a Feydeau farce.

The Maxim's magic, somehow, incredibly, survives, as ageless as the naked ladies on the walls, who gaze languorously on giddy tourists and noisy parvenus. Nowadays Maxim's is most Maxim's at midday, when the Parisian elite gather for lunch. And despite our carping, it remains the most romantic spot in town to celebrate a love affair, an anniversary, a divorce . . . any occasion when Champagne and violins are *de rigueur.*

A la carte: 500F (lunch), 800F (dinner).

12/20 L'Obélisque

(Hôtel de Crillon)
10, pl. de la Concorde - 42 65 24 24
M. Roche. Open until 10:30 p.m. Closed Sat. dinner, Sun. & Aug. No pets. Telex 290241. Cards: V, AE, DC, MC.

From his kitchens at Le Grand Véfour, André Signoret plans and directs food operations at the Crillon's luxurious quick-service restaurant, which has been redecorated by Sonia Rykiel, with paneling and velvet banquettes. You can expect a stylish clientele and fast-moving cuisine: sea trout with purée of leeks, mushroom lasagne, grilled chicken with carrot confit, excellent chocolate desserts.

A la carte: 230-250F. Menu: 170F.

Au Petit Montmorency

5, rue Rabelais - 42 25 11 19,
45 61 01 26
MM. Bouché. Open until 10:15 p.m. Closed Sat., Sun. & Aug. Air cond. Pets allowed. Cards: V.

It's like running an obstacle course when you turn off avenue Matignon into rue Rabelais, where the Israeli Embassy, through no fault of its own, makes life miserable for riverside businesses. Imagine: Barricades and police patrols are your introduction to a gastronomic experience. It's much easier if you come via the rue du Colisée. In any case, the talent of owner/chef Daniel Bouché, the hospitality of his wife, Nicole, and the serene ambience of their restaurant are well worth the detour. We were the first to applaud them, and we won't be the last to call Bouché not only engaging and disarmingly modest but also a most imaginative chef. Sometimes, however, his imagination plays tricks on him—a risk worth taking to develop one's abilities. Again he has presented us with several delectable creations: artichoke soup with fresh mushrooms accompanying foie gras on toast rounds, chervil-flavored custard with lobster tails, roast spiced lotte garnished with vanilla-flavored potatoes au gratin (don't grimace, this odd-sounding combination tastes wonderful), cod soufflé, pot-au-feu of beef and a potato pancake flavored with horseradish, and an incredible potato stew with pimientos. The desserts, particularly the chocolate soufflé with vanilla ice cream and the walnut "mal-brûlée," Bouché's version of crème brûlée, will make you his fan forever. You really ought to sample the cooking of this extraordinary chef, who would be doing a booming business on any other street.

A la carte: 350-700F.

Prince de Galles

(Hôtel Prince de Galles)
33, av. George-V - 47 23 55 11
M. Ferchaud. Open daily until 10:30 p.m. Air cond. Garden dining. No pets. Telex 280627. Cards: V, AE, DC.

Like the 140 rooms, with magnificent, wall-to-wall mosaic tile bathrooms and majestic art deco suites, the restaurant in this old hotel was refurbished from scratch by the Marriott people and is now unrecognizable. The 1930s patio has become a winter garden of soft lighting that extends to the dining room, with its paneling, autumn-colored fabrics and comfortable armchairs. Chef Dominique Cécillon, who used to assist Joël Robuchon, has added to this peaceful setting a cuisine that is sober but appetizing and unpretentious. In addition to the matchless fixed-price lunch menu and an extraordinary Sunday brunch served in the main dining room, there is a short list of selections that includes sea-perch ravioli with essence of truffle, whole steamed salmon with ginger, marinated beef filet and a host of exciting "nouvelle pâtisserie" desserts. The wine list still lacks affordable bottles.

A la carte: 400F. Menus: 190F (Sunday brunch only), 240F (Thursday only), 165F.

⑭ Les Princes

(Hôtel George-V)
31, av. George-V - 47 23 54 00

M. Bonnetot. Open until 11 p.m. Closed July 17-Aug. 20. Air cond. Garden dining. Parking. Pets allowed. Telex 650082. Cards: V, AE, DC, MC.

Competition from the Prince de Galles hotel next door, which Marriott recently spent a fortune redecorating, has pressured the new manager of the George-V to make some long-deferred improvements in the great dining hall (round tables and theater-like draperies), where the babble of millionaires mingles with the murmur of fountains in a most charming interior garden. The cooking has changed radically since Pierre Larapidie was brought in. This talented chef (formerly at Clovis) stripped away overnight a 50-year record of pompous culinary pageantry with such dishes as his taboulé of lobster, filet of sea bass with black pepper, roast calves' liver with puréed onions, and soufflé of red fruit pulp. There's a new fast-service grill in the gallery.

A la carte: 600F. Menus: 250F (weekday lunch only), 360F, 490F.

⑯ Alain Rayé

49, rue du Colisée - 42 25 66 76

M. Rayé. Open until 10:30 p.m. Closed Sat. lunch & Sun. Air cond. Pets allowed. Cards: V, AE, DC.

When Savoie's reigning chef moved to Paris in 1986, it was generally believed that fame and glory would soon follow. Yet it took a few years for success to come; only recently has Rayé managed to fill his soberly elegant dining room. An able, inventive chef, Rayé offers a short but enticing choice of subtle dishes that are quite personal. Try the oysters in lettuce and a lemon cream sauce, a ramekin of lobster with a crépinette of crab and leeks, semicooked salmon with artichokes in hazelnut oil, a superb saddle of rabbit stuffed with eggplant and baked in a pastry, deliciously crusty brains with creamed tomatoes, excellent calves' liver with Swiss chard and turnips, and a few first-rate desserts (a pistachio-chocolate soufflé and a mouth-watering concoction of dates, nuts and brown sugar).

The best wines are available—Didier, the young sommelier, is friendly and knowledge-able—but they don't come cheap. On the other hand, the 205-franc fixed-price menu, served at both lunch and dinner, is a steal.

A la carte: 380-600F. Menus: 205F, 330F, 420F.

⑬ Régence-Plaza

(Hôtel Plaza-Athénée)
25, av. Montaigne - 47 23 78 33

M. Cozzo. Open daily until 10:30 p.m. Air cond. Garden dining. Parking. No pets. Cards: V, AE, DC, MC.

From ocean liner to grand hotel, chef Barnier, at the helm for 25 years, has dropped anchor but now wants to revive (though cautiously) his "aristocratic" repertoire, with a few concessions to the modern style—carpaccio with lemon grass, spicy tartare of sea perch, lobster ravioli with a basil-flavored cream sauce. An Italian influence has also crept in: Ravioli with asparagus and osso buco appear alongside calves' liver and grapes flamed in Armagnac and rolled slices of sole in a lobster sauce. The skillful, meticulous cooking and remarkable wines result in an explosive bill that rockets among the gilt-edged paneling in the château-size dining room and the flower-decked patio, where a fashionable international crowd parks its haunches in the summertime.

A la carte: 600-700F. Menu: 290F (Sunday lunch only).

12/20 Relais-Plaza

(Hôtel Plaza-Athénée)
21, av. Montaigne - 47 23 46 36

M. Cozzo. Open until 1 a.m. Closed Aug. 1-28. Air cond. Parking. Pets allowed. Cards: V, AE, DC, MC.

We're told that the smart set pays no attention to food, that what matters is having a regular table, knowing the maître d' and the waiters and surrounding yourself with the kind of people you wouldn't be ashamed to invite to your own home. The Relais-Plaza fits into this scheme perfectly. Who cares if the cooking is ordinary (except the beef in aspic) and the tab unreasonable? Some people will accept just about anything to be among kindred spirits who smell good and don't mistake a Karajan for a caravan of Jordan almonds. There's a special treat for those who like it: At the back of the 1930s ocean liner–style room sits a harpist who dispenses her syrup along with the iced cakes at teatime.

A la carte: 350-600F. Menu: 280F (dinner only, wine incl.).

12/20 Le Saint-Germain

74, av. des Champs-Elysées
45 63 55 45

M. Hasegawa. Open until 10 p.m. Closed Sat. & Sun. Air cond. Parking. No pets. Telex 641566. Cards: V, AE, DC, MC.

Inside is a cheerful, spacious decor, even though it's tucked away below the street-level shopping arcade. The fixed-price lunch menu ought to bring in more customers: It includes an apéritif, appetizers, a plate of smoked fish, a lamb chop seasoned with thyme, dessert, coffee and a demi-carafe of red wine.

A la carte: 250-280F. Menus: 165F (lunch only, wine incl.), 250F (dinner only, wine incl.).

⑬ Saint-Moritz ❀

33, av. de Friedland - 45 61 02 74

M. Raichon. Open until 10:15 p.m. Closed Sat. & Sun. Air cond. Pets allowed. Cards: V, AE, DC, MC.

The prices are pretty steep, and the single menu/carte forces you to spend almost 300 francs with wine. But this is a luxury neighborhood, and the cuisine of Alain Raichon, who offers several specialties of his native Jura, is genuine and plentiful: excellent thick, perfectly pink foie gras marinated in vin jaune (yellow wine), roast pigeon (slightly overdone) with chanterelles, a good selection of ripe cheeses and pleasant desserts. The attractive decor is reminiscent of a mahogany-paneled English club room, with the addition of pretty pink tablecloths. Friendly waitresses look after you.

Menu/carte: 280F.

12/20 Savy ❀

23, rue Bayard - 47 23 46 98

M. Savy. Open until 11 p.m. Closed Sat., Sun. & Aug. Pets allowed. Cards: V.

Find yourself a seat at the end of the narrow corridor (called the "dining car," as at Maxim's) in the paneled dining room and order some of père Savy's hearty regional (Aveyron) fare: knuckle of ham with lentils, Auvergne-style calves' liver or Auvergne sausage with a purée of green peas. Friendly,

cheerful atmosphere.

A la carte: 250F.

11/20 Soma

10, rue du Commandant-Rivière
43 59 46 40

M. Gupta. Lunch only. Closed Sat. & Sun. Air cond. Telex 670416. Pets allowed. No cards.

Open five days a week for lunch only, Soma is the fast-service annex to next-door neighbor Indra. The spotless interior in pale tones complements the light, popular Indian cuisine: fritters, curries and raw vegetables.

A la carte: 130F. Menus: 45F, 69F.

12/20 Suntory

13, rue Lincoln - 42 25 40 27,
45 25 47 11

M. Hermitte. Open until 11:30 p.m. Closed Sat. lunch & Sun. Air cond. No pets. Cards: V, AE, DC.

At this luxury Japanese address with a sushi bar in the basement, the polite staff includes cooks who work expertly in plain view, making sashimi, teppanyaki, tempura and the like.

A la carte: 300-400F. Menus: 305F, 315F, 320F, 385F.

⑬ La Table de l'Astor

(Hôtel Astor)
1, rue d'Astor - 42 65 80 47

M. Bidamant. Open until 9:30 p.m. Closed Sun. lunch & Sat. Pets allowed. Telex 642737. Cards: V, AE, DC, MC.

Formerly open only for private luncheon parties during the week, this elegant restaurant, whose 1930s decor lies hidden beyond the hotel's entrance hall, is now serving dinner as well. All the better, for the management is diligent and maintains high standards of service, and the new chef, Michel Legrand, is no novice. For proof, try his duck liver with raw spinach, stir-fried lobster with crisp vegetables, salmon cooked on one side only with chives, and good desserts. The fixed-price lunch menu is generally fine.

A la carte: 300F. Menus: 160F (dinner only), 210F (weekday lunch only).

Taillevent
19
15, rue Lamennais - 45 63 39 94
M. Vrinat. Open until 10:30 p.m. Closed Sat., Sun., Feb. school vacation & July 21-Aug. 20. Air cond. No pets. Cards: V.

It looks like the great plan to revamp Taillevent didn't come off. The young genius who was to take over the kitchen had second thoughts and never showed up. But that doesn't prevent owner Jean-Claude Vrinat from playing, as usual, to capacity crowds of Parisians and foreign gourmets in his historic building. In the nobly proportioned dining room, amid glorious woodwork, rich draperies, fine paintings and the blue banquettes we continue to dislike almost as much as the *niches à bibelots*, elegantly clad diners from the world of business and politics are served by attentive yet reserved waiters (who, thank heavens, are trained *not* to describe in flowery language the food on the plate they've placed before you).

These days Taillevent's cuisine seems more workmanlike than inspired, but the dishes are refined, sauces are light, and everything is cooked with split-second timing. There is a slip-up every now and again (a lamb's trotter is not at its best when enveloped in puff pastry), but on the whole we dote on such dishes as a salad of lamb's lettuce and red mullet with black olives, sauced with a keenly flavored emulsion of olive oil and anchovy. And the giant prawns with fresh pasta, the potatoes stuffed with a lobster ragoût, the wild-mushroom terrine and the spinach-and-rabbit tourte fragrant with summer savory are all irresistible preludes to such desserts as frozen nougat with lime-blossom honey, crème brûlée with orange zest and vanilla-plum tart.

Taillevent's highly praised cellar remains the repository of voluptuous Burgundies, luscious Bordeaux and delectable Côtes-du-Rhône, and an appealing selection of the relatively inexpensive wines that Jean-Claude and Sabine Vrinat take such pleasure in discovering.

A la carte: 650F and up.

12/20 **Le Val d'Or**
28, av. Franklin-Roosevelt
43 59 95 81
M. Rongier. Lunch only. Closed Sun. & Dec. 23-Jan. 2. Cards: V.

Géraud Rongier has a gift for locating excellent little wines (they're priced from 6 to 10 francs a glass) to drink with his delicious open-face cold-cut sandwiches. A few well-prepared hot dishes are served in the basement, but the most popular, and fun, place to be is the crowded bar at street level.

A la carte: 200F.

NINTH ARRONDISSEMENT

11/20 **L'Assiette au Boeuf**
20, bd Montmartre - 47 70 91 35
See Sixth Arrondissement.

14 **Auberge Landaise**
23, rue Clauzel - 48 78 74 40
M. Morin. Open until 10 p.m. Closed Sun. Pets allowed. Parking. Cards: V, AE, DC.

In these two pretty rooms, the tables are well spaced and dressed in impeccable linens. Around these tables are found hearty, happy business people enjoying southwestern French classics, notably a superb pipérade (a type of omelet), duck confit with delicious parsleyed potatoes and heaping portions of flawless cassoulet. Chef/owner M. Morin also prepares a thick cut of calves' liver for two and a hot foie gras with grapes. Mme. Morin bestows a warm greeting in the setting of white-stone walls and false beams that could almost pass for the real thing. Good, sturdy wines of the region, with the accent on Bordeaux, and an impressive array of Armagnacs.

A la carte: 250F.

11/20 **Bistro de la Gare**
38, bd des Italiens - 48 24 49 61
See Sixth Arrondissement.

12/20 **Le Boeuf Bourguignon**
21, rue de Douai - 42 82 08 79
Mme. Nattier. Open until 10 p.m. Closed Sun. & Aug. Terrace dining. Pets allowed. No cards.

Checkered tablecloths and white walls covered with movie posters dominate the house,

THE BEST
IN AIR TRAVEL

The best of the U.S.A. is connected with the best of France on Air France direct flights from New York, Washington D.C., Philadelphia, Boston, Chicago, Houston, Los Angeles, San Francisco.

Air France offers the best means to reach France in comfort and style. With Concorde the first supersonic commercial airliner, symbol of technical perfection and elegance, Air France is the only airline linking France to the U.S.A. in just 3 hours and 45 minutes. On board Air France has selected the finest meals and the most reputed wines and champagnes.

For Reservations
in the U.S.A.:
CALL 1 (800) AF PARIS
1 (800) 237-2747
in New York City:
(212) 247-0100
or contact your travel agent

AIR FRANCE

including the newly added dining room. Nathalie Nattier, star of the famous film *Les Portes de la Nuit* (*The Gates of Night*), is still running the kitchen, which turns out good Parisian home-cooking that favors ragoûts and bourguignons.

A la carte: 130-150F. Menu: 54F (wine incl.).

10/20 Chartier

7, rue du Faubourg-Montmartre
47 70 86 29

M. Lemaire. Open daily until 9:30 p.m. No pets. No cards.

Sadi Carnot was president of France in 1892 when Chartier opened its doors to ordinary hungry folks. In 1989, there's not a wrinkle in the admirable decor, and the cuisine is as philanthropic as ever.

A la carte: 60F.

12/20 Le Grand Café Capucines

4, bd des Capucines - 47 42 75 77
MM. Blanc. Open daily 24 hrs. Air cond. Terrace dining. Pets allowed. Cards: V, AE, DC.

The magic of the grand Parisian boulevards is resuscitated in the brilliance and gaiety of this room, whose new Belle Epoque decor is even more comfortable and sparkling than before. The food is good if you choose from the standard brasserie items: seafood, duck confit and pigs' feet. The fine cellar is strong in Loire wines.

A la carte: 250F.

12/20 Mövenpick

(Café des Artistes)
12, bd de la Madeleine - 47 42 47 93
M. Van Maenen. Open daily until 11:45 p.m. Air cond. Pets allowed. Cards: V, AE, DC, MC.

The decor conceals the lines and angles of this basement restaurant arranged around a pool. It's extravagant yet offers typically Swiss fast-forward service and five types of fixed-price menus, ranging from a gala breakfast to a full meal (excellent meats and oysters, spectacular frozen desserts) to a sandwich and salad. The wine bar is unusually good, and the list features frequent specials.

A la carte: 100-300F. Menus: 198F (Tuesday and Thursday only), 150F.

⑬ Les Muses

(Hôtel Scribe)
1, rue Scribe - 47 42 03 40
M. Antoine. Open until 10:30 p.m. Closed Sat., Sun., holidays & Aug. Air cond. Parking. No pets. Telex 214653. Cards: V, AE, DC, MC.

Chef Christian Massault's new menu is a brief, intelligent selection of seasonal classics, exhibiting a deft touch. Witness the confit de foie gras pleasantly balanced with tart apples, the ample pot-au-feu of sole and shrimp, and the thick slice of rosy calves' liver with onions and potatoes. In other words, this is warm and generous cooking, served by a nicely inconspicuous staff in an elegant setting that was recently redone (wainscoting, smoky mirrors). Fine selection of wines.

A la carte: 300F. Menus: 290F (dinner only, on special order), 175F.

⑭ Opéra Restaurant

(Café de la Paix)
3, pl. de l'Opéra - 47 42 97 02
M. Meyruils. Open daily until 11 p.m. Closed Aug. Air cond. Pets allowed. Telex 220875. Cards: V, AE, DC, MC.

The brochure states that the tableware is magnificent, the service and wine cellar superb, and the Napoléon III decor—designed by Charles Garnier, architect of the Paris Opéra—unmatched. This says nothing of the sumptuously elegant dining room, restored at great expense to its former gilded splendor, the comfortable chairs and pleasant lighting, the sparkling silverware and incredible collection of wines that makes up one of the finest cellars in the capital. The clientele, perhaps simply in contrast to all this, does not always measure up. The service, on the other hand, is exquisitely honed and discreet. So it's all the more a pity that we are forced to report that the cooking of the nationally recognized chef, Gil Jouanin, is becoming rather dull. The wonderful ingredients, the bountiful servings and his panache are not enough to disguise a certain lassitude in the kitchen. You would think this is the cooking of a chef who has lost interest, or one who isn't allowed to do what he wants (except in the dessert department, where all is still marvelous and superbly done). Taste the cold soup of shrimp, cucumbers, queen scallops and clams (though it's diminished by too much cold), the noteworthy seafood assortment and the salmis of duckling with wild mushrooms. A little more effort and they'll be back to two toques.

A la carte: 500F.

⑬ Pagoda

50, rue de Provence - 48 74 81 48
MM. Tan Dinh. Open until 10:30 p.m. Closed Sun. & Aug. Air cond. Pets allowed. Cards: V.

For nearly twenty years, Pagoda's old chef Tang has been serving good, reliable Chinese cooking—not overly imaginative, but really delicious when he puts his heart in it. And his heart was in it when we had our last meal here: crab-claw fritters; crusty, fragrant spring rolls; and Peking duck, marvelously crisp and rendered of its fat. There's more room between the tables now, and co-owner/hostess Rosine is as cordial as ever.

A la carte: 200F. Menus: 95F (lunch only), 58F.

12/20 Le Quercy ❣

36, rue Condorcet - 48 78 30 61
M. Simon. Open until 9:30 p.m. Closed Sun., holidays & Aug. Pets allowed. Cards: V, AE, DC.

Both the marvelous Rocamadour cabécou (little goat cheeses), and the highly recommended Quercy cassoulet with duck confit appear on the "suggested" menu of this beguiling restaurant with a country-inn decor. You'll also find excellent charcuterie, which Mme. Simon "imports" from the Quercy region.

A la carte: 230F. Menu: 128F.

⑯ La Table d'Anvers

2, pl. d'Anvers - 48 78 35 21
MM. Conticini. Open until 10:30 p.m. Closed Sun. & week of Aug. 15. Air cond. Pets allowed. Cards: V.

At a time when the return to classic cuisine is giving many chefs an alibi for their lack of initiative and imagination, chef Christian Conticini and his brother, Philippe, a first-rate pastry chef, are there to remind us that the ktichen is also a place for invention, creation and the discovery of novel taste sensations.

You'll share our enthusiasm when you visit this contemporary dining room, decorated in modish tones of gray, and start salivating over a menu full of original, unprecedented dishes. The appetite is piqued by such suggestions as compote of rabbit with chestnuts, accompanied by the animal's sautéed liver in a rémoulade sauce; salmon baked atop firm, flavorful potatoes; cream of celery with cèpes and a walnut purée; and a terrine of hog jowls, blood sausage, arugula and beets. Narrowing down the choices is no small matter.

Seduction isn't everything, of course—the dishes must stand or fall on their own merits. Of all the offerings we sampled, only one sounded a false note, and only in its garnish: The braised turnips escorting a marvelous pig's trotter were overpowered by a coating of coarse mustard. But every other aspect of the meal proved the kitchen's artistry in combining textures and vivid flavors (if you don't like spices, pick another restaurant!). Only a top-drawer talent could pair delicate coquilles St-Jacques with chewy cockles and a peppery mayonnaise fragrant with tarragon, or garnish a crusty-skinned salmon with vanilla-scented peas. Conticini is a virtuoso. He turns a slice of tuna, set on a flaky crust and complemented with peppers, black olives, leeks and capers, into a minor masterpiece. A simple purée of potatoes becomes a rare treat, and a veal blanquette, with crisp mushrooms and a few pungent fried melissa leaves in a smooth sauce, is a paragon of creative cookery. Brother Philippe's praline friantines, chocolate-coffee croquettes, pistachio and hazelnut sponge cake and walnut cake au gratin are stellar conclusions to a feast that, in a fancier neighborhood, would easily command twice the price. We are happy to award this talented pair an extra point in this edition.

A la carte: 280-350F. Menus: 170F (weekday lunch only, wine incl.), 160F, 195F, 230F, 275F.

11/20 Taverne Kronenbourg

24, bd des Italiens - 47 70 16 64
M. Blan. Open daily until 3 a.m. Air cond. Terrace dining. Pets allowed. Cards: V, AE, MC.

Sauerkraut is king in this spacious, comfortable, lively place that has one of the last café orchestras, along with good Alsatian wines, first-rate grilled pigs' feet béarnaise, fresh seafood and excellent service.

A la carte: 180F. Menu: 64F.

TENTH ARRONDISSEMENT

12/20 Brasserie Flo

7, cour des Petites-Ecuries
47 70 13 59

M. Bucher. Open daily until 1:30 a.m. Air cond. Pets allowed. Telex 281396. Cards: V, AE, DC.

With its authentic, lovingly maintained 1900s decor, Flo is a lively spot famous for its formidable sauerkraut, foie gras, fresh seafood and pastries served straight from the oven. A genuine, ever-fashionable brasserie.

A la carte: 200F. Menu: 113F (wine incl.).

13 Casimir

6, rue de Belzunce - 48 78 32 53

M. Pujol. Open until 10 p.m. Closed Sat. lunch & Sun. Terrace dining. Parking. Pets allowed. Cards: V, AE, DC.

Plastered with famous wine labels, the decor is a bit bush-league and not overly cheerful, but it is inviting and well suited to this provincial corner of Paris, which you reach on foot via a steep, narrow street. The owners are delightful hosts, and Barthélemy Pujol flits in and out of the dining room in his chef's toque. His cooking seems to hover between two styles: bass with kiwis and excellent andouillette. The daily specials always turn up a few pleasant surprises, and the wine list has great treasures.

A la carte: 280-300F. Menu: 170F (wine incl.).

15 Chez Michel

10, rue de Belzunce - 48 78 44 14

M. Tounissoux. Open until 10 p.m. Closed Fri., Sat., 2 weeks in Feb. & 1st 3 weeks of Aug. Air cond. Pets allowed. Cards: V, AE, DC.

It isn't the lobster salad with kiwi, or the rather stingy fixed-price menu for 170 francs, or even the ragoût of lobster and mushrooms for 305 francs that sends us running to Michel Tounissoux's place, where the frightening checks cast an aura of grand luxury over the small, ultra-provincial dining room. But let's give him credit for recently reducing the price of several wines, making it possible to have something to drink for 100 francs or less. As for the food, it remains pretty much the same: classic cuisine that is well prepared and solidly

anchored in such standbys as lobster omelet, grilled turbot, John Dory with a purée of greens, sliced beef with béarnaise sauce, chicken with mushrooms, and honey-flavored ice cream with a dash of Chartreuse.

A la carte: 400F. Menu: 170F (weekday lunch only).

13 La Grille

80, rue du Faubourg-Poissonnière
47 70 89 73

M. Cullerre. Open until 9 p.m. Closed Sat., Sun. & 8 days in Feb. & Aug. Cards: DC.

The menu rarely changes, ditto the prices and the quality of the cooking. In other words, the mouth-watering specialties served by chef/owner Yves Cullerre in his old-fashioned corner bistro behind iron railings have neither aged nor wilted. First and foremost is the magnificent whole turbot for two, grilled to perfection and served with a superb beurre blanc, as well as good herring filets, a so-so andouillette and heaping portions of broiled or pan-fried meat. Good Loire wines and a warm, friendly reception from co-owner Geneviève.

A la carte: 200-250F.

12/20 Julien

16, rue du Faubourg-Saint-Denis
47 70 12 06

M. Bucher. Open daily until 1:30 a.m. Air cond. Pets allowed. Telex 281396. Cards: V, AE, DC.

Julien is the fifth feather in M. Bucher's cap (Terminus Nord and Boeuf sur le Toit are among his others), and it is breathtakingly lovely, with its 1890s brasserie decor and good food based on a menu common to its sister houses.

A la carte: 230F. Menu: 121F (wine incl.).

14 Le Louis XIV

8, bd St-Denis - 42 08 56 56

M. Flottes-Descombes. Open until 1 a.m. Closed Mon., Tues. & May 31-Sept. 1. Parking. Pets allowed. Cards: V, AE, DC.

Watching squab, quail, legs of lamb and chickens turn on the spit in the center of the rather quaint 1950s-style restaurant; seeing your chateaubriand broiled to order; singeing your eyebrows in the heat of the charcoal grill; eating lobster Thermidor or lobster au gratin with your fingers—that's what dining is all about in this big, busy bistro where the tables practically rub against one another. It's lively, noisy, sometimes mad and always congenial. If you really want a good meal, order the excellent oysters, a large grilled sole, scallops or the seafood pasta. If it's hunting season, try one of the wild-game dishes for which this restaurant is known.

A la carte: 300F. Menu: 185F.

⑬ Le New Port
79, rue du Faubourg-Saint-Denis
48 24 19 38

M. Fargeau. Open until 11 p.m. Closed Sat. lunch & Sun. Air cond. Pets allowed. Cards: V, AE.

After two years in this yacht-club setting, Francis Fargeau made a clean break from the old image of this veteran bistro well known to the denizens of Parisian nightlife. His new decor, enlivened with Dufyesque watercolors, is more comfortable and inviting than that at the mother branch, Les Algues in the Gobelins district. Le New Port welcomes seafood lovers who don't want their dinner ruined by astronomical bills. Prices are reasonable and everything is fresh and appetizing: salmon in puff pastry with cream of watercress, pike simmered with vegetables, fresh cod à la ratatouille. The desserts are making progress as well, and the wines are good. The toque is still warranted.

A la carte: 260-280F. Menus: 85F, 120F.

12/20 Paris-Dakar
95, rue du Faubourg-Saint-Martin
42 08 16 64

MM. Mamadou & Aziz. Open daily until 1 a.m. Pets allowed. Cards: V.

Two Senegalese men and their wives have transformed this former crêperie into an authentic little African restaurant presenting a short menu of true African classics: fish fritters, a poached fish stew (tiep-bou-dienn, the national dish) and chicken yassa (lemon-marinated and spicy).

A la carte: 160-180F.

⑬ La P'tite Tonkinoise
56, rue du Faubourg-Poissonnière
42 46 85 98

M. Costa. Open until 10 p.m. Closed Sun., Mon. & Aug. 1-Sept. 15 & Dec. 20-Jan. 6. Pets allowed. Cards: V.

Michel Costa continues to serve native Tonkinese dishes, just as his father did, only he's Frenchified them a bit. His is an authentic yet personal cuisine, more seasonal than is customary in Vietnamese restaurants: crab with braised asparagus, a crisp fried cake made of seven vegetables, mérou (grouper) in a sweet-and-sour ginger sauce, stuffed duck "Lotus." Henri Costa, Michel's father, greets you warmly; the friendly, congenial atmosphere is reinforced by a loyal following of Indochinese expatriates.

A la carte: 200F.

12/20 Terminus Nord
23, rue de Dunkerque - 42 85 05 15

M. Bucher. Open daily until 12:30 a.m. Air cond. Terrace dining. Pets allowed. Telex 281396. Cards: V, AE, DC.

There's nothing exciting or stylish about a neighborhood around a rail terminal, but Jean-Paul Bucher (who also owns Flo, Julien, Vaudeville, etc.) is magician enough to pack his brasserie every night with a fashionable clientele, who love the clever Belle Epoque–Gay Nineties setting and the cooking, which is wholesome and reliable: seafood, foie gras, choucroute and wines by the pitcher.

A la carte: 200-250F.

ELEVENTH ARRONDISSEMENT

⑬ Astier
44, rue Jean-Pierre-Timbaud
43 57 16 35, 43 38 25 56
M. Picquart. Open until 10 p.m. Closed Sat.,
Sun., holidays, Aug., 2 weeks in May & 2 weeks
end Dec. Air cond. Pets allowed. Cards: V.

Owner/chef Michel Picquart, who wanders
through his popular, crowded corner bistro
(recently refurbished), is always in one of two
moods: jovial or grouchy. And though it sets
the mood at Astier, it has no effect on the
surprising amplitude of his cuisine and menu.
The terrines are superb, the salads seasonal, the
home-cooking strictly classic, and the breast of
duck with cream of foie gras and the beef filet
in Cahors wine well prepared. Excellent choice
of little-known growers' wines.
Menu: 100F.

⑭ La Belle Epoque
(Holiday Inn)
10, pl. de la République - 43 55 44 34
M. Lutz. Open daily until 10:30 p.m. Air cond.
Terrace dining. Parking. Pets allowed. Telex
210651. Cards: V, AE, DC, MC.

Surely it can't be much fun for a talented
cook to work for a conference center like the
Holiday Inn; Patrice Trincali is finding this
out. Sadly, everyone seems to ignore him—except us, and we persist in admiring the freshness and individuality of his dishes: salad of
snails and frogs' legs with sherry, whole roast
salmon and a feuilleté of sweetbreads. We can
understand his going through a slump now
and then, for what cook wouldn't suffer from
the critics' indifference? The desserts are superb, and the menu for dinner-dances is exceptional. Another point is warranted for the
exquisite prawn ravioli with coriander, the
salad of lobster and potatoes with sour cream

and the red mullet in a tapenade cream sauce.
The king-size 1930s decor is chilly but comfortable.
A la carte: 300F. Menus: 180F (lunch only,
wine incl.), 230F (dinner only).

⑬ Le Chardenoux
1, rue Jules-Vallès - 43 71 49 52
M. Souvrain. Open until 11 p.m. Closed Sat.
lunch, Sun. & Aug. Terrace dining. Parking.
Pets allowed. Cards: V, AE.

The new owner is reviving this inviting turn-
of-the-century neighborhood bistro. The authentic period decor, with its serpentine
marble counter, wildly ornate carved moldings
and acid-etched mirrors, is perfectly charming.
The classic cuisine is simple, fresh and uncomplicated: appetizing specials (blanquette of veal
or lamb, petit salé of pork, stuffed cabbage),
excellent and hard-to-find shepherd's pie,
stuffed tomatoes, genuine miroton (ragoût)
and delicious lean boudin with sautéed potatoes and apples. Prices are quite reasonable,
even on the good selection of growers' wines.
A la carte: 180-200F. Menu: 150F (wine
incl.), 120F.

12/20 Chez Fernand
(Les Fernandises)
17, rue de la Fontaine-au-Roi
43 57 46 25
M. Asselinne. Open until 10:30 p.m. Closed Sat.
lunch, Sun. & Aug. Air cond. Pets allowed.
Cards: V.

M. Fernand, a good old Norman boy,
knows the secret of friendly feasts that gladden
the heart but don't sadden the purse. In this
unpretentious neighborhood pub with a coun-
try-tavern decor, you can stop by for a friendly

drink bolstered by a plate of pork, sausage, tripe, codfish au gratin, roast lamb, cider-basted duck or skate wing with excellent house-made Camembert. Fast-service annex next door.

A la carte: 180-200F. Menu: 95F.

🍳 Chez Philippe

15 106, rue de la Folie-Méricourt
43 57 33 78

M. Serbource. Open until 10:30 p.m. Closed Sat., Sun. & Aug. Air cond. Pets allowed. Parking. Cards: V.

What looks like a village café is really a grand old Paris bistro that was familiar to merrymakers 100 years ago. The cooking is the best kind: generous, fresh, technically solid and free of modern clichés. After the food, the next best thing about this veteran neighborhood eating place is its owner: plump, gentle, quick-witted Philippe Serbource. Then there's the unpretentious interior, with low-hanging beams and a restful atmosphere, which attracts a steady stream of customers who like to slip off their jackets (but not their caps!) and relax. At the bar, Serbource uncorks magnificent Burgundies (at reasonable prices) for tasting, which stimulates conversation and an appetite for charcuterie, foie gras, rabbit stew, a near perfect goose cassoulet, an enormous rib steak marchand de vin and the best paella around. Desserts are less spectacular (good clafouti and pastries). Prices are climbing.

A la carte: 280-330F.

🍴 Le Péché Mignon

13 5, rue Guillaume-Bertrand
43 57 02 51

M. Rousseau. Open until 10 p.m. Closed Sun., Mon., Feb. school vacation & Aug. Air cond. Parking. Pets allowed. Cards: V.

Daniel and Evelyne Rousseau have gradually transformed this modest bistro in a working-class district into a sleek, elegant interior with raspberry-velvet accents and tulip-shaped sconces. There are comfortable banquettes, round and oval tables with pretty settings and a general ambience of good taste that complements the personal, flexible, seasonal menu: sauté of mixed fish in Sauternes, filet of roast brill with thyme leaves, filet of beef with garden vegetables (from which garden?). The six-course gourmet menu, well worth its fixed

price, provides a good tour of the house specialties. Enticing desserts (apple feuilleté, chocolate fondant).

A la carte: 280F. Menu: 190F.

🍴 Le Picotin

13 13, rue de la Pierre-Levée
43 57 34 63

M. Malherbe. Open until 10 p.m. Closed Sat., Sun., Aug. 4-Sept. 3 & Dec. 23-Jan. 2. No pets. Cards: V, AE.

M. Malherbe's cooking is light, fresh and meticulous, and we hope this toque he has earned won't inflate his prices. On the menu are fragrant duck foie gras, filet of pike in a light basil sauce with delicious baby vegetables, and an excellent chocolate-and-orange charlotte. Adequate reception and service. The graceless, chilly interior is illuminated by a huge bay window with net curtains.

Menus: 85F (lunch only, wine incl.), 150F.

🍴 Le Repaire de Cartouche 🏵

14 8, bd des Filles-du-Calvaire
47 00 25 86

M. Pocous. Open until 10:30 p.m. Closed Sat. lunch, Sun. & July 25-Aug. 20. Pets allowed. Cards: V, AE.

Jovial, mustachioed Raymond Pocous (who has just opened a wine bar, Les Bacchantes, that serves charcuterie and daily specials opposite his Cartouche Edouard VII) does a fine job with down-to-earth, honest country fare. The pleasure of eating is doubled by the reasonable prices, and the wine chosen from a wide selection of moderate-to-humble representatives won't ignite the bill. Southwestern specialties include ventrèche (smoked pork brisket), marvelous sausage and ham, hot or cold home-made duck foie gras, feuilleté of snails or mussels, sauté of duck confit, farm cheeses from the Pyrénées and tourtière landaise (not consistently good). Sturdy wood furnishings and excellent Armagnac.

A la carte: 230-250F. Menu: 90F (weekdays only).

🍳 A Sousceyrac 🏵

15 35, rue Faidherbe - 43 71 65 30
M. Asfaux. Open until 10 p.m. Closed Sat., Sun. & Aug. Air cond. Parking. Pets allowed. Cards: V, AE.

The specialties of Quercy used to occupy center stage on the long handwritten menu at this old-fashioned, handsomely oak-paneled restaurant. But after 40 years, Gabriel Asfaux has stepped down and passed the crown to his son Patrick, who prefers high-quality Paris bistro fare to regional cuisine. Among the best dishes are Sousceyrac cassoulet (Wednesday and Friday), marvelous goose or duck foie gras, duck breast with wild mushrooms and, in hunting season, superb, rarely found hare à la royale. The rest of the menu includes such standard bistro items as andouillette, grilled pigs' feet, braised sweetbreads, pan-fried beef forestière and a daring and delicious combination of lamb's sweetbreads and lobster. Gabriel is in and out of the kitchen and dining room, where another son, Luc, acts as sommelier. The cordial, close-knit relationship between father and sons surely is an added attraction. Cahors is served in small pitchers or showcase bottles.

A la carte: 250-300F.

12/20 Le Wei-Ya

49, rue de Lappe - 43 57 62 58
Mme. Suen. Open until 11 p.m. Closed Sun. & Aug. No pets. Cards: V.

The owner/chef teaches a course in Chinese civilization every morning at the University of Paris (where he is on the faculty), and every night he practices, for his French friends, the fine art of Cantonese and Pekingese home cooking, which was handed down to him by his grandmother.

A la carte: 120F. Menu: 45F (weekdays only).

TWELFTH ARRONDISSEMENT

⑬ Chez Marcel

7, rue St-Nicolas - 43 43 49 40
M. Trottet. Open until 9:30 p.m. Closed Sat., Sun., holidays & Aug. Pets allowed. Cards: V.

Bottles of Beaujolais, Muscadet and Cassis (added to dry white wine to make kir) are automatically brought in. You can eat all you want of the rabbit terrine with prunes; the smoked cured beef comes in portions big enough for three; and the vanilla-chocolate dessert is so thick and creamy that people often ask for a second helping. Tradespeople and office workers rub elbows at Chez Marcel, the old-time bistro with leather banquettes and etched glass, where everything is tasty, well made and pleasantly served.

A la carte: 200F. Menu: 130F.

12/20 Le Drainak

18, av. Ledru-Rollin - 43 43 46 07
MM. Drai. Open until 10:45 p.m. Closed Sat. lunch & Sun. Terrace dining. Pets allowed. Cards: V, AE, DC.

The brothers Drai run this authentically restored 1900 bistro efficiently but have switched from home-style dishes to such things as gratin of prawns and zucchini, fricassée of sole and foie gras with fresh pasta. The new menu is not bad but pricey.

A la carte: 300F. Menus: 65F, 145F.

⑮ La Gourmandise

271, av. Daumesnil - 43 43 94 41
M. Denoual. Open until 10 p.m. Closed Sat. lunch, Sun., March 19-27 & Aug. 6-28. Pets allowed. Cards: V, AE.

Alain Denoual is a chef who prefers to stick to his stove and not to parade his toque among the customers. His angular dining room is tidy and comfortable, and he feels that the basic, old-fashioned decor—pink-velvet banquettes and well-lighted, attractively set tables—is fresh enough. The emphasis is on classic cuisine with a distinctively modern style. Denoual is a meticulous cook and technician (he worked at Tour d'Argent, Maxim's and Laurent, among others), a solid all-around professional who handles meats and variety cuts (superb sweetbreads and veal kidney with rice and essence of truffle) as imaginatively as he does fish (excellent salmon with crab mousse). Precise timing and expert seasoning transform an ordinary mackerel with aromatic herbs, or a terrine of leeks vinaigrette, or a filet of brill with chervil into extraordinary dishes. Desserts are not quite up to these standards. The menu is well balanced and prices are holding steady.

A la carte: 250-300F. Menus: 165F (weekday lunch only), 260F (dinner only).

12/20 Le Jardin de la Gare

48 bis, bd de Bercy (Gare de Paris-Bercy) - 43 40 82 48

M. Chazal. Open daily until 9:30 p.m. Garden dining. Parking. Pets allowed. Cards: V.

While you wait for your high-speed train or a Verdi opera at the sports palace, this garden restaurant stop atop the railroad station will serve you fast-cooked but well-prepared meals supervised by the Chazal kitchen team (which also operates Le Train Bleu in the Gare de Lyon): calf's-feet salad, andouillette with herbs and grilled steak.

Menu: 69F.

(16) Au Pressoir

257, av. Daumesnil - 43 44 38 21

M. Séguin. Open until 10 p.m. Closed Sat., Sun., Feb. school vacation & Aug. 1-27. Air cond. Parking. Pets allowed. Cards: V.

Henri Séguin's originality lies in his being *truly* original, which can't be said of too many others. Not only does his menu change frequently (and he offers a half dozen seasonal daily specials that don't even appear in print), but at least half the menu is devoted to dishes you've never eaten anywhere else—but which you'll surely see weeks later in other eating spots. Few restaurants can maintain the inventive spirit that rules this comfortable, unpretentious dining room, which could pass for a neighborhood bistro in spite of the carpeting and oak-paneled walls. It's best to come with an open mind; you might be offered a salad of fricasséed pigs' ears, puréed cod with asparagus, flaked bass with anise butter and carrot soufflé, orange-flavored veal kidney with a mushroom mousse, a gratin of prunes and pink grapefruit, or double-chocolate banana mousse. Everything is quite good, delicately flavored and beautifully presented. Son Jean-Jacques keeps the service humming and takes good care of the wine cellar. This meal is worth its price.

A la carte: 350-500F. Menu: 300F (menu dégustation).

(13) La Sologne

164, av. Daumesnil - 43 07 68 97

M. Médard. Open until 10:30 p.m. Closed Mon. dinner, Sun. & 1 week at Christmas. Air cond. Terrace dining. Parking. Pets allowed. Cards: V, AE.

M. Médard is fond of hunting, and during the season his menu of wild-game dishes rings out like a hunting cry for the entire neighborhood to hear. Excellent classic cuisine with an unrivaled array of prestigious traditional sauces: saddle of hare Saint-Hubert, wild pig sauce poivrade, roast leg of venison Grand-Veneur, tenderloin of yearling roe deer with a sauce Soubise and so forth. The "modernized" cuisine is not quite as distinguished when the hunting season is over.

A la carte: 250-350F.

12/20 La Tour d'Argent

6, pl. de la Bastille - 43 42 90 32

M. Solignac. Open daily until 1:15 a.m. Air cond. Terrace dining. Pets allowed.Cards: V, AE, DC.

This is no fraudulent annex of Claude Terrail's world-famous restaurant, but rather an old-time brasserie updated in keeping with the urban renewal efforts in the Opéra-Bastille neighborhood. The owner comes from the Aveyron region and knows his business: seafood, choucroute and daily specials. The food is generally good, not too expensive and served with a smile.

A la carte: 200-300F.

(13) Le Train Bleu

20, bd Diderot (Gare de Lyon, 2nd floor) - 43 43 09 06

M. Chazal. Open daily until 10 p.m. Pets allowed. Cards: V, AE, DC.

According to interior decorator Slavik, you need a neck brace to properly appreciate the ornate extravagance of this gilded 1900s monument, with its elaborately carved ceilings and woodwork, its frescoes and mammoth draperies, its leather and brass decorations. The cuisine is not quite so high-flying. The menu rarely digresses from its programmed Paris-Lyon-Mediterranean circuit, including a medley of competent dishes (brill with sorrel, duckling with peaches) and a few remarkable ones (leg of lamb, milk-fed veal chop Foyot with noodles). The excellent service can be even faster if necessary for hurried travelers.

A la carte: 300F and up. Menus: 195F (weekday lunch only, wine incl.), 220F (dinner only).

⑯ Au Trou Gascon ☺
40, rue Taine - 43 44 34 26

Mme. Dutournier. Open until 10 p.m. Closed Sat., Sun., July 28-Aug. 26 & last week of Dec. Parking. Air cond. Pets allowed. Cards: V, AE, DC.

Alain Dutournier has moved out, but his wife, Nicole, runs the place—with boundless competence, one might add—and loyal pa-

trons are now enjoying the cuisine of Bernard Broux, who cooks like a born-and-bred Gascon. Foie gras, sausage, farmer's ham, mushroom pâté with parsley juice, mutton stew with white beans, salmon with smoked bacon, roast fowl with mushroom juice and squab with broad beans—these and other dishes come rolling out of the kitchen of this former coachman's bistro. The original carved moldings and Belle Epoque charm remain in place. Excellent fixed-price business lunch. Claude Tessier, the maître d' and sommelier, will provide you with wines from all over at civilized prices.

A la carte: 350-500F. Menus: 190F, 390F.

THIRTEENTH ARRONDISSEMENT

12/20 Boeuf Bistrot
4, pl. des Alpes - 45 82 08 09

MM. Amice & Garnier. Open until 10:30 p.m. Closed Sat. lunch & Sun. Terrace dining. Pets allowed. Cards: V, AE, DC.

A whiff of the Left Bank along the Butte-aux-Cailles, this amusing, meticulous, imaginative cuisine has beef as its theme: cured, with marrow bones and vegetables; tartare; filet; braised. You can order Beaujolais by the glass, and your bill won't suffer for it.

A la carte: 180-200F. Menu: 89F.

12/20 Fortune des Mers
53, av. d'Italie - 45 85 76 83

M. Remond. Open until 12:30 a.m. Closed Sun. & Mon. Terrace dining. Pets allowed. Telex 270352. Cards: V, AE, DC.

This combined fish market, restaurant, brasserie, bar and grill is devoted to seafood in a range of prices. Fish prepared simply is the best choice, and portions are generous.

A la carte: 120-300F. Menu: 86F (wine incl.).

⑬ Les Marronniers
53 bis, bd Arago - 47 07 58 57

M. Lorenzatti. Open until 11 p.m. Closed Sun. & July 29-Sept. 7. Terrace dining. Pets allowed. Cards: V, AE, DC, MC.

This version of an "old-fashioned" establishment, with floral wallpaper and framed repro-

ductions, is too provincial for words. It opens onto a delightful terrace shaded by tall chestnut trees that line the boulevard. Mme. Lorenzatti is a charming hostess, the waitresses are most obliging, and Gilbert Lorenzatti's cooking makes up in hearty, bold and flavorful dishes what it lacks in finesse. The excellent growers' wines include a dreamy Bourgueil.

A la carte: 280F.

⑭ Le Petit Marguery
9, bd de Port-Royal - 43 31 58 59

MM. Cousin. Open until 10:15 p.m. Closed Sun., Mon., Aug. 1-Sept. 2 & Dec. 23-Jan. 3. Pets allowed. Cards: V, AE, DC, MC.

Michel and Jacques in the kitchen, Alain in the dining room—the three Cousins get along like brothers! It's a pleasure to watch them hard at work pleasing the contingent of lively, jovial regulars who appreciate the congenial atmosphere and fine cooking. The red-and-pink interior opens onto a pleasant sidewalk terrace, the staff is good-natured, and the wines are excellent and inexpensive (65 francs for a superb Bourgueil from Paul Maître). The cuisine is fresh and obviously seasonal, as the menu changes daily (handwritten in purple ink, of course). Choose from superb terrines, the best game dishes in the city, pan-fried mushrooms bordelaise, roast skate with ginger and mint leaves, delicious milk-fed roast lamb fragrant with marjoram and delicate dessert pastries.

A la carte: 250-300F. Menu: 250F (menu dégustation).

⑬ Les Vieux Métiers de France

13, bd Auguste-Blanqui - 45 88 90 03, 45 81 07 07

M. Moisan. Open until 10:30 p.m. Closed Sun. & Mon. Air cond. Pets allowed. Cards: V, AE, DC, MC.

The comically ultra-modern decor's accent is on fake stonework and beams on the ground floor of a modern building bordering the Butte-aux-Cailles. The cooking is genuine, however, and even though he's not much of an explorer, Michel Moisan certainly makes an effort to update his classic cuisine. Try one of the terrines, grilled salmon with fresh noodles, sea scallops beurre blanc and beef tenderloin in wine . . . which brings us to the wines (not to be forgotten!). The list is extraordinary in length and quality, including splendid aged port. And note that chef Moisan is a superb pastry cook.

A la carte: 350F. Menu: 195F.

FOURTEENTH ARRONDISSEMENT

⑬ Les Armes de Bretagne

108, av. du Maine - 43 20 29 50, 43 22 01 67

M. Boyer. Hours & closings vary. Air cond. Parking. Pets allowed. Cards: V, AE, DC, MC.

After a bad period, this once-impressive little restaurant has regained its toque with its delicious seafood classics, such as fricassée of abalone and pan-fried sole with beurre blanc. The service is flamboyant and a bit affected, and the reception warm and friendly. The quite pleasant, comfortable Second Empire setting boasts large tables and roomy banquettes.

A la carte: 350F.

⑬ L'Assiette

181, rue du Château - 43 22 64 86

Mme. Lucette. Open until 10:30 p.m. Closed Mon., Tues. & Aug. Pets allowed. Cards: V, AE, DC.

Lulu from the Basque country, her beret pulled down over her ears, keeps turning out heaping plates of first-class bistro fare: rillettes (cold paste) of mackerel, homemade pâté of poultry and foie gras or wildfowl, cured duck, veal kidneys in mustard sauce. These dishes suit her temperament as well as the old-fashioned butcher-shop decor—not to mention the tastes of her plate-cleaning customers. There are several delicious desserts, such as rhubarb-apple crumble and île flottante (floating island), and good wines from the Touraine. It's too bad that it has gotten so expensive, and that the service is so hopelessly slow.

A la carte: 280-300F.

12/20 Le Bistrot de la Gaîté

20, rue de la Gaîté - 43 22 86 46

M. Reissinger. Open daily until 11 p.m. Air cond. Parking. Pets allowed. Cards: V, AE, DC.

This place is among the last of those good old popular bistros, where patrons of the now-defunct Bobino music hall used to come to celebrate after the show. Plain, honest decor and a good standard cuisine: marinated herring, lamb stew, skate with hazelnut butter. Good little wines from the countryside.

A la carte: 180-200F. Menu: 76F.

⑯ La Cagouille

12, pl. Brancusi - 43 22 09 01

M. Allemandou. Open until 10:30 p.m. Closed Sun., Mon., Aug. 12-Sept. 4 & Dec. 22-Jan. 2. Terrace dining. Parking. Pets allowed. Cards: V.

Gérard Allemandou, with his Neptune beard and Bacchic belly, offers the freshest fish and shellfish in town (in company with Le Duc and Le Divellec). This jovial native of Charentes embarked on his culinary career with no more equipment than a gargantuan appetite, a few good tips on supply sources and extraordinary talent. He claims he has none, but what else would you call his ability to prepare fish as if he invented the species? It makes one lose patience with all those false purveyors of "grande cuisine" who smother seafood in layers of butter or pastry or stuffing and have yet to discover the real taste of black scallops from the Brest harbor, gilthead seasoned with herbs, flaked skate sauce gribiche (tangy mayonnaise sauce) or silver hake with mustard sauce. Where does Allemandou go to get the marvelously fresh creatures whose names are inscribed daily on the blackboard? No farther than Rungis, the Paris market complex, where he performs his purchasing miracles twice a week. There are a few desserts (the dark-chocolate fondant and a flat apple tart are excellent) and a limited selection of good wines, but the collection of Cognacs from local growers is remarkable. Just one small gripe we'd like to get off our chest: The welcome and service in this small (60-seat), clean-lined, noisy restaurant are about as friendly as . . . a cold fish.

A la carte: 400-500F.

12/20 La Coupole

102, bd du Montparnasse
43 20 14 20

M. Bucher. Open daily until 2 a.m. Cards: V, AE, DC.

Habitués old and new of this Montparnasse landmark all voice strong opinions about its recent refurbishment, commissioned by new owner Jean-Paul Bucher, head of the Flo brasserie empire. We wonder how many of those critics are aware that the "new" Coupole is actually a near-perfect facsimile of the old Coupole, as it looked on opening night in 1927? The brown velvet banquettes, gold-flecked green pillars, lemonwood *boiseries* and art deco lights have all been restored to their former splendor; the famous murals (none of which, alas, are by Foujita, Kisling, Chagall or the others who made La Coupole their headquarters in the twenties) are freed at last from layers of grime. Considering that the staff must greet and serve nearly 4,000 clients a day, it's a minor miracle that the food manages to be as good as it is—fine, fresh crabs, oysters and prawns, and such creditably handled brasserie classics as foie gras in a Riesling aspic, sumptuous choucroutes, fried whiting with tartar sauce, roast leg of lamb, grilled pig's tails and ears, andouillette and much more. With a cool carafe of the house Riesling, the tab won't leave you gasping. Our only gripe is that the place is as noisy as Bedlam; but then again, bright lights, stylish crowds and loud chatter have always been part of La Coupole's mystique.

A la carte: 250F.

Le Duc

243, bd Raspail - 43 20 96 30

M. Minchelli. Open until 10:30 p.m. Closed Sat., Sun. & Mon. Pets allowed. Telex 204896. No cards.

Paul Minchelli is one of the rare chefs who understands that when it comes to fish, less is more. His minimalist approach brings out flavors of unsurpassed purity, so unusual that from time to time patrons accustomed to the neutral, aseptic taste of fish that's been kept on ice indignantly send a superb bass or John Dory back to the kitchen; they don't realize that the "smell" to which they object is the smell of the sea! Minchelli, however, doesn't always man the stove at Le Duc, since he has other fish to fry in the restaurants he and his brother, Jean, own in Geneva and the Seychelles. Luckily his assistant, Tony, a cook of Italian-Scottish descent, has Minchelli's techniques down pat; we dare you to guess who's in the kitchen from what's on your plate.

A food writer recently confided that she hates fish—except at Le Duc. We, on the other hand, adore seafood, but we share her belief that it doesn't get much better than in this dining room. In fact, we would—almost—trade Robuchon's sublime sesame sole for Le Duc's turbot or sea bass cooked with brilliant simplicity (and not a trace of fat) between two Pyrex plates placed over a plate of boiling water. A few seconds later (timing is crucial here), the fish is sprinkled with sea salt and served forth. *Et voilà!*, pure perfection—as long, of course, as the fish is as irreproachably fresh as Le Duc's. But that dish isn't the only string to Minchelli's culinary bow. Sample his coquilles St-Jacques sautéed in palm oil for precisely three seconds, tiny clams with thyme, crisp, irresistible beignets of lotte, squid, lobster and langoustines, poached lobster or lobster with orange, or delectable red mullets grilled whole with their innards intact. Accompany all this with a crisp Muscadet from Métaireau, a Meursault-Charmes or—why not?—a Château Margaux, and you will know unalloyed bliss—until the fatal moment when the check arrives. And remember: This is not an eat-now, pay-later proposition, for Le Duc has the audacity to not accept credit cards.

A la carte: 450-800F.

14 Aux Iles Marquises

15, rue de la Gaîté - 43 20 93 58

M. Thery. Open until midnight. Closed Sat. lunch & Sun. Pets allowed. Cards: V, AE.

This narrow little restaurant shaped like a railroad car, with its funny shrimp-colored paintings, large mirrors and pretty nautical frescoes, represents the past glory of Montparnasse (in its heyday led by Edith Piaf). The food was never good until recently (1985), when Mathias Théry opened his fine seafood restaurant. Some of the main courses are no less than brilliant: crown of frogs' legs with watercress and hazelnut oil, and crab flan in the shape of a quenelle with a fine, thick, highly seasoned sauce. Excellent desserts (paper-thin tarts, millefeuilles with red fruit or citrus fruit) are provided by Mme. Théry, a rather timid but charming hostess, whose father is M. Demund, the great pastry chef in Bordeaux. The wine list and fixed-price menus are ideal, only one shouldn't have to ask for them when the à la carte menu is brought around.

A la carte: 300F and up. Menus: 110F, 140F.

12/20 Le Jéroboam

72, rue Didot - 45 39 39 13

M. Bon. Open until 10 p.m. Closed Mon. dinner & Sun. Pets allowed. Cards: V, AE.

This big, bright, attractive modern bistro on two levels, with red bricks and woodwork, is mobbed day and night for its buffet and daily specials (potted duck thighs, roast wild boar with noodles) and its shrewd wine list. The waitresses smile gamely but are clearly overwhelmed by the hectic pace.

A la carte: 150F.

15 Lous Landés ✿

157, av. du Maine - 45 43 08 04

M. Rumen. Open until 11 p.m. Closed Sun. Air cond. Terrace dining. Pets allowed. Cards: V, AE, DC.

Ever since Georgette Descat, first lady of the Landes region in Paris, took off her apron, Lous Landés hasn't been the same. Jean-Pierre, her son, took over the kitchen for a while but recently made his own departure. Fortunately, the place couldn't have fallen into better hands: Hervé Rumen gave up his tiny dining room, Le Croquant (in the fifteenth arrondissement), for this large one, which is now practically unrecognizable in its new green outfit of plumage-decorated fabric that goes nicely with the coffee-bean curtains. The Descats' collection of bric-à-brac was amusing if coarse; the new decor is simple, friendly and quietly elegant.

The Landes isn't far from Périgord, and regular customers won't feel homesick having to choose from a shorter but still distinctly southwestern menu of duck foie gras served with brioche-like toast and truffles, farmer's ham, fricassée of wild mushrooms, cured breast of duck with foie gras sauce, pigeon in Madiran with coriander, cassoulet and knuckle of lamb with garlic juice. Rumen's simple, generous cuisine will be beyond reproach once he drops the habit of undercooking both his vegetables and his meats. There are a few good desserts (spiced apple tart, macao with dark chocolate and dark rum), a limited selection of wines, including the excellent Cahors from Gilis, and reasonable prices.

A la carte: 250-300F. Menu: 240F.

12/20 L'Olivier-Ouzerie

9, rue Vandamme - 43 21 57 58

M. Mavrroïdakos. Open until 11 p.m. Closed Sun. & July 30-Sept 3. Pets allowed. Cards: V.

This new and agreeable little Greek tavern is remarkable for its spotless tables, fresh interior decoration (facing a verdant patio) and satisfying cuisine: tarama, cucumbers in cream, grape leaves, moussaka, Greek-style cod. Pleasant, inexpensive white retsina.

A la carte: 150F. Menus: 49F (lunch only, wine incl.), 68F.

15 Pavillon Montsouris

20, rue Gazan - 45 88 38 52

M. Courault. Open daily until 10:30 p.m. Garden dining. Parking. Pets allowed. Cards: AE, DC.

It used to be a delightful place, but the food was no good. It's still delightful, and now the food is great. There's no doubt about it: Jean-Michel Bouvier, the young chef who's taken over the kitchens, is a good one. He might even turn out to be excellent. With Senderens and Guérard for teachers, he could have done worse, but Bouvier isn't here to repeat their lessons. Owner Yvan Courault, who was once with the Grand Véfour, is determined to revive this "historic" pavilion that has played host to

Lenin, Trotsky, Mata Hari, Henri (Le Douanier) Rousseau, Braque and Prévert, but he doesn't intend to do it by engraving the customers' checks in gold leaf. From the start, he adopted and stuck with the policy of a single menu/carte for 210 francs, feeling that at that price, people weren't likely to complain as long as the cooking was decent.

This distinctive greenhouse is so charming, with its pink walls and flower-shaped lamps, that you scarcely notice what's on your plate. But Bouvier's cuisine is not merely decent—it's brilliant. In a great restaurant, people would willingly pay twice as much for it. A miracle? Nothing of the sort—simply a rational approach to modern cooking. In concert with such restaurateurs as José Lampreia of La Maison Blanche, Bouvier has grasped the fact that one can serve good food for less than a fortune. It just takes a little thought: You have to rule out such costly items as truffles, foie gras and lobster and be creative with less-costly ingredients. On the menu this translates to a superb terrine of calf's feet with green peppers, warm skate filets on a bed of mixed salad with sherry vinegar, salmon trout with a highly seasoned oil-and-vinegar dressing, raw tuna steak, braised oxtail with cabbage, roast stuffed wild duck and a splendid platter of three raviolis filled with calf's feet, pork and lamb, the raviolis' distinct flavors are exceptionally delicate. We have one small suggestion for Bouvier: If he used less concentrate and more juice in his sauces, his cooking would be even better.

Following a first course and a main dish, a delectable bittersweet-chocolate marquise with coffee syrup or an almond-cream layer cake with cherries arrives, and for 250 or 300 francs, including an excellent Chinon, you've got a steal in one of the liveliest, loveliest settings in Paris.

Menu/carte: 210F.

FIFTEENTH ARRONDISSEMENT

12/20 L'Amanguier
51, rue du Théâtre - 45 77 04 01
See Second Arrondissement.

Bistro 121
121, rue de la Convention
45 52 52 90
Mmes. Moussié. Open until 10:30 p.m. Closed Sun. dinner, Mon., July 14-Aug. 15 & Dec. 22-29. Air cond. Pets allowed. Cards: V, AE, DC, MC.

After 25 years on the scene, there's not a wrinkle on the calf's head sauce gribiche (tangy mayonnaise sauce), duck liver with verjuice (the juice of unripened grapes), casserole of stuffed chicken or wild hare à la royale (type of custard). Chefs from the Quercy region have come and gone, but the good Moussié ladies carry on, making the rounds of their restful dining room, with frilly lamps lighting each table.

André Jalbert, who energizes the chic clientele with dollops of truffle, warm leeks vinaigrette, duck confits and beef skirt steak in mustard sauce, and José, the bubbly Portuguese sommelier who delivers the finest Burgundies and Bordeaux, have been too busy to celebrate their years of service. Only that annoying little extra zero now clinging to the original 40-franc menu reminds you that it's time to turn your clock ahead.

A la carte: 400F. Menu: 250F (wine incl.).

11/20 Le Bistro Champêtre
107, rue St-Charles - 45 77 85 06
M. Dorr. Open daily until 11 p.m. (11:30 p.m. weekends). Air cond. Terrace dining. Pets allowed. Cards: V.

The menu that has made this bright, flower-decked restaurant such a success has expanded to include several hearty dishes, such as lotte with sea urchin coral and roast saddle of lamb with tarragon essence. Affordable, well-planned wine cellar.

A la carte: 130F. Menus: 135F (wine incl.), 63F.

12/20 Yvan Castex
2, rue Langeac - 48 42 55 26
M. Castex. Open until 10 p.m. Closed Sun. Pets allowed. Cards: V, AE.

The many-membered Castex family—mother, father, two sons and their wives—arrived recently from Tours to take over this cozy restaurant. Unfortunately, the once-good cooking has proved disappointingly dull and careless of late. Perhaps Yvan Castex has been affected by the increasingly grand atmosphere—classical music and overdone appointments—but whatever the reason, his cuisine features overly thick shellfish ravioli, a wilted and unattractive salad of scallops, and an uninteresting sole bonne femme. Only the excellent desserts remain at one-toque level.

A la carte: 300F. Menus: 135F (wine incl.), 220F.

Les Célébrités
(Hôtel Nikko)
61, quai de Grenelle - 45 75 62 62
M. Sekihara. Open daily until 10 p.m. Air cond. Parking. Pets allowed. Telex 260012. Cards: V, AE, DC, MC.

Those noble busts of Roman emperors leering down at your calf's tongue sauce gribiche (tangy mayonnaise sauce) may remind you of something. In fact, their twin brothers sit atop the columns in Robuchon's dining room. This is not surprising, since the same Japanese owners funded the decor that so delighted future culinary genius Joël Robuchon when he cooked here.

Since taking over these kitchens, Jacques Sénéchal isn't turning out the same style of cuisine that he did for twelve years at the Tour d'Argent, nor has he slipped into the "sub-Robuchon" category. He has a distinct talent all his own, which produces some superb, highly elaborate (and horrendously expensive) preparations—too elaborate on occasion—as well as exquisite sauces. (The most recent menu no longer included the Japanese-style cod, and we can't say we're sorry, because the sake-based sauce and mouth-puckering seaweed were more than we could handle.)

There are fewer Japanese (who regard the Nikko as their home away from home) than French in this panoramic dining room overlooking the Seine, and the latter tend to order the excellent foie gras, roast langouste (spiny lobster) with mushrooms, sea scallops with truffles, chevreau (kid) with mild garlic or superb lamb with tarragon cream sauce, all of which, along with Jean-Paul Cauvin magnifi-

cent desserts, make Les Célébrités one of the finest hotel restaurants in Paris.

A la carte: 500-800F. Menus: 220F and 260F (lunch only), 540F, 640F.

Charly de Bab-el-Oued
215, rue de la Croix-Nivert
48 28 76 78, 45 31 35 92
See Seventeenth Arrondissement.

12/20 Le Ciel de Paris
(Tour Montparnasse)
33, av. du Maine - 45 38 52 35
M. Dufresne. Open daily until midnight. Air cond. Pets allowed. Telex 804418. Cards: V, AE, DC, MC.

Paris, vaporous and alluring, stretches out 300 yards below. The kitchen tries hard, and visitors from the countryside who flock to this immense glass cage perched high in the clouds are flabbergasted. Try the veal terrine laced with parsley and the desserts from Lenôtre.

A la carte: 250F. Menu: 135F.

Le Clos Morillons
50, rue des Morillons - 48 28 04 37
MM. Delacourcelle & Leguay. Open until 10:15 p.m. Closed Sat. lunch & Sun. Air cond. Pets allowed. Cards: V.

Philippe Delacourcelle has made great progress of late, and this restaurant, which he took over from Pierre Vedel a few years ago, is regaining its stature with a cuisine that is at once personal and improvised. The curried celery flan is a marvelous blend of contrasting flavors, the rabbit stew is tender and seasoned with a superb ginger sauce, the soy-flavored sauce accompanying the steamed salmon is a model of delicacy, and the rhubarb cake (actually a flan) topped with red-fruit sauce reminds us that this former pupil of Morot-Gaudry was also a pastry chef at Fauchon. Philippe's brother, Marc, puts out a short list of selected Loire wines (on the "discover the Loire Valley" menu; you may order them by the glass). The service staff is singularly aloof, but the new decor is more comfortable, with attractive round tables and a spacious, subdued interior lined with old photographs and mirrors.

A la carte: 260F.

⑬ Le Croquant

28, rue Jean-Maridor - 45 58 50 83

M. Bigot. Open until 10:30 p.m. Closed Sun., Mon. dinner & Aug. Pets allowed. Cards: V, AE, DC.

Hervé Rumen, the likable "croquant" (peasant) who made this restaurant so successful with his fine southwestern cuisine, has gone and opened Lous Landés (fourteenth arrondissement). The new chef's cooking, however, is uneven and lacks finish but is interesting nonetheless. The Norman oysters and mushrooms are disappointing, but the John Dory with shallots is nicely done. Several good Norman specialties are to be had, as well as excellent vanilla ice cream. Prices (including those of the modest cellar) are very fair, and Mme. Bigot, who greets you and takes care of the service all by herself (for now), is charming.

A la carte: 260-300F. Menus: 160F (lunch only), 230F.

⑬ Didier Délu

85, rue Leblanc - 45 54 20 49

M. Délu. Open until 10:30 p.m. Closed Sat., Sun. & Dec. 23-Jan. 2. Pets allowed. Cards: V, AE, DC.

Bocuse, Lameloise and Chapel have a few grateful pupils. One of them is Didier Délu, who honors their lessons on his menu and their faces on his walls. The new half-modern, half-nostalgic decor is pleasant and lively, but we were left with a few lingering question marks concerning the food after our last visit. Délu knows how to do fish, roll out flaky pastry and whip up a sauce, but his rabbit terrine with fines herbes, for example, was lackluster. You'll also find grilled red mullet with tomato pulp, a feuilleté of sweetbreads with glazed carrots, unusual whiskies, a good selection of wines and attractive fixed-price menus, if rather small portions.

A la carte: 300F and up. Menus: 150F (lunch only), 200F (dinner only, wine incl.).

⑭ Erawan

76, rue de la Fédération - 47 83 55 67

M. Napaseuth. Open until 10:30 p.m. Closed Sun. & Aug. Air cond. No pets. Cards: V, AE.

This is the best Thai cooking in Paris: colorful, fragrant, light and exciting, a happy blend of Chinese, Indian and Malayan influences. Specialties range from the shrimp soup with lemon grass and pimientos, the heavenly prawns (marinated in galanga, a fragrant root), the chicken wings stuffed with pork, crab and water chestnuts, the fish soup with celery, to the tender, subtle oven-browned flan with coconut milk. Hot or iced tea is the perfect beverage to set off such delicately spiced fare.

A la carte: 220-250F. Menus: 79F (lunch only), 158F, 164F, 175F.

⑬ La Gauloise

59, av. de la Motte-Picquet
47 34 11 64

M. Aphécetche. Open until 11 p.m. Closed Sat. & Sun. Terrace dining. Pets allowed. Cards: V, AE.

La Gauloise's savvy clientele consists of well-known sports personalities, like Yannick Noah, and politicians (including Mitterrand) whose faces decorate the walls of this long dining room. The staff seems to take this as license for arrogant behavior. The new owners have changed neither the menu nor the decor—the latter a not exactly unpleasing affair in light brown, and the former basic bistro food, a little overdone and overpriced: tuna rillettes, excellent fish court bouillon with a velouté of mussels, good lemon tart. Fine selection of Bordeaux, enjoyable terrace dining on the boulevard and fearsome prices.

A la carte: 300-350F.

⑭ Kim-Anh

15, rue de l'Eglise - 45 79 40 96

M. Kim-Anh. Dinner only. Open until 11:30 p.m. Closed April 2-10 & July 16-30. Pets allowed. No cards.

Kim-Anh fled to Paris from Saigon, where he imported American automobiles and a famous brand of French Cognac. This charming, articulate, pipe-smoking man has arranged his tiny dining room tastefully to accommodate twenty diners in an intimate, elegant setting of white woodwork, wicker panels, black walls and pleasant lighting. Flowers, white napkins and decorated chopsticks contribute to the refined atmosphere.

The lilliputian kitchen is his wife's territory. In split seconds, she prepares the tangy dishes sprinkled with fresh herbs and subtle spices that make Vietnamese cooking so appealing. Every dish is a revelation for the taste buds: light, crunchy nems, served in a nest of assorted greens and mint leaves (green on the outside, lavender inside, imported from Vietnam), with the compelling flavor of lemon grass; bo-bun, composed of sautéed shredded beef in a mixture of stir-fried green vegetables with vermicelli, peanuts and shallots marinated in vinegar; caramelized langoustines served with a remarkably fragrant Thai rice; stuffed crab; glazed duck; and a delicious creamed corn with coconut that, for a change, makes one eager to try a dessert in a Vietnamese restaurant. Even the coffee is good! Reservations are a must for this small room.

A la carte: 230-300F. Menu: 158F.

⑬ Les Lutins

29, av. de Lowendal - 47 83 51 22

M. Lancry. Open until 10:30 p.m. Closed Sun. dinner, Mon. & Sept. 15-Oct. 3. Pets allowed. Cards: V, MC.

Two young men are partners: One acts as host and the other mans the kitchen, turning out respectable everyday cooking. Fresh, seasonal, high-quality ingredients mark the cuisine of this new restaurant, which deserves more recognition. Try the boned squab with turnips and the sponge biscuit with farm cheese. Desserts and prices require lighter treatment.

A la carte: 250-300F. Menu: 110F.

La Maison Blanche

⑰ 82, bd Lefebvre - 48 28 38 83

M. Lampreia. Open until 11 p.m. Closed Sat. lunch, Sun. & Mon. Air cond. Pets allowed. Cards: V.

When other restaurants are half empty, José Lampreia's place is mobbed. His recipe is simple: talent, taste, good looks (journalists like the latter, as do customers), a ready smile, not taking oneself too seriously and a willingness to slave ten hours a day.

You must also understand three things. Number one is that a restaurant is a pleasure dome. And when you enter this all-white room—walls, tablecloths, even the 300 flowers that poke their heads out of one colossal vase—you suddenly become younger, more streamlined than in many eating places that make you

feel ancient. La Maison Blanche quite simply reflects the trend of the times without being trendy. Number two is that diners don't want to spend a fortune even if they can afford to. The trick is to avoid luxury items, rely on seasonal produce and rack your brain to transform everyday ingredients into something special. If you want to use foie gras, use just enough to "grease" a superb potato cake moistened with a bit of truffle juice. How about sea urchins? Fill them with chopped pigs' feet for a divine combination. The third rule is to surprise your guests with innovative dishes that are in keeping with classic cuisine. You can see that Lampreia, working in a glass-bound kitchen dressed in immaculate white, never indulges in extravagant preparations.

This sophisticated Portuguese chef has a rustic streak in his veins—a smart peasant with good taste! He has won our admiration for his salad of calf's head; his turbot and whipped potatoes with olive oil; his sea bream, its skin all crusty with spices, garnished with raisin semolina; his velvety oven-browned rabbit; his parsleyed steak with potatoes au gratin; his marvelous desserts (gingered pear compote, praline-glazed macaroon, caramel leaves with red fruit, rhubarb tart with vanilla ice cream); and the excellent ordinary wines, ranging from 70 to 100 francs (and up, of course).

A la carte: 400-500F. Menu: 250F (lunch only).

⑯ Morot-Gaudry

8, rue de la Cavalerie - 45 67 06 85

M. Morot-Gaudry. Open until 10:30 p.m. Closed Sat. & Sun. Air cond. Terrace dining. Pets allowed. Cards: V.

If asked to name ten Paris restaurants we'd like to revisit, we wouldn't choose some of the more celebrated and highly rated ones, but Morot-Gaudry would definitely be on our list. Why do we love it? Because it's run by such an endearing couple. Jean-Pierre is smart and down-to-earth, unlike some of the celebrity chefs whose heads have grown too swollen to make it through their kitchen doors. His wife is gracious and smiling, the perfect hostess. Also, there's the picturesque setting of this 1930s converted garage, where you dine in an elegant mirrored room or on a verdant little terrace overlooking the rooftops. By craning your neck, you can glimpse the Eiffel Tower, which seems planets away. And we love it because of the discerning clientele (which comes here to dine rather than to be seen), the wine cellar (where great and not-so-great bottles are given equal place) and, of course, the constant care lavished on the cooking by Jean-Pierre.

His sweetbreads with mushrooms, veal kidney roasted whole in its own fat and Barbary duckling in Hermitage white wine are evidence of his mastery of classic principles. And when Jean-Pierre injects the sunny, herbal flavors of Provence into his creations, it conveys a style all his own. The chocolate desserts are delectable, as are the miniature fruit tarts and the caramelized apple in a light cream sauce. And the "businessman's lunch" is a spectacular bargain.

A la carte: 380-500F. Menus: 200F(lunch only, wine incl.), 300F, 420F (wine incl.).

Olympe

17 8, rue Nicolas-Charlet - 47 34 86 08
Mme. Nahmias. Open until midnight. Closed Sat. lunch, Sun., Mon., Aug. 1-20 & Dec. 24-Jan. 2. Air cond. Pets allowed. Cards: V, AE, DC.

Once a wasteland at lunch (though crammed to the rafters at dinner), Olympe is now a choice Parisian venue for a midday feast. Magic? No—the turnaround was just a question of dollars and cents. Dominique Nahmias (alias Olympe) had the bright idea to introduce a 200-franc fixed-price lunch offering a choice of fifteen starters and entrées, homey desserts and a little selection of charming wines tariffed at about 70 francs. Businessfolk who entertain here at lunch know they won't look like cheapskates to their guests, who can enjoy prawn bouillon with ravioli, crunchy calf's-brain beignets with capers or succulent rabbit terrine with pickled vegetables, followed by rosy slices of Pauillac lamb or a robust civet of suckling pig with macaroni and Swiss chard.

After a period of desertion by the fickle Parisian public, the restaurant is now operating full blast in the evening. The stylish crowd adores Olympe's clever, lively cuisine, modern yet rooted in tradition. Olympe got the message that people were tired of hefty tabs, stilted service and bowing maître d's. So she turned to less costly ingredients of equally high quality—and found that her old customers came back en masse, enchanted by checks that totted up to 350 to 400 francs, rather than twice that.

The food *chez* Olympe is hearty and bursting with earthy flavors: duck ravioli with wild mushrooms, chestnut-flour galette with spinach and woodland mushrooms, skate and potatoes pepped up with coriander, and roast rabbit with artichokes perfumed with pesto. So adieu, foie-gras-this and truffle-that! And believe us: You'll never miss them.

A la carte: 350-400F. Menu: 200F(lunch only).

12/20 Le Petit Mâchon

123, rue de la Convention
45 54 08 62
Mme. Moussié. Open until 10:30 p.m. Closed Sun., Mon. & July 25-Aug. 20. Terrace dining. Pets allowed. Cards: V.

This is one of Slavik's most handsome recreations of an old-time bistro, and it's devoted to the cuisine of the Lyon area, just like its main branch next door (Bistro 121): rosette de Lyon (pork sausage), tripe, knuckle of ham with lentils and every Beaujolais in the book.

A la carte: 160-180F. Menu: 75F.

La Petite Bretonnière ☙

15 2, rue de Cadix - 48 28 34 39
M. Lamaison. Open until 10 p.m. Closed Sat. lunch, Sun. & Aug. Parking. Pets allowed. Cards: V, AE.

Alain Lamaison is a smart man. Rather than underwrite the decorating trade, he preferred simply to make his tiny dining room more comfortable and cozy and to keep his prices down. By choosing raw salmon with parsley cream sauce, gâteau landais with truffle juice, caramelized grapefruit and a half liter of Madiran for 250 francs, you can enjoy a wonderful meal for 250 francs. For a trifle more, you can sample the innovative southwestern cuisine of this 28-year-old chef, who has a most engaging style: foie gras, terrine of duck, oyster soufflé gratiné, roast duck with mushrooms and apple tarte. There's a good choice of affordable wines from all over. Warm reception from Georgia Lamaison.

A la carte: 250-300F.

12/20 Pizzéria Les Artistes

98, bd de Grenelle - 45 77 79 70
MM. Dessez & Verrières. Open until 10:45 p.m. Closed Sun. & year-end holidays. Air cond. Terrace dining. Pets allowed. Cards: V, AE.

For the best pizza in Paris and pasta by the yard with every imaginable sauce and herb (if there are three of you, order the assortment), this is the required stop. Excellent fixed-price menu and an amusing collection of customers packed into a room under the elevated Métro.

A la carte: 160F. Menus: 57F, 99F.

⑬ Raajmahal
192, rue de la Convention
45 33 29 39, 45 33 15 57

M. Kassam. Open daily until 11 p.m. Air cond. Pets allowed. Telex 692151. Cards: V, AE, DC.

Amin Kassam will never end his days on a bed of nails. Not satisfied with having recycled this former bathhouse on the rue de la Convention into a temple of North Indian cuisine, this flamboyant Bengali is now franchising a chain of takeout restaurants that are entirely predesigned, from the microwave ovens to the shape of the dining seats. Add to that an extensive business in spices, basmati rice, tea and coffee, and you can understand why Kassam is a busy man. A little too busy, it seems, when things don't run smoothly in his maharajah's palace with fishbowl lighting through a glass roof, when the service is confused and when the deliciously fragrant cooking is off its mark. But since he takes such pride in his profession, he's sure to heed our advice and tighten the screws on his operation.

Specialties include meat-filled samosas, marinated lamb or chicken with mint and pimientos en brochette broiled over charcoal in the tandoor oven, monumental lamb's-knuckle curry, biryanis of meat or fowl soaked in a diabolic sauce with at least twenty spices, and bread (both leavened and unleavened), all so delicious that it more than makes up for the unabashed simplicity of the Indian desserts.

A la carte: 200-280F. Menu: 79F (weekday lunch only).

⑯ Le Relais de Sèvres
(Hôtel Sofitel Paris)
8-12, rue Louis-Armand - 40 60 30 30, 40 60 33 66

M. Ciret. Open until 10 p.m. Closed Sat., Sun., Aug. & 1 week at Christmas. Air cond. Parking. Pets allowed. Telex 200432. Cards: V, AE, DC, MC.

We're still waiting for chef Roland Durand to strike out on his own, as we're sure he someday will. But he's a cautious one, not eager to launch his own place unless he's certain he can succeed. This award-winning cook, admired for his ability, his experience and his professionalism, is *chef des chefs* for the Sofitel hotel group. He is equally comfortable arranging a reception for a thousand guests or training the young talents who win raves for the chain's kitchens all over France. Now wouldn't you think that Sofitel would reward this hardworking, serious chef with a dining room decor worthy of his exquisite food?

The dishes Durand has prepared for us fell just short of the three-toque level: hot duck pâté baked in potato dough, crusty herbed snails, fresh cod stuffed with crab, oven-baked sea bream with pressed olives and macaroni gratin, calf's-head fricassée with mushrooms, rump of rabbit baked tandoori-style. This is distinguished, distinctive cooking—a far cry from traditional hotel dining—that is firmly rooted in classic and regional repertoires (Durand is from the Ardèche region). And his desserts prove once again that the best, most imaginative pastry chefs are now in the restaurant business. His b'stilla of cinnamon-flavored pears, crown of hot caramelized apples, and compote of vanilla-flavored rhubarb and ginger-glazed nougat are truly magnificent. There's an excellent fixed-price business lunch, and the many wines priced at or around 100 francs (red Sancerre, Bourgueil, Crozes-Hermitage, Pelouse) are far superior to bottles you'll find elsewhere at twice the price.

A la carte: 360-450F. Menu: 295F (lunch only), 250F.

⑭ Aux Senteurs de Provence
295, rue Lecourbe - 45 57 11 98, 45 58 66 84

M. Dell'omo. Open until 10 p.m. Closed Sun., Mon. & Aug. 2-22. Cards: V, AE, DC.

Léonardo Dell'omo, the cordial owner of this neighborhood bistro, and his new chef, Christophe Agemeister, may not be the most likely candidates for promoting Provençal cuisine, but they do a good job of it. And now, alongside the bouillabaisse, aïoli (served on Wednesdays), bourride (on request) and lamb daube are a number of new and inventive dishes, such as a terrine of skate wing stuffed with capers and fresh herbs, and some beautiful prawns simply poached in a nicely scented fish coulis. The excellent desserts, however, remain on the rustic side. Good wines from Provence and excellent service under the baton of Dell'omo, who was maître d' at Lucas-Carton in its glory days.

A la carte: 300-350F. Menus: 160F to 180F.

⑬ Uri

5, rue Humblot - 45 77 37 11
M. Cho-Ran-Ke. Open until 10:30 p.m. Closed Sun. & Aug. Air cond. No pets. Cards: V.

The chef for many years at the luxurious but disappointing Séoul, M. Cho finally opened his own place—or rather, "our place," which is what "uri" means. Two thousand Koreans in Paris have taken him to their hearts, and rightly so, because his fresh, appetizing cuisine reveals the unsuspected riches of an unfamiliar culinary tradition: chopped duck roll steamed in a cabbage leaf, deviled salad of raw skate, beef ragoût sauce piquante and exquisite soups, into which you dunk your white rice, as the French do their bread. Cordial reception by Mme. Cho and her son.

A la carte: 230F.

⑮ Pierre Vedel

19, rue Duranton - 45 58 43 17
M. Vedel. Open until 10:15 p.m. Closed Sat., Sun., 2 weeks in July & 1 week at Christmas. No pets. Cards: V.

Still one of the best values in town: Including wine (and Pierre Vedel knows how to select it), the average price of a meal can still be kept around 250 francs. That's the key to the record

success of this very Parisian bistro. Decorator Slavik's familiar hand can be detected in the white walls, fans, mirrors and old photos. Adored by his customers, Vedel—the nicest amateur weight-lifter you'll ever meet—ladles out hearty portions of mackerel filets, poached eggs in red wine, bourride "the way they make it down home" (he comes from Sète, like his old pal Georges Brassens, the singer), calf's head, duckling with turnips, and île flottante (floating island).

A la carte: 250F.

12/20 Le Western

(Hilton)
18, av. de Suffren - 42 73 92 00
M. Baillet. Open daily until 11 p.m. Terrace dining. Pets allowed. Parking. Cards: V, AE, DC, MC.

The Tex-Mex frenzy has hit Paris, thus re-kindling interest in good ol' Le Western, where many Parisians got their first taste of real T-bone steak and guacamole. The recently spruced-up decor is a match for any of the newfangled "cowboy" places springing up nowadays in Les Halles and elsewhere, and the new chef has even snuck a few contemporary dishes onto the menu, alongside the steaks and barbecued spareribs. Some traditional French specialties are also offered (the *suggestion du chef* changes weekly) as well as an attractive business lunch menu. The wine list features a judiciously chosen selection of French and Californian vintages.

A la carte: 250-300F. Menus: 180F, 210F (wine incl.).

SIXTEENTH ARRONDISSEMENT

11/20 Auberge du Bonheur

Bois de Boulogne, Allée de Longchamp
42 24 10 17
M. Menut. Open until 11 p.m. Closed Sat. (off-seas.) & Feb. Garden dining. Parking. Pets allowed. Cards: V.

At this excellent little place in the Bois, you sit in the shade of 100-year-old chestnut trees, eat crisp salads and grilled meats and sip pleasant growers' wines at reasonable prices. You couldn't ask for a more pleasant experience.

A la carte: 180-200F. Menu: 100F (wine incl.).

11/20 Brasserie Stella

133, av. Victor-Hugo - 47 27 60 54
M. Guerlet. Open until 1:30 a.m. Closed Aug. Terrace dining. Cards: V.

The oyster bar poking out onto the sidewalk attracts the fashionable set from this fashionable neighborhood until late at night. The cheerful, boisterous crowd appreciates the good, solid home-cooking (pot-au-feu, smoked pork and the like).

A la carte: 200F.

(14) Paul Chène

123, rue Lauriston - 47 27 63 17

M. Chène. Open until 10:30 p.m. Closed Sat., Sun., July 30-Sept. 2 & Dec. 24-Jan. 3. Air cond. Parking. Pets allowed. Cards: V, AE, DC.

The outward appearance of a nice little neighborhood restaurant often hides its true character, just as the names of certain dishes leave diners puzzled (mackerel in Muscadet wine, fried "angry" silver hake). However, at Paul Chène it's the tastiest mackerel and the best "angry" hake, plus marvelous terrines, a real potted chicken Henri IV, goose confit with celestial parsleyed potatoes, and mouth-watering desserts like grandma used to make (apple fritters with currant jelly and caramel-flavored île flottante). The big problem is that this nice little neighborhood restaurant charges an arm and a leg. Everything is delicious and abundant, but before you can blink an eye your bill is up to 400 francs, and folks complain that that's too steep for a rustic, old-fashioned place where all you've eaten is rabbit afloat in a Riesling aspic and garnished with french fries (but delicious ones, to be sure), or daube of beef with wine and onions.

A la carte: 400F.

(15) Conti

72, rue Lauriston - 47 27 74 67

M. Ranvier. Open until 10:45 p.m. Closed Sat. & Sun. Air cond. Pets allowed. Cards: V, AE.

Fine cooking in a light, modern vein: French with Italian styling or vice versa. Michel Ranvier gives his own subtle interpretations to ravioli (stuffed with cabbage and chopped sweetbreads), lasagne (with foie gras and herbs vinaigrette), scampi (superb miniature lobsters grilled with basil), polenta (with curried lamb) and a masterpiece sabayon (with port wine). Everything is beautifully presented and served with typical Italian courtesy in a maroon-colored interior under a Murano chandelier. Try the generous pasta sampler, fettuccine with black truffles or the feathery-light Mascarpone cake. Excellent French and Italian wines.

A la carte: 350F.

(14) L'Estournel

(Hôtel Baltimore)

1, rue Léo-Delibes - 45 53 10 79

M. Lo Monaco. Open until 10 p.m. Closed Sat., Sun., Aug. & holidays. Air cond. Telex 611591. Cards: V, AE, DC, MC.

The decor of this circular hotel dining room is one of the few in Paris unlikely to develop early wrinkles. The crimson walls, Decaris paintings and simple, elegant furnishings recall the carefree atmosphere of posh prewar restaurants that never seem to go out of style. We wish the same could be said for the cooking, but with a rich international business clientele who are probably not the most demanding gourmets, chef Henri Boutier has not been kept on his toes. He has accustomed us in the past to more precise and subtle results than the overcooked hot oysters, jarring crab ravioli with orange sauce, overly honeyed duck breast and the needless, half-cooked apples in the exquisite rhubarb pastry. We must withdraw, therefore, our second toque. As always, however, you can expect an excellent wine list and impeccable service.

A la carte: 400F and up. Menu: 215F.

(13) Fakhr el Dine

30, rue de Longchamp - 47 27 90 00

M. Bou Antoun. Open daily until midnight. Air cond. Parking. No pets. Cards: V, AE, DC.

Upper-crust Lebanon in a jolting blend of white beams and paneling, beige fabrics and soft lighting. Local color need not apply! The doorman makes a mockery of traditional Lebanese hospitality and is likely to send you packing if you don't have a reservation and aren't from one of the rich families that come here to feed their nostalgia for the old country. Small, medium and large mezze (27 cold, 18 hot) are, in the opinion of those in the know, the best in Paris. After tasting the hummus (purée of chickpeas in sesame oil), moujaddara (purée of lentils), baba ghanouj (purée of eggplant with lemon), fatayers (pastry filled with chopped meat and spinach), kébbé (meatballs) and rkakat (cheese puff pastry), all of which make it pointless to read the rest of the menu (so-so brochettes, stuffed chicken and the like), we agree. The pastries are so light and flaky that you'll be lulled into thinking that you didn't really just consume a week's worth of calories.

Expect expensive wines—which doesn't mean they're all good—and a check of about 300 francs with a half bottle of ksara (a Lebanese wine) and a glass of arak.

A la carte: 300F. Menus: 136F (lunch only), 130F.

Faugeron
18 52, rue de Longchamp - 47 04 24 53
M. Faugeron. Open until 10 p.m. Closed Sat., Sun., Aug. & Dec. 23-Jan. 3. Air cond. Parking. No pets. Cards: V.

Of all the period menus concocted to honor the Bicentennial of the French Revolution, Faugeron's was undoubtedly the best. Henri Faugeron's milk soup with onions and croutons, delicately spiced rabbit, pigeon poached in court bouillon and (a personal invention) "decapitated" potatoes stuffed with milk-poached sweetbreads were so delicious that we hope he will keep them in his repertoire. Faugeron, the chef who introduced us to soft-boiled eggs with truffle purée and hot goat-cheese salads, is in tip-top form these days. Though he isn't a slave to novelty, his handsomely presented menu changes often enough to pique our curiosity and our appetite on every visit. Of course, our taste buds are always happy to reacquaint themselves with Faugeron's house-smoked salmon, turbot in red wine, oxtails cooked for ten hours and garnished with meltingly good carrots, and his many other signature dishes. But at our last meal he outdid himself, regaling our palates with a rare and subtle succession of flavors: first, an exceptionally delicate asparagus bavarian, followed by veal shins in a Sauternes sauce touched with curry and sweet onions (destined, we hope, to become a house classic) and one of the best desserts we've tasted in some time: a sugar-free apple charlotte bathed in vanilla custard. So it is surely no accident that Henri and Gerlinde Faugeron's spacious blue-and-saffron dining room is more crowded than ever with patrons who seem mightily pleased to be there. Faugeron was one of the first *grands restaurants* in Paris to offer a fixed-price business lunch, and an appealing and generous one it is, including an appetizer, a fish and a meat course and

dessert. Jean-Claude Jambon, wine steward *extraordinaire*, will propose some excellent affordable wines to accompany your meal. If, on the other hand, you feel inclined to splurge on a superlative bottle, he'll obligingly produce one from his fabulous cellar.

A la carte: 600F and up. Menus: 290F (lunch only), 455F.

Jean-Claude Ferrero
16 38, rue Vital - 45 04 42 42
M. Ferrero. Open until 10:30 p.m. Closed Sat. (except Sat. dinner in winter), Sun., April 28-May 21 & Aug. 11-Sept. 3. Parking. Pets allowed. Cards: V, AE, DC.

Jean-Claude Ferrero is now a happy man, owner of a cozy Second Empire house; a lovely dining room full of happy patrons who are coddled by his charming wife, Andrée; a vest-pocket garden with a fountain; and an upstairs room for twenty diners with a view of a flowery patio. He also has peace of mind—or something like it, for Ferrero is a restless spirit. This athletic-looking man devotes himself exclusively to one sport: cooking. City streets may not be the ideal location for a country lad born and bred in Briançon, where he used to gather mushrooms and hunt rabbits; now he must wait for nature to come to him. Since Ferrero's head is always brimming with ideas for new concoctions, dining is never a bore on the rue Vital. Langoustines sautéed with nut oil and lime juice (without salt or pepper), filet of bass with bacon and spinach, salt-cod stew, prune and truffle sorbet . . . the list goes on and on. He adores working with mushrooms and truffles, which he adds to every sauce; in season, he celebrates with special "all-mushroom" (550 francs) and "all-truffle" (550 to 600 francs) menus, which have become a tradition with Parisian gourmands.

Several of our recent meals here merited three toques, but others fell short—the good ideas were poorly executed. Though we know he's a cussed individualist, we suggest that Ferrero hire a trusty sous-chef to work side by side with him and help cope with the growing numbers of clients.

A la carte: 400F and up. Menu: 220F (lunch only).

⑭ Le Grand Chinois

6, av. de New-York - 47 23 98 21,
47 23 99 58

*Mme. Tan. Open until 11 p.m. Closed Mon. &
Aug. Pets allowed. Cards: AE, DC.*

Colette Tan is Cambodian, and she's polished to the tips of her long fingernails. A
member of the family that operates Tan Dinh
(seventh arrondissement), her shared interest
in collecting great Bordeaux wines is understandable. These wines accompany some excellent dishes, such as shrimp with stir-fried
vegetables, steamed Chinese cabbage with
crab, glazed duck roasted on the spit and
minced pigeon. The ultra-red, typically Chinese decor is cluttered but comfortable and
permanently furnished with the poshest Chinese clientele in Paris.

A la carte: 250F and up. Menu: 110F (lunch
only).

⑯ La Grande Cascade

Bois de Boulogne, near the Longchamp
racetrack - 45 27 33 51

*M. Menut. Open until 10:30 p.m. Lunch only
Nov. 1-April 14. Closed Dec. 20-Jan. 20. Gar-
den dining. Parking. Pets allowed. Cards: V,
AE, DC.*

The iron-and-glass marquee of this graceful
pavilion tucked away in the forest spreads its
wings like a giant dragonfly speared on a pin.
In summer, the spacious terrace, which seats
120 people, is one of the most beguiling outdoor dining spots in Paris. Until recently,
though, the interior was another story. But
André Menut and decorator Dominique
Honnet have created an elegant, lighthearted
pastiche, using yard upon yard of draped fabric,
tons of bright paint, gold leaf and droll furnishings. The restaurant's foyer and bar look
coquettishly fresh, while the dining room is
arrayed in bouquets of rococo curlicues.

Whether you settle outside under the pretty
parasols or inside beneath the ornate ceiling
and glass roof, the service is impeccable, ably
directed by André Menut and his son. This
stylish Belle Epoque establishment, a favorite
of Colette's, is best known for its consistently
fine classic cuisine produced with a light touch
by chef Jean Sabine. It may not be what you'd
call creative cookery, but it is dependably fresh,
tasty and surprisingly simple for such a posh

address: fondant of rabbit with Chablis and
herbs, fish poached in seaweed and basil,
sweetbreads in truffle butter and a tart of caramelized green apples. Sumptuous wines.

A la carte: 500-700F. Menu: 240F (lunch
only).

⑰ Patrick Lenôtre

28, rue Duret - 45 00 17 67,
45 00 20 45.

*M. Lenôtre. Open until 11 p.m. Closed Sat.
lunch & Sun. Pets allowed. Cards: V, AE, DC.*

His family name is practically a household
word; now he wants to be a celebrity in his own
right—"do his own thing," as he puts it.
Lenôtre, a nephew of Gaston Lenôtre, served
as chef at Le Pré Catelan for years and, more
recently, at Les Jardins Lenôtre on the
Champs-Elysées before buying Guy Savoy's
old restaurant: a small, elegant dining place
with light paneling, walls the color of marbled
foie gras and a mirror in the back to create the
illusion of space. Mauro Fratesi, who used to
work at La Marée and Laurent, manages the
dining room and presents guests with their
menus, the caliber of which instantly places this
restaurant among the finest in town: salmon
marinated with parsley and white nettles, cold
filets of sole en gelée (too bad the aspic was
flavorless), sea trout with squid and fennel,
excellent braised saddle of hare, beef flank with
marrow, a magnificent hot soufflé of tropical
fruits, sabayon flavored with tea and rhubarb,
and delicious homemade breads, petits fours
and chocolates. All told, it's a well-balanced,
mouth-watering repertoire that ought to make
Lenôtre II a gastronomic idol. We would,
however, like to see a few more affordable
wines on the list, but Patrick Lenôtre is clearly
no advocate of moderate prices. Another point
in this edition.

A la carte: 350-550F. Menus: 220F (lunch
only), 260F and 460F (weekday dinner only).

⑯ Michel Pasquet

59, rue de La Fontaine - 42 88 50 01,
45 20 13 38

*M. Pasquet. Open until 10:45 p.m. Closed Sat.
lunch, Sun., July 15-Aug. 15 & Dec. 23-27. Air
cond. Pets allowed. Cards: V, AE, DC.*

Something's out of order at Michel
Pasquet's place. And that's too bad, for he's a

talented chef. The gaps are between his elaborate cuisine, the would-be service on a grand scale (it doesn't work because there's not enough help) and the pleasant decor without any real style, in which the good elements (attractive pink banquettes, subdued lighting, handsome dinnerware) share center stage with the not-so-good (fake flowers and just the wrong shade of green wallpaper). This sense of disorder, compounded on the night of our visit by clusters of empty tables, doesn't do justice to the expert cooking, confirmed once again by a delicious plate of escargots in pastry; ravioli filled with lobster and leeks and sauced with a remarkable soy butter; a thick, tender turbot with chive butter; and excellent sweetbreads. Though the flavor of our desserts was slightly muddled, the petits fours were flawless. And the price was right. The 280-franc fixed-price menu has great variety, and the 160-franc lunch is a real bargain.

A la carte: 350F. Menus: 160F (lunch only), 300F.

Le Petit Bedon

38, rue Pergolèse - 45 00 23 66
M. Marchesseau. Open until 10:15 p.m. Closed Sat., Sun. & Aug. Air cond. Pets allowed. Cards: V, AE, DC.

Christian Ignace has forsaken his pretty little restaurant and his upscale (but well-bred!) clientele, leaving everything in the hands of veteran chef Pierre Marchesseau, author of some 40 cookbooks. A jolly, pot-bellied kitchen pro ("Le Petit Bedon" means "the little paunch," so what could be more appropriate?), Marchesseau has slanted the menu toward classic dishes with clear, uncomplicated flavors. He's not one for bold combinations or creative cooking. Fresh crab Tante Louise, mussels au gratin, rack of lamb with scalloped potatoes, casseroled veal kidney with mustard sauce, Bresse chicken braised in vin jaune with morels—that sort of thing is more up his alley. It may sound heavy, but Marchesseau is blessed with a light touch. Even a dish as daunting in prospect as red mullet with onions and a duck-liver fondue turns out to be delicious and eminently digestible. Chef Marchesseau has a sweet tooth as well: The menu lists no fewer than twenty desserts. Though we found the chocolate fondant with coffee sauce a bit cloying, the cherry fondant with Champagne (ask

for it without the Champagne) is admirable, and the chocolate profiteroles filled with honey, pistachios and caramel ice cream delight the pretty people who chat picturesquely in a dining room that belongs in the pages of *House and Garden*. Service is ably directed by Daniel, formerly of Lamazère; prices are in keeping with the fashionable neighborhood.

A la carte: 350-600F. Menu: 200F (lunch only).

La Petite Tour

11, rue de la Tour - 45 20 09 31, 45 20 09 97
M. Israël. Open until 10:30 p.m. Closed Sun. & Aug. Pets allowed. Cards: V, AE, DC.

Freddy Israël, who was tired of his cramped quarters on the rue de l'Exposition, recently bought this sleepy old neighborhood restaurant. He hasn't had the time to change the too-dainty decor, but his wife's warm reception, the comfortable banquettes and his good cooking calmed our impatience. The modest, polished cuisine rarely repeats itself (it will in time) and is light and meticulously prepared: lobster bisque, fresh duck-liver maison, sea urchin soufflé (a few spines wandered into our preparation), a remarkable mustard-flavored veal kidney, and desserts still in the development stage. No fireworks, but no blunders either. Just good, solid, reliable dishes that the fashionable Passy crowd eats up.

A la carte: 300F and up.

Le Pré Catelan

Bois de Boulogne, rte. de Suresnes 45 24 55 58
M. Lenôtre. Open until 10 p.m. Closed Sun. dinner, Mon. & Feb. school vacation. Garden dining. Parking. Pets allowed. Telex 614983. Cards: V, AE, DC.

For years the food at Uncle Gaston's hadn't been anything to write home about—either at his place on the Champs-Elysées or here, where Denis Bernal presides as chef. But now, this 33-year-old cook, trained by Michel Guérard, along with his assistant and fish chef, is quietly but steadily weaning the house away from its "restaurant" cuisine. His dishes aren't just pretty to look at, they are flavorful, hearty and have real personality. For example, the firm-fleshed rock lobster in a delicate paprika sauce, the bouquet of lobster with baby vegetables, rock mullet "buttered" with its liver, lotte tail in a pistachio cream sauce, pan-fried filet of turbot steeped in vanilla and fresh mint and lightly sauced with beurre blanc, baron of rabbit with herb-stuffed ravioli and a dish that you rarely find in Paris, an exquisite goose filet mignon with "kitchen tobacco" (the name invented in the seventeenth century for powdered dried mushrooms).

Since top French chefs like Jean Bardet, Michel Trama, Pierre Gagnaire and Jacques Chibois have conditioned us to recognize truly outstanding desserts, we are all the more critical of Lenôtre's repertoire, knowing as we do that in his time he revolutionized French pastry making. Everyone has copied his gâteau opéra and worn out his mousse recipes. Of course, the napoleon with caramelized pastry cream, soufléed crêpes with bitter cherries and vanilla ice cream, and apricot rice suprême are fine desserts. But if the Lenôtre pastry squad really means to impress, they'll have to do it a lot more, and not merely repeat tried-and-true recipes. Lenôtre pastries are often oversugared, and we are beginning to tire of it. What we never tire of is the perennial charm of the Belle Epoque dining room, with its frieze designed by Caran d'Ache and, bordering the park, the marvelous terrace thick with greenery. Colette Lenôtre provides the reception, and the service is regal, if a trifle solemn.

Since the Bois de Boulogne is just outside the door, ask Denis Bernal or his assistant to tell you his secret places to find mushrooms (boletus and morels), not to mention the fat truffle he rooted out, in true Périgord style.

A la carte: 600-800F. Menu: 580F.

12/20 Le Presbourg

3, av. de la Grande-Armée
45 00 36 40, 45 00 24 77
M. Chaunion. Open daily until 1 a.m. Terrace dining. Pets allowed. Cards: V, AE, DC.

Le Presbourg's amusing, comfortable terrace, designed like a greenhouse, faces the Arc de Triomphe. The cooking attempts a variety of styles: delicious calf's head, hearty choucroute with pigs' knuckles, and a confused blend of fresh cod and oysters. Good wines by the pitcher and excellent service.

A la carte: 300F. Menu: 92F.

Robuchon   Cuisinier du siècle

19.5 32, rue de Longchamp - 47 27 12 27
M. Robuchon. Open until 10:15 p.m. Closed Sat., Sun. & July. Air cond. Parking. Pets allowed. Cards: V.

Joël Robuchon is a great artist, but he's no prima donna—unlike so many of his egotistic confrères who take themselves for Michelangelo. Perhaps we journalists are partly responsible for the inflated egos. Yet how is it that the most gifted chef in France has managed not to be tainted by the praise heaped upon him by the press? Simply because deep down, Robuchon, who is far less timid than legend would have it, has remained an exacting craftsman. To the endless, delirious acclaim he responds simply with more discipline and effort.

Like some others, he could give private lessons all over the globe, "supervise" a menu in Los Angeles and another in Tokyo, sell "consultations" right and left or waste time suing colleagues for stealing his recipes. Instead, he prefers to teach young cooks, to help out his friends in the profession and to manage his 45-seat restaurant with an iron hand. Don't dream of disturbing Robuchon at mealtimes. Any columnist who gets the bright idea of telephoning him during those sacred hours is told that the call will be returned later—quite the opposite of the celebrated chefs who come crawling whenever the media whistle. But if you could watch Robuchon at work in the kitchen, you'd understand his attitude. He seems to have eyes all over his head; he doesn't miss even the smallest detail, and he won't let a single plate enter the dining room without his approval. How many "great" chefs take that trouble these days?

We might as well go ahead and say it: For our money, Robuchon is the best. He has taken traditional French cooking and contemporary cuisine and melded them in a way that has inspired a whole generation of chefs. In a word, Robuchon is the pivotal figure on the gastronomic scene today. At the risk of wounding his genuine modesty, the Gault Millau guide, which is now celebrating its twentieth birthday and which was the first to recognize Robuchon's genius, wishes to pay a special homage to this singular chef. By giving him a rating of 20 out of 20? No, only the good Lord could give himself a mark like that, and only on one of his better days! By naming

Robuchon "chef of the year"? Everybody knows that he has been the best every year. So why don't we just go ahead and declare him *cuisinier du siècle*, or "chef of the century" (perhaps in tandem with Fredy Girardet and Paul Bocuse, who also have serious claims to that honor)?

A title like that is a weighty responsibility. But you will admit that he earned it, and you may want to heap him with even greater honorifics, on the frabjous day when your name reaches the top of the waiting list and you sit, along with 44 other diners, in Robuchon's dainty, beflowered, pale-green dining room. Your pleasure will then be attended to by a staff of 35 cooks, waiters, maître d's and busboys, all of whom make this little gem of a restaurant the very best in France. Service is dignified but simple, overseen by Jean-Jacques, Robuchon's dining room manager since the Nikko days. Thankfully, no obsequious waiter will ask you a hundred times if you're enjoying your meal.

Each Saturday, Robuchon uses his day off to try out his latest ideas. His palate is infallible; when a dish gains his approval, you can be certain that it is absolutely perfect, neither needing nor lacking a milligram of salt, herbs or spice. His most recent strokes of inspiration included a dish of "smothered" spider crab, whose delicate essence was enhanced, not masked, by black pepper, thyme, green bell pepper, saffron, a pinch of curry, diced mushrooms and zucchini; langoustines cooked alive in a bouillon based on four or five types of mushrooms, a dish with an incredibly deep and powerful flavor; sole with sesame seeds that did away with our long-held prejudice against complex fish dishes; and two apparently ordinary dishes transformed by the Robuchon magic into unforgettable experiences: a ragoût of duck giblets with lentils and a simply roasted Bresse chicken, its juices saturating a garnish of macaroni and truffles. This isn't just gastronomy, dear readers, this is high art. Like the tarte au chocolat, with a crust invisible to the eye but delectably present on the tongue.

We'll wait until next time to talk about Robuchon's fried whiting with herb butter, his simmered pig's head, his sweet-and-sour venison mignonnettes, his crème brûlée and his cellar's white Chinon and other grandiose bottles (tended by sommelier Antoine Hernandez), which can boost your bill to astronomic heights. We hope our message has come through loud and clear—Joël Robuchon is not the least talented chef in town!

A la carte: 600-800F and up. Menu: 790F.

⑭ Sous l'Olivier
15, rue Goethe - 47 20 84 81

M. Warnault. Open until 10:30 p.m. Closed Sat., Sun. & holidays. Terrace dining. Pets allowed. Cards: V.

The southern cuisine of this former Italian restaurant acquired a northern accent under the guidance of its new owner/chef, William Warnault, from Picardie. We miss the terrine of duck Amiens-style, the smoked eel with horseradish and the other home-style specialties that seem to have disappeared from his menu, probably deemed not worthy of this chichi neighborhood. We'll content ourselves instead with the exquisite galette of calf's feet with a tangy watercress sauce, calves' liver pan-fried in its own juices and seasoned with an astonishing clove sauce, buttered potatoes and a perfect Calvados sorbet. All this warrants an extra point, but the waitresses definitely need to shape up. There's a bright, comfortable blue-and-white decor on two levels.

A la carte: 250-300F. Menu: 150F (dinner only).

⑭ Le Sully d'Auteuil
78, rue d'Auteuil - 46 51 71 18

M. Brunetière. Open daily until 10:30 p.m. Air cond. Terrace dining. Pets allowed. Cards: V, AE.

The most cheerful, luxurious and cozy railroad-station buffet in France (owned by the SNCF, the French rail system). This delightful Belle Epoque lodge at the Auteuil train depot, with its ivy-covered terrace and fresh, gilt-edged decor (salmon-tinted Japanese wallpaper, thick carpeting, Louis XVI armchairs, elegant dinnerware), owes its success not to enterprising railroad management but solely to the long-term efforts of a seasoned professional. That's Michel Brunetière, whose 45 years in the kitchen haven't dulled his boyish enthusiasm. He passes among the tables cracking jokes for the politicians and theater people who enjoy the cordial reception (Brunetière's son-in-law doubles as host and sommelier), fine service and excellent food. Brunetière's imagination sometimes carries him overboard; nobody would object if he removed a number of puzzling, ill-defined entries from his over-loaded à la carte menu or omitted the ham and melted cheese that asphyxiate his beautifully seasoned lamb filet with coriander. Desserts are clever but tend to be too sweet or too dense (like the apricot torte). Prices are pretty stiff.

A la carte: 380-400F.

16 Le Toit de Passy

94, av. Paul-Doumer - 45 24 55 37

M. Jacquot. Open until 10:30 p.m. Closed Sat. lunch, Sun. & Dec. 28-Jan. 9. Air cond. Terrace dining. Parking. Pets allowed. Cards: V.

In his rooftop restaurant, chef/owner Yannick Jacquot prepares a cuisine character-ized by precise, distinct flavors: salad of pigeon and beans with purslane (an herb-weed for salads) in an exquisite hazelnut oil vinaigrette, John Dory filets with artichokes poivrade, rock lobster with citrus butter, parsleyed lamb with an eggplant compote and Brittany squab in salt pastry—not to mention a half dozen good desserts, including a millefeuille with red fruits, and a broad selection of wines. Don't expect affordability—you're also paying for a view of the Eiffel Tower.

A la carte: 400-500F. Menus: 225F and 270F (lunch only), 395F.

13 Tsé Yang

25, av. Pierre-Ier-de-Serbie
47 20 68 02

M. Tong. Open daily until 11 p.m. Cards: V, AE, DC.

This lavishly decorated opera set came, in sections, straight from Hong Kong. Along with the elegant porcelain dinnerware, flashy cutlery and collection of ivories in display cases, this Far Eastern Versailles has cost M. Tong a small fortune, which he is rapidly recouping by charging the highest prices in town for Chinese food. But the luxury-hotel crowd in this neigh-borhood and the Mideast oil magnates don't seem to notice. The cuisine is meticulously prepared with the freshest ingredients—shark's-fin soup, roast duck with Chinese tea, sautéed shrimp with a spicy sauce—and choice wines are available.

A la carte: 350F. Menu: 195F.

14 Vi Foc

33, rue de Longchamp - 47 04 96 81

M. Té Vépin. Open until 10:45 p.m. Closed Aug. 11-28. Air cond. Parking. Pets allowed. Cards: V, AE, DC.

M. Té travels all over the world and brings back recipes for his kitchen. It's a rare Asian restaurant in which you can eat regularly with-out repeating a dish—but here you can sample from an ever-changing list of such items as a salad of fresh mangoes and sea scallops, egg-plant stuffed with crab and shrimp, giant shrimp with mild pepper and duck with plum sauce. You'll find a distinguished Asian decor and good everyday wines, but the checks are getting daunting.

A la carte: 250-300F. Menu: 100F (lunch only).

Vivarois

19 192, av. Victor-Hugo - 45 04 04 31

M. Peyrot. Open until 9:45 p.m. Closed Sat., Sun. & Aug. Air cond. Pets allowed. Cards: V, AE, DC.

For ages now, as anyone who's read our reviews over the years could perceive, we've been itching to give Claude Peyrot that elusive fourth toque. We've watched the man's im-mense talent develop and mature for so many years; in fact, we were among the first to wander into his restaurant on a fine day almost 25 years ago. But recently we were perplexed to hear that Peyrot planned to drop everything, fly off to Marrakech and learn the secrets of Moroccan cuisine! Another time he threatened to retire to a remote corner of his native Ardèche. What next? we wondered. Time passed, and Peyrot calmed down. He stayed in his kitchen, creating dish after dish full of brio and invention, making his customers swear that he had attained a state of grace. Now we ask you: How could we keep back the fourth toque? The answer is, we can't. Here it is, Claude, and we hope it will persuade you to forgo foreign adventures and stick to your stove.

Peyrot may be the only chef in creation who doesn't babble on to his clients about the composition of his sauces or how hard it is to find decent help these days. No, he prefers to chat about God or death or psychoanalysis (he's a renegade Lacanian himself), anything rather than listen to praise of his marvelous cuisine. Lately, his painful timidity seems to have abated a bit; he still doesn't enjoy compliments, but he hides his embarrassment.

Nowadays Vivarois is full almost every evening, and we suspect that the elegant crowd doesn't show up just to admire the restaurant's rather forbidding decor (American cherry paneling, gray marble, abstract paintings). Word has surely spread that the food is divine. There's a bracing terrine of sardines with a black-olive coulis, salt cod in a spicy crust, bass stuffed with raw lobster and scallops, a succulent pig's trotter enveloped in caul fat, an unsurpassed version of chicken with morels and a very personal reading of that culinary chestnut, lièvre (hare) à la royale (Peyrot's includes tart, bright-tasting quince). This chef's technique is flawless; proportions and cooking times are calculated with extreme precision.

Sommelier Jean-Claude Vinadier, he of the sparkling glance and mischievous mustache, will produce the perfect partner for every course—from the first appetizer through the final, irresistible dessert—from Vivarois's prodigious wine cellar. Jacqueline Peyrot oversees all the proceedings with a kindly, maternal eye.

A la carte: 550F and up. Menu: 315F (lunch only, wine incl.).

SEVENTEENTH ARRONDISSEMENT

12/20 L'Amanguier
43, av. des Ternes - 43 80 19 28
See Second Arrondissement.

Apicius
122, av. de Villiers - 43 80 19 66
M. Vigato. Open until 10 p.m. Closed Sat., Sun., Feb. school holidays & Aug. Air cond. Parking. Pets allowed. Cards: V, AE.

In some restaurants the food is good but you feel uncomfortable; in others the food is second-rate but you feel relaxed. It's difficult to find comfort and good dining under one roof. At Apicius, however, you'll find the best of both worlds. The Paris carriage trade knows it, and at lunch and dinner, it packs the pastel dining room, where blond, fragile Madeleine Vigato waits to greet her guests.

Apicius is a fashionable restaurant, though it's not a social gathering spot where one comes to be seen. Rather, it's a place to sit back and enjoy its "rejuvenated" classic cuisine, designed not so much to dazzle the eyes as to tempt the palate with light sauces and natural flavors. We read somewhere that Jean-Pierre Vigato is on his way to stardom—sheer nonsense, considering that this tall, athletic-looking hulk of a man, who's actually rather timid, doesn't enjoy mixing with the public. His habitat is his kitchen, and he hasn't wasted his time there. Among other things, he has developed the budding talent that was manifested at Grandgousier at the foot of Montmartre. Today, he creates a short à la carte menu, plus several daily specials, all of which are based on sound principles of contemporary cooking, with excursions into hearty regional fare. His wife will enthusiastically describe them all for you. For instance, his "marbled" blend of sweetbreads and lobster; his medley of white fish, cooked separately, with olive oil (a good example of southern French cooking); his whole roasted scallops, firm and savory, with shallots and parsley; his John Dory with honey and vinegar (a contemporary blend of flavors); and his magnificent side of salmon, barely cooked through, with herbs and leeks. There are also such sturdy meat dishes as lamb tenderloin en crépinette with green cabbage, boned roasted pigs' feet in parsley-flavored juices, and calf's head lightly rubbed with lemon, which drives calf's head lovers wild.

Of the desserts (they are among the best in town), we most like the coffee gratin with lemon-cream glaze, a superb blancmange with almond milk, and an all-bittersweet-chocolate creation. If you want to sample some of the treasures of the small but choice cellar, consult Marc Brockaert, the knowledgeable, amusing sommelier we remembered from Guy Savoy and later Le Divellec. It's time for a third toque.

A la carte: 400-650F.

16. La Barrière de Clichy
1, rue de Paris, 92110 Clichy
47 37 05 18

M. Le Gallès. Open until 10 p.m. Closed Sat. lunch & Sun. Air cond. Pets allowed. Cards: V, AE, DC, MC.

When Gilles Le Gallès took over this restaurant at the age of 30, it was a shambles. He repainted and refurbished it from cellar to attic with the help of decorator Michel Lussot and made it into a place of great charm and intimacy: pink and white tones, flowered fabrics and colorful lithographs. When he finally reopened, word traveled and the mink and chinchilla brigade flocked to investigate. They were delighted by the fine, light cuisine—hot oysters with coriander, squid stuffed with duck liver accompanied by a zucchini purée, mushrooms with cabbage and almonds, a superb John Dory with olives, filet of bass with walnuts, a bravura tenderloin of lamb with goat cheese—served in a relaxed setting.

A la carte: 300-350F. Menus: 245F (lunch only, wine incl.), 330F.

13. Le Bistrot d'à Côté
10, rue Gustave-Flaubert - 42 67 05 81
M. Rostang. Open until 10:15 p.m. Closed Sat. lunch, Sun. & Aug. 1-15. Terrace dining. Pets allowed. Cards: V.

Next door to his own restaurant, Michel Rostang opened this pleasant bar and grocery, in which he serves home-cooking in the styles of Lyon and Paris: excellent duck rillettes and terrines, macaroni au gratin (so-so), andouillette (on the dull side) and delicious tripe. Modest wines and simple, friendly service.

A la carte: 180F.

15. La Braisière
54, rue Cardinet - 47 63 40 37
M. Vaxelaire Open until 10:15 p.m. Closed Sat., Sun., holidays, Feb. school vacation, May 1-8 & Aug. Pets allowed. Cards: V, AE.

Pinkish-beige walls, cretonne curtains, elegant tables (too close together) and attentive service: Bernard Vaxelaire's restaurant fits the perfect image of a large, prosperous Parisian bistro. This impression is confirmed by the confident, consistent cooking turned out for the past five years by a brilliant graduate of the hotel school in Strasbourg. The cuisine is resolutely modern in execution rather than inspiration. Vaxelaire values harmony over audacity; he loves fine products, precise timing and minimal sauces, but he's not interested in having a creative fling. All the same, his menu keeps in tune with the times, as evidenced by the tomatoes stuffed with snails and wild herbs, center cut of salmon cooked on one side, lotte bourguignon with tiny ravioli, and fondant of sweetbreads and squab. Desserts are wonderfully light, there's a large selection of wines, and prices are reasonable for such high quality.

A la carte: 350F. Menu: 185F (wine incl.).

13. Charly de Bab-el-Oued
95, bd Gouvion-Saint-Cyr
45 74 34 62

M. Driguès. Open daily until midnight. Air cond. Pets allowed. Cards: V, AE, DC.

This is the patriarch of the Charly chain that began some twenty years ago. In those days, along with the couscous decor you got a free performance by the boss, a delightful Algerian-born Frenchman who went from table to table regaling customers with Bab-el-Oued stories. Then Bernard Driguès became a businessman and became scarce here. Times have changed. Now a Japanese makes the couscous—which is excellent, light and distinctively garnished. In addition, there is lamb en brochette (méchoui), Algerian b'stilla, good tajines (stew) and ultra-rich pastries. Warm reception and impeccable service.

A la carte: 200-250F.

15. Chez Augusta
98, rue de Tocqueville - 47 63 39 97
M. Berton. Open until 9:30 p.m. Closed Sun., Aug. & holidays. Pets allowed.
Cards: V, AE, DC.

One of the best fish restaurants in town, Chez Augusta already had that reputation when Marcel Bareste was in charge, and it has moved up a notch since Didier Berton came along a few years ago. He updated the menu and spruced up the decor. Wisely, he has kept (and improved) certain house favorites that regular customers have been ordering for the past 25 years: the superb bouillabaisse with potatoes, simmered mutton tripe and trotters, and rack of lamb roasted in its own juices with potatoes Sarladaise (sliced and baked with goose fat). The menu changes every three months, not so much to reflect the market season as to refresh the repertoire. Thus, you can sample the delicious Augusta salad with seasonal shellfish, salmon with chives and first-rate langouste (spiny lobster) in court bouillon, and you can feast on exquisitely light, not-too-sweet desserts—the chocolate-and-cherry "delight" or the macaroon-and-pistachio creation. The splendid cellar holds great Bordeaux, rare Champagnes and good medium-priced wines.

A la carte: 400F.

(14) Chez Georges

273, bd Pereire - 45 74 31 00

M. Mazarguil. Open until 11:30 p.m. Closed Aug. Terrace dining. Pets allowed. Cards: V.

This is the best of Parisian family bistro atmosphere, noisy and fun, with all kinds of wonderful-smelling platters parading past your nose, borne by regiments of fast-moving if disorganized waiters. There is the roast lamb, a monument of smoked pork, a trainload of beef ribs, whole loins of roast pork and more. Cabbage, lentils, gratin dauphinois (one of the best in town), white beans and spinach accompany these robust entrées, which are carved tableside by adroit practitioners of the art. Chez Georges represents dependable, copious home-cooking and country-style fare at its best. Great little local wines, and the bill is always reasonable.

A la carte: 250F.

Clos Longchamp

(17) (Hôtel Méridien)
81, bd Gouvion-Saint-Cyr
40 68 34 34

M. Coulon. Open until 10:30 p.m. Closed Sun. Air cond. No pets. Telex 290592. Cards: V, DC, MC.

Wanting by no means to encourage absenteeism among head chefs, we admit nevertheless the pleasure of discovering, after a fine meal, that the boss is not in the kitchen that evening. If the orchestra plays just as well in his absence, it is indicative of how completely he

has molded them in his image (although he shouldn't make a habit, as some do, of proving it!).

Jean-Marie Meulieu had taken the night off when we dined at Clos Longchamp recently. Having known him for some time before he came here, we were delighted by what we found and could scarcely believe he had produced such a meal—and produced it second-hand, as it were. The execution was perfect, and the meal was exactly like a meal prepared when he is in attendance, from the duck liver with Beaumes-de-Venise, to the frogs' legs wrapped in spinach leaves and moistened with a Thai-style spicy sauce with fresh ginger, to the blanquette of sole with citronella, to the young rabbit stuffed with its liver mixed in herbs in a red-wine sauce that was the height of intensity and delicacy. We do not wish a broken leg upon chef Meulieu, but if he had to leave his pots for a few days, diners would have nothing to worry about.

The wine service by Didier Bureau is flawless, as is his ability to uncover hidden gems from the cellar, such as the 1983 Aloxe-Corton white from Sénard or the Vosne-Romanée les Suchots from Confuron. As for the decor, the split-level dining room with its equestrian frieze is not in any danger of making architectural history, and the deep booths force the serving staff to practically lie down on the table to serve those seated in the back. On the other hand, the newly redone garden does provide a pleasing backdrop. And besides, it is the chef, not the interior decorator, that we are rewarding with a third toque.

A la carte: 450-700F. Menus: 230F (weekday lunch only), 420F (weekday dinner only).

(15) Michel Comby

116, bd Pereire - 43 80 88 68

M. Comby. Open until 10:30 p.m. Closed Sat. (except dinner June-Oct.) & Sun. Terrace dining. Pets allowed. Cards: V, AE, DC.

The atmosphere is well behaved but not boring, the laughter muffled, the conversation in whispers, and you'll find the requisite sparkling silverware, fresh flowers and fine china—in short, this place has all the trademarks of an upscale private club. Michel Comby came here a few years ago with his maître d' and sommelier in tow, and the compliments began to pour in soon after, for which he was grateful after enduring years of neglect tending the ovens at

Lucas-Carton in its dog days. The service under his wife's direction is alert, low-key and on the rapid side, much to the satisfaction of the business lunch trade (it's not quite so active at night). And the cuisine is classic from start to finish, with modern overtones of lightness. Some of the old dishes from Lucas-Carton appear on the menu, such as the rich ballotines and the famous sole with a mushroom duxelles. The snails with Chablis, the marvelous hot Lyon sausage, the boned frogs' legs in puff pastry and the crusty glazed apples are star productions well worth our toques. The cellar is small, select, fairly priced.

A la carte: 350-400F. Menus: 175F (lunch only), 235F

12/20 Dessirier

9, pl. du Maréchal-Juin - 42 27 82 14, 43 80 50 72

M. Robinet. Open daily until 12:30 a.m. Terrace dining. Parking. Pets allowed. Cards: V, AE, DC.

The best oysters in Paris have a standing contract with this 100-year-old brasserie, which has been transformed over the years into a luxuriously appointed restaurant. You can eat them year-round—from the best sources, opened and presented by a professional. Nevertheless this is not the wonderful seafood restaurant it once was. But if you ignore the prices and keep your attention instead on the silk-lined surroundings, the marvelous shellfish, and the simpler fish dishes, such as filet of sole or grilled salmon steak, you'll leave with memories of a nice evening. Excellent wines are served by the carafe (petit Chablis or Brouilly).

A la carte: 400F. Menu: 150F (wine incl.).

Epicure

22, rue Fourcroy - 47 63 34 00

M. Péquignot. Open until 10:15 p.m. Closed Sun. Pets allowed. Cards: V.

The Péquignots, a most civilized, engaging couple, have given up chasing two rabbits through the same field. They've sold their annex on rue Cardinet and are working full time in this restaurant. The modern, impersonal dining room, though awkwardly geometric and harshly lit, is comfortable, with small, well-dressed tables. Mme. Pequignot moves among these tables tirelessly, eager to please. The fixed-price lunch menu is remark-

able: for example, a generous portion of foie gras, slightly cooked, in a fragrant aspic; followed by excellent homemade ravioli or minced veal kidney seasoned with coriander; and a thin, crisp apple tart. More or less the same menu applies at dinner and costs more; you can also order from the à la carte dishes developed by Alain Bergounioux, a former protégé of Dutournier's at Trou Gascon (oxtail in aspic with horseradish sauce, salad of smoked eel in a peppered vinaigrette). Lots of agreeable little wines sell for about 100 francs.

A la carte: 300-350F. Menus: 175F (lunch only), 195F (dinner only).

Epicure 108

108, rue Cardinet - 47 63 50 91
46 22 77 28

MM. Tourette & Goujon. Open until 10:30 p.m. Closed Sat. lunch, Sun. & holidays. Pets allowed. Cards: V, MC.

A new owner, a new chef and presto! We hear rounds of applause for this attractive "dining car" restaurant done in soothing shades of beige and pink. Chef Jean-Christophe Beaugon's credentials are minimal, but he is fast building a reputation for himself and his simple yet subtle cuisine, which is marked by clear, delicate flavors. Like the former owners, the Péquignots, the new management offers a single, changing à la carte menu and some of the same dishes: lamb's tongue with aromatic salad, a ruddy breast of duck flavored with honey, salmon steak with lentils and, for dessert, a flaky rhubarb turnover with caramel sauce. Good cellar with pleasant Loire wines and a memorable Brouilly.

A la carte: 185F.

L'Etoile d'Or

(Hôtel Concorde-La Fayette)

3, pl. du Général-Koenig - 47 58 12 84

M. Houin. Open until 10:30 p.m. Closed Aug. Air cond. Pets allowed. Telex 650892. Cards: V, AE, DC, MC.

The nightly piano music and formal dinner dancing on Fridays make this restaurant a great place to come for a romantic dinner and a chance to sample chef Joël Renty's contemporary cuisine. Try his salad of red mullet in hazelnut oil, northern cod in a soy sauce with chives, braised beefsteak with shallots, and honey-glazed nougat with apricot purée; the "symphony" of five chocolates is much too sweet. If it is all nicely done but lacks, well, inspiration, might that not be due to his having to supervise a staff of 80 across two restaurants and giant banquet rooms? The wine list holds several good values for about 100 francs, but that won't guarantee a merciful check, so it may be best to stick with the fixed-price menus, which are generous and attractive. Stylish modern decor and pretty brass lanterns.

A la carte: 400-600F. Menus: 198F (lunch only), 325F.

12/20 Goldenberg

69, av. de Wagram - 42 27 34 79

M. Goldenberg. Open daily until 11:30 p.m. Air cond. Terrace dining. Pets allowed. Cards: V.

This is the place to come for pickled herring, pike caviar, stuffed carp, Yiddish-style cassoulet and kosher Beaujolais. You'll immediately feel like part of the family in twinkly-eyed Patrick Goldenberg's nostalgic, amusing Paris delicatessen.

A la carte: 180-200F. Menu: 98F (wine incl.).

12/20 La Gourmandine

26, rue d'Armaillé - 45 72 00 82

M. Dumonteil. Open until 10:15 p.m. Closed Sun., Mon. & Aug. 15-30. Pets allowed. Cards: V, AE, DC.

The cuisine of M. Dumonteil, a diploma-studded chef, makes only the barest concessions to current fashion. The nearly perfect fixed-price menu includes, for example, a seasonal salad, curried fowl or stuffed pigs' trotters with foie gras and mushrooms, cheese, an excellent dessert and a regional wine. The nice wines are informatively listed.

A la carte: 250F. Menus: 145F (lunch only, wine incl.), 195F (weekdays only).

15 Guyvonne

14, rue de Thann - 42 27 25 43

M. Cros. Open until 10 p.m. Closed Sat., Sun., July 7-Aug. 1 & Dec. 22-Jan. 8. Terrace dining. Pets allowed. Cards: V.

For years this has been a quiet neighborhood eating spot, spared the turbulence of social success both by the moody reserve of the Monceau district and by owner Guy Cros's restrained ambition. The decor suggests a stylish little country inn, and your fellow diners will be informed food lovers, most likely regular customers who come to eat some of the finest cooking in town. And Cros never disappoints, especially with seafood, which he loves to prepare and to verbally describe for his guests: for example, grilled langouste (spiny lobster) with fresh artichokes, red-clawed crayfish that you won't find anywhere else in Paris (en cocotte with Chablis), oysters and clams with spinach and a few chanterelles, and pan-fried salmon with endives and watercress butter—evidence that he watches for seasonal products to come to market. Add to this impromptu menu a few excellent meat dishes, such as saddle of rabbit with chives, and old-fashioned desserts that melt in your mouth (superb fruit compotes). The prices are modest for such a high standard of quality.

A la carte: 350F. Menu: 195F.

13 Laudrin

154, bd Pereire - 43 80 87 40

M. Billaud. Open until 10:30 p.m. Closed Sat. & Sun. Air cond. Pets allowed. Cards: V, AE.

For the last 30 years, courtesy-conscious M. Billaud has been managing this lovely little yacht of a restaurant, with its mixture of nautical and Louis XVI decor and its comfortable booths. Chefs have come and gone; the present one maintains the high and (like the menu) unvarying standard of the bourride of lotte, Savoie-style beef rib steak Bercy and the remarkable "tripes de la Mère Billaud" (sliced thin). Plenty of fine wines are served in magnums (you pay only for what you drink).

A la carte: 300F and up.

16 Maître Corbeau

6, rue d'Armaillé - 42 27 19 20

MM. Giral et Guillet. Open until 10:30 p.m. Closed Sat. lunch, Sun., Feb. 12-20 & July 30-Aug. 21. Air cond. Pets allowed. Cards: V, AE, DC.

No longer content after fifteen years to preen its plumage in the obscurity of Ezy-sur-Eure, Maître Corbeau abandoned its thinning clientele recently and flew off to Paris, where it built a nest in the former Maisonette Russe. The latter has been rendered unrecognizable, with its light-oak woodwork, white lace tablecloths and the delicate flower arrangements that bespeak the fine taste of the superb hosts, Michel Guillet and Paul Giral.

En route, Maître Corbeau had the good

fortune to snare chef Julien Vasquez, formerly the number-two man at Duc d'Enghien. Chef Vasquez still seems shy in his new setting, but that can't last long—not when his first-rate talent is signalled by such dishes as prawn soup, featuring an intensely flavored vegetable broth; snail ravioli with licorice and sweet garlic on a bed of artichoke hearts; turbot (a shade over-done) with a green-olive sauce made with a flawless veal-and-rabbit reduction; and veal kidneys roasted in their fat, accompanied by an exquisite polenta with rosemary. The crème brûlée sported too much brown sugar, but the hazelnut-and-pistachio glazed nougat and the mocha brittle are great desserts. The wine list is superb, boasting some very good Bordeaux at humane prices, and the 250-franc fixed-price menu (including wine) and fairly priced à la carte menu have kept full one of the most attractive dining rooms in the best-fed neigh-borhood in Paris. It's all the more strange, therefore, that one of our trusted friends had the misfortune of waiting unconscionably long for his dinner, which eventually featured over-cooked fish and which undoubtedly ruined his evening.

A la carte: 350F and up. Menu: 150F (lunch only), 190F, 250F (wine incl.).

Le Manoir de Paris

⟨17⟩ 6, rue Pierre-Demours - 45 72 25 25
M. Vandenhende. Open until 10:30 p.m. Closed Sat., Sun. & July 9-31. Air cond. Park-ing. Pets allowed. Cards: V, AE, DC.

They talked about redecorating for three years, and it finally happened. This is classy stuff: Tiffany ceiling, mirrored pilasters, intri-cately carved white woodwork, flowers and greenery all over the place and, on the tables, little pink lamps that send out a seductive glow and put a sparkle in women's eyes. Pierre Pothier, who refurbished Maxim's, has done a great job here for Denise Fabre and Francis Vandenhende. Le Manoir, which never had anything going against it save its unappealing interior, has become one of the most attractive eating places in Paris. Chef Philippe Groult agrees. At one point he was ready to pack up and leave, complaining that the decor fell far short of the cuisine, but he soon unpacked his bags. Don't count on his being around forever, though; he'll open his own place one of these days unless they make him a partner.

Whatever the future brings, we have Pothier's remodeling to thank for perpetuating the cooking of one of Joël Robuchon's most gifted pupils. The cuisine even seems to have improved (not the first time that decor has affected a chef's morale), with more precise and substantial flavors. The calf's-foot aspic with a hint of truffle is incredibly subtle, the feuilleté of hot foie gras with spiced potatoes is lavish, and the ravioli stuffed with thyme-scented rabbit asserts the dignity of this perva-sive pasta product, subjected nowadays to sauce baths of every description and color. Chocolate-truffle cake, orange meringue and caramelized vanilla-and-chocolate ice cream are among the mouth-watering desserts. Ex-cellent wines selected by Francis's brother are served by jovial Rémy Aspect, and the faultless service is under the baton of Charles Madeira, the solid, smiling pillar of Le Manoir.

A la carte: 400-600F. Menus: 310F (lunch only, wine incl.), 395F (menu dégustation).

⟨15⟩ Alain Morel

123, av. de Wagram - 42 27 61 50
M. Morel. Open until 10:30 p.m. Closed Sat. lunch & Sun. Terrace dining. Pets allowed. Cards: V.

Alain Morel has taken over these odd-shaped, dreary but comfortable premises, with off-white walls and the type of Louis XVI moldings you find in older apartments in the Ternes district. The atmosphere needs a dose of cheer, the waiters are young and polished, and the prices are appalling.

Some of Morel's less-charitable colleagues have called him a "swellhead"; we, on the other hand, find this thirtysomething chef anxious, eager to do well and rather modest. Take his menu, for instance, on which a sweetbreads salad, salmon with soy sauce and filet of lamb in pastry appear just that way, instead of dressed up in elaborate descriptions. This in itself would not be of great interest if the dishes didn't turn out to be so remarkable. Our latest sampling included potato salad with semi-cooked duck foie gras, lamb moussaka (a good way to utilize wonderful summer vegetables and tender morsels of lamb), and roast turbot in all its natural splendor, with nothing more than a touch of walnut-oil vinaigrette. For dessert we enjoyed that audacious pastry cone filled with seasonal fresh fruit in place of tradi-tional raspberries or wild strawberries (the leafy frame really isn't necessary) and marvelous licorice ice cream with a muscular flavor. A terrace is open for meals in summer.

A la carte: 400-500F. Menu: 130F.

Paul et France
27, av. Niel - 47 63 04 24

M. Romano. Open until 10:30 p.m. Closed Sat., Sun. & July 14-Aug. 15. Air cond. No pets. Cards: V, AE, DC.

Do we dare admit that we miss the old haphazard but cozy decor, now that Paul et France looks like every other place around: pale woodwork, salmon-colored upholstery and smoky mirrors? Luckily, the southern vitality of Georges Romano and his smiling wife, Suzanne, and the mild euphoria of a fair- and foul-weather following make up for it, and a Paul et France meal today is still a feast in miniature. Romano drifts among the tables describing his dishes in mouth-watering detail, dishes that reflect his temperament: sunny, colorful, simple, generous and delicious. His menu never stands still—he's a soccer fan and likes to keep things moving. His "market-basket cuisine" sets the kitchen humming, running from crab-filled ravioli to red mullet with oyster butter, from brill with red butter to turbot with cream of parsley, from braised lobster with noodles to breast of duck with truffle butter, from chocolate fondant to an extraordinary wild-blackberry sorbet. A little more attention needs to be paid to details, lest the food end up like the now-impeccable decor: boring. The ravioli at our most recent meal was oversauced, and the sweetbreads unattractively paired with regrettable pleurote mushrooms. Good wines are selected by an experienced sommelier.

A la carte: 350F. Menus: 250F (lunch only, wine incl.), 300F, 380F.

Le Petit Colombier
42, rue des Acacias - 43 80 28 54, 43 80 08 61

M. Fournier. Open until 10:30 p.m. Closed Sun. lunch, Sat. & Aug. 1-17. Air cond. Parking. Pets allowed. Cards: V.

While head of the Paris Association of Restaurateurs, Bernard Fournier also managed his own restaurant and kitchens. Now that he has stepped down as president, he is be able to devote more time to his passion: cooking. No one knows better than Fournier how to roast a wild partridge or a well-aged cut of beef or how to make a classic coq au vin de Bourgogne. These delectable dishes are served in a pleasantly old-fashioned country inn with brass fixtures, pewterware and flower bouquets. You can also order molded pike, squab with no seasoning other than salt and pepper, a delicious chevreau (kid) with wild thyme, tasty desserts (blancmange with almond milk, chocolate fondant with a coffee crème brûlée topping) and the very best wines from a 35,000-bottle cellar. A meal at Le Petit Colombier is as soothing as a ride through the French countryside.

A la carte: 280-400F. Menu: 200F (lunch only, wine incl.).

Pétrus
12, pl. due Maréchal-Juin
43 80 15 95

Mme. André & M. Berneau. Open until 11 p.m. Closed Aug. 6- Sept. 6. Air cond. Terrace dining. Parking. Pets allowed. Cards: V, AE, DC, MC.

If you order six Charente or New Zealand oysters, a feuilleté of hogfish with basil butter, a splendid cabbage stuffed with rock lobster and sponge cake with an almond-caramel frosting, you will have tasted the best of Gilbert Dugast's cooking. This excellent chef, with saltwater in his blood and the ocean at his fingertips, would select these dishes for himself if he were paying the bill. Every morning, 50 kilograms of fish are deposited on his doorstep and scarcely make it to the refrigerator before getting snapped up by eager diners. They know that the best poached turbot, grilled bass and sole meunière, in their natural state, can be found in this decidedly unstylish but warm and inviting dining room.

After a superb platter of cheeses come the several good desserts: île flottante (floating island), coffee parfait and the sponge cake with almond-caramel frosting. Jean Frambour, president of the national association of wine stewards, attends to your gullet; Jean Berneau and Monique André look after your comfort; and all you have to worry about is paying a check that rides the high seas, though at a relatively reasonable speed.

A la carte: 350-550F.

Michel Rostang

19 20, rue Rennequin - 47 63 40 77
*M. Rostang. Open until 10:15 p.m.
Closed Sat. lunch (& dinner in seas.), Sun.,
holidays & Aug. 1-16. Air cond. Pets allowed.
Telex 649629. Cards: V, MC.*

Boyish, charming Michel Rostang isn't one
to philosophize about the metaphysics of ravioli or chase after flattering comments from the
press. Far from shy, he knows just how good
he is, but he prefers not to shout about it.
Rostang is both a craftsman—constructing his
dishes as meticulously as a cabinetmaker as-
sembles a fine piece of furniture—and an artist.
It takes solid technique, a refined palate and
considerable ambition to produce dishes of
such purity, with clear, distinct flavors. And the
remarkably consistent results are appreciated
by his admirers. Unlike some of his celebrated
colleagues, Rostang has no ups and downs, no
"inspired" moments followed by nothing-
goes-right days.

Maybe we've taken him for granted over the
years, accustomed as we are to enjoying almost
anything he serves us. Now we wonder why it
took us so long to award Rostang the fourth
toque he so richly deserves (and which, unlike
some others, he has never claimed as his due).
It could be that toques and stars just aren't
important to him. No matter—he'll make of it
what he will.

The way we see it, something recently
"clicked" *chez* Rostang. Did his talent suddenly
mature? Or did we? In any event, we were
bowled over by the seemingly effortless virtuosity of such dishes as baked turbot enhanced
with wild-mushroom jus, caramelized shallots
and a touch of vinegar; Bresse-bred guinea-
fowl, simply roasted with slow-stewed tomatoes (as sweet and addictive as candy); a sauté
of tiny Louisiana crawfish backed up by a
powerfully flavorful shellfish sauce; a salad of
lotte livers coated with a crunchy cornmeal
crust and spiced with juniper (to be consumed
in small portions, however, for its richness cloys
quickly); red mullet in a subtle sauce of its own
liver and raw sorrel; and young pigeon seductively combined with four types of garlic
(stewed, baked, broiled and in a flan).
Rostang's cheese board features a stunning
selection of goat cheeses and ripe, creamy
Saint-Marcellin. Desserts are equally spectacular: "French toast" garnished with a caramelized peach and perfumed with crème de cacao,
warm rhubarb tart with shaved almonds, cold
caramel soufflé on a creamy foundation flavored with Earl Grey tea. Alain Rozatti looks
after the prestigious, costly wine cellar (at our
last meal, we selected a sumptuous Puligny-
Montrachet "La Truffière" '82 and Chave's
fabulous red Hermitage). The solicitous presence of young Mme. Rostang helps soften the
shock of a towering check.

A la carte: 500-600F and up. Menus: 240F
(lunch only), 440F, 495F.

Guy Savoy

19 18, rue Troyon - 43 80 40 61,
43 80 36 22
*M. Savoy. Open until 10:30 p.m. Closed
Sat. (except lunch Oct. & Easter), Sun. & July
14-Aug. 5. Air cond. Parking. No pets. Cards:
V.*

His fourth toque hasn't swelled Guy Savoy's
head, but it may have contributed to a further
blooming of his enormous talent. What a marvelous, admirable meal he served us the other
day! Just listen: an unctuous cream of lentils
(an apotheosis for that humble legume) served
as a backdrop for big, tender prawns passed
quickly over the fire; John Dory cooked gently
in coriander juice was a paragon of pure, clear
flavor from the garden and the sea; Bresse
chicken (so tender we could barely resist eating
it with our fingers) came to the table bearing
a bouquet of young vegetables, sparked by a
sprinkling of coarse salt and a fillip of vinegar.
Then followed a cup of consommé—pure essence of chicken—to clear the palate and prepare it for the excitement of dessert: macaroons
with tart cherries, vanilla crème brûlée, praline
feuilleté . . . any of them is sure to dissuade you
from asking for "just coffee and the check,
please."

No one would deny that Guy Savoy is a
thoroughly modern chef. Yet what lends his
repertoire its peculiar charm is his fidelity to
the tastes of his childhood. It's as if the memory
of his mother's market basket, filled with garden vegetables, farmyard poultry and pork,
continues to inspire him in his quest for the
authentic, natural flavors he combines in so
personal a manner. We're thinking of his potato purée with garlic and chive juice, which
turns a lowly dish of sautéed pollack into a royal
treat, or the green beans in onion juice that
metamorphose a dish of smoked eel, or the

beets and cream of parsley that transform an ordinary mussel soup. Savoy improvises brilliantly with textures and tastes that all come together with disconcerting *justesse*. His cooking is seamless, his virtuosity appears effortless.

Guy Savoy makes no concessions to popular taste. He follows his own path, cooking only what he and his wife like to eat. But there are enough kindred spirits around to keep his beige, green and white dining room filled for every lunch and dinner service. Wine service is orchestrated by Eric Mancio, a young sommelier who "chants" his cellar with a storyteller's art. You can rely on—and here the pleasure ends—a resounding bill.

A la carte: 500F and up. Menu: 400F (lunch only), 575F.

🍴 Sormani
4, rue du Général-Lanzerac
43 80 13 91

M. Fayet. Open until 10:30 p.m. Closed Sat., Sun., Aug. 1-24 & Dec. 23-Jan. 3. Air cond. No pets. Cards: V.

One of the finest and most brilliant Italian cuisines in Paris is produced by a Savoie-born Parisian, Pascal Fayet. For many years this remarkable chef was in charge of a good Italian restaurant, Conti, and having an Italian grandmother (whose name adorns the signboard) hasn't hurt. The delicacies you'll taste here seem to have been meticulously planned and executed, yet not a hint of this effort dilutes the bold and happy union of flavors. You'll find superb seafood pizza, tomatoes stuffed with spiny lobster, remarkably subtle red mullet in olive oil and basil, chaud-froid of salmon in tomato sauce and elaborate desserts to round off a perfect meal—provided you don't make the mistake of ordering the risotto with white truffles, which is curiously dry and lumpy. The bright-blue decor is a trifle chilly but chic (attractive tables, Louis XV armchairs, flowers galore); the service is low-key and vigilant.

A la carte: 400F. Menu: 350F (menu dégustation).

🍴 La Toque
16, rue de Tocqueville - 42 27 97 95

M. Joubert. Open until 9:30 p.m. Closed Sat., Sun., July 22-Aug. 20 & Dec. 23-Jan. 1. Air cond. Pets allowed. Cards: V.

Jacky Joubert certainly didn't learn interior decorating from Michel Guérard, with whom he trained. His tiny bistro is virtually crushed under the weight of velvet draperies and clutter, so it's best to rivet your eyes on the plates (which are breathtakingly elegant) and, more important, on what they contain. This excellent chef can't be faulted when it comes to stuffing his guests with a compote of duck in vegetable aspic, saffron-seasoned hogfish, snails fricassée, roast lamb with thyme, casserole of beef with shallots, caramel-glazed soufflé and dainty pastries (which certainly don't need their coatings of powdered sugar). While everyone complains of the stingy portions that come with modern cuisine, here it's the prices that are small. For about 500 francs for two, with a good wine, you can enjoy an excellent meal.

A la carte: 230-300F. Menu: 190F.

EIGHTEENTH ARRONDISSEMENT

🍴 A. Beauvilliers
52, rue Lamarck - 42 54 54 42

M. Carlier. Open until 10:45 p.m. Closed Mon. lunch, Sun. & Aug. 26-Sept. 11. Terrace dining. No pets. Cards: V, MC.

The best New Year's Eve parties in Paris, the most lavish flower arrangements, the prettiest terrace, the most adorable private salon (on display under glass are bridal bouquets from past wedding receptions), the most romantic restaurant, the most eclectic clientele. What else can we say, except that owner/chef Edouard Carlier is as crazy as ever. Crazy about parties, which he will organize at the drop of a hat, to honor his fellow cooks, to salute the new wine from Montmartre's vineyards or to celebrate birthdays. Even if you're not a "club member," you feel part of the fun in this converted bakery nestled against the Butte Montmartre, transformed into a pleasure dome by soft lighting, antique portraits and prints and a profusion of flowers.

Leaning on what looks like a Napoléon III counter, Carlier receives his guests with approving grunts, while his partner, Micky, checks the tables set with sparkling silverware to make sure that nothing is amiss. Michel Deygat, a tall, athletic-looking fellow who trained at the Nikko under Robuchon, then at Faugeron, doesn't venture onstage—he never leaves the kitchen. And that's where you'll find him, preparing standard dishes from his repertoire and developing new ones. There's no doubt that he is responsible for the reawakening of Beauvilliers, which was dozing on its laurels. You'll agree when you taste his boned rabbit braised in white Burgundy and seasoned with chopped parsley, fresh artichoke bottom with crab, poached egg with sautéed mushrooms, lamb's brains with bacon and sherry vinegar, and his remarkable roasted turbot with veal juice and roast filet of lamb with tarragon and Provençal vegetables (an Antoine Beauvilliers recipe that dates back to 1814). Begin with a glass of sherry (Carlier is crazy about it and stocks the finest sherries in town), then rely on sommelier Georges Bertet to help you choose from a vast collection of Bordeaux and Côtes-du-Rhône to suit everyone's taste.

A la carte: 500-700F. Menus: 175F (lunch only), 300F (lunch only, wine incl.).

⑭ Clodenis
57, rue Caulaincourt - 46 06 20 26
M. Gentes. Open until 10:30 p.m. Closed Sun. & Mon. Pets allowed. Cards: V.

Deny Gentes, who was one of the most enthusiastic chefs in Paris ten years ago, seems to have retreated from his highly creative beginnings. On the plus side, this has helped him maintain consistency in producing a set repertoire (which a Japanese chef is entrusted to repeat faultlessly day in and day out) using the finest ingredients. The decor has improved a good deal, and you'll never see a waiter drop as much as a spoon on the carpet. For all these reasons Clodenis remains one of the best eating places in this popular tourist area, especially when the warm weather comes and you can sit out on the delightful sidewalk terrace. Taste the smoked salmon maison perfumed with anise, cracked Brittany crab, brandade of cod the way they make it in Nîmes, hot foie gras with potatoes and feuilleté of red fruits.

A la carte: 350F. Menus: 180F (lunch only), 220F (dinner only).

11/20 La Crémaillère 1900
15, pl. du Tertre - 46 06 58 59
M. Bailly. Open daily until 12:30 a.m. Air cond. Garden dining. Pets allowed. Telex 232435. Cards: V, AE, DC.

This magic garden and charming 1900s-style place is located scarcely beyond reach of the noisy and touristy place du Tertre. Oyster bar and good, honest brasserie fare. Piano music at night.

A la carte: 180-200F. Menu: 77F.

⑮ Les Fusains
44, rue Joseph-de-Maistre
42 28 03 69
M. Mathys. Dinner only. Open until midnight. Closed Sun., Mon. & Sept. Terrace dining. Cards: V.

Bernard Mathys prefers to be known as a new chef rather than a former actor. As informed as he is engaging, this amateur cook has the right idea: He'll make more waves in the kitchen than in the theater, where he had a brief run. Cooking, it turns out, is his thing. Like most self-taught people, he throws himself into it heart and soul. More surprising is the degree of professional discipline Mathys brings to everything he does, beginning with his duties as host in his own dining room, with its cozy, candlelit tables and casual yet elegant atmosphere. There is only one menu—a fixed-price one—and it changes nightly, or quite often, according to the market. His dishes are simple and executed with great clarity. The other day we had a duck foie gras appetizer followed by a marvelously light salad of scallops and mushrooms; a fricassée of fresh chanterelles that tasted of the woods; and a precisely grilled salmon steak, moist and velvety, on a bed of tender sea fennel; followed by perfectly ripened cheeses and a pastry spree of apricot tarts, gratin of wild strawberries and hazelnut financière (small cake). Wines are expensive, but once you taste something as delectable as the Saint-Emilion Les Abeilles at 140 francs, you'll feel that they're practically giving them away.

Menu: 270F.

⑬ Grandgousier

17, av. Rachel - 43 87 66 12

M. Marzynski. Open until 10 p.m. Closed Sat. lunch, Sun. & 2 weeks in Aug. Parking. Pets allowed. Cards: V, AE, DC, MC.

A quiet bourgeois establishment, Grandgousier presents food that's good and consistent if not distinctive: fisherman's salad (raw fish perfumed with ginger and pink pepper), filet of red mullet (overcooked) in a delicate curry sauce and desserts that have made some progress (blancmange and a chocolate marquise). Nice wine list with stiff prices.
A la carte: 260F. Menu: 135F.

12/20 Le Maquis

69, rue Caulaincourt - 42 59 76 07

M. Lesage. Open until 10 p.m. Closed Sun. & Mon. Terrace dining. Pets allowed. Cards: V.

M. Lesage, who owns the nearby Clodenis, keeps an eye on quality and prices at Le Maquis, which has an amusing terrace decor. His extraordinary fixed-price menu and his market-basket à la carte dishes pack the house for lunch and dinner: brandade of cod, osso buco, scallop salad and feuilleté of lobster tails. Wine from the Gard region is served in carafes.
A la carte: 200F. Menu: 57F (lunch only, wine incl.).

NINETEENTH ARRONDISSEMENT

⑮ Au Cochon d'Or

192, av. Jean-Jaurès - 46 07 23 13

M. Ayral. Open daily until 10:30 p.m. Air cond. Pets allowed. Cards: V, AE, DC, MC.

Despite the blood sausage with puffed potatoes, the incomparable calf's head and the best meats in Paris served in truckload portions, the Cochon d'Or is no longer a "bistro," at least not in the sense it used to be when the meat butchers were here at Villette and the atmosphere was rough and zoo-like. Long ago the comfortable, homey decor and enlarged floor space (the immense wine cellar is spectacular) transformed it into a chic restaurant. Meat lovers and fans of hearty country fare like to come here for the filet mignon, the remarkable pigs' feet sauce Choron and the finest cuts. Still, if you look closely at the new urban clientele attracted by the gigantic cultural projects mushrooming just across the way, and if you carefully study the pretty menu (superb foie gras, delicately treated fish), you're bound to catch the whiff of smug trendiness pervading these sullen outskirts of the capital.
A la carte: 400F. Menu: 210F.

12/20 Dagorno

190, av. Jean-Jaurès - 46 07 02 29

M. Abatécola. Open daily until midnight. Air cond. Cards: V.

The new brasserie look of the old Dagorno isn't exactly subtle, but it is cheerful and inviting. The cooking has yet to find its stride, and andouillette from Duval doesn't belong in such a posh setting. Nonetheless, you can expect some excellent dishes, whatever they are, along with good wines and faultless service.
A la carte: 300F. Menu: 150F (wine incl.).

⑮ Au Pavillon Puebla

(Christian Vergès)
Parc des Buttes-Chaumont
42 08 92 62

M. Vergès. Open until 10 p.m. Closed Sun. & Mon. Garden dining. Parking. Pets allowed. Cards: V.

If you're an amateur decorator, you're bound to make mistakes, even if you have good taste. That's the story behind this Napoléon III hunting lodge near the entrance to the Buttes-Chaumont park. Revived after years of neglect, it became a little jewel—overpolished, as it turns out, since it's a jewel that would look better if it were left to glow in its own light. But on sunny days, the rooms and the winter garden remain charming reminders of the romantic past.

Not long ago we reported that Christian Vergès had come into bloom in this interior designed by him and his wife. The words were barely out of our PCs when he completely ruined our next meal with all kinds of elaborate, boring gimmickry. The next time around we were luckier; despite pokey service, the wrong check delivered and errors in the "right" check, we rediscovered the fine flavors of this self-made chef's elegant cuisine. The large, handsome menu includes stuffed baby calamari, hot curried oyster ravioli, poached lobster with leeks, oxtail miroton, tournedos of duck with foie gras (not very convincing), leg of lamb with chanterelles and nice desserts. The bill is no picnic, but there's a good fixed-price menu for 200 francs at lunch that attracts a steady stream of business people.

A la carte: 350-500F. Menu: 200F.

TWENTIETH ARRONDISSEMENT

12/20 Le Bistrot du 20e

44, rue du Surmelin - 48 97 20 30
M. Bihoues-Lechevallier. Open until 10 p.m. Closed Sat., Sun. & July. Pets allowed. Cards: V, AE.

This cute little restaurant in an old butcher shop features good, solid classic cuisine. Try the smoked salmon, charcuterie from the Landes and feuilleté of sweetbreads.

A la carte: 180-200F. Menus: 150F (dinner only, wine incl.), 80F.

12/20 Le Courtil

15, rue St-Blaise - 43 70 09 32
M. Azincourt. Open until 10 p.m. Closed Sun., Mon., March 28-April 1 & Aug. 1-26. Pets allowed. Cards: V.

A jazz duo on Tuesday evenings livens up this winsome restaurant. With a pocket-size garden in the rear, Le Courtil serves a modern cuisine with an accent on vegetables (seafood salad, duck confit and Gamay wine in pitchers).

A la carte: 180F.

THE SUBURBS

ARGENTEUIL
95100 Argenteuil - (Val d'Oise)

(13) La Closerie Périgourdine ❁

85, bd Jean-Allemane
39 80 01 28
M. Senot de la Londe. Open until 10 p.m. Closed Sat. lunch, Sun. dinner & Mon. Pets allowed. Cards: V, AE, DC.

Maguy and Frédéric Senot de la Londe, the owners of this dark, rustic, suburban restaurant, are strong believers in truffles, cèpes, foie gras, preserves and the other delicacies of the Périgord. The homemade duck-wing jambon is delicious, the portions of duck liver, also homemade, are generous (you can take some home for an extravagant price), and the feuilleté desserts are beautiful. Contrary to what might be feared, this cuisine (especially the sauces) is as light as can be. There is also a good selection of Cahors and Bordeaux wines.

A la carte: 300F. Menus: 135F and 170F (wine incl.), 110F.

ASNIERES
92600 Asnières - (Hauts-de-Seine)

(13) L'Ecurie

4 bis, Grande-Rue-Charles-de-Gaulle
47 90 91 30
M. Fontaine. Open until 10 p.m. Closed Sat. lunch, Sun., Feb. 9-15 & Aug. 9-31. Pets allowed. Cards: V.

A veteran from Le Train Bleu at the Gare de Lyon, André Fontaine has given his tiny bistro next to the Asnières bridge the country-like ambience of his dreams, complete with cart-wheels, artificial stones and rough, white plaster. Everything is neat, clean and cheerful, and the kitchen has a genuinely festive air. The fixed-price lunch menu is especially generous; all the menus, in fact, are reasonably priced. Try the brill in a crab bouillon, the noisettes of lamb with garlic and tarragon and the banana gratin in passion-fruit juice. The wine selection is also good.

A la carte: 250F. Menus: 115F.

BOUGIVAL
78380 Bougival - (Yvelines)

⑭ L'Huître et la Tarte
6, quai Georges-Clemenceau
39 18 45 55

M. Delaveyne. Open until 10 p.m. Closed Sun. dinner, Mon. & Aug. Pets allowed. Cards: V.

L'Huître et la Tarte's success has been astounding, and it is not likely to end soon. While Le Camélia, next door, is too often sadly empty, these tables, pushed close together in pleasant surroundings of pine and cashmere fabric, are much in demand at both lunch and dinner. It must be said that M. Delaveyne scored brilliantly when he opened this restaurant/shop, where the freshest and finest seafood is served at unbeatable prices: oysters year-round, smoked or marinated Norwegian salmon, a confit of exquisitely fresh anchovies, mussel soup, a gratin of macaroni with shellfish, seafood omelets, cod aïoli, a finely ripened Camembert worth its weight in gold, a delicious white cream cheese and a choice of tarts. You won't find lobster, crayfish or any exceptional fish that would weigh heavily upon the check, but you will find creative seafood dishes at freshwater prices: appetizers for 38 to 58 francs, six oysters with grilled sausages for 60 francs, entrées for 48 to 63 francs and tarts for 29 francs.

A la carte: 180-250F.

BOULOGNE-BILLANCOURT
92100 Boulogne-Billancourt (Hauts-de-Seine)

⑭ L'Auberge
86, av. Jean-Baptiste-Clément
46 05 22 35

M. Veysset. Open until 10 p.m. Closed Sun. & Aug. 6-31. Pets allowed. Cards: V, AE, DC, MC.

Although he is experimenting more and more seriously with modern cuisine, the talented Jean-François Veysset has nevertheless remained loyal to the wholesome regional specialties from the Franche-Comté, for which he is famous (winter stew, Jésus de Morteau and so on). And he does not mind borrowing from

neighboring provinces. His two young chefs are completely at ease with the recipes, which, despite their diversity, all share the lightness of a precise, graceful execution. The wonderful fixed-price menu is as popular as ever, and we can understand why—you choose from wild-rabbit rillettes with hazelnuts or assiette maraîchère; perch and eel pochouse (fish stew) or calf's knuckle with fresh pasta; a cheese plate from Cantin's; and cream of honey and almond milk. The well-stocked cellar houses some excellent Bordeaux wines, along with many good labels for less than 100 francs.

A la carte: 300F. Menu: 180F.

⑬ L'Avant-Seine
1, rond-point Rhin-et-Danube
48 25 58 00

M. Pautrat. Open until 10 p.m. Closed Sun. & Mon. Air cond. Pets allowed. Cards: V.

Gérard Vié's Boulogne annex (he owns Les Trois Marches in Versailles) is as pleasant as ever. Pierre Pardaillon, the young award-winning sommelier, is gone, but he has left behind a cellar in good standing (and an ample selection by the glass). As for the cuisine, it is still magnificent for the price. The 103-franc fixed-price menu, for instance, offers a duck mousse with salad, a fricassée of young fowl and a pear millefeuille with pistachios.

A la carte: 300F. Menus: 103F, 155F.

⑯ Au Comte de Gascogne
89, av. Jean-Baptiste Clément
46 03 47 27

M. Charvet. Open until 10:30 p.m. Closed Sat. lunch, Sun. & Aug. 6-22. Air cond. Garden dining. Pets allowed. Parking. Cards: V.

Gérard Vérane has entrusted his airy greenhouse and his fashionable clientele of socialites and tycoons to Henri Charvet, late of Aix-en-Provence. Predictably, the restaurant went through a roughish shakedown period that, according to our readers, affected the quality of the welcome and service, formerly flawless under the voluble, charming Vérane. The kitchen needed some time to get the kinks out, too. Our second visit proved that considerable progress has been made. Chef Charvet, who had wavered between the southwest (Vérane's legacy) and Provence (his personal repertoire) has come down in favor of the latter. His new menu has the sunny, fragrant, rustic accent of the Midi, though it includes a half dozen preparations featuring foie gras and duck confit (hence the restaurant remains Au Comte de Gascogne, not Au Comte de Provence). Nonetheless, Provence inspires the menu's best offerings, such as exquisite baby artichokes à la barigoule, thick asparagus dressed with a sparkling grapefruit vinaigrette, ethereal ravioli stuffed with oxtail, carrots and celery root, a sprightly sauté of minted morels and fava beans—what a delightful pairing of textures!—alongside a thyme-scented lamb filet, red mullet baked with tender fennel, lobster fricassée with bacon and snow peas, casserole-roasted squab with a lentil ragoût, and saddle of rabbit with a herbed-and-spiced stuffing of its liver and kidneys, accompanied by fresh pasta. In sum, this a savory collection of keenly flavored dishes easily earns a pair of toques.

Patrice Marchand, the young sommelier, is certain to take tender care of the cellar built up by Vérane and to renew its riches as necessary. We thank him for ferreting out an exceptional '82 Bourgogne Aligoté from Jean-Pierre Diconne, which even a veteran oenophile might have mistaken for a classy Chassagne-Montrachet.

A la carte: 450-700F.

12/20 Le Poivre Vert

1, pl. Bernard-Palissy - 46 03 01 63
M. Vérane. Open daily until 11:30 p.m. Air cond. Cards: V.

This cheerful, attractive, small, unpretentious annex of Au Comte de Gascogne is located in a lovely green setting. The fixed-price menu includes an appetizer and an entrée (noisette of lamb in tarragon sauce). Try the delicious grilled andouillette and the duck confit. Dessert (nothing extraordinary) and wine are not included in the price.

Menu: 80F.

CHATEAUFORT

78530 Buc - (Yvelines)

La Belle Epoque

10, pl. de la Mairie - 39 56 21 66
M. Peignaud. Open until 9:30 p.m. Closed Sun. dinner, Mon., Aug. 12-Sept. 6 & Dec. 23-Jan. 5. Garden dining. Pets allowed. Cards: V, AE, DC.

The grumbling, opinionated yet immensely likable Peignaud, a native of Berry, is quite a character. It's always a pleasure to see him in the cheerful 1900s-style clutter of his old inn overlooking the Chevreuse valley. He acquired a taste for Brittany from his good friend Delaveyne and recently bought a house in the Finistère. So don't be surprised to see, next to the calf's head (the obligatory postwedding course in Berry), a Vendée squab, a tail of young rabbit "mère-grand," a soft goat curd, a pan of delicious small marinated sardines, a pollack with tasty potatoes from Goyen, a John Dory, a lobster steamed in seaweed or a salad of damselfish from Cherbourg (insufficiently seasoned), to which Peignaud adds a touch from his own region: exquisite melon grown in Berry's ancient peat bogs. Nor has this countryman forgotten his ties to Japan (he was chef at Maxim's in Tokyo), which find expression in his sweet peppers in an Oriental marinade, his effiloché of ray in a sour sauce with soybean sprouts, or his wakame, a Japanese seaweed that, once cooked, tastes much like green beans grown in the ocean. Peignaud's cuisine, however, remains essentially classical and cannot be noted for lightness. The desserts are good, especially the peaches with orange blossoms and the glazed nougat in a raspberry sauce. Among the Burgundies and Bordeaux, some delightful wines from the Loire valley accompany this somewhat baroque cuisine, which blends the flavors of Berry, Asia and Brittany in a delightful harmony.

A la carte: 350-400F.

CHENNEVIERES-SUR-MARNE

94430 Chennevières-sur-Marne (Val-de-Marne)

L'Ecu de France

31, rue de Champigny - 45 76 00 03
M. Brousse. Open until 9:30 p.m. Closed Sun. dinner, Mon. & Sept. 4-11. Terrace dining. No pets. Parking. Cards: V.

Smart and spruce for long, this old place has begun to fall into neglect. The exterior is shabby and dilapidated, and the large provincial dining room, with its drab colors and faded carpet, is beginning to look antiquated. Still, one's eyes may feast on the Marne river and its cool greenery, as well as on the terrace close to the water that gives this restaurant its inimitable charm. The more modern dishes are decreasing in number, and the preparation is sometimes hasty. The well-prepared feuilleté is excessively garnished with long asparagus stems (instead of just the tips); slices of a rather bland lamb are cut too thin; but the pastries (if looks alone count) are appealing. The toque is proffered on probation.

A la carte: 330-350F.

CLICHY
92110 Clichy - (Hauts-de-Seine)

⑭ La Bonne Table
119, bd Jean-Jaurès - 47 37 38 79
M. Berger. Open until 8 p.m. Closed Sat. lunch, Sun. & Aug. 15-Sept. 15. Air cond. Pets allowed. Cards: V.

Gisèle Berger, a sincere, straightforward, generous woman, prepares a feminine cuisine in a simple and cheerful setting that suits her beautifully. The menu doesn't change much, but this self-made woman from Savoie is so charming that the lobster lasagne, the fish cassoulet (with fish sausages!), the fish choucroute, the eggplant stuffed with shellfish and the classic bouillabaisse assure lasting pleasure. René Berger keeps an excellent selection of shellfish. The wines (like everything else) are expensive.

A la carte: 400F.

COURBEVOIE
92400 Courbevoie - (Hauts-de-Seine)

⑭ La Safranée sur Mer
12, pl. des Reflets - 47 78 75 50
M. Ferreira. Open until 10:30 p.m. Closed Sat., Sun., Aug. & Dec. 24-Jan. 2. Air cond. Terrace dining. Pets allowed. Parking. Cards: V, AE, DC.

The top executives working in Courbevoie's business world for a long while have made La Safranée sur Mer their port of call. The clientele is almost exclusively male, and the setting somehow calls to mind the dining room of a luxurious private yacht anchored in some Mediterranean harbor. On sunny days, you can sit at a table under the tricolored umbrellas on the

La Défense square, reveling in the bird's-eye view of the Arc de Triomphe. The new chef and new owner know how to make the most of a menu composed primarily of superb seafood: grilled red mullet, bouillabaisse, salmon braised in dill and so on. The dessert cake, a combination of raspberry mousse and Cointreau on a génoise shell, is disappointing, but the wine list is superb.

A la carte: 500F. Menus: 280F, 300F.

⑭ Les Trois Marmites ۞
215, bd St-Denis - 43 33 25 35
M. Faucheux. Open until 10 p.m. Closed Sat., Sun., March 20-28 & Aug. 1-28. Pets allowed. Parking. Cards: V.

After cooking splendid bistro specialties at Pierre Traiteur's for many years, Marc Faucheux has created—in the midst of these modern, noisy, rather spiritless suburbs—a quaint and charming café where one feels immediately at ease. The handwritten menu revives the best themes from Pierre's: delicious jambon persillé, enchanting terrines, estofinado (poached cod with potatoes) from the Rouergues, green cabbage with bacon and the famous "boeuf à la ficelle ménagère" (beef suspended on a string and poached in broth) with tasty vegetables. The cellar holds the best vintages of Bourgueuil, Sancerre, Pouilly Fumé and Beaujolais. A young, pretty waitress ensured perfect service on our visits there.

A la carte: 330F.

CROISSY-BEAUBOURG
77200 Torcy - (Seine-et-Marne)

⑬ Hostellerie de l'Aigle d'Or
8, rue de Paris - 60 05 31 33, 60 05 22 24
M. Giliams. Open until 9 p.m. Closed Sun. dinner & Mon. Garden dining. Pets allowed. Parking. Cards: V, AE, DC.

The Eurodisneyland developers need only drive a few kilometers to enjoy the shade of this old house, with its terrace overlooking a flower garden and the Croissy pond. The owner is an elegant, charming woman, the clientele is prosperous, and the wine lovers are plentiful (thanks to the wonderful cellar). Chef Hervé Giliams has taken tremendous pains with his cuisine, although it expresses itself in the not-so-appealing style of a slick hotel: salade des Princes (lobster, foie gras . . .), lobster blanquette in Champagne, filet of veal in a sauce of honey and morel juice. Service is excellent.

A la carte: 300-400F. Menus: 150F (weekdays only), 340F (weekend and holiday dinner only), 200F.

ENGHIEN
95880 Enghien - (Val d'Oise)

🧑‍🍳 Duc d'Enghien
16

3, av. de Ceinture - 34 12 90 00

M. Kéréver. Open until 10:30 p.m. Closed Sun. dinner, Mon., Jan. 4-10 & July 31-Aug. 27. Air cond. Telex 607842. Terrace dining. Parking. Pets allowed. Cards: V, AE, DC.

It would surprise us if the new owners were to bid farewell to a chef of Kéréver's caliber. No, they are intelligent enough to give him a setting worthy of his talent, which we confirmed once again by tasting his exquisite ravioli filled with tourteau (crab) covered with a strong crab sauce and a sprig of chervil, his extremely subtle ramekin of crayfish and mushrooms (though it could perhaps have been a bit more seasoned), his excellent fresh pasta with seafood and basil and his sensational turbot, which is roasted in buttered paper with lardons, small onions, young carrots and coriander. The à la carte menu features delicious sea bass, pan-fried in its skin, superb roast duck from Challans in a gravy of its own juice and liver, magnificent pan-fried rib of beef with marrow gravy, and divine desserts, including praline Paris-Brest with coffee sauce, unjustly forgotten by today's pâtissiers.

Most noteworthy among the offerings of the very good cellar (where the prices of even the greatest Bordeaux are not astronomical) is Hugel's rare Alsatian Pinot Noir, which could easily be confused with a beautiful Burgundy. Under the management of a maître d' who possesses a rare graciousness and skill, the service is nothing short of excellent.

A la carte: 500-750F. Menus: 325F (lunch only, wine incl.), 360F.

JUVISY-SUR-ORGE
91260 Juvisy-sur-Orge - (Essonne)

🧑‍🍳 Le Pays d'Oc 🌓
13

2, rue de Draveil - 69 21 50 62

M. Fort. Open daily until 10 p.m. Terrace dining. Pets allowed. Parking. Telex 690316. Cards: V, AE, DC, MC.

The Forts, who also manage the excellent Minotaure in the Hôtel California (see Paris Hotels, Eighth Arrondisement), prepare a simple, substantial, generous cuisine in this old and comfortable mariners' inn overlooking the Seine. The specialties include fish and dishes from southern France: beautiful seafood in season, foie gras, well-made winter cassoulet, fish soup from Saint-Raphaël and grilled meats. The fixed-price menus are most appealing, and the ambience and garden decor of this hospitable place are consistently elegant. Meals are served on a pleasant terrace in the summer.

A la carte: 250F. Menus: 85F, 120F, 170F.

LEVALLOIS-PERRET
92300 Levallois-Perret - (Hauts-de-Seine)

🧑‍🍳 Gauvain
14

11, rue Louis-Rouquier - 47 58 51 09

MM. Hude & Guillermou. Open until 10 p.m. Closed Sat., Sun. & Aug. 5-20. Air cond. Cards: V.

With only ten dishes on the fixed-price menu, which changes at least once a week, you can make your choice quickly and painlessly. The first formula entitles you to two dishes plus cheese and dessert, the second one to three dishes. No additions, no extras, no surprises—that is, except for one, and it's a big one. All the food, prepared by Jean-François Guillermou, a veteran from Maxim's, is deliciously simple, modern and light, whether you choose the warm oysters with leeks, the fricassée of lotte with bacon, the veal kidney with Meaux mustard or the rib of beef gros sel. Finish with the admirable marquise au chocolat. This is a great little place. We have found it both both lively and reliable on all of our visits. It was converted from a bakery shop, and its attractive decor is charming, bright and cheerful, and the service is always with a smile. Menus: 175F, 210F.

LIVRY-GARGAN
93190 Livry-Gargan - (Seine-Saint-Denis)

⑭ **Auberge Saint-Quentinoise**
23, bd de la République - 43 81 13 08, 43 81 74 01

M. Nicoleau. Open until 10 p.m. Closed Sun. dinner, Mon. & Jan. 15-Feb. 10. Terrace dining. Pets allowed. Cards: V.

Michel Nicoleau, who was an assistant chef at Oliver Sr.'s Grand Véfour, then chef at Oliver Jr.'s Bistrot de Paris, can prepare many great dishes, but he is particularly good with the generous, simple, yet devilishly savory provincial cuisine so famous at his last employer's: pot of "petit-gris" (small snails) in a golden crust, fresh cod with bacon and sautéed cabbage, lamb's tongue in piquante sauce, suckling lamb with sweet garlic and so on. The decor has been redone, and the courtyard garden is quite pleasant during Livry-Gargan's hot summers. The small wine list is nice, and the service, professional.

A la carte: 300F and up. Menus: 135F and 185F (weekday lunch only), 175F (weekday dinner only), 200F and 250F (weekends and holidays only).

LES LOGES-EN-JOSAS
78350 Les Loges-en-Josas - (Yvelines)

⑬ **La Ferme des Loges**
Porte des Loges - 30 24 97 77

M. Woltz. Open until 9 p.m. Closed Sun. dinner, Mon. & Aug. 14-29. Air cond. Garden dining. Hotel: 6 stes 780-890F; 49 rms 470-670F; half-board 750-780F. Parking. Cards: V, AE, DC.

This large group of aristocratic buildings, once used as the "stables of the King's farm," is in the middle of a charming park where tables are set in summer. The park is, in fact, far more cheerful than the large, rather dreary country-

style dining room. After an extremely promising beginning, young chef Eric Schneider's cuisine seems to have weakened a bit. His salade gourmande is adequate but stingy. The delicious noisettes of lamb are a touch overcooked, though they're served with a perfect zucchini gratin. And a good millefeuille with wild strawberries is given new life with a rhubarb sauce (though there is a bit too much cream topping it). The wine cellar is well stocked, particularly with Bordeaux.

A la carte: 350F. Menus: 190F, 240F, 320F.

MAISONS-LAFFITTE
78600 Maisons-Laffitte - (Yvelines)

⑭ **Le Laffitte**
5, av. de St-Germain - 39 62 01 53

M. Laurier. Open until 9:30 p.m. Closed Tues. & Sun. dinner, Wed. & Aug. Pets allowed. Cards: V, AE.

His three "Rabelaisian" fixed-price menus win André Laurier a crown. The most expensive of the trio, with foie gras and lobster, plus fish, meat, cheese and dessert courses, may seem like a challenge to put away in one sitting, but Laurier is such a gifted cook that the meal goes down quite easily. The check, however, doesn't. The less daring ought to know that the so-called small menu is not exactly a consolation prize, and that the à la carte menu abounds in fine entrées, such as the salmon from Scotland with garden sorrel and the veal kidney sautéed in Pouilly wine. The cellar holds some excellent country wines for about 80 francs. The old-fashioned decor is pleasant.

A la carte: 280-300F. Menus: 200F, 270F, 300F.

⑯ **Le Tastevin**
9, av. Eglé - 39 62 11 67

M. Blanchet. Open until 10 p.m. Closed Mon. dinner, Tues., Feb. school vacation & Aug. 16-Sept. 10. Garden dining. Pets allowed. Parking. Cards: V, AE, DC.

The name of Michel Blanchet's restaurant alludes to his passion for fine wines. For the past fifteen years he has done such a good job collecting bottles that today his cellar is one of the best stocked in the Paris area. And next to these great aged labels is a number of more modest vintages, priced well below 100 francs (a rosé Rully, for example, or a delicious red Menetou). This is all for the best, as the opportunities to spend money are not lacking in this well-to-do, bourgeois millstone house, built on the green edge of the Maisons-Laffitte park. Try the fondant of lobster, the marinière of palourdes (clams) with saffron, the turbot roasted with shallots in a meat juice, the sautéed langoustines or the escalopes of sweetbreads with creamed asparagus and truffles, all of which are prepared by this discreet and charming cook, whose command of sauces and preparations is nothing short of extraordinary. The solemn beige dining room is lightened with beveled mirrors that reflect a lovely flowering garden where meals are served in summer, just like in the country.

A la carte: 400F.

La Vieille Fontaine
8, av. Grétry - 39 62 01 78
Mme. Letourneur & M. Clerc. Open until 10:30 p.m. Closed Sun., Mon. & Aug. Garden dining. Pets allowed. Cards: V, AE, DC.

Designer Elisabeth Malhettes opted for sobriety and discretion: mirrors, tons of flowers, black-lacquered armchairs upholstered in a splendid cashmere, walls of red and gray moiré and, above the park, an exquisite white winter garden. The effect is utterly charming. At the same time, longtime patrons of this grand white Napoléon III establishment will retain the comforting feeling that they aren't out of place.

Manon Letourneur's gracious smile flourishes in these ideal surroundings, and François Clerc's cooking has rediscovered a harmony and confidence of execution that for a time had seemed to waver. In any event, the new menu left us with favorable impressions, with its millefeuille of oysters and foie gras, oxtail-and-mutton sausage, marinière of lobster with watercress butter, oursinade of bass with fresh pasta, coquilles St-Jacques with vanilla and ginger, lamb's brains with coconut milk and

curry, pot-au-feu with Pomerol and duck ragoût with apricots. Clerc, assisted by Gilles Angoulvent, has gone beyond revising his cooking; he's created something totally original. His current efforts remind us that long before he became famous for his restaurant, he was a great chef. His new desserts—apple charlotte en brioche, a delicious pudding or cheese with cassis and raspberries—add just the right finish to a delightful meal, which is accompanied by perfect wines recommended by Hervé Besle, the young wine steward. Excellent menu/carte (a fixed-price menu with à la carte–style selections) at lunch.

A la carte: 450-800F. Menu/carte: 190F.

MEUDON
92190 Meudon - (Hauts-de-Seine)

Relais des Gardes
42, av. du Général-Galliéni
45 34 11 79
M. Oudina. Open until 10 p.m. Closed Sun. dinner, Sat. & Aug. Terrace dining. Pets allowed. Cards: V, AE, DC.

Although Paris is quite close to Meudon, the Relais des Gardes seems hundreds of kilometers away. So soothing is the large dining room, with its tall fireplace, its etchings and its longstanding provincial clientele, that it takes us far away from the customary suburban bistros. Pierre and Simone Oudina manage this 200-year-old restaurant, which was patronized by the hunters and horse guards of the royal domain during the reign of Louis XV, with simplicity and graciousness. It's surely a fine place to be, as evidenced by the 40-year tenure of chef Daniel Bertholom. His cuisine is seasoned in a bourgeois or regional style, but it's much lighter, and noted for its generosity and simplicity. The charlotte of young rabbit en gelée and fresh herbs is delightful, as is the fish soup from Glénan, the filet of Charolais beef in wine and the pot-au-feu of duck à la saintongeaise. It is all accompanied by some voluptuous wines that aren't as expensive as one might think. The dinner menu/carte, with apéritifs and Champagne included, is enticing.

A la carte: 350-380F. Menus: 280F (wine incl.), 180F.

NEUILLY-SUR-SEINE
92200 Neuilly-sur-Seine - (Hauts-de-Seine)

⑬ Carpe Diem
10, rue de l'Eglise - 46 24 95 01
M. Coquoin. Open until 9:45 p.m. Closed Sat. lunch, Sun., May 1-8 & Aug. 6-27. Pets allowed. Cards: V, DC.

In this small, pleasant, smartly decorated room, Serge Coquoin, a veteran from the Casino Royal in Evian, creates a lively, original, tasty cuisine—for example, the chevreau (kid) aspic with herbs, the salad of lamb's sweetbreads with a sea urchin vinaigrette, the millefeuille of salmon and oysters, the carp stew with Parma ham, the sautéed filet of lamb with pine nuts, the braised rabbit tail with asparagus tips, the crépinettes (flat sausages) of pigs' feet and lamb's sweetbreads with foie gras, as well as some excellent desserts, including a crème caramel with cherries. The fixed-price menu, for 145 francs, is lovely.

A la carte: 300-350F. Menu: 150F.

12/20 Le Chalet
14, rue du Commandant-Pilot
46 24 03 11
M. Brun. Open until 11 p.m. Closed Sun. Pets allowed. Cards: V.

In this old chalet-style restaurant, you can feel free to put both elbows on the wooden table and tuck a paper napkin under your chin. The grilled meats are good, the Raclette generous. The wine is served in pitchers, and the customers are congenial.

A la carte: 180-200F. Menus: 65F, 100F and 170F (wine incl.).

12/20 La Chevauchée
209 ter, av. Charles-de-Gaulle
46 24 07 87
M. Valero. Open until 10:30 p.m. Closed Sat. lunch, Sun. & Dec. 26-Jan. 2. No pets. Cards: V, AE, DC.

This is one of the best little places in town. The dining room is cozy, the prices reasonable, and the cuisine has some nice "olé olé" touches

(gazpacho, paella, crème catalane). The small fixed-price menu is astounding.

A la carte: 230-250F. Menus: 140F, 170F.

12/20 Chez Livio
6, rue de Longchamp - 46 24 81 32
M. Innocenti. Open until 10:45 p.m. Closed Sat. & Sun. in Aug. & Dec. 23-Jan. 2. Garden dining. Pets allowed. Cards: V.

This charming trattoria in beautiful Neuilly has been famous for a quarter of a century. The small but thick pizzas are unrivaled; the osso buco and pasta, perfect. Springtime dining on the large patio with an open ceiling proves especially delightful. An épicerie is located next door.

A la carte: 160-180F. Menu: 125F (wine incl.).

⑯ Jacqueline Fénix
42, av. Charles-de-Gaulle - 46 24 42 61
Mme. Fénix. Open until 10 p.m. Closed Sat., Sun., July 27-Sept. 3 & Dec. 22-Jan. 3. Air cond. Pets allowed. Cards: V, AE.

Iced tureen of salmon, salmon caviar, quail eggs and new potatoes, a slice of warm foie gras with a shallot spread, roasted langoustines with watercress, sole and vegetables en papillote with tarragon, grilled filet of duckling from Ganders, warmed cheese, marbré of bitter chocolate, lime and grapefruit paillettes . . . and all of this for less than 295 francs! It's a gift, in fact, from the beautiful Jacqueline to the ravenous public-relations people who come out here to discuss deals over lunch and return for personal pleasure at dinner. But don't be afraid: The advertising/PR agents aren't the only ones occupying the grounds. People come from just about everywhere to this flowery, very feminine atmosphere to savor the beautiful and tasty cuisine prepared by Albert Corre, formerly the sous-chef here under Michel Rubod. He also has perpetuated the style of the original creations of his former boss—a rémoulade of smoked salmon and duck with orange, a terrine of eel filets and chanterelles, a millefeuille of young rabbit with eggplant and rosemary, red mullet with duck or cod liver, and veal kidneys with crispy leeks. And one won't easily forget the classic Pauillac lamb with garlic and potatoes or the delicious country-style rib of veal casserole. As for the desserts—from the marbré of bitter chocolate to the hot waffles and madeleines with jam—they're just about unforgettable.

A la carte: 400-500F. Menu: 295F (menu dégustation).

⑬ Les Feuilles Libres
34, rue Perronet - 46 24 41 41
Mme. Guillier-Marcellin. Open until 10:30 p.m. Closed Sat. lunch, Sun. & Aug. Air cond. Terrace dining. Pets allowed. Cards: V, AE, DC.

A brand-new little restaurant whose provincial charm will seduce you. This corner of Neuilly seems remote from Paris, and the small, square windowpanes, red floor tiles and banquettes give the place the air of an English teahouse. The proprietor, though not a cook, has exceptionally discriminating tastes, and his advice is always well taken. As for Patrice Hardy, the young chef, we have met him before at various toque-winning restaurants. The simple yet enticing fixed-price menu includes a half bottle of Muscadet or Bordeaux, a fondant of cauliflower with spices in a sauce we found a bit dull, delicious filet mignon of pork en croûte, and a perfect iced nougat in raspberry sauce. We award Les Feuilles Libres a small toque for its promising debut.

A la carte: 250F. Menus: 150F (lunch only), 230F (wine incl.).

⑮ Jenny Jacquet
2, pl. Parmentier - 46 24 94 14,
46 24 39 42
M. Jacquet. Closed Sat. lunch & Sun. No pets. Cards: V.

Having made the leap from the sixteenth arrondissement to Neuilly, Jenny Jacquet has landed on his feet once again. The decor of the former Truffe Noire is still not exactly inspiring, but it doesn't matter; we have eyes only for the fine cuisine of this Tours native, who makes full use of the time he spent at Papa Augereau's stoves in Rosiers-sur-Loire. That's where his taste for true country flavors, slowly simmering stews and refined sauces comes from (his "beurre nantais" is one of the best in the Paris area). Jacquet changes his menu every two months; if you happen to see his duck foie gras with Chaume wine, his pike mousseline

with beurre blanc, his brill cooked with mushroom crumbs, his fricassée of sweetbreads with hazelnuts or his breast of duck with hot liver and celery, don't pass them up. There are no more than five or six desserts, always delicious (Jacquet spent several years at Lenôtre's), and the wines from the Loire, though few in number, are exquisite.

A la carte: 280F.

⑬ La Tonnelle Saintongeaise ⬧⬧
32, rue Vital-Bouhot - 46 24 43 15
M. Girodot. Open until 10 p.m. Closed Sat., Sun., Aug. 1-20 & Dec. 23-Jan. 5. Air cond. Garden dining. Pets allowed. Cards: V.

On sunny days, lunch here along the Seine feels almost like a garden party. When Joël Girodot opens his lovely terrace under the chestnut trees, the Ile de la Jatte becomes as beautiful as Cythera. Nicole Girodot makes dishes as beautiful as the setting: fricassée of snails, fish soup from Saintonges, young rabbit cooked in Pineau wine, small rounds of hot chèvre marinated in Cognac and her own versions of other delicious specialties from Charentes. The attractive dining room has been newly decorated with wood and stone.

A la carte: 250F. Menu: 200F (summer weekdays and on the terrace only).

ORLY
94396 Aéroport d'Orly - (Val-de-Marne)

⑭ Maxim's
Aérogare d'Orly-Ouest - 46 87 16 16
M. Janisson. Open daily until 10 p.m. Air cond. Pets allowed. Telex 201389. Cards: V, AE, DC.

A comfortable grill serves as the anteroom to this twin of the Maxim's on rue Royale. With its exceptional fixed-price menu—country terrine of young rabbit with prunes and Armagnac, roasted meats (a beautiful, thick sirloin with marrow in a bordelaise sauce), lamb stewed with tomatoes and basil, cheese and salad, and a cart of desserts and pastries served with the best coffee to be found at the airport; all accompanied by an excellent wine, perhaps a Champigny or a fine Muscadet—it is one of the best places these suburbs have to offer. You'll feel as though you have wings, just like the huge Boeings on the runways before you. Next door, at the deep-red banquettes in the lively decor of Maxim's II, you'll have to pay a bit more to sample the paillasson of potatoes (like a potato pancake) topped with an escalope of duck liver, the lobster salad in walnut oil or the red mullet with saffron and olive oil. The cuisine is prepared by chef Jean Jorda, who is increasingly determined to abandon the chichi repertoire of the past. The cellar is most handsome, and the service consistently meets its high standards.

A la carte: 400F (250-350F at the Grill). Menu: 220F (in the Grill only, wine incl.).

LE PERREUX
94170 Le Perreux - (Val-de-Marne)

⑮ Les Magnolias
48, av. de Bry - 48 72 47 43
M. Royant. Open until 10 p.m. Closed Sun., April 2-10 & Aug. 7-21. Pets allowed. Cards: V, AE, DC.

Les Magnolias is a small suburban house with vivid colors reminiscent of Utrillo's paintings. The facade has just been repainted, and the interior will surprise you with its majestic decor: walls covered in burgundy linen, flourishing green plants, tables partitioned by light balustrades and elegant young waiters fluttering about in striped gray jackets. Gérard Royant, the chef/owner, takes the orders himself and keeps an eye on the service (according to our readers, he doesn't much care to be contradicted). The cuisine is original and on the whole quite well prepared, with an interesting fixed-price menu (but the à la carte dishes are costly): light zakuski (Russian hors d'oeuvres), a loaf of escargots in beurre blanc astutely seasoned with fresh herbs, breast of duck in a good wine sauce and delicious crêpes stuffed with raspberries. The wine cellar is small but perfect.

A la carte: 350F.

PONTOISE
95300 Pontoise - (Val d'Oise)

⑮ Le Jardin des Lavandières
28, rue de Rouen - 30 38 25 55
M. Decout. Open until 9:30 p.m. Closed Sat. lunch, Sun., holidays, July 14-Aug. 15 & Dec. 23-Jan. 4. Air cond. Pets allowed. Cards: V, AE.

A murky stream running behind the parking lot testifies to the presence of a distant garden and the washerwomen who used to come here. It's enough to send those Parisians and Cergy natives, starved for a taste of the countryside, into pastoral dreaminess. When you step inside this old, still-charming house close to Notre-Dame, Chantal Decout's simple gracious smile greets you. Flowers fill the vases and decorate the walls, and with the beamed ceilings, the peaceful lighting and the atmosphere of natural freshness, you would indeed think you were in the country.

Jean-Louis, Chantal's husband, who once worked with Faugeron, cooks with as much attention and precision as a clock maker. Applying his genius to the finest of seasonal produce, without concocting extravagant combinations, he creates light, simple, yet elegant dishes whose flavors impress with their candor: salad of young leeks with truffles and foie gras, seafood and spinach en papillote, quail tourte with cabbage and grapes, lasagne of young rabbit and morels, and a waffle with wild strawberries. We have only one reproach for these delicious meals: One can't return too often, because the checks, although justified, climb quickly (the beautiful, expensive wine list is partially to blame), and Jean-Louis has not yet thought to offer his admirers the alternative of a smaller fixed-price menu.

A la carte: 300-350F.

LE PORT-MARLY
78560 Le Port-Marly - (Yvelines)

⑬ Auberge du Relais Breton
27, rue de Paris - 39 58 64 33
M. Chaumont. Open until 10 p.m. Closed Sun. dinner, Mon. & Aug. 10-Sept. 30. Garden dining. Pets allowed. Cards: V, AE.

Fifteen minutes from the porte Maillot and just a few steps from one of the most delightful landscapes along the Seine stands this old, thoroughly rustic inn, whose decor is reminiscent of Brittany. In its charming, intimate, leafy garden, one is served a lovely, lightly classical cuisine: hot oysters in Champagne, braised sole in lobster sauce, breast of duck with walnut butter. The beautiful desserts come from Flo-Prestige (whose owner is one of the inn's former managers).

A la carte: 250F. Menus: 195F (wine incl.), 149F.

⑬ Le Lion d'Or
7, rue de Paris - 39 58 44 56

M. Cluzel. Open until 10 p.m. Closed Tues., Wed., March 1-15 & Sept. 1-15. Terrace dining. Pets allowed. Cards: V, AE.

Jean-Paul Cluzel, upon reaching 50, locked up his business, slipped the key under the door and left to study cooking with André Guillot, Jung, Darroze and Vié. Today he is an accomplished chef: serious, skillful, in full command of his techniques and original as well, as are all self-made people. That's why a visit to his old, quasi-historic inn (it appears in Sisley's painting *The Flooding of Port-Marly*), is always full of lovely surprises. Try the blancmange (jellied almond cream) of fowl, the duck cassoulet with beans, the small stuffed quails, the stuffed lamb and the exquisite farmers' cheeses from the Auvergne. Françoise Cluzel, a full-blooded native of Anjou, has collected some marvelous wines from her region. The terrace by the water is delightful.

A la carte: 250-300F. Menu: 120F, 220F.

LE PRE-SAINT-GERVAIS
93310 Le Pré-Saint-Gervais (Seine-Saint-Denis)

⑭ Le Pouilly-Reuilly
68, rue André-Joineau - 48 45 14 59

M. Thibault. Open until 10 p.m. Closed Sun., holidays & Aug. No pets. Parking. Cards: V, AE, DC.

We seem to be out in the country, in Père Thibault's native region of the Sologne, which abounds in wild game; but we're also in the land of chicken with crayfish, of andouillette in Pouilly wine, of paupiettes of Morvan-style ham (the way François Mitterrand likes it) and of fried fish. Actually, we're in a suburban restaurant with a high-tech, pale-colored decor and an extraordinarily cordial and friendly atmosphere. This place is one of the very few in which the noble bistro tradition survives. The black-aproned service, the exquisite little wines and Rolande's melting smile win out over the bad rustic imitations. So why on earth doesn't

the owner serve any tarte tatin? He is, after all, a native of Lamotte-Beuvron, where it was invented. He replaces it brilliantly, however, with a magnificent giant coffee éclair.

A la carte: 280-330F.

PUTEAUX
92800 Puteaux - (Hauts-de-Seine)

⑬ Les Deux Arcs
34, Cours Michelet (La Défense 10) 47 76 44 43

M. Chevauche. Open daily until 10 p.m. Terrace dining. No pets. Parking. Telex 612189. Cards: V, AE, DC, MC.

Les Deux Arcs is an oasis of peace and comfort in a depressing environment of concrete and asphalt. The modern, cheerful decor is a perfect success, the staff courteous, the cuisine serious and good, and small touches of refinement can be found everywhere: roses on the tables, Echiré butter, delicious rolls. The terrine of fowl livers is flavorful, as is the duck confit with sautéed potatoes and the daube of beef, although its sauce, boiled down too far, is a little bitter. The iced nougat is perfect, and the Chinon wine from Gosset is delicious but too expensive.

A la carte: 300F and up. Menu: 270F (lunch only).

⑮ Gasnier 😊
7, bd Richard-Wallace - 45 06 33 63

M. Gasnier. Open until 9:30 p.m. Closed Sat., Sun., holidays, Feb. school vacation & June 29-Aug. 2. Air cond. Pets allowed. Cards: V, AE, DC.

The area may not be exciting, nor the angular decor much fun, but Hubert Gasnier's Parisian heart contains a wealth of happiness. His cuisine from the southwest of France remains tremendously spirited, and his marvelous foie gras, charcuterie and fowl come from the best Basque and Béarn suppliers. His à la carte menu is graced with as much cordiality and warmth as one could wish for between Mont-de-Marsan and Castelnaudary. He takes great care to lighten his sauces, simplify his recipes and refine this earthy cuisine. For example, there is the perfectly balanced mesclun salad with foie gras and sweetbreads; the plump, tender aiguillettes of duck served with savory cèpes and chanterelles; the astounding cassoulet de Castelnaudary; and the andouillette braised in Jurançon wine. Maïté Gasnier's desserts, particularly her light, crusty apple feuilleté, are a perfect finish to these festive meals. And we mustn't forget the great wines and fabulous Armagnacs from the cellar.

A la carte: 300-350F. Menu: 240F (wine incl.).

LE RAINCY
93340 Le Raincy - (Seine-Saint-Denis)

⑭ Le Chalet des Pins
13, av. de Livry - 43 81 01 19

M. Aumasson. Open until 9 p.m. Closed Sun. dinner (July: Closed Sun. & Mon. dinner & Tues.; Aug.: Closed Sat. lunch, Sun., Mon. & Tues. dinner). Garden dining. Pets allowed. Cards: V, AE, DC.

The cooking of Fernande de Oliveira has all the virtues of a good feminine cuisine: generosity, forthright flavors, lightness and a careful technique. The raw salmon and sardines in raspberry vinegar, the émincé of lobster with fresh mint, the calf's head with fresh tomato, the roast salmon with truffle juice, the young rabbit with coriander and the excellent pastries (warm pear feuilleté) all have a degree of freshness and originality that goes beyond expectations. The rose-and-beige lacquered decor is elegant. Reasonable prices and a cellar rich with wines and spirits.

A la carte: 280-300F. Menu: 110F.

ROISSY-EN-FRANCE
95700 Roissy-en-France - (Val d'Oise)

⑭ Maxim's
Aéroport Charles-de-Gaulle
48 62 16 16

M. Champagnac. Lunch only. Air cond. Pets allowed. Telex 240270. Cards: V, AE, DC.

The concrete interior of Terminal 1 on the main floor, the mix of Boeings and business people, the chrome-pipe decor—none of this evokes the fancy, refined atmosphere promised by the restaurant's sign. Nevertheless, Maxim's is one of the better restaurants in the Paris region. Yet it is not necessarily one of the most expensive, provided you keep to the adjacent grill, which serves salads, appetizers and meats along with fish grilled over charcoal. The food in the restaurant, although it is still technically superior to most, has lost its interest and individual accent. We therefore have removed a point, though one still dines reasonably well here, particularly on Jacques Legrand's fixed-price menu, which he bases on his morning shopping. For example, he might offer a small salad of salmon and watercress followed by sea bass with basil, aiguillettes of duck in Santenay wine, excellent cheeses, a tray of splendid light pastries, and coffee. When you add a perfect Côtes-du-Rhône or a fruity red Sancerre (the cellar is exceptional), your check will scarcely exceed 300 francs per person. It's certainly worth doffing your hat for such seriousness and quality. The service is faultless.

A la carte: 450-500F. Menus: 220F (in the Grill only, wine incl.), 250F.

ROMAINVILLE
93230 Romainville - (Seine-Saint-Denis)

⑮ Chez Henri
72, rte. de Noisy - 48 45 26 65

M. Bourgin. Open until 9:30 p.m. Closed Sat. (except dinner off-seas.), Sun. & holidays. Air cond. Pets allowed. Parking. Cards: V.

The large, comfortable bistro of the faunlike and Rabelaisian Henri Bourgin may be as warm as its environment of suburban warehouses is icy and gloomy, but this has not been sufficient cause to draw large crowds to the grayish Romainville avenue, which features the city's refuse and a gas station as its major attractions. However, Bourgin is a remarkable cook, whose creativity and broad technical ability are rare indeed. Using his incredible knowledge of natural produce, he creates dishes whose appearance may not always be attractive, but which are truly original and admirably rich in flavor: quiche of fresh morels in truffle juice, a navarin of lotte with peas and baby onions, roasted John Dory with potatoes and baby carrots, leg of young rabbit with smoked bacon served on baby turnip tops. When leaving Chez Henri, you'll feel that you've never before tasted this type of cuisine. Nowadays, that's quite a compliment to pay a chef. The feuilleté desserts are enchanting, and the wine cellar is impressive.

A la carte: 400F. Menu: 200F.

RUNGIS
94150 Rungis - (Val-de-Marne)

(13) La Rungisserie
20, av. Charles-Lindbergh
46 87 36 36

M. Holzmann. Open daily until 11 p.m. Air cond. No pets. Parking. Telex 260738. Cards: V, AE, DC, MC.

Something new has happened to this huge building in the deserted zone between Rungis and Orly. For one thing, it is now rather elegant, despite the huge buffet of appetizers, erected like a catafalque under a blue-black linen cloth. For another, new chef Christian Petetin is cooking imaginative, clever dishes that would merit two toques were it not for the lack of seasonings (even in such country dishes as the calf's-foot salad). This may be due to the demands of an international clientele with an unsophisticated palate. So, for the time being, this restaurant's main attraction is its exceptional fixed-price menu: an infinite selection of appetizers and cold courses (as much as you can eat) and a special of the day or a grilled meat, followed by cheeses and desserts. Wine and coffee are included.

A la carte: 300F. Menu: 162F (weekdays only, wine incl.), 185F (weekdays only) and 75- 200F.

SAINT-CLOUD
92210 St-Cloud - (Hauts-de-Seine)

12/20 La Désirade
2, bd de la République - 47 71 22 33
M. Cogé. Open daily until 10 p.m. Air cond. Terrace dining. Pets allowed. Parking. Telex 631618. Cards: V, AE, DC, MC.

The green and pink fabrics and cream-colored wood lattices on the first floor of the new Hôtel Quorum form a pleasant, exotic setting for the attractive waitresses in khaki dresses. Choose the remarkable fixed-price menu,

which changes every day; perhaps it will include the egg casserole with ratatouille, the loin of pork with sage and the excellent Paris-Brest. The wine list needs expansion.

A la carte: 280F. Menu: 120F.

SAINT-DENIS
93200 St-Denis - (Seine-Saint-Denis)

(13) Mélody
15, rue Gabriel-Péri - 48 20 87 73
M. Balat. Open daily until 11:30 p.m. Air cond. Pets allowed. Cards: V.

Everything is new—first and foremost the prices, which have been cut in half; then the decor, now with big mirrors, paintings and small, crimson-velvet chairs; but especially the food, which is prepared in the best of the genuine, generous bistro style. Michel Balat has been extremely successful in carrying out his courageous, small "cultural revolution." No doubt many of his fellow restaurateurs would find the solution to their problems by following his example. Of course, they would have to do it the right way and prepare such dishes as the delicious herrings in oil, the perfect hot saucisson and the tender leg of lamb with beans that melts in your mouth. The wine list is good (Cabernet is served in carafes).

A la carte: 160-180F. Menu: 60F.

SAINT-GERMAIN-EN-LAYE
78100 St-Germain-en-Laye - (Yvelines)

(14) Cazaudehore
1, av. du Président-Kennedy
34 51 93 80, 39 73 36 60

MM. Cazaudehore. Open until 10 p.m. Closed Mon. (except holidays). Garden dining. Pets allowed. Parking. Telex 696055. Cards: V, MC.

The Cazaudehores—father and son—have undertaken a huge renovation project at their beautiful large house in the middle of the woods. The new dining room wallpaper is fresh and tastefully floral. An immense veranda opens up directly onto the garden, which is a most delightful place to be: seated on the comfortable green chairs surrounding tables adorned with pink tablecloths, enjoying the cool shade of the old trees during the day and the light of the authentic Parisian street lamps

at night. The chef's tasty cuisine, classical but light, is commendable and offers plenty of specialties from the southwest of France: tripe à la paloise (broiled tripe with green beans and potatoes), salmon roasted in olive oil and dill, lamprey à la bordelaise, lobster à la nage, loin of lamb with rosemary and on and on and on. The check mounts quickly, due to the selective wine list and the absence of a fixed-price menu.
A la carte: 350-500F.

Pavillon de la Croix de Noailles
Carrefour de Noailles - 39 62 53 46
M. Nakoniecznyj. Open until 9:30 p.m. (10 p.m. in summer). Closed Mon. dinner, Tues. & Feb. Garden dining. Pets allowed. Cards: V, AE.

This attractive eighteenth-century hunting lodge is built next to the most crowded intersection in the forest. But, surrounded as it is by splendid ancient oaks, the Pavillon is still delightful, particularly in summer, when meals are served in the lovely garden under parasols. The hospitality is good, the waitresses are delightful, and the cuisine is still as light and well prepared as ever. We will, however, penalize it slightly for its lack of versatility and its indifference to the changing market and seasons. For instance, the mesclun salad with ray in raspberry vinegar is good but the greens aren't varied enough, and the aiguillettes of roast duckling are delicious but are served with large peas instead of the promised fresh beans. The tutti-frutti tart is a bit messy, but fresh and good.
A la carte: 350-400F. Menu: 145F (weekdays only).

12/20 Restaurant des Coches
7, rue des Coches - 39 73 66 40
M. Corbel. Open until 10:15 p.m. Closed Sun. dinner, Mon. & Aug. 10-20. Air cond. Terrace dining. Pets allowed. Parking. Telex 699491. Cards: V, AE, MC.

Only the decor is still charming; everything else here has become so slipshod. The service is clumsy and condescending and the kitchen has fallen away: boring scallop salad, skeletal beef ribs with reheated potatoes, and desserts that are made too quickly (though the tea sorbet with prunes and cinnamon is good). No toque in this edition.
A la carte: 300F. Menus: 98F (lunch only), 190F, 250F.

SAINT-OUEN
93400 St-Ouen - (Seine-Saint-Denis)

Chez Serge
7, bd Jean-Jaurès - 40 11 06 42
M. Cancé. Closed Sun. & Aug. Pets allowed. Cards: V.

Mme. Cancé has left her stove, so Serge himself is in charge of the kitchen. The à la carte menu is short, but this is not a criticism, for it is versatile and uses fresh, seasonal produce purchased daily (with the exception of the marvelous foie gras in a Sauternes aspic, the calf's head and the homemade persillé, which are served year-round). Everything is delicious, honest and simply prepared, just like at home: calf's knuckle printanière, fresh cod with orange, real civet de lapin, and fricassée of Bresse chicken in truffle juice. The wine cellar is one of the most wonderful in these suburbs—not because of the number of bottles it holds, but because of its excellent selection and prices (twelve years ago, Serge made this restaurant famous when he won an award for the best wine selection). The provincial bistro decor may be unexciting, but the lively crowd lends a cordial atmosphere.
A la carte: 300-400F.

Le Coq de la Maison Blanche
37, bd Jean-Jaurès - 40 11 01 23, 40 11 67 68
M. François. Open until 10 p.m. Closed Sun. Terrace dining. Pets allowed. Cards: V.

Le Coq is a big suburban bistro, as warm as the suburbs are gloomy, with a monumental white facade on the street corner that isn't exactly enticing. But the vast interior is cordial, with chocolate-brown drapes, a merry clientele of foremen and manufacturers and a young, vigorous and funny boss supervising a friendly staff. At the end of World War II, people came here to eat coq au vin à la Escoffier. Today the food, which has been prepared by André Gamon from Lyon for the past 30 years, is predominantly bourgeois and hearty. Generous, frank and seasonal: the jambon persillé, the terrine of skate with basil and a tomato coulis, the lobster salad with watercress, the perfectly grilled sole, the Loiret kid roasted with herbs, the numerous grilled meats (the pigs' trotters with sautéed potatoes are outstanding) and the chef's or granny's tasty desserts, including brioche with crème caramel. The Beaujolais is superb and the wine cellar well stocked.

A la carte: 250F.

VERSAILLES
78000 Versailles - (Yvelines)

See also "Versailles" in the Out of Paris chapter.

12/20 Brasserie du Boeuf à la Mode
4, rue au Pain - 39 50 31 99
M. Vié. Open daily until 12:30 a.m. Pets allowed. Cards: V.

The Brasserie du Boeuf à la Mode is one of the latest additions to Gérard Vié's friendly little gourmet empire. A gifted former assistant chef at Les Trois Marches prepares anoverwhelming successful and delicious jambonneau of duck, an excellent boudin (blood sausage) with apples and a perfect chocolate terrine, all of which won't cost you more than 150 francs with a half bottle of Sancerre or Champigny wine.

A la carte: 160F.

14 Le Potager du Roy
1, rue du Maréchal-Joffre - 39 50 35 34
M. Letourneur. Open until 10 p.m. Closed Sun. & Mon. Air cond. Pets allowed. Cards: V.

Here, in the redecorated dining room of Gérard Vié's old Trois Marches, which has been extended by a pleasant closed terrace, Philippe Letourneur serves two miraculous daily fixed- price menus that rate among the best in the region. The larger one includes a delectable pâté of blond liver or a mousse of coquilles St-Jacques, followed by veal kidneys in mustard sauce, cheeses and delicious eggnogs with cassonade (soft brown sugar). The wine list composed by Les Trois Marches's sommelier should offer more half bottles.

A la carte: 300F and up. Menus: 105F, 150F.

14 Le Rescatore
27, av. de St-Cloud - 39 50 23 60
M. Bagot. Open until 10 p.m. Closed Sat. lunch & Sun. Air cond. Pets allowed. Cards: V, AE.

The enterprising patron of this restaurant, the sunniest and merriest in Versailles, draws his inspiration almost exclusively from the freshest possible seafood. The large windows, whose handrails are beautifully wrought, open onto avenue de Saint-Cloud, and the big, round tables are set in discreet elegance in the lovely, freshly wallpapered dining room. The cuisine provides many unexpected, original and (most of the time) happy combinations: the fricassée of scallops with Sauternes, the roasted oysters with slices of rare duck breast, the lotte with fresh ginger and the soufflé of sole with baby vegetables. All the dishes taste natural, and our only negative word is that Jacques Bagot stays too long with his creations instead of changing his à la carte menu more often.

A la carte: 300-400F. Menu: 225F (weekday lunch only).

13 Trianon Palace
1, bd de la Reine - 39 50 34 12
M. Marcus. Open daily until 9:30 p.m. Terrace dining. No pets. Parking. Telex 698863. Cards: V, AE, DC, MC.

This imposing old luxury hotel, built in 1912 in the Palace of Versailles's park, was recently refurbished. The magnificent main floor looks even more aristocratic than before, and the ambience of comfort and luxury is pleasant indeed, particularly in summer, when the high windows open onto the superb terrace. The cuisine of Jean-Jacques Mathou, an impressive collector of diplomas, is proof of a job well done. His delicious ravioli stuffed with supions (cuttlefish) and zucchini, his royal sea bream cooked to perfection with soft garlic, and his turbot pleasantly enhanced by fennel and purple olives win him one toque. The service is excellent.

A la carte: 450F. Menus: 190F (weekdays only), 260F (holidays only), 220F.

18 Les Trois Marches
3, rue Colbert (pl. du Château)
39 50 13 21
M. Vié. Open until 10 p.m. Closed Sun. & Mon. Garden dining. Pets allowed. Cards: V, AE, DC, MC.

With extreme discretion, Gérard Vié has built himself a small kingdom (in Versailles he has Le Potager du Roy, Le Quai No. 1 and La Brasserie du Boeuf à la Mode, and in Boulogne, L'Avant Seine). This realm allows him to offer Les Trois Marches's clients the luxury of a historic building (it once belonged to the Gramont family), a garden for summertime dining, excellent service and cooking whose delicacy and finesse are reaffirmed year after year.

These proper surroundings add so much to the pleasure of Vié's dishes—dishes that were once compromised by rather muddled flavors but are now quite precise. Some of the newer creations on Vié's menu include cold lobster with crushed tomatoes marinated in olive oil and ginger, rabbit in aspic with leeks, duck foie gras au rancio (a wine liqueur), fresh cod with cabbage and bacon, turbot in meat juices with potato galettes, and roast leg of baby lamb with garlic. Each is proof of a talent in full bloom. And everything surrounding these main dishes is equally exquisite: The bread is marvelous, the cheese tray is stupendous, and the canapés, petits fours and coffee—particularly the Jamaican roast—are all sumptuous. Food fit for a prince, right under the rays of the Sun King.

A la carte: 500-700F. Menus: 230F (weekday lunch only), 325F, 435F.

IN NEARBY LE CHESNAY

⑬ Le Chesnoy
24, rue Pottier - 39 54 01 01

M. Baratin. Open until 10 p.m. Closed Sun. dinner & 1st 3 weeks in Aug. Air cond. Pets allowed. Parking. Cards: V, AE, DC.

The career of George Torrès, Le Chesnoy's chef, is marked by the number of good, solid seafood places he has left behind—Le Chalut, Les Glénan, Marius et Jeannette. So it's not surprising that his fresh cod with aromatic spices and his flan of coquilles St-Jacques with asparagus are particularly successful. But his seasonal à la carte menu (offering a wide choice of vegetables) lists just as many meat entrées, including an excellent croustillant of duck in a pear-caramel sauce. To sum up, this excellent establishment, located close to the shopping center, is the best in Le Chesnay. M. Baratin doesn't try to impress you; he is a charming man who greets his clients like old friends. The dining room, decorated with mirrors and

brown lacquer, is comfortable.

A la carte: 280F. Menu: 150F.

LE VESINET
78110 Le Vésinet - (Yvelines)

⑯ A la Grâce de Dieu
75, bd Carnot - 34 80 05 44

M Ballester. Open daily until 10 p.m. Air cond. Pets allowed. Cards: V.

Daniel Ballester, a native of Bougival and a student of Jean Delaveyne (that's why, being a perfectionist, he never stops experimenting), worked until recently in a delightful restaurant in the village of Follainville, near Mantes. Not long ago, he bought an old brewery located between Chatou and Saint-Germain and redecorated it in a plain style. But here, at Le Vésinet, he wanted to strike it rich and fill his already-crowded restaurant, so he devised a unique menu/carte for 110 francs. With a half bottle of good Beaujolais, your check won't exceed 145 francs—yes, you read correctly—and your meal will be out of the ordinary. The fresh ingredients Ballester uses are perfect (he goes to Rungis's central market four nights a week), the food is amusing and savory, and the presentations are simple yet always elegant. One may choose from a selection of ten appetizers, including a compote of rabbit en gelée, small marinated mackerel, beef shoulder with a tomato mousse, scrambled eggs with chanterelles, and fresh pasta with mussels; four fish dishes, including papillote of coalfish with herbs, salmon with sorrel, ray with fresh mint and turbot with an embeurrée of cabbage (this last dish will cost you an additional 35 francs); six meat dishes, including a civet of duck with fresh pasta, pigeon crépinette and leg of mutton with couscous; and six desserts, including a heavenly strawberry millefeuille. Let's add that the short wine list has been remarkably well composed by Guy Renvoisé and that the service is attentive. In conclusion, we suggest that you hurry and visit this restaurant to see what work, heart and talent can get you for 110 francs.

Menu/carte: 110F.

HOTELS

INTRODUCTION

P aris hotels rooms come in every possible style, size and price range. The one feature they all share is that you'll have to book early to get exactly what you want. Our selection ranges from sumptuous suites to far humbler lodgings, but note that certain hoteliers put as high a price on charm or modern facilities as others do on pure luxury, so don't assume that "charming" means "cheap." The prices quoted include taxes and service.

Hotels are classified as follows: Luxury, First Class, Charming, Large & Modern, Practical, Airport, and The Suburbs.

RESERVATION SERVICE

Les Hôtesses de Paris can arrange a same-day reservation in any Parisian or French hotel. The service costs 15 to 45 francs, depending on the hotel. These friendly hostesses also provide tourist information for Paris and France. All you need to do is drop in (don't telephone) at one of the locations listed in *Basics* under Tourist Information.

NO ROOM AT THE INN?

If your every attempt to find a hotel room has failed, you needn't panic. Here are two companies that can track down a room for you or even rent you a high-class studio or apartment. The latter come with every guarantee of home comforts, security and such options as maid, laundry and repair services. Prices range from 450 to 2,500 francs and up, depending on the size and accommodations. Town houses and houseboats are available as well! Just contact Paris-Séjour-Réservation, 90, avenue des Champs-Elysées, 75008 (42 56 30 00), Monday through Friday 9 a.m. to 7 p.m.,

Saturday 10 a.m. to 6 p.m.; or Paris Bienvenue, 10, avenue de Villars, 75007 (47 53 80 81), Monday through Friday 9 a.m. to 8 p.m., Saturday and Sunday 10 a.m. to 7 p.m.

RENTAL APARTMENTS

At the apartments listed below, you'll enjoy the same service you would find in a hotel, for a lower price. Rates vary from 450 to 765 francs per night for a studio for two.

•Orion Les Halles, 4, rue des Innocents, 1st arrondissement, 45 08 00 33.

•Orion La Défense, Paris-Porte de Neuilly, 92700 La Défense, 47 78 15 01.

•Flatotel International, 14, rue du Théâtre, 15th arrondissement, 45 75 62 20.

•Flatotel Porte de Versailles, 52, rue d'Oradour-sur-Glane, 15th arrondissement, 45 54 93 45.

•Les Citadines-Montparnasse, 67, av. du Maine, 14th arrondissement, 43 27 14 24.

•Les Citadines-Trocadéro, 29 bis, rue Saint-Didier, 16th arrondissement, 47 04 88 22.

•Les Citadines-Austerlitz, 27, rue Esquirol, 13th arrondissement, 45 84 13 09.

SYMBOLS & ABBREVIATIONS

Our opinion of the comfort level and appeal of each hotel is expressed in the following ranking system:

Very luxurious

Luxurious

Very comfortable

Comfortable

Very quiet

Symbols in red denote charm.

Rms: rooms
Stes: suites
Seas.: season
Air cond.: Air conditioning
Half-board: rate per person for
room, breakfast and one other meal
(lunch or dinner)

Credit Cards
  AE: American Express
  DC: Diners Club
  MC: MasterCard (Eurocard)
  V: VISA (Carte Bleue)

LUXURY

Beverley Hills

8th arr. - 75, rue de Berri - 43 59 55 55
Open year-round. 10 stes 9,400-30,000F (per week). TV. Parking. Telex 643868. Cards: V, AE, DC, MC.

This is a residence designed for Texas millionaires and sheiks: total electronic surveillance, huge apartments with dining rooms and all imaginable amenities. Piano bar and restaurant.

Le Bristol

8th arr. - 112, rue du Faubourg-Saint-Honoré - 42 66 91 45
Open year-round. 45 stes 4,400-7,685F. 155 rms 1,380-2,330F. TV. Air cond. Heated pool. No pets. Parking. Telex 280961. Cards: V, AE, DC, MC.

The elegance of its decor (genuine period furniture, as well as lovely imitations), the comfort of its rooms, the luxury of its suites and the quality of its clientele make Le Bristol one of the rare authentic luxury hotels in Paris (as well as one of the most expensive). There are ultra-modern conference rooms, a small heated swimming pool on the seventh-floor terrace and extremely spacious rooms with magnificent marble bathrooms and superb Louis XVth– and Louis XVIth–style furniture. An extraordinary restaurant (Le Bristol) opens onto the lawn and the flowers of a large garden. The staff is both cordial and impressively trained.

Claridge-Bellman

8th arr. - 37, rue François-Ier
47 23 54 42
Open year-round. 42 rms 550-1,150F. TV. No pets. Telex 641150. Cards: V, AE, DC.

Though rather small (only some 40 rooms), the Bellman has made the best possible use of the lovely decor—paintings, precious ornaments, antique furniture—it inherited from the Claridge. Its pleasant rooms are soundproofed by double windows. The smaller attic rooms (on the seventh floor) are delightful. Restaurant: Le Relais Bellman.

George V

8th arr. - 31, av. George-V
47 23 54 00
Open year-round. 59 stes 2,950-11,380F. 292 rms 1,640-2,590F. TV. Air cond. Pets allowed. Parking. Telex 650082. Cards: V, AE, DC, MC.

The new management has succeeded perfectly in instilling new life and spirit into this "monument in decline." The bar and the restaurant (Les Princes; both open onto a delightful patio) have been redecorated, and the rooms have been renovated with as much concern for the elegance of the decor as for the modernism of the comfort (electronic panels located at the head of the beds allow guests to close the venetian shutters, control both the television and the air conditioning, call room service and so on). The lounges and the corridors, however, are faded, dull and depressing, and need attention. There are some precious objects (such as an admirable Regency clock), paintings (*Vase of Roses* by Renoir) and tapestries (from Flanders) estimated by Sotheby to be worth some 40 million francs. These and the elevator, with its plate glass, and the Galerie de la Paix, with its red and black marble, still radiate that George V charm. Perfect reception; attentive floor service. Restaurant: see Les Princes, eighth arrondissement.

Grand Hôtel

9th arr. - 2, rue Scribe - 42 68 12 13
Open year-round. 33 stes 3,500-7,150F. 482 rms 1,160-1,740F. TV. Air cond. Pets allowed. Parking. Telex 220875. Cards: V, AE, DC, MC.

The renovation of this grand hotel, built in 1862, is now complete (it follows the gorgeous work done on the Café de la Paix and the Opéra restaurant, which was decorated by Garnier). In the past ten years, this monumental Second Empire structure has recovered all the luster it had had when Empress Eugénie, on the arm of the banker Pereire, opened it— along with the additional comfort of the most contemporary equipment available, offices for business people, superb relaxation rooms, ultra-modern conference rooms, a sauna and much more. Excellent bar. Restaurant: see Opéra Restaurant, ninth arrondissement.

Hôtel Balzac

8th arr. - 6, rue Balzac - 45 61 97 22
Open year-round. 14 stes 2,500-5,000F. 56 rms 1,250-1,600F. TV. Air cond. Pets allowed. Parking. Telex 290298. Cards: V, AE, DC, MC.

One of the most recently opened little hotels in Paris, the Balzac has 70 rooms and suites that have been completely renovated and are spacious, quiet and discreet. Their soft pastel decor, their well-designed lighting, their comfortable furniture and their roomy beds ensure a truly lovely stay. The service is flawless. Restaurant: Le Sallambier.

Hôtel de Crillon

8th arr. - 10, pl. de la Concorde
42 65 24 24
Open year-round. 41 stes 3,500-15,000F. 148 rms 1,600-2,000F. Half-board 350F (plus room). TV. Air cond. Pets allowed. Parking. Telex 290204. Cards: V, AE, DC, MC.

The Crillon is the last of the Parisian luxury hotels to have remained authentically French: with its inner courtyards; terraces overlooking the most beautiful square in the world; superb salons; rooms that, though not always immense or well soundproofed, are exquisitely decorated; and the most beautiful suites one could hope for. Their windows overlook the place de la Concorde or the rue Boissy-

---

Prices for rooms and suites are per room, not per person. Half-board and full-board prices, however, are per person.

---

d'Anglas, and bathrooms are completely re-done in marble. Let's not forget the well-trained staff. Yes, the Hôtel de Crillon has reestablished its link with the elegant and intimate ambience of years past (Louis XVIth–style furniture, silk drapes, pastel walls and woodwork ornamented with gold leaf, well-hidden minibars). Relais et Châteaux. Restaurants: see Les Ambassadeurs and L'Obélisque, eighth arrondissement.

Hôtel Lotti

1st arr. - 7, rue de Castiglione
42 60 37 34
Open year-round. 5 stes 3,740-4,620F. 123 rms 1,120-1,980F. TV. Air cond. Pets allowed. Telex 240066. Cards: V, AE, DC, MC.

This elegant hotel is very popular with the members of the Italian aristocracy. Each of the rather spacious rooms, whose comfort is worthy of their clientele, is uniquely decorated and offers outstanding facilities. The restaurant, the lobby and all the rooms were recently renovated.

Inter-Continental

1st arr. - 3, rue de Castiglione
42 60 37 80
Open year-round. 62 stes 2,940-9,085F. 393 rms 1,497-2,138F. TV. Air cond. Pets allowed. Telex 220114. Cards: V, AE, DC, MC.

Garnier, the architect of the Opéra, designed this vast hotel; three out of its seven immense and spectacular salons are ranked for their high standards. With its remarkably equipped conference rooms, it answers perfectly to the business world's needs; and as for charm and comfort, you'll find them both in the lovely patio filled with flowers, in the decor and the incomparable loveliness of many of the rooms (though some are tiny and gloomy), as well as in the small singles located in the attic, from which there is a fine view of the Tuileries. The suites (with Jacuzzi) are luxurious. Three restaurants: La Rôtisserie Rivoli, Le Café Tuileries and La Terrasse Fleurie (in summer).

Lancaster

8th arr. - 7, rue de Berri - 43 59 90 43
Open year-round. 8 stes 2,990-6,325F. 51 rms 1,380-2,070F. TV. Air cond. in 30 rms. Pets allowed. Parking. Telex 640991. Cards: V, AE, DC, MC.

Once you recover from the immense, breathtaking bouquet of flowers in the lobby, you'll notice that the general setting—furniture, draperies, paintings, ornaments—isn't really as refined and luxurious as you would wish. The small inner garden, with its flowers, fountains and statues (meals are served there on sunny days), lends an unexpected rural touch to this hotel located only a few steps from the Champs-Elysées. The rooms and suites all have period furniture and double windows; the decor, on the whole, is like something out of an interior design magazine. Excellent reception; attentive and punctual service. The small conference rooms have fine equipment.

Marriott Prince de Galles

8th arr. - 33, av. Georges-V
47 23 55 11
Open year-round. 30 stes 2,800-5,500F. 141 rms 1,400-2,200F. TV. Air cond. No pets. Parking. Telex 280627. Cards: V, AE, DC, MC.

A coldly distinguished, Empire-style establishment rich in draperies and signed furniture. The rooms are decorated in a variety of styles (the finest ones are those furnished in a contemporary or 1930s style, with mosaic-tile retro bathrooms); their old fireplaces have been preserved, so you can treat yourself to the luxury of a fire in winter. Others have delightful balconies ideal for breakfast. Individual air conditioning; efficient soundproofing; video programs. Flowered terraces and pleasant patios. Restaurant: Le Panache.

Meurice

1st arr. - 228, rue de Rivoli
42 60 38 60
Open year-round. 36 stes 3,440-9,500F. 151 rms 1,440-2,350F. TV. Air cond. in 120 rms. Pets allowed. Telex 230673. Cards: V, AE, DC, MC.

The Meurice has undergone substantial renovation these past few years. Most recently, the admirable salons on the main floor were redone; the rooms and suites (which offer a view of the Tuileries) were outfitted with air conditioning and tastefully redecorated; and the pink marble bathrooms are now ultra-modern and superb. The Meurice remains one of the best and most frequented grand hotels in Paris. There is a restaurant in the basement.

Plaza Athénée

8th arr. - 25, av. Montaigne
47 23 78 33
Open year-round. 42 stes 4,950-8,240F. 220 rms 1,750-3,740F. TV. Air cond. Pets allowed. Parking. Telex 290082. Cards: V, AE, DC, MC.

At the Plaza, one finds nothing but discretion, efficiency and friendly courtesy. The rooms and suites are bright, generous in size and stocked with every available (or about-to-be-made-available) piece of hotel equipment. The rooms overlooking avenue Montaigne are perfectly soundproofed. At about 11 a.m., the guests staying here gather in the bar (where Mata Hari was arrested); and, from 4 p.m. to 7 p.m. in particular, you'll see them in the gallery (of which Marlene Dietrich was particularly fond). Two restaurants, Le Relais and Le Régence (see Restaurants, eighth arrondissement), are located just across from the wonderful patio, where tables are set in the summer among cascades of geraniums and ampelopsis vines. Dry-cleaning services are provided, as well as a beauty salon, Dow Jones agency and so on.

Raphaël

16th arr. - 17, av. Kléber - 45 02 16 00
Open year-round. 35 stes 1,950-5,000F. 53 rms 950-1,700F. Half-board 805-1,105F. TV. Pets allowed. Telex 610356. Cards: V, AE, DC, MC.

Built during those wild years between the two World Wars, the Raphaël has maintained an atmosphere of relative privacy behind its freshly repainted facade. The Oriental rugs (authentic, according to the management) strewn upon the marble floors, along with the columns, woodwork, old paintings and period furniture, make it a luxurious palace; and while it may not be particularly charming, it is tranquil. The fairly spacious rooms (all with two beds) are luxuriously furnished in various styles and are equipped with modern bathrooms, small bars, flower terraces and a view of Paris.

Résidence Maxim's de Paris
8th arr. - 42, av. Gabriel - 45 61 96 33
Open year-round. 39 stes 3,000-20,000F. 4 rms 1,800-2,000F. TV. Air cond. Pets allowed. Parking. Telex 642794. Cards: V, AE, DC.

Pierre Cardin himself designed the hotel of his dreams: He completely remodeled the interior of this bourgeois building opening onto the gardens of the Champs-Elysées. And the result is the most radically luxurious hotel created in Paris in a very, very long time. Needless to say, the rates of this little wonder deliberately exceed the means of most mortals. Restaurant.

Ritz
1st arr. - 15, pl. Vendôme
42 60 38 30
Open year-round. 45 stes 5,300-39,410F. 143 rms 1,995-2,650F. TV. Air cond. Heated pool. Pets allowed. Parking. Telex 220262. Cards: V, AE, DC, MC.

The most famous hotel in the world has turned to state-of-the-art modernism, but without in the least betraying the distinctive character that won the Ritz its reputation. In other words, even if nowadays you can change the video program or make a phone call without leaving your very bed or Jacuzzi tub (Charles Ritz was the first hotel owner to provide private bathrooms for his clients), nothing has altered the pleasure of stretching out on a wide brass bed surrounded by signed furniture. Add to that a full view of one of the most famous squares in the world, in an atmosphere of old-fashioned luxury so distinguished that a new word (ritzy) had to be invented for it. Recent improvements include an eighteen-meter swimming pool, a squash court, a gym and a heliport on the roof. Res-

taurant (see L'Espadon, first arrondissement); grill; several bars; summer terrace.

Royal Monceau
8th arr. - 35-39, av. Hoche
45 61 98 00
Open year-round. 33 stes 3,600-12,000F. 186 stes 1,750-2,550F. TV. Air cond. Heated pool. Pets allowed. Parking. Telex 650361. Cards: V, AE, DC, MC.

The atmosphere is quite Parisian at this respectable, discreetly elegant palace, given refinement with a certain moderation. The rooms are brilliantly decorated and have magnificent marble bathrooms. Extras include a fashionable piano bar, a spacious health club (which has a sauna, Jacuzzi, swimming pool and massage), outstanding ultra-modern conference rooms and a well-equipped "business club." The rooms overlooking the charming flowered patio are the most sought after by the hotel's habitués. Two restaurants: see Le Carpaccio and Le Jardin, eighth arrondissement.

Saint-James et Albany
1st arr. - 202, rue de Rivoli
42 60 31 60
Open year-round. 4 stes 1,500-2,000F. 203 rms 650-1,200F. TV. No pets. Parking. Telex 213031. Cards: V, AE, DC, MC.

Rated a "Residence-Hôtel," the Saint-James et Albany has studios, two-room apartments, suites and duplexes equipped with kitchenettes; they overlook a courtyard or an inner garden, and are perfectly quiet. Renovation should be complete on 40 of the rooms by now. There's a sauna, a bar with background music and a restaurant, Le Noailles.

Scribe
9th arr. - 1, rue Scribe - 47 42 03 40
Open year-round. 11 stes 3,200-5,000F. 206 rms 1,330-2,200F. TV. Air cond. Pets allowed. Parking. Telex 214653. Cards: V, AE, DC, MC.

The Scribe's Napoléon III facade is contemporary with the Palais Garnier, but its lobby, salons, bar, dining room (in the basement) and all six floors were completely redone several years ago. The rooms, suites and duplexes (with high ceilings; they include a room on the terrace, a living room that also serves as a dining room/office, a bathroom, dressing room and two entrances), are uniformly decorated in a lovely ocher and China red. The rooms on the street have double windows and either contemporary or Louis XVIth–style furniture; the ones on the courtyard are furnished with Louis-Philippe-style pieces and offer perfect tranquility. All the rooms provide color TVs and video programming. Room service is available 24 hours a day. Restaurants: Le Jardin des Muses and Les Muses, see Restaurants, eighth arrondissement.

 Warwick

8th arr. - 5, rue de Berri - 45 63 14 11
Open year-round. 4 stes 3,150-7,300F. 144 rms 1,500-1,980F. TV. Air cond. Pets allowed. Parking. Telex 642295. Cards: V, AE, DC, MC.

A new hotel whose bright, spacious rooms are designed more for relaxing and living in than for a quick stopover. Efficient soundproofing and air conditioning. There is an attractive bar with piano music in the evening and pleasant rooftop terraces. Room service 24 hours a day. Restaurant: see La Couronne, eighth arrondissement.

 Westminster

2nd arr. - 13, rue de la Paix
42 61 57 46
Open year-round. 20 stes 2,810-3,540F. 80 rms 1,250-1,820F. Half-board 250F (plus room). TV. Air cond. Pets allowed. Parking. Telex 680035. Cards: V, AE, DC, MC.

Recent and extensive renovation has completely transformed this charming little luxury hotel. Its lobby now is splendid and luxurious; its bar (with piano) is more than comfortable; its conference rooms are superbly equipped; and its air-conditioned rooms are impeccably modernized. Restaurant: Le Céladon.

FIRST CLASS

 Ambassador-Concorde

9th arr. - 16, bd Haussman
42 46 92 63
Open year-round. 7 stes. 298 rms 650-1,500F. Half-board 135F (plus room). TV. Air cond. in 50 rms. Pets allowed. Parking. Telex 650912. Cards: V, AE, DC, MC.

Several rooms are ultra-modern, but most have been renovated in a fine retro style that better suits this establishment—they include painted wooden beds, lovely green and gold wallpaper and antique furniture. There is a hair salon for men and women in the hotel, as well as a gift shop and restaurant.

Astor

8th arr. - 11, rue d'Astorg
42 66 56 56
Open year-round. 128 rms 740-840F. TV. Telex 642737. Cards: V, AE, DC, MC.

Marble, dark-oak woodwork, inviting leather sofas and huge vases of flowers year-round. The Astor's rooms are gorgeous, with their pale-green or beige wall hangings and stylish furniture. English bar. Restaurant: see La Table de l'Astor, eighth arrondissement.

Baltimore

16th arr. - 88 bis, av. Kléber
45 53 83 33
Open year-round. 1 ste 1,600-2,000F. 118 rms 700-1,280F. TV. Air cond. in 19 rms. Pets allowed. Telex 611591. Cards: V, AE, DC, MC.

Six fine meeting rooms are located in the basement; the largest and most luxurious is the former vault room of the Banque Nationale de Paris. The 120 comfortable rooms were completely renovated in 1985 with a sober elegance that is well suited to the district and the tastes of the clientele. Restaurant: see L'Estournel, sixteenth arrondissement.

Castille
1st arr. - 37, rue Cambon
42 61 55 20

Open year-round. 14 stes 1,000-1,800F. 62 rms 700-1,280F. TV. Pets allowed. Telex 213505. Cards: V, AE, DC, MC.

The rooms and the superb duplexes of this small hotel are bright, hospitable and impeccably equipped. Bar, restaurant.

Château Frontenac
8th arr. - 54, rue Pierre-Charron
47 23 55 85

Open year-round. 4 stes 1,000-1,200F. 99 rms 680-760F. TV. No pets. Parking. Telex 660994. Cards: V, DC, MC.

An excellent hotel whose rooms have been redecorated in either a classic or modern style, with a great deal of care taken to ensure their comfort and privacy. The soundproofing is good, but the rooms overlooking the rue Cérisole are still the quietest. Restaurant: Le Pavillon Russe.

Concorde Saint-Lazare
8th arr. - 108, rue Saint-Lazare
42 94 22 22, 42 93 01 20

Open year-round. 324 rms 650-1,500F. TV. Pets allowed. Parking. Telex 650442. Cards: V, AE, DC, MC.

Slavik and Sonya Rykiel have combined their talents to restore the spacious lobby and the billiard room (ten tables). The result: a hotel that offers modern comforts without sacrificing tradition. Large bathrooms. American bar. Restaurant: see Café Terminus, eighth arrondissement.

Garden Elysée
16th arr. - 12, rue Saint-Didier
47 55 01 11

Open year-round. 48 rms 700-1,300F. TV. Air cond. No pets. Parking. Telex 648157. Cards: V, AE, DC, MC.

Located in a brand-new building set back from the street and facing a flower garden, this hotel offers elegant, unusually spacious rooms, all overlooking the garden (where breakfast is served on warm days). The decor is fresh and modern, and the equipment is particularly fine (satellite television, individual safes, Jacuzzi). No restaurant.

Hôtel du Louvre
1st arr. - Pl. André-Malraux
42 61 56 01

Open year-round. 10 stes 2,200-2,600F. 202 rms 880-1,900F. Half-board 125-200F (plus room). TV. Air cond. in 180 rms. Pets allowed. Parking. Telex 220412. Cards: V, AE, DC, MC.

From the door of the Hôtel du Louvre, one can see the Gardens of the Palais-Royal, the Louvre and the Tuileries. The guest rooms, under high ceilings, offer the decor and all the conveniences one expects from such a chain. The restaurant, the bar, the lobby and the second floor were recently redecorated.

Lutétia
6th arr. - 45, bd Raspail - 45 44 38 10

Open year-round. 18 stes 2,200-2,800F. 275 rms 840-1,600F. TV. Air cond. in 150 rms. Pets allowed. Parking. Telex 270424. Cards: V, AE, DC, MC.

Sonya Rykiel has given the Lutétia a brand-new retro look. The twelve banquet rooms, bearing extremely pompous names ("Babylone," "Pompéi"), range from the very small to the very large and are decorated in gold, gray and purple tones with art deco frescoes and period chandeliers. As for the rooms, most of them have also been given a completely fresh look in the art deco style. Restaurants: see Brasserie Lutétia and Paris, sixth arrondissement.

Méridien
17th arr. - 81, bd Gouvion-Saint-Cyr
40 68 34 34

Open year-round. 15 stes 3,700-8,000F. 995 rms 1,060-1,750F. TV. Air cond. Pets allowed. Parking. Telex 290952. Cards: V, AE, DC, MC.

The Méridien is the largest hotel in Western Europe, and one of the most exciting ones in Paris. The rooms are small but remarkably equipped. There are boutiques, travel agencies, a bar, three restaurants (including the excellent Clos Longchamp—see Restaurants, seventeenth arrondissement), a coffee shop, vast conference rooms, a sauna, massages and a discothèque. Brunch is very popular on Sundays (with jazz music by Claude Bolling).

B&D de Vogüé

Escape to a Chateau in France . . .

Choose from:

- over 90 private Chateaux throughout Europe from $80/night

- 200 Villas and country houses from $500/week

- 300 Private apartments in PARIS from $90/night

- Luxury barge cruising from $975/person with Barge About France/Quiztour

BRASH, BOLD GUIDES
TO THE BEST OF THE VERY BEST

Also available:

Montalembert

7th arr. - 3, rue de Montalembert
45 48 68 11, 45 48 61 59
Open year-round. 61 rms 560-780F. TV in 15 rms. Pets allowed. Telex 200132. Cards: AE, MC.

An intelligent management is discreetly modernizing this old eight-story townhouse; it regularly renews the upholstery and carpeting in the rooms, all the while preserving the lovely 1930s style. The bar (Le Décameron) is the rendezvous of the top Paris publishers. The guests include many Americans and Italians, along with writers from everywhere; some of them seem almost to have made Montalembert their permanent residence. No restaurant.

Napoléon

8th arr. - 40, av. de Friedland
47 66 02 02
Open year-round. 38 stes 1,290-3,350F. 102 rms 550-1,290F. TV. Pets allowed. Parking. Telex 640609. Cards: V, AE, DC, MC.

The decor is Empire style, and the comfort, equipment and service are all impeccable. The large rooms have a classic though not very cheerful decor. The pleasant banquet rooms (L'Etoile, for example) are much in demand for receptions and conferences. Restaurant: Napoléon.

Park Avenue

16th arr. - 55, av. R-Poincaré
45 53 44 60
Open year-round. 16 stes 1,000-1,800F. 89 rms 700-1,280F. TV. Air cond. Pets allowed. Parking. Telex 643862. Cards: V, AE, DC, MC.

Behind the facade of the former mansion of designer Baguès hides this all new establishment in a little corner of English countryside. Its beautiful rooms are done in a '30s style, with kitchenettes. Restaurant: Le Relais du Parc.

Pont-Royal

7th arr. - 7, rue de Montalembert
45 44 38 27
Open year-round. 5 stes 1,900-3,000F. 75 rms 760-1,300F. TV. Air cond. Pets allowed. Telex 270113. Cards: V, AE, DC, MC.

Business types and movie actors have taken over the rather spacious and classic (but not

terribly attractive) rooms where writers—from Faulkner to Sagan—once stayed. On the ninth floor, three rooms have terraces with views of all of Paris. Restaurant.

Pullman Saint-Honoré

8th arr. - 15, rue Boissy d'Anglas
42 66 93 62
Open year-round. 1 ste 1,015F. 111 rms 560-730F. TV. Pets allowed. Telex 240366. Cards: V, AE, DC, MC.

Comfortable, luxurious and functional: This well-renovated hotel consists of seven stories of identically furnished, pleasant, modern rooms with impeccable bathrooms. Seven duplexes are located on the seventh floor; there is one suite on the eighth floor. The bar is open from 10 a.m. to 2 a.m. No restaurant.

Pullman Windsor

8th arr. - 14, rue Beaujon
45 63 04 04
Open year-round. 6 stes 1,950-2,200F. 129 rms 800-1,650F. TV. Air cond. Pets allowed. Parking. Telex 650902. Cards: V, AE, DC, MC.

This solid, austere building (built in 1925) hides a remarkably comfortable hotel, whose facilities (ultra-modern equipment for the business clientele) are constantly being improved. The rather large, bright rooms include sober, functional furniture (with minibars, color TVs and video programming). Room service. Restaurant: see Clovis, eighth arrondissement.

Régina

1st arr. - 2, pl. des Pyramides
42 60 31 10
Open year-round. 130 rms 640-1,900F. TV. Pets allowed. Parking. Telex 670834. Cards: V, AE, DC, MC.

Across from the Tuileries is one of the city's most venerable luxury hotels, with immense rooms, precious furnishings (Louis XVI, Directoire, Empire) and—a practical addition—double-glazed windows. The grandiose lobby is graced with handsome old clocks that give the time of all the great European metropolises. A quiet bar and a little restaurant that opens onto an indoor garden are pleasant places to idle away an hour.

Résidence Bassano

16th arr. - 15, rue de Bassano
47 23 78 23

Open year-round. 10 stes 1,450-1,950F. 23 rms 750-950F. TV. Pets permitted. Air cond. Parking. Telex 649872. Cards: DC.

Housed in a building of Haussmann vintage, these high-class accommodations offer impeccable, thoughtfully designed and equipped guest rooms, enhanced with black-and-white art deco furniture. Among the amenities are a sauna, Jacuzzi and 24-hour room service.

Rond-Point de Longchamp

16th arr. - 86, rue de Longchamp
45 05 13 63

Open year-round. 58 rms 520-600F. TV. Air cond. Pets allowed. Telex 620653. Cards: V, AE, DC.

A decent hotel with modern rooms, double-glazed windows and an attentive reception. There is an elegant restaurant with a fireplace, as well as a billiards room.

Royal Saint-Honoré

1st arr. - 13, rue d'Alger - 42 60 32 79
Open year-round. 1 ste 1,200F. 77 rms 597-754F. TV. Pets allowed. Telex 680429. Cards: V, AE, DC, MC.

The Royal Saint-Honoré offers excellent, comfortable, quite peaceful rooms; those located on the upper floors have pleasant balconies. Bar and conference rooms on the second floor; restaurant.

San Régis

8th arr. - 12, rue Jean-Goujon
43 59 41 90

Open year-round. 10 stes 2,000-3,600F. 34 rms 1,000-2,000F. TV. Air cond. No pets. Telex 643637. Cards: V, AE, DC.

This exquisite hotel, one of the most luxurious in Paris, was totally renovated and modernized in 1986. It boasts splendid period furniture, delicate fabrics, a discreet and refined decor, sumptuous bathrooms and lots of space, light and character. The staff is irreproachable. Restaurant.

Splendid Etoile

17th arr. - 1 bis, av. Carnot
47 66 41 41

Open year-round. 3 stes 920F. 54 rms 580-820F. TV. Air cond. in 10 rms. No pets. Telex 280773. Cards: V, DC, MC.

The Splendid Etoile features about 60 well-maintained, comfortably furnished, good-size rooms, all with double windows; some of the windows afford views of the Arc de Triomphe. The bathrooms are perfectly equipped. Attractive small salon. Restaurant: Le Pré Carré.

Terrass Hôtel

18th arr. - 12, rue Joseph-de-Maistre
46 06 72 85

Open year-round. 13 stes 870-1,000F. 93 rms 570-860F. Half-board 570-740F. TV. Air cond. in 4 rms. Pets allowed. Telex 280830. Cards: V, AE, DC, MC.

Located on the slopes of the Montmartre hill, the Terrass offers a majestic, unsurpassable view of almost all of Paris. Its comfortable rooms are regularly redecorated in a luxurious style. The seventh floor features a terrace garden with a summer bar. Restaurant: Le Guerlande.

La Trémoille

8th arr. - 14, rue de La Trémoille
47 23 34 20

Open year-round. 14 stes 2,070-5,290F. 97 rms 1,230-2,200F. TV. Pets allowed. Parking. Telex 640344. Cards: V, AE, DC, MC.

Cozy comfort, antique furniture, luxurious bathrooms, balconies filled with fresh flowers and service worthy of a grand hotel. Several duplexes are brand new and remarkably comfortable. There is a delightful dining room/salon that's heated by a wood fire in winter. Restaurant.

Victoria Palace
6th arr. - 6, rue Blaise-Desgoffe
45 44 38 16
Open year-round. 110 rms 585-780F. TV.
No pets. Telex 270557. Cards: V, AE, DC, MC.

This is a decorous, elegant and intimate little hotel. Above an immense lobby, you'll find quiet rooms with double-glazed windows and flowered wallpaper; all have attractive bathrooms in marble. Bar and restaurant.

CHARMING

Abbaye Saint-Germain
6th arr. - 10, rue Cassette
45 44 38 11
Open year-round. 4 stes 1,200-1,400F. 44 rms 600-800F. No pets.

  Set back from the street, this serene hotel located between a courtyard and a garden has charming, elegantly decorated rooms; the most delightful ones are on the same level as the garden. No restaurant.

Agora
1st arr. - 7, rue de la Cossonnerie
42 33 46 02
Open year-round. 29 rms 250-450F. TV in 8 rms. No pets. Cards: AE.

In the heart of the pedestrian district of Les Halles, these rooms are exquisitely decorated and well soundproofed. Lovely pieces of period furniture and engravings are everywhere; the cleanliness is impressive. No restaurant.

Alexander
16th arr. - 102, av. Victor-Hugo
45 53 64 65
Open year-round. 2 stes 1,200F. 60 rms 550-830F. TV. No pets. Telex 610373. Cards: V, AE.

  This is a comfortable and peaceful establishment, with a lobby paneled in light wood and superbly equipped and furnished rooms (the ones overlooking the courtyard are especially quiet). Two suites can accommodate two, three or four people. The reception is most courteous. No restaurant.

Angleterre
6th arr. - 44, rue Jacob - 42 60 34 72
Open year-round. 3 stes 660-730F. 26 rms 500-660F. TV. No pets.Cards: V, AE, DC.

Hemingway once lived in this former British Embassy building, which surrounds a patio decorated with flowers. Its impeccable rooms have been completely renovated; some are quite spacious, with high wood-beamed ceilings, and you'll sleep soundly in the immense beds. Luxurious bathrooms. There is a brand-new bar, as well as salon (with piano).

Aramis Saint-Germain
6th arr. - 124, rue de Rennes
45 48 03 75
Open year-round. 42 rms 375-600F. TV. No pets. Telex 205098. Cards: V, AE, DC.

These new, well-soundproofed and delightfully decorated rooms have soft lighting, modern equipment and perfect bathrooms. The service is especially attentive; room service (for breakfast) is available at all hours. No restaurant.

Atala
8th arr. - 10, rue Chateaubriand
45 62 01 62
Open year-round. 2 stes 1,050F. 47 rms 650-870F. TV. Pets allowed. Telex 640576. Cards: V, AE, DC.

The cheerfully decorated rooms and suites open onto a garden and offer perfect comfort and new marble bathrooms. L'Atalante, the bar and restaurant, is also open to visitors. Excellent service.

Banville

17th arr. - 166, bd Berthier
42 67 70 16

Open year-round. 39 rms 450-480F. TV. Pets allowed. Telex 643025. Cards: V, AE.

A fine small hotel, with flowers decorating the window sills and bright, cheerful rooms, all of which are made soundproof with thick carpeting—even found in the marble bathrooms. No restaurant.

Bradford

8th arr. - 10, rue Saint-Philippe-du-Roule
43 59 24 20

Open year-round. 2 stes 650F. 46 rms 480-570F. No pets. Parking. Telex 648530. Cards: V.

The large, bright rooms are meticulously clean and often pleasantly furnished; the staff is discreet and efficient; and there is a comfortable little Louis XVI salon. Four more rooms with showers were being built at the time of this writing. No restaurant.

California

8th arr. - 16, rue de Berri - 43 59 93 00
Open year-round. 3 stes 1,800-2,500F. 176 rms 860-1,230F. TV. Telex 660634. No cards.

The management has recently and successfuly turned this place around. The rooms are redone in extremely good taste, and open onto a quiet patio. Ornately frescoed restaurant.

Colbert

5th arr. - 7, rue de l'Hôtel-Colbert
43 25 85 65

Open year-round. 2 stes 1,200-1,450F. 38 rms 500-790F. TV. No pets. Telex 260690. Cards: V, AE.

Nearly half the rooms in this aristocratic eighteenth-century house look out upon Notre-Dame through their small-paned windows. The rooms are small and quite simply decorated; the bar, while large, is somewhat boring. The hotel was completely renovated in 1988. No restaurant.

Colisée

8th arr. - 6, rue du Colisée
43 59 95 25

Open year-round. 44 rms 430-630F. TV. Air cond. in 11 rms. Pets allowed. Telex 643101. Cards: V, AE, DC, MC.

Half the rooms were redecorated in 1988. Those whose numbers end with an "8" are more spacious than the others; the attic rooms on the top floor have wooden beams. There's a salon/bar but no restaurant.

Corona

9th arr. - 8, cité Bergère - 47 50 52 96
Open year-round. 4 stes 780F. 56 rms 450-550F. TV. Pets allowed. Telex 281081. Cards: V, AE, DC.

In a handsome complex of 1930s-era buildings (all renovated) on the cité Bergère, these lovely, hospitable rooms include elegant gnarled-elm furniture and an unsurpassable view of the artists' entrance to the Théâtre des Nouveautés. No restaurant.

Danemark

6th arr. - 21, rue Vavin
43 26 93 78

Open year-round. 15 rms 500-630F. TV. Air cond. Telex 202568. Cards: V, AE, DC.

This small hotel, located in front of the rue Vavin's famous bathhouse, was completely renovated in 1987. Its refined, modern rooms have pleasant lighting, elegant wood furniture and gray marble bathrooms. Breakfast is served in the lovely cellar. No restaurant.

Les Deux Iles

4th arr. - 59, rue Saint-Louis-en-l'Ile
43 26 13 35

Open year-round. 17 rms 480-585F. TV. Pets allowed. Telex 375974. No cards.

This newly repainted hotel, like many buildings on the Ile-Saint-Louis, is a lovely seventeenth-century house. You'll sleep close to the Seine in small, pretty rooms decorated with bright Provençal fabrics. No restaurant.

Duc de Saint-Simon

7th arr. - 14, rue Saint-Simon
45 48 35 66

Open year-round. 5 stes 1,100-1,250F. 24 rms 700-1,000F. No pets. Telex 203277. No cards.

Back from the street, and between two gardens, sits this quiet, elegant building from the nineteenth century. Redone and modernized a few years ago, it features exposed beams and period furniture, as well as a pleasant bar downstairs. No restaurant.

Ducs d'Anjou

1st arr. - 1, rue Saint-Opportune
42 36 92 24

Open year-round. 38 rms 280-460F. TV. Pets allowed. Cards: V, AE.

Located on the delightful small place Sainte-Opportune, this ancient building has been restored from top to bottom. The rooms are small (as are the bathrooms) but quiet; those overlooking the courtyard are a bit gloomy. No restaurant.

Duminy-Vendôme

1st arr. - 3, rue du Mont-Thabor
42 60 32 80

Open year-round. 79 rms 390-800F. TV. No pets. Telex 213492. Cards: V, AE, DC, MC.

Duminy-Vendôme's rooms have impeccable bathrooms and lovely wallpaper; those on the sixth and seventh floors have slightly sloping ceilings. A small summer patio is located on the main floor.

Etoile-Pereire 🌲🍸

17th arr. - 146, bd Pereire
42 67 60 00

Open year-round. 5 stes 810-850F. 21 rooms 410-580F. TV. No pets. Parking. Telex 305551. Cards: V, AE, DC, MC.

Located at the back of a quiet courtyard, these spacious rooms have just been redecorated (the duplexes under the rooftop are the most attractive). More than twenty different varieties of delicious jams are served at breakfast. Both the atmosphere and service are charming and cheerful. No restaurant.

Family Hôtel

1st arr. - 35, rue Cambon
42 61 54 84

Open year-round. 1 ste 1,000F. 25 rms 300-450F. Pets allowed. Cards: V, AE.

This is a small, quiet, well-maintained hotel. Ask for Room 50 on the sixth floor, which offers a view of the Vendôme column; or for Room 41, with its retro furniture. The rooms

facing the street have double-glazed windows, so you'll sleep soundly. The rates are reasonable for the district. No restaurant.

Gaillon Opéra

2nd arr. - 9, rue Gaillon
47 42 47 74

Open year-round. 1 ste 630F. 25 rms 460-630F. TV. Pets allowed. Telex 215716. Cards: V, AE, DC.

This delightful little 26-room hotel (all have bathrooms and minibars) opened in 1983. There are plants everywhere and period furniture in an elegant setting, as well as a patio with flowers. No restaurant.

L'Hôtel

6th arr. - 13, rue des Beaux-Arts
43 25 27 22

Open year-round. 2 stes 2,300-2,700F. 25 rms 850-1,700F. TV. Air cond. Pets allowed. Telex 270870. Cards: V, AE, DC.

The little effort given to renovation explains the slightly faded character of the rooms in this delightful Directoire-style building—whether it's the room once occupied by Oscar Wilde, the Imperial room (decorated in a neo-Egyptian style), the Cardinale room (in purple and violet) or that once occupied by Mistinguett (on the fourth floor), which contains the art deco furniture from her Bougival home. The seventh floor houses two lovely suites. In the piano bar (open from 7:30 p.m. to 1 a.m.), you are sure to find a congenial clientele. Restaurant: see Le Bélier, sixth arrondissement.

Hôtel du Collège de France 🌲🍸

5th arr. - 7, rue Thénard - 43 26 78 36
Open year-round. 2 stes 870-970F. 25 rms 420-450F. TV. No pets. Cards: AE.

The simple rooms of Hôtel du Collège de France, located on a quiet little street, are wallpapered in light-brown or green tones; the most pleasant of them, located on the sixth floor, have wooden beams, half-timberings and a view of the towers of Notre-Dame. No restaurant.

Hôtel du Jeu de Paume

4th arr. - 54, rue Saint-Louis-en-l'Ile
43 26 14 18

Open year-round. 9 apts 1,200-1,500F. 23 rms 650-820F. TV. Pets allowed. Cards: V, AE, DC.

This is a seventeenth-century residence with a splendid wood-and-stone interior, and featuring a glass elevator to the rooms. There is a sunny little garden, and light food is available.

Hôtel Moulin Rouge
9th arr. - 39, rue Fontaine
42 81 93 25
Open year-round. 3 stes 650-800F. 47 rms 370-540F. TV. Pets allowed. Telex 660055. Cards: V, AE, DC.
A hotel full of charm and surprises, with its seductive Pompeiian-style lobby and large rooms (some of them are extended by a small terrace overlooking the inner courtyards). An excellent buffet-style breakfast is served until noon. No restaurant.

Les Jardins d'Eiffel
7th arr. - 8, rue Amélie - 47 05 46 21
Open year-round. 5 stes 800-1,100F. 34 rms 400-590F. TV. No pets. Parking. Telex 206582. Cards: V, AE, DC.
The small, cozy, well-soundproofed rooms were redone in 1986; they include outstanding equipment (hairdryers, individual safes, color TVs, minibars . . .). Convenient individual parking spaces are provided; there is also a small but charming inner garden. Many services. No restaurant.

Lenox (Montparnasse)
14th arr. - 15, rue Delambre
43 35 34 50
Open year-round. 6 stes 800F. 46 rms 380-490F. TV. No pets. Telex 260745. Cards: V, AE, DC, MC.
Everything is spanking new inside the Lenox, a three-year-old hotel in the heart of Montparnasse; its suites and rooms are bright and cheerful. There is no restaurant, but light meals are served at the bar until 2 a.m.

Lenox (Saint-Germain)
7th arr. - 9, rue de l'Université
42 96 10 95
Open year-round. 2 stes 780F. 32 rms 395-550F. TV. No pets. Telex 260745. Cards: V, AE, DC, MC.

These petite but most attractive rooms were recently renovated with elegant wallpaper and stylish furniture; numbers 22, 32 and 42 are the most enchanting. The top floor includes two duplexes with exposed beams and flower-filled balconies. No restaurant.

Lutèce
4th arr. - 65, rue Saint-Louis-en-l'Ile
43 26 23 52
Open year-round. 23 rms 480-620F. TV. No pets. Telex 375974. No cards.
A tasteful, small hotel for the lovers of Paris, this handsome old house has some twenty rooms with whitewashed walls, wooden ceiling beams and lovely bright fabrics. The bathrooms are small but modern and impeccable. No restaurant.

Majestic 🌲🍷
16th arr. - 29, rue Dumont-d'Urville
45 00 83 70
Open year-round. 3 stes 1,300F-1,500F. 27 rms 630-900F. TV. Pets allowed. Telex 640034. Cards: V, AE, DC, MC.
Richly furnished rooms (some with dressing rooms) and suites in the Louis XV and Directoire styles. All have been (or are soon to be) renovated; soundproofing and air conditioning were recently installed throughout the hotel. On the top floor, a lovely penthouse features a small balcony filled with flowers. No restaurant.

Les Marronniers 🌲🍷
6th arr. - 21, rue Jacob - 43 25 30 60, 43 29 88 10
Open year-round. 37 rms 285-455F. No pets. No cards.
Set back a bit from the rue Jacob, this hotel has a small garden where breakfast is served. Chose a room just above this garden, or one of the rather bizarre but absolutely delightful (and bright) attic rooms on the seventh floor, which have views of the belfry of Saint-Germain-des-Prés. No restaurant.

Odéon Hôtel
6th arr. - 3, rue de l'Odéon
43 25 90 67

Open year-round. 34 rms 550-700F. TV. No pets. Telex 202943. Cards: V, AE, DC.

The highly rated Odéon Hôtel, located on a small, strategic street between the Odéon theater and the square of the same name, has some 30 rather small but appealing and well-equipped rooms (all have marble bathrooms). No restaurant.

Passy Eiffel
16th arr. - 10, rue de Passy
45 25 55 66

Open year-round. 50 rms 410-500F. TV. Pets allowed. Telex 612753. Cards: V, AE, DC, MC.

Five stories of spotless, comfortable rooms (though not all equally attractive); a pleasant breakfast room faces a tiny, glassed-in inner garden. No restaurant.

Pavillon de la Reine
3rd arr. - 28, pl. des Vosges
42 77 96 40

Open year-round. 23 stes 1,100-1,800F. 30 rms 800-900F. TV. Air cond. Pets allowed. Telex 216160. Cards: V, AE, DC, MC.

The air-conditioned rooms, duplexes and suites, all equipped with marble bathrooms, are tastefully decorated; they artfully blend authentic antiques with lovely copies. They overlook either the place des Vosges and its garden or a serene inner patio filled with flowers. The charm of the setting almost makes up for the frosty reception. No restaurant.

Queen's Hôtel
16th arr. - 4, rue Bastien-Lepage
42 88 89 85

Open year-round. 22 rms 230-470F. TV. No pets. Cards: V, AE.

About twenty rather petite but delightful, modern, quiet and comfortable rooms hidden behind a lovely white facade with flower-filled balconies. Excellent reception. No restaurant.

Regent's Garden Hotel
17th arr. - 6, rue Pierre-Demours
45 74 07 30

Open year-round. 1 ste 700-800F. 39 rms 475-825F. TV. Pets allowed. Parking. Telex 640127. Cards: V, AE, DC, MC.

This handsome Second Empire bourgeois building, just a stone's throw from the place de l'Etoile, offers huge rooms with high molded ceilings and lovely rustic furniture (but some of the rooms—especially the ones on the street—are rather noisy and a bit rundown). Lovely large flower garden. No restaurant.

Relais Christine 🌳
6th arr. - 3, rue Christine - 43 26 71 80

Open year-round. 13 stes 1,150-1,700F. 38 rms 980F. TV. Air cond. Telex 202606. Cards: V, AE, DC, MC.

This sixteenth-century cloister was transformed into a luxury hotel in the early 1980s. Its spacious, comfortable, quiet rooms (all air-conditioned) include marble bathrooms. Courteous reception. No restaurant.

Relais Saint-Germain
6th arr. - 9, carrefour de l'Odéon
43 29 12 05

Open year-round. 1 ste 1,595F. 9 rms 935-1,155F. TV. Air cond. Pets allowed. Telex 201889. Cards: V, AE, DC, MC.

About ten large rooms, all different from one another, are marvelously decorated in a refined and luxurious manner, with superb furniture, lovely fabrics, exquisite lighting and beautiful, perfectly equipped marble bathrooms. The tall, double-glazed windows open onto the lively Odéon intersection. You will

Any time of year except August, Paris's hotels can be reserved well in advance. Make your reservations early and be prepared to send a deposit.

surely fall in love with Paris staying here. No restaurant.

Résidence du Bois 🌳

16th arr. - 16, rue Chalgrin
45 00 50 59

Open year-round. 3 stes 1,355-2,175F. 16 rms 940-1,320F. TV. Pets allowed. No cards.

The rooms of this small Napoléon III residence, all furnished in various period styles, are larger than the ones found in modern hotels; they overlook a delightful garden. The comfort is outstanding, and the service is efficient, discreet and impeccable. No restaurant. Relais et Châteaux.

Riboutté-Lafayette

9th arr. - 5, rue Riboutté

Open year-round. 24 rms 350-380F. TV. Pets allowed. Parking. Cards: V, MC.

This small and charming hotel faces rue La Fayette and is located within walking distance of the Opéra, the Bourse and the *grands boulevards*. Its quiet rooms are small and attractive and have all been renovated. Very hospitable staff.

Saint-Dominique

7th arr. - 62, rue Saint-Dominique
47 05 51 44

Open year-round. 35 rms 350-490F. TV. Pets allowed. Telex 206968. Cards: V, AE, DC, MC.

This most modest of the three "Centre Ville" hotels is also the most charming, and the location is excellent. Its rooms are delightful, homey and comfortable. No restaurant.

Saint-Louis

4th arr. - 75, rue Saint-Louis-en-l'Ile
46 34 04 80

Open year-round. 21 rms 410-510F No cards..

The simple but stylish rooms of this delightful house (in which an elevator has recently been installed) have been freshly repainted and furnished with new beds and flowered drapes. The modern bathrooms have attractive blue-gray and brown tiles. No restaurant.

Sainte-Beuve

6th arr. - 9, rue Sainte-Beuve
45 48 20 07

Open year-round. 1 ste 1,300F. 22 rms 600-1,000F. TV. No pets. Telex 270182. Cards: V, AE.

Sainte-Beuve's quite pleasant rooms (especially the attic rooms on the seventh floor) are fairly well decorated (lovely furniture and fabrics, but what ugly carpets!). Lots of comfort; fine equipment; delicious breakfasts. No restaurant.

Solférino

7th arr. - 91, rue de Lille - 47 05 85 54

Closed Dec. 23-Jan. 3. 1 ste 535F. 32 rms 227-535F. TV in 15 rms. No pets. Telex 203865. Cards: V.

Simple rooms with fresh colors, a lovely little salon, a balcony where breakfast is served and charming ornaments everywhere: The Solférino is both relaxing and pleasantly antiquated. Friendly reception. No restaurant.

Suède 🌳

7th arr. - 31, rue Vaneau
47 05 18 65, 47 05 00 08

Open year-round. 1 ste 850F. 40 rms 441-693F. TV in 5 rms. No pets. Telex 200596. Cards: V, AE, MC.

The Suède offers attractive Empire-style rooms and one soberly and pleasantly decorated suite. From the fourth floor and up you'll have a view of the foliage and the parties given in the Matignon gardens. No restaurant. Bar and snack service from 6:30 a.m. to 10 p.m.

Varenne

7th arr. - 44, rue de Bourgogne
45 51 45 55

Open year-round. 24 rms 370-500F. TV. Pets allowed. Telex 205329. Cards: V, AE.

You have to make reservations well ahead of time for the pleasure of staying in one of the flower-filled rooms at this provincial little hotel, which includes an attractive salon and a delightful patio where breakfast is served on sunny days. No restaurant.

LARGE & MODERN

 Concorde–La Fayette
17th arr. - 3, pl. du Général-Koenig
45 58 12 84
Open year-round. 27 stes 2,800-5,600F. 963 rms 850-1,450F. TV. Air cond. Pets allowed. Parking. Telex 650892. Cards: V, AE, DC, MC.

The Concorde–La Fayette is immense: It includes the Palais des Congrès and its 4,500 seats; banquet rooms that can accommodate 2,000; 60 boutiques; four movie theaters; two discothèques; and 1,500 parking places. Its 1,000 tiny rooms offer all the modern amenities available, including magnetic locks, color TVs, adjustable air conditioning, soundproofing, minibars and clock radios. The top floor (the "executive floor") features the Top Club, which includes luxurious rooms and personalized service. Panoramic bar, Plein Ciel, decorated by Slavik. Three restaurants, including L'Etoile d'Or (see Restaurants, seventeenth arrondissement).

Frantour Berthier Brochant
17th arr. - 163 bis, av. de Clichy
42 28 40 40
Open year-round. 648 rms 290-390F. Half-board 280F. TV. Pets allowed. Telex 660251. Cards: V, AE, MC.

These twin hotels with a common restaurant and lobby house pleasant rooms (with free cribs for infants); self-serve or à la carte breakfasts are served in the restaurant. Group dinners can be held for up to 220 persons.

 Frantour Suffren
15th arr. - 20, rue Jean-Rey
45 78 61 08
Open year-round. 10 stes 760-1,500F. 397 rms 455-490F. TV. Air cond. Pets allowed. Parking. Telex 204459. Cards: V, AE, DC, MC.

The Frantour Suffren is a large, modern hotel located next to the Seine and the Champ-de-Mars. Its rooms are small, but comfortable and functional. Restaurant (Le Champ-de-Mars); bar; discothèque.

Hilton
15th arr. - 18, av. de Suffren
42 73 92 00
Open year-round. 9 stes 5,000-8,600F. 453 rms 1,100-1,950F. TV. Air cond. Pets allowed. Parking. Telex 200955. Cards: V, AE, DC, MC.

The city's first postwar luxury hotel is still living up to Hilton's high standards. Rooms are spacious, service is courteous and deft, and children—of any age!—can share their parents' room for free. Closed-circuit TV shows recent films, and on the premises are two restaurants (including Le Western; see Restaurants, fifteenth arrondissement) and the Toit de Paris bar, with its admirable view and evening tapas (see "Rendezvous Spots" in Bars & Cafés).

Holiday Inn (Porte de Versailles)
15th arr. - 69, bd Victor - 45 33 74 63
Open year-round. 90 rms 650-1,030F. TV. Air cond. Pets allowed. Parking. Telex 260844. Cards: V, AE, DC, MC.

The well-designed, air-conditioned (with individual controls) and soundproofed rooms all offer modern comfort; their remarkable bathrooms are equipped with radios, hairdryers and magnifying mirrors. Beautifully furnished restaurant.

Holiday Inn (République)
11th arr. - 10, pl. de la République
43 55 44 34
Open year-round. 7 stes. 333 rms 950-1,200F. TV. Air cond. Pets allowed. Parking. Telex 210651. Cards: V, AE, DC, MC.

The architect Davioud, who designed the Châtelet, built this former Modern Palace in 1866. Today it belongs to the largest hotel chain in the world, which completely restored and modernized it in 1982. The rooms and suites are functional, pleasant and well soundproofed; the most attractive ones overlook the floral inner courtyard. Pleasant brasserie, La Belle Epoque (with dinner-dancing; see Restaurants, eleventh arrondissement); piano bar.

Mercure Paris-Bercy
13th arr. - 6, bd V.-Auriol
45 82 48 00
Open year-round. 1 ste 960F. 87 rms 470-530F.
TV. Pets allowed. Parking. Telex 205010.
Cards: V, AE, DC, MC.
Just across the Seine from the new Finance
ministry at Bercy, this is one of the chain's
newest branches. Good-size rooms, pretty
enough, are well-insulated; some have terraces.
Bar open until midnight, and restaurant.

Méridien Montparnasse
14th arr. - 19, rue du Cdt-Mouchotte
43 20 15 51
Open year-round. 30 stes 2,750-4,500F. 920 rms
950-1,050F. TV. Air cond. Pets allowed. Park-
ing. Telex 200135. Cards: V, AE, DC, MC.
This hotel, crammed with lush plants and
shrubbery, is decorated in a handsome, modern style. The functional rooms are comfortable and pleasant (though their ceilings are low
and the corridors seem endless). Three restaurants; bar; boutiques.

Nikko de Paris
15th arr. - 61, quai de Grenelle
45 75 62 62
Open year-round. 22 stes 3,000-9,000F. 757 rms
945-1,550F. TV. Air cond. Heated pool. Pets
allowed. Parking. Telex 260012. Cards: V, AE,
DC, MC.
The ceilings on the Nikko's 31 floors are
pitted with small concavities, giving the hotel
much the appearance of an immense beehive.
You can opt either for vaguely Japanese-style
or modern, ultra-functional rooms; their large
porthole windows overlook the Mirabeau
bridge. On the six upper floors are the luxury
Arc-en-Ciel restaurant, 61 conference rooms,
heated swimming pool with sauna, gym room
and massage are also available. The bar has a
pleasant view. Restaurants: Brasserie du Pont
Mirabeau; Les Célébrités (see Restaurants, fifteenth arrondissement).

Novotel Bercy
12th arr. - 85, rue de Bercy
43 42 30 00
Open year-round. 1 ste 900F. 130 rms 530-560F.
TV. Air cond. Pets allowed Cards: V, AE, DC,
MC.
This all-glass structure, right next door to
the big Bercy arena, has handicapped access,
bar and restaurant.

Novotel Paris Les Halles
1st arr. - pl. Marguerite-de-Navarre
42 21 31 31
Open year-round. 14 stes 850-1,250F. 271 rms
665-705F. TV. Air cond. Pets allowed. Telex
216389. Cards: V, AE, DC, MC.
This ultra-modern building constructed of
stone, glass and zinc is located in the heart of
the former Les Halles market. Its rooms offer
perfect comfort, but their air conditioning
(alas!) prevents one from opening the windows. The restaurant is open from 6 a.m. to
midnight, and there is a bar on a terrace. The
conference rooms can be tailored to size by
means of movable partitions. Travel agency.

Pullman Saint-Jacques
14th arr. - 17, bd Saint-Jacques
45 89 89 80
Open year-round. 14 stes 1,345-1,515F. 786 rms
905-1,012F. TV. Air cond. Pets allowed. Telex
270740. Cards: V, AE, DC, MC.
The Pullman Saint-Jacques is the Parisian
mega-hotel closest to Orly and Old Paris; it has
800 very small rooms with tiny but comfortable bathrooms. With its shopping galleries,
nineteen conference rooms, beauty salon, entertainment (games; tours of Paris), bars and
restaurants, its atmosphere is reminiscent of an
airport.

Résidence Monceau
8th arr. - 85, rue du Rocher
45 22 75 11
Open year-round. 1 ste 760F. 50 rms 514-546F.
TV. No pets. Telex 280671. Cards: V, AE, DC.
The Résidence Monceau opened in the
summer of 1987 following a complete renova-

tion. All its rooms have private bathrooms, color TVs, minibars and automatic alarm clocks. Good privacy; breakfast is served on a patio. No restaurant.

Sofitel Paris Invalides

7th arr. - 32, rue Saint-Dominique
45 55 91 80

Open year-round. 4 stes 2,900F. 108 rms 1,170-1,430F. TV. Air cond. Pets allowed. Parking. Telex 250019. Cards: V, AE, DC, MC.

Located behind the Palais-Bourbon, this is an intelligently designed hotel of modest dimensions and sober decor. All the rooms, renovated in 1987, have soft lighting and agreeably functional furniture. Restaurant: see Le Dauphin, seventh arrondissement.

Sofitel Paris

15th arr. - 8, rue Louis-Armand
45 54 95 00

Open year-round. 2 stes 1,400-2,100F. 633 rms 700F. TV. Air cond. Heated pool. Pets allowed. Parking. Telex 200432. Cards: V, AE, DC, MC.

Thirty-seven meeting and conference rooms (with simultaneous translation available in five languages) are connected to a central administration office. The hotel also features recreational facilities (exercise room, sauna and a heated swimming pool with sliding roof on the 23rd floor) and a panoramic bar. The rooms, all equipped with magnetic closing systems, are modern and comfortable, though a bit tiny. Restaurant: see Le Relais de Sèvres, fifteenth arrondissement.

PRACTICAL

Alison

8th arr. - 21, rue de Surène
42 65 54 00

Open year-round. 35 rms 330-560F. TV. No pets. Telex 640435. Cards: V, AE, DC, MC.

The 35 modern, functional rooms, as well as the lobby with its deep leather sofas and the breakfast room in the basement, are all decorated in orange, beige and brown tones. The bathrooms are impeccably clean. No restaurant.

Ambassade

16th arr. - 79, rue Lauriston
45 53 41 15

Open year-round. 38 rms 330-430F. TV. No pets. Telex 613643. Cards: V, AE, DC, MC.

The rooms behind a lovely facade (recently repainted) are decorated with printed wallpaper and lacquered rattan furniture and are equipped with small gray-marble bathrooms. Their double windows overlook the street. No restaurant.

Bergère

9th arr. - 34, rue Bergère - 47 70 34 34
Open year-round. 136 rms 380-660F. TV. Telex 290668. Cards: V, AE, DC, MC.

All the rooms (most of which overlook a courtyard garden) have been freshened up and modernized, including the bathrooms. The setting is modern and simple. Fine equipment.

Capitol

15th arr. - 9, rue Viala - 45 78 61 00
Open year-round. 4 stes 800F. 42 rms 420-480F. TV. Air cond. No pets. Telex 202881. Cards: V, AE.

This new hotel with its white stone facade offers cleverly arranged, eminently comfortable rooms, all decorated with muted fabrics and modern gray wood furniture. Cordial reception. No restaurant.

Centre Ville Etoile

17th arr. - 6, rue des Acacias
43 80 56 18

Open year-round. 16 rms 450-700F. TV. Pets allowed. Telex 206968. Cards: V, AE, DC, MC.

Attractive contemporary rooms with minitels (electronic telephone directories), satellite TV and excellent bathrooms. Breakfast served in a quiet salon. Restaurant: Le Cougar.

Commodore

9th arr. - 12, bd Haussman
42 46 72 82

Open year-round. 11 stes 1,250-1,800F. 151 rms 650-1,150F. TV. Pets allowed. Telex 280601. Cards: V, AE, DC, MC.

This excellent traditional hotel is located a few steps away from the new Drouot auction house and its parking lot. All rooms are decorated in a 1930s style (which is when the hotel was built). Restaurant: Le Carvery.

Courcelles

17th arr. - 184, rue de Courcelles
47 63 65 30

Open year-round. 42 rms 490-580F. TV. Pets allowed. Telex 642252. Cards: V, AE, DC, MC.

All the rooms here are equipped with remote-control color TVs, direct phone lines, clock-radios and minibars. The most attractive ones are decorated in green with floral wallpaper. The furniture is modern; the bathrooms are flawless. Small salon/winter garden, bar.

Le Cours de Vincennes

1st arr. - 61, rue de la Voute
43 45 41 38

Open year-round. 12 stes 700F. 35 rms 435F. TV. Pets allowed. Telex 215050. Cards: V, AE, DC, MC.

A brand-new, delightful hotel with comfortable and well-furnished modern rooms.

Elysées-Maubourg

7th arr. - 35, bd de Latour-Maubourg
45 56 10 78

Open year-round. 2 stes 700F. 28 rms 450-650F. TV. Air cond. Pets allowed. Telex 206227. Cards: V, AE, DC, MC.

The 30 brand-new rooms are decorated without much originality, but they are superbly equipped and very comfortable. There is a Finnish sauna and a cafeteria in the basement, a bar and a flower-filled patio. No restaurant.

Etoile

17th arr. - 3, rue de l'Etoile
43 80 36 94

Open year-round. 25 rms 405-570F. TV. Pets allowed. Telex 642028. Cards: V, AE, DC, MC.

L'Etoile is perfectly located between the place de l'Etoile and the place des Ternes. Its ultra-modern decor is inviting; its large salon includes a small bar and a library. No restaurant. Courteous reception.

Fondary

15th arr. - 30, rue Fondary
45 75 14 75

Open year-round. 20 rms 285-330F. TV. Telex 206761. Cards: V, AE.

An excellent neighborhood address, with rooms still almost like new (they were completely redone in 1985), which feature a pleasant pastel decor, attractive fabrics and simple bamboo furniture. Good service and pleasant salon/bar. No restaurant.

Hôtel de Neuville

17th arr. - 3, pl. Verniquet
43 80 26 30, 43 80 38 55

Open year-round. 2 stes 800F. 26 rms 455-595F. TV. Pets allowed. Telex 648822. Cards: V, AE, DC, MC.

The former owner of Quai d'Orsay has just opened this lovely hotel on a quiet square. Its simple rooms are tastefully decorated with lovely floral fabrics and are equipped with fine bathrooms. Pleasant salon/winter garden and basement restaurant, Les Tartines.

Hôtel Pierre

17th arr. - 25, rue Théodore-de-Banville - 47 63 76 69

Open year-round. 50 rms 530-660F. TV. Pets allowed. Parking. Telex 643003. Cards: V, AE, DC, MC.

The Hôtel Pierre is a Mapotel-Best Western and features a spacious lobby, a small salon opening onto an inner garden and 50 standard, admirably equipped rooms, plus a conference room and a dining room, where a generous buffet breakfast is served. No restaurant.

Le Jardin des Plantes

5th arr. - 5, rue Linné - 47 07 06 20
Open year-round. 33 rms 300-490F. TV. Pets allowed. Telex 203684. Cards: V, AE, DC, MC.

This hotel, facing the Cuvier fountain, has appealing, delightfully decorated brand-new rooms. On the sixth floor, the flower-filled terrace overlooks the Jardin des Plantes. No restaurant.

Kléber

16th arr. - 7, rue de Belloy
47 23 80 22
Open year-round. 1 ste 796-840F. 21 rms 560-645F. TV. Pets allowed. Parking. Telex 612830. Cards: V, AE, DC, MC.

This impeccable little hotel has about twenty rooms spread over six floors, all equipped with double-glazed windows and lovely bathrooms. Decor is modern but warm. Bar, no restaurant.

Latitudes Saint-Germain

6th arr. - 7-11, rue Saint-Benoît
42 61 53 53
Open year-round. 117 rms 540-700F. TV. Pets allowed. Telex 213531. Cards: V, AE, DC, MC.

This spacious hotel, opened in 1987, is located in the heart of Saint-Germain-des-Prés; it used to be a printing shop, and its gracious turn-of-the-century facade has been preserved. The large rooms are well equipped, elegant and part of a matchless setting designed, in the words of the management "for a charming stay amid the chic et choc of Paris." The shock: the list of extra charges, but the chic is real, except for the pretentious piano bar. No restaurant.

 ## Le Laumière

19th arr. - 4, rue Petit - 42 06 10 77
Open year-round. 54 rms 135-270F. Pets allowed. Cards: V.

This fine, modern small hotel is located a few steps away from the Buttes-Chaumont, in a district where modern hotels are not exactly plentiful. Well soundproofed and good moderate rates. No restaurant.

Lenox Monceau-Courcelles

17th arr. - 18, rue Léon-Jost
46 22 60 70
Open year-round. 5 stes 950-1,200F. 13 rms 450-490F. TV. No pets. Telex 649949. Cards: V, AE, DC, MC.

This former bordello has been totally renovated. Its rooms are on the small side, but they're tastefully decorated and furnished. A large duplex on the top floor has a lovely terrace. Breakfast is served on the patio in summer. No restaurant.

Magellan

17th arr. - 17, rue Jean-Baptiste-Dumas
45 72 44 51
Open year-round. 75 rms 410-435F. TV. Pets allowed. Parking. Telex 644728. Cards: V, AE, DC, MC.

Business people will appreciate the serenity and comfort of the rooms (all have new bedding and furniture) in this peaceful hotel, particularly those overlooking the garden, where breakfast is served in summer and on warm days. No restaurant.

Nouvel Hôtel 🌲

12th arr. - 24, av. du Bel-Air
43 43 01 81
Open year-round. 28 rms 250-450F. TV in 22 rms. Pets allowed. Telex 240139. Cards: V, AE, DC.

The rooms of the Nouvel Hôtel are serene and attractive (the loveliest is number nine, on the same level as the garden). A pleasant little piano room is ornamented with a 1920s frieze. Inviting patio with flowers. No restaurant.

Ouest Hôtel

17th arr. - 165, rue de Rome
42 27 50 29, 42 27 21 44
Open year-round. 50 rms 180-290F. TV. Pets allowed. Cards: V.

This cozy establishment has thick carpeting, efficient double windows and modest, modern rooms. No restaurant.

Perreyve

6th arr. - 63, rue Madame
45 48 35 01

Open year-round. 30 rms 248-350F. TV. No pets. Telex 205080. Cards: V, AE.

Near the Luxembourg Garden and its foliage, the 30 comfortable rooms of the Perreyve have small but spotless bathrooms. There is a small provincial salon on the main floor. No restaurant.

Regyn's Montmartre

18th arr. - 18, pl. des Abbesses
42 54 45 21

Open year-round. 22 rms 280-350F. Pets allowed. Telex 650269. Cards: V, DC, MC.

Each of the rooms in this excellent renovated hotel has a direct telephone line, radio, color TV and bathroom; the decor is simple but pleasant. Lovely view. No restaurant.

Rennes-Montparnasse

6th arr. - 151 bis, rue de Rennes
45 48 97 38, 45 48 85 02

Closed Aug. 41 rms 340-430F. TV. Pets allowed. Telex 250048. Cards: V, AE, DC, MC.

A small, modern, well-located and well-maintained hotel. Its rooms at the back (about ten) are perfectly quiet, but those on the rue de Rennes are rather noisy. Excellent equipment (such as individual safes). No restaurant.

Royal Médoc

9th arr. - 14, rue Geoffroy-Marie
47 70 37 33

Open year-round. 41 rms 480-530F. TV. No pets. Telex 660053. Cards: V, AE, DC.

Ten minutes away from the Opéra and close to the main boulevards, this modern, functional building (with direct telephone lines and a multilingual staff) near the Bourse (the Stock Exchange) is perfect for international business types. No restaurant.

La Tour d'Auvergne

9th arr. - 10, rue de La Tour d'Auvergne - 48 78 61 50

Open year-round. 25 rms 300-480F. TV. No pets. Telex 281604. No cards.

This hotel was entirely renovated in 1986, each room with a decor from a different period; all are furnished with four-poster beds and double-glazed windows. A fine little establishment. Restaurant.

Trocadéro

16th arr. - 21, rue Saint-Didier
45 53 01 82

Open year-round. 23 rms 405-570F. TV. Pets allowed. Telex 643164. Cards: V, AE, DC, MC.

The management of the L'Etoile hotel (see above) also supervises this small, serene hotel, which was completely renovated in 1986. The rooms are simple but are quite comfortable, and the bathrooms are well equipped (they each include hairdryers). No restaurant.

Urbis Paris Jemmapes

10th arr. - 12, rue Louis-Blanc
42 01 21 21

Open year-round. 1 ste 700-1,100F. 48 rms 359-430F. TV. Pets allowed. Telex 211734. Cards: V, MC.

This brand-new business hotel is well designed and perfectly tailored for a busy clientele attending conventions and seminars. The rooms (which we found to be on the chilly side) are modernly and soberly decorated. Excellent equipment. Generous breakfasts are served. No restaurant.

Utrillo

18th arr. - 7, rue A.-Bruant
42 58 13 44

Open year-round. 30 rms 200-300F. TV. No pets. Telex 281550. Cards: V.

Located behind rue Lepic in a still-typical Montmartre district, this building, which used to rent furnished rooms, has been totally renovated. The new rooms feature freshly whitewashed walls, and the upholstery and bedding are done in cheerful fabrics. Clean and hospitable. No restaurant.

Welcome Hôtel
6th arr. - 66, rue de Seine
46 34 24 80
Open year-round. 30 rms 225-380F. No pets. No cards.

You can almost forget the busy intersection of the nearby boulevard Saint-Germain behind the quiet-enhancing double windows in these small, bright, tidy rooms. And if you want a taste of the bohemian life, you'll find it on the seventh floor (you can take the elevator!) where you will discover a quaint wooden-beamed attic. No restaurant.

Le Zéphyr
12th arr. - 31 bis, bd Diderot
43 46 12 72
Open year-round. 52 rms 320-440F. TV. Air cond. No pets. Telex 216398. Cards: AE, DC, MC.

This charming new hotel, painted all in white, has been renovated in the art deco style. It offers quite pleasant, well-equipped rooms, as well as conference rooms. Restaurant.

AIRPORT

ORLY

Altea Paris-Orly
94547 Orly Aérogare - Orly-Ouest
46 87 23 37
Open year-round. 200 rms 355-435F. Half-board 90-300F. TV. Air cond. Pets allowed. Parking. Telex 204345. Cards: V, AE, DC, MC.

The comfortable rooms are done in bright, lively colors; the plumbing is of good quality. The staff is more numerous than efficient. Tennis and golf facilities should be operational by the time you read this. Restaurant.

Hilton International Orly
94544 Orly-Aérogare - Aérogare
d'Orly-Sud - 46 87 33 88
Open year-round. 376 rms 680-910F. TV. Air cond. Pets allowed. Parking. Telex 250621. Cards: V, AE, DC, MC.

The rooms at this Hilton are as functional as they are comfortable, and the hotel is located very close to the airport (free shuttle). The conference facilities are exceptional. Restaurant: La Louisiane.

Mapotel d'Occitanie
91260 Juvisy-sur-Orge - 2, rue de Draveil - 69 21 50 62
Open year-round. 29 rms 230-439F. TV. Pets allowed. Parking. Telex 690316. Cards: V, AE, DC, MC.

All the rooms are tastefully decorated in a modern style, and are well maintained. Some have pleasant views of the River Seine. The service here is excellent. Restaurant: see Le Pays d'Oc, Juvisy-sur-Orge.

Pullman Paris-Orly
94150 Rungis - 20, av. Charles-Lindbergh- 46 87 36 36
Open year-round. 2 stes 850F. 204 rms 565-820F. TV. Air cond. Pool. Pets allowed.

The perfectly soundproofed and air-conditioned rooms at the Pullman Paris-Orly, each complete with color television and direct-dial telephone, offer all the comfort you can expect of this hotel chain. There is also a continuous shuttle service to the airport, a panoramic bar, sauna, shops and new luxury rooms (called the "Privilège" rooms). Restaurant: see Le Rungisserie, Rungis.

ROISSY CHARLES-DE-GAULLE

Holiday Inn
95700 Roissy-en France - 1, allée du Verger - 49 88 00 22, 39 88 00 22
Open year-round. 240 rms 640-880F. Half-board 835F. TV. Air cond. Pets allowed. Parking. Telex 695143. Cards: V, AE, DC, MC.
The rooms are large, bright and well equipped. There is a health club (gym, sauna, whirlpool), a free shuttle to the air terminals (from 6 a.m. to 1 a.m.) and a restaurant.

Sofitel
95713 Roissy-en-France Cédex
Aéroport Charles-de-Gaulle
48 62 23 23
Open year-round. 8 stes 1,200F. 344 rms 595-825F. TV. Air cond. Heated pool. Tennis. Pets allowed. Parking. Telex 230166. Cards: V, AE, DC, MC.
Located facing the runways, Sofitel is equipped with all the amenities one expects of this chain—everything from a disco, a heated pool and a sauna to a restaurant and coffee shop.

THE SUBURBS

NORTHERN SUBURBS

Le Grand Hôtel
95800 Enghien - 85, rue du Général-de-Gaulle- 34 12 80 00
Open year-round. 3 stes 750-800F. 48 rms 390-565F. Half-board 460-660F. TV. Heated pool. Parking. Pets allowed. Telex 697842. Cards: V, AE, DC.
Though massive and unattractive, this building is located in a charming park. The rooms are spacious and comfortable, and the decor and furnishings here are done in a distinctive, classical fashion. Restaurant.

Paris Penta Hotel
92400 Courbevoie - 18, rue Baudin
47 88 50 51
Open year-round. 494 rms 510-640F. TV. Telex 610470. Cards: V, AE, DC.
A hymn to concrete. The comfort level is high and continually undergoing improvement. There is a shuttle-bus service to the RER (rapid regional transit). Bar and restaurant.

WESTERN SUBURBS

Château de la Jonchère
78380 Bougival - 10, côte de la Jonchère
39 18 57 03
Open year-round. 2 stes 1,000-1,500F. 45 rms 550-1,000F. TV. Pets allowed. Telex 699491. Cards: V, AE, DC, MC.
Twenty minutes away from the place de l'Etoile, in the middle of the verdant countryside and under new management, Château de la Jonchère boasts luxurious, lovely suites. At the other end of the park is a quite comfortable 40-room hotel (Hôtel du Parc de la Jonchère) under the same management. Restaurant.

Dauphin
92800 Puteaux - 45, rue Jean-Jaurès
47 73 71 63
Open year-round. 30 rms 345-360F. TV. Pets allowed. Tennis. Parking. Telex 615989. Cards: V, DC, AE, MC.
In the lovely reception room of the Dauphin, generous buffet breakfasts are served, and the rooms are serene and comfortable. Free shuttle to the RER station.

Eden Hôtel

78000 Versailles - 2, rue Ph.-de-
Dangeau - 39 50 68 06

*Open year-round. 24 rms 175-250F. TV. No
pets. Telex 698958. Cards: V, AE.*

Located on a fairly quiet street near the
police station, equidistant from the train station and the palace, the Eden Hôtel features
24 newly decorated and modernized rooms.
No restaurant.

La Forestière

78100 Saint-Germain-en-Laye - 1, av.
du Président-Kennedy
34 51 93 80, 39 73 36 60

*Open year-round. 6 stes 820F. 24 rms 560-650F.
TV. Pets allowed.*

Located in a large flower garden on the
border of a forest, La Forestière has 24 recently
renovated rooms and suites furnished with
beautiful antique furniture; the walls are enlivened with fresh pastel colors. Relais et
Châteaux.

Hôtel Quorum

92210 Saint-Cloud - 2, bd de la République
47 71 22 33

*Open year-round. 58 rms 360-390F. TV. Air
cond. Pets allowed.*

Everything, from the communal areas to the
private rooms, is spanking new and brightly
decorated in an elegant, modern, simple style;
the rooms are large, with gray-marble bathrooms. Guests are cordially greeted. Restaurant: see La Désirade, Saint-Cloud.

Le Pavillon Henri-IV

78100 Saint-Germain-en-Laye - 21, rue
Thiers - 34 51 62 62

*Open year-round. 3 stes 2,200F. 42 rms 400-
1,400F. Half-board 820F. TV. Pets allowed.
Parking. Telex 695822. Cards: V, AE, DC, MC.*

Nothing has been spared to make the 42
large rooms and suites of Le Pavillon Henri-IV
extremely comfortable. The banquet rooms
are magnificent (they were recently rated as

ancient monuments), as is the incredible view
of the immense park. Restaurant.

Princesse Isabelle

92800 Puteaux - 72, rue Jean-Jaurès
47 78 80 06

*Open year-round. 1 ste 900F. 28 rms 510-530F.
TV. Pets allowed. Tennis. Parking. Telex
613923. Cards: V, DC, AE, MC.*

The rooms of this new hotel, very close to
La Défense, are beautifully decorated and
equipped with Jacuzzis or multijet showers.
Some of the rooms are on the same level as the
flowering patio. Free chauffeured-car shuttle
to the RER station or to the Pont de Neuilly.
No restaurant.

Neuilly Park Hôtel

92200 Neuilly-sur-Seine - 23, rue
Madeleine-Michelis - 46 40 11 15

*Open year-round. 24 rms 440-530F. TV. Pets
allowed. Telex 612087. Cards: V, AE, MC.*

This luxurious, elegant building, the newest
of the small Neuilly hotels, has exquisite, well-
furnished rooms, and its prices are excellent.

Sofitel Paris–La Défense 🏶

92800 Puteaux - 34, cours Michelet
(La Défense 10) - 47 76 44 43

*Open year-round. 1 ste 3,200F. 149 rms 950-
1,150F. Half-board 1,155F. TV. Air cond. Pets
allowed. No cards.*

This latest addition to the chain, decorated
with golden mirrors and light marble, has a
warm atmosphere. The quiet rooms have superb pink marble bathrooms. Service is outstanding, and breakfast is delicious. Well
equipped for conferences. Restaurant: see Les
Deux Arcs, Puteaux.

Syjac Hôtel

92800 Puteaux - 20, quai de Dion-
Bouton- 42 04 03 04

*Open year-round. 4 stes 850-1,200F. 29 rms
380-710F. TV. No pets. Telex 614164. Cards: V,
AE, DC.*

This is a new building that escaped the
triumphal style of architecture that character-

izes its concrete neighbors at La Défense. The rooms are pleasant, huge and perfectly equipped. In addition, there is a pretty interior courtyard and a superb free sauna. The hotel has no restaurant, but there is the possiblity of room service.

▲▲ Trianon Palace
78000 Versailles - 1, bd de la Reine
39 50 34 12

Open year-round. 10 stes 1,785-2,990F. 110 rms 490-1,110F. Half-board 503-766F. TV in 95 rms. Pets allowed. Heated pool. Tennis. Cards: V, AE, MC.

Half of the Trianon Palace's rooms were recently modernized; all the furniture was changed and an underground swimming pool and two tennis courts were being completed when we went to press. This old, neoclassical deluxe hotel has been transformed into a superb contemporary jewel. Restaurant: see Trianon Palace, Versailles.

▲▲ Le Versailles
78000 Versailles - 7, rue Saint-Anne
39 50 64 65

Open year-round. 48 rms 310-380F. TV. Pets allowed. Parking. Telex 689110. Cards: V, AE, DC.

Next to the entrance of the Palace of Versailles and across from the Palais des Congrès, the location of Le Versailles is excellent. No restaurant.

BARS & CAFES

PUBS

Académie de la Bière
5th arr. - 88 bis, bd de Port-Royal
43 54 66 65
Open 3:30 p.m.-2 a.m. Closed Sun. & Aug. No cards.

As the name suggests, those dedicated to the immortal delights of Gambrinus (the mythical king/inventor of beer) gather here to clink mugs into the night. University types from the neighborhood sit alone resting their eyes on the collections of bottles and labels that adorn the walls. The wooden benches are a bit hard, and at busy times elbows get pressed pretty close together, but these quibbles are small beer compared to the house brew, drawn perfectly under the practiced eye of a true artist of the tap, Pierre Marion.

Bar Belge
17th arr. - 75, av. de Saint-Ouen
46 27 41 01
Open 3:30 p.m.-1 a.m. Closed Mon. No cards.

One of the fourteen lovely beers on tap is a Lindermans kriek and a Lambic Vieux Bruges (14 francs), and the superb list of bottled beer is topped by the famous Judas-sur-Lie (38 francs). But we found the tavern itself to be downright tacky, sitting glumly across the street from the Gare du Nord. The hurry-up service didn't help much. And the atmosphere is as unappetizing as the fare: frankfurters and fries (30 francs), onion soup (24 francs). You could always take a large group of friends along, to assure the friendly pub-like ambience that is so thoroughly lacking.

Au Général La Fayette
9th arr. - 52, rue La Fayette - 47 70 59 08
Open 11 a.m.-3 a.m. (Sat. 3:30 p.m.-3 a.m.) Closed Sun. Cards: V.

A coat of paint, a few improvements and a fairly new terrace are all that it took to rejuvenate this former jewel of Parisian bars. Early each day, great trainloads of foreign visitors unloading at Gare du Nord and Gare de l'Est, each thirsting mightily for a Guinness, tumble through the door. The collection of odd bric-a-brac is not enough to hide the beauty of the old woodwork adorning the rococo interior. There are a dozen beers on tap, hundreds by

the bottle and some solid nourishment as well, making this a good spot for a zippy lunch.

Le Gobelet d'Argent (Chez Tong)
1st arr. - 11, rue du Cygne - 42 33 29 82
Open 4 p.m.-1 a.m. Parking: Forum des Halles. No cards.

This is *the* place in town for Guinness and loads of Irish ambience.

La Gueuze
6th arr. - 19, rue Soufflot - 43 54 63 00
Open noon-2 a.m. Closed Sun. & July 9-31. Parking: Soufflot. Cards: V.

Going down a long paneled corridor, one is surprised by the ultimate size of this immense but discreet establishment located halfway between the Pantheon and the Luxembourg Gardens. From the nearby Sorbonne, teachers and students alike flock here at noon and in the evening. The classic array of beers is sufficiently inclusive to satisfy any lover of fine suds. Of the bountiful food offered here, we prefer the herbed white cheese, which you spread on slices of hearty bread and wash down with a solid Duvel beer.

Le Manneken-Pis
2nd arr. - 4, rue Daunou - 47 42 85 03
Open noon-4 a.m. (Sat. 7 p.m.-4 a.m.). Closed Sun. Parking: Marché Saint-Honoré. Cards: V.

The "little king of Brussels" set up shop here a few years ago, gallantly undaunted by its American neighbor, the famous Harry's Bar. In this corner of Paris, where the yen is king, this little place evidently has had difficulty sheltering itself from the winds of inflation. Still, we've never regretted the 36 francs spent for the kriek Eylenbosh or the 38 francs for the Pope's 1880 from England. Belgian beers are clearly in the majority here, including several rare brews and the traditional lager by the pitcher. The cooking is wholeheartedly Belgian, to an extent one doesn't always find even on the other side of the border: mussels, waterzooi (traditional Flemish stew), carbonade (beef stew from Argentina) and more. Some evenings the atmosphere can become downright warm—overheated, some might say—but that's the tradition of the rue

Daunou. The cellar downstairs offers a quiet refuge.

La Micro-Brasserie

2nd arr. - 106, rue de Richelieu
42 96 55 31
Open 11 a.m.-1 a.m. Closed Sun. Parking: Opéra, Bourse. Cards: V, AE.

This is a novelty in Paris: a bar/restaurant/brasserie. Yes, the house beer is brewed on the premises, in huge copper vats that are a big part of the interior decor. To accompany the beer, the establishment offers astonishingly light fare utilizing various forms of the hops: prime rib "marchand de bière," filets of rockfish cooked in pale beer and so forth. For 68 francs, the fixed-price menu offers a choice of a main dish and either a first course or a dessert. Some excellent cheeses from the north and east of France can be found here. It's too bad that the postmodern decor, in salmon and black, tends to be cold and noisy, for overall this is a very successful experiment.

Kitty O'Shea

2nd arr. - 10, rue des Capucines
40 15 00 30
Open noon-1:30 a.m. Closed 1 wk. Christmas-New Year's. Parking: Marché Saint-Honoré. Cards: V, AE, DC.

This all-green pub was the pathfinder for the more recent Jameson restaurant, which joined it on this corner near the place Vendôme. Kitty doesn't have any culinary ambitions; you come here to put down a few Smithwicks and Guinnesses, served on tap at ideal temperature and pressure—"like in Dublin." Both the staff and the clientele are largely female and English-speaking. The smoked salmon, the chicken pie and the Irish coffee never fail to be everything the regulars expect them to be. The decor, which is half-bar, half-dining room, has its charm. But you can't be in too much of a hurry or too picky about the selection.

Pub Saint-Germain

6th arr. - 17, rue de l'Ancienne-Comédie
43 29 38 70
Open daily 24 hours. Parking: Mazarine, Saint-Sulpice. Cards: V, AE, DC, MC.

Witness the sad outcome of an ill-advised marriage: This unique pub, home to many great and honorable beer-drinking associations, is one of the finest specialized establishments in all of France. With 24 beers on tap, it holds the European record—and that doesn't even count the unrivaled 450-bottle beer list maintained here. But now these storied walls boast innumerable copper plaques displaying the names of the knights of Gambrinus and other valiant organizations, and the place has turned into the quintessential brasserie. This changeover has succeeded, but it has been a Pyrrhic victory—Pub Saint-Germain now hosts a mob of beautiful bingers, at hearing-impairment decibel levels, and serves them foul, indigestible fare. Even a tourist would blush. The taste of Pub Saint-Germain's beer has gone flat.

La Taverne de Nesle

6th arr. - 32, rue Dauphine
43 26 38 36
Open daily 7 p.m.-5 a.m. Parking: Mazarine. No cards.

More than 400 beers and seventeen krieks (a Belgian brew) are served in this tavern, where you can pass a good part of an evening, as long as you can put up with the noise of the last-round revelers who drift in after energetic soirées in the area. The video entertainment makes a good attempt to thwart all conversation. We prefer to come here around 8 p.m. for an apéritif, such as the good draft beer, and a relaxed chat or a glance at a video number.

The Twickenham

7th arr. - 70, rue des Saints-Pères
42 22 96 85
Open 9 a.m.-2 a.m. (Sat. 6 p.m.-2 a.m.). Closed Sun. & Aug. Parking: Saint-Sulpice, Saint-Germain. Cards: V.

Who could claim to be able to bring together in the same place such literary notables as Alain Minc, Lucien Bodard, Bernard-Henri Lévy, Jean-Claude Fasquelle and Arthur Miller? The answer is limited to two men in Paris—Henri and Jacques, who run The Twickenham, the literary bar that presided over the birth of Editions des Femmes, a prestigious women's publishing house and bookstore. The Twickenham also continues to administer to the thirsts of other publishers. They gather here around 6:30 every evening except Saturday (when the place is given over to shoppers and tourists). One other thing you ought to know: The establishment is named after the great rugby stadium in Britain, so following big matches in Paris, the final timeout is conducted here.

RENDEZVOUS SPOTS

Le Bar à Huîtres
14th arr. - 112, bd du Montparnasse
43 20 71 01
Open daily noon-2 a.m. Cards: V, AE.
   The center of this great, classic Montparnasse shellfish café is its high circular counter. You can perch here at any hour of the day to taste the array of oysters and white wines, all of which are reasonably priced. We particularly like the "deep sea" Breton oysters, the number-five belon oysters and the delicious "butterflies" of Marennes, washed down with a glass of Saint-Vran. The shellfish are opened right in front of your eyes, and around the bar the conversation normally runs to the inexhaustible subject of . . . oysters.

Bar Alexandre
8th arr. - 53, av. George-V - 47 20 17 82
Open daily 8 a.m.-2 a.m. Parking: Georges-V. Cards: V, AE, DC, MC.
   The decor is warmed with wood, leather and a vague accent of ships and the sea. Pretty women, journalists, gentlemen of the turf and travel agents come here for a scotch, a beer or their 7 p.m. glass of Champagne. Amiability is the house rule here.

Bar de Holiday Inn (Les Trois Bornes)
11th arr. - 10, pl. de la République
43 55 44 34
Open daily 11 a.m.-1:30 a.m. Parking: rue de Malte. Cards: V, AE, DC, MC.
   A good place for doing business in the place de la République area, with comfortable armchairs and the spectacle of the place pleasantly removed. You can order a tequila sunrise (47 francs) and enjoy the rare treat of a bar that doesn't cut you off completely from the life of the city outside. With plenty of American tourists and business people, the bar does a brisk business in ice cubes and nightcaps.

Bar de l'Hôtel (Le Bélier)
6th arr. - 13, rue des Beaux-Arts
43 25 27 22
Open daily 24 hours. Parking: rue Mazarine. Cards: V, AE, DC, MC.
   A half dozen tables, a few stools, the gentle sound of a fountain, warm colors, a cheeky bartender . . . and the cocktails—such as the Blier (vodka, Curaçao, grenadine, fruit juices)—are good, too. It's quite a pleasant spot to end an evening.

Bar du Concorde–La Fayette (Plein Ciel)
17th arr. - 3, pl. du Général-Koenig
47 58 12 84
Open daily 11 a.m.-2 a.m. Parking: Palais des Congrès. Cards: V, AE, DC, MC.
   Everything here is organized to take advantage of the commanding panoramic view of Paris and of the axis that connects the two arches (the Arc de Triomphe and the huge new arch at the La Défense complex). The little crescent-shaped sofas are a nice touch in the room, which is flatteringly stretched out along the windows. This, of course, rules out table-to-table communication, so the thing to do here is sit back under the turning fans and enjoy the house mixed drinks or one of the 24 Champagnes. The clientele is a hodgepodge of tourists and business people staying at the hotel, participants from conferences taking place at the nearby Palais des Congrès and couples who aren't concerned with finding a discreet hideaway. We like the recent innovation of serving top Champagnes by the glass, on a changing basis. On the cocktail list, lovers of Pineau Charentes (a French sherry) will welcome the Cagouillard Pineau mixed with a choice of such concoctions as vodka, crème de cassis, tonic or vermouth. And the lover of fine spirits will thrill to the eight vodkas available, including Pieprzowka, flavored with pepper and pimento.

Bar du George-V
8th arr. - 31, av. George-V - 47 23 54 00
Open daily 11 a.m.-1:30 a.m. Parking: Georges-V. Cards: V, AE, DC, MC.
   The clientele comes from top-drawer conferences, seminars and other such gatherings. Where are the movie stars you'd expect to see? The atmosphere is a little chilly in this otherwise comfortable bar, which opens onto a series of little salons where you can have a quiet conversation while sipping a whisky se-

lected by Monsieur Jacques, who is fluently conversant on the subject.

Bar du Meurice (Le Meurice)

1st arr. - 228, rue de Rivoli - 42 60 38 60
Open daily 10 a.m.-2 a.m. Parking: Vendôme. Cards: V, AE, DC, MC.

You don't come here for the bar but, inevitably, to sip tea amid this Pompadour decor that embodies so well what Madame herself would have loved

Bar du Méridien (Le Patio)

17th arr. - 81, bd Gouvion-Saint-Cyr
47 58 12 30
Open daily 7 a.m.-2 a.m. Parking: Méridien. Cards: V, AE, DC, MC.

This large space is done predominantly in beige and black tones. The crowd is loyal to this lively, international bar for its cheerful, quick service. It's true that the cost of a morning cup of coffee is a bit steep, but round about 6 in the evening, when the pianist sets to work (to be replaced later in the evening by one or another excellent jazz orchestra), the cocktails are flawless. All in all, it's astonishing to realize that you can actually pass a pleasant moment right next door to the huge, bustling Porte Maillot. Try the house specialties: the Bleu Méridien (vodka, Curaçao, pineapple juice and lemon) and the Ecume des Nuits (bourbon, Grand Marnier, orange juice and grenadine) or one of the ample selection of whiskies.

Bar du Raphaël

16th arr. - 17, av. Kléber - 45 02 16 00
Open daily 11 a.m.-midnight. Parking: Foch. Cards: V, AE, DC, MC.

Reminiscent of the exquisite luxury hotels the English frequented in Italy during the nineteenth century, Bar du Raphaël happily remains a graceful institution. There is opulence and refinement in the bronze sculptures, the carved wood, the carpets and the cocktails. Somewhat of a secret and very expensive, the bar is a most useful watering hole for stars seeking a respite from their admiring throngs.

Bars du Hilton (Le Bar Suffren, Le Bar du Toit de Paris)

15th arr. - 18, av. de Suffren - 42 73 92 00
Open daily 11 a.m.-12 a.m. (Le Bar Suffren), 6 p.m.-2 a.m. (Le Bar du Toit de Paris). Parking: Suffren. Cards: V, AE, DC, MC.

Le Bar Suffren manages to maintain a relaxed, friendly atmosphere—no mean feat in this sort of place. Big-business types from nearby offices meet here to discreetly settle deals. Meanwhile, up on the tenth floor, wealthy foreign visitors unwind in the Toit de Paris bar, sipping cocktails made by Christian Viel, mixmaster extraordinaire, and enjoying a splendid view of the Eiffel Tower. From 8 p.m. to midnight, a tasty assortment of tapas is served (40 francs), making Le Bar du Toit de Paris a fine place to finish an evening.

Bars du Ritz (Le Cocktail Room, L'Espadon, Le Bar Hemingway)

1st arr. - 15, pl. Vendôme - 42 60 38 30
Open daily 11 a.m.-3 a.m. Parking: Vendôme. Cards: V, AE, DC, MC.

To see and be seen is the fun of this place, and it's rather ethereal fun at that. Nevertheless, there's some excitement for the taste buds, too; the seasonally changing cocktail inventions, in addition to the grand classics, are excellent (70 to 80 francs). And in the rich wine cellar lurk some true marvels, such as the 1906 Da Silva port (410 francs), an 1858 Cognac (1,400 francs), an 1878 Armagnac (920 francs) and the superb house Chablis (40 francs per glass).

Bars du Sofitel Paris (Choiseul, Montgolfier)

15th arr. - 8, rue Louis-Armand
40 60 30 30
Open daily 8:30 a.m.-1 a.m. (Choiseul), 6 p.m.-2 a.m. (Montgolfier). Parking: Sofitel. Cards: V, AE, DC.

The Choiseul and Montgolfier bars (famous for their nightly jazz) are the only more-or-less quiet (or appropriately lively) spots in this neighborhood surrounding the huge exhibition complex known as the Salons of the Porte de Versailles. It's a good meeting spot, and you needn't fear being overwhelmed by a tidal wave of show visitors and exhibitors.

Le Berkeley
8th arr. - 7, av. Matignon
42 25 47 79, 42 25 72 25
Open daily 9 a.m.-2 a.m. Parking: Rond-Point des Champs-Elysées. Cards: V, AE, DC, MC.

At this oasis of quiet near the Champs-Elysées traffic circle, you'll find tea in the afternoon and piano music at night. In addition, simple food is served. The clientele is very Right Bank: politicians, buyers and sellers of luxury goods, journalists and advertising execs.

Café Costes
1st arr. - 4-6, rue Berger (pl. des Innocents)
45 08 54 39
Open daily 8 a.m.-2 a.m. Parking: Forum des Halles. No cards.

There are those who love famous designer Philippe Starck and his postmodern cult-by-default of steel and glass. And there are those who unreservedly despise all that. In any case, you'll find the Starck look here, and you'll find it expensive. The clientele is composed of an inexhaustible supply of young people of seemingly all kinds, including, toward 10 p.m. or so, pretty women shopkeepers from the hip boutiques of the area.

Le Chapman
2nd arr. - 27, rue Louis-le-Grand
47 42 98 19
Open 11 a.m.-2 a.m. Closed Sun. Parking: Paramount Opéra. Cards: V, AE.

Bernard Bionaz, formerly of Harry's Bar, brings together in his café two loves: golf and cocktails. There is light food available at lunch, wines by the glass and a happy-hour special of a free second glass between 5 p.m. and 7 p.m.

Closerie des Lilas
6th arr. - 171, bd du Montparnasse
43 26 70 50
Open daily 10:30 a.m.-2 a.m. Parking: Montparnasse. Cards: V, AE, DC, MC.

Sure, this place once saw the likes of Hemingway and Gide, and now Jean-Edern Hallier

sits at his own table by the door. But there is also a superb decor, particularly inviting in warm weather with the laurel-enclosed terrace, the high-class, polished service and the excellent cocktails. So don't pass up the pleasure of sitting on the moleskin banquettes, where so much good taste lounges about being seen. Snobby and expensive? You bet. But remember, you're not out for a beer at the neighborhood tavern.

La Coupole
14th arr. - 102, bd du Montparnasse
43 27 09 22
Open daily 8 a.m.-2 a.m. Cards: V.

The new owner, Mme. Bucher of the Bucher chain, has promised that she won't change this hallowed monument to the glory days of Montparnassian artistic and creative life. Or rather, she won't change its spirit—naturally, she'll make logical improvements to the flesh of the place: freshening the decor, adding some photographs and decorations from its heyday and improving the morbidly unflattering lighting. Soon, therefore, artists and writers will once again be able to seek inspiration around the bar or spend the evening in contemplation and discussion. And, as before, the lovely sidewalk terrace will fill up with pretty people, pensive artists and Japanese tourists.

Les Deux Magots
6th arr. - 6, pl. Saint-Germain-des-Prés
45 48 55 25
Open 7:30 a.m.-2 a.m. Closed 1 wk. in Jan. Parking: Saint-Germain. No cards.

Over there, a group of Japanese tourists is sipping the famous "old-fashioned chocolate"—thoroughly whipped and made from chocolate bars melted in milk. Beneath the chandeliers and the sign reading *boulevard Saint-Germain*, a German couple is putting away the fresh, long Comté cheese sandwiches. The Beaujolais from Brouilly, the coffee, the Muscadet and the salads are all of good quality, with prices to match. The legends may have gone, but nonetheless you'll really feel like you're in Paris.

Le Flore

6th arr. - 172, bd Saint-Germain
45 48 55 26
Open daily 7:30 a.m.-1:30 a.m. Parking: Saint-Germain. No cards.

The intent was to modernize, but the uncomfortable result is that this old café, once the hangout of poet Apollinaire, is passing from one era to another. It was once a gay, chic café, and now it's become a brasserie where advertising and publishing types, tourists and business people eat fast lunches of eggs and beer. The food is lighter and cheaper than across the street at Lipp, and anybody can get in.

Le Flore en l'Ile

4th arr. - 42, quai d'Orléans - 43 29 88 27
Open 10 a.m.-1 a.m. Closed Jan. Parking: Pont-Marie, Hôtel de Ville. No cards.

Here you'll find the excellent Berthillon brand of ice cream, a nicely redone decor, a salon-de-thé atmosphere and one of the best views of Paris and Notre-Dame, all in one spot.

Le Forum

8th arr. - 4, bd Malesherbes - 42 65 37 86
Open 11:30 a.m.-2 a.m. (Sat. & Sun. 5:30 p.m.-2 a.m.). Parking: Madeleine. No cards.

This is the archetypal French-style rendezvous bar, with its perfect service, lovely decor (even the cocktail shakers are a work of art) and stern policy of discretion. At about seven in the evening, couples of various sorts drift in for an intimate chat before heading home to west Paris. The 150 cocktails and the selection (one of the best in Paris) of scotch whiskies are accompanied by olives and peanuts. The armchairs are comfortable, and the touch of nostalgia in the decor isn't objectionable—there's a bit of the spirit and style of the '30s hanging about in this corner of the place de la Madeleine. Take advantage of it, along with a Zytnia vodka made from pure rye (60 francs), a Highland Park Orkney malt (70 francs) or a mixed drink (57 francs).

Le Fouquet's

8th arr. - 99, av. des Champs-Elysées
47 23 70 60
Open daily 9 a.m.-2 a.m. Parking: Georges-V. Cards: V, AE, DC, MC.

The radio, television, movie and publicity folk are still using this bar as their meeting spot. In the afternoon you'll find Italian, Japanese and/or Lebanese visitors filling the sidewalk tables; in the evening, toward midnight, Le Fouquet's is sometimes an end-of-a-hard-day haven for the golden lads of local journalism.

La Mousson

4th arr. - 2, rue Jean-Beausire - 42 71 85 20
Open daily 7 p.m.-1:30 a.m. Parking: Bastille. Cards: V.

Boasting pickles, wicker, ferns and the new Bastille "in" crowd, Le Mousson is a jumping joint after 9:30 p.m. or so.

Le Normandy

1st arr. - 7, rue de l'Echelle - 42 60 30 21
Open daily 11 a.m.-midnight. Cards: V, AE, DC.

In these Chesterfield armchairs you won't find the preen-and-be-seen set but rather the confidential murmerings of journalists and those enjoying a pre–Comédie Française drink along with discreet, virtuoso service. Women alone can feel at ease here, and the cocktails made by Serge, Jean and Xavier are as fine as the other elements of this lovely old hotel bar—be it the Changy (gin, grapefruit juice and wild strawberries, for 48 francs) or a Rusty Nail. There is a fine choice of brandies, featuring Cognacs from Delamain and a superb Armagnac 1957, Cuvées Normandie.

Pub Sir Winston Churchill

16th arr. - 5, rue de Presbourg
45 00 75 35
Open daily 8 a.m.-2 a.m. Parking: Foch. Cards: V, AE, DC, MC.

This attractive stop is just a stone's throw from the Arc de Triomphe. With its long bar, copper-trimmed stools and piano bar, it has a very British feel to it, though the interior is actually the work of Slavik, the well-known Parisian decorator. The whisky selection (including Bushmill's for 52 francs) is of unquestionably high quality, "Grandma's" apple pie (37 francs) is a toothsome delight, and the choice of wines by the glass is truly interesting (Meursault, 40 francs; Mercurey blanc, 35 francs). But despite these good things, the place still gets a trifle boring in the evening, partly because the crowd is sparse in an environment that was designed to be packed. This may be due to the service, which we have found to border on the rude (the cashier didn't seem to like to be disturbed during her mealtime and didn't care who heard her say so).

Le Sélect

6th arr. - 99, bd du Montparnasse
45 48 38 24
Open daily 8 a.m.-2 a.m. Parking: Montparnasse. Cards: V.

This is just the place to watch the possibly infamous rehabilitation of that well-known landmark, La Coupole, across the street. It's also just the place to come for a last-minute rendezvous before a seafood dinner in the neighborhood. It's extremely select, of course, with service and comfort at their finest.

Le Train Bleu

12th arr. - Gare de Lyon, 20, bd Diderot, 2nd floor - 43 43 09 06
Open daily 11 a.m.-10 p.m. Parking: Bercy. Cards: V, AE, DC, MC.

This otherwise classic bar serves (via decent waiters) the standard repertoire. The decor is stunning: The ceiling is perhaps the most beautiful of its kind in all of Paris, and the woodwork is positively majestic. And now, the TGV (high-speed train line) has returned what had disappeared from Paris's train stations: a cosmopolitan European atmosphere where one hears Italian, English and even the Swiss French of the wealthy Genevan women who hop up to Paris for the day to see their (haute couture, of course) dressmakers. We even know of a regular client, a businessman from Lyon, who is in the habit of arranging all his appointments here so that from the time he arrives on the TGV in the morning and leaves in the evening, he never has to set foot on the pavement. The drinks here are more than potable, and the seats comfortable.

Trianon-Palace

6th arr. - 1 bis, rue de Vaugirard
43 29 88 10
Open 11 a.m.-3 p.m. & 5:30 p.m.-10 p.m. Closed Sat. & Sun. Parking: Soufflot, Ecole de Médecine. Cards: AE, V, DC.

All it takes to transform an ordinary, decent hotel bar into a Parisian "must" is for a queen bee to set up shop there. In this case, it's the three well-known Françoises (Verny, Sagan and Mallet-Jorris), who take their cocktails dry and their chit-chat free of rough edges. Trianon-Palace makes an ideal setting for an intellectual tryst. Please be advised to read the latest by or about the above-mentioned queen bees before entering, just in case. . . .

Le Vaudeville

2nd arr. - 29, rue Vivienne - 42 33 39 31
Open daily 7 a.m.-2 a.m. Parking: Bourse. Cards: V, AE, DC, MC.

Across the street from the stock exchange, next to the French wire services and near the Club Méditerranée headquarters, this place serves as a much-needed neighborhood meeting spot. Another link in the Bucher chain, it offers (besides meals) a pleasant decor, a comfortable bar and flawless service. It is particularly good for breakfast.

TEA ROOMS

A Priori-Thé

2nd arr. - 35-37, passage Général-Vivienne
42 97 48 75
Open noon-7 p.m. (Sun. 1 p.m.-7 p.m.). No cards.

We would be hard pressed to come up with a prettier or more charming spot in Paris than the passage Général-Vivienne. You slip beneath its glass roof, which is supported by bas-relief carved goddesses and horns of plenty, to reach this honey-colored room (the bit of a terrace out front is marked by its rattan armchairs). If the passage itself has become chic, A Priori-Thé has fully retained the relaxed, country feel that has always been its charm. From noon until 3 p.m. the regulars, people from the nearby fashion houses, lunch on interesting cold platters (bulghur salad, cheese-and-herb terrine, eggs with cheddar cheese and so forth) or on the uneven hot specials (good sautéed chicken livers, indigestible macaroni and cheese). From 3 p.m. on, Peggy, Polly, Bonnie and Terry, the owners, serve creations from their pastry menu, which owes some items to American influence (brownies and cheesecake); others are lovely reinterpretations of the classics made by the gifted and creative Moroccan pastry chef. A nice selection of teas is available, including such rare ones as cherry and hazelnut. Brunch is served on Saturday and Sunday: eggs with cheddar or tomato, fruit salad, pastry, bread, jam, butter and coffee or tea (110 francs).

Angélina

1st arr. - 226, rue de Rivoli - 42 60 82 00
Open daily 9:30 a.m.-7 p.m. Cards: V, AE, DC.

This is it, the high-water mark of posh Paris society—or at least it used to be. Angélina still appears to be *the* elegant tea room in town, a kingdom of elderly grande dames in green hats. But has it really maintained its once-lofty social position? Not according to the afore-mentioned grande dames, who chide it for its increasingly common clientele—the rich young bourgeois in their leather jackets and the young ladies just out of their fashionable convent schools, smoking and squalling. And perhaps these newcomers *are* out of place in this room, which, with its bronzed moldings, cream-of-tomato-colored pilasters and faded Côte d'Azur frescoes, has always had a certain provincial air, even if it is noticeably tired. It may have been that the decor went unnoticed at the turn of the century, when there was a brilliant, chic clientele to capture one's atten-tion. In any case, even Angélina's detractors would prefer the vague charms of this room to the back salon, which is a sort of modern add-on, sad and discreet. And there are the capricious waitresses, some of whom now wear—we thought we'd never see it here—black skirts. In other words, things change, even a tea room's clientele.

But for those with a soft spot in their hearts for this sort of place, there's still plenty of charm in the heavy, textured curtains that cover the windows, the wealth of gilded plaster molding and the incessant ballet of the waitresses carrying the silver trays and the tra-ditional fine white china. Society ladies still come here, as do bankers from the place Vendôme, who shed a bit of their eternal dignity in the company of starlets. And the prices are still up there in the stars, particularly at noon, when you'll pay 230 francs for the rack of lamb and 100 francs for the most modest daily special. One unfortunate development is the precipitous decline of the now-doughy Mont Blanc (the classic dessert of chestnut purée with crème chantilly) and the scarcely

presentable pastry tray (even if the chocolate is still exquisite). But you don't come here to feast; rather, you come to appreciate the het-erogenous—that is to say, Parisian—atmo-sphere, not to mention the elderly but still coquettish ladies, whose coffee is served with chocolates (16 francs).

L'Arbre à Cannelle

1st arr. - 57, passage des Panoramas
45 08 55 87
Open 11 a.m.-6:30 p.m. Closed Sun. Parking: Bourse. No cards. Take-out pastries & tarts.

This splendid, Second Empire tea room re-placed François Marquis's famous chocolate shop of the nineteenth century. While tearing out the walls in the course of renovation, the owners of the tea room discovered a fascinating decor: a floor composed of black, brown and white marble triangles, carved woodwork, etched-glass mirrors and paintings done on ceramic and wood panels. To our great good fortune, they left it intact. The napkins, table-cloths and cushions are all done in the cinna-mon color of the walls. And the refinement of the rooms themselves is accentuated by the superb china, the beautiful glassware and the lovely presentation of dishes. Old ladies in mink and young ladies in Hermès come here to have tea (thirteen varieties) and the delicious accompanying homemade cakes and pies: apple-cinnamon, pear-chocolate, coconut-ba-nana. Special mention goes to the apple crumb cake topped with crème fraîche. At lunchtime we've seen more men than we've ever seen in a tea room; L'Arbre is located near the stock exchange, and its servings are generous. While brokers talk, we like to eavesdrop while enjoy-ing one of the various quiches (31 francs) and salads (try the mixed salad with smoked trout, 41 francs). Even heavy eaters are not forgotten: They can feast on mixed platters of charcuterie, mozzarella cheese, cold vegetables, salad and croutons, which are available all afternoon. Regulars order the daily specials (veal kidneys with fresh noodles, for example, for 58 francs). In short, this is a fine spot to know about. The Saturday brunch (served from noon to 6 p.m., 80 francs) includes fresh fruit juices; tea, coffee or chocolate; a choice of quiche (cheese, gar-den vegetables, Provençal) or eggs (scrambled, hard- or soft-boiled); and cakes, pies and other desserts.

L'Auberge du Bonheur
16th arr. - Bois de Boulogne, av. de
Longchamp (behind Grande Cascade)
42 24 10 17
*Open noon-11 p.m. (Oct.15-April 15 until 6
p.m.). Closed Sat. in winter. Cards: V.*

This little country inn in the heart of the Bois
de Boulogne has the special attraction of a
lovely terrace for long summer evenings. But
the Auberge is a treat in winter, too, when you
can squeeze into a comfortable banquette after
a stroll in the Bois de Boulogne park. These
former stables have been done over prettily:
exposed beams, red-and-white-checked curtains, lots of plants and a smartly turned-out
service staff. In this utterly cozy little spot,
grandmas catch up with their little darlings
over a cup of tea (12 francs, but from a bag)
and a treat, perhaps a tart (28 francs) or ice
cream (25 francs). At noon, people who work
near the Bois join the regulars (the place is a
bit hidden) for the daily special (70 francs).
Worth noting are the house specialties: juicy
grilled salmon and good cuts of meat.

Bereley's
6th arr. - 35, rue du Dragon - 45 48 91 08
*Open noon-11 p.m. Closed Sun. Parking: Saint-
Germain. Cards: V. Tea served 3 p.m.-6 p.m.*

Pining for New York? You'll find it right
here in Paris. All sorts of people hang out here:
Americans, students, nice Saint-Germain-des-
Prés gentlewomen. The tea selection sticks to
the classics (20 francs); they're served by the
glass, accompanied by pound cake (20 francs),
toasted brioche (25 francs) or delicious brownies (30 francs). The meals served at noon and
in the evening have a made-in-America taste: a
75-franc meal composed of a zakuski platter
(Russian hors d'oeuvre starting with caviar and
running the gamut, traditionally accompanied
by vodka), an assortment of house specialties
and chicken livers. Sadly, something is missing
in this picture: The greeting and the service are
slipshod.

Boissier
16th arr. - 184, av. Victor-Hugo
45 04 87 88
*Open 9 a.m.-7 p.m. (Sat. & Sun. until noon).
No cards.*

Located right in the arid stretches of the
sixteenth arrondissement, this elegant, traditional tea room, which is refined but not

snobby, inviting but not wildly expensive, is no
mirage. Tulips in delicate blue china vases
reflect spots of color onto the creamy walls.
From the windows, you looks onto the square
Lamartine. Inside, little girls in kilts and white
ankle socks down the house specialties: enormous chocolate candies and apple tarts made
of delicate layer pastry (17 and 13 francs).
Their mothers, no doubt more concerned with
their figures, order mushroom salads in olive
oil (25 francs) or the superb "Marceau" platter,
composed of Parma ham, mozzarella, tomatoes and raw mushrooms (60 francs) and a
glass of Château de Lussac 1981 (18 francs).
The new proprietor has undeniably rejuvenated the establishment. From noon to 3 p.m.
a daily special is served (65 francs); in the
morning (after 9 a.m.) breakfast dandies—
croissants; buttered toast; coffee and tea—are
served. The service is smiling and attentive, the
prices are more than reasonable, and the food
is chic but good. This is the house of treats in
these parts.

La Boulangerie Saint-Philippe
8th arr. - 73, av. Franklin-Roosevelt
43 59 78 76
*Open 7:30 a.m.-7:30 p.m. (Sun. 8 a.m.-7 p.m.).
Closed Sat. & Aug. Cards: V.*

Just opposite the Saint-Philippe church, this
tea room/bakery has been in business for more
than 100 years. On Sunday, famous people
come to pay tribute to the tarte tatin served
warm with big cups of crème café (delicious
but a little too sweet for our taste) and to eat
in the comfortable cafeteria decorated in somber autumn tones. During the week, office
personnel lunch in grand style on skewered
lamb, melon with ham or home-cooked goose
liver. For dessert, we love the macaroons, the
Black Forest cake, the chocolate-covered cookies scented with Grand Marnier or, better still,
croissants, brioches and toasted buns served
with delicious butter, jams and tea. Service by
friendly waitresses.

La Boutique à Sandwichs
8th arr. - 12, rue du Colisée - 43 59 56 69
*Open 11:45 a.m.-11:30 p.m. Closed Sun. &
Aug. Cards: V.*

On the second floor of this restaurant, you
might see a few famous faces seated together
around Raclette, vegetable soup and other
modest but honest dishes. For our part, we
remain loyal to the ground floor, where the

best sandwiches in Paris are served, featuring shrimp, chicken and smoked ham. There is an excellent corned beef served hot or cold with horseradish, pickles and Poilane bread that could compare to any good New York deli's. This is one of the better spots in Paris.

Café Noir (La Passion du Fruit)

5th arr. - 71, quai de la Tournelle
43 26 04 02
Open daily 11 a.m.-2 a.m. Parking: Maubert-Saint-Germain. No cards.

This gray-and-black room has a beamed ceiling, photographs of celebrities lining the walls and two TVs showing video clips. The clientele is young, the greeting is lively, and the menu (limited in winter) offers cocktails, hot and cold drinks, house pastries, desserts and various salads and fruit salads. Ten or so kinds of teas are served to wash down either a plate of Roquefort on toast (29 francs) or a bitter-chocolate cake (29 francs). A new sidewalk terrace allows a better view of the ongoing student traffic. Brunch is 93 francs.

Carette

16th arr. - 4, pl. du Trocadéro
47 27 88 56
Open 8 a.m.-7 p.m. Closed Tues. & Aug. Parking: av. Georges-Mandel. Cards: V, AE.

Carette is famous for its macaroons—chocolate, vanilla, lemon—and its coffee (20 francs). The wealthy heirs and heiresses of the avenue Mozart like to come here to chat. But now the younger generation is joining them, and dandies and hipsters, busy comparing the number of cylinders in their motor-scooter engines, abound. The result is an unholy racket in which to try to appreciate a cup of tea. You can try to hide inside, but the tables are tiny and jammed together. Fortunately, Carette is also a pastry shop and caterer, so you can stop by, pick up some macaroons and go home to eat them in peace.

Casta Diva

8th arr. - 27, rue Cambacérès - 42 66 46 53
Open 11:30 a.m.-6:30 p.m. Closed Sun. Parking: Malesherbes. No cards.

These two quite chic white rooms under the arcades, with their spacious alcoves and heavy pistachio-colored curtains, shelter a posh, well-shopped-for clientele. The furniture, all in mahogany, is richly evocative of the Empire. Even the salads are rich, and tasty to boot, such as

the preserved-chicken-gizzards representative (58 francs). The desserts uphold the house standards very well, from the apple délice with Calvados (18 francs) to the chocolate mousse cake (30 francs). The tea list features such rare selections as the Pettiagala or the Gielle (19 francs). Everything here is done with high polish. If Napoléon had ever gotten off Saint Helena, it wouldn't have been a bit surprising to see him show up here.

Les Champs-Mesnil

16th arr. - 15, rue Mesnil - 47 55 96 44
Open 9 a.m.-7:30 p.m. Closed Sun. No cards.

To get to the tea room in this health establishment, you go down a corridor lined with books bearing such titles as *Diabetes and Malnutrition*. Fortunately, the tea room itself bears no resemblance to the refectory of an order of vegetarian monks; rather, it is more evocative of a traditional Provençal homestead, with its bunches of lavender on the rough stucco walls, bouquets of dried herbs, copper pots and large flowered tablecloths. Chef Michel Brugeron is a lively fellow who's full of energy. He continues to make his old-fashioned pastry, finishing each cake by hand and never using artificial colors, and he sweetens his tarte tatin (22 francs) naturally with apple juice. This tarte tatin is one of nature's miracles, a marvel of delicate crust with just the right amount of sweet. The chocolate (which Jacques Chirac, the mayor of Paris, comes to buy) is delicious, and the Auvergne-style potato-and-ham pie is quite tasty (served with a vegetable salad or purée of vegetables for 40 francs). Tea is 10 francs; hot milk with honey and cinnamon, 12 francs. From noon until 3 p.m. the house offers some finely prepared, delicious main dishes, often based on the fish that the owner buys himself in Norman ports. An excellent address to know. Remember to make reservations for lunch.

La Charlotte de l'Isle

4th arr. - 24, rue Saint-Louis-en-l'Isle
43 54 25 83
Open 2 p.m.-8 p.m. Closed Mon. & Tues. Parking: Notre-Dame. No cards. Take-out pastries.

Tea tins piled everywhere, posters, paintings, old mirrors, hats, bouquets of dried flowers and, yes, even a piano: Such are the elements of this wonderful, artistically disordered decor. For fifteen years Sylvie Langlet has been turning out excellent chocolate, spice and fruit cakes in this magical spot, and giving them names like Next-to-Nothing or the Crazy Florentine (truffles, raisins and orange rind, 12 francs). These poems in pastry accompany her spice tea or any of the 30 other choices. And there is more lovely art at work in the presentation: small etched trays, old teapots and cups, silver carafes for the hot water, even a sugar pot that doubles as a little statue. Hot chocolate lovers will be more than happy with Langlet's old-fashioned version, which carefully preserves the flavor of the chocolate (12 francs). This dollhouse of a tea room is as favored by Parisians as it is by their friends from the provinces.

La Chocolatière

6th arr. - 5, rue Stanislas - 45 49 13 06
Open noon-6:30 p.m. Closed Sat. & Sun. No cards.

At lunch and teatime, television people (channel TF1 is close by), high schoolers (Lycée Stanislas is next door) and Luxembourg Garden strollers all find themselves together in this cozy spot. At lunchtime, the ambience is jazzy, with efficent service making possible a quick lunch of a salad (32 to 39 francs) or a quiche (34 francs). Or you can order the 52-franc formula, which features tabouli, a mixed salad and apple sauce or white cheese, washed down with a small carafe of rosé (14 francs) or cider (13 francs). For afternoon snacks, there is caramel tea (19 francs) with dark-chocolate cake, or old-fashioned hot chocolate, served in a china chocolate pot, with crème fraîche and a glass of ice water on the side (28 francs). This goes nicely with the hot apple and almond fondant (22 francs) or light pound cake—homemade, of course.

Christian Constant

7th arr. - 26, rue du Bac - 42 96 53 53
Open daily 8 a.m.-8 p.m. Parking: Pont-Royal. Cards: V.

The white walls and ivory armchairs accentuate the lovely shades of brown of the best hot chocolate in Paris. And there is a wide variety of them: extra bitter, bitter ganache, Mexican spice and so forth. All are heavenly—so good that you forget even the excellent prices. The only problem is the constraint imposed by the walls; there just isn't enough room; there's always a wait. You can pass the time at the Adrien Maeght gallery just up the street, and then return refreshed in spirit to refresh the rest

of you with a cup of tea (served with honey, 22 francs). You'll also find a pleasing range of pastries to eat in or take out (13 to 16 francs) and lovely chocolates at 380 francs per kilo. And we can't forget to mention the homemade jams and good-quality brandies and wines. The clientele comes from the neighborhood, regulars of all ages but of similarly good breeding, all of whom are watched after by the all-seeing, motherly madame who owns the establishment.

Coquelin Aîné

16th arr. - 1, pl. de Passy
45 24 44 00, 42 88 21 74
Open 9 a.m.-6:30 p.m., pastry shop 9 a.m.-7:30 p.m. (Sun. until 1 p.m.). Closed Sun. & Mon. Parking: Passy. No cards.

Coquelin Aîné—what a truly Parisian treat. Yes, my dear, we know exactly where we are the moment we enter this tea room and see Hermès scarves closing Burberry raincoats. The crowd is snobby, and the sweet little things from the Janson-de-Sailly school for girls come for tea (tea bag, 18 francs) and a tart, éclair, meringue or the house favorite, macaroon (12 francs). Unfortunately, the place is noisy, the service jostling and the seating cramped. At noon the shopkeepers from the rue de Passy come to eat salads and pâtés for 40 francs, or they order the 85-franc fixed-price luncheon, comprising a salad and a main dish. And not only is this is a great pastry shop, but it's also the home of a famous caterer.

Cotton Flag

1st arr. - 45, rue de Richelieu - 42 96 09 58
Open noon-3:30 p.m. & 7:30 p.m. Closed Sun. & Mon. evening. Parking: Pyramides. No cards. Take-out pastries. Lunch reservations advised.

If it's good old what-dreams-are-made-of cheesecake that you crave, you won't find it anywhere as good as it is here, where they use their own cream cheese and follow a secret recipe, stored on computer and originating from the United States. Toward midnight, the chic place des Victoires in-crowd gathers here to sup in a pristine decor of grays and yellows, featuring an American bar. A 75-franc fixed-price menu is offered at lunch (smoked-salmon tart, chopped steak and a choice of desserts, including the renowned cheesecake, apple pie, brownies, pecan pie and chiffon pie). In the evening another fixed-price menu (115 francs) will bring you spinach salad, pork ribs and dessert. The fresh salmon steak grilled over beechwood is worthy of particular attention. One of the most authentic American-style brunches served in Paris, if not also one of the best, is available on Saturday from noon until 4 p.m. (for 115 francs): fresh fruit juices, coffee, tea or hot chocolate, pancakes with a homemade syrup of mixed red berries and pecans, a big platter of smoked salmon, pastrami, homemade brioche, sausages, scrambled eggs, potato pancakes and salad, followed by pastry or fruit salad for dessert.

A la Cour de Rohan

6th arr. - 59-61, rue Saint-André-des-Arts 43 25 79 67
Open noon-7:30 p.m. (Sun. 2:30 p.m.-7:30 p.m.). Closed Mon. & 2nd wk. of Aug. Parking: Mazarine, Ecole de Médecine. No cards.

Tucked in the Rohan passage, which runs from the place de l'Odéon to the rue Saint-André-des-Arts, you'll find a cozy tea room that's as charming as a private home: dishes from Cocteau, Louis XVI furniture and old Limoges china. The only jarring notes are the waxed tablecloths and the stainless-steel flatware. These details are unfortunate, but they certainly won't prevent you from having a pleasant time, particularly if you choose a table on the second floor. Most of the food made here—reliable eggplant caviar (39 francs), many varieties of quiche (48 francs)—is quite good. Beware, however, of the concrete scones (28 francs). The tea list, on the other hand, is a strong point (18 francs). The reception is rather affected and a tad snobby, the conversations are all in low tones, and the ambience is strictly well-to-do. None of this deters the students, who constitute the regulars, or the Japanese tourists off the street from coming in.

Dalloyau

6th arr. - 9, pl. Edmond-Rostand 43 29 31 10
Open 9:30 a.m.-6:40 p.m. (Sun. until 6:15 p.m.). Cards: V.

Dalloyau will always be Dalloyau. Nothing changes: The same grandmothers from the sixth arrondissement chat together or bring their grandchildren in for a treat, the same schoolgirls sit telling each other schoolgirl stories, and the same young couples smile timidly at each other after a walk around the Luxembourg Gardens, which you can see from the windows. The conscientious serving staff offers

a substantial choice of teas (17 francs), fruit juices (17 francs), good hot chocolate (5.50 francs), delicate pastries (13 to 19 francs) and sumptuous ice cream concoctions (35 to 45 francs). If you wish you can order lunch, which runs to such dishes as rumpsteak (78 francs), seafood brochettes (76 francs) and scallops (84 francs). But, frankly, people come here for the tea, even if the lunch special does change each week.

Aux Délices

17th arr. - 39, av. de Villiers - 47 63 71 36
Open 9 a.m.-6:45 p.m. Closed Mon. No cards.

Aux Délices is nothing short of an institution. The grand chandelier is hung so high up in the vault of the ceiling that it looks small. The huge room, tiled in blue and sienna, has a distinct rust-and-ocher flower pattern on the walls, woodwork, painted ivory and endless mirrors. Its austere dignity and slightly tired air of nobility make it a splendid spot for elderly women, who sip the good if slightly bitter coffee (9.50 francs) and never notice the celebrities. A tip: The vanilla and chocolate macaroons are incredibly light. The tables are a bit rickety, but the neighborhood is nice and quiet, and the place is well run by the new manager, Charles Ragueneau. A product of the Lausanne Hotel School, and a true professional, he strolls confidently through his domain, perhaps more respected than liked by the staff, whose efficiency he has restored. There are cakes and pastries, as well as smoked-salmon slices (49 francs per 100 grams) and a small egg with caviar (150 francs). The daily specials are delicious. Breakfast is 32 francs; tea, 16.50 francs.

Djarling

15th arr. - 45, rue Cronstadt - 45 32 47 17
Open noon-7 p.m. Closed Sat. No cards.

Come teatime, the pretty teacups on the red cashmere tablecloths sit patiently waiting to be filled with one of the fifteen varieties (the classics plus more rare blends, including representatives from Kenya, 14 francs) that the house offers. No snooty chic, just a relaxed atmosphere. All the tea accompaniments have been seen to: pound cake (12 francs), scones (15 francs for two) and a fancier cake (23 francs). If your appetite is larger, you can order a "special" salmon (40 francs), a salad and pâté (21 francs) and a daily special (old-fashioned veal stew, for example, 38 francs). Sunday brunch, served from noon to 7 p.m., gives you three choices: The Petit Djarling comprises tea, coffee or hot chocolate, fruit juice, two hard-boiled or fried eggs on toast, vegetable salad or cheese and scones with butter and jam. The "fitness" brunch presents tea or coffee, fresh-squeezed orange juice or lemonade, cereal, two hard-boiled eggs, vegetable salad and an unsweetened fruit compote. And then there's the Grand Djarling, which, in addition to the Petit's offerings, includes salmon.

Le Dos de la Baleine
4th arr. - 40, rue des Blancs-Manteaux
42 72 38 98
Open daily 8 p.m.-3 a.m. No cards.

If this is the Whale's Back (*Le Dos de la Baleine*), where's the Giraffe's Neck (Le Cou de la Girafe)? Why, out in the high-rise suburbs, silly. Henri Béhar, who was already running the restaurant at the Théâtre des Amandiers, opened this place in the heart of the Marais district a few years ago. Its huge room is broken up by columns, decorated with the necessary amount of natural materials to make it comfortable (wooden tables, for example) and mixed with the necessary fashionable details (ceiling fans, big Expressionist paintings) for ambience. If the decor is not exactly suited to your banker uncle, at least you won't have to take out a loan to pay your tab. Despite the parading blue-jeaned waiters, carrying little blue stuffed whales in their back pockets, this hip eatery is the antithesis of the typical snob joint where you pay plenty to eat nothing. Neighborhood theater students join the night owls of the area for the good, nicely interpreted traditional cooking. We suggest you try the scrambled eggs with tarragon (35 francs), fricassée of kidneys (82 francs), poached haddock (65 francs) and a bottle of Bourgogne Passetoutgrain (67 francs).

Les Enfants Gâtés
4th arr. - 43, rue des Francs-Bourgeois
42 77 07 63
Open daily 9 a.m.-7 p.m. Cards: V.

The ambience is soft, the lighting is subdued, and the round tables and deep armchairs are arranged between tall ivory-painted columns beneath whirling ceiling fans. A fairly classy joint, Les Enfants Gâtés could pass for the bar of a Roman palazzo. Swedish students and young Americans while away the hours here, buried in the piles of magazines the house

makes available. The menu is amusing, a cartoon of a somber detective tale that provides clues to the contents of the Durand salad (ham, Gruyère, corn, tomato and egg), the Dupont (tuna, hearts of palm, tomato) and the Blake and Mortimer (cucumber and egg). The fixed-price lunch menu, on the other hand, is no mystery (quiches or salad, with a pastry, beverage and coffee, 70 francs). There are twenty kinds of tea, including an exquisite Russian Imperial blend. Or you can accompany the dark-chocolate cake (31 francs), tart Bourdaloue (29 francs) or pound cake (25 francs) with a glass of Champagne (40 francs). It's all good and plenty generous. If you're an adult, this is a great place to be a spoiled child (*enfant gâté*). There are several brunch possibilities priced from 65 to 165 francs. The "large brunch" features fresh fruit juice, hard-boiled eggs, open-face sandwiches, croissants, butter and jam, blinis, salmon, tea, coffee or chocolate and the pastry of the day.

Eurydice
4th arr. - 10, pl. des Vosges - 42 77 77 99
Open noon-7 p.m. (summer until 11 p.m.). Closed Mon. & Tues. Parking: 16, rue Saint-Antoine. No cards.

After a trip to the Victor Hugo house or the Picasso Museum, culture vultures like to gather at Eurydice. The neoclassical decor enlivened with ocean-liner accents includes walls done in trompe l'oeil, metal chairs and marble tables. It's all very up-to-date, down to the Italian glass plates. The tea room is fairly empty before 6 p.m. or so, when trysting couples arrive for a steaming cup (six varieties) and a little cake (walnut, chocolate or cheesecake, 27 francs). The quality is strictly average, and the menu is sparse. The emphasis here is on speed; you won't find fresh-squeezed fruit juices, for example, because they take too long to make. From noon until 3 p.m. on weekdays, there is an express fixed-price lunch (55 francs) featuring white cheese, a gratin dish and coffee. Another fixed-price menu is offered for 69 francs: liver pâté, gratin or salad and dessert. And you can order something savory or sweet at any time. On Sunday, brunch is served from noon to 5 p.m. including (for 60 francs), orange juice, fried eggs with basil on toast, homemade apple sauce with prunes and raisins, Ceylon tea or coffee and the house brioche served hot.

Fanny Tea

1st arr. - 20, pl. Dauphine - 43 25 83 67
Open 1 p.m.-7:30 p.m. (Sat. & Sun. 3:30 p.m.-8 p.m.). Closed Mon. & Aug. Parking: Pont-Neuf. Cards: V.

Emily Post would have loved these rickety little tables and the white porcelain vases that house a rotation of peonies, roses, marigolds and tulips, which appear according to some natural law no more immutable than the one that drives Fanny to turn out her pound cake and chocolate cake day in and day out. So have a seat in one of the snug little armchairs while you think of something primly witty to say. The hostess will bring you, with a melancholy smile, excellent tea and some crunchy little goodies to nibble on. As you leave you may cast a misty-eyed glance in the direction of Simone Signoret, who always seemed so removed from this sort of crude snobbishness.

Fauchon

8th arr. - 24, pl. de la Madeleine
47 42 60 11
Open 9:45 a.m.-6:30 p.m. Closed Sun. Cards: V, AE, DC.

Though atrociously noisy and cramped, this is undoubtedly the best self-service cafeteria in Paris. Customers have to stand up while eating the excellent sandwiches and such honorable dishes as the vegetable tart and tagliatelle au gratin. At teatime, you can choose from twenty different cakes. And there are excellent fruit and vegetable juices and coffees so fragrant that Fauchon's president comes here for an after-lunch demitasse.

La Fourmi Ailée

5th arr. - 8, rue Fouarre - 43 29 40 99
Open noon-7 p.m. Closed Tues. Parking: Notre-Dame. Cards: V, MC.

From the outside, La Fourmi Ailée looks like a bookstore. Inside, why, it is a bookstore, but one that artfully conceals a tea room—a blissfully intimate, down-home tea room. Waiting for you on a rustic sideboard sit a spice cake (two slices, 25 francs) and a Norman tart (25 francs). Wisps of steam rise from the spouts of a mixed assortment of teapots set on the tables (sixteen types of tea, 15 francs). The composed salad with goat cheese (40 francs) and the hard-boiled eggs with toast points (20 francs) are so tasty they would disappear without dirtying the silver knives and forks if it were not for

nice Parisian society reminding us to mind our manners. Brunch, served both Saturday and Sunday from noon to 7 p.m., comes in three versions—70 francs, 80 francs and 95 francs. The midsize one comprises tea, fruit juice, an omelet, a salad and an assortment of cakes (scones, buns, muffins).

Les Fous de l'Ile

4th arr. - 33, rue des Deux-Ponts
43 25 76 67
Open noon-3 p.m. & 7 p.m.-11 p.m. Closed Aug. Parking: Maubert-Saint-Germain. Cards: V, MC.

The upper levels above this large, windowed room are lined with books, china is displayed in glass cases, and here and there black-and-white photographs hang. It's a busy place, very relaxed and pleasant, with a student atmosphere. The clientele is young, cosmopolitan and at ease, and the waiters officiate in T-shirts and jeans. A variety of teas are offered, including Sakura (green tea flavored with cherry) and Caraibes (Indian, Ceylon and Caribbean flowers) at 15 francs. The house pastries at 25 francs include the chocolate roulé (truffles and whipped cream). Ice cream, sorbet, fruit juice, and various alcoholic drinks round out the possibilities. Daily specials consist of eggplant caviar (30 francs), stuffed cabbage (42 francs) and Québec stew (45 francs).

Institut du Monde Arabe

5th arr. - 23, quai Saint-Bernard
46 34 25 25
Open noon-10 p.m. Closed Sun. evening & Mon. Parking: Institut du Monde Arabe. Cards: V.

Having tea on the ninth floor of the Arab World Institute, even if it's made from a bag (13 francs), has its charm. The setting is all steel and glass, and the view of Paris is superb. For lunch, there are such dishes as shish kebab (66 francs), and for dinner, a minced avocado and smoked salmon with Noilly butter (90 francs). In the afternoon, it feels more like a high-class bar, but an agreeable one, particularly while eating a floating island (21 francs) or baklava (25 francs).

Le Jardin

7th arr. - 100, rue du Bac - 42 22 81 56
Open noon.-10:30 p.m. Closed Sun. No cards.

You wend your way through a health-food store stuffed with the customary assortment of grains, jams and spice cakes from the Indies, down the aisles past macrobiotic literature and books on herbal cures, and suddenly you find yourself in an elegant interior garden. The stone floor, the indirect lighting, the garden furniture and the parasols all add to the ambience: You've found the country in the city. Assorted salads, gratin dishes and meat pies are all fresh and carefully done—but rather dull. The vegetarian menu (at 63 francs) includes a first course, a grain dish and a dessert. Tea is served, we shudder to say, from the bag. Fortunately, the chocolate truffle is well prepared (desserts range in price from 24 to 30 francs). Who comes here? Young-at-heart grandmothers, bespectacled postadolescents and frugal singles. The atmosphere isn't riotously jovial, but at least you can smoke and drink wine. Evidently, we are not among the house loyalists.

Ladurée

8th arr. - 16, rue Royale - 42 60 21 79
Open 8:30 a.m.-7 p.m. Closed Sun. Parking: Madeleine. Cards: V, AE.

The cherubs on the faded frescoes, the plush red carpet, the dark-oak woodwork and the round tables in veined black marble are all part of the charm of this tiny institution, which is always full as a tick. Especially Saturdays, when the lovely ladies from lovely neighborhoods put down their Hermès shopping bags for a few minutes to enjoy a macaroon or two. During the week, from 11:30 a.m. until 3 p.m., lunch, which consists chiefly of omelets (32.20 francs), chicken quarters (46 francs) or such daily specials as cassoulet (86.25 francs), is served. There is a large choice of attractive pastries (11.80 francs) and, of course, the famous raspberry, chocolate or vanilla macaroons (13.80 francs). The hot chocolate is good (20.70 francs). The minuscule sandwiches (salmon or crab, 10.40 francs) will empty your wallet long before they fill your stomach. That is the chief sin of places that would be "gourmet," and this is the only place it is allowable.

Le Loir dans la Théière

4th arr. - 3, rue des Rosiers - 42 72 90 61
Open noon-7 p.m. (Sun. 11 a.m.-7 p.m.). Closed Mon. & Aug. No cards.

Young women as graceful as nymphs ferry bulbous teapots among the low sofas. A faint feeling of nostalgia, a faded carpet, old armoires from Normandy, soft lights, frescoes on the walls—these elements always make us feel like we're back in our aunt's parlor out in the provinces. The atmosphere is quaint and a tad intellectual. The place is run on a kind of cooperative basis, and since the waiters and cooks are constantly changing, it is impossible to suggest any items in particular. The clientele, which is more bourgeois and conventional than the place itself, tends to favor the straightforward pastries and the hazelnut cake called Alice's Secret (though we've found it to be rather heavy). The salads bear such names as "Gay" (corn, carrots, eggs, pine nuts) and "Not Sad" (endives, walnuts, blue cheese). The service, although a little too whirly, is friendly and engaging. Sunday from 11 a.m. to 7 p.m. is reserved for brunch, in four variations. We've tried the two *classique* meals—fruit or vegetable juice, tea, coffee or hot chocolate, croissants or toast (50 francs)—and the *Bon Goût*—fruit juice, tea, coffee or hot chocolate, croissants, toast, two hard-boiled eggs and cereal or cheese.

Lord Sandwich

1st arr. - 276, rue Saint-Honoré
40 15 98 66
Open 9 a.m.-5 p.m. Closed Sat. & Sun. Cards: V, AE. 2 other branches: 15, rue Duphot - 1st arr. - 42 60 55 94, open at 11 a.m., closed Sun.; parking, Vendôme; caterer & home delivery available; 134, rue du Faubourg-Saint-Honoré - 8th arr. - 42 56 41 68, open at 11 a.m.

By now, no doubt everyone is familiar with the tale of John Montagu, Lord Sandwich, who had a passion for all-night card games and who accidentally invented the sandwich one night toward dawn, when he ordered his butler to bring him a slice of ham between two slices of bread to avoid getting the cards greasy. This Lord Sandwich offers some of the best-tasting such creations in Paris, along with the greatest selection (70 versions, ranging from 20 to 50 francs). These range from simple BLTs to a sophisticated compilation of pastrami, lettuce, mozzarella, bacon and tomato. Vegetarians and weight-watchers have an array of twenty salads to choose from (19 to 33 francs). The wildly hungry will appreciate the platter of ham, potato salad, celery, walnuts, grapes, cheese, tomato and bread. At tea time, the American pies are good, but the tea is sold by the bag and the other beverages arrive in plastic bottles. The cafeteria format is reminiscent of a fast-food outfit, but at least on the second floor there is a sort of garden-style dining room for Parisians and less-hurried tourists. It's too bad the management doesn't soften the rough edges, because the food is really quite good.

Maison du Chocolat

8th arr. - 52, rue François-Ier - 47 23 38 25
Open 9:30 a.m.-7 p.m. Closed Sun. Parking: Georges-V. Cards: V, MC.

Both haven and heaven for the truly devout—chocoholic, that is—can be found here. Maison du Chocolat is a tea room that lives up to its name by serving neither tea nor coffee, only hot chocolate. And the house drink has only one fault: It's too small. Made just a few hours ahead, poured from a hot chocolate pot into Limoges china cups, the divine stuff comes in five incarnations: Guayaquil, a classic and elegant brew; Caracas, bitter, full-bodied, recommended for true lovers of chocolate; Brésilien, lightly flavored with coffee; Seville, spiced with a bit of cinnamon; and Bacchus, which leaves you dreaming of the Antilles. All come accompanied with whipped cream on the side and cost 25 francs. You can also try the worthy chocolate frappé, with either ice cream or sorbet. If you're still not sated, try one of the pastries, perhaps the pleyel or the ganache with macaroons (19 francs), or a little assortment of fifteen chocolates lovingly dreamed up by Robert Linxe.

Marais Plus

3rd arr. - 20, rue des Francs-Bourgeois
42 72 73 52
Open 10 a.m.-midnight (Sun. 10 a.m.-7 p.m.). No cards.

The canaries are chirping, the cabbage-shaped water carafes are sitting pretty in the middle of tables that look onto a private courtyard garden, the tree branches are brushing against the windows. The charm of this friendly, light-filled place is due in part to its relaxed, straightforward atmosphere and in part to its hybrid nature as bookstore/tea room. The waitresses remind us of ever-so-kindly elves who would never think of saying anything if you seated yourself alone at a table set for four, or if you came at lunchtime and ordered nothing but a slice of cake (23 to 30 francs) and tea (13 francs, from a lovely list), or if you lingered at the table while leafing through the art books from the adjoining bookstore. You'll be sorely tempted by the brownies and the walnut cake, which sit enthroned on a honey-colored sideboard, but don't let them make you forget the other interesting creations, such as the orange and the chocolate cakes. An array of salads and quiches are available at any hour: quiche with a raw vegetable salad is 33 francs, and warm goat cheese, bacon and croutons on greens is 37 francs. The hot daily specials are always very original but not always successful (39 francs). There is also Gamay wine (10 francs) and fruit wines (12 francs). Marais Plus is open until midnight, and regulars can get a discount with a *carte de fidélité*. On Sunday the 65-franc lunch features an artichoke/tomato omelet, ham, pastries, fresh fruit juice and tea, coffee or chocolate.

Mariage Frères

4th arr. - 30-32, rue du Bourg-Tibourg
42 72 28 11
Open 11 a.m.-7:30 p.m. Closed Mon. Parking: Hôtel de Ville. Cards: V, AE.

A jungle of teas, teapots, teacups, tea balls—Mariage Frères is, in short, a tea-ocracy. For more than a century it has sold tea, 350 kinds of it, from the strongest Imperial Slavic blends to the most delicately perfumed varieties. Non-smokers may station themselves at a table on the ground floor beneath the exotic palms and the ceiling fans. Those dedicated to tobacco as well as tea leaves climb, at their own risk, the steep stairs to a place in which they will be welcomed. Everybody is kept happy here. The teas, prepared with filtered water, are served at the appropriate temperatures in insulated infusion-style teapots, and the waiters respect the ritual of tea. Watching them wheel between the tables, impeccably garbed in something vaguely Indian, one wonders when they have time to read their Kipling. Delicate house pastries valiantly accompany these sublime teas. A grand number of brunch items are served on Sunday.

La Marine

6th arr. - 59, bd du Montparnasse
45 48 27 70
Open daily 7 a.m.-2 a.m. No cards.

Thankfully, the sanitizing and bleaching of the once-colorful Montparnasse area has not yet reached La Marine; it still retains its folkloric charm—even if little except the varnished tables and copper portholes remains of the nautical motif. A big sign (which we've translated for you) announces OUR JOB IS TO SERVE A GOOD BEER, SO LEAVE US THE CHOICE AND HAVE NO FEAR, thereby setting the tone: Beer is queen here. Dark, light or amber, it is accompanied at any hour by Nuremburg sausages or weitwurst (or a combination plus apples and fries, 35 francs), or mussels in beer sauce (27 francs).

La Nuit des Thés

7th arr. - 22, rue de Beaune - 47 03 92 07
Open noon-7 p.m. Closed Sun. Parking: Montalembert. Cards: V.

The decor is rich: white lacquer, pink upholstery, mercury mirrors, damask tablecloths, antique furniture and watercolors on the walls. The welcome is distracted if you aren't a regular, but the clientele is noticeably at ease, chatting about such weighty topics as dog pedigrees, boating and the latest literary successes. Meanwhile, they're nibbling on salads and main-dish pies and tarts of all sorts, all of very high quality: leeks in puff pastry (58 francs), a bowl of Champagne with either peaches or raspberries (37 francs) and vegetable juices (25 francs). A variety of teas is available, as is brunch on Sunday in either 85-franc or 110-franc arrangements, the difference being a savory tart included in the latter.

Olsson's

8th arr. - 62, rue Pierre-Charron
45 61 49 11
Open daily noon-midnight. Cards: V, AE.

Located in the former Crédit Municipal building, with its high ceilings and gilded moldings, Olsson's features a very Swedish-looking decor and demure blond waitresses. The attractive and copious "Olsson" dish is composed of salmon, herring, homemade mustard, almonds, mussels, homemade bread, fish roe and more. The pastries are filling and, like everything else here, expensive.

Le Paradis du Fruit

4th arr. - 1, rue des Tournelles
40 27 94 79
Open daily 11:30 a.m.-1:30 a.m. Parking: Pl. de la Bastille. Cards: V. 2 other branches: 27, quai des Grands-Augustins - 6th arr. - 43 54 51 42; 28 bis, rue Louis-le-Grand - 2nd arr. - 42 65 54 67.

A lighted, blinking sign points the way to paradise lost, or at least this edition of it, along the quays of the Seine, where fruit concoctions

come at you in waves of orange and purple. Under the purring ceiling fans, in front of walls splattered with kitschy frescoes depicting fruit and animal phantasms, you can fortify yourself with a light-hearted vitamin cure before assaulting the Musée d'Orsay. Try the carrot-pineapple Bronzette cocktail or the Clin d'Oeil, which is composed of carrot and orange juices. For the anemic, the J'Assure cocktail of mango, carrot and lemon ought to do the trick (25 francs). Small appetites are assuaged by the generous mixed salads, nicely presented and ranging from 22 francs to 29 francs. If that isn't enough, you can continue with ice creams and pastries, a real pleasure to look at as well as to taste (the pirogue, for example, a coconut-milk-and-lychee-nut creation, 38 francs). A choice of frozen desserts (between 33 francs and 40 francs) features the special date-and-walnut and cinnamon-and-walnut ice creams. Hot quiches also are available (35 to 40 francs), as well as a large selection of Mariage Frères teas (16 francs). The friendly greeting and smiling service complete the genteel ambience here. You can even get a glass of Champagne for just 25 francs. Sunday brunch comes in two versions: 35 francs for tea, coffee, toast and orange juice; 58 francs for all that plus cheese and crackers, hard-boiled eggs and white cheese.

La Pâtisserie Viennoise

6th arr. - 8, rue de l'Ecole-de-Médecine
43 26 60 46
Open 9 a.m.-7 p.m. Closed Sat. & Sun. No cards.

Medical and literature students are among the enlightened crowd who fill up the seats of this citadel of the Latin Quarter, its seats worn smooth and shiny by generations of devotion. La Pâtisserie Viennoise opened in 1928, and to date the youthful ambience remains as tasteful as the cakes are tasty—the strudel and the poppy-seed cake (called the *flanni*) are among our favorites. The teas are perfect and the Viennese hot chocolate is a dream; they all marry beautifully with a croissant or a raisin brioche. Everything is made on the premises and everything is good. There's only one drawback: The place is always packed. But so what—just pile on in or find a stool at the bar. It's worth it: The good feeling in the place can take you right out of Paris and into the heart of Vienna.

Rose-Thé

1st arr. - 91, rue Saint-Honoré

42 36 97 18

Open noon-6:30 p.m. Closed Sat. & Sun. Parking: Les Halles. No cards.

Your grandmother from Philadelphia would love it here: paintings on the walls, subdued lighting, antique furniture, green plants and a sideboard displaying some luscious-looking cakes. The mistress of the place (nowhere near a grandmother's age) wanted to re-create the cozy feeling of a parlor in a large house in the provinces. And she has done so with an emphasis on refinement; witness the needlepoint and dried flowers on every table and the old teacups. Tea lovers will certainly fall for the rose-thé, an exquisite blend of Bulgarian rose with a touch of jasmine and lotus. Devotees of something more solid will find no fault with the old-fashioned rich chocolate cake made from chocolate bars (22 francs). And the hot chocolate is not to be missed (24 francs). Between noon and 2 in the afternoon, the regulars, including the antiques dealers of the neighborhood, come to nibble on the gratin dishes, the various quiches and the famous meat pie. In summer a sheltered terrace allows you to soothe the stresses of such refined consumption with a spot of calm in the madding heart of Paris.

Smith & Son

1st arr. - 248, rue de Rivoli - 42 60 37 97

Open 10:15 a.m.-6 p.m. Closed Sun. Cards: V.

Sporting needlepoint blouses and little black aprons tied with wide ribbons, the waitresses at Smith & Son are pale, coolly shy and very British looking. Under the low ceilings adorned with griffins, behind the stained-glass windows bearing coats of arms, reading VERITAS, you'll think yourself in Kent County. Young Richard the Lionhearts in Shetland sweaters bring their pretty damsels here to pledge their troth over the excellent apple pie (25 francs). Stylish grandmothers in plumed, green felt hats reserve their favorite tables near the fireplace, in the alcove and, preferably, in the nonsmoking section. The game is to avoid the crowds that come up from Smith's bookstore by the back stairwell. What is unavoidable are the paper table settings, like a snack bar's, which appear at lunchtime and are about as incongruous as a plastic cup on the Round Table. Soon after those place settings are laid, the fans of the little 78-franc fixed-price lunch (pâté, roast chicken or eggs and bacon, apple tart and a beverage) arrive in droves, along with the lovers of the 50-franc Smith salads (crudités, egg-and-mayonnaise, ham).

The waitresses brave this onslaught with dignity until about 3 in the afternoon, when the dining room regains its cloister-like tranquility and teatime sets in. The tea, served with scones, muffins or cucumber sandwiches, is poured steaming into the cups. God bless the Queen, or whoever is responsible for this blessed rite!

Breakfast is served daily from 9:30 a.m. until noon. The 50-franc Continental breakfast comprises fresh-squeezed orange juice, coffee, tea or hot chocolate and toasted tea cakes or muffins with marmalade or preserves; the 65-franc traditional breakfast brings you fried or poached eggs with bacon, sausage or fried tomato, toasted muffin, jam or marmalade, fresh orange juice and coffee, tea or hot chocolate).

Le Stübli

17th arr. - 11, rue Poncelet - 42 27 81 86

Open 10 a.m.-6:30 p.m. Closed Sun. & Mon. Parking: Ternes. Cards: V.

In the ground-floor shop you can choose from among the best Viennese pastries in Paris—éclairs (15.40 francs), Black Forest cake (22.50 francs) and, of course, apple strudel (24 francs). On the second floor, in the warm atmosphere of an Austrian chalet, all of these pastries and more can be tasted along with a hot chocolate, a cup of Viennese coffee (19.50 francs for a large cup) or even tea (15 francs). It's *Stüblime!* And in case you're really hungry, don't worry—there's a Bavarian salad (21.60 francs), a Baltic platter (22.80 francs) and the Stübli, a plate of hot beef sausage and potato salad (34.50 francs).

Sweet et Faim

5th arr. - 1, rue de la Bûcherie

43 25 82 16

Open daily 10 a.m.-2 a.m. Parking: Maubert. No cards.

This certainly is an eclectic spot: restaurant, tea room and jazz club all in one cellar room. The decor is prosperous if a bit banal, and the service is lively. In summer it's tourist-filled, in winter, Parisian-filled. There's quite a choice of à la carte dishes (John Dory filet in sorrel, 79 francs; boneless duck breast with blueberries, 85 francs) and a daily special at 49 francs. Fixed-price menus are available for 119 francs and 179 francs. The Baltic platter (49 francs) that we tried on our last visit was quite fresh, the homemade raspberry charlotte (32 francs) excellent, and the chocolate marquise delicious. There's a pretty sidewalk terrace on the place Frédéric-Sauton. The California brunch on weekends is rather expensive at 149 francs, but it does include Champagne and smoked salmon.

Tarte Julie

14th arr. - 8, rue Jolivet - 43 20 70 34
Open 11:30 a.m.-6 p.m. Closed Sun. Cards: V.

This is the prettiest of the Julie chain, with its blue and white ceramic tiles, cute lacework, mauve, flowered tablecloths and pine sideboards. It vaguely resembles a Moorish candy shop, but it's getting a little worn, with graying walls and yellowing floor tiles. Nevertheless, it's still a good spot for broke students, and the trees of pretty little Jolivet Square outside make everything inside seem just fine, except perhaps the mediocre lemon and berry tarts (16 to 20 francs). On the other hand, the salads aren't bad (we particulary enjoy Julie's special tuna, 40 francs). There are six types of tea (14 francs), more than the choice of wines, which bear such inane names as "Julie's Folly" (43.50 francs per bottle, 28 francs per half bottle). The welcome is kindly and down-to-earth, and the small shop sells tarts to go.

Tarte Julie

16th arr. - 5, rue Mesnil - 47 04 69 03
Open daily 9:30 a.m.-7:30 p.m. No cards.

The pink counters and sideboards and the red and pink plastic table settings are set off by the wooden tables, which furnish the rustic note that makes Julie Julie. This tarteria has the advantage of being good-size, and the tarts are well presented, even if the sweet ones (in particular the tarte Julie, made of plums and apricots, 16 francs) are nothing special. You can also order some interesting à la carte specialties, such as the goat-cheese tart with fresh mint and hazelnuts (25 francs). From noon to 3 p.m., pizzas and salads are served.

The Tea Caddy

5th arr. - 14, rue Saint-Julien-le-Pauvre
43 54 15 56
Open noon-7 p.m. (Tues. 3 p.m.-7 p.m., Sun. 1 p.m.-7:30 p.m.). Parking: Notre-Dame. No cards.

This place has a marked country feel about it, with exposed ceiling beams and colored glass squares in the windows. It's famous for its warmth and reasonable prices, and its clientele tends to be young and international (we overheard Swedes discussing with Parisians in English the relative merits of Australian cinema). The gratin of vegetables and ham (40 francs) or the scrambled eggs with spinach and bacon (45 francs) can be complemented by any of the six or seven types of tea. The pastry list has an English and Austrian accent: chocolate Sachertorte, Linzertorte with cinnamon and raspberries, fruit pies with cream. Unfortunately, the quality is uneven.

Tea Follies

9th arr. - 6, pl. Gustave-Toudouze
42 80 08 44
Open daily noon-10 p.m. No cards.

The refurbishment did away with the '30s-style facade. Those who used to hide behind the green carved shutters must now wear sunglasses, for a big window is all that separates Tea Follies from the shady little square outside. Another change, an air-filtering device, allows one to breathe more easily in the smokers' dining room (another area is reserved for non-smokers). The white walls are enlivened with watercolors, and the friendly service remains professional to the hilt. At noon, the savory tarts, the famous chicken pie or the boneless duck breast with peaches gets to the table in record time. In the afternoon, young ladies murmur demurely in front of their full teas (with scones, 43 francs). One has to wonder how they keep their slender shapes in the face of such divine pastries as the chocolate-and-chestnut Archéchois (28 francs) and the airy caramel meringue (31 francs). Sunday brunch (48 francs) is a presentation of orange juice, three kinds of scones, toast, butter, jam and coffee or tea; for 89 francs, an assortment of fish and vegetables and a spinach soufflé or savory tart are added to the above.

Thé Cool

16th arr. - 10, rue Jean-Bologne
42 24 69 13

Open daily noon-7 p.m. Parking: Passy. No cards. Take-out pastries.

The pun in the name is perfectly appropriate for this place, a haven of relaxed calm in the middle of a busy neighborhood. Michele and Marie-Claude always provide a warm welcome, leading us into a tea room that resembles a garden, where the cakes you see in the window do indeed reign supreme. The stressful part is making the difficult decisions—between the apple crumble (30 francs), the lemon meringue pie (32 francs), the chocolate truffle (32 francs) and the fruit tarts. The only solution is to select the chocolate marquise bathed in crême anglaise (32 francs). For the more healthful among us, there is a 170-franc fixed-price lunch and fresh-fruit and vegetable juices (18 francs). The regulars often lunch on the gratin preparations (35 francs), the salads (38 francs) or the savory tarts (35 francs).

For those who live for teatime, the choice of 30 teas is stunning. We suggest trying the unusual fixed-price Special Tea, which includes scones, pound cakes, butter cakes, honey, butter, jam and tea for 45 francs. After making the rounds of the shops on rue de Passy in the afternoon, tea at Thé Cool is the perfect treat. Brunch is a weekend affair—noon until 4 p.m. on Saturday and 11 a.m. to 4 p.m. on Sunday. Four menus are offered, ranging from 60 francs to 185 francs. The Brunch Royal, for example, at 135 francs, is composed of fresh-fruit or vegetable juices, tea, coffee or hot chocolate, brioches, scones, pound cake, butter, honey, jam, salmon roe, smoked Norwegian salmon, Parma ham or preserved beef, a green salad and cereals.

Thé au Fil

2nd arr. - 80, rue Montmartre - 42 36 95 49
Open noon-6 p.m. Closed Sat. No cards.

From the apricot walls covered with posters and the flowered tablecloths, we knew immediately we were in a tea room. But the liveliness of the place is much more suited to a neighborhood bistro at happy hour. The tea list is exceptional, the atmosphere convivial but not pretentious, and the lovely salads are quite reasonably priced (37 francs for a big platter of ham and raw vegetables). The woman who owns the place, Irit Spiro, is a Parisian Betty Boop with a sharp wit. The pastries are for the most part unremarkable, running to such things as brownies, cheesecakes and a cake weirdly christened, "For my love." Says Spiro, "I call it that because it is made in such a fashion that it is always fresh." Fresh maybe, but if truth be told, her love's a little dry. On Saturday and Sunday, the English-style brunch comes in two versions. For 70 francs: fruit juice, soft-boiled eggs with bacon or poached eggs Dijon style, a sweet or savory tart and tea or coffee. For 95 francs: fruit juice, apple pancakes with honey syrup or scones or toast with jam, soft-boiled eggs on smoked salmon or eggs Florentine, a pastry tray and coffee, tea or hot chocolate.

Toraya

1st arr. - 10, rue Saint-Florentin
42 60 13 00

Open 10 a.m.-7 p.m. Closed Sun. Cards: V, MC.

Once we step through the black door that bears the emblem of a tiger, we feel very far away from Paris. The black lacquer, orange velour and bamboo plants—along with the silence, the accents and the courtesy of the Japanese staff—are also transporting. You might, however, be a little disconcerted by the acrid taste of the green tea, which is served on a tray that is itself a work of art. Or by the pastries with their transcendant, poetic names: In spring you'll be offered the toyamazakura ("the cherry trees on the far mountain"), in summer the semi no ogawa ("the red fish") and in winter the matso no yuki ("snow-covered pines"). Each of these exotic delights (20 francs) bears a resemblance to its name. Strange, very strange, is the colorless agar-agar (gelatin substitute) topped with an aduki bean paste. The waiter may suggest a monaka (crunchy rice and aduki) or a yokan, which is made from agar-agar paste. The staff will probably tell you that Japanese pastry has something for all five senses: the pleasure of the sound of the name, the treat for the eyes, the pleasant contact of the red-bean paste with the tongue and teeth, and the pleasing sound of the rice crunching. There remains then only to define the pleasure of the taste. Well, it must be delicious—after all, Toraya has been the chosen supplier to the Emperor of Japan since 1789.

Verlet

1st arr. - 256, rue Saint-Honoré
42 60 67 39
Open noon-6:30 p.m. & coffee and tea sales 9 a.m.-7 p.m. Closed Sun. & Mon. Parking: Pyramides. No cards.

At Verlet, it isn't Champagne or the proximity of your beloved that goes to your head, but rather the delicious aromas of tea and coffee. Once inside the door and in the presence of sacks and sacks of both of these earthly delights, we lose all desires except to be seated and served a steaming cup of *something*. This is one of the best places in Paris for either tea or coffee. Seated on the old small chairs, in an all-wood decor dating from 1880 (including the original telephone and the old gas hookup), coffee devotees sip Jamaican, an excellent mocha or the house blend, Grand Pavois. For tea drinkers, there are more than 30 varieties, including a nicely perfumed Chinese tea called White Flowers and, of course, the famous Darjeeling, which seems particularly soft and subtle here. There are little Viennese-style pastries (17 francs) if you want a snack, and croque monsieurs (16.50 francs) and white-cheese and fruit compotes for a quick lunch.

WINE BARS

1929

11th arr. - 90 bis, rue de la Roquette
43 79 71 55
Open daily 11 a.m.-2 a.m. (Sun. 7 p.m.-2 a.m.). Parking: Pl. de la Bastille, Voltaire. Cards: V.

This bistro is now enough in fashion that we feel obliged to administer some well-deserved knocks. The wines are poorly selected, and though the people serving them are charming, they really know nothing about them. Otherwise—and that's a big otherwise for a wine bar—1929 has what it takes to be a pleasant spot. The clientele comprises starving artists mixed with other great communicators from the lofts in the neighborhood. The decor is neon and old zinc, the cooking is bistro-style, and the arrival of rock pianist Vincent "Gratounet" Ferniot is a spectacular coup for the house. It's rather close to Bastille (with its new hip scene) for our taste, and too far from the times its name celebrates.

L'Astrolabe

94130 Orly - Aérogare d'Orly-Ouest
46 87 16 16
Open daily 4:30 p.m.-10 p.m. Parking: Aérogare. Cards: V.

The wines here, you'll quickly discover, were not selected with any great originality. But there are also good open-faced sandwiches and a few hot plates to choose from. Morgon from Duboeuf, Gamay from Sauvignon, Cahors from the house of Rigal and Latour's version of Monthélie . . . the salesmen got here first, obviously. But then they're often here anyway, waiting for a plane. Now when will Charles de Gaulle airport at Roissy get a wine bistro? So far only Orly and Mérignac airports have acted on this good idea.

Bar du Caveau

1st arr. - 17, pl. Dauphine - 43 54 45 95
Open 8:30 a.m.-8 p.m. Closed Sat. & Sun. Parking: Pont-Neuf. No cards.

Lawyers, it seems, will always be lawyers. And lawyers can always be found at Bar du Caveau, pleading their cases over glasses of Bordeaux. In winter, when the interior of this well-heeled establishment gets a bit cramped, their verbal antics can wax tiresome. You may prefer sitting quietly with a Parisian daily, presented in the old reading-room style on a thin pole, or simply to enjoy a salad, an open-faced sandwich and a glass of one of the excellent Bordeaux selected by the management, which also runs the restaurant next door. In summer the tiny sidewalk terrace on the place Dauphine is a treat.

Bar du Sommelier (Intercontinental)

1st arr. - 3, rue de Castiglione - 42 60 37 80
Open daily 9 a.m.-2 a.m. Parking: Vendôme. Cards: V, AE, DC.

The bar of this soul-less hotel is trying to pass itself off as something more than it is by offering wines by the glass, with the traditional open-faced-sandwich menu to accompany them. Naturally, these carry the same intergalactic prices that govern everything else here:

140 francs for a plate of foie gras, 33 francs for a glass of simple Bordeaux. But the choice of wines is honest and reliable, from the proprietary Rully '80 to the Riesling. A word of warning to unaccompanied young women: Expect dark looks from the staff.

Bistrot de l'Auberge de France

1st arr. - 1, rue du Mont-Thabor
42 60 68 70
Open noon-6 p.m. Closed Sat. & Sun. Parking: Saint-Honoré, Vendôme. Cards: V, AE, MC.

The wine cellar of this restaurant near the place de la Concorde, with its neo-Gothic decor and sign announcing CHAMPAGNE OF PARIS, has been transformed into a wine bar. You can get a glass of good Cahors red wine for 7 francs to complement the country-style dish of the day (for example, lamb chops, for 45 francs).

Le Bistrot du Sommelier

8th arr. - 97, bd Haussmann - 42 65 24 85
Open noon-2:30 p.m. & 7:30 p.m.-10:30 p.m. Closed Sat. morning & Sun. Parking: Pl. Saint-Augustin. Cards: V, AE, DC.

Despite the name, this is hardly a bistro; it's more like a classic-style restaurant. But there's certainly a sommelier: Philippe Faure-Brac, chosen Best Sommelier of France in 1988. His own predilection is for wines from the Rhône valley, of which he is a native, and "Bordeaux from the other side of the river" (St. Emilion, Pomerol). But that hasn't kept him from stocking his cellars with the riches of France. At lunchtime the crowd of neighborhood regulars does not permit attentive tasting, but in the evening, the head of the establishment is available to assist in any number of fascinating research projects. You can, for example, enjoy a tour of little-known sweet wines starting from Gaillac through Australian Cabernet Sauvignon to white wines of Rully and late-harvest Alsatians. No concessions are made to accessibility or easy drinking: Here you'll find neither Sancerre nor Beaujolais nor Muscadet. It is a little expensive, and certainly very serious, but it is a required course for anyone majoring in Wine in Paris.

Blue Fox

8th arr. - Cité Berryer, 25, rue Royale
42 65 10 72
Open noon-3 p.m. & 7 p.m.-10:30 p.m. Closed Sat. evening & Sun. Parking: Madeleine. Cards: V, MC.

Steven Spurrier, known from New York to Bordeaux for his knowledge of wine, was the Blue Fox's original founder. (These days his own wine shop and "academy of wine" are just around the corner.) At first, it had everything going for it as a wine bar, including two nice dining rooms and a lovely terrrace for warm weather. But the Blue Fox nevertheless went down a hole; at our last visit, its salads were as overchilled as its wines, the incompetence of the service was exceeded only by its sloth, and the size of the checks was as stunning as the tables' lack of size. These dubious delights were being enjoyed by a snobby crowd and some down-and-outers who claimed there wasn't much choice in this neighborhood. Evidently Spurrier got tired of it and was crafty enough to sell.

Aux Bons Crus

1st arr. - 7, rue des Petits-Champs
42 60 06 45
Open 8 a.m.-10 p.m. Closed Sat. & Sun. Parking: Bourse. No cards.

This is actually a wine shop and a wine bar, with a few tables in back. The traditional wine-seller's apron serves as a waiter's uniform, and the daily wines available by the glass are posted on the wall. The prices are astonishingly low: A Bourgogne Aligoté white wine sells for 5 francs by the glass. And it's good, as are the Muscadet, the Sancerre and the many Côtes-du-Rhône representatives. The food runs to simple cold dishes made according to the founding edict of the establishment in 1905. It comes either on the plate (cold ham) or in the can (tuna à la catalane). The universal goes-with-everything accompaniment is the cold lentil salad (of course the lentils are cooked). The clientele is youngish—scholars working in the nearby Bibliothèque Nationale, actors and bank employees share the space nicely.

La Boutique des Vins

8th arr. - 31-33, rue de l'Arcade
42 65 27 27

Open noon-3 p.m. & 7 p.m.-midnight. Closed Sun. Parking: Madeleine, Malesherbes. Cards: V, AE, DC, MC.

Here in a quiet alley, we came upon a well-cared-for place, well suited for a clientele looking for a bit of calm in this bustling business neighborhood (it is also quite close to the Saint-Lazare train station and the big department stores). In other words, La Boutique des Vins is a perfect spot for a successful wine bar and simple restaurant. But we found the amateurish service and the inconsistent cooking impossible to overlook. This is one stop we're tired of making.

Le Chai de l'Abbaye

6th arr. - 6, rue de Buci - 43 26 68 26
Open daily 8 a.m.-5 a.m. (Sun. 10 a.m.-11 p.m.). Parking: Mazarine. No cards.

Having been refurbished, this corner café well known to the nighttime denizens of Saint-Germain has lost in atmosphere what it has gained in flash. The wine list is undeniably long and the by-the-glass service fairly inclusive, but nonetheless it is clear that imagination is not management's strong suit. *Business* is the business here. Still, it's always pleasant to stop for a glass of Vouvray (14 francs). In this expensive and overrun neighborhood, one tends to be less picky than usual.

La Cloche des Halles

1st arr. - 28, rue Coquillière - 42 36 93 89
Open 8 a.m.-9 p.m. (Sat. 9:30 a.m.-6 p.m.). Closed Sun. Parking: Les Halles. No cards.

The wooden clock is still there, a small replica of the bronze one that used to ring to signal the closing of the huge central markets. The bistro itself has gracefully survived the great changes in the area. Serge Lesage, who recently took over the reins, is scrupulously maintaining tradition. There are always several special dishes in addition to the excellent open-faced sandwiches and good wines bottled on the premises. At lunchtime, a bit of patience is in order; people stand three deep around the bar, a friendly mix of hipsters elbow-to-elbow

with police inspectors, notaries and pretty female shopkeepers. Fully refreshed, you'll have spent a few dozen francs at most.

Le Coude-Fou

4th arr. - 12, rue du Bourg-Tibourg
42 77 15 16

Open daily noon-4 p.m. & 6 p.m.-2 a.m. (Sun. 6 p.m.-2 a.m. only). Parking: Hôtel de Ville. Cards: V.

This place doesn't empty out until late, mostly because the customers feel so at home here. Conversations flow freely among the big and little tables. The cooking is simple and straightforward (blood pudding, poultry dishes and the like). If you prefer the bar to a table, the wines by the glass (from 7 francs) and the cold cut platters (35 francs) will keep you happy and speed you on your promenade through the Marais. The house usually offers about 30 wines, half of them by the glass. The Côtes-du-Rhône wines and those from the Loire are well chosen, and on occasion there are some nice little wines from the Savoie.

Au Duc de Richelieu

2nd arr. - 110, rue de Richelieu
42 96 38 38

Open 7 a.m.-5:30 a.m. Closed Aug. Parking: Bourse, Drouot. Cards: V.

Just about everybody gets over here sooner or later . . . it's open until 3 a.m., the simple Parisian decor is the real thing, and the food is good and filling. "Everybody" includes journalists, starving night owls and actors and, at lunch, bankers and people from the nearby headquarters of *Le Monde*. At the counter you can eat guillotines, open-faced ham sandwiches on delicious Poilane bread. As for wine, you have entered one of the temples of Beaujolais. The owner of the bar happens to also be a vineyard proprietor in the Beaujolais village of Fleury. But before ordering his wine, ask him if it is a propitious season for it—if the wine is still "working" (he is on his honor on this point), he will steer you toward a lovely Saint-Amour or a Morgon with a few years on it. You won't be disappointed.

L'Ecluse

1st arr. - rue Mondétour - 47 03 30 73
Open daily noon-2 a.m. Parking: Les Halles.
Cards: V. Other branches: see text below.

"Our clientele is trendy, aware, laid-back and chic. They drink top-shelf, sparingly, and they spend money, because that's their style." So says the boss of the group that owns—in conjunction with the Nicolas wine shops—this Paris-wide chain of wine bars. Started and made successful originally by Georges Bardawil and a reporter from *Paris-Match*, the basic formula remains unchanged. Bordeaux wines are served exclusively, ranging from a little Barsac (the junior neighbor of Sauternes) to a white Graves to the Grands Crus. L'Ecluse makes extensive use of the recent inert-gas replacement devices that allow an opened wine to be maintained in a perfect state for up to ten days. This allows for a top château by the glass (for 60 francs and up) to be offered each week. The food is prepared off-premises in a "laboratory," vacuum-packed and distributed to the six (soon to be nine) establishments throughout Paris: salad of cucumber and fromage blanc, foie gras, thin-sliced red meats, chocolate cake. This fare was a striking novelty when introduced ten years ago, but it hasn't changed since, except for the prices, whose rise has in turn given rise to a reputation (as yet undeserved) as a glitter trap. But the ingredients are still of top quality, down to the bread and condiments, and selected with evident care. The red-velour seating is comfortable, and the clientele pleasant. Our minor complaints include lax service (at the Madeleine branch) and a certain chilliness (at the Opéra branch). Our favorite remains the original address, the tiny, beautifully redone bistro near Saint-Michel. Other branches: 15, quai des Grands-Augustins, sixth arrondissement, 46 33 58 74; 15, place de la Madeleine, eighth arrondissement, 42 65 34 69, parking, Madeleine; 64, rue François-Ier, eighth arrondissement, 47 20 77 09, parking, Georges-V; 4, rue Halévy ou Hachette Multistore, ninth arrondissement, 47 42 62 33, parking, Opéra.

A L'Etoile du Berger

1st arr. - 7, rue Berger - 42 33 16 87
Open 11:30 a.m.-2 a.m. Closed Tues. evening.
Parking: Forum des Halles. No cards.

The new owners, into whose hands this well-known bistro has passed directly from the master's, haven't done anything to affect the enjoyable ambience. And there's still Beaujolais (16 francs) and those good old open-faced sandwiches.

Au Franc Pinot

4th arr. - 1, quai de Bourbon - 43 29 46 98
Open 11:30 a.m.-2:30 p.m. & 6:30 p.m.-11:30 p.m. Closed Sun. & Mon. Parking: Hôtel de Ville. No cards.

This is one of the oldest taverns on the banks of the Seine, and you couldn't ask for a more picturesque spot. The lower levels (the cellars purportedly descend to river-bottom level) are reserved for dining, but the ground-floor entry, with its centuries-old walls, is a comfortable wine bar. Loire wines figure prominently, but the selection of them veers very little from the standard array available in other such establishments. More interesting is the choice of brandies and Armagnacs, not to mention the old plum brandy from Périgord. The service is charming, and the open-faced sandwiches at the bar delicious. Overall the place may be rather stodgy, and pricey, but this is, after all, the Ile-Saint-Louis, and it's been here for 350 years.

Ma Bourgogne

8th arr. - 133, bd Haussmann - 45 63 50 61
Open 7 a.m.-8:30 p.m. Closed Sat., Sun. & July or Aug. Parking: Haussmann-Berri. Cards: V.

Ma Bourgogne is the meeting spot for the Rabelais Academy and the panel of judges that awards the "Best Pot of Beaujolais" prize. In other words, Beaujolais reigns supreme here, bought in Beaujolais and bottled by the owner, Burgundy-born Louis Prin. Since Prin also serves some of the best charcuterie of his region (such as a melt-in-the-mouth ham) and good home-cooking (veal stew), his is always a full house. If you go there for lunch, be sure to take the opportunity to taste his red Burgundies—the name of the place demands it. His Hautes-Côtes-de-Beaune possesses a rare finesse. And the prices, considering the quality and the nieghborhood, remain affordable.

Jacques Mélac

11th arr. - 42, rue Léon-Frot - 43 70 59 27
Open 9 a.m.-7:30 p.m. (Tues. & Thurs. until later). Closed Sun., Mon. & July 15-Aug. 15. Parking: bd Voltaire. No cards.

The proud father of a new vineyard, Jacques Mélac is brimming with joy. Just thinking about his first vintage on his new property in Lirac is enough to set his mustache quivering and his ever-present suspenders snapping. Over the years he has kept in training by vinifying the harvest from his vines against the wall here, making the Château Charonne that which he sells at auction for the price of Lafite. In his bistro, one of the most successful ones around, you can choose between Chinon, Cahors, Chignin or Coteaux-du-Layon. You'll do well to avoid the Chinon white, rare but overdone, and the Saint-Joseph, which the staff has a tendency to push. Yes, it's a little crowded and rambunctious, and the staff can be condescending, but it's impossible to resist the temptation now and then to pass an afternoon or an evening in this wine temple. It's worth the trek even for the simple but excellent fare—the blue-cheese omelet, the tripe from Aveyron or the plate of charcuterie from Rouergue. Reservations are not accepted, so either come early or come prepared to wait. But waiting is no hardship with all the nice little white wines there are to sample.

Le Millésime

6th arr. - 7, rue Lobineau - 46 34 22 15
Open 10 a.m.-1 a.m. Closed Sun. & holidays. Parking: Saint-Sulpice. No cards.

Take this as an SOS sent out to all lovers of good wine and friendly bistros: You owe it to yourself to discover the *zinc* (bar) of Chico Selce, whose white mustache is wilting from the lack of business. His efforts deserve more; he is turning himself inside out to bottle and sell wonderful local wines as well as rare appelations from all over, and he sells them at prices that know no competition. And for Selce, "from all over" means going as far as Turkey or Chile. Meanwhile his array of charcuterie and preserved goodies, showing the same fine care, is equally peerless in the wine-bar field. What other wine list offers a large glass of Coteaux-du-Languedoc La Clappe for 12 francs, or some other equally interesting wine for a similar price. Success surely ought to have sought Selce out by now, but only a few barflies seem to know about this address tucked behind the former Saint-Germain open market. We suggest you take by storm this citadel of wine-loving Paris and give the pretty murals the viewing that such an establishment merits.

Le Petit Bacchus

6th arr. - 13, rue du Cherche-Midi
45 44 01 07
Open 10 a.m.-8 p.m. (Mon. 10 a.m.-1 p.m. & 3 p.m.-8 p.m.). Closed Sun., Mon. & Aug. 1-15. Parking: Bon Marché, Saint-Germain. Cards: V, MC.

This wine shop/bistro has rejoined the empire that Englishman Steven Spurrier, the head of all non-French wine experts in Paris, is reassembling. A simple formula is at work here: some stools, plates of charcuterie, wines by the glass chosen from Spurrier's vast cellars, and excellent cheeses. And, of course, there's the obligatory, delicious Poilane bread (and you know it's fresh—Poilane himself is headquartered just across the street).

Petrissans

17th arr. - 30 bis, av. Niel - 42 27 52 03
Open 11:30 a.m.-9 p.m. Closed Sat., Sun. & Aug. Parking: Ternes. Cards: V, AE.

This wine shop, one of the most prestigious in Paris, will soon be 100 years old. Down through the years, a cavalcade of literati and bon vivants have drunk the good wines and Champagnes of Martin Petrissans and his descendants. Currently, Christine, the great-granddaughter, and her husband, a former lawyer who left the bar (so to speak), run the establishment. Among the enormous number of choices: By the glass the selections range from a 1986 Graves from Borie-Manoux to a Châteauneuf-du-Pape 1979 from Vidal-Fleury, not to mention the exclusive Champagne from Chigny-les-Roses, ranked Premier Cru (vintage 1983). The dining room, 26 seats and a bar, has an attractive English atmosphere. There are lovely plates of charcuterie served at all hours, and at lunchtime a hot special of excellent quality (duck breast in honey, stewed fatted fowl), in addition to cold salmon and more. It's all classic, refined and, well, select.

La Plume

5th arr. - 151 bis, rue Saint-Jacques
43 26 12 10
Open noon-2:30 p.m. & 7 p.m.-10:30 p.m. (Fri. & Sat. until 11 p.m.). Closed Sun. Parking: Soufflot. Cards: V.

A stone's throw from the Sorbonne, this chic but cheap eatery that blends Lebanese (kafta) and French (poultry) influences is transforming itself into a wine bar as well. The wine cellar is well stocked and demonstrates some originality. A body can eat here, and very well at that, for 120 francs, including a half bottle of Loire or Beaujolais wine.

Puzzle

6th arr. - 13, rue Princesse - 46 34 55 80
Open noon-2 a.m. Closed Sun. Parking: Saint-Sulpice. Cards: V.

At this annex to Castel, we're growing kind of tired of the modern, metallic interior, all in the fashionably obligatory gray. But the big shots of the area who come by here toward 1 in the afternoon for a glass tend to warm up the place. The service staff is extremely cordial, and the cooking light and well done: filets of poultry and beef bourguignon, among them. The wine list grants particular attention to the region down toward the Rhône Valley and is served by the glass upon request. Figure on 200 francs for a meal.

Le Rallye (Bernard Péret)

14th arr. - 6, rue Daguerre - 43 22 57 05
Open 9:30 a.m.-8:30 p.m. (Sat. 8 a.m.-7 p.m.). Closed Sun., Mon. & Aug. Parking: Saint-Jacques. Cards: V, MC.

With all the little food shops along this street, we always work up quite a hunger and thirst. But Bernard Péret is here to remedy that, as were his father and grandfather, with mountain sausage and a fine glass of Morgon. The wine cellar is immense—the shop side sells wine right out onto the sidewalk—but the bistro is tiny, six tables and a *zinc* (bar counter), offering about fifteen wines by the glass. English connoisseurs in Paris, who consider the Chenas and the Beaujolais nouveau the best available, can often be found here toward the end of the business day, elbow-to-elbow with the butcher and the baker.

La Royale

14th arr. - 80, rue de l'Amiral-Mouchez 45 88 38 09
Open 7:30 a.m.-8:30 p.m. (Sat. 7 a.m.-5 p.m.). Closed Sun. & Aug. No cards.

A gentleman from the Auvergne was conquered by a young woman from the Loire, and by her region as well. One of the results of the marriage is one of the best bistros in Paris, located in this unlikely neighborhood behind the Gare Montparnasse. The owner offers a Chinon Ligré from his own vineyard, a wine

that requires a few years in order to show well—but then what a show! Or you can sample a very good Saumur-Champigny that has not undergone the same rise in price and drop in quality that this trademark has widely suffered. And there are always the Vouvrays, the Saumurs, even Beaujolais. At noon the tables fill with sales reps and other connoisseurs drawn by Yvette's stews and hearty fare: veal chops with cauliflower au gratin, beef bourgignon with fresh noodles and much more.

Le Rubis

1st arr. - 10, rue du Marché-Saint-Honoré 42 61 03 34
Open 7 a.m.-10 p.m. Closed Sat. & Sun. No cards.

It was a long time ago, at this very spot, that old Gouin first raised the banner for good wine and excellent cold cuts. In his honor, the regulars, from firemen to fashion plates, continue to call the place by its old name, Chez Léon. After all, the menu has never veered off course, and the selection of wines is as good as ever, though there are some who say they notice some weaknesses in the Beaujolais. On the other hand, the white Côtes-du-Rhône and the wines from the Loire remain at the peaks of their respective categories. The food includes a daily hot special (andouillette, for example, at 36 francs) in addition to the customary array of open-faced sandwiches and cheese and cold-cut platters. The real problem of the place is its size; it's just too small to handle all the devotees who continually fill the place up. In the summer, after having done elbow-to-elbow combat to get a glass of wine and a plate of food from the bar, you can take them out onto the sidewalk, where upended wine casks serve honorably as tables.

Le Sancerre

7th arr. - 22, av. Rapp - 45 51 75 91
Open 8 a.m.-9 p.m. (Sat. until 5 p.m.). Closed Sat., Sun. & Aug. Parking: Champ-de-Mars. No cards.

Reserve a table if you want to eat lunch here; in a fancy neighborhood where good bistros are rare, this one fills up fast. And it doesn't lack for personality, especially that of the owners, the Mellot family. They also own the Domaine de la Moussière vineyard in Sancerre, and they sell their wine here direct from the sheds. Andouillette (sausage) and crottin de Chavignol (small, round goat cheeses) are the rule here, but then they always have been, even before that sort of thing was in style. And don't be put off by the slick window dressing out front—Le Sancerre is very comfortable.

Tabac de l'Institut

6th arr. - 21, rue de Seine - 43 26 98 75
Open 9:15 a.m.-7 p.m. Closed Sun. & Aug. Parking: Mazarine. No cards.

From the outside, it's just another news-and-tobacco shop with a long row of tables in the back. But upon entering, you find yourself in a dark, wood-paneled, quiet bar, where you can taste some excellent wines: Macon-Viré, various Beaujolais and Sauvignons and so forth. This is a surprising address—right in the middle of the School of Fine Arts neighborhood—for an intimate conversation.

La Tartine

4th arr. - 24, rue de Rivoli - 42 72 76 85
Open 8 a.m.-10 p.m. (Wed. noon-10 p.m.). Closed Tues. & 3 wks. in Aug. Parking: Hôtel de Ville. No cards.

It's easy to picture Trotsky here, seated at the tables in the back or with his elbows up on the big marble bar, in a debate with his cronies over a glass of red. His followers, and his opponents, still come to listen for his echoes and to mix with the varied crowd on this end of the rue de Rivoli in the Marais. The wine selection is wonderful—about 50 choices by the glass, ranging from Côtes-du-Rhône to the Loire and finally to Bordeaux. There are a few good glasses of Burgundy as well, but undoubtedly the center of gravity here is in Bordeaux. In any case, all can be tasted for 10 francs or less. At noon you'll find a daily hot special, and, of course, open-faced sandwiches (tartines) are served at any time.

Taverne Henri-IV

1st arr. - 13, pl. du Pont-Neuf
43 54 27 90
Open 11:30 a.m.-9:30 p.m. Closed Sat., Sun. & Aug. 15-Sept. 15. Parking: Dauphine. No cards.

For more than 30 years the fruits of Beaujolais, Montlouis and the greater and lesser Bordeaux vineyards have been flowing through this old so-called tobacco counter. It continues to fill with advertising types, travel agents, publishers, journalists, lawyers and so forth, not to mention the tourists and the boatloads fresh from excursions on the Seine. Behind the counter—or seated with one of the regulars—you'll find the owner, Robert Cointepas, loud and ruddy-faced, and his wife, the daughter of a wine maker. Cointepas knows how to buy wine even better than he knows how to sell it. Selecting his wines in October in the vineyards, he knows the art of presenting them in top shape all year, including the Beaujolais in its traditional pint "pot." The standard open-faced sandwiches are of good quality, and fine charcuterie and wines are available for takeout.

Le Val d'Or

8th arr. - 28, av. Franklin-Roosevelt
43 59 95 81
Open 7:30 a.m.-9 p.m. (Sat. 11 a.m.-6 p.m.). Closed Sun. & 1 wk. Christmas-New Year's. Parking: Rond-Point des Champs-Elysées. Cards: V.

Géraud (not Gérard, thank you) Rongier, who hails from deep in the Auvergne, is one of the grand masters of the wine profession. He trains good wine stewards and some excellent colleagues, such as Serge Lesage, who now runs Rongier's former establishment, La Cloche des Halles. Several years ago Rongier took over this unknown little bistro near Saint-Philippe-du-Roule, and with his personal renown, it has attracted a wide following. At midday, it's filled with advertising execs, civil servants from the Ministry of the Interior, fashion-industry women and television folk from the nearby TV business centers. One of the old Gallic guard of the wine profession, Rongier has harsh words for many of the upstarts who are invading it. And it's hard to argue with him when you taste his selection from the Loire, his Côte-de-Brouilly, his Mâcon-Clessé, his Bordeaux or his Aloxe-Corton. All of these are offered at highly competitive prices, rarely exceeding 10 francs for a glass. As for more solid sustenance, Rongier himself prepares ham cooked on the bone, rillettes and cheeses that he ages himself. He is a model of his kind. The dining experience is a classic one (a little too much so, perhaps), with, of course, a superb wine list.

Verre à Soif

4th arr. - 2, rue des Hospitalières-Saint-Gervais - 48 04 57 04

Open daily 6 p.m.-midnight. Parking: Hôtel de Ville. Cards: V, MC.

It isn't easy to find this little street off the rue des Rosiers near rue Vieille du Temple, but if you study your map of the Marais for a moment, you won't regret the effort. This is a wonderful, friendly bistro. Along with French, Spanish is spoken here, featuring a Latin American accent. And you'll discover good wines from Chile, Romania and California, guided if you wish by the ready help of the owners. The food is plentiful and made from quality ingredients: salmon, hot sausages and so forth. We have a weakness for the spinach empañadas, particularly if washed down by the Chilean Concha y Toro, a superb Cabernet Sauvignon from 1983. Figure about 150 francs for a fine meal that includes, for dessert, a luscious tarte tatin.

Au Vin des Rues

14th arr. - 21, rue Boulard - 43 22 19 78

Open 9:30 a.m.-10 p.m. (Wed. & Fri. until later). Closed Sun. morning & Mon. No cards.

Jean Chanrion sold the Moulin de la Boulange to open this place. Combined with the recent takeover of the nearby Cagouille by another fine specialist, and the established presence of Bernard Peret, the opening virtually transforms the neighborhood into a wine-lover's crossroads. The atmosphere of this Everyman's bistro is only bolstered by the qualities we expect of Chanrion: the excellent choice of Beaujolais and Macon and the daily hot-food specials made from the best ingredients. Ah, the baked andouillette with a little white wine. . . .

Willi's Wine Bar

1st arr. - 13, rue des Petits-Champs

42 61 05 09

Open noon-11 p.m. Closed Sat. & Sun. Cards: V, MC.

The Englishman who founded this establishment is probably the best connoisseur in Paris (among the English, that is) of wines from the Côtes-du-Rhône, which, of course, figure prominently on his wine list both in quality and number. We never grow weary of trying new ones, red and white. At the bar, Williamson has a habit of offering discoveries from other regions, such as Italian Piedmont selections, wines from Madeira or sweet wines from all over. The marble and blond-wood dining room is comfortable and frequented by an unobjectionable crowd: bankers and art buffs at noon, tony regulars at night. You can figure 200 francs for dinner, including the pleasant, genteel service.

NIGHTLIFE

CABARETS

Alcazar

6th arr. - 62, rue Mazarine - 43 29 02 20
Open 8 p.m.-2 a.m. Closed Sun. & July 17-end Aug. Parking: valet. Cards: V, AE, DC, MC. Dinner show: 8 p.m., later show: 10 p.m. Cover: 350F (show & Champagne), 510F (show, wine & dinner).

It is now smooth sailing for this once-leaky vessel of the night. Newcomer Dominique Comte is at the helm of the twenty-year-old establishment and is determined to set sail toward new successes. "Either that or I quit," she threatens. There is a smooth-talking emcee, fleet-footed dancers and a young, with-it service team.

Crazy Horse Saloon

8th arr. - 12, av. George-V - 47 23 32 32
Open daily 8:45 p.m.-2 a.m. Parking: Georges-V and valet. Cards: V, AE, DC, MC. 2 shows: 9 p.m. & 11:35 p.m.; Fri. & Sat. 3 shows: 8 p.m., 10:30 p.m. & 12:50 a.m. Cover: show & 2 drinks 350F, 420F, 470F (depending on seating); bar with 2 drinks 190F (no reservation).

Here ye, here ye, the Crazy Horse has had a facelift! Come and see its newly decorated interior, complete with sophisticated laser show. Chic women dispose of their skimpy attire with barely a shrug and a wink. This is strictly soft-core striptease.

Folies Bergères

9th arr. - 32, rue Richer - 42 46 77 11
Open 9 p.m.-11:30 p.m. Closed Mon. Parking: Lafayette. Cards: V, MC. Show: 9 p.m. Cover: 72-361F.

It's worth a trip just to see the great hall—but sadly, the show is a pale rendition of its former self. This oldest and once most prestigious of dinner theaters is serving up fare that would be considered unsophisticated in Kalamazoo. In an attempt to revive the follies, the management has opened a bar and serves up drink and dancing in the hall.

Le Lido

8th arr. - 116, av. des Champs-Elysées
45 63 11 61
Open daily 8 p.m.-2 a.m. Parking: Georges-V. Cards: V, AE, DC, MC. 2 shows: 10 p.m. & midnight. Cover: 365F (show & Champagne), 530F (dinner, show & Champagne).

"The greatest show on earth" is pretty tame these days but still a lot of fun. Large girls parade with military precision in various stages of undress. The technical tricks are heart-stopping; be ready for lots of feathers and furs and some of the most astonishing sights in Paris.

Le Moulin Rouge

18th arr. - 82, bd de Clichy - 46 06 00 19
Open daily 7:30 p.m.-2 a.m. Parking: pl. de Clichy, Hôtel Ibis. Cards: V, AE, DC. Dinner show: 8 p.m.; later shows: 10 p.m. & midnight. Cover: 365F (show & Champagne), 530F (dinner, show & Champagne).

You've all seen the movie; now you can see the real, incomparable thing. Tradition is everything here, and the Doris girls, the famous cancan dancers, scrupulously respect it. Twice a night, seven nights a week, they energetically flash their covered bottoms; only bosoms may be bared. Debbie de Coudreaux leads the revue, and songs are French. This is old-fashioned, unchanged, *gai Paris*. Thank heavens!

Le Paradis Latin

5th arr. - 28, rue du Cardinal-Lemoine
43 25 28 28
Open 8:30 p.m.-12:30 a.m. Closed Tues. Parking: valet. Cards: V, AE, DC, MC. Dinner show: 8 p.m.; later show: 10 p.m. Cover: 365F (show & Champagne), 530F (dinner, show & wine or Champagne).

What can be said about a sticky-sweet show led by dancers who look like a nice bunch of sorority sisters? That this place is obviously part of the European tour package, judging by the clients? Some pluses: Ursuline Kaison, a singer from Chicago, fun-loving waiters and Mister Sergio, the house emcee who could liven up a funeral. Nevertheless, this magnificent theater built by Gustave Eiffel deserves better.

DISCOS

Les Bains

3rd arr. - 7, rue du Bourg-l'Abbé
48 87 01 80
Open midnight-dawn. Cards: V, AE. Restaurant. Cover: 120F.

To date, many night birds have perched here to dry their wings and wet their beaks. Under new management, Les Bains (once known as Les Bains-Douches) has lost its showers and gained some lovely bathers. Unknowns from the worlds of show biz, advertising and fashion rub shoulders with the lofty likes of Roman Polanski and Jack Nicholson. In order to get through the door, jealously guarded by Marylin, it helps to have a Siren on your arm, to be naturally crazy and wildly elegant, to be an habitué or to have a card. This is a steamy jungle teeming with contented wild things.

Le Balajo

11th arr. - 9, rue Lappe - 47 00 07 79
Open 11 a.m.-5 a.m. Closed Tues. & Wed. Cards: V. Cover: 100F.

Keep boredom at bay by taking a twirl at the Balajo. Cohosts Serge and Albert have made this a popular landmark for ballroom dancing and nightclubbing in the Bastille area. Tables nestle neatly around a well-waxed dance floor and the oh-so-kitsch decor sends a shiver down the spines of nostalgia lovers. Real and not-so-real Parisians sway around the long bar—which can be difficult to reach at prime time—to marvelous rhythms. Monday mixes current music with more traditional tunes. Thursday is dedicated to swing, mambo, cha-cha, accordion bands, soul and occasionally pop (and admission for women is free).

Le Bus Palladium

9th arr. - 6, rue Fontaine - 48 74 54 99
Open 11:30 p.m.-dawn. Closed Mon. No cards. Cover: 110F.

Remember when men wore long hair and bell-bottoms? That's about when the old Bus started its journey. There's still the same doorman, and he's still letting lucky passengers board the Bus with grace. Show-biz types, the "in" crowd and arrogant dudes hole up here with pretty girls. A carefully studied cool look sets the tone. It's a little down at the heels, but Josy, who's been in charge for the last twenty years, drives this bus with a taxi driver's skill.

La Locomotive

18th arr. - 90, bd de Clichy - 42 57 37 37
Open 11 p.m.-6:30 a.m. (Sat. & Sun. until 7 a.m.). Closed Mon. Cards: V. Cover: 50F, Fri. & Sat. 90F (free for women on Sun.).

Night lovers adore the Locomotive. It's so big you can get lost in it, and it draws the rockers like moths to a flame. The menu is unchanged since the great days of rock 'n' roll . . . in the '60s this was the land of the Who, the Rolling Stones, the Kinks and many others. Today the Locomotive is back on track and running around three floors. Top floor: American bar, billiards, video screen. Going down, ground floor: a bar stretching into infinity and a huge dance floor with electronic games at one end. Going down, down, to the basement: the Moulin Rouge's old boilers are on show to the curious. From 1 a.m. good rock music prevails. The deejay knows his stuff. On Sunday, women rockers get in free.

La Nouvelle Eve

9th arr. - 25, rue Fontaine
45 26 76 32, 48 74 69 25
Open Fri. 11 p.m.-5 a.m. (Nov.-end April 12:30 p.m.-5 a.m.). Closed July & Aug. Parking: rue Mansart. Cards: V, AE, DC. Cover: 100F.

Friday night is yuppie night at La Nouvelle Eve. This is where moneyed youth find refuge from the more garish nightspots, where they can dance *le rock* and the mamba. This Pigalle nightclub, which resembles a cream-topped Viennese pastry, is a high temple of kitsch.

To discover more hoofers' hot spots, see "Latin Clubs" and "Private Clubs" later in this chapter.

Le Palace

9th arr. - 8, rue du Faubourg-Montmartre
42 46 10 87

Open 11 p.m.-dawn. Cards: V, AE. Cover: 120F, weekdays before midnight 65F.

Since the departure of the revolutionary and elegant Fabrice Emaer, the old theater of the Faubourg-Montmartre has fallen into legend. Life at the Palace is not what it was, even though a few luminaries still pop in for a late-night drink at the bar. Let's hope the new management will be able to pump new blood into old veins.

Studio A

8th arr. - 49-51, rue de Ponthieu
42 25 12 13

Open 11 p.m.-dawn. Closed Sun., Mon. & Tues. Cards: V. Cover: 90F.

Since its inception in spring 1987, Studio A has made something of a splash. The surprise skits: singers, dancers and strippers rarely fail to be entertaining, and the club is a fantastic melting pot of creatures of the night, with some spillage from Régine's next door. Invention, derision, some kindness and a true musical patchwork. It's quite a mix!

JAZZ CLUBS

Caveau de la Huchette

5th arr. - 5, rue de la Huchette
43 26 65 05

Open 9:30 p.m.-2 a.m. (Fri. until 3 a.m. & Sat. until 4 a.m.). No cards. Cover: 45F, Fri. & Sat. 55F, drinks from 15F.

This is a true temple of jazz, situated in a cellar in the Latin Quarter. There is an orchestra, smoke, young tourists, eternal students and a few veteran dancers with a real sense of rhythm for bebop and slow dance. Whether you're bent on seduction or simply in search of nostalgia, Huchette has the right aura. Enough, one hopes, in this postbicentennial of the French Revolution, to forget that under Danton and Robespierre, this underground cellar once served as a tribunal where traitors were sentenced to death.

Jazz Club Lionel Hampton

17th arr. - 81, bd Gouvion-Saint-Cyr
47 58 12 30

Open 10 p.m.-2 a.m. Closed Sun. Cards: V, AE, DC, MC. Cover: 110F.

Lots of jazz and pop greats have passed through here, including Fats Domino, Monty Alexander, John Hendrix, the Come Busy orchestra. Sunday brunch features music by the likes of Claude Bolling and his orchestra, and every night from 6 p.m. to 10 p.m., jazz pianist Danny Revel livens up the eats and drinks.

Le Montana

6th arr. - 28, rue Saint-Benoît - 45 48 93 08
Open 6:30 p.m.-5 a.m. Closed Sun. No cards. Cover: 80F.

Le Montana, founded in the golden age of jazz at Saint-Germain-des-Prés, is a well-known address for jazz lovers. Rotating groups and players include Stardust, Brazilian-born Emmanuelle Le Prince and modern jazz pianist René Urtreger, who was once a permanent fixture but now takes his turn along with the rest. The live music stops at 2 a.m., but you can linger into the dawn.

New Morning

10th arr. - 7-9, rue des Petites-Ecuries
45 23 51 41

Open 9 p.m.-1:30 a.m. No cards. Concert: 9:30 p.m. Cover: 110F.

A great jazz location, New Morning features such prominent musicians as Pharaoh Sanders, Gary Burton, Chet Baker, Lionel Hampton and Archie Shepp. The club's 400-seat auditorium makes for surprisingly comfortable seating. You won't find much better in Paris.

Le Petit Journal Montparnasse

14th arr. - 80, av. du Maine - 43 21 56 70
Open 9 p.m.-2 a.m. Closed Sun. & Mon. Cards: V. Cover: 80F.

Le Petit Journal Montparnasse features jazz musicians Manu di Bango and Guy Marchand, among others. Its sister establishment at 71, boulevard Saint-Michel, also features the Claude Bolling trio, saxophonist Benny Waters and plenty more. Both these clubs have constantly rotating players and offer a good, solid selection of contemporary and classical jazz.

LATIN CLUBS

La Chapelle des Lombards
11th arr. - 19, rue de Lappe - 43 57 24 24
Open 10:30 p.m.-5 a.m. Closed Sun., Mon. & Tues. Cards: V. Cover: 70F, Fri. & Sat. 80F; extra drink from 40F.

This is the land of rum punch, Latino music, the samba and the tropics. It is here that sunshine breaks through gray Paris skies. The beat is hot, real hot. Come mingle with the reggae crowd—they're onto a real good thing, and they know it.

L'Escale
6th arr. - 5, rue Monsieur-Le-Prince
43 54 63 47
Open 11 p.m.-4 a.m. No cards. Cover: 60-85F.

Every night is fiesta night at L'Escale, where Paris's South American colony congregates. Latino music is in and is drawing a younger generation to join ranks with exiles and other nostalgia seekers who favor country songs and folklore. There is a tiny stage where groups play their respective country's music. Everything's included (even the bossa nova), and there's absolutely no favoritism involved. Since 1964, the Los Muchucambos group has been a favorite in this offbeat cellar. Disco almost put the place out of business, but it has most definitely bounced back!

Le Tango
3rd arr. - 13, rue au Maire - 42 72 17 78
Open 11 p.m.-dawn (Sun. 10 p.m.-dawn). Closed Mon. & Tues. No cards. Cover: 40-70F.

Thanks to Serge Kruger, Afro-Latin music is back, alive and well, on Wednesday to Friday in this old dance hall. Black and white members of the Paris African scene flock here to warm their hearts to sounds of the beguine, the calypso and the salsa. Rich or poor, the effect on the dance floor is the same. If you're the type who hates nightclubs, empty noise, fashion and hit parades but likes unforeseen encounters and the cha-cha, let yourself go for one last tango in Paris.

Les Trottoirs de Buenos Aires
1st arr. - 37, rue des Lombards
42 33 58 37
Open 10:30 a.m.-1 a.m. Closed Mon. Parking: Les Halles. Cards: AE. 2 shows: 8:30 p.m. & 10:30 p.m. Afternoon tango lessons. Cover: 90F, extra drink from 25F.

Itinerant musicians have brought back the one-and-only true Milagra. Real tango lovers come to this concert-café to listen to passionate and plaintive notes borne out of exile, and amateurs come here also to drink.

PRIVATE CLUBS

Castel-Princesse
6th arr. - 15, rue Princesse - 43 26 90 22
Open 9 p.m.-dawn. Closed Sun. Parking: Saint-Sulpice. Cards: V, AE, DC. 2 restaurants. Cover: drinks 65-120F.

But for the rare exception, this is strictly members-only. The Castel gang numbers 3,000 and constitutes a private community of honored members, diplomats (always impressive), overseas residents and affiliated members who belong to another exclusive club. Life members pay through the nose to be set apart from the night's vulgar rabble. To join this late-night coterie, you need to have two sponsors, a file on your life history, 3,000 francs (to cover the application) and an additional 1,800 francs (annual fee). Only 50 new members are admitted per year. Now, if you are still interested, good luck!

Keur Samba

8th arr. - 79, rue de La Boétie - 43 59 03 10
Open midnight-dawn. Cards: V, AE. Cover: drinks 120F.

Le Keur takes off when many are just beginning to think about going to sleep. Slow nights go on until 7 or 8 in the morning, but some nights go on until 11 . . . tomorrow. This establishment is a melting pot of races and music. You're met at the door by a lion that lights up and N'Diaye Kane, who watches over her little universe. The African jet set, fashion models, happy-go-lucky youth and business sorts all share whisky and a table. By 3 in the morning, diners give way to predators of the night. Keur Samba is different and alluring.

Régine's

8th arr. - 49, rue de Ponthieu - 43 59 21 60
Open 10 p.m.-dawn. Cards: V, AE, DC. Restaurant. Cover: drinks 140F.

The envious (those who get turned away at the door) bad-mouth it. Régine's friends, the silk-tie-and-satin-culottes brigade, ignore the critics and continue to spend large sums of money with total insouciance. As for Régine, she's done the honorable thing and joined the crusade against drugs. And she now owns one of Paris's venerable culinary temples, Ledoyen. Innovations are in the offing—keep an eye on this place.

Olivia Valère

8th arr. - 40, rue du Colisée - 42 25 11 68
Open 10 p.m.-dawn. Cards: V, AE, DC, MC. Restaurant. Cover: drinks 140F.

Thanks to lots of panache and sleepless nights, Olivia Valère has launched her club up into the lofty ranks of hot Parisian nightspots. There is a piano bar for intimacy, a discreet and comfy restaurant and a disco club for the energetic. The question now: Is Olivia Valère really the reigning queen of the night? It's not an easy choice. Nightclubbers are quite demanding, after all. What is essential is to be seen . . . and Olivia's club excels at that, in its own inimitable way.

SHOPS

ANTIQUES

ANTIQUES CENTERS

La "Nouvelle" Cour aux Antiquaires
8th arr. - 54, rue du Faubourg-Saint-Honoré - 47 42 43 99
Open 10:30 a.m.-6:30 p.m. Closed Sun., Mon. & July 20-Sept. 5. Parking: Madeleine, Concorde. Cards: V, AE.

Aspects of the art and antiques market are brought together in these little, highly polished boutiques. Eighteen shops combine to offer inlaid furniture of the seventeenth through nineteenth centuries, paintings, engravings, ceramics, jewelry and quality knick-knacks for a refined clientele.

Le Louvre des Antiquaires
1st arr. - 2, pl. du Palais-Royal
42 97 27 00
Open 11 a.m.-7 p.m. Closed Mon. Parking: Louvre. No cards.

Le Louvre des Antiquaires, a marketplace for objets d'art, is the greatest success of its kind in France and probably the world. The former Magasins du Louvre department store has been beautifully redone and now houses some 250 dealers on three levels. These merchants are the most select, professional and scrupulous in the trade, if not the most famous. There isn't a single piece offered for sale whose authenticity and quality is not absolutely assured. Of course, the prices reflect this. Everything is represented—from art deco objects to eighteenth-Century furniture, from nineteenth-century minor masters to ship models, from old porcelain to rare stamps and from bronzes of animals to lead soldiers. In addition, Le Louvre des Antiquaires provides a delivery service, a club, exhibition halls and bars. Its annual exhibitions are mounted around selected themes on the second floor.

Village Saint-Paul
4th arr.
Closed Tues. & Wed. Parking: Cité des Arts. No cards.

A new area of antiques dealers was inaugurated between the rue Saint-Paul and the rue Charlemagne about ten years ago. Starting out

with 60 stores (several dozen others have since opened for business), the sector stocks eighteenth-century and Empire furniture and objects from the 1900–1930 period.

FRENCH ANTIQUES

ART NOUVEAU, ART DECO & 1930s

Maria de Beyrie
6th arr. - 23, rue de Seine - 43 25 76 15
Open 10:30 a.m.-1 p.m. & 2 p.m.-7 p.m. (Mon. 2 p.m.-7 p.m.). Closed Sun. Parking: Saint-Germain. No cards.

Lovely items from the turn of the century can, as always, be found in this shop, as well as the great names from the years 1925–1930: Legrain, Rousseau, Printz, Ruhlmann and others. And that is not to mention the architect-designed furniture, particularly that made of metal, from 1925 to 1950. You will also find the creations of the union of modern artists, run by René Herbst with Le Corbusier, Chareau, Mallet-Stevens, Charlotte Periand, Eileen Gray and others to whom we owe the foundation of the contemporary arts. There is a palpable nineteenth-century charm to this store, particularly in its renewed interest in Romanticism.

Denis Bosselet
6th arr. - 34, rue de Seine - 43 26 29 26
Open 11 a.m.-1 p.m. & 2 p.m.-7 p.m. Closed Sun., Mon. & Aug. 1-Sept. 15. Parking: Mazarine. Cards: V, AE.

The window of this shop is a striking display, in strong colors, of the work of Italian artists of the '50s who broke with tradition and created an entirely new approach to design. Denis Bosselet opened this gallery in 1984 to present his rigorous selection of the best artists, mostly Italian, in each of the decorative arts: ceramics, glass, furniture and so forth. These days he specializes more and more in abstract painting of the period from 1950 to 1980.

Jean-Jacques Dutko

6th arr. - 5, rue Bonaparte - 43 26 96 13
Open 10:30 a.m.-12:30 p.m. & 2:30 p.m.-7 p.m.
Closed Sun., Mon. & Aug. Parking: Saint-Germain. Cards: AE.

Dutko was one of the early promoters of art deco, particularly at the Biennial Paris Show. Clustered all around him are the best signatures of the period. His giant store (on two floors) is the very image of that period, mixing cubist and post-cubist painters, Daum vases, sculpture by Léger and, increasingly, paintings and drawings by Masson (whose prices he has driven considerably higher).

Alain Lesieutre

1st arr. - 356, rue Saint-Honoré
42 60 68 62
Open 12:30 p.m.-8 p.m. Closed Sat. & Sun. Parking: Pl. Vendôme. Cards: AE. Other branch: 32, allée Riesener, Louvre des Antiquaires - 1st arr. - 42 97 28 63, open 11 a.m.-7 p.m., closed Mon.; parking, Louvre.

An inexhaustible collection of art nouveau and art deco objets d'art: "dragonfly" vases, glass sculptures by Gallé, silver trays by Lalique, enameled bottles by Feuillâtre and other such marvels. Lesieutre is the supplier to a demanding clientele of dealers. It's worth a detour to see the window display of ivory and bronze pieces, a specialty of the house, and several Bugatti sculptures—though the prices may knock you over.

Félix Marcilhac

6th arr. - 8, rue Bonaparte - 43 26 47 36
Open 10 a.m.-noon & 2:30 p.m.-7 p.m. (Sat. 3 p.m.-7 p.m.). Closed Sun. & Aug. Parking: Saint-Germain. No cards.

Félix Marcilhac is one of the big boys in art deco, and recognized far and wide for his expertise in other areas. He sells to the grandest museums in the world, and his top-quality objects attract a rich-and-famous clientele.

Eric Philippe

1st arr. - 25, galerie Véro-Dodat
42 33 28 26
Open 2 p.m.-7 p.m. Closed Sun., Mon. & Aug. Parking: Louvre. No cards.

Experienced in fashion design for haute couture, Eric Philippe and his wife are familiar with the problems of form and materials, which gives a peculiar accent to the exhibitions organized here. Since 1980 business has been conducted here, in one of the most beautiful *passages* in Paris. Furniture from the period from 1900 to 1950 is selected according to the house's own unique ideas. Nevertheless, one observes a marked preference for the "Viennese Secession" (Hoffman) and for the Belgian school (Henri Van de Velde). The prices are most often reasonable.

Le Roi Fou

8th arr. - 182, rue du Faubourg-Saint-Honoré - 45 63 82 59
Open 10:30 a.m.-7 p.m. Closed Sun. & Aug. Parking: Pl. des Ternes. Cards: V, AE.

Alexandre Mai has accumulated a considerable pile of all sorts of objects from 1880 through 1930: furniture, bronzes, ivories, porcelain, clocks, jardinières (flower stands) and art deco chandeliers. If you are willing to rummage a bit, your efforts will often be rewarded. In addition, there are several exhibitions of contemporary art each year.

DIRECTOIRE, EMPIRE, RESTORATION & CHARLES X

Au Directoire

7th arr. - 12, bd Raspail - 42 22 67 09
Open 10:30 a.m.-noon & 2:30 p.m.-7 p.m. (Mon. 2:30 p.m.-7 p.m.). Closed Sun. & Aug. Parking: Saint-Germain. No cards.

In 1982 Thierry Winsall opened this store on the boulevard Raspail, where the Dubreuil family once sold Empire furniture. He maintained his own specialty from his former store on the rue de Grenelle: the end of the eighteenth century through the beginning of the nineteenth, featuring desks, bookcases, commodes, bronzes, lamps and, his special interest, chairs. There is lots of mahogany, and the prices are sufficiently reasonable to attract other, mostly foreign, dealers.

Jean-Louis Grouillé

7th arr. - 46, rue du Bac - 45 48 13 29
Open 10:30 a.m.-12:30 p.m. & 2:30 p.m.-7 p.m. (Sat. 2:30 p.m.-7 p.m.). Closed Sun., Mon. & Aug. Parking: Bon Marché. No cards.

A discreet but first-rank establishment, this shop run by Jean-Louis Grouillé and his wife houses a collection of French, English and

American furniture and objects from the early nineteenth century and before. Their pieces are often quite curious and interesting, and as full of unexpected charm as an afternoon spent nosing around the Left Bank.

Raoul Guiraud

7th arr. - 90, rue de Grenelle
45 48 11 82, 42 22 61 04
Open 10 a.m.-12:30 p.m. & 2:30 p.m.-7 p.m. Closed Sun. & Aug. Parking: Pl. des Invalides. No cards.

The tradition here is eclectic: mahogany furniture of northern Europe produced between 1800 and 1830. The objects celebrate the pleasure of beauty married to utility, such as scientific instruments, marine objects, various knickknacks and curiosities. A separate branch is maintained at the Marché Paul-Bert, where paintings are the specialty.

Imbert

8th arr. - 157, rue du Faubourg-Saint-Honoré - 45 63 54 89
Open 10 a.m.-5 p.m. Closed Sat., Sun. & July 15-Sept. 15. Parking: Haussmann. No cards.

The store window may not be much, but inside, the sizable stock of blond-wood furniture (Restoration and Charles X), bronzes and opalines are all of the finest quality.

Mancel-Coti

7th arr. - 42, rue du Bac - 45 48 04 34
Open 10 a.m.-6 p.m. Closed Sun. & Mon. morning & Sat. in June & Aug. Parking: Saint-Germain. No cards.

This is an old establishment known for its furniture, clocks and porcelain of the Directoire, Consulate and Empire periods. Its clients are connoisseurs, including Prince Murat and the Legion of Honor museum.

Renoncourt

6th arr. - 1-3, rue des Saints-Pères
42 60 75 87
Open 10 a.m.-noon & 2:30 p.m.-7 p.m. Closed Sun. Parking: Saint-Sulpice, Saint-Germain. No cards.

The tradition here is the grand and the classic of the Empire, Restoration and Charles X periods. The objects are of the highest quality, and the Renoncourts are generous in sharing their charm and their extensive knowledge.

LOUIS-PHILIPPE, NAPOLEON III & LATE NINETEENTH CENTURY

Calvet

9th arr. - 10, rue Chauchat - 42 46 12 36, 47 70 87 03
Open 9:30 a.m.-12:30 p.m. & 2 p.m.-6:30 p.m. or by appt. Closed Sun. & Aug. No cards.

Calvet is the third generation of specialists in furniture built during the Second Empire (according to eighteenth-century style; the best cabinetmakers of the period were those who worked in this style). Calvet is still supplier to the president of the Ivory Coast.

Madeleine Castaing

6th arr. - 21, rue Bonaparte - 43 54 91 71
Open 10 a.m.-1 p.m. & 3 p.m.-7 p.m. (Mon. 10 a.m.-1 p.m.). Closed Sun. Parking: Saint-Germain. No cards.

Madeleine Castaing, a renowned decorator, friend to painters, patron of Soutine, was one of the very first to rediscover these fragile little furniture pieces and objects of the Second Empire, which she sells at imperial prices. She also carries a substantial inventory of her own carpeting and fabrics.

Andrée Debar

1st arr. - 2, allée Germain, Louvre des Antiquaires - 42 97 28 08
Open 11 a.m.-7 p.m. Closed Mon. Parking: Louvre. No cards. Other branch: 142, rue du Bac - 6th arr. - 42 60 33 45; parking: Bon Marché, Sèvres-Babylone.

The furniture and knickknacks here are of a quality that justifies their serious prices. Madame Debar, a former actress, has become a leading expert on Second Empire antiques. She also sells furniture and objects from the turn of the century.

Galerie Bellier

7th arr. - 7, quai Voltaire - 42 60 74 72
Open 10 a.m.-12:30 p.m. & 2 p.m.-7 p.m. Closed Sun., Mon. & Aug. No cards.

Jean-Claude Bellier is one of the best-known modern art experts in Paris. Bellier presents the great masters of the nineteenth and twentieth centuries, the Impressionists and post-Impressionists and those famous from the 1920s, particularly Vuillard, who was Bellier's godfather.

MEDIEVAL & RENAISSANCE

Jacqueline Boccador

7th arr. - 22, rue du Bac - 42 60 75 79
Open 10 a.m.-7 p.m. Closed Sun., Mon. morning & Aug. Parking: Solférino. No cards.

Often called to act as expert witness to the courts of Paris and the Customs Service, Jacqueline Boccador combines her remarkable familiarity with antiques of the Middle Ages with an equally profound knowledge of products of the Renaissance. An author as well, she is responsible for several superb scholarly works, and she has the ability to communicate what she knows as she describes with passion her furniture, statues and tapestries to her customers. There is an atmosphere of mystery about her store, and soft music plays while you are making all kinds of discoveries, like Gothic fireplaces, for instance.

Charles et Philippe Boucaud

7th arr. - 25, rue du Bac - 42 61 24 07
Open 9:30 a.m.-12:30 p.m. & 2 p.m.-7 p.m. Closed Sun. & Aug. Parking: Solférino. Cards: AE.

The tradition of maintaining the highest levels of expertise and quality was established by the founder of this house; today it is maintained by Madame Charles Boucaud and her son Philippe, who rank among the top European specialists of not only pewterware but also porcelain pharmacy jars from the fifteenth to the nineteenth centuries, and sculpture of the classical period. The Boucauds put out a fully documented catalog of French pewter and, from time to time, help edit technical publications for specialists.

Edouard et Gabriel Bresset

7th arr. - 5, quai Voltaire - 42 60 78 13
Open 10 a.m.-12:30 p.m. & 2:30 p.m.-7 p.m. (Mon. 2:30 p.m.-7 p.m.). Closed Sun. & Aug. Parking: Solférino. Cards: AE. Other branch: 197, bd Saint-Germain - 6th arr. - 45 48 18 24, open at 2:30 p.m.; parking: Saint-Germain.

No one will dispute the fact that these people are the world's top specialists in medieval statuary, whether in wood or stone, unpainted or polychrome. They also own some Gothic tapestries, which they sell to major museums, and a huge collection of paintings, furniture and carved wood—wonderful cabinets encrusted with tortoiseshell or ebony—and bronze, ivory and enameled sculpture from the

Middle Ages and the Renaissance. When you visit, be sure to explore the superb vaulted cellars on the quai Voltaire.

Jean-Claude Edrei

7th arr. - 8, rue de Beaune - 42 61 28 08
Open 10:30 a.m.-7:30 p.m. Closed Sun. & Aug. Parking: Solférino. Cards: AE, DC.

Here is a huge, beautiful store dedicated in part to the classical period and in particular to china and pewterware, for which it is well known as a dealer of the highest quality. You also can find representative tapestries and some furniture from the sixteenth century up until the Regency period, and even pieces from the seventeenth and eighteenth centuries.

Antony Embden

7th arr. - 15, quai Voltaire - 42 61 04 06
Open 10:30 a.m.-12:30 p.m. & 2:30 p.m.-7 p.m. Closed Sun., Mon. & Aug. Parking: Solférino. No cards.

Here is a rich center of Renaissance sculpture in bronze, marble and ivory, as well as some exquisite old china and a wide selection of high-quality objects from the sixteenth and seventeenth centuries.

Marc Lagrand

7th arr. - 25, rue de Bourgogne
45 51 47 16
Open 10 a.m.-12:30 p.m. & 2 p.m.-7 p.m. (Mon. 2 p.m.-7 p.m.). Closed Sun. & July 20-Sept. 2. Parking: Pl. des Invalides. No cards.

The Lagrand family has been inviting connoisseurs to discover their collection of good and lovely pieces—the classical period and Louis XIII—which they have been gathering with patience, purpose and perseverance since 1890. Marc more than upholds the tradition.

Robert Montagut

7th arr. - 15, rue de Lille - 42 60 29 25
Open 10:30 a.m.-12:30 p.m. & 2:30 p.m.-7 p.m. (Mon. 2:30 p.m.-7 p.m.). Closed Sun. & Aug. Parking: Solférino. Cards: AE.

There isn't much furniture but there is a great deal of taste in this shop, which is dominated by paintings, bronzes, knickknacks and extraordinary objects. This former pharmacist from Toulouse never fails to mount his annual exhibition dedicated to his favorite theme: pharmacy paraphernalia. In addition to being beautiful, all the objects are documented.

Perpitch

7th arr. - 240, bd Saint-Germain

45 48 37 67

Open 10 a.m.-7 p.m. Closed Sun. & Aug. Parking: Saint-Germain. No cards.

With 40 years of experience, Antoine Perpitch is known as a great expert of the Flemish and Italian Renaissance, as well as of French Gothic and of medieval statuary. Louis XIII chairs, credenzas and tables, including some enormous monastery pieces, and tapestries of the sixteenth and seventeenth centuries are on display in his vast store, superbly situated on the corner of the rue du Bac.

SEVENTEETH & EIGHTEENTH CENTURIES

Didier Aaron

8th arr. - 118, rue du Faubourg-Saint-Honoré - 47 27 17 79

Open 9:30 a.m.-6:30 p.m. Closed Sat., Sun. & Aug. Parking: Haussmann, Rond-Point. No cards.

Whether it be in London, New York or Paris, Didier Aaron's collection of eighteenth-centuryinlaid furniture and objets d'art is brilliant. At the head of the pack of antiques dealers in Paris, he is also a formidable figure on the international market.

Antiquités de Beaune

7th arr. - 14, rue de Beaune - 42 61 25 42

Open 10:30 a.m.-12:30 p.m. & 2:30 p.m.-7 p.m. (Mon. 2:30 p.m.-7 p.m.). Closed Sun. & Aug. Parking: Solférino. No cards.

An excellent specialist in regional productions of the eighteenth century in cherry, maple, sycamore and walnut, Horowitz also offers a large selection of porcelain from the eighteenth and early nineteenth centuries.

Aveline

8th arr. - 20, rue du Cirque - 42 66 60 29

Open 9:30 a.m.-7 p.m. Closed Sun. & Aug. Parking: Rond-Point des Champs-Elysées. Cards: V, AE, DC, MC.

Here is a venerable establishment whose furniture of "museum quality" is indeed often purchased by the big museums (the Louvre, the Getty, the Compiègne, to name but a few). Jean-Marie Rossi is also known for his collection of high-quality curiosities that are always both beautiful and strikingly original. Bob Benamou competently manages the nine-

teenth-century-painting department. After-sales repairs or trade-ins are guaranteed.

Bernard Baruch Steinitz

9th arr. - 4, rue Drouot - 42 46 98 98

Open 9 a.m.-5 p.m. & by appt. (Sat. noon-5 p.m.). Closed Sun. & Aug. No cards.

An inveterate traveler in search of unusual objects, Steinitz has been set up here near the Hôtel Drouot since 1982. His store on two floors gives the impression of an eighteenth-century city mansion still intact. The quality of the pieces is beyond question, and the merchandise reflects an eclectic taste. In his workshops, 30 select artisans maintain the highest tradition of restoration. The prices, oh my, the prices. Let's just say they're in the highest tradition also. But it's worth a visit simply for the visual pleasure.

La Cour de Varenne

7th arr. - 42, rue de Varenne - 45 44 65 50

Open 10 a.m.-12:30 p.m. & 2 p.m.-6:30 p.m. Closed Sun., Mon. & Aug. Parking: Sèvres-Babylone. No cards.

This lovely shop opens onto not only the street but also a beautiful inner courtyard, around which are found the former outbuildings of the residence of Madame de Staël. Claude Levy has accumulated some real treasures: clocks and seventeenth- and eighteenth-century furniture, which will be looked after by a top-flight, house-calling artisan if necessary. In fact, according to Claude, this shop has the "best after-sales service in the world." Despite lunar prices, his perfect, quality merchandise is sold to the four corners of the globe. On the ground floor, a gallery is dedicated almost exclusively to nineteenth-century painting.

Fabius Frères

8th arr. - 152, bd Haussmann - 45 62 39 18

Open 9:30 a.m.-12:30 p.m. & 2:30 p.m.-6 p.m. Closed Sat., Sun. & Aug. Parking: Haussmann. No cards.

Since 1867 the Fabiuses have been antiques dealers in Paris—it goes from father to son (except when a son named Laurent recently became France's prime minister). Its clients are museums and the high and mighty who appreciate their collection of furniture and objects from the seventeenth and eighteenth centuries. And that's not to mention their holdings of Empire productions or their recent forays into significant painting and sculpture of the nineteenth century, principally that of Barye and Carpeaux.

Galerie Camoin-Demachy

7th arr. - 9, quai Voltaire - 42 61 82 06
Open 10 a.m.-7 p.m. Closed Sun. & Aug. Parking: Solférino. No cards.

This is perhaps the most beautiful antiques store in Paris. Here you will witness a magnificent presentation of no-less-magnificent pieces. Alain Demachy has done things just right, and his plan is ambitious: to bring together rare and lovely furniture of the eighteenth and nineteenth centuries, including Russian, Italian and Austrian products, with objets d'art and decorative art from diverse periods and styles. The result is a striking effect of luxury and of a world in which fantasy plays an important role in the judgment of taste. Marie-Christine Delcourt runs a spirited presentation of nineteenth-century art in a recently added gallery department.

Galerie Perrin

7th arr. - 3, quai Voltaire - 42 60 27 20
Open 10 a.m.-1 p.m. & 2 p.m.-7 p.m. (Mon. 2 p.m.-7 p.m.). Closed Sun. & Aug. Parking: Solférino. No cards. Other branch: 98, rue du Faubourg-Saint-Honoré - 8th arr. - 42 65 01 38; parking: Rond-Point des Champs-Elysées.

Jacques Perrin can be counted among the big boys in this business. In a flamboyant decor of lacquer and black aluminum, he stages his presentation of some of the most spectacular pieces of the seventeenth and eighteenth centuries, which are prized by oil sheiks and American billionaires equally: Boulle commodes, Mazarin desks and other signed masterpieces of the period.

Gismondi

1st arr. - 2, pl. du Palais-Royal
42 97 01 90
Open 9:30 a.m.-7:30 p.m. (Mon. 2 p.m.-7:30 p.m.). Closed Sun. & Aug. Parking: Pyramides. No cards. Other branch: 20, rue Royale - 8th arr. - 42 60 73 89; parking: Concorde, Madeleine.

Already well known among collectors for his Antibes shop, Gismondi has taken over and rejuvenated the prestigious location on the place de Palais-Royal, which was once occupied by the famous dealer Bensimon. With a pronounced predilection for spectacular baroque objects, such as sumptuous German and Italian cabinets, gilded bronzes and pieces by

Boulle overlaid with copper and tortoiseshell, he presents a magnificent variety of objects, and paintings, from the seventeenth and eighteenth centuries. And the posh, theatrical ambience with Italian undertones is itself something to behold.

Kraemer

8th arr. - 43, rue de Monceau
45 63 24 46, 45 63 31 23
Open 9 a.m.-7 p.m. Closed Sun. Parking: Haussmann. No cards.

Evidently it is possible to be one of the world's top experts on the French seventeenth and eighteenth centuries, to sell to museums and top-flight collectors a range of furniture, chairs, bronzes and objets d'art and yet to remain humble. For such are the accomplishments of Philippe Kraemer. His mind-boggling gallery could itself be considered a museum.

Jean de Laminne

8th arr. - 148, bd Haussmann - 45 62 08 15
Open 10 a.m.-6 p.m. Closed Sat., Sun. & Aug. Parking: Haussmann. No cards.

Since 1937, Jean de Laminne has been showing, in his 2,000-square-foot space, beautiful furniture of the eighteenth century. Now he works with his son. Devotees of Regency furniture in ebony or black wood with copper finework won't go wrong with purchases of his commodes and mirrors, which still bear their original patina.

Etienne Lévy

8th arr. - 178, rue du Faubourg-Saint-Honoré - 45 62 33 47
Open 9:30 a.m.-12:30 p.m. & 2 p.m.-6:30 p.m. Closed Sun. & Aug. Parking: Haussmann, Georges-V. No cards.

Claude Lévy learned from working with his father, and now he and his wife run this high-class shop along with their other store, the Cour de Varenne. They are fond of items that possess some degree of originality, such as mechanical tables and writing tables with ornamental quartz inlay. Otherwise, this is a shop where you can regularly find the works of the great cabinetmakers of the eighteenth century, Jacob, Weisweiler, Leleu and so forth. And, of course, there are always some seventeenth-century masterpieces lying around.

Michel Meyer

8th arr. - 24, av. Matignon - 42 66 62 95
Open 10 a.m.-1 p.m. & 2 p.m.-7 p.m. (Mon. 2 p.m.-7 p.m.). Closed Sun. & Aug. Parking: Rond-Point des Champs-Elysées. No cards.

Meyer grew up in a sultan's palace of antiques, and it shows. The ever-replenished stock of furniture and objects from the eighteenth century reflect a fondness for chiseled bronzes and mounted objects. With his excellent reputation, Meyer is an influential figure in the Paris biennial shows.

Maurice Segoura

8th arr. - 20, rue du Faubourg-Saint-Honoré - 42 65 11 03
Open 9 a.m.-7 p.m. Closed Sun. & Aug. Parking: Madeleine, Concorde. No cards.

Segoura is another big name in Parisian antiques dealing. Its three floors of furniture, objets d'art and spectacular decorative arts are destined for an international clientele and for prestigious private collections. He has also carved out a bit of a specialty in the works of French painters Greuze, Watteau, Fragonard, which are scattered here and there in the shop, and set off the beautiful furniture.

FOREIGN ANTIQUES

AFRICAN, OCEANIC & PRE-COLUMBIAN

Arts des Amériques

6th arr. - 42, rue de Seine - 46 33 18 31
Open 10:30 a.m.-7 p.m. Closed Sun., Mon. & Aug. Cards: V, AE.

Within this friendly little shop is an enormous selection of pre-Columbian art, primarily from Mexico, Costa Rica and Colombia. Every object is sold with a photograph and a certificate of authenticity.

Galerie Carrefour

6th arr. - 141, bd Raspail - 43 26 58 03
Open 9 a.m.-12:30 p.m. & 2:30 p.m.-6:30 p.m. Closed Sun. & Aug. 1-15. No cards.

Monsieur Vérité (that's his real name) has stockpiled here a huge, diverse but well-selected welter of mostly African objects: Ibéji, Yorouba, and Dan masks, Ibo statues, Achanti bronzes, Sénoufo doors, Akan jewelry, Baoulé

statuettes and so forth. The range of prices is as wide as the turnover is high. In addition, there's a department of Mediterranean Basin antiques (displaying about 300 objects).

Galerie Mermoz

8th arr. - 6, rue Jean-Mermoz - 43 59 82 44
Open 10 a.m.-noon & 2 p.m.-7 p.m. Closed Sun. & Aug. No cards.

This is a highly specialized store of the finest sort. It is well known at all the Paris shows on account of its rigorously selected array of pre-Columbian works. Prices to match.

BRITISH

British Import

92200 Neuilly - 23, bd du Parc, Ile-de-la-Jatte - 46 37 27 75
Open 11 a.m.-7 p.m. (Sun. 3 p.m.-7 p.m.). Closed Aug. Cards: AE. 2 other branches: 4, allée Topino, Louvre des Antiquaires - 1st arr. - 42 97 29 57, open 11 a.m.-7 p.m., closed Mon. & Aug., parking, Louvre; 78, av. de Suffren, Swiss Village - Sous-Sol, No. 3 - 15th arr. - 45 67 87 61, open 11 a.m.-12:30 p.m. & 2 p.m.-6:30 p.m., closed Tues., Wed. & Aug., parking, pl. Joffre.

This establishment has just one specialty: English furniture of the seventeenth, eighteenth and nineteenth centuries, primarily in mahogany. At the Isle de la Jatte (a popular subject of Seurat) location, there's a restoration workshop for customers. Approximately 100 pieces arrive every few months.

Andrée Higgins

7th arr. - 54, rue de l'Université
45 48 75 28, 45 48 56 92
Open Wed.-Sat. 9:30 a.m.-1 p.m. & 2 p.m.-7 p.m. Closed Aug. Parking: Solférino. No cards.

She was one of the first to introduce Paris to the taste for things English. She chooses her furniture of the eighteenth and nineteenth centuries with the utmost care. The rediscovery of the colonial style has filled her shop with lovely Chinese lacquer-panel tables and secretaries, such as those in fashion in England at the turn of the century. On our last visit, we also spotted some lovely French furniture of the seventeenth and eighteenth centuries. The stock is always changing, and presentations can be made at home.

Aliette Massenet

16th arr. - 169, av. Victor-Hugo
47 27 24 05
Open 10 a.m.-6:30 p.m. (Sat. until 6 p.m.). Closed Sun. & Aug. Parking: Victor-Hugo. No cards.

Every month the charming owner, Aliette, takes delivery of British specialties such as furniture and nineteenth-century objects, tea services, table settings for fish courses, porcelains, sports engravings, silver and bronze frames, pipe holders and costume jewelry.

FAR EASTERN

Bernard Captier

7th arr. - 25, rue de Verneuil - 42 61 00 57
Open 11 a.m.-7 p.m. Closed Sun., Mon. & Aug. No cards.

The price-quality ratio in this shop belonging to a specialist in Japanese antiques is quite fair. Perhaps it's because he is one of the few Paris dealers to travel to Japan several times a year in search of nineteenth-century objects and furniture (chests, commodes), which he restores in Paris for his wife to sell. (Note: He will also buy them back at the selling price plus inflation.) China and Korea are also represented, and on our last visit, we noticed some very handsome screens.

Beurdeley

7th arr. - 200, bd Saint-Germain
45 48 97 86
Open 2 p.m.-7 p.m. Closed Sun., Mon. & July 14-Sept. 1. No cards.

An expert if ever there was one, Jean-Michel Beurdeley is recognized as one of the great specialists of Far Eastern art. He supplies the big museums, and though you'll rarely see him in Paris, his gallery continues to bring together some of the best work of China and Japan.

La Boutique du Marais

4th arr. - 16, rue de Sévigné - 42 74 03 65
Open 10:30 a.m.-1 p.m. & 2 p.m.-7 p.m. (Sun. 2 p.m.-7 p.m.). Closed Mon. Cards: V, AE, DC, MC.

From opium pipes to Japanese cupboards (Tansu), Marie-Anne Baron specializes in works from India, China and Japan. Recently, though, the artisanship of India is giving way more and more to the antique furnishings of China and Japan. New exhibition space can be found on the second floor.

Compagnie de la Chine et des Indes

8th arr. - 39, av. de Friedland - 45 63 83 28
Open 9:30 a.m.-noon & 2 p.m.-6:30 p.m. Closed Sun., Mon. & Aug. No cards.

Ah, to discover the entire Far East under one roof. A top-notch selection of Chinese porcelain, pottery, furniture, Indian and Khmer sculpture, paintings and screens is displayed on three floors. Some of the objects are truly museum quality, and the head of the shop, Jean-Pierre Rousset, can be counted on for wise counsel.

Gérard Lévy

7th arr. - 17, rue de Beaune - 42 61 26 55
Open 2 p.m.-7 p.m. Closed Sun. & Aug. Cards: V, AE.

Lévy is a most reliable guide to the art of China, Cambodia, Japan, Korea and Thailand, and in his pretty shop we've encountered some ardent collectors. He sells important pieces to museums, but there are always more accessible items as well—always of a refined and high quality. Lévy is also devoted to old photography and is an official expert on the subject.

Loo

8th arr. - 48, rue de Courcelles
45 62 53 15, 42 25 17 23
Open 9 a.m.-12:30 p.m. & 2:30 p.m.-6:30 p.m. Closed Sun. & Aug. No cards.

Generally, it is only the specialized or the brave that venture into this unique pagoda of treasures, converted from an old rococo hotel where Charles Dickens once stayed. But Janine Loo is no dragon, and a visit to her shop is worth going out of your way. Just ring the bell calmly, take the "Chinese" elevator up, and you've arrived. Piles of rare and beautiful items are jammed onto three huge floors of this quasi-museum: lacquered screens, Hindu carvings, porcelain and knickknacks, Ming vases, Han statuettes and Tang horses. Loo also offers made-to-order contemporary furniture of a Chinese-inspired design.

Jan et Hélène Lühl

6th arr. - 19, quai Malaquais - 42 60 76 97
Open 2 p.m.-7 p.m. Closed Sun., Mon. & Aug. No cards.

These great collectors of engravings will infect you with their enthusiasm. The shop is located in the former gallery of the famous Ernest Le Veél (whose collection was dispersed in three historic auctions at the Hôtel Drouot), and they have developed an international reputation. They have it all—even culinary etchings from Japan.

Yvonne Moreau-Gobard

6th arr. - 5, rue des Saints-Pères
42 60 88 25
Open 10 a.m.-12:30 p.m. & 2 p.m.-7 p.m. Closed Sun. & Aug. No cards.

The wife of the great expert Jean-Claude Moreau-Gobard, Yvonne offers a complete and reliable array of archaeological objects from China, India and Cambodia. The number of pieces displayed here is as impressive as their quality.

Orient Occident

6th arr. - 5, rue des Saints-Pères
42 60 77 65
Open 10 a.m.-12:30 p.m. & 2 p.m.-7 p.m. Closed Sun. & Aug. No cards.

As unassuming and media-shy as possible, Jean-Loup Despras, who reads hieroglyphs like we read the funnies, is an ace specialist of Egyptian antiques. He shares the shop with Yvonne Moreau-Gobard, a first-rate expert on Indian and Far Eastern arts. Gobard's bronzes, pottery and ceramics are on display.

Janette Ostier

3rd arr. - 26, pl. des Vosges - 48 87 28 57
Open 2 p.m.-7 p.m. Closed Sun., Mon. & Aug. No cards.

This charming little boutique is primarily devoted to Japanese art; included are drawings, etchings, pictures, painted screens, masks, and lacquered boxes. Janette Ostier organizes some wonderful shows, which generally are accompanied by richly illustrated and fully documented catalogs.

ISLAMIC

Arts de la Perse et de l'Orient

6th arr. - 21, quai Malaquais - 42 60 72 91
Open 10:30 a.m.-12:30 p.m. & 2:30 p.m.-7 p.m. Closed Sun. & Aug. No cards.

Monsieur and Madame Kevorkian are two of France's top specialists in Middle Eastern art. They have a magnificent collection of Islamic ceramic work, in addition to miniatures, diverse objects and some exquisite bronzes.

Philippe et Claude Magloire

4th arr. - 13, pl. des Vosges - 42 74 40 67
Open 1 p.m.-6 p.m. Closed Mon. Cards: V, AE.

Claude and Philippe Magloire, who are geologists and collectors as well as experts attached to the Court of Appeals of Paris, spent ten years in Iran. In 1981, they opened a gallery in the place des Vosges to introduce and promote Iranian art, a refined but little-understood tradition in the West. Treasures such as bronzes from Louristan, Islamic ceramics (from Nishapur) and antique rugs form a good collection of Asian art and archaeology.

Jean Soustiel

1st arr. - 146, bd Haussmann - 45 62 27 76
Open 9 a.m.-1 p.m. & 2 p.m.-7 p.m. Closed Sat., Sun. & Aug. No cards.

Nineteen eighty three marked the 100th anniversary of this gallery; four generations of the family have tended shop here. Jean Sousteil, a highly regarded expert among his colleagues, runs one of the most famous and reputable galleries in the world. He is also the author of an exhaustive study of Islamic ceramics, which has become the collector's bible.

MEDITERRANEAN

Nina Borowski

7th arr. - 40, rue du Bac - 45 48 61 60
Open 10 a.m.-12:30 p.m. & 2 p.m.-7 p.m. (Sat. 10 a.m.-noon & 2 p.m.-7 p.m.). Closed Sun. & Aug. No cards.

Daughter of the great Borowski of Basel, this erudite and charming young woman exhibits a significant quantity of pottery, vases, bronzes and marbles of Greek, Roman and Etruscan origin. Her selection of archaeological artifacts changes every year. It's possible to find small Greek terracotta pieces at reasonable prices.

Galerie Samarcande

6th arr. - 13, rue des Saints-Pères
42 60 83 17
Open 10 a.m.-noon & 2:30 p.m.-7 p.m. Closed Sun. & Aug. Cards: V, AE, DC.

Paris has a new archaeology gallery; visitors can find gold and silver jewelry, as well as everyday objects and artifacts from Greece, Rome, Egypt, Islam and Asia.

Mythes et Légendes

4th arr. - 18, pl. des Vosges - 42 72 63 26
Open 10 a.m.-12:30 p.m. & 2 p.m.-7 p.m. (Mon. 2 p.m.-7 p.m.). Closed Sun. & Aug. 13-27. Cards: V, AE. Other branch: 12, rue de Sévigné - 3rd arr. - 42 72 35 43.

Whether from Egypt, Rome, the Far East or pre-Columbian America, Michel Cohen, father of Gilles Cohen, displays about 200 objects every month, from Egyptian amulets to some rare and important Cambodian finds. He offers a certificate of expertise and a mail-order catalog.

A la Reine Margot

6th arr. - 7, quai de Conti - 43 26 62 50
Open 10:30 a.m.-1 p.m. & 2 p.m.-7 p.m. (Mon. 3 p.m.-7 p.m.). Closed Sun. Cards: V, AE, DC.

This is the oldest gallery of its kind in Paris. These days more and more space is being devoted to archaeology. Gilles Cohen, the proprietor, puts on excellent exhibits each year and publishes fine catalogs. There are, as always, medieval, haute epoque and seventeenth-century departments.

Simone de Monbrison

6th arr. - 22, rue Bonaparte - 46 33 13 77
Open 2:30 p.m.-7 p.m. Closed Sun., Mon. & Aug. No cards.

You can always find a fine, and sometimes spectacular, selection of beautiful early-Greek and Etruscan art pieces here, as well as Roman and Egyptian objects. Simone de Monbrison is virtually an institution in her field. Her clientele, more and more informed, is interested not only in smiling Venuses and Tanagra statuettes but also in the works of earlier civilizations of the Mediterranean Basin. The gallery features regular exhibits and a worthy selection of technical literature.

RUSSIAN

Artel

6th arr. - 25, rue Bonaparte - 43 54 93 77
Open 10:30 a.m.-12:30 p.m. & 2 p.m.-7 p.m. Closed Sun., Mon. & Aug. No cards.

If the supply of objets d'art from czarist Russia is increasingly rare, the demand remains high. Keeper of Russian and Greek icons ranging in origin from the fifteenth to the nineteenth century, Marine Cuttat also sees to the restoration of these pieces.

A la Vieille Cité

1st. arr. - 350, rue Saint-Honoré
42 60 67 16
Open 11:30 a.m.-6:30 p.m. (Mon. 1:30 p.m.-6:30 p.m.). Closed Sat., Sun. & July 14-Sept. 1. No cards.

This very Louis Philippe-style decor showcases a treasury of silverwork, beautiful icons, Fabergé pieces, porcelain, Russian painting and a collection of delicately worked Easter eggs.

SPECIALISTS

BANKING, STAMPS & STOCKS

Le Marché aux Timbres

8th arr. - Av. des Champs-Elysées, Carré Marigny
Open Thurs., Sat., Sun. & holidays 10 a.m.-6 p.m. No cards.

On the right side of the Champs-Elysées near the corner of Marigny and Gabriel avenues, 70 licensed sellers set up booths along the sidewalk and the alleyways. They are there almost all day buying, selling and exchanging.

Numistoria

2nd arr. - 49, rue Vivienne - 42 33 93 45
Open 11 a.m.-7 p.m. (Sat. by appt.). Closed Sun. & July 14-Aug. 31. No cards.

This huge and constantly changing presentation of all kinds of bank notes is run by Guy Cifré, and offers everything from stocks and bonds to coins and old deeds. There's no place like it this side of Ali Baba's cave.

BRONZES

Fred Guiraud

16th arr. - 9, rue de Belloy - 47 04 33 86
Open 10 a.m.-7:30 p.m. (Sat. noon-7:30 p.m.). Closed Sun. & Aug. No cards.

Guiraud presents a collection of bronze animal statues from famous sculptors of the nineteenth century: Barye, Frémiet, Moigniez, Pompon, Bugatti. Only period pieces are sold here—nonmodern recastings. Neverthless, it pays to keep your eyes open, for there are a lot of counterfeit objects. He also provides homes for nineteenth-century seascapes in oil, gouache and watercolor, displayed amid wall clocks from the Directoire, Empire and Restoration periods.

Moatti

6th arr. - 77, rue des Saints-Pères
42 22 91 04
Open 9:30 a.m.-12:30 p.m. & 2 p.m.-7 p.m. (Mon. 2 p.m.-7 p.m.) and by appt. Closed Sun. & Aug. No cards.

In a mansion on the rue des Saints-Pères, this dealer shows almost exclusively by appointment only. In his collection of bronzes and collectors' items, you'll find what connoisseurs consider to be among the most finely selected pieces in the world. In the plush and highly discreet atmosphere, the prices are whispered in a way that suggests that art is beyond any valuation. Every piece must first pass a three-part scrutiny verifying its authenticity, quality and rarity. An item purchased at Moatti bears the additional value of the worldwide renown of the establishment.

CAMERAS

Aux Fontaines de Niepce et de Daguerre

18th arr. - 20, rue André-del-Sarte
42 54 27 13
Open 10:30 a.m.-5:30 p.m. Closed Sun., Mon. & Aug. Cards: V, AE.

This superb store, with its Second Empire decor, is home to the best-known if not the greatest antique-photographic-equipment specialist in Paris. Within the walls of this vast quasi-museum, Monsieur Bomet has amassed a fine collection of seemingly every sort of apparatus. He adds unceasingly to his treasure horde, and his collectors include the king of Belgium, no less. Bomet's crown jewels include the obscure eighteenth-century grandfather to all cameras, the drawing box; the first Eastman, from 1885; and a rare Sigrist stereoscope. In all there are close to 500 pieces,

displayed with the daguerrotypes and ambrotypes also collected by Bomet.

Galerie Octant

1st arr. - 10, rue du 29-Juillet - 42 60 68 08
Open 2:30 p.m.-7 p.m. Closed Sun., Mon. & school holidays. No cards. Other branch: 6, rue du Marché-Saint-Honoré - 1st arr. - 42 60 68 08

A careful but copius collection of prints, ranging from works from photography's shadowy beginnings to the touching pictorial records of the mad '20s and '30s.

Garnier-Arnoul

6th arr. - 39, rue de Seine - 43 54 80 05
Open 11 a.m.-12:30 p.m. & 2 p.m.-7 p.m. Closed Sun. No cards.

Here is the store for the devout and the crazed, a store full of stars. It seems to stock a photo of every stage artist you could dream of.

Photo Verdeau

9th arr. - 14-16, passage Verdeau
42 70 51 91
Open Tues.-Fri. 9 a.m.-1 p.m. & 2 p.m.-7 p.m. Closed Feb. & Aug. No cards.

This shop belongs to a great specialist in the field and contains a grand array of antiques and curiosities for every budget: folding "tourist" cameras with holders for the gelatine-bromide glass plates (from 1,000 to 2,000 francs), "detective" models, such as those Zola was fond of (500 to 1,000 francs):, with earlier wood cameras fetching 3,000 francs and more. On our last visit, we also saw a 1925 Pathé Baby projector, in working condition, of course, and a substantial collection of silent films, including Harold Lloyd and newsreels put out by Pathé Gazette from 1926 to 1939, all priced according to vintage.

Don't plan to do much shopping in Paris in August — a great many stores shut down for the entire vacation month.

CLOCKS & WATCHES

J.-P. Rochefort
7th arr. - 14, rue des Saints-Pères
42 96 60 05
*Open 2 p.m.-7:30 p.m. Closed Sun. & Aug.
Cards: V, AE.*

Rochefort is one of the big names among dealers of antique clocks. He manages to accumulate in his elegant shop the loveliest (and most expensive) examples of table clocks from the sixteenth and seventeenth centuries, perpetual clocks and rare models created by some of the best clockmakers in Geneva, Chaux-de-Fonds and Franche-Comté. Of particularly worthy note are the cuckoo clocks, the songbirds in cages and the astronomic clocks.

CHESTS & BOXES

Alain Bidegand
7th arr. - 27, rue de Varenne - 42 22 78 55
Open 2:30 p.m.-7 p.m. Closed Sun., Mon. & Aug. No cards.

Only the most lovely inlaid objects in precious wood—chests, writing cases, toiletry objects, cigar boxes, glove boxes, jewel boxes, perfume boxes—make it into this shop. Many of the pieces bear the stamp of a well-known cabinetmaker of the nineteenth century.

Coffrets et Flacons
1st arr. - 7, rue de Castiglione - 42 96 33 81
Open 11 a.m.-1 p.m. & 2 p.m.-7 p.m. Closed Sun. Cards: V, AE.

Here, it's the bottle not the wine, the flask not the brandy, that matters. The collection of rare chests dates from the Renaissance to the present day, and includes flasks and glasses, of the highest quality, from the eighteenth century.

Nicole Kramer
1st arr. - 5, allée Desmalter, Louvre des Antiquaires - 42 97 29 36
Open 11 a.m.-7 p.m. Closed Mon. Cards: V, AE, DC.

This pretty shop belongs to a fine specialist of her kind. She displays a number of small eighteenth-century French boxes, as well as a variety of other objects (surgical instruments, for example).

COINS & MEDALS

Emile Bourgey
9th arr. - 7, rue Drouot
47 70 35 18, 47 70 88 67
Open 9 a.m.-noon & 2 p.m.-6:30 p.m. (Sat. 9 a.m.-noon). Closed Sun. & Aug. No cards.

Located in an apartment across the street from the sales room of the famous antiques exhibition center, the Hôtel Drouot, Emile Bourgey's offices have maintained the plush, discreet ambience of an earlier age. For over 30 years, everything here has been dedicated to coin collecting: the exquisite display cases, the library of several thousand titles on the subject and the attention that Bourgey and/or his daughter provide to initiate clients into the kingdom of numismatics.

Numismatique et Change de Paris
2nd arr. - 3, rue de la Bourse
42 97 53 53, 42 97 56 85
Open 9 a.m.-5:30 p.m. Closed Sat., Sun. & Aug. No cards.

While he reserves the trade in collectors' pieces for his boutique, at this address Jean Vinchon leaves his daughter in charge of buying and selling gold coins, ingots, tokens, old bills and bank notes. Gold pieces are sealed into transparent plastic sachets in the presence of the buyer, a unique procedure that provides a valuable guarantee. If you are interested in selling gold here, you should know that there is a 10 percent commission.

Jean Vinchon
2nd arr. - 77, rue de Richelieu
42 97 50 00
Open 9 a.m.-noon & 2 p.m.-6 p.m. Closed Sat., Sun. & Aug. No cards.

Jean Vinchon is not only one of the most ardent coin experts in the world, he also has been among the first to recognize that coin collecting is more than a hobby or an esoteric specialty. He has worked diligently for its acceptance as a discipline of art. In the felt-lined atmosphere of his shop, great collectors argue the merits of individual coins worth fortunes, while Vinchon advises those interested in lesser coins with the same careful attention.

CRYSTAL & GLASS

L'Arlequin

4th arr. - 13, rue des Francs-Bourgeios
42 78 77 00

Open noon-7 p.m. Closed Sun., Mon. & July 14-Sept. 1. No cards.

This is the kind of shop that gets handed around from family to family when the little one has broken a few of the best glasses or the stopper to the carafe has mysteriously disappeared. L'Arlequin stocks hundreds of styles from every period (the house specialty is nineteenth century), and at a wide range of prices.

La Brocante de Marie-Jeanne

17th arr. - 17, rue Laugier - 47 66 59 31
Open 11 a.m.-7 p.m. Closed Sun., Mon. & Aug. No cards.

Among all the glasses and crystal, sold in sets or individually, and the liqueur decanters and the toiletry accessories, it would be surprising if Marie-Jeanne Schuhmann couldn't find that out-of-the-ordinary tiny carafe you've been hunting for. But if she can't, you can console yourself with some beautiful art deco vases, or perhaps a nice lamp or lovely bedside carafe.

Galerie Altero

7th arr. - 21, quai Voltaire, 42 61 19 90
Open 10:30 a.m.-12:30 p.m. & 2:30 p.m.-7 p.m. (Mon. 2:30 p.m.-7 p.m.). Closed Sun. & Aug. No cards.

This is another one of those places worth seeing even if you are not a devotee; seventeenth-century furniture and eighteenth-century glass cases function as the decor for the display of glasses and carafes from all periods from Louis XIV to Napoléon III.

Phillipe Leroux et Jacques Badin

7th arr. - 16, rue de Beaune - 42 61 18 24
Open 2 p.m.-7 p.m. Closed Sun., Mon. & Aug. Cards: AE.

Are they partial to old glassware here? No, more than that, they are are militant promoters of it. The two regularly roam Europe uncovering the rarest examples of glass from Venice, Bohemia, England and seventeenth- and eighteenth-century France.

CURIOS & UNUSUAL OBJECTS

Air de Chasse

7th arr. - 8, rue des Saints-Pères
42 60 25 98

Open 10 a.m.-1 p.m. & 2 p.m.-7 p.m. (Mon. 2 p.m.-7 p.m.). Closed Sun. & Aug. No cards.

Here in Jeanine Gerhard's shop is everything you can imagine that in some way or other is connected with hunting or shooting: eighteenth-, nineteenth- and twentieth-century prints, knickknacks, bronze animal statuettes, duck decoys, birds in terracotta.

Atelier 12

7th arr. - 12, rue des Saints-Pères
42 60 81 00

Open 10 a.m.-5 p.m. Closed Sun. No cards.

Birds and painted shells, turtle shells made into other objects, ostrich eggs—you'll either like them or you won't. But the shop window is a spectacular enough reason itself to visit.

Le Bain Rose

6th arr. - 90, rue de Rennes - 42 22 55 85
Open 10:30 a.m.-1:30 p.m. & 2:30 p.m.-7 p.m. Closed Sun., Mon. & Aug. Cards: V, AE.

This is the store for antique washbasins and stands, which sell for between 10,000 and 40,000 francs. That may seem a little high, but everything works: the faucets, the basin, the drain. You can also find pedestal-type sinks for lower prices, or settle for some antique decorative bathroom tiles.

Brocante Store

6th arr. - 31, rue Jacob - 42 60 24 80
Open 10:30 a.m.-7 p.m. Closed Sun. & Mon. No cards.

Amid the pretty English antiques is a veritable heap of charming objects, including little chests, instruments and lamps.

Brugidou-Malnati

7th arr. - 17, rue de Grenelle - 42 22 61 04
Open 10:30 a.m.-12:30 p.m. & 2:30 p.m.-7 p.m. Closed Sun. & Aug. Cards: V.

There are some beautiful and astonishingly crafted objects among a welter of things from a great number of periods. Bernard Brugidou is a specialist in copper, scientific instruments, old books and country furniture, in addition to buying and selling used furniture. He runs the establishment in an efficient and honest manner. He'll even tell you the price he hopes to get for the piece that he is buying from you.

Le Cabinet de Curiosité
7th arr. - 23, rue de Beaune - 42 61 09 57
Open 2 p.m.-7 p.m. Closed Sun. & Aug. Cards: V, AE, DC.

With the same passion and kindly manner of her late husband, a man of rare modesty and wonderful curiosity, Madame Jean Herbert is carrying on his work. The scientific instruments, games, tools, old wooden objects and everything else in her shop has been chosen with taste to satisfy one aim: to charm the eye and the spirit. It is always a joy to go rummaging about in this lovely shop.

Comoglio
6th arr. - 22, rue Jacob - 43 54 65 86
Open 9 a.m.-12:30 p.m. & 2:15 p.m.-6:45 p.m. Closed Sun. & Aug. No cards.

This shop was the supplier for, among others, Jean Cocteau and Christian Bérard—not to mention the numerous set designers for stage, screen and television who still come here to rent or to buy unique decor elements: woodwork, stained glass, wallpaper and furniture. This is a house of surprises, full of discoveries waiting to be made.

Dugrenot
1st arr. - 18, rue de Montpensier
42 96 02 43
Open Tues.-Fri. 2 p.m.-6 p.m. & by appt. No cards.

This honorable establishment, founded in 1856, displays a pronounced taste for baroque, as well as strange objects and furniture, antique or modern. From a carved stone box from India to a Louis XIV secretary, you can never quite predict what you will come across on any given visit to Dugrenot.

Fanfan la Tulipe
6th arr. - 55, rue du Cherche-Midi
42 22 04 20
Open 3:30 p.m.-7 p.m. Closed Sun. & Aug. No cards.

André Holland is a versatile expert in the fields of historical objects, coats of arms and other heraldic paraphernalia, and equipment for smokers. One is as likely to find nineteenth-century candelabra as Creil china or elegant canes (a new specialty for Holland). He is also a great connoisseur of playing cards, from the Renaissance to 1930.

Galerie 13
6th arr. - 13, rue Jacob - 43 26 99 89
Open 2:30 p.m.-7 p.m. Closed Sun. No cards.

At one time a specialist in old games, Martine Jeannin is now more interested in charming decorative objects. She carries wood carvings from the eighteenth century, overmantels and folding screens alongside whimsical and strange items, such as bird cages, romantic baubles, embroidery, expensive turned-wood objects from the Florentines or Louis XIV and naive art.

Galerie Jacques Casanova
1st arr. - 25, galerie Montpensier
42 96 23 52
Open noon-7 p.m. Closed Sun. & Aug. No cards.

The shop is dedicated to the decidedly unusual—curious and bizarre objects of all sorts, including the erotic, items of witchcraft and modern paintings and drawings inspired by strange themes, can be found here. We dare not fail to mention the most singular piece in the collection: a robot dog made of wire that obeys vocal commands and can urinate on command.

Magnolia
7th arr. - 78, rue du Bac - 42 22 31 79
Open 10 a.m.-7 p.m. Closed Sun. Cards: V, AE.

This congenial depot of bric-a-brac is adorned by a display of turn-of-the-century bridal bouquets (1,000 to 1,500 francs). In addition, we've also come across chromolithographs, busts in plaster or bronze, pill boxes, powder boxes, engraved flasks, old jewelry (from 1,500 to 35,000 francs), baptismal medals (300 francs) and several beautiful art deco wall clocks.

Alain et Emmanuel Thiriot
16th arr. - 29, rue de la Tour
45 04 46 54
Open 10:30 a.m.-7:30 p.m. (Sat. & Mon. 2 p.m.-7:30 p.m.). Closed Sun. No cards.

Originality and quality are the guiding standards of the selection of these two brothers, whose taste is decidedly eclectic. On our last visit we came upon a beautiful piece of furniture from the '50s next to a lovely Chinese cabinet, a ship model from the turn of the century beneath a large decorative lacquered panel signed by Jouve. Don't come here looking for something practical; everything is devoted to the decorative arts, and everything has a certain flair about it. But stop by frequently—you won't be disappointed.

Yveline
6th arr. - 4, rue de Furstenberg
43 26 56 91
Open 11 a.m.-6:30 p.m. Closed Sun. & Aug. No cards.

This charming little shop on a delightful square sells a little bit of everything—from wooden mannequins to furniture and lamps of all periods and styles. These objects never grow dull and are always decorative.

FABRICS

Aux Fils du Temps
7th arr. - 33, rue de Grenelle - 45 48 14 68
Open 2 p.m.-7 p.m. Closed Sun. & Aug. No cards.

In an early-nineteenth-century decor, Marie-Noëlle Sudre sits pretty amid her treasures: bolts and bolts of old fabric from all over the planet. These representatives are piled up like the crates of an explorer back from a long voyage through time and space; in Sudre's case, it is from the eighteenth century to the 1950s. If you're looking for something specific, you should call ahead—Sudre will have things ready when you arrive.

Juliette Niclausse
9th arr. - 50, rue La Bruyère - 48 74 11 49
Open 2 p.m.-5 p.m. & by appt. Closed Sat. & Sun. No cards.

Juliette Niclausse has been technical advisor to the national historical trust for 27 years. She is also the author of several works on tapestries and old fabric. So it's no surprise that this collector of rare fabrics and gowns of the eighteenth century has a strong, ready grasp of the subject. This gentlewoman prefers to receive clients by appointment.

FANS

Duvellroy
6th arr. - 6, rue de la Michodière
47 42 55 77
Open 2 p.m.-7 p.m. Closed Sun. & Aug. No cards.

Has the fan come back into fashion, thanks to Karl Lagerfeld? It certainly has its admirers, who ought to be very happy that Michel Maignan has given a second lease on life to the house of Duvellroy, the prettiest store for elegant whimsies in Paris.

Georges Antiquités
1st arr. 26, rue de Richelieu
42 61 32 57
Open 10:30 a.m.-6:30 p.m. (Sat. by appt.). Closed Sun. No cards.

A most refined presentation of ivory objects and various collectibles. From every period from Louis XIV to Louis-Philippe comes a display of fans made of tortoiseshell, lace, feathers, mother-of-pearl, tulle with sequins, finely worked bone, painted parchment, donkey skin and more. Prices vary drastically.

FIREPLACES

Michel Elbaz (S.C.A.D.)
10th arr. - 29 bis, rue de Rocroy
45 26 40 00
Open 9:30 a.m.-6:30 p.m. (Sat. until 12:30 p.m.). Closed Sun. & Aug. No cards.

Elbaz's selection of fireplaces from the seventeenth century through 1900 come mainly in marble, and prices start at 1,500 francs. Also through this savvy dealer, you can obtain older examples in stone or wood. A wide range of attractive prices.

Fernandez-Blanchard
11th arr. - 36, rue Sedaine - 47 00 67 59
Open 10 a.m.-5 p.m. Closed Sat., Sun. & Aug. No cards.

The selection is enormous, and the fireplaces are all beautiful old specimens in marble, wood and often Burgundian stone. There are also some garden fountains, and restoration service is provided.

Jean Lapierre

3rd arr. - 58, rue Vieille-du-Temple
42 74 07 70
Open 11 a.m.-7:30 p.m. Closed Sun., Mon. &
Aug. No cards.

Oak doors, parquet floors, stairs and other old elements are sold either as they are or nicely restored. But the chief attraction is the stonework from (primarily) the Mâcon area: fireplaces in their entirety or in separate pieces, mostly eighteenth century, as well as some interesting carved well copings. In short, this is the place to go if you're looking for any manner of stone objects and sculpture from the eighteenth century, even (the occasional) terracotta tiles. If you happen to be in the vicinity of Mâcon, stop by Sennecé-les-Mâcon to see the main store and Jean Lapierre's fascinating exhibition hall (16 - 85 36 01 08).

Pierre Madel

6th arr. - 4, rue Jacob - 43 26 90 89
Open 3 p.m.-7 p.m. Closed Sun., Mon. & Aug.
No cards.

The impressive array of wrought iron from the seventeenth century to 1900 includes and specializes in fireplace tools: pokers, ash pans, mechanical roasting spits and so forth.

FOLK ART

Pierre-G. Bernard

8th arr. - 1, rue d'Anjou - 46 65 23 83
Open 10:30 a.m.-6 p.m. & Sat. by appt. Closed
Sun. & July 10-Aug. 31. No cards.

Here you'll find original objects and documents in the domain of science, industry and commerce. M. Bernard is an ardent student and collector of trades and crafts, especially old tools and all that pertains to the history of the table (be it for writing or for eating). From a Gallo-Roman cooking pot to an old-fashioned cake mold, there's a panoply of antique objects and rare documentary literature on such subjects as wine making. Yet another specialty is scale models of machinery.

Galerie d'Art Populaire

7th arr. - 10, rue de Beaune - 42 61 27 87
Open 2:30 p.m.-7 p.m. Closed Sun. & Aug.
Cards: V, AE, DC.

This gallery, located on the site of the barracks of Richelieu's gray Musketeers, is filled with a nice smell of furniture wax. It is filled with beautiful old country furniture, wrought

iron and folk art objects, such as butter molds, salt boxes and sheep collars.

L'Herminette

1st arr. - 4, allée Germain, Louvre des Antiquaires - 42 97 28 09
Open 11 a.m.-7 p.m. Closed Sun. & Mon.
Cards: V, AE, DC.

A fine, highly specialized establishment that features the art of ironwork, locks and old tools. Prices range from 200 to several thousand francs.

JEWELRY

Jacqueline Subra

6th arr. - 51, rue de Seine - 43 54 57 65
Open 11 a.m.-noon & 2 p.m.-6:30 p.m. Closed
Sun., Mon. & Aug. Cards: V, AE.

Whether from the end of the nineteenth century, art nouveau, art deco or the 1950s, the jewelry of Jacqueline Subra is always of the best quality, in both materials and design. Displayed in her windows are excellent examples of the style of each period.

Pierre Barboza

1st arr. - 356, rue Saint-Honoré
42 60 67 08
Open 10 a.m.-6:30 p.m. Closed Sat. (except Nov.
& Dec.) & Aug. Cards: V, AE.

Annette Gribe, the shop's manager, makes no secret of
her fascination with the eighteenth century, or her passion for long earrings of the nineteenth century, and still less for her love of the diversity of colors in semiprecious stones. Her faithful clientele has complete confidence in her and her ability to take a few unwearable jewels and work wonders. And what's more, she does it for surprisingly reasonable prices.

Garland

2nd arr. - 13, rue de la Paix - 42 61 17 95
Open 10 a.m.-1 p.m. & 2 p.m.-6:30 p.m. Closed
Sun. & 10 days in mid-Aug. Cards: V, AE, DC.

The proprietress, Minouche, never sells one of her rare and antique jewels without a twinge of regret. She is the queen of antique jewelry in Paris; some of the pieces that have passed through her shop are such treasures as the bracelet offered to Sarah Bernhardt by the czar and a superb nineteenth-century necklace that belonged to King Farouk. Recently, her husband, Bernard Messager, a former craftsman at

Cartier, has joined the force and makes contemporary jewelry that is sold in the shop.

C. Gustave

1st arr. - 416, rue Saint-Honoré
42 60 14 38
Open 10:30 a.m.-6:30 p.m. Closed Sat. (except Nov. & Dec.), Sun. & Aug. Cards: V, AE, DC.

This is the oldest boutique in the neighborhood; it is also the first in Europe to import cultured pearls. On the fringes of the international chic zone, Faubourg-Saint-Honoré, it has some lovely old bargains, stones of a quality you do not see anymore and pieces signed by Van Cleef and Boucheron.

Michel Périnet

8th arr. - 420, rue Saint-Honoré
42 61 49 16
Open 11 a.m.-7 p.m. Closed Sun. No cards.

The decor of this shop resembles a 1920s jewel box. Michel Périnet employs stunning taste in the selection of his magnificent jewels from the Charles X, Second Empire, art nouveau (Lalique), art deco and 1940s (Cartier, Boucheron, Van Cleef) periods. It is located just across the way from the illustrious house of Kugel, and the prices here hold their own, as does the quality.

MINERALS, GEMS & SHELLS

Claude Boullé

6th arr. - 28, rue Jacob - 46 33 01 38
Open 10:30 a.m.-12:30 p.m. & 2 p.m.-7 p.m. Closed Sun. & Aug. mornings. No cards.

Boullé is a top specialist in the field with a taste for rare and unique minerals. Among the famous who are collectors of "pretty stones" and frequent this shop are André Breton, Roger Caillois and Vieira da Silva. Beautiful limestone bowls from Tuscany, marble from Bristol, jasper from Oregon, sandstone from Utah . . . the list seems endless.

Michel Cachoux

6th arr. - 16, rue Guenegaud - 43 54 52 15
Open 11 a.m.-7 p.m. Closed Sun., Mon. & Aug. Cards: V, AE, DC.

Michel Cachoux generally puts on a dazzling show. Several times a year he is off to Brazil, the United States, Madagascar or simply down to the Alps, in search of his treasures. We still remember the one-ton amethyst geode he exhibited several years ago. These days he is

also going in for fossils and objects in hard stone, such as boxes and jewelry. And his prices are, if anything, falling. His regular exhibits feature themes and are highly interesting.

Deyrolle

7th arr. - 46, rue du Bac - 42 22 30 07
Open 9 a.m.-12:30 p.m. & 2 p.m.-6:15 p.m. (Sat. until 5 p.m.). Closed Sun. No cards.

A fabulous shop, this sumptuous mansion houses an astonishing array of minerals of every size and description. In addition, there are displays of shells, fossils, butterflies, botanical specimens and stuffed animals—from partridges to polar bears.

Sciences, Art et Nature

5th arr. - 87, rue Monge - 47 07 53 70
Open 10 a.m.-6:30 p.m. Closed Sun. & Mon. No cards.

Inheritor of the famous house of Boubee, founded in 1846 but now defunct, Françoise Morival still deals in the treasures of the natural world: among her teeming collections are minerals, fossils, shells, rare insects and other delights of taxidermy. Each piece sold is accompanied by an identification card that verifies its unique-object status.

MIRRORS & FRAMES

Georges Bac

6th arr. - 37, rue Bonaparte - 43 26 82 67
Open 9 a.m.-noon & 2 p.m.-6:30 p.m. Closed Sun. & Aug. No cards.

Museums and major art dealers have known for a long time about the impressive inventory of gilded wood frames, consoles and mirrors from the seventeenth and eighteenth centuries housed in this gallery, which enjoys the highest reputation.

Marguerite Fondeur

7th arr. - 24, rue de Beaune - 42 61 25 78
Open 2 p.m.-6:30 p.m. Closed Sun. & end of July-Sept. 8. No cards.

There is no risk of getting stuck with a tricked-up phony cherub from the Italian or Spanish trade here in this fine old establishment founded by Madame Fondeur's parents. But to acquire a lovely gilded-wood piece or a mirror from the eighteenth century, with full proof of authenticity, involves a significant investment. There are also lovely, if not gilded, furniture, chairs and objects of the period.

Lebrun

8th arr. 155, rue du Faubourg-Saint-
Honoré - 45 61 14 66
*Open 9:30 a.m.-12:30 p.m. & 2 p.m.-6:30 p.m.
Closed Sat., Sun. & Aug. No cards.*

Mirrors, consoles, barometers and sculpted
wood all can be found here in addition to some
magnificent frames from the fifteenth to the
nineteenth century that constitute one of the
largest collections in Paris. Interestingly, the
establishment was founded as recently as 1947.
The restoration work is top-notch.

Navarro

6th arr. - 15, rue Saint-Sulpice
46 33 61 51
*Open 2:30 p.m.-7 p.m. Closed Sun., Mon. &
Aug. No cards.*

This establishment is founded on the love of
fine objects. Mirrors, barometers and gilded
wood from the seventeenth, eighteenth and
nineteenth centuries are graciously lent out for
"home trial" before purchasing. Certificates of
authenticity, as well as an inventory that covers
price ranges (and attracts an international clientele), are available upon request.

MUSICAL INSTRUMENTS

André Bissonnet

3rd arr. - 6, rue du Pas-de-la-Mule
48 87 20 15
*Open 2 p.m.-7 p.m. Closed Sun. & Aug. No
cards.*

Brother of the famous butcher Jean
Bissonnet, André—himself a butcher for
years—was seized by a passion for antique
musical instruments, which he knows how to
play very well. He has created from his former
butcher shop, whose decor is intact (other than
the added pieces), one of the more amusing
and astonishing boutiques in all of Paris.

Alain Vian

6th arr. - 8, rue Grégoire-de-Tours
43 54 02 69
*Open 9:30 a.m.-noon & 2 p.m.-7 p.m. Closed
Sat., Sun. & Aug. No cards.*

This famous shop is a mecca for the collector
and the curious alike. Alain Vian, expert to the
Customs authority and specialist in stringed
instruments, woodwinds and brass, has expanded into music boxes, calliopes, old accor-
dions, automatic violins, even cameras. But his

beloved favorite is his Barbary player organ; he
manufactures the playing rolls himself.

OPALINE WARE

Au Petit Hussard

7th arr. - 5, rue de Beaune
42 61 29 86
*Open 2:30 p.m.-6:30 p.m. Closed Sun. & Aug.
No cards.*

One treads very carefully in this little boutique. It is completely dedicated to opalines,
sulfides, Romantic porcelain and portraits of
children and notables from the early nineteenth century. Quality and prices rival each
other for highest position.

Hugette Rivière

1st arr. - 4, allée Riesener, Louvre des
Antiquaires - 42 97 28 36
*Open 11 a.m.-7 p.m. Closed Sun. & Mon. No
cards.*

The kingdom of opalines bears all the charm
of the Romantic era in its pink, mauve and
pigeon-breast-colored glory. We also found
Paris porcelains, jewelry and small furniture
from the Second Empire period.

PEWTER & BRASS

Jean Monin

7th arr. - 7, rue du Bac - 42 61 13 90
*Open 10 a.m.-12:30 p.m. & 2 p.m.-7 p.m.
(Mon. 2 p.m.-7 p.m.). Closed Sun. & Aug.
Cards: AE.*

There are few specialists on the subject of
pewter, but Jean Monin is clearly one of the
best. The manifestations of his expertise—
tumblers, goblets, harvest platters, soup por-
ringers and pitchers—are all of a high
decorative quality to equal, say, seventeenth-
century silver.

PORCELAIN & CHINA

Antiquités pour la Table

1st arr. - 170-172, galerie de Valois
42 96 32 30
*Open 1 p.m.-7 p.m. Closed Sun. & Mon. No
cards.*

Represented here are styles of china service
from the beginning of the nineteenth century
through the 1930s: Limoges, Gien,

Sarreguemines, Creil, as well as various Paris manufacturers—in every conceivable shape, color and price range.

Hélène Fournier-Guérin

6th arr. - 25, rue des Saints-Pères
42 60 21 81
Open 11 a.m.-12:30 p.m. & 2:30 p.m.-6:30 p.m. (Mon. 2:30 p.m.-6:30 p.m.). Closed Sun. & Aug. Cards: AE.

Here is a tasteful selection of porcelain and pottery primarily from the eighteenth century, and primarily from the houses of Moustiers and of La Compagnie des Indes. Also: painted pottery from Marseille, Strasbourg, Rouen and Nevers. This show is run by certified experts.

Galerie des Thériaques

94220 Charenton - 2, rue de l'Embarcadère
43 76 18 73
Open 9 a.m.-noon & 1 p.m.-6 p.m. Closed Sat., Sun. & Aug. No cards.

Monsieur Brachet, head of a pharmaceutical-supply house headquartered on the outskirts of Paris, will make sure you're supplied with every sort of apothecary device, instrument, object or accessory—old or new, even made-to-measure—you could imagine. There is a well-run showroom of such wares: pots and jars of every description, style and use (oil, salves, leeches), as well as watercolors, tripods, cuspidors, microscopes, and mortars.

L'Imprévu

6th arr. - 21, rue Guénégaud - 43 54 65 09
Open 2:30 p.m.-7 p.m. Closed Sun. & Aug. 1-Sept. 15. No cards.

It's all here, under the sign of the unexpected. As expected, right away a specialty is apparent: poured ceramicware, brightly colored and fashioned in relief, such as those pieces that flourished in the last 30 years or so of the nineteenth century. Among the genre: dessert plates, asparagus plates, oyster plates, plates from Salins, Sarreguemines, Clement, Longchamp and plates created by Delphin Massier at Vallauris. Then there's the house's stock of nineteenth-century printed plates from such manufacturers as Creil-Montereau, Choisy-le-Roi and Sarreguemines. And finally, the house's little specialty, tromp l'oeil platters adorned with fish or reptiles in the style known as "Bernard Palissy." Recently L'Imprévu has begun to deal in Second Empire objects and furniture.

Lefebvre et Fils

7th arr. - 24, rue du Bac - 42 61 18 40
Open 10:30 a.m.-noon & 2:30 p.m.-6:30 p.m. Closed Sun. & July 14-Aug. 31. Cards: AE.

Parisian society come here for their pottery, porcelain and sculpture from the sixteenth to the eighteenth century. This old establishment is run by the leading expert in antique ceramicware and celebrated its centennial in 1980. Lefebvre proudly lists among its former clients Victor Hugo and Marcel Proust.

Nicolier

7th arr. - 7, quai Voltaire - 42 60 78 63
Open 10:30 a.m.-noon & 2:30 p.m.-6:30 p.m. (Mon. 2:30 p.m.-6:30 p.m.). Closed Sun. & July 14-Aug. 31. No cards.

For three generations, this establishment has been presenting an astounding collection of pottery from the ninth to the nineteenth century: Iranian pottery, seventeenth-century china, decorated ceramicware from the Italian Renaissance (Urbino, Gubbio), vases, platters and statuettes in pottery and porcelain from all over Europe, including Delft, Sèvres, Saxony, Rouens, Moustiers, Nevers and Chantilly. Of course, all of it is of the best quality and in perfect condition. All sales are accompanied by a certified guarantee.

Florence Rousseau

7th arr. - 9, rue de Luynes - 45 48 04 71
Open 2 p.m.-6:30 p.m. Closed Sun., Mon. & Aug. No cards.

A green and floral theme, following the curving lines of art nouveau, runs markedly through this shop. Florence Rousseau, the owner, is more an admirer of the calmer art deco pottery. In any case, her store is so filled with china, porcelain and silver that, as she tells us, at one time she was unable to close her shutters. Lovely gift possibilities run the price gamut from 1,000 to 10,000 francs.

Trésors du Passé

8th arr. - 131, rue du Faubourg-Saint-Honoré - 42 25 05 39
Open 10 a.m.-7 p.m. Closed Sat., Sun., Mon. mornings & Aug. No cards.

Beautiful old pottery from the seventeenth and eighteenth centuries, including Sèvres porcelain and high-quality china, is available here. The walls are adorned with a number of eighteenth-century prints in black and white and in color, as well as drawings.

Vandermeersch
7th arr. - 27, quai Voltaire - 42 61 23 10
Open 10 a.m.-12:30 p.m. & 2 p.m.-6:30 p.m. Closed Sun., Mon. & Aug. Cards: V, AE, DC.

One of the founders of the Paris biennial shows, Pierre Vandermeersch was a major figure in the world of antiques. His son, Michel, is carrying on the business in a new store on the ground floor of the Villette mansion (where Voltaire died). The stock is limited but of the highest quality. His other store, on the rue de Beaune, is a good deal more eclectic.

RUGS & TAPESTRIES

Achdjian et Fils
8th arr. - 10, rue de Miromesnil
42 65 89 48, 42 68 07 71
Open 10 a.m.-12:30 p.m. & 2 p.m.-7 p.m. Closed Sun. & Aug. Cards: V, MC.

It is Berdj Achdjian, the son, who receives by appointment collectors looking for old and rare rugs. But both father and son tend to the gallery. Here, for excellent prices, you can find every manner of old Oriental rug: Caucasian, Armenian, Chinese and Turkish. Competent specialists, Achdjian has some rare gems in its collection, dating back to the sixteenth century, to complement the modern and highly decorative rugs.

Benadava
8th arr. - 28, rue de la Boétie - 43 59 12 21
Open 9:30 a.m.-6:30 p.m. Closed Sun. & Aug. No cards.

Specialists in the three activities going on here: restoration, appraisal and cataloging of rare rugs from the Far East. In addition, Benadava carries tapestries from Flanders and Aubusson, even from Gobelins, as well as a sizeable collection of European rugs from Spain, France and Portugal.

Jacqueline Boccara
8th arr. - 184, rue du Faubourg-Saint-Honoré - 43 59 84 63
Open 10 a.m.-1 p.m. & 2 p.m.-6:30 p.m. Closed Sun., Mon. & Aug. No cards.

No need to look any further for that tapestry you have been wanting to hang in your apartment. From the Middle Ages, the Renaissance, the neoclassical or the age of Enlightenment, Jaqueline Boccara has them. She supplies tapestries to the big European sales and auctions as well as to museums. If there is something she doesn't have, she will find it for you. And she also displays an array of collector's items and old drawings that she sells for reasonable prices.

Chevalier
7th arr. - 15, quai Voltaire - 42 60 72 68
Open 10 a.m.-6:30 p.m. (Sat. 11 a.m.-6:30 p.m.). Closed Sun. & Aug. Cards: V.

You'll think you're in a gracious private home, with all the woodwork and soft lighting. The establishment was founded in 1917, and today two of the grandsons who carry on the restoration work of the rugs and tapestries. Certified experts, the Chevalier team sells pieces of the highest quality, be they Oriental or European. The rugs are complemented by a fine selection of cushions, which aren't always easy to locate.

Lefortier
8th arr. - 54, rue du Faubourg-Saint-Honoré - 42 65 43 74
Open 10:30 a.m.-12:30 p.m. & 2 p.m.-6:30 p.m. Closed Sat., Sun. & Aug. No cards.

When an establishment of this quality is about to turn 100, it may safely be regarded as an institution. Heads of state come here from all over the world for gifts of state, and for appraisals of old rugs. Madame Potignon-Lefortier, who steers the destiny of the house, is expert for the Customs department and for the Court of Appeals of Paris.

Robert Mikaeloff
8th arr. - 23, rue de la Boétie - 42 65 24 55
Open 9 a.m.-noon & 2 p.m.-7 p.m. Closed Sun. & Aug. No cards.

To get the full effect of Robert Mikaeloff and his passion for his silk rugs from Tabriz, or his rarest Keshans, you must see him in action. It is more accurate to say that he *stages* his rugs rather than exhibits them. For the needs of his clients, he maintains a restoration service.

Remember that if you spend 1,200 francs or more in a store, you are entitled to a full refund of the value-added tax (VAT). See "Basics" for details.

Yves Mikaeloff

8th arr. - 10-14, rue Royale - 42 61 64 42
Open 10 a.m.-7 p.m. Closed Sun. & Aug. No cards.

In the Mikaeloff family, the passion for rugs knows no bounds; as a result, the environment in which they are sold is as sumptuous as we've ever imagined, let alone actually seen. To buy a rug is not a simple commercial act but an expression of love. The ambience is Oriental, the decor plush, and the prices . . . well, when in love, one doesn't keep count.

SCIENTIFIC & NAUTICAL INSTRUMENTS

Art et Marine

8th arr. - 8, rue de Miromesnil
42 65 27 85
Open 11 a.m.-7 p.m. (Sat. 2:30 p.m.-6 p.m.). Closed Sun. & July 14-Aug. 31. Cards: V, AE, DC.

Jean-Noël Marchand-Saurel is the sort of expert who knows about everything from shipowners' large-scale ship models to tiny models in ivory from Dieppe. All those suffering from unrequited love or nostalgia of things marine come here to obtain dioramas, sperm whale teeth, eighteenth- and nineteenth-century hourglasses, and old ships in a bottle (1,200 to 3,000 francs and up). Restoration services are provided.

Balmès-Richelieu

3rd arr. - 21, pl. des Vosges - 48 87 20 45
Open 10 a.m.-noon & 2 p.m.-7 p.m. (Mon. 2 p.m.-7 p.m.). Closed Sun. & Aug. No cards.

Here are some of the most beautiful marine articles in Paris. Nevertheless, Monsieur Balmès's grand specialty remains clocks and scientific instruments from the sixteenth to the nineteenth century.

Alain Brieux

6th arr. - 48, rue Jacob - 42 60 21 98
Open 10 a.m.-1 p.m. & 2 p.m.-6:30 p.m. Closed Sun. & Aug. Cards: DC.

One finds here astrolabes (compact instruments used to observe the position of celestial bodies before the invention of the sextant) certainly, but collectors the world over come here seeking medical and scientific antiques: wooden anatomy models, anatomical tables, surgical or optical instruments. Brieux takes great care in his selections, and is currently one of the important figures in his field.

Galerie Atlantide

1st arr. - 3, rue Sauval - 42 33 35 95
Open 11 a.m.-8 p.m. Closed Sun., Mon. & Aug. Cards: V, AE.

The exhibits in this store constitute a veritable marine history. And there are also the obligatory but handsome ships in bottle and scale-model reproductions of various marine-world objects. This shop also provides a restoration service for ship models and paintings.

Olivier Roux-Devillas

6th arr. - 12, rue Bonaparte - 43 54 69 32
Open 10 a.m.-noon & 2 p.m.-7 p.m. (Mon. 2 p.m.-7 p.m.). Closed Sun. No cards.

A superb shop with the lovely patina of ageless age, it presents a remarkable collection of marine, optical and scientific instruments. There are also old charts, documents and works on scientific and geographical subjects.

SILVER & GOLD

Bacstreet

7th arr. - 1, rue du Bac - 42 61 24 20
Open 10 a.m.-6:30 p.m. Closed Sun., Mon. & July 15-Aug. 31. No cards.

Though the jewelry here is certainly romantic and contemporary, the shop is known primarily for its lovely French and English silver, nicely presented, from the second half of the nineteenth century.

J.P. de Castro

4th arr. - 17, rue des Francs-Bourgeois
42 72 04 00
Open 10:30 a.m.-1 p.m. & 2 p.m.-7 p.m. (Sun. 11 a.m.-1 p.m. & 2 p.m.-7 p.m.). Closed Mon. No cards.

This is a magical place for lovers of old silver. It's full of delightful objects to give or to keep, all at reasonable prices. The recent enlargement of the shop now permits display of one of the largest arrays of silver in Paris. Every style is represented: Victorian, Napoléon III, bistro and classic. Collectors in search of the hard-to-find piece will find happiness here in the forms of samovars, chafing dishes, rare tableware and so forth.

Eléonore
8th arr. - 18, rue de Miromesnil
42 65 17 81
Open By appt. Closed Sat., Sun., July & Aug.
No cards.

Claude-Gérard Cassan and Sophie de
Granzial are walking catalogs of French silver—from the Renaissance to the 1880s—and
they offer a remarkable range of old silver and
curiosities. The two regularly exhibit their best
pieces at the Paris shows: stamped silver from
the eighteenth century with full documentation. They also provide restoration work.

A l'Epreuve du Temps
7th arr. - 88, rue du Bac - 42 22 11 42
Open 10 a.m.-6 p.m. Closed Sun. Cards: V, AE.
If you're in the mood for shopping for
charming old pieces, little boxes, knickknacks
and period jewelry, and at reasonable prices,
this is the spot. Restoration services, as well as
the fabrication of silver-plated flatware, are also
available.

Joséphine
6th arr. - 1, rue Bonaparte - 43 26 49 73
Open 10 a.m.-12:30 p.m. & 2:30 p.m.-6 p.m.
Closed Sun., Mon. & July 18-Aug. 31. No cards.
The variety, taste and magnificence of the
pieces selected from the eighteenth century to
the present by Claude Dubois will knock you
out. She is, without rival, the queen of the trade
in goldwork.

Jacques Kugel
8th arr. - 279, rue Saint-Honoré
42 60 86 23, 42 60 19 45
Open 10 a.m.-1 p.m. & 2:30 p.m.-6:30 p.m.
Closed Sun., Mon. & Aug. Cards: V, AE.
Devotees the world over speak with pride
simply for having had the good fortune to visit
this illustrious establishment and witness one
of the most magnificent displays of goldwork
ever assembled. Since Jacques passed on,
Nicolas and Alexis (his two sons) have carried
the torch. Here is royal silver, princely plates,
even paintings, furniture and all sorts of objects
of great curiosity and, as always, beauty.

Suger
1st arr. - 151, rue Saint-Honoré, Louvre
des Antiquaires - 42 97 28 69
Open 11 a.m.-7 p.m. Closed Sun. & Mon.
Cards: V, AE, DC.
Suger is one of the few houses in Paris to
carry on the trade of goldwork (exclusively),
from 1800 to 1950. Inheritors of the house of
Puiforcat goldsmiths, it boasts a significant
inventory of pieces, particularly from the
1920s, bearing the signatures of Tetard, Jean
Dupres and, of course, Puiforcat. The clientele
is composed largely of British buyers and other
such connoisseurs.

Au Vieux Paris
2nd arr. - 4, rue de la Paix - 42 61 00 89
Open 10 a.m.-12:30 p.m. & 2 p.m.-6:30 p.m.
(Mon. 2 p.m.-6:30 p.m.). Closed Sun. & Aug.
No cards.
Founded in 1849, this is the oldest establishment of its kind in Paris. Michel Turisk has
a reliable eye for old gold and presents a selection of old work, such as gold boxes from the
Regency and Empire periods and watches and
objects of interest from the seventeenth, eighteenth and nineteenth centuries.

TOYS, GAMES & DOLLS

Jacques Bittard–Les Drapeaux de France
1st arr. - 34, galerie Montpensier
40 20 00 11
Open 10:30 a.m.-6:30 p.m. Closed Sun. & Mon.
No cards.
Monsieur Roussel is not only one of the last
great artisans of toy soldiers and historic figurines, he is also a dealer for major manufacturers DOM, Pixie, CBG-Miguet and MDM.

Robert Capia
1st arr. - 24-26, galerie Véro-Dodat
42 36 25 94
Open 10 a.m.-7 p.m. Closed Sun. No cards.
This expert, known far and wide by collectors, and also an advisor to the Customs service, is the foremost specialist in antique dolls.
He has set up shop in one of the most forgotten

passages of Paris, the Véro-Dodat gallery, which was opened in 1826 by charcutiers Véro and Dodat. His dolls are all signed by the top names of yesteryear (Jumeau, Steiner, Bru, Rohmer, Gaultier, Schmitt) and are available for rental. The prices are high but justified by the quality. Also stocked here is just about anything to make youthful dreams come true: ivory dominoes, construction sets illustrated by lithographs and some mechanical toys. The workshop takes care of all after-sales service. We also particularly enjoyed the large selection of phonograph cylinders that played Sarah Bernhardt and Enrico Caruso for us.

La Maison de Poupée

6th arr. - 40, rue de Vaugirard
46 33 74 05
Open 2:30 p.m.-7 p.m. Closed Sun. & Aug. Cards: V.

Françoise du Rot Hazard opened this shop (actually more like a cross between a museum and a store) in 1980 out of sheer love for dolls. All are period pieces and almost all are accompanied by their original trousseaus. You can find the first dolls in celluloid, from the beginning of the nineteenth century, games, small theaters, puppet shows, dollhouse table settings in porcelain and magnificent dollhouses.

Monsieur Renard–Au Beau Noir

6th arr. - 6, rue de l'Echaudé - 43 25 70 72
Open 10:30 a.m.-1 p.m. & 2 p.m.-7 p.m. (Mon. 2:30 p.m.-7 p.m.). Closed Sun. & Aug. Cards: V.

Antique games and mechanical toys are the house specialties. Monsieur Renard has old dolls from famous makers (Bru, Jumeau and others) and games from the second half of the nineteenth century. Several times a year he gathers together exhibits of unusual items mixed with some naive paintings from the nineteenth century.

Au Petit Mayet

6th arr. - 10, rue Mayet - 45 67 68 29,
43 06 61 22
Open 11 a.m.-7 p.m. Closed Sun. No cards.

The home of the big specialist in old toys: trains, soldiers, boats, cars. Monsieur Lepage

is devoted to his field and conveys his enthusiasm winningly. We can't wait for Christmas.

Polichinelle

18th arr. - 20, rue André-del-Sarte
42 55 85 65
Open By appt. Closed Sun. & Aug. Cards: V.

François Theimer specializes in the appraisal, restoration and sale of nineteenth-century dolls in ceramic, wax or papier-mâché, with all the accompanying paraphernalia. These delicate but expensive individuals (5,000 to 100,000 francs) will also be taken care of by the workshop if they're ailing. The shop also puts out its own magazine, *Polichinelle*, at an annual subscription rate of 280 francs. And if furniture is needed, the upper floors of the shop are stacked with dollhouses, furniture, dresses, shoes, gloves umbrellas and hats from all periods.

Aux Soldats d'Antan

7th arr. - 12, rue de l'Université
42 60 89 56
Open 10:30 a.m.-noon & 2:30 p.m.-7 p.m. Closed Sun. & Aug. No cards.

Mademoiselle Stella was one of the first and remains one of the best in the antique-toy-soldier business, adding to this specialty an excellent knowledge of and collection of chivalric medals and insignias.

Le Temps Libre

7th arr. - 9, rue de Verneuil - 42 60 26 73
Open 2:30 p.m.-7:30 p.m. Closed Sun. & Aug. 15-Sept. 15. No cards.

There are plenty of out-of-the-ordinary gift ideas in this friendly jumble, where they say singer Serge Gainsbourg sticks his head in now and then. You'll find all sorts of doll furniture, Lehmann toys in metal and stacks of games.

Don't plan to do much shopping in Paris in August — a great many stores shut down for the entire vacation month.

Prices start at 20 francs and run to more than 10,000 francs for some of the mechanical toys.

La Tortue Electrique

5th arr. - 7, rue Frédéric-Sauton
43 29 49 28
Open 2 p.m.-7 p.m. Closed Sun. & Mon. No cards.

The electric turtle referred to in the shop's name is actually an obstacle-course game. Stacked into this shop opposite Notre-Dame are games of strategy or skill, chess pieces, puzzles, tops, target games and antique coin-activated games, to boot.

Vieille France

1st arr. - 364, rue Saint-Honoré
42 60 01 57
Open 10 a.m.-6:30 p.m. Closed Sun. No cards.

This place more than lives up to its name (which, of course, translates as "Old France"); it is packed with lovely sets of the kings of France, heroes of the Old Order, military paintings, medals and insignias, old flags and more. The France of yesteryear lives again, here among miniatures of the great moments of its history.

UMBRELLAS & WALKING STICKS

Antoine

1st arr. - 10, av. de l'Opéra - 42 96 01 80
Open 10 a.m.-7 p.m. Closed Sun. Parking: Pyramides. Cards: V, MC.

In 1745 Monsieur and Madame Antoine moved up from the Auvergne and set themselves up at either end of the Pont-Neuf and rented out umbrellas to bridge-crossing pedestrians. In 1760 they opened a shop in the galleries of the Palais-Royal, specializing in canes, umbrellas and parasols. Today the worthy descendant of this dynasty, Madame Lecarpentier Purorge, offers a collection of old umbrellas, canes and crops, and enjoys the steady stream of artists that come through her shop.

Lydia Bical

92200 Neuilly - 31, rue de Chartres
46 24 14 30
Open 3 p.m.-7:30 p.m. Closed Sun., Mon. & July 13-Sept. 1. No cards.

This remarkable spot features hundreds of canes produced in the years preceding 1930:

canes by Dandy with gold knobs, canes carved by doughboys in the trenches, canes identifying the owner as a Dreyfus supporter, canes depicting George Clemenceau. Then, of course, there are the sword canes, rifle canes, cosh canes (a weighted weapon similar to a blackjack) and professional canes (undertakers and police, among them). And we must not forget the absinthe canes, the blowgun canes, fire-starting canes and the rather salacious model with a set of mirrors that permits the voyeur to peek beneath ladies' skirts.

Madeleine Gély

7th arr. - 218, bd Saint-Germain
42 22 63 35
Open 9:30 a.m.-7 p.m. Closed Sun. & Mon. No cards.

Madeleine Gély offers hundreds of canes in astonishing forms—from antique canes and collector's items to utilitarian canes and ceremonial canes. Equally fascinating are the dual-function canes, such as watch/canes, pipe/canes, cigarette holder/canes, horse measurer/canes and a whiskey cane with the original flask, stopper and glass intact.

WEAPONS

Aux Armes de France–Charles Marchal

8th arr. - 3, rue de Miromesnil
42 65 72 79
Open 10 a.m.-noon & 2 p.m.-7 p.m. Closed Sat., Sun. & July 15-Aug. 31. No cards.

This display is one of the best known among those who savor collectible military objects and arms. There are fewer naval objects than there have been in the past, but there is still a formidable selection of lead soldiers.

Patrice Reboul

1st arr. - 6, allée Riesener, Louvre des Antiquaires - 42 97 28 93
Open 11 a.m.-1 p.m. & 2 p.m.-7 p.m. Closed Sun. & Mon. Cards: V, AE.

This narrow little shop is stuffed to brimming with enough curiosities to fascinate anyone. Medals (prices start at 50 francs) and delightful miniature replicas of hats of the Napoleonic era done during the Second Empire by Charles Sandre, toymaker to the Imperial household (5,000 to 10,000 francs) are among some of delights that can be found in this unusual shop.

AT YOUR SERVICE

BABY-SITTERS

Ababa

15th arr. - 8, av. du Maine - 45 49 46 46
Open 7:45 a.m.-9 p.m. (offices).

Ababa leaves us agaga: It comprises Ababa "show" (organizing children's parties), Ababa "granny" (elderly ladies' companions), Ababa "clean" (housecleaning, particularly day-after-party cleanup), Ababa "grosses têtes" (tutorial support in all subjects), Ababa "commensal" (practicing foreign languages) and Ababa "tonus" (getting in shape). Although we haven't yet had the opportunity to personally try every one of their services, the word-of-

---

AU PAIRS

Two reliable au pair services are L'Accueil Familial des Jeunes Etrangers, 23 rue du Cherche-Midi, 6th arr., 42 22 50 34; and L'Arche, 7 rue Bargue, 15th arr., 42 73 43 39.

---

mouth reports are excellent. There is a fixed price of 300 francs per month or 750 francs quarterly plus hourly charges (for example, babysitting at 24 francs an hour or housecleaning help at 30 francs an hour).

BEAUTY & HEALTH

Beauty Spot

9th arr. - 16, rue des Martyrs - 45 26 46 39
Open 8 a.m.-8 p.m. (by appt. only).

Seven days a week these ladies will come to you to perform their magic: facials, hairdos, makeup jobs—whether it's your wedding day or you just feel like being beautiful without lifting a finger. These are professionals who are accustomed to plying their craft in homes and can adapt to whatever situation they find. Prices, according to services, range from 200 to 1,500 francs.

Paris Top Services

8th arr. - 6, rue de Greffhule - 42 88 58 99
Open 6 a.m.-8 p.m. Closed Aug. 5-25.

Beauticians and chiropractors are ready, after a simple phone call, to come to your place and give massages and herbal facials. They are adept at shiatsu and other forms of massage, as well as depilation and mud packs. Prices run according to services (generally from 300 to 500 francs).

SOS-Kiné

7th arr. - 11 bis, rue Chomel - 45 49 99 99
Open daily 24 hours.

These are certified masseurs offering therapeutic, relaxation or athletic massages. We tried them once in an emergency, on Bastille Day morning, and someone appeared at our doorstep in 30 minutes (he thankfully, carefully and competently proceeded to put an ornery vertebra back in its rightful place).

CLOTHING REPAIR

Mermoz Retouches

8th arr. - 21, rue Jean-Mermoz
42 25 73 36
Open 9 a.m.-6 p.m. Closed Sun., Mon. & Aug.

This is an address to hold on to, since good alterations specialists are so rare. Nothing daunts them, whether it's a matter of lengthening, shortening or inserting shoulder pads. Prices are made according to estimate.

DRY CLEANERS

Delaporte

8th arr. - 62, rue François-Ier - 43 59 82 11
Open 9 a.m.-7 p.m. (Sat. until 5 p.m.). Closed Sun. Parking: François-Ier, Georges-V.

The Delaporte dry-cleaning shop is owned by Jean-Claude Lesèche, a famous name in Paris dry cleaning. His mother taught him everything, on the job, and he was an excellent student. All the tailors and dressmakers on avenue Montaigne call on him.

Huguet

16th arr. - 47, av. Marceau - 47 20 23 02,
47 23 81 39
Open 9 a.m.-7 p.m. Closed Sat. & Sun.

Behind the imposing facade lies a Belle
Epoque shop interior that is home to seemingly perfect dry-cleaning services, which are
relied upon by the haute couture neighbors
and all the Paris celebrities, at astonishingly
reasonable prices (wedding gown, 400 francs;
suit, 100 francs), including free delivery. And
there's an extra attraction: hand-washed and
ironed men's shirts for 30 francs.

HIRED HANDS

Connexion Services

8th arr. - 172, bd Haussmann - 42 93 68 08
Open 9 a.m.-8 p.m. Closed Sat. & Sun.

Thibault de Saint-Vincent and Tristan Aug-
ier de Moussac have been encroaching on the
terrain of the Ludéric firm for a couple of years
now. And, after all, you can't blame them.
These two young men, recent business-school
graduates, offer services designed for "companies that are inundated daily by a multitude of
problems" and for those "men and women of
action who don't have time to waste on both-
ersome details." Bravo! This means that they
take care of housekeeping, errands, deliveries
and, in short, all those unexpected minor
emergencies that come up. The two also have
a proclivity for "redecorating and refurbishing." Concerning the latter, estimates are free
and the tradesmen and artisans are hand-
picked. Prices are available upon request, and
a yearly subscription option is available, at 600
francs, which saves 20 percent on the fees. The
only hitch is that the two young entrepreneurs
seem to be snowed under themselves; on the
day of our appointment they canceled and
never returned the call.

Ludéric

16th arr. - 20, rue Pétrarque - 45 53 93 93
*Open 9 a.m.-1 p.m. & 2 p.m.-6 p.m. Closed Sat.,
Sun. & 1 wk. in Aug.*

The "Ludéricians" all look like their boss,
Olivier Maurey: stylishly preppy, chic, glowing
with health and bursting with enthusiasm.
Begun in 1975, this is the best known of the
multiservice agencies, and it remains true to its
founding dictum, "Everything is possible."

You can ask of the rapidly growing company
just about anything. At first, when it was
Ludéric Service, they baby-sat, shopped,
chauffeured, served, dog-sat and so forth.
Some years later Ludéric Evénement joined
the family, organizing receptions and promo-
tional events. Then came Ludéric Traiteur (caterer), when hungry Ludéric bought up a
caterer and pastry outfit. Since then we've seen
Haute Tension (for launching new products),
Le Repérage Français (providing locations for
filming or parties), Kiosque Théâtre (15, place
de la Madeleine, for last-minute tickets), Boutique Ludéric (for caviar, salmon and Champagne at low prices), Forum Voyages (a travel
agency) and, lastly, a bit of madcap, the historic
bistro L'Ami Louis that Ludéric bought to
preserve it intact. All horizons are met, but
surely by the time you read this Ludéric will no
doubt have created a new service to meet the
needs of some new client. The only question
that remains is whether Ludéric can continue
to cater to individual needs in the face of its
growing corporate clientele and as they expand
to the provinces and overseas. We'll let you
know in a year or two. The yearly membership
(620 francs for individuals, 1,550 francs for
corporate accounts) provides access to all services (for example, baby-sitting at 25 francs per
hour, housecleaning at 36 francs per hour).

HOME DELIVERY

BREAKFAST

Mille Break First

12th arr. - 7-9, pl. Abel-Leblanc
43 45 76 53
Open daily 24 hours. Free delivery.

Ordered the night before, breakfast is delivered any time from 7 a.m. to 1 p.m. There are
all sorts of fixed formulas, including the traditional continental breakfast (180 francs for
two), the "brunch" (260 francs for two) and
the "morning after," which includes a revital-
izing cocktail of white wine, grape juice, Alka-
Seltzer and a small bottle of Perrier, plus
grapefruit juice (60 francs). There are breakfast
or brunch menus for company and group functions. Newspapers and cigarettes come free
with orders priced at 580 francs and up.

DRINKS

Bacchus
42 38 04 73
Open daily 24 hours.

If you order by Minitel before 2:30 p.m., delivery within 24 hours is assured. And there doesn't seem to be much missing from the roster: all varieties of wine, liquor, liqueurs, Champagne and all the literature that goes with such—wine guides, reference works and so forth. A bottle of Perrier-Jouët is 135 francs; delivery is 85 francs (the only telephone orders accepted are those totaling more than 600 francs).

FOOD

Martin Alma
8th arr. - 44, rue Goujon - 43 59 28 25
Open noon-2:30 p.m. & 7 p.m.-11 p.m. (Sun. noon-2:30 p.m.). Closed Mon. 30F delivery charge.

This place prepares some classy couscous, the best in Paris we're promised, as well as the traditional Moroccan tahines. On Wednesday the tradition turns to paella. This is not an express delivery service like some of its counterparts but rather a high-quality caterer with the advantage of evening delivery. The only hitch is that delivery is for a minimum of four persons, and the price per averages about 185 francs.

Les Gustatifs Modernes
15th arr. - 56, rue Falguière - 43 22 00 00
Open noon-2:30 p.m. & 7 p.m.-11:30 p.m. (Sat. & Sun. 7 p.m.-11:30 p.m.). 24-hour ordering, free delivery.

According to some surveys, 40 percent of Parisians are urbane young professionals for whom the traditional service of a meal has lost its ritual meaning. That is, intensely active lives and meals that suit the moment, such as pizza one evening, a home-cooked meal the next. Targeting this slice as their clientele, Les Gustatifs Modernes gives them what they want. Fast (30 to 45 minutes), friendly and not overpriced, the staff delivers such tasty good salads as tomato, cucumber, goat cheese and endive leaves or lettuce with smoked trout, radishes, cheese, avocado and shrimp. Or, if you prefer, a chicken fricassée with tarragon, sole cooked in Chablis, a blanquette or a curry of veal, all well prepared and followed by deli-

cious desserts. Everything is light but copious. A la carte meals are priced between 120 francs and 150 francs, fixed-price menus are available at 90 francs, 100 francs and 110 francs. By the same token, carefully done luncheon formulas can be delivered to the office. The salad lunches are not up to the rest.

Jacques Hesse
15th arr. - 16, rue Saint-Charles
45 77 77 83
Open 10 a.m.-2 p.m. (companies only), 6 p.m.-11:30 p.m. By Minitel, 3615 code Jacques Hesse. Free delivery.

This French banker worked on Wall Street before making the return to France ten years ago. His reorientation was bumpy, as he found French life lacking comfort and common sense. In a few months he had thrown over banking and launched a home-delivery service. Today Hesse delivers to companies and individuals, changes his menu daily, and comes up with exciting specials, like the bachelor platter for the month of August. Service is fast and efficient. But the portions are skimpy and the quality-price ratio is more and more favoring price (120 to 180 francs per person).

La Pomme de Pain
8th arr. - 22, rue de la Pépinière
43 87 29 30
Open 11 a.m.-6 p.m. (ordering 10 a.m.-5 p.m.). Closed Sat. & Sun. 50F delivery charge, free for 200F and over.

You have no time to prepare something decent to eat, so you order a sandwich or a quiche and a beer. It may not be great for the diet, but at least La Pomme de Pain fare is quite tasty. Only the prices are a bit of a problem: 50 francs for delivery of tabs less than 200 francs (free delivery for above that); sandwiches cost 15 to 25 francs; salads, about 28 francs.

Slice
6th arr. - 62, rue Monsieur-Le-Prince
43 54 18 18
Open daily 11:30 a.m.-2:30 p.m. & 6:30 p.m.-midnight.

Here is the real American enormous pizza with a crunchy thin crust, served with brownies and a large soda. Sounds great, right? Not if the pizza is undercooked, or the delivery person forgets the brownies, or if you order the regretable vinegary cabbage they dare to deem cole slaw. The prices aren't bad: 200 francs for two includes pizza, cole slaw and brownies. Delivery for orders of 90 francs and up.

Wenchow

3rd arr. - 55, rue au Maire - 42 74 72 54
Open daily 9 a.m.-11 p.m.

This is Chinese take-out, or bring-to (as the name translates): batter-fried shrimp, Cantonese raviolis, almond chicken and Peking beef, with the house tea, of course. Frankly, it's not bad, perfect for when we're suddenly struck by an overwhelming urge for eggrolls. . . .

FRUIT BASKETS & FLOWERS

Exotic Center

11th arr. - 3 bis, bd de Charonne
43 48 77 20, 43 48 24 49
Open 10 a.m.-8 p.m. Closed Sun. Parking: Nation.

Pineapples, mangoes, old rum, tea: Antillean baskets for delivery come in five sizes, starting at 300 francs. This is for someone searching for that special, unusual basket gift.

Interfruit Service

17th arr. - 89, av. de Wagram - 47 63 10 55
Open 9 a.m.-7 p.m. Closed Aug. 50F delivery charge.

Baskets of in-season or exotic fruit are nicely done up and delivered. Interfruit has swiftly become a classic in its field (about 450 to 500 francs for a lovely basket).

Téléfleurs France

10th arr. - 15, rue Martel - 48 24 00 13
Open 8:30 a.m.-6 p.m. Closed Sun.

This chain of florists delivers anywhere in France, with 3,000 shops at your service.

MISCELLANY

Le "22" Les Services à Domicile

6th arr. - 40, rue du Dragon - 42 22 22 22
Open daily 24 hours.

If you have decided to stay put in your quarters and live the lazy life, you should write this telephone number down in red. Le "22" delivers everything: the menus of certain restaurants (without a surcharge), groceries, beverages, fruits and vegetables. And it can arrange for repairs, baby-sitting and housecleaning. In short, there doesn't seem to be a limit to the services offered. All you need to do is pick up the phone and dial.

SWEETS

Intergâteaux

Minitel: 3615 code GATO
24-hour ordering. 68F delivery charge (60F minimum order).

This establishment attempts to deliver pastry and chocolates (with a message if you like) anywhere in Paris, or for that matter, all over France. This company promises to deliver within 24 hours.

LAUNDRY

Blanchisserie Soret

8th arr. - 25, rue Royale, cité Berryer, 3rd floor - 45 65 77 28
Open 7:30 a.m.-7 p.m. Closed Sat., Sun. & Aug.

The bachelor's savior, Jean Soret, like his father and his grandfather before him, takes great care of gentlemen's wardrobes, including cleaning them by hand. From simple shirts (29.50 francs) to evening shirts (95 francs) and from silk pajamas (100 francs) to nightshirts (16 to 25 francs), Soret cleans everything and delivers to your home.

Louyot

7th arr. - 4, rue Perronet - 42 22 15 26
Open 8 a.m.-noon & 1:30 p.m.-6:30 p.m. Closed Sat. & Sun.

Ah, Madame Louyot, your clientele is the most intellectual that a laundry has ever known. But then again, what a laundry it is! Right out of Zola, with its cast irons, the huge table in the middle of the shop, the laundry hanging above and the warm steam and smell of cleanliness that permeate the place. Madame Louyot is not only an artisan of clean linen but also a guardian of a tradition. And, what is even more rare, the rest of the help is charming and friendly as well.

Vendôme

1st arr. - 24, rue du Mont-Thabor
42 60 74 38
Open 8 a.m.-5 p.m. Closed Sat., Sun. & Aug.

Madame Nicole has replaced Madame Elise in the management of the Vendôme laundry. Other than that, nothing here has changed. Just as in the previous century, the laundry maids here wash by hand, using soap flakes, and hand-iron delicate finery, Chantilly lace and all. A cambric handkerchief is laundered for 8 francs, but a baptismal robe costs 500 francs. Vendôme also takes care of embroidered tablecloths and men's shirts, and, perhaps happiest of all, they deliver.

LOCKSMITHS

Jacques Rouge
14th arr. - 30, rue Delambre - 43 20 67 81
Open 8 a.m.-noon & 1 p.m.-5:30 p.m. Closed Sat. & Sun.

He can copy or make up any key, old or otherwise—be it to your Louis XVI commode or your two-car garage. He also installs anti-theft door reinforcement and double-glazed windows. Prices follow estimates.

MAID SERVICE

Maison Service
16th arr. - 10, rue Mesnil - 45 53 62 30
Open 9 a.m.-noon & 2 p.m.-6 p.m. Closed Sat. & Sun.

You ought to know from the start that the personnel here are top-notch—and temporary. The woman who deigns to respond to the telephone will inform you in no uncertain terms that Maison Service hires only French from France between 30 and 60 years old, possessing five years of certified experience and excellent references, and ready to serve "a privileged social class." If that sounds like it fits the bill, you will pay 90 francs perhour for someone to do your ironing, your cleaning, your cooking, all for a minimum of four hours. Ladies' companions and governesses can be procured on the same basis, for four or five months, but be advised that these grand ladies of household help have never heard of volume discounts.

Molly Maid
15th arr. - 62, rue des Morillons
42 50 46 26
Open 9 a.m.-7 p.m. Closed Sat. & Sun.

First comes the evaluation and the estimate. If you are happy with Molly Maid's price, then the cleaning commando arrives, in uniform, thank you very much, with full equipment. Brooms up, forward, march! Everything is vacuumed, swept, dusted, washed, waxed and put away. The Molly Maids don't take on huge

jobs or unusually heavy work, but they are quite simply the queens of housework.

RENT-A- . . .

BICYCLE

Bicyclub
17th arr. - 8, pl. de la Porte Champerret
47 66 55 92
Open 9 a.m.-1 p.m. & 2 p.m.-6 p.m. Closed Sat. morning & Sun. Other branches.

These bikes are just right for pedaling through the huge wooded parks on the edge of Paris. Adult bikes (with baby seats available) and children's models (training wheels available) can be rented for 55 francs for the day.

BOAT

Navig France
17th arr. - 172, bd Berthier - 46 22 10 86
Open 9 a.m.-7 p.m. Closed Sat. & Sun.

Little barges, nine meters by three meters, that sleep six are available here, for about 7,680 francs a week (in season). Weekend prices equal 60 percent of the charge for a week. A boat license is preferred. Departures from Saint-Maur.

CAR

JKL
16th arr. - 23, av. de Neuilly - 47 47 77 00
Open 8:30 a.m.-7 p.m. Closed Sun.

Make your dream come true—at least for a day or a weekend: a Testarossa, Porsche 911 Carrera, Jaguar, Rolls-Royce, even a Range Rover. For a weekend, it will cost you from 6,900 to 11,000 francs, depending on the model.

Murdoch
16th arr. - 59, av. Marceau - 47 20 00 21
Open 9 a.m.-7 p.m. Closed Sun. 24-hour ordering.

The American-style limousine comes furnished with unflappable chauffeur, telephone and bar, perfect for gliding quietly down the avenues. It's VIP service for the VIP in your life, or perhaps just for splashy arrivals at big parties. The cost? Just 400 francs per hour for a Mercedes, plus 8 francs per kilometer after the first ten kilometers.

FORMAL OUTFIT

Eugénie Boiserie
9th arr. - 32, rue Vignon - 47 42 43 71
*Open 10 a.m.-noon & 1 p.m.-6 p.m. Closed Sun.
& Mon.*

In business for over 30 years, Eugénie Boiserie carries a stunning collection of haute-couture gowns for hire (700 francs, plus a 1,000-franc deposit). The vast selection of dresses is hidden away in the back of the store (the front is given over to old-fashioned gift items), where they are shown to customers by appointment. No accessories are available, but alterations can be arranged.

Le Cor de Chasse
6th arr. - 40, rue de Buci - 43 26 51 89
*Open 9 a.m.-noon & 1:30 p.m.-6 p.m. Closed
Sun. & Mon.*

Famous since 1875 and loved by several generations of Parisians, this stylish shop hires out morning clothes, top hats, tuxedos and other formal apparel for men (rental fees range between 600 and 700 francs). Shirts and accessories are offered for sale, and alterations are handled by expert tailors.

Les Costumes de Paris
9th arr. - 21 bis, rue Victor-Massé
48 78 41 02
*Open 9:30 a.m.-1 p.m. & 2 p.m.-6:30 p.m.
Closed Sun. & Mon.*

Among the charming, droll and zany costumes fit for the fanciest fancy-dress ball is an enchanting collection of evening gowns by Loris Azzaro, Thierry Mugler, Diamant Noir and others, in sizes 36 to 44 (which roughly translates to American sizes 6 to 14). All these gowns are in excellent condition. The price for rental runs 500 to 2,000 francs.

Velleda
10th arr. - 206, rue Lafayette - 42 41 81 93
Open 10 a.m.-7 p.m. Closed Sun.

What, absolutely nothing to wear to the masquerade ball? You must check out the in-

*Don't plan to shop on Sundays —
the vast majority of Paris
stores are closed.*

credible selection of costumes and disguises at Velleda; people have been known to rent the shop's bridal "costume" to wear to their own wedding! Just as authentic are the medieval get-ups and the swingy, beaded Roaring Twenties gowns. Rates run to 400 francs for a weekend rental, plus a deposit of 1,500 to 3,000 francs.

HELICOPTER

Hélicap
25th arr. - 4, av. de la Porte-de-Sèvres
45 57 75 51
Open 9 a.m.-7 p.m. Closed Sat. & Sun.

See Paris and La Défense from the air, or Versailles and its surroundings, or take a trip to the Château d'Esclimont for dinner, touching down on the lawn out front. The possibilities are endless: the cliffs at Etretat on the Norman coast, Mont Saint-Michel, the castles on the Loire. By now you're probably wondering what the price for such trips could be. . . . Versailles for 300 to 15,600 francs (five people) makes a very nice gift.

PLANE

Euralair
Le Bourget - Aéroport du Bourget
48 35 95 22
Open daily 24 hours. Parking: Euralair.

This is a wonderful service if you have the means, and we mean the means! A Mystère Falcon 20 is yours for 18,600 francs per day, to which you add 5,825 francs per hour of flying time, as well as lodgings for the two pilots and the stewardess if you are gone more than two days. Should a Mystère be too small, ask for one of the three Boeing 737s they keep in the stables.

SHOE REPAIR

Central Crépins
3rd arr. - 48, rue de Turbigo - 42 72 68 64
*Open 8:30 a.m.-7 p.m. Closed Sat. morning,
Sun. & Aug.*

Bags, suitcases, saddles and clothes, Central Crépins repairs everything in leather. Discounts are available to regulars with a membership card.

Coordonnerie Vaneau
7th arr. - 44, rue Vaneau - 42 22 06 94
Open 9 a.m.-1 p.m. & 2 p.m.-7 p.m. Closed Sun. Parking: Bon-Marché. 5 other branches: 34, rue Jean-Mermoz - 8th arr.; 35, rue de Lonchamp - 16th arr.; 8, rue Mignard - 16th arr.; 51, bd Gouvion-Saint-Cyr - 17th arr.; 37, rue de Chézy - Neuilly. (Call 42 22 06 94 for information.)

The best for the finest. Vaneau is where the finest feet of Paris, shod by Lobb, Weston or Aubercy, go to have work done. It is sturdy, artisanal shoe repair, for prices running from 250 francs to 500 francs. Free pickup and delivery with a membership card.

A l'Exactitude
9th arr. - 28, rue Rodier - 48 78 03 10
Open 8 a.m.-12:30 p.m. & 1:45 p.m.-7 p.m. Closed Sun. & Mon. Parking: Anvers.

Jean-Paul Pigeon works for Weston shoemakers, and repairs all reputable makes.

BEAUTY

BEAUTY SALONS

Jacqueline Bravo
16th arr. - 19, av. de la Grande-Armée
45 00 25 02
Open 9 a.m.-8 p.m. Closed Sun. No cards.

This strikingly handsome, all-new establishment encourages fitness as well as beauty with a wide range of treatments and exercise classes, including slimming or calisthenics (100 to 295 francs) with a certified physical therapist, water therapy, sauna and tanning. Skin-care services include treatments for before and after plastic surgery (190 francs), skin repair for overenthusiastic sunbathers (295 francs) and facials to brighten smokers' dulled complexions (195 francs). Hair care and styling are also available, as well as leg waxing, pedicures, and the list goes on. This all-under-one-roof approach is quite practical for the busy but well-groomed woman.

Carita
8th arr. - 11, rue du Faubourg-Saint-Honoré - 42 65 79 00
Open 9 a.m.-7 p.m. Closed Sat. & Sun. Parking: Madeleine. Cards: V, AE, DC, MC. Men's services available.

Carita's famous name now belongs to Shiseido, the Japanese cosmetics company. Completely redesigned by the divine Andrée Putmann, the salon's luxurious but minimalist decor in tones of beige and brown is functional and simply stunning. The ground floor is now occupied by a reception area and private rooms. The salon's cadre of hair stylists practice their art on the upper floor, where other beauty services are also dispensed (stars and other bigwigs are pampered in royally appointed private booths). Carita treatments have fully earned their excellent reputation; expert beauticians can impart a permanent curl to eyelashes or shape eyebrows and lips with a special tattooing technique (2,500 and 3,000 francs, respectively). A "day of beauty" can be yours for 2,000 francs. Marc is the man to call for an incredible antistress leg-and-foot massage, the beneficial effects of which extend to the entire body. Classic Carita facials last about an hour, and cost 400 francs. A last note: Paris's chic Japanese population swears by Carita's shiatsu massage (450 francs for an hour and a half of pure bliss).

Jeanne Gatineau
8th arr. - 52, rue du Faubourg-Saint-Honoré - 42 65 52 52
Open 10 a.m.-6:30 p.m. (Mon. noon-6:30 p.m., Sat. 9 a.m.-2 p.m.). Closed Sun. Parking: Malesherbes. Cards: V, AE, DC.

This well-regarded establishment offers its clients a warm atmosphere and stimulating, effective beauty treatments. Serious body care includes a massage and collagen mask for the bust that yields impressive results (450 francs). Sagging skin invariably responds to the "toni-ionic" treatment that employs a muscular stimulation machine (250 francs). The tired and bleary can treat themselves to an entire day of beauty care (dietetic lunch included) for a mere 1,800 francs; women on the run will appreciate the "beauty-express" service (160 francs), and a special treatment offer is available to the younger set for a reasonable sum (165 francs).

Guerlain

6th arr. - 29, rue de Sèvres - 42 22 46 60

Open 9:30 a.m.-6:45 p.m. (Sat. until 7 p.m.).
Closed Sun. Cards: V, MC. Other branch: 68,
av. des Champs-Elysées - 8th arr. - 43 59 31 10.

Guerlain is tops in beauty care. At the Champs-Elysées location, expert technicians dispense the very latest skin-care treatments—they'll even restructure your wrinkles—you can rest assured that your face is in the very best hands. So lie back and enjoy the luxurious surroundings while the excellent Issima line of skin products is applied to your skin for a relaxing hour and a quarter (about 350 francs). Be sure to stop at the perfume counter to try some of the enchanting house fragrances.

Lancôme

8th arr. - 29, rue du Faubourg-Saint-Honoré - 42 65 30 74

Open 10 a.m.-7 p.m. (Wed. 1 p.m.-7 p.m.).
Closed Sat. & Sun. Parking: Madeleine. Cards:
V, AE, DC.

Isabella Rossellini's haunting beauty projects Lancôme's public image, but top aesthetician Béatrice Braune (director of the Lancôme institute) is the woman behind the scenes here who makes sure the products deliver what they promise. An exclusive "beauty computer" measures the skin's smoothness, elasticity, moisture level and degree of dryness and/or oiliness, then produces a prescription for personalized skin care. Services offered in the institute's handsome, comfortable salons include a Niosome treatment, a bioenergizing massage and body sloughing followed by a lymphatic drainage massage. One's wallet is lightened to the tune of 300 or 400 francs, depending on the type of treatment chosen.

Ingrid Millet

8th arr. - 54, rue du Faubourg-Saint-Honoré - 42 66 66 20

Open 9 a.m.-6 p.m. Closed Sun. Cards: V, AE,
DC.

Madame Millet doesn't eat the quantities of caviar she buys; no, she slathers it (in cream form) on her clients' faces. Her specialized skin-care services include a facial mask/tonic/rejuvenation treatment (365 francs), an energizing facial (520 francs) and an all-over body treatment with a particularly effective sloughing action (750 francs). The salon's soothing green-and-white decor makes it an oasis of calm and relaxation on the busy Faubourg-Saint-Honoré.

Jeanne Piaubert

8th arr. - 129, rue du Faubourg-Saint-Honoré - 43 59 36 46

Open 9 a.m.-6 p.m. Closed Sat. & Sun. No
cards.

The Jeanne Piaubert beauty institute is backed up by a laboratory that specializes in body-care products. The institute applies the treatments according to a time-tested method in order to model the body's contours: electrical muscle stimulation is followed by massage. A vitamin-based cream and a specially formulated vitamin capsule to be taken orally complete the program. For new mothers, or women who have lost a lot of weight, the system strengthens and tones flaccid tissues. In short, the method can work wonders if one enters into it with determination. Body treatments cost 250 francs; a twenty-session subscription sells for 2,950 francs.

Sothys

8th arr. - 128, rue du Faubourg-Saint-Honoré - 45 63 98 18

Open 9:30 a.m.-7:30 p.m. (Thurs. until 9 p.m.,
Sat. 10 a.m.-5 p.m.). Closed Sun. Parking:
Hôtel Bristol. Cards: V, AE, DC. Men's services
available.

How luxurious! How chic! In Sothys's fifteen private booths (all equipped with cellular phones), a capable staff dispenses a wide variety of beauty treatments, ranging from deep facial cleansing to slimming techniques (which include baths in highly carbonated water paired with hydromassage). It's quite tickly and pleasant, take our word for it. (Prices go from about 200 to 400 francs.)

Helena Topiol

39 58 86 86

By appt. only. No cards.

Madame Topiol is a strong-minded, energetic beauty specialist who plies her trade in collaboration with a team of medical experts. She shuns all hoopla (no advertising!) and approaches her work with great seriousness. She will soothe and rejuvenate you with 90 minutes of massage, dead-cell sloughing, purifying masks, electromassage and sensible advice ("Drink more water, get more sleep, work less"). A maternal type, she coddles her customers with magic fingers. Treatments are tariffed in the neighborhood of 400 francs.

EPILATION

Ella Bache
2nd arr. - 8, rue de la Paix - 42 61 67 14
Open 10 a.m.-6 p.m. (Sat. 9 a.m.-5 p.m.). Closed Sun. No cards.

Cold wax is Ella Bache's secret weapon against unwanted hair. The treatment starts with a mentholated disinfecting lotion, then waxing and the application of a soothing moisturizing cream. Prices? Legs, 108 francs; bikini line, 64 francs; underarms, 38 francs.

Institut Georges-V
8th arr. - 12, av. Georges-V - 47 23 49 77
Open 9 a.m.-7 p.m. Closed Sat. & Sun. No cards.

Nary an unwanted hair will survive once Antoinette gets through with you. For 23 years she has been removing unwanted hair from heavenly bodies. The salon is unprepossessing (just two rooms on the fifth floor), but the service and products are first-rate. Antoinette swears by a special pale-pink bees' wax, made just for her by an unnamed skilled artisan; and her far-famed technique leaves legs smooth and silky for at least three weeks. By appointment only, from 150 francs.

HAIR SALONS

Patrick Alès
8th arr. - 37, av. Franklin-Roosevelt
43 59 33 96
Open 9 a.m.-6 p.m. (Wed. 10 a.m.-6 p.m.). Closed Sun. & Mon. Parking: Rond-Point des Champs-Elysées. No cards.

Young Patrick Alès is the mind behind the excellent "Phyto" line of hair treatments. Formerly a stylist with Carita, Alès developed the products in his spare time (in his garage, no less) with the help of his friend and collaborator, Olga. She tried each formula on herself, and numbered them according to how many times each had been tested (shampoo S88: 88 trials). Today, Alès continues to come up with new products at his estate in Provence, while Olga runs the Paris salon.

Alexandre
8th arr. - 3, av. Matignon - 42 25 57 90
Open 9:30 a.m.-6:30 p.m. Closed Sun. & Mon. No cards.

Even if it's only once in your life, you really should visit this lovely old art deco salon, where socialites and celebrities have been elegantly coiffed for years and years. Alexandre is so passionate about hair that he has devoted a museum to it! Formal styles for weddings and gala evenings are a specialty.

Atelier Lyne Bertin
1st arr. - 78, rue Jean-Jacques-Rousseau
42 36 04 59
Open 10 a.m.-7 p.m. (Tues. 12:30 p.m.-9:30 p.m.). Closed Sun., Mon. & 3 wks. in Aug. No cards.

Svelte and elegant Lyne Bertin is a sculptor at heart, a hairdresser by avocation. She looks at each head of hair as she would a block of clay to be modeled: the results are beautifully precise hairstyles.

Bruno
6th arr. - 15, rue des Saints-Pères
42 61 45 15
Open 9:30 p.m.-7 p.m. Closed Sun. & Mon. No cards.

Ever since he opened his New York salon, Bruno (the hairstyling hero of many a fashion magazine) hasn't been seen much in Paris. His salon is now overseen by Régis, a charming young man to be sure, but he doesn't always realize that this season's pet cut and styling may not work with every customer's hair, or flatter her face. Some women may only feel secure if they know that their hair is coiffed in the latest fashion; but others among us prefer that the stylist ask our opinion before he starts to snip!

Camille Darmont
16th arr. - 61, rue de la Tour - 45 03 10 99
Open 10 a.m.-7 p.m. (Thurs. 6 p.m.-8 p.m., Sat. 10 a.m.-1 p.m. & 2 p.m.-7 p.m.). Closed Sun. Cards: V.

Camille Darmont, who holds diplomas in dermatology and pharmacy, for many years was the principal assistant of hair guru René Furterer. Now on her own, she is one of the most esteemed hair specialists in Paris. A two-hour treatment in her salon includes a thorough massage of head, neck and shoulders to improve circulation, followed by a mud pack and a hot-towel wrap. The client's individual hair problems are then treated with products formulated by Madame Darmont herself. A session of this serious hair care costs 300 francs for women, 200 francs for men.

Jean-Louis David International
8th arr. - 47, rue Pierre-Charron
43 59 82 08
Open 10 a.m.-7 p.m. (Wed. 11 a.m.-7 p.m.). Closed Sun. Parking: valet. No cards.

Businessman/coiffeur Jean-Louis David has done it again. His most recent venture, on the rue Pierre-Charron, is always swarming with heads eager to wear the latest JLD style. We must say, he is a first-rate manager, and he knows how to keep his customers satisfied, notably with innovative ideas like Quick Service for women in a hurry (dry cut, mousse and gel, you're out in twenty minutes), or the Mistershop (same principle, for men). Jean-Louis David International, the top-of-the-line division, charges 354 francs for a shampoo, cut and style, while the "diffusion" sector, less chic, charges 245 francs for the same services. Star stylists to ask for are Valérie (she specializes in show-biz types) or Maryse, Guy or Laurent for men.

Jacques Dessange
8th arr. - 37, av. Franklin-Roosevelt
43 59 33 97, 43 59 50 08
Open 9:30 a.m.-6:30 p.m. Closed Sun. & Mon. No cards. 15 other branches.

With commendable concern for his customers' hygiene, Jacques Dessange has decreed that a brand-new brush be used for each client. Efforts have also been made to warm up what was once a pretty uppity, stiff reception. But best of all, the stylists no longer systematically impose Master Dessange's latest creation on every head that passes through the salon's front doors. Women are charged 280 to 330 francs for a shampoo, cut and style; men's tariffs range from 200 to 240 francs.

René Furterer
8th arr. - 15, pl. de la Madeleine
42 65 30 60
Open 9 a.m.-6 p.m. Closed Sun., holidays & Sat. in Aug. Parking: Madeleine. Cards: V.

Back when permanents meant frizz, and hairstyles were inevitably the product of rollers and pincurls, René Furterer virtually invented, singlehandedly, the science of hair care. Now retired, he leaves an impressive legacy: an institute that bears his name, where scientific hair treatments continue to be formulated by the Pierre Fabre laboratory. Simone Vasconi, who heads up the institute, is a respected expert in her field. If you are lucky enough to get an appointment with her, you won't regret it. She offers clear explanations, technical advice and a treatment program that may include massage or plant-based rinses. Sessions last from 25 to 45 minutes, at a cost of 250 francs. One is never urged to buy more than two or three products, which are always reasonably priced. For our money, René Furterer is the best hair-care institute in Paris.

TURKISH BATHS

The city's best-known hammam (and perhaps the best for an introduction to the luxury of the Turkish bath) is the Hammam Saint-Paul at 4, rue des Rosiers, 4th arr. (42 72 71 82); fee—85 francs. Exotic, but with minimal facilities, the Cleopatra Club is for women only and located at 53, boulevard de Belleville, 11th arr. (43 57 34 32); fee—50 francs. The oldest hammam in Paris also boasts a sauna, massage and beauty salon: Les Bains d'Odessa, 5, rue d'Odessa, 14th arr. (43 20 91 21); fee—73 francs. For all the pleasures of a hammam plus the services of a professional beautician, there's Plage 50, at 50, Faubourg-Saint-Denis, 10th arr. (47 70 06 64); fee—90 francs. And for authentic atmosphere, try the Hammam de la Mosquée, at the Paris Mosqué, 39, rue Geoffroy-Saint-Hilaire, 5th arr. (43 31 18 14); fee—56 francs. All (except the Cleopatra Club) are open to both men and women, but at different times. Call for information.

Marianne Gray
6th arr. - 52, rue Saint-André-des-Arts
43 26 58 21
Open 9:30 a.m.-7 p.m. (Sat. until 6 p.m., Fri. 11 a.m.-9 p.m.). Closed Sun. Cards: V, MC.

Marianne Gray is a cheerful, unpretentious salon where natural-looking styles are the order of the day. The massage that precedes the shampoo is sheer heaven, and reason enough to make an appointment with Marianne, Sendera or (for men) Claude.

Léonor Grey
9th arr. - 57, rue de Châteaudun
45 26 57 63
Open 9:30 a.m.-6:30 p.m. (Thurs. until 8:30 p.m.). Closed Sun. & Mon. No cards.

With the help of her husband, a chemist who formulates her products, Léonor Greyl works wonders on dull, lifeless hair with her various powders, freeze-dried roots, wheat-germ oil and sundry other secret ingredients. But make no mistake: there's nothing hocus-pocus about her hair-care treatments (shampoo, manual and electric massage, scalp packs and the list goes on), and they yield excellent results. Women pay 280 to 310 francs; men 180 to 200 francs.

Harlow
16th arr. - 70, rue du Ranelagh
45 24 04 54
Open 9:30 a.m.-6:30 p.m. Closed Sun. & Mon. No cards. 2 other branches.

Many women want a good haircut that doesn't require elaborate upkeep. For them, Harlow and company have come up with wash-and-wear hair. The salon's atmosphere is relaxed, and service is fast. A shampoo and styling is 110 francs; with a cut, the price is 260 francs.

Jean-François Lazartigue
8th arr. - 5, rue du Faubourg-Saint-Honoré
45 65 29 24
Open 9 a.m.-6:30 p.m. Closed Sun. Cards: V, AE, DC.

Decorated in tonic tones of green and white, the Lazartigue salon presents the highest standard of creature comforts. Each private booth boasts a telephone and an individual closet (including, of course, a lock for your fur). The staff is perfectly charming, too. There's just one hitch: for an examination and an assessment of your hair problems, treatments and a "pre-scription" for Lazartigue products, the bill will come to something over 1,000 francs! Now for that kind of money, wouldn't you think that the ingredients would be listed on the label of the hair-care products you've been strong-armed into buying? We suppose that Monsieur Lazartigue wants to keep his "miracle" formulas secret.

Jean-Marc Maniatis
8th arr. - 18, rue Marbeuf - 47 43 30 14
Open 9:30 a.m.-6:30 p.m. Closed Sat. & Sun. Parking: François-Ier. No cards.. 2 other branches.

His first clients were photo stylists from the fashion press; they raved about the Maniatis technique of precision scissoring one tiny section of hair at a time for chic, superbly shaped cuts. His reputation grew, and now Maniatis is one of the city's best-known coiffeurs. The stylists who work with him are well trained and fast; they do a lot of work for celebrities, models, journalists and so on. The salon is friendly, noisy and always busy. Be prepared to wait. A shampoo, cut and styling cost 435 francs for a woman, 243 francs for a man.

Mod's Hair
11th arr. - 9, rue Saint-Sabin - 43 38 90 78
Open 10 a.m.-7 p.m. Closed Sun. & Mon. No cards. 2 other branches.

At its salon near the Bastille, Mod's Hair caters to the younger crowd, with saucy, fashionable styles. The walls of the salon are decorated with the work of talented artists, giving you something to contemplate besides your face in the mirror. "Training Day" provides a special value: a cut by an aspiring coiffeur for only 30 francs; normally, a shampoo, cut and style go for 278 francs.

Alexandre Zouari
16th arr. - 1, av. du Président-Wilson
47 23 79 00
Open 9:30 a.m.-6:30 p.m. Closed Sun. Parking: valet. No cards.

Celebrities seem to appear wherever you look in this luxurious (but ever-so-slightly gaudy) salon: their PR people insist that Alexandre Zouari is the very last word in hairstyling for the rich and famous . . . well, now we know! Figure on spending 225 francs for a shampoo and blow-dry styling, and throw in another 200 francs for a cut.

MANICURE & PEDICURE

Carita
8th arr. - 11, rue du Faubourg-Saint-Honoré - 42 65 79 00
Open 9 a.m.-7 p.m. Closed Sat. & Sun. Parking: Madeleine. Cards: V, AE, DC, MC.

Entrust your feet to Monsieur Ho, and he will work his brand of Oriental magic to make your tired tootsies new again (288 francs). Ask for Sophie or Kekko if you want an expert "French manicure": white polish is applied to the very end of the nail, resulting in an impeccably groomed finish (but don't even contemplate it unless your hands are in perfect condition).

Institut Laugier
17th arr. - 39 bis, rue Laugier
42 27 25 03
Open 10 a.m.-7 p.m. Closed Sun. & Aug. Cards: V.

The best manicures and pedicures in Paris are performed at the Institut Laugier. Hands are cared for on the ground floor, where the exclusive Supernail treatment is yours for the asking, as are vitamin baths and artificial nails for both sexes (just 38 francs per nail). Downstairs, feet are pampered with massage, vibrating baths, pumice stones and a skin-sloughing treatment (120 francs). Before they leave, clients are strongly encouraged to purchase a whole slew of (effective, but costly) products to prolong the benefits of the salon's treatments.

Institut Yung
9th arr. - 22, rue Caumartin - 47 42 20 63
Open 9 a.m.-7 p.m. Closed Sun. No cards.

No mere cutters or scissors are used here: Monsieur Yung's pedicure equipment is limited to a simple series of steel blades of varying lengths with more or less sharp points. In just 30 minutes, his fancy footwork will rid you of calluses, bumps, corns and dead skin. Treatment and polish cost just 100 francs.

L'Onglerie
9th arr. - 26, rue Godot-de-Mauroy
42 65 49 13
Open 10 a.m.-8 p.m. (Mon. & Sat. until 7 p.m.). Closed Sun. Cards: V, DC, MC.

The house specialty is American-style artificial nails, made of the same tough resins used in dentistry. These nails are absolutely "unchewable," besides being revolting tasting (280 francs for ten). Complete manicure and pedicure services are also offered.

Revlon
8th arr. - 95, ave. des Champs-Elysées - 47 23 71 44
Open 9:45 a.m.-7 p.m. Closed Sat. & Sun. Parking: Georges-V. No cards.

Revlon's reputation for nail care is worldwide and well deserved. The institute on the Champs-Elysées employs four medically certified pedicurists, as well as seven manicurists who will take your hands in hand and make them as lovely as they possibly can be. The house products are excellent and most effective. Manicures are tariffed at 145 francs (165 francs with a hot-cream treatment), pedicures at 210 francs.

PERFUME

L'Artisan Parfumeur
7th arr. - 84 bis, rue de Grenelle
45 44 61 57
Open 10 a.m.-7 p.m. Closed Sun. Cards: V, AE, DC. 2 other branches.

Jean Laporte's shops look like stage sets, rich with gilt and velvet drapery. The fragrances he devises are equally voluptuous, based on musk, gardenia, rose iris . . . not, we emphasize, the sort of scents worn by shrinking violets. His two best-sellers are L'Eau du Grand Siècle (280 francs) and L'Eau du Navigateur. Quite popular as well are the aromatic pomanders that diffuse Laporte's heady perfumes (180 to 350 francs and 595 francs) and an exquisite selection of gift items: jewelry, fans, combs and other decorative trifles.

Comptoir Sud-Pacific

2nd arr. - 17, rue de la Paix - 42 61 74 44
Open 9:30 a.m.-7 p.m. Closed Sun. Cards: V, AE, DC, MC.

Josée Fournier has a passion for Polynesia. She was the first to market Monoï oil in Paris some years ago, and followed up that initial success with a line of perfumes that recall her beloved Pacific islands, perfumes with such delicious names as Cherry Vanilla (said to be a favorite with film star Isabelle Adjani), and Barbier des Iles (a kind of Bay Rum). The scents also come in the form of candles (200 francs), spray and diffusers (250 francs). A line of exotic cosmetics, travel toiletries and bath fragrance is the most recent addition to Comptoir's considerable inventory.

Dyptique

6th arr. - 34, bd Saint-Germain
Open 10 a.m.-7 p.m. Closed Sun. & Mon. Cards: V, AE.

Dyptique is now over twenty years old, but the shop doesn't show its age. The marvelous, exclusive fragrances marketed by Desmond Knox-Leet and Yves Couestant are as appealing as ever; their L'Ombre dans l'Eau is a perennial bestseller (295 francs). You'll find all the house scents available in candle form (95 francs), and there is also a pretty selection of Shetland lap robes.

Annick Goutal

1st arr. - 14, rue de Castiglione
42 61 52 82
Open 9:30 a.m.-7:30 p.m. Closed Sun. Cards: V, AE, DC, MC. 3 other branches.

In less than a decade, Annick Goutal has created a highly successful line of perfumes, opened four boutiques and won the European prize for excellence (as Rolls-Royce, Dior and Tiffany's had done before her). Her delicate, fruity fragrances are sold in their own elegant boutiques decorated in beige and gold tones. Our favorite scent is the deliciously citrusy Eau d'Hadrien (175 to 270 francs; perfume, 450 francs). Goutal's soaps, bath oils and scented pebbles make wonderful gifts (145 to 350 francs).

Grain de Beauté

6th arr. - 9, rue du Cherche-Midi
45 48 07 55
Open 10:30 a.m.-7 p.m. Closed Sun., Mon. morning & Aug. Cards: V, MC.

Traditional English furniture and chintzes make an appropriate setting for traditional English scents by such renowned perfumers as George F. Trumper, Penhaligon's and Floris, whose toilet waters, soaps, potpourri, and other fragrant miscellanea are showcased here.

Patchouli

6th arr. - 3, rue du Cherche-Midi
45 48 96 98
Open 10 a.m.-7 p.m. Closed Sun. Cards: V. 5 other branches.

The Patchouli shops, all decorated alike in white, gold and bordeaux, are good sources of prestigious cosmetics (Estée Lauder, Shiseido, Lancaster and others) sold at attractive prices (the shop's membership card entitles holders to a 20 percent reduction). Patchouli's sales staff makes every effort to sell the customer the products that best meet her needs (they don't just push merchandise from firms that pay fat commissions).

Shu-Uemura

6th arr. - 176, bd Saint-Germain
45 48 02 55
Open 10 a.m.-7 p.m. (Mon. 11 a.m.-7 p.m.). Closed Sun. Parking: Saint-Germain. Cards: V, AE, DC, MC.

A Japanese-style decor of wood and glass is the handsome setting for these no-less-handsomely packaged cosmetics. Members of the friendly staff provide professional-quality makeup lessons, with no obligation to buy.

Silver Moon

8th arr. - 12-14, ave. des Champs-Elysées
45 62 94 55
Open 10 a.m.-7 p.m. Closed Sun. Cards: V, AE, DC. Discounts available. 5 other branches.

A wide range of cosmetics and perfumes is sold at reasonable prices in Paris's five Silver Moon shops. Two of the branches also provide beauty services (hair removal, facials and such).

Sur Place
6th arr. - 12, pl. Saint-Sulpice - 43 26 45 27
Open 10 a.m.-7 p.m. (Mon. 1 p.m.-7 p.m.).
Closed Sun. Cards: V, AE, DC.
Pretty toiletries and bath accessories at reasonable prices.

TANNING SALONS

Les Bahamas
17th arr. - 45 bis, rue des Acacias
46 22 82 00
Open 10 a.m.-9 p.m. (Sat. until 8 p.m.). Closed
Sun. Cards: V.
Ventilators to beat the heat, adjustable sunlamps and free Monoï-based tanning cream are just a few of the little extras that make this establishment stand out from the rest of the pack. The decor is a delight: palm trees and fine, white sand. Open late.

Les Comptoirs du Soleil
8th arr. - 51, rue de Ponthieu - 42 89 19 19
Open 9 a.m.-10 p.m. (Sun. 1 p.m.-6 p.m.).
Cards: V, MC.
Not only can you prepare a tan for your vacation in a Les Comptoirs tanning booth—twenty minutes (85 francs, bust; 100 francs, body)—you can plan your holiday as well, thanks to their in-house travel agency.

Institut Fémina
6th arr. - 27, rue des Grands-Augustins
46 33 72 32
Open 9 a.m.-8 p.m. (Thurs. until 8:30 p.m.).
Closed Sun. Cards: V, AE, DC, MC.
The institute's two self-service tanning booths are appointed with the latest and most sophisticated tanning equipment, allowing you to tan all over, on both sides (think of a waffle iron). An in-house beauty center features Phytomée cosmetics and fitness products, as well as a small hair salon. Prices are among the lowest in Paris (50 francs for U.V.).

THALASSOTHERAPY

La Boutique de la Mer
8th arr. - 183, rue du Faubourg-Saint-Honoré - 42 56 44 29
Open 10 a.m.-7 p.m. Closed Sun. & Sat. in Aug.
Cards: V.
Done up in the appropriately maritime colors of navy blue and white, this beauty center showcases products based on sea plants manufactured by the Phytomer company. Trained staff members perform such refreshing, rejuvenating treatments as seaweed wraps, packs and plasters, and seawater hydromassage. The client's well-being and overall fitness are as much a concern here as matters of appearance. A session of seawater therapy is available for 245 francs.

Institut Thalgo
1st arr. - 41, rue Saint-Honoré
48 04 70 33
Open 10 a.m.-7 p.m. Closed Sun. Cards: V.
Is that really the invigorating scent of the sea wafting from a former monastery in the middle of Paris? Strange but true. The "Pacific" in this case is a huge tub of seawater, wherein clients are massaged from head to toe with jets of seawater. As they step out of their ocean, rosy and refreshed, Patricia applies seaweed packs or gives seaweed massages, as they prefer. Not your run-of-the-mill beauty treatment! Body care: 250 francs. Facial: 200 francs.

BOOKS & STATIONERY

ART

Arenthon
6th arr. - 3, quai Malaquais - 43 26 86 06
Open 8:30 a.m.-12:30 p.m. & 3 p.m.-7 p.m.
Closed Sun. & Aug. Cards: V, AE, DC.
The proprietors of this shop at 3, quai Malaquais have been purveying printed matter (but not under the same name) since the eighteenth century. Current owner Lucien Desalmand tends toward illustrated volumes and original engravings, many of them rare (by Fernand Léger and Hans Bellmer), plus albums on various painters. Also featured are rare books with illustrations by Max Ernst, Matta and other major surrealist artists, as well as chic and pricey gift items (foulards, puzzles .)

Artcurial

8th arr. - 9, av. Matignon - 42 99 16 19

Open 10:30 a.m.-7:15 p.m. Closed Sun., Mon. & 1st 3 wks. in Aug. Parking: Rond-Point des Champs-Elysées. Cards: V, AE, DC.

The ground floor of this well-lit, pleasant bookshop is a lively contemporary art gallery. On show are bronzes and drawings by the likes of Salvador Dali and Giorgio De Chirico, plus original jewelry and engravings. The first-floor bookshop boasts some 8,000 works on painting, sculpture, drawing, architecture, graphics, design, photography and crafts, as well as a fine selection of books (primarily Japanese) on fashion and textiles.

Jullien Cornic

8th arr. - 29, av. Matignon - 42 68 10 10

Open 9 a.m.-6 p.m. Closed Sat., Sun. & Aug. Parking: Hôtel Bristol. Cards: V, AE, DC.

The Jullien Cornic bookshop has been collecting art books from Napoleonic times to the present since 1946. Its inventory of nearly 10,000 volumes includes works on fine and commercial arts from all over the world. Featured are detailed catalogs and books on such artists as Pablo Picasso, Edgar Degas and Honoré Daumier, and reference books on the history of costume, textiles, furniture, ceramics, ivory and other collector's items.

ENGLISH-LANGUAGE

Attica 1

6th arr. - 84, bd Saint-Michel
46 34 16 30, 43 25 96 31

Open 10 a.m.-7 p.m. (Mon. 2 p.m.-7 p.m. & Sat. 10 a.m.-1 p.m.). Closed Sun. Parking: Soufflot. Cards: V, MC. 2 other branches: Attica 2, 34, rue des Ecoles - 5th arr. - 43 26 09 53, parking, Maubert-Saint-Germain; Attica 3, 23, rue Jean-de-Beauvais - 5th arr. - 46 34 16 30, parking, Maubert-Saint-Germain.

At the three Attica shops, all located in central Paris, you can pick up books in English. Attica 1 features foreign-language teaching materials (English and 40 other languages); Attica 2 sells a wide range of English and American books at good prices; and Attica 3 specializes in children's books in English and travel guides (mostly related to English-speaking countries).

Brentano's

2nd arr. - 37, av. de l'Opéra - 42 61 52 50

Open 10 a.m.-7 p.m. Closed Sun. Parking: Pl. du Marché Saint-Honoré. Cards: V.

Freshly remodeled, Brentano's is still a favorite among Americans in Paris for its remarkable array of American, English and French books, periodicals, records and postcards. Bestsellers of the week are always displayed at the entry. And there is also a large children's-book section.

Galignani

1st arr. - 224, rue de Rivoli - 42 60 76 07

Open 9:30 a.m.-7 p.m. Closed Sun. Parking: Vendôme. Cards: V, MC.

Galignani, purported to be the oldest English bookshop on the continent, was established in 1810 on the rue Vivienne by Giovanni Antonio Galignani, descendant of the famous twelfth-century publisher from Padua, Italy. In the mid-1800s Galignani moved to the rue de Rivoli, near the terminus of the Calais-Paris, and the shop has passed from father to son and so on down the line. Featured are English, American and French hardcovers and paperbacks, plus a sizable selection of art and children's books.

Le Nouveau Quartier Latin

6th arr. - 78, bd Saint-Michel - 43 26 42 70

Open 10 a.m.-7 p.m. Closed Sun. Parking: Soufflot. No cards.

The Nouveau Quartier Latin carries a wide selection of English, American, Spanish and German literature, plus dictionaries and paperbacks in English (over 10,000). Also featured are books on painting, design, architecture, photography, graphics and music. An entire section is given over to books on teaching or learning English. The adjacent room is equipped so that you may listen to and watch audiotapes and videotapes before purchasing them. The book-ordering service is fast and efficient, and sales go on throughout the year. Catalogs are available.

Shakespeare and Company

5th arr. - 37, rue de la Bûcherie - No phone

Open 11 a.m.-midnight. No cards.

Shakespeare and Co. on the quai by Notre-Dame is the late-night favorite of buyers and browsers in search of secondhand English and American books.

W. H. Smith

1st arr. - 248, rue de Rivoli - 42 60 37 97
Open 9:30 a.m.-7 p.m. (Sat. until 7:30 p.m.).
Closed Sun. Parking: Concorde. Cards: V. En-
glish tea room (see Tea Rooms).

This is the closest thing to the perfect self-service bookstore: it is easy to locate almost any item among the over 8,000 English and American titles, from cookbooks to travel guides to children's books, records, cassettes. . . . The selection of periodicals is vast, and you can take out a subscription to just about any newspaper or magazine in the world at Smith's specialized subscription service. Upstairs is a delightful tea room where you can relax and peruse your purchases (when business is slow). The staff is efficient and friendly . . . and very British.

The Village Voice

6th arr. - 6, rue Princesse - 46 33 36 47
Open 11 a.m.-8 p.m. (Mon. 2 p.m.-8 p.m.).
Closed Sun. No cards.

Nowadays the Village Voice controls the turf once so jealously guarded by Silvia Beach's original Shakespeare and Co.—a mecca for Americans in Paris, especially writers, journalists and literary types. The Village Voice was recently remodeled, and though the quaint coffee shop in the corner is gone, poetry readings and book-signing parties are still frequent. While the selection of titles is small, it is well chosen. The open-timbered upper floor is an art gallery well worth a visit.

FILM & PHOTOGRAPHY

La Chambre Claire

6th arr. - 14, rue Saint-Sulpice
46 34 04 31
Open 10 a.m.-7 p.m. (Mon. 2 p.m.-7 p.m.).
Closed Sun. No cards.

This bookshop is given over entirely to photography—with some 5,000 editions, it is the official supplier to several of the world's greatest museums. A truly remarkable place.

Ciné Doc

9th arr. - 43-45, passage Jouffroy
48 24 71 36
Open 10 a.m.-7 p.m. Closed Sun. Parking:
Drouot. No cards.

This flea market–style shop in the delightful passage Jouffroy boasts an admirable jumble of publications pertaining to the cinema, plus posters, postcards and original photographs. The interesting displays in the shop windows change often and add to the already lively ambience.

FOOD & COOKING

La Librairie Gourmande

5th arr. - 4, rue Dante - 43 54 37 27
Open 10 a.m.-7 p.m. (Sun. 2:30 p.m.-7 p.m. &
summer 10 a.m.-noon & 1 p.m.-7 p.m.). Cards:
V, MC.

At La Librairie Gourmande you will find a mouth-watering array of cookbooks, for amateurs and pros alike, as well as works on the history of French and foreign cooking (some volumes date to the sixteenth century). Vast collections treating traditional and nouvelle cuisine, recipes by Balzac and Dumas, plus a wide range of works on enology make this one of Paris's most appetizing bookshops. You can bank on a warm welcome and excellent service from owner Geneviève Baudon.

Edgar Soete

7th arr. - 5, quai Voltaire - 42 60 72 41
Open 10 a.m.-noon & 2 p.m.-6:30 p.m. Closed
Sat., Sun., Aug. & 1st wk. in Sept. Parking:
Saint-Germain. No cards.

At Edgar Soete's bookshop, you can spend hours happily browsing, embroiled in questions regarding anything edible or potable that has ever been poured, put into a pot or crossed a cutting board. Anything that has been written up, photographed or drawn in the thousands of volumes on display here. But we're sorry to report that the prices of these delectable works on enology and gastronomy are for the most part pretty hard to stomach!

Le Verre et l'Assiette

5th arr. - 1, rue du Val-de-Grâce
46 33 45 96
Open 10 a.m.-12:30 p.m. & 2:30 p.m.-7:30 p.m.
(Sun. & Mon. 2:30 p.m.-7:30 p.m.). Cards: V,
AE, DC.

Too many chefs may well spoil the broth, but they certainly don't spoil Le Verre et l'Assiette. Feast your eyes on the window display: a potpourri of books and accessories pertaining to gastronomy and enology—from unique corkscrews to rare editions on Celtic cooking. This is the bookshop most frequented by famous chefs, gourmets and brothers of the grape. In addition to the thousands of volumes on food and wine, there is a fine selection of gift ideas (the wine taster's ideal traveling case, for example). *Bon appétit!*

GENERAL INTEREST

Gibert Jeune

5th arr. - 23-27, quai Saint-Michel
43 54 57 32
Open 9:30 a.m.-7:15 p.m. Closed Sun. Cards: V. 2 other branches: 5, pl. Saint-Michel - 5th arr.; 15 bis, bd Saint-Denis - 10th arr.

This multistory emporium of books is renowned for its special sales and secondhand hardcovers and paperbacks. A fine selection of English and American books.

La Hune

6th arr. - 170, bd Saint-Germain
45 48 35 85
Open 10 a.m.-midnight (Mon. 2 p.m.-midnight & Sat. 10 a.m.-7:30 p.m.). Closed Sun. Parking: Saint-Germain. Cards: V, AE, DC, MC.

La Hune is a favorite among Paris intellectuals, bibliophiles and browsers. It stays open late and stocks an impressive array of books on architecture, contemporary art and design, as well as classics and contemporary literature. The mezzanine is given over to the graphic arts, photography, theater and cinema. One of the city's finest.

Librairie Delamain

1st arr. - 155, rue Saint-Honoré
42 61 48 78
Open 10 a.m.-7 p.m. Closed Sat. in Aug., Sun. & 1 wk. in mid-Aug. Parking: Palais-Royal. Cards: V, AE, DC, MC.

Delamain is the oldest bookstore in France, founded in 1710 under the arcades of the Comédie-Française. About 100 years ago the original shop burned down, and Delamain was forced to move to its current location on the rue Saint-Honoré. Thousands of volumes on French literature, travel, history and art (French only) are available new or used. The first floor is given over to the graphic arts, photography, film and theater.

FNAC

1st arr. - Forum des Halles - 42 61 81 18
Other branches: 136, rue de Rennes - 6th arr. - 45 44 39 12, 26; ave. de Wagram - 8th arr. - 47 66 52 50

FNAC is the biggest bookstore chain in Europe, with a low-price policy that means you can read more for less: French books sell for 5 percent under standard retail, while foreign editions are discounted by a hefty 20 percent. Miles of shelves are packed with a vast and varied stock of volumes ranging from do-it-yourself manuals, cookbooks and guides to high-brow fiction, poetry and philosophy. The stores are huge and densely packed with book-loving humanity, particularly on weekends. The sales staff is qualified and knowledgeable, though it often seems like they are rarer than first editions (which means, however, that one can browse here for hours undisturbed!).

La Librairie des Femmes

6th arr. - 74, rue de Seine - 43 29 50 75
Open 10 a.m.-7 p.m. (summer noon-7 p.m.). Closed Sun. Cards: V.

This is not a feminist bookshop. It is a publisher/bookseller's showcase that highlights books written by or about women (and many books by men, too!). The first-floor sales area is one of the most attractive in Paris—sunny, spacious and user-friendly. The shop also organizes photo and engraving exhibits.

Librairie du Muséum d'Histoire Naturelle

5th arr. - 36, rue Geoffroy-Saint-Hilaire - 43 36 30 24
Open 10 a.m.-6:30 p.m. Closed Mon. morning. No cards.

This charming little shop features more than 10,000 works on the natural sciences (in several languages). It has recently been remodeled and is now managed by specialists affiliated with the natural history museum. You will find nature guides, works on gardening, ecology, history and much more, plus a large children's-book section.

La Maison du Dictionnaire

14th arr. - 98, bd Montparnasse
43 22 12 93
Open 9 a.m.-6:30 p.m. Closed Sat. & Sun. No cards.

This one-of-a-kind shop features more than 3,000 dictionaries (general, technical and special-interest) in more than 100 languages. Even more astounding is the Pivothèque reading room, open to the public, in which you may sit and browse through any book before buying it.

RARE BOOKS

Jean Cluzel
6th arr. - 61, rue de Vaugirard
42 22 38 71
Open 2 p.m.-6:30 p.m. Closed Sun., Mon. & Aug. No cards.
This is one of the few Paris bookshops that specializes in eroticism. Represented are all the big names in French literature, from Guy de Maupassant and Charles Baudelaire to Alexandre Dumas and Victor Hugo. Their intimate works on objects of affection, love and love-making are shelved in the "Enfer," or "Inferno," section. Also featured are works on the occult, plus mainstream literature.

Courant d'Art
6th arr. - 79, rue de Vaugirard
40 11 43 88
Open 10 a.m.-7 p.m. Closed Sun. No cards.
Art is the passion of bookseller Marie-Josée Grandjean. Her rue de Vaugirard shop is a showcase for books on art—from studies and monographs of painters, sculptors and artisans, to sales catalogs from Christie's, Sotheby's or Drouot (France). On display is a large collection of engravings, reproductions, exhibition catalogs, back issues of art magazines and all sorts of other unfindables. Not to mention the noteworthy collection of books on cinema and photography. In addition to her shop, Grandjean runs a stand at the Saint-Ouen flea market (from 9 a.m.-6 p.m. on Saturday, Sunday and Monday; Marché Jules-Vallès, 40 11 43 88).

L'Envers du Miroir
6th arr. - 19, rue de Seine - 43 54 00 85
Open noon-7 p.m. Closed Sun., Mon. & Aug. Parking: Mazarine. No cards.
As its name suggests, L'Envers du Miroir is indeed a through-the-looking-glass experience . . . where you'll find the cream of the crop of surrealist writers poets of the twentieth century: Breton, Crevel, Char, Michauz, Cocteau and Peret. There's also a fine collection of first

editions, plus quality editions by such publishers as Actes Sud, Fata Morgana and Clivages.

Librairie du Cygne
6th arr. - 17, rue Bonaparte - 43 26 32 45
Open 10 a.m.-noon & 2 p.m.-7 p.m. Closed Sun. & Aug. No cards.
The Librairie du Cygne seems to have tumbled out of a Blazac novel. The ancient oak bookcases of this austere shop groan with signed first editions and illustrated works by the greats—Stendhal, Molière, Anatole France, Maupassant, Zola and Hugo. A must shop for any bibliophile.

Librairie du Pont-Neuf
6th arr. - 1, rue Dauphine - 43 26 42 40
Open 9:30 a.m.-noon & 2 p.m.-6:30 p.m. Closed Sun., Mon. & Aug. No cards.
This charming shop run by the Coulet brothers features a nineteenth-century reading room whose shelves are packed with first editions, illustrated works and reprints by Carteret, Vicaire and Pia. The lovely setting, just across from the Pont-Neuf, and one of the best selections of antiquarian books in Paris make the Librairie du Pont-Neuf a must-visit for bibliophiles and curious browsers alike.

STATIONERY

Armorial
8th arr. - 98, rue du Faubourg-Saint-Honoré - 42 65 08 18
Open 9:30 a.m.-6:30 p.m. Closed Sun. Parking: Rond-Point des Champs-Elysées. Cards: V, AE, DC.
The desk sets and other sophisticated accessories crafted by this prestigious firm can be found in the offices of many cabinet ministers and executives with refined tastes.

L'Art du Bureau
4th arr. - 47, rue des Francs-Bourgeois
48 87 57 97
Open 10:30 a.m.-7 p.m. Closed Sun. Cards: V, AE.
L'Art du Bureau has everything for the office, but not just any office . . . the hip, fashionable, witty desk accessories and stationery have been chosen with the high-style, high-profile executive in mind.

Cassegrain

8th arr. - 422, rue Saint-Honoré
42 60 20 08
Open 9:30 a.m.-6:30 p.m. Closed Sun. Cards: V, AE.

This venerable institution on the rue Saint-Honoré, founded in 1919, is aiming to update its image (while preserving its reputation for fine engraving, of course). A new line of "youthful" leather accessories has been introduced: brightly colored lizard date and address books, boxes covered with marbleized paper, more boxes and picture frames in burled elm and amusing gadgets for children. Cassegrain is one of the rare sources in France for the legendary notebooks from Smythson of Bond Street (bible paper, sewn bindings, leather covers—they cost a fortune, but they're worth it). Another Cassegrain store is located at 81, rue des Saints-Pères, in the sixth arrondissement.

Les Crayons de Julie

3rd arr. - 10, passage de l'Horloge
42 71 60 17
Open 10:30 a.m.-7:15 p.m. (Mon. until 7:45 p.m.). Closed Sun. Cards: V, AE, DC, MC.

Traditionalists who still write (literally) letters and thank-you notes love to browse in this cozy, English-style shop for old-fashioned fountain pens and pretty stationery.

Dupré Octante

8th arr. - 141, rue du Faubourg-Saint-Honoré - 45 63 10 11
Open 9 a.m.-12:30 p.m. & 1:30 p.m.-6:15 p.m. Closed Sun. Cards: V.

Every illustrator and graphic designer in Paris can be found, at one time or another, in this vast stationery shop in the Faubourg-Saint-Honoré. A considerable assortment of letter papers in lovely, exclusive colors is on view, as well as a full range of office accessories. In the equally vast shop nearby on the rue d'Artois is a complete line of drawing materials—from pencils to computer software. You can expect to find even the most arcane art supplies, but don't expect service with a smile from the staff, who we found to be rather surly.

Elysées Stylos Marbeuf

8th arr. - 40, rue Marbeuf - 45 25 40 49
Open 9:30 a.m.-7 p.m. Closed Sun. & Aug. Cards: V, AE, DC.

If it's a fountain pen you're seeking, this is the place. The selection of famous French and imported brands is quite astonishing; repairs are also performed here (though no gimcrack pens will be considered). The solid-gold pens and luxurious gold and silver desk accessories make sumptuous, impressive gifts.

Maquet

8th arr. - 45, rue Pierre-Charron
47 20 27 19
Open 10 a.m.-6:30 p.m. Closed Sat. & Sun. No cards.

Founded in 1841 by the man who invented the envelope, Maquet has an enviable reputation as a prestigious engraving firm. The shop also offers custom-made, hand-tooled desk sets crafted from antique leathers—the height of elegance for any office.

Marie-Papier

6th arr. - 26, rue Vavin - 43 26 46 44
Open 10:30 a.m.-7 p.m. Closed Sun. Cards: V.

Marie-Paule Orluc launched the trend of fashionable stationery when she opened her enchanting little shop, where all the different papers are conveniently displayed on the walls at eye-level. We don't know of anyone who offers a wider choice of colored letter and note papers, albums, folders and boxes; each season brings a new crop of marvelous hues. Unfortunately, there are just a few catches here: the merchandise is extremely expensive, the atmosphere very high-hat and the salespeople we found hard put to hide their annoyance when a customer walks through the door.

Montorgueil

1st arr. - 34-36, rue Montorgueil
40 26 84 39, 42 36 71 12
Open 11:30 a.m.-7:30 p.m. Closed Sun., Mon. & Aug. Cards: V, AE, DC.

All the high-class, handmade papers sold here are packaged in gorgeous trompe-l'oeil boxes (*faux* wood, *faux* marble and burled elm). Those who crave the very best of everything will love the gilt-edged writing paper, made up in the color of your choice.

Mélodies Graphiques

4th arr. - 10, rue du Pont-Louis-Philippe
42 74 57 68
Open 11 a.m.-7:30 p.m. Closed Sun. & Mon. Parking: Lobeau, Pont-Marie. Cards: V, AE.

This pretty boutique, done up in blond wood, showcases desk accessories covered in marbleized paper. The papers, ten styles in all, are made by the well-known Florentine firm, Il Papiro, according to sixteenth-century methods. A selection of unusual decorative objects—carnival masks and such—is also sold.

Papier Plus
4th arr. - 9, rue du Pont-Louis-Philippe
42 77 70 49
Open 12-7:30 p.m. Closed Sun. & Mon. Parking: Pont-Marie, Lobeau. Cards: V.

Both this shop and Mélodies Graphiques, which adjoins it, carry quality stationery, but each has its specialty. In Papier Plus, you'll find writing paper sold by the kilo, blank notebooks, photograph albums and files, in a host of pastel shades. Mélodies Graphiques, its more artistic counterpart, sells reams of drawing paper, sketch pads and colored pencils in a rainbow of wonderful hues.

Sennelier
7th arr. - 3, quai Voltaire - 42 60 29 38
Open 9 a.m.-noon & 2 p.m.-6 p.m. Closed Sun. Cards: V, AE, DC.

Appropriately located next to the Ecole des Beaux-Arts, Sennelier has, in its 100-year-old life, sold tons of art supplies to many well-known and aspiring artists. Here they find the best brands of paints and pigments, paper and sketch pads of excellent quality, canvas, easels and framing equipment.

Stern
9th arr. - 47, passage des Panoramas
45 08 86 45
Open 9:30 a.m.-12:30 p.m. & 1:30 p.m.-5:30 p.m. Closed Sat. & Sun. No cards.

Stern started out in 1830, when the *grands boulevards* were the epicenter of elegant Parisian life. Now known throughout the world as engraver to royalty, aristocrats and people of taste, Stern carefully conserves its traditions of using the finest papers, all made and engraved by hand. The firm has models available for every type of visiting or business card, invitations and announcements, but Stern's draftsmen can also produce designs to your specifications.

TRAVEL

Le Tour du Monde
16th arr. - 9, rue de la Pompe - 42 88 58 06
Open 10 a.m.-1 p.m. & 2 p.m.-7 p.m. Closed Sun. & Mon. Parking: Passy. No cards.

Travel-book buffs take note: Jean-Etienne and Edmonde Huret have earned their reputation as the Sherlock Holmes(es) of the book world. Their shop is chockablock with hard-to-find, out-of-print and rare works on the far-flung and the right-next-door. They also stock a fine selection of children's books.

CHILDREN

BOOKS

L'Arbre à Livres
6th arr. - 76, bd Saint-Michel - 43 26 59 93
Open 10 a.m.-7 p.m. (Mon. 2 p.m.-7 p.m.). Closed Sun. Parking: Saint-Sulpice. Cards: V, AE.

The shelves of this bookshop groan with books chosen for the quality of both their text and illustration in English, German, Italian, Portuguese, Arabic and Vietnamese (and whenever possible, their French equivalent)—a unique find in France. A lot of the books are bilingual, sometimes trilingual. There's every-thing from traditional fairy tales to contemporary works. The philosophy behind the shop is to help children of all nationalities and races understand other cultures. An association called the Friends of l'Arbre à Livres is composed of teachers, writers and illustrators crusading for children's early education of foreign languages. This is a worthy institution that deserves all the support it can muster.

Chantelivre
6th arr. - 13, rue de Sèvres - 45 48 87 90
Open 10 a.m.-7 p.m. Closed Sun., Mon. & 2 wks. in Aug. No cards.

Enter here, all you bibliophiles in short pants and smocked dresses. Among the some 10,000 titles to choose from are illustrated story books, fairy and folk tales and novels, as well as records and educational games. In a back corner of the shop is an area open for children—to draw, look at books or listen to a story.

INFANTS & SMALL CHILDREN

CLOTHING–BUDGET

Till
15th arr. - Centre Beaugrenelle
54 75 76 17
Open 9:30 a.m.-7 p.m. (Mon. 2 p.m.-7 p.m.). Closed Sun. Cards: V. 5 other branches.

You can be sure that you will get your little darlings properly shod here. Till, the most important chain in Europe of its kind, hires only experienced salespeople and will not sell any shoes that haven't been impeccably finished. Kids' tennis shoes have spongy linings, babies' shoes are reinforced and finished in leather. Till staff will explain to you that children's feet have special requirements, and that successive generations need bigger and bigger shoes. There are 300 designs displayed—from moccasins to dress shoes to sandals and slippers. This is a serious shoe-shopping stop.

CLOTHING–CLASSIC

Bonpoint
7th arr. - 67, rue de l'Université
45 55 63 70
Open 10 a.m.-7 p.m. Closed Sun. Cards: V, AE. 3 other branches.

Marie-France Cohen and her sister, Dominique Swildens, were the first to dare introduce Parisian-yuppie fashion. Their styles are suited essentially for French yuppie children, but without too much chi-chi. For the last few years, Bonpoint has been trying to lower prices and maintain its renowned high quality. Pants are lined so they won't itch, hems are huge, and cloth is of first-rate quality. A blouse runs about 300 francs; a pair of Bermuda shorts, so well cut that they grow with the child, is also about 300 francs; and a pleated or quilted skirt is about 340 francs. The boutique specializes

in children's formal dress: white gloves, hats and other such romantic attire . . . ravishing!

Cacharel
8th arr. - Galerie du Claridge, 74, av. des Champs-Elysées - 45 63 23 09
Open 10 a.m.-7:30 p.m. (Mon. 11:30 a.m.-7:30 p.m.). Parking: Rond-Point des Champs-Elysées. Cards: V, AE, DC.

Cacharel carries parkas, jackets and blazers, as well as pleated skirts, Bermuda shorts and dresses for children ages 4 to 18 years old. Girls look fetching in Liberty dresses, and boys handsome in the striped shirts. A note of warning: Clothes are cut small, so remember to oversize when buying.

Jacadi
17th arr. - 60, bd de Courcelles
47 63 55 23
Open 10 a.m.-7 p.m. Closed Sun. Cards: V. 8 other branches.

Jacadi's growth and success has been mind-boggling. In eight years, some 27 shops have sprung to life. What's the system? Competitive prices and amusing styles. Bermuda shorts sell for about 105 francs; a coat, 350 francs. And there are lots of accessories as well as the recent addition of a child-care department.

Tartine et Chocolat
8th arr. - 89, rue du Faubourg-Saint-Honoré - 42 66 36 39
Open 10 a.m.-7 p.m. Closed Sun. Parking: 1, rue Rabelais. Cards: V, AE, DC.

The famous little blue stripes that made the brand a success have survived, though these days they represent only 3 percent of the collection. Aside from the clothes, Tartine et Chocolat also sells lots of other amusing items. We recommend the new eau de cologne, P'tit Senbon, in its pretty antique bottle.

CLOTHING–LUXURY

Baby Dior
8th arr. - 28, av. Montaigne - 47 23 54 44
Open 9:30 a.m.-6:30 p.m. Closed Sun. Parking: François-Ier. Cards: V, AE, DC.

If you can afford to buy an entire set of baby clothes, wonderful; if you can't . . . at least let yourself get one, teeny, little shirt with a ruffle (400 francs), a pair of sheets for the cradle or a dressing gown. The booties (170 francs) make a darling baby present, and there are also some other nice items—picture frames (595 francs) and silver cups from about 1,300 francs.

La Châtelaine

16th arr. - 170, av. Victor-Hugo
47 27 44 07

Open 9:30 a.m.-6:30 p.m. (Sat. 9:30 a.m.-12:30 p.m. & 2:30 p.m.-6:30 p.m.). Closed Sun. & Mon. Parking: Victor-Hugo. Cards: V.

This is the most luxurious children's clothing shop in Paris. Dresses, vests and shirts are perfectly finished, and the babywear is the finest, most elegant in all of Paris. It is designed exclusively for La Châtelaine by Molli, a Swiss lingerie firm. Clothes for any age group can be custom-made and will be delivered free of charge; alterations, too, are done gratis. This isn't so surprising when you consider that a size-five Liberty dress is priced at 1,000 francs.

Nina Ricci

8th arr. - 39, av. Montaigne - 47 23 78 88
Open 10 a.m.-6:30 p.m. (Sat. 10 a.m.-1:15 p.m. & 2:15 p.m.-6:30 p.m.). Closed Sun. Parking: François-Ier. Cards: V, AE.

This is for those who dream of a haute-couture set of baby clothes. Here such a jumpsuit sells for 400 francs, pajamas for 480 francs. There are pretty pillowcases as well, and, of course, everything is labeled.

CLOTHING–TRENDY

Chantal Goya

6th arr. - 17, rue du Cherche-Midi
45 48 74 37

Open 10:30 a.m.-1 p.m. & 2 p.m.-7 p.m. Closed Sun. Parking: Saint-Sulpice. Cards: V, AE, DC.

Singer Chantal Goya's store for girls will have grannies drooling over clothes for their little darlings. Nothing for boys or babies.

Naf-Naf Enfant

2nd arr. - 33, rue Etienne-Marcel
42 36 15 28

Open 9:30 a.m.-6:30 p.m. Closed Sat. & Sun. Parking: Forum des Halles. Cards: V.

If you like jogging suits, sweatshirts and dungarees, trot along to Naf-Naf. Everyone knows it as much for its styles as for its recent advertising campaign: piglets in a display of doubtful taste. We think you could do better elsewhere, and price-wise, too!

Petit Faune

6th arr. - 33, rue Jacob - 42 60 80 72
Open 10:30 a.m.-7 p.m. (Mon. 2:30 p.m.-7 p.m.). Closed Sun. Parking: Saint-Germain. Cards: V, AE.

Sylvie Loussier no longer designs for Petit Faune, but her spirit is there in the flowered dresses and hand-knitted baby clothes. As for the prices, they really do defy good sense.

Sonia Rykiel Enfants

6th arr. - 8, rue de Grenelle - 42 22 43 22
Open 10 a.m.-7 p.m. (Mon. 2 p.m.-7 p.m.). Closed Sun. Parking: Saint-Germain. Cards: V, AE.

It took becoming a grandmother for Sonia Rykiel to realize she had nothing for her darling little Lolia and Tatiana, her two granddaughters. So she got her own daughter, Natalie, to oversee a children's line. And it's a success. Clothes are enbroidered with gold-colored teddies, there's plenty of sharp red, violet, gray and fuchsia jersey, long sweaters over miniskirts and elegant jogging outfits. Now mommies can have carbon-copy little Rykiels.

SHOES

Bonpoint

7th arr. - 86, rue de l'Université
45 49 20 11

Open 10 a.m.-7 p.m. Closed Sun. Parking: Montalembert. Cards: V, AE.

Having outfitted your children at Bonpoint No. 67, what could be easier than crossing the street to outfit their little footsies? There are black Paraboots (extremely difficult to find anywhere else), pastel-colored ballet slippers, tennis shoes and boots.

Cendrine

6th arr. - 3, rue Vavin - 43 54 81 20
Open 9:30 a.m.-12:30 p.m. & 2 p.m.-7 p.m. (Mon. 2 p.m.-7 p.m.). Closed Sun. & 3 wks. in Aug. Parking: Montparnasse. Cards: V.

Has your child got delicate or hard-to-fit feet? Well, if so, Cendrine is the place to go. Not that these shoes are orthopedic. On the contrary, these are classic styles, but Cendrine will fit your baby with a half-sole or advise you on the best model to buy. Anxious mothers emerge confident that their children are correctly shod.

Froment Leroyer

16th arr. - 50, rue Vital - 42 24 82 70
Open 9:45 a.m.-7 p.m. Closed Sun., Mon. & 2 wks. in Aug. Cards: V, MC. 3 other branches.

Thank you, Mr. Froment Leroyer, for all the shoes we grew up in. We hope you'll still be there for our children and for our grandchildren with your Start-Rite sandals, your leather slippers, your blue booties with laces, your canvas sandals—all those unchangeable children's styles that have become reassuring symbols of continuity. Here one can find everything from classics to the more avant-garde styles in children's shoes.

JUNIORS & TEENS

CLOTHING

Charles Chevignon

2nd arr. - 5, pl. des Victoires - 42 36 10 16
Open 10:15 a.m.-7 p.m. Closed Sun. Parking: Saint-Eustache. Cards: V, AE, DC.

Charles Chevignon pioneered the threadbare, wrinkled leather look and has lost no time translating it into his sportswear line. Heavy canvas, leather and cotton tend to predominate. It all would have been quite nice, but it appears that good taste lost out to an overdose of insignias and badges. Nevertheless, the Chevignon image is reinforced by watches, belts, leather goods and so on. Prices fluctuate between modest and prohibitive.

Chipie

6th arr. - 49, rue Bonaparte - 43 29 21 94
Open 10:30 a.m.-7 p.m. (Mon. 11:30 a.m.-7 p.m.). Closed Sun. Parking: Saint-Germain. Cards: V, AE. 3 other branches.

The brand's motto: "Quality and fun since 1967." Well, if that's supposed to mean that the *fun* comes from the label being pasted all over the front of the clothing, and the *quality* is in the cloth (which doesn't appear to be able to make it from one season to the next). . . . But who cares? This is carefully coded fashion for kids who want to look like all their friends. Trench coats, bomber jackets and jeans are signed Jean Elbas and René Reynes. This duo

will shortly be relaunching the Fiorucci line. Prices are high; service is pushy.

Creeks

1st arr. - 98, rue Saint-Denis - 42 33 81 70
Open 11 a.m.-8 p.m. (Mon. 11:30 a.m.-8 p.m.). Closed Sun. Parking: Les Halles, Saint-Eustache. Cards: V, AE.

The third Creeks shop to open in Paris's Les Halles area was designed by (who else but?) Philippe Starck. Marble, granite and chrome predominate, and the huge spaces are filled by blasting FM music. People buy what they recognize: old friends include the Chevignon, Liberto, Levi's, Paraboot and Bowen brands. Creeks aims essentially at the 15- to 25-year-old age group, and prefers them svelte.

Fiorucci

1st arr. - 34, rue Saint-Denis
42 33 85 08, 42 36 85 63
Open 10:30 a.m.-7:30 p.m. Closed Sun. Parking: Forum des Halles. Cards: V, AE, DC.

This is the Paris link of the Elio Fiorucci chain and stocks such brands as Appaloosa, Classic Nouveau (for men only) and, as of late, Landlubber, which was much appreciated in the 1960s.

Marithé et François Girbaud

2nd arr. - 38, rue Etienne-Marcel
42 33 54 69
Open 10:30 a.m.-7:30 p.m. Closed Sun. Parking: Saint-Eustache. Cards: V, AE, DC.

This Tower of Babel–like boutique is full of mobiles and video pictures of fashion shows. Funereal salespeople, crazy prices and questionable styles cannot detract from its phenomenal success, which is due in part to the seasonal metamorphosis imposed by the design community on sacrosanct denim. Fashioned this way and that, the common blue jean has undergone innumerable mutations. We think the manufacture is a bit hasty, considering the high prices. And in our humble opinion, a bit less pretension wouldn't hurt.

Ixi: Z Galerie Kent et Curwen

2nd arr. - 48-50, Général Vivienne
42 97 49 03
Open 10:30 a.m.-7 p.m. Closed Sun. Parking: Bourse, Saint-Eustache. Cards: V, AE.

Phonetically, *Ixi: Z* means *exercise.* Designed in Japan exclusively for Parisians, the jogging clothes, sportswear collection and coordinated accessories—all pleasant, comfortable and original—come in sharp colors. Large sizes and low prices are available.

New Man

6th arr. - 10-12, rue de l'Ancienne-Comédie - 43 54 77 54
Open 10 a.m.-7:30 p.m. Closed Sun. Parking: Mazarine. Cards: V, AE, DC.

The two stores have recently been redecorated and, by offering extra-large men's sizes, are enjoying a a new clientele. Big and little men are now given the chance to dress in denim, gabardine and cotton or *cupro*, a new seductive fiber mix. Suits, jackets, pants and shirts are sold at reasonable prices (1,100 francs for a suit).

Stefanel

6th arr. - 54, rue de Rennes - 45 44 06 07
Open 10 a.m.-7:30 p.m. Closed Sun. Parking: Saint-Germain. Cards: V, AE, DC. 3 other branches.

A Benetton competitor, this Italian brand goes in for naval styles, pastel-colored knitwear, a preppy or executive look, junior sportswear and cottonwear—for a young clientele. Prices are modest, styles are seasonal. And they throw in pleasant service, too.

SHOES

Free Lance

1st arr. - 22, rue Mondétour - 42 33 74 70
Open 10:30 a.m.-7:15 p.m. Parking: Forum des Halles. Cards: V, AE.

Lost amid a haze of graffiti and multicolored walls, rows of pumps valiantly display themselves to a devoted clientele who try—alas, in vain—to ignore the glacial welcome of the creature who passes as salesperson. There are also real Doc Martens, their colored deviation, Bozo-the-clown style, as well as pretty ballet slippers, hobnailed boots and leather sandals. May not be the most comfortable of shoes, but that's not what's important here.

Gelati

6th arr. - 20, rue du Cherche-Midi
48 07 15 15
Open 11 a.m.-7 p.m. (Mon. 2 p.m.-7 p.m.). No cards.

This is Italian fashion at its most fun and inventive. Prices are reasonable (from 400 francs) for some brash, vivid-colored shoes with square toes and small heels. Shoes that are destined to be worn with absolute intensity will probably last for just one season.

Charles Kammer

2nd arr. - 4, pl. des Victoires - 42 36 31 84
Open 10 a.m.-7 p.m. Closed Sun. Parking: Saint-Eustache. Cards: V, AE, DC.

The decor is Pompeii-baroque. Krammer's creations mix British new-wave tendencies and decorative impertinence. The result: polka-dot laces in black and white or madras. It's not very expensive at 600 francs, but it's not very solid, either (but that's not the point!).

TOYS

Ali Baba

7th arr. - 29, av. de Tourville - 45 55 10 85
Open 10 a.m.-1 p.m. & 2 p.m.-7 p.m. Closed Sun. Parking: Pl. Joffre. Cards: V.

Ali Baba has three floors of quality games and toys for children of all ages. The basement level is a kingdom of scale models and electric trains. The ground floor is devoted to card and board games. Do not miss the superb collection of hand-painted tin soldiers.

Multicubes

15th arr. - 110, rue Cambronne
47 34 25 97
Open 10 a.m.-1:30 p.m. & 3 p.m.-7 p.m. Closed Mon. & July 20-Aug. 20. Cards: V, MC. Other branch: 5, rue de Rivoli - 4th arr. - 42 77 10 77 - open 10 a.m.-7 p.m., closed Sun, no cards.

Every year sees a new collection from Erzgebirge, the land of wooden-toy makers. Some of the toys are pure marvels and quite pricey, coveted by the old and young alike. There are mobiles, yo-yos, model farms and animals, as well as dolls with real hair made by Kathe Kruse (a Bauhaus disciple); prices start at 1,000 francs. Don't miss the Christmas pyramid in carved wood. There are also lots of decorations from Germany and Scandinavia.

Au Nain Bleu

8th arr. - 406-410, rue Saint-Honoré
42 60 39 01
Open 9:45 a.m.-6:15 p.m. Closed Sun. Parking: Vendôme. Cards: V, AE, MC.

Don't be put off by the 32,000-franc price tag on the miniature Bugatti in the window.

This illustrious shop does have other wonderful and less expensive toys to tempt you. Down in the basement, old friends like Mickey Mouse and Babar live, and you can hop a ride on some fine rocking horses, some of which boast real leather trappings. There's a great variety of dolls and accessories, plastic and china doll services, lots of remote-control cars and motorcycles and a costume and makeup section. The cost for baby cradles, complete with toys for tiny tots, start at about 800 francs.

L'Oiseau de Paradis
7th arr. - 211, bd Saint-Germain
45 48 97 90
Open 9:30 a.m.-7 p.m. Closed Sun. Parking: Bon Marché. Cards: V, AE, DC.

This is the traditional toy shop *par excellence*, chockablock from floor to ceiling. Tricycles, rocking toys and scooters hang from the rafters, and we're always greeted with a smile, no matter what we've come to buy. Apart from the standard variety of toys, there are some fine tin soldiers, handmade wooden puzzles and a collection series of miniature cars.

La Pelucherie
8th arr. - 84, av. des Champs-Elysées
43 59 49 05
Open 10 a.m.-midnight (Mon. until 7:30 p.m. & Sun. 11:30 a.m.-8 p.m.). Parking: Georges-V. Cards: V, AE, DC. Expeditions worldwide.

A boon for night owls, this kingdom of soft toys stays open until midnight. You'll find everything here from the tiniest teddy bear to a gargantuan elephant in every color of the rainbow. There's also a section for newborns that sells darling baby clothes. La Pelucherie delivers within Paris and all over the world.

Si Tu Veux
2nd arr. - 62, Général-Vivienne
42 60 29 97
Open 11 a.m.-7 p.m. Closed Sun. & Mon. Cards: V.

Right next to the famous children's shop is this space reserved for nostalgic grownups. Remember those teddy bears stuffed with straw (135 francs for the smallest)? Well, you can get those here as well as painted tin toys, little china services and cardboard dolls.

Si Tu Veux
2nd arr. - 68, Général-Vivienne
42 60 59 97
Open 11 a.m.-7 p.m. Closed Sun. & Aug. Parking: Bourse. Cards: V. Mail-order sale catalog.

Nestled cozily in the heart of this lovely gallery is a gold mine for children's parties. Games and toys are attractive and reasonably priced. There are wooden blocks, washable dolls, a great choice of marbles and a panoply of items with which to play. For children's birthdays and party occasions, there are ready-to-wear as well as ready-to-make costumes (from 110 francs for a kit), easily removable play makeup, hats, magic wands and party kits for 185 francs.

CLOTHING

DISCOUNT

L'Annexe
6th arr. - 48, rue Saint-Placide
45 48 82 85
Open 10 a.m.-7 p.m. (Mon. noon-7 p.m.). Closed Sun. Parking: Bon Marché. Cards: V, AE, MC.

Looking for bargains in men's name-brand clothing? Savvy shoppers put this address high on their list. L'Annexe sells designs by Thierry Mugler and Jean-Paul Gaultier, English mens-wear from Hyde Park and suits by Structure. Shirts are priced as low as 50 francs. Since new stock is constantly arriving, it's worthwhile to drop by for a look-see whenever you're in the neighborhood.

Boutique Sosy
6th arr. - 11, rue Saint-Placide
42 22 62 10
Open 10 a.m.-7 p.m. Closed Sun. & Mon. Cards: V, MC.

Bright, youthful clothing by Carroll is sold here at a discount; prices start at 79 francs (420 francs for an outfit). The stock changes every ten days, so if you see something you like, it's smart to snap it right up.

Chercheminippes
6th arr. - 109, 110 & 111, rue du Cherche-Midi - 42 22 53 76
Open 10:30 a.m.-7 p.m. Closed Sun. & July 8-Aug. 28. No cards.
Here, on the fashionable rue du Cherche-Midi, is clothing for the entire family at cut-rate prices. Some of the garments are secondhand, others have slight imperfections, but they are generally in good condition, with designer labels to boot. If you've got a closet full of good-quality clothes that you no longer care to wear, bring them to Chercheminippes for sale on consignment.

BARGAIN CITY

Discounters hawking clothes and shoes for men, women and children are clustered on the rue Saint-Placide in the 6th arr. For manufacturers' outlets, head to the rue d'Alésia, 14th arr. Number 74 is Dorotennis, with Dorothée Bis just next door at number 76. Stock and Stock II are good bets for bargains, at numbers 80 and 92; Cacharel is a mere stone's throw away at 114. For fine Italian footwear at unbeatable prices, check out the rue Meslay, 3rd arr. Discount houses sit cheek-by-jowl with the most prestigious names in tableware on the rue de Paradis, 10th arr. Remember, though, that rooting out a good buy requires considerable time and patience!

La Clé des Champs
9th arr. - 38, rue de Rochechouart
42 80 32 85
Open 10 a.m.-7:30 p.m. Closed Sun. & Mon. in Aug. Cards: V, MC.
This store is excellent source for ski, tennis and windsurf equipement (and other sporting goods), sold at a considerable discount.

Le Dépôt des Grandes Marques
2nd arr. - 15, rue de la Banque
42 96 99 04
Open 10 a.m.-7 p.m. Closed Sun. Cards: V.
Rack after rack of designer menswear is set out for your inspection at this first-floor shop near the stock exchange. All the best labels are represented: Renoma, Cerruti, Louis Féraud, Jacques Fath and more, priced at an average of 40 percent under normal retail. Suits, jackets, pants, shirts and ties make up the stock. On a recent visit, we saw a Renoma silk suit (with label) from the current collection selling for 2,950 francs, a Cacharel silk tie for 130 francs, a Harris tweed jacket for 1,150 francs, a pure cashmere jacket for 2,500 francs. Take note that the most complicated alterations will be done by in-house tailors. Lots of stockbrokers invest their clothing budgets here, but so do many executives and political types who recognize a good deal when they see one.

Dépôt-Vente de Paris
20th arr. - 81, rue de Lagny - 43 72 13 91
Open 9:30 a.m.-7:30 p.m. Closed Sun. No cards.
Modern and antique furniture, knickknacks and bric-a-brac, dishes, jewelry, used appliances . . . everything but clothing can be bought or sold on consignment (the fee is 25 percent) at this vast old warehouse. Professionals generally cream off the best of the jewels and antiques, but if they've got a sharp eye, even nonpro shoppers can come up with some interesting bargains. New stock arrives daily.

Les Deux Portes
16th arr. - 35, rue de l'Annonciation
45 25 31 97
Open 10 a.m.-6:30 p.m. (Mon. 2 p.m.-6:30 p.m.). Closed Sun. No cards.
Designer fabrics for the home (curtains, upholstery, wallpapers) and top-of-the-line

household linens are sold at extremely attractive prices at the four Paris Deux Portes shops. Many items are manufacturers' closeouts, others are the firm's own exclusive designs. Also available is a line of sofas, custom-made draperies and a decorating service.

Deuxième Souffle
24th arr. - 61, bd de Vanves - 46 55 78 95
Open 10 a.m.-7 p.m. Closed Sat. & Sun. Cards: V.

Sporting goods may be swapped, bartered and otherwise exchanged at this shop in a suburb just south of Paris. Used equipment is sold for about half its original price.

Dewal Chaussures
6th arr. - 40, rue Saint-Placide
45 48 94 84
Open 10 a.m.-7 p.m. (Mon. 1 p.m.-7 p.m.). Closed Sun. No cards. Other branch: 33, rue du Four - 6th arr. - 43 25 26 77.

Founded some 25 years ago, Dewal is the dean of discount-shoe shops on the rue Saint-Placide, where cut-rate stores and bargain basements abound.

Halle Bys
2nd arr. - 60, rue de Richelieu
42 96 65 42
Open 10:30 a.m.-7 p.m. Closed Sun. Parking: Bourse. Cards: V, MC.

This vast, skylit emporium dates from the nineteenth century, but the fashions on sale here are absolutely up-to-the-minute. You'll find clothes for the entire family, priced at 20 to 50 percent under retail. Women's labels include Pierre d'Alby, Capucine and Toupie; for men, there are designs by Dior and Yves Saint Laurent. New stock arrives about every two weeks, and prices are even lower in the bargain basement.

Kid's
6th arr. - 19, rue Saint-Placide
45 48 74 25
Open 10 a.m.-7 p.m. (Mon. noon-7 p.m.). Closed Sun. & 2-3 wks. in Aug. Parking: Bon Marché. Cards: V, DC, MC.

Prices for Levis won't seem low to Americans (almost $50 for a pair of 501s), but the jeans and denimwear by European manufac-turers offer a lot of style for the money. Frequent special sales and bins of cut-rate clothing placed alluringly just outside the door make Kid's one of the better bets on the rue Saint-Placide.

Marché Saint-Pierre
18th arr. - 2, rue Charles-Nodier
46 06 56 34
Open 9:15 a.m.-6:30 p.m. (Mon. 1:30 p.m.-6:30 p.m.). Closed Sun. & Mon. in Aug. & Sept. No cards.

"None priced lower!" "Sensational bargains!" "Special one-day sale!" Such are the slogans (which we've freely translated for you) that lure crowds of shoppers into the Marché Saint-Pierre, the foremost fabric discount market in Paris. On the ground floor, look for cottons priced as low as 8 francs per meter (approximately three feet) and tulle in every imaginable color (13 francs per meter). The second floor is devoted to silk, velvet, satin (27.50 francs per meter) and felt (perfect for lining drawers and closets). Upholstery and decorating fabrics are grouped on the third floor, while terry cloth, muslin, linen and other household fabrics occupy the fourth floor. Up there as well are ready-made linen aprons (30 francs) and dishcloths (4 francs). Before you leave, look out from the store and admire the fabulous unobstructed view of Sacré-Coeur.

Le Mouton à Cinq Pattes
6th arr. - 19, rue Grégoire-de-Tours
43 29 73 56
Open 10:30 a.m.-7:30 p.m. (Mon. 2 p.m.-7:30 p.m.). Closed Sun. Cards: V, AE, MC. Other branch: 8-10, rue Saint-Placide - 6th arr. - 45 48 86 26 - closed at 7 p.m.; parking: Boucicaut.

You can actually find clothes for 10 francs, 30 francs or 50 francs in the stores' huge sidewalk bargain bins—whether you'd actually want to wear them is another question. Inside, racks hold quantities of label-less cut-rate clothing. The stock is constantly changing, and we have heard that designers' press collections find their way here. But don't ask the staff—they are decidedly unhelpful.

Réciproque

16th arr. - 95, 103 & 123, rue de la Pompe
47 04 82 24
*Open 10 a.m.-6:45 p.m. Closed Sun., Mon. &
last wk. of July & Aug. Cards: V.*

Thrifty ladies of the jet-set, show-biz and
business worlds bring the clothes they no
longer want (but can't bear to give away—how
do you think they got so rich?) to Réciproque.
Manager Nicole Morel displays only the finest
designer clothing from recent collections, all
of it in excellent condition. The spacious, quiet
store is a delightful place in which to browse;
the ambience is anything but thrift shop.

Tony Boy

6th arr. - 33, rue Saint-Placide
45 48 34 07
*Open 10 a.m.-7 p.m. (Mon. 1 p.m.-7 p.m.).
Closed Sun. Cards: V, MC.*

Here is cheap and cheerful kidswear, sold at
a considerable discount.

Tropico

6th arr. - 4, rue des Canettes - 43 54 66 61
*Open 10:30 a.m.-7:15 p.m. (Mon. 1:30 p.m.-
7:15 p.m.). Closed Sun. Parking: Saint-Sulpice.
Cards: V, AE, DC, MC. Other branch: 16, rue
Saint-Placide - 6th arr. - 42 22 10 90, open Mon.
at 1 p.m., closed at 7:30 p.m. Cards: V.*

The Tropico stores are a good source for
pretty, inexpensive shoes that are always in step
with the latest fashion trends.

EYEWEAR

Gualdoni

16th arr. - 65, rue de Passy - 46 47 40 27
*Open 9 a.m.-7 p.m. (Mon. 2:30 p.m.-6:30 p.m.).
Closed Sun. & Mon in winter. Parking: Passy.
Cards: V, AE, DC. 2 other branches.*

Gualdoni specializes in tortoiseshell. The
prices vary according to thickness and color;
the darker the frame, the cheaper the price
(about 3,000 francs). Lighter frames can cost
as much as 25,000 francs. Come down to earth
with the eye-catching Silhouette brand, the
top-of-the-line in imitation tortoiseshell (from
1,200 to 1,600 francs). Colored plastic frames
are cheaper still, while wooden frames retail for
1,500 francs. There's a children's section as

well as a selection of designer frames (Lafont,
Cartier, Vuarnet and so forth).

Mikli

4th arr. - 1, rue des Rosiers - 42 71 01 56
*Open 11 a.m.-7 p.m. (Mon. 2 p.m.-7 p.m.).
Closed Sun. Cards: V, AE, DC.*

Mikli, with its soothing blond-wood interior
and comfortable armchairs, is the latest place
to shop for eyeglasses. And the selection is
grand indeed. Mikli once went in for extravagant and provocative frames in large voluptuous shapes, à la Hollywood. A glance at the
new collection shows that Mikli is becoming
more classical (straightforward round frames),
yet incorporating some technical innovations,
such as a combination of metal and plastic in
matte or glossy colors. Allow a two- to ten-
day turnaround for a pair of glasses, depending
on how much work is involved. And you can
expect to pay between 500 francs for classic
frames and 3,000 francs for a pair of more
sophisticated spectacles.

Optique Marceau

16th arr. - 37 av. Marceau - 47 20 55 90
*Open 10 a.m.-7 p.m. (Sat. until 6:30 p.m.).
Closed Sun. & Mon. No cards.*

Shattered eyeglasses! Thanks to Pascal
Vansteenberghe and his enormous glass and
frame stock, you need not panic. Your eyeglasses can be replaced or repaired in one hour.
Unless, of course, you're unfortunate enough
to break them on Sunday or Monday when the
shop is closed.

Optique Mazet

6th arr. - 10, rue de Buci - 43 26 28 25
*Open 9:30 a.m.-7 p.m. (Mon. 2:30 p.m.-7 p.m.).
Closed Sun. & 1 wk. in Aug. Parking: Maza-
rine. Cards: V, AE, DC.*

This boutique has had a facelift and has
bounced back into the limelight with a luxurious selection of eyeglass frames presented on
velvet trays, just like at the jewelers! The service
is exquisite. These hip but chic frames—by
Cartier and such farsighted designers as Montana and Anne-Marie Beretta (2,200 francs).
There are also Jean Lafont frames for the more
thrifty (500 francs). All the models are exclusive designs, so you get first choice. You will
also find the latest models from the United
States. Don't leave the shop without a trip to

the first floor, where all the frames are priced at 150 francs. There's nothing wrong with them; they're simply six-month-old stock.

Pouilloux

8th arr. - 28, rue Boissy-d'Anglas
42 65 86 10
Open 9 a.m.-6:30 p.m. (Mon. 2:30 p.m.-6:30 p.m.). Closed Sun. & 2 wks. in Aug. No cards.

Inventor of the famous Vuarnet ski and sunglasses and the Nautilux glasses for fishing, windsurfing and other nautical sports.

FOR HIM & HER

DESIGNERS

Armani

8th arr. - 6, pl. Vendôme - 42 61 55 09
Open 10 a.m.-7 p.m. Closed Sun. Parking: Vendôme. Cards: V, AE, DC.

Armani's Parisian outpost is a cathedral of mirrors, furnished with cubical seating crafted of glowing wood: a cross between an Egyptian mausoleum and a hall of mirrors—and just as disorienting! Armani has a couple thousand stores all over the planet, and hundreds of thousands of faithful customers: it's a marketing miracle, really, since the price (for example) of an off-the-rack Armani suit is about the same as a ticket on the Concorde from Paris to New York! But do go in for a look-see (the sales staff may not seem glad to see you, but never mind them), and bring plenty of money in case you find something irresistible. If you can't bear to leave the shop empty-handed, there's always the Armani cologne; it's far more reasonably priced than the clothes. A few Left Bank boutiques now offer a selection of the Emporio Armani line. Try Oliver or Maximilien, both on the boulevard Saint-Germain.

Anne-Marie Beretta

6th arr. - 24, rue Saint-Sulpice
43 29 84 04
Open 10:30 a.m.-12:30 p.m. & 2:30 p.m.-7 p.m. (Mon. 2:30 p.m.-7 p.m.). Closed Sun. Parking: Saint-Sulpice. Cards: V, AE, DC.

Dame Beretta goes in for rigorously architectural geometrics. No artifice, please! Con-stants include large shoulders and a defined waistline around which she builds her design. She wants women to look up-to-date but with no frills. Though she's somewhat on her own in this vision of the future, and her prices are on the high end, we suggest you give her her due and check it out. At the back of the bunker-like boutique is a somewhat retiring menswear corner.

Adolfo Dominguez

1st arr. - 2, rue Catinat - 47 03 40 28
Open 11 a.m.-7 p.m. (Mon. 2 p.m.-7 p.m.). Closed Sun. Parking: Saint-Eustache. Cards: V, AE, DC.

Spaniard Adolfo Dominguez's style takes up where a waning yen for Japanese style left off. Handbags are made primarily of synthetic materials in funereal colors, and there is false promise of Latin style, which is highly priced and minimally displayed. The little-to-nonex-istent welcome is proffered by surly attendants. Surely the Spanish merit a better ambassador of their creative skills.

Jean-Paul Gaultier

2nd arr. - 6, rue Vivienne - 42 86 05 05
Open 10 a.m.-7 p.m. (Sat. 11 a.m.-7 p.m.). Closed Sun. Parking: Bourse. Cards: V, AE, DC.

The welcome is astonishingly courteous, the clothes are pressed together in glass wardrobes, accessories gleam . . . there is electricity in the air. The salespeople know what they're about. Clothes are maliciously classic and extremely provocative: rubber sweaters, tight-knit T-shirts, shoes with astrakhan trimmings. There is also the new Junior Gaultier line for smaller budgets. It is impossible to take yourself seriously here.

Michel Léger

2nd arr. - 22, pl. du Marché Saint-Honoré
42 60 47 90
Open 10 a.m.-7 p.m. Closed Sun. Parking: Saint-Honoré. Cards: V, AE, DC.

Michel Léger's talents surface equally in his designs for men and women. He blends an exclusivity of style with the use of such quality materials as thick cottons lined with alpaca for coats, a wool-silk mix for suits, and viscose for knitwear. His style is elegant, comfortable, classic and . . . urban. You won't find anything sporty here. Prices start at 2,400 francs for a coat. The service and the welcome, like the well-lit boutique, is warm.

Missoni

7th arr. - 43, rue du Bac - 45 48 38 02
Open 10 a.m.-7 p.m. Closed Sun. Parking: Montalembert. Cards: V, AE, DC.

This conservative yet sumptuous collection of fashion aimed primarily at those who love contrasting colors, changing textures, new forms, mossy mohair and glazed linen.

Montana

1st arr. - 3, rue des Petits-Champs
40 20 02 14
Open 10:10 a.m.-7 p.m. Closed Sun. Parking: Bourse. Cards: V, AE, DC. 2 other branches.

Claude Montana cultivates an ambiguous look—his style is fierce and arid; he goes in for stark silhouettes bedecked with accessories (like the metal belts). Double knits, quilted cottons, elasticized waists, wide belts and large-shouldered blousons appear from one collection to the next and remain the trademark of the Montana style of the future. The boutiques are uncomfortably bare, prices are stable (3,500 francs for a jacket, 1,300 francs for a knit sweater), and attendants are courteous, worth mentioning because it is increasingly rare these days. All three of his stores carry a superb collection of leather clothing.

Thierry Mugler

8th arr. - 49, av. Montaigne - 47 23 37 62
Open 10 a.m.-7 p.m. Closed Sun. Parking: François-Ier. Cards: V, AE, DC.

Thierry Mugler's new premises, in blinding blue, look a bit like something from outer space. A master of such materials as whipcord, jersey, piqué and gabardine, he goes in for strict lines with no frills. His high-waisted pants flatter even overabundant hips; colors are generally muted but will flare into electric blue, tobacco brown or even pine-green. Prices, too, are fiery: 1,000 francs for a knit sweater, 3,700 francs for a cardigan in wool gabardine. Just look at it as an investment; the Mugler style is already beyond fashion.

Sonia Rykiel

6th arr. - 4-6-8, rue de Grenelle
42 22 43 22
Open 10 a.m.-7 p.m. Closed Sun. Parking: Bon Marché–Velpeau. Cards: V, AE, DC. Other branch: 70, rue du Faubourg-Saint-Honoré - 1st. arr. - 42 65 20 81.

Sonia Rykiel's fringe of flamboyant red bangs hides a piercing look. This pioneer-cum-diva of fashion has turned the rue de Grenelle on the Left Bank into Rykiel-land. Her style began as ultra-feminine, all soft silhouettes draped in striped jerseys. Now her empire has grown, and the Rykiel-land population now includes men and children. Her famous outside stitching has given way to a more dressy and structured look, dominated by the color black. She will shortly be moving to new, nearby premises.

Angelo Tarlazzi

6th arr. - 74, rue des Saints-Pères
45 44 12 32
Open 10 a.m.-7 p.m. Closed Sun. Parking: Saint-Germain. Cards: V, AE, DC. Other branch: 67, rue du Faubourg-Saint-Honoré - 8th arr. - 42 66 67 73. See also Menswear.

Tarlazzi creates sexy, provocative designs for women with splashes of bright colors in prodigiously worked materials. Prices are stiff, but, thankfully, there is the Bataclan line to temper the whole. This is fiery fashion that frightens off some—still, try slipping into a trompe l'oeil suit. You may never take it off. . . .

Valentino

8th arr. - 17-19, av. Montaigne
47 23 64 61
Open 10 a.m.-7 p.m. Closed Sun. Parking: Georges-V, François-Ier. Cards: V, AE, DC.

Like Caesar, another famous Roman before him, Valentino came, saw and conquered the world of French fashion. Celebrities and commoners alike flock to his 120 boutiques in search of classic styles in everything from socks to eyeglasses. The *V* sign on your ankle or your nose could change your outlook on life. Though they're very expensive, be careful—we are always easily seduced by his creations and lose all control. . . .

Gianni Versace

6th arr. - 67, rue des Saints-Pères
45 44 09 52

Open 10 a.m.-7 p.m. (Mon. noon-7 p.m.).
Closed Sun. Parking: Bon Marché–Velpeau.
Cards: V, AE, DC.

Versace's home in Paris is an imposing two-level structure of gray granite, glass and white stone. Versace inherited his talent for couture from his mother, but his genius for fashion design is all his own. With every collection, Versace manages to introduce a marvelous new fabric: glazed linen, for example, or a subtle mix of linen and silk that looks like suede. The detailing and craftsmanship, the "fall" of every fabric and the definition of every line make these clothes and accessories a pleasure to wear. Whether your look is classic or contemporary, the skilled sales staff will offer judicious advice. The prices, alas, keep Versace out of reach for many of his admirers. Men's suits, for example, start at about 6,000F. Accessories are more accessible, of course, as are the fragrance and (very effective) skin-care products.

Workshop by Yohji Yamamoto

6th arr. - 4, rue du Dragon - 42 22 59 22
Open 11 a.m.-7 p.m. (Mon. 1 p.m.-7 p.m.).
Closed Sun. Parking: Saint-Germain. Cards: V,
AE, DC.

In the wake of Issey Miyake and his clones, here comes Yohji's Workshop—but with a difference: he also makes clothes for men. Using high-quality materials, he achieves a purity of line and classic forms that result in discreet elegance at reasonable prices.

READY-TO-WEAR

Agnès B.

16th arr. - 17, rue Pierre-Ier-de-Serbie
47 20 22 44

Open 10:30 a.m.-7:30 p.m. (winter until 7 p.m.). Closed Sun. Cards: V, AE. Other branch: 13, rue Michelet - 6th arr. - 46 33 70 20.

Above all, Agnès B. designs an ageless collection of fashionable clothing that virtually anyone can live with; her Paris shops suit mother and daughter alike. These are comfortable, easy styles at affordable prices: jogging outfits, sweatshirts and sweaters for a sporty look, lots of stripes and, for more dressy encounters, silk and linen outfits.

Cerruti 1881

8th arr. - 27, rue Royale - 42 65 68 72
Open 10 a.m.-7 p.m. Closed Sun. Parking: Madeleine. Cards: V, AE, DC.

Nino Cerruti runs this family business, which was established in 1881. His self-appointed role is to keep alive the tradition of the Italian suit—as classy as a Ferrari, with its unusual color combinations and the use of top-quality cloth, such as silk, linen or soft wools. Prices vary between 4,000 and 16,000 francs. A few years ago, Cerruti launched a woman's collection; it hasn't proved to be as successful as it might have been. Perhaps the line, clothes for the "executive woman" (rather austere suits, crisp blouses), is too severe. There are also lingerie and sportswear lines for both men and women.

Charvet

1st arr. - 28, pl. Vendôme - 42 60 30 70
Open 9:45 a.m.-6:45 p.m. Closed Sun. Parking: Vendôme. Cards: V, AE, DC, MC.

Charvet is an institution. It has been serving the same clientele from generation to generation. Clients' measurements are kept for decades, so the faithful can order their shirts and whatnot by telephone and have them delivered. Whether you're in search of twenty fine Egyptian cotton shirts or a simple pair of cuff links, the welcome and deference extended to you will be the same. The women's styles are classical (severe suits and blazers). Another classic is the paisley silk dressing gown, a gift for him that she will wear. Prices are steep.

Kenzo

1st arr. - 3, pl. des Victoires - 42 36 81 41
Open 10 a.m.-7 p.m. (Mon. 11 a.m.-7 p.m.).
Closed Sun. Parking: Bourse. Cards: V, AE.
Other branch: 16, bd Raspail - 7th arr. - 42 22 09 38.

Kenzo was the first of the Japanese designers in Paris. Now he's everywhere. He designs for the whole family, has a collection of bed and bathroom linens and accessories such as watches and eyeglasses. He's also jumped into sportswear. Colors, soft shapes, billowing shirts are his trademark. The annual sales lower prices by as much as 50 percent.

Mettez

8th arr. - 12, bd Malesherbes - 42 65 33 76
Open 10 a.m.-7 p.m. Closed Sun. Parking: Madeleine, H. Bergson-Laborde. Cards: V, AE.

This venerable old establishment has moved to new premises but has not lost its faithful clientele, most of which come from the world of politics or the theater. Since 1947 Mettez has consistently found buyers for the linen hunting and hacking jacket, as well as the Austrian jackets by Gieswen or Staff. Knickers, capes and velvet pants abound, as do Gloverall duffle coats.

Old England

9th arr. - 12, bd des Capucines
47 42 81 99
Open 9:30 a.m.-6:30 p.m. (Mon. 9:30 a.m.-12:30 p.m. & 2 p.m.-6:30 p.m.). Closed Sun. Parking: Madeleine, Galeries Lafayette. Cards: V.

The only English thing about this shop is its name. Yuppieware includes blazers, jackets, suits, raincoats and sweaters designed for young executives. At the top of the monumental staircase and emblazoned with England's royal coat of arms is the womenswear (blouses, cashmeres and kilts) and children's (conservative) department. On the ground floor you can find Derek Rose pajamas in lovely stripes, Mason and Pearson brushes, and Floris or Atkinson eau-de-toilettes. The advice of the tailors is invaluable. You would do well to listen. A rare spot indeed!

Renoma

16th arr. - 129 bis, rue de la Pompe
47 27 13 79
Open 10 a.m.-7:30 p.m. Closed Sun. Parking: Victor-Hugo. Cards: V, AE, DC.

Renoma is a blast from the past. From the '60s, to be precise, when it flourished. Today it's caught its breath and bounced back, thanks to the futuristic decoration of its huge floor space broken up into different levels. The collection gives one a rather painful sense of déjà vu. Are these copycat styles or just the latest fashion? Summer suits look suspiciously like Armani, button details just like Yamamoto, the leather-goods collection could be Mulberry.

The Jazz line launched in 1983 is a real cocktail of Latin and Anglo-Saxon styles concocted with some humor. Unfortunately, atmosphere wins over quality. The upcoming sportswear collection may help to revise our judgment.

Scapa of Scotland

6th arr. - 71, rue des Saints-Pères
45 48 99 44, 45 44 18 50
Open 10 a.m.-7 p.m. Closed Sun. Parking: Saint-Germain. Cards: V, AE.

Brian Redding designs these strictly classical collections brightening them with a touch of pastel or a colorful ribbon. You can deck yourself out from head to toe at a reasonable price. The sportswear, chic and attractive, is well complemented by the nice, discreet service.

Ventilo

2nd arr. - 25, rue du Louvre - 42 33 18 67
Open 10:30 a.m.-7 p.m. (Mon. 2 p.m.-7 p.m.). Closed Sun. Parking: Saint-Eustache. Cards: V, AE.

The Armand Ventilo and Brothers shop is bathed in restful light. The La Colline collection makes up the basic theme of the ground floor. Softly styled menswear can be found on the first floor along with sober womenswear. The White and Wood collection is located on the second level, while the Nouvelle Maison de Thé dominates the shop as a whole, and offers a haven of tranquility with 932 varieties of teas. Nice staff and moderate prices.

AND ALSO . . .

Aquascutum

1st arr. - 10, rue de Castiglione
42 60 09 40
Open 10 a.m.-7 p.m. Closed Sun. Parking: Vendôme. Cards: V, AE, DC.

Burberrys

8th arr. - 8-10, bd Malesherbes
42 66 13 01
Open 9:30 a.m.-6:30 p.m. Closed Sun. Parking: Madeleine. Cards: V, AE, DC. 2 other branches: 55, rue de Rennes - 6th arr. - 45 48 52 71; 56, rue de Passy - 16th arr. - 42 88 88 24.

Delaunay
6th arr. - 159, bd Saint-Germain
45 48 37 80
Open 10 a.m.-7 p.m. Closed Sun. Parking:
Saint-Germain. Cards: V, AE, DC.

Jaeger
8th arr. - 5, rue du Faubourg-Saint-Honoré
42 65 22 46
Open 10 a.m.-7 p.m. Closed Sun. Parking: Mad-
eleine, Concorde. Cards: V, AE, DC.

Ralph Lauren
8th arr. - 2, pl. de la Madeleine
42 86 90 83
Open 10 a.m.-7 p.m. Closed Sun. Parking: Mad-
eleine. Cards: V, AE, DC.

MENSWEAR

BELTS

Losco
6th arr. - 45, rue Mazarine - 46 34 14 15
Open 10:30 a.m.-7:30 p.m. (Mon. 2 p.m.-7
p.m.). Closed Sun. & Aug. No cards.

This burgeoning boutique boasts nothing but belts and interchangeable buckles.

DESIGNERS

Arnys
7th arr. - 14, rue de Sèvres - 45 48 76 99
Open 10 a.m.-7 p.m. Closed Sun. Parking: Bon
Marché–Velpeau. Cards: V, AE, DC, MC.

The windows of this house of fashion seem more like studies in monochromes than eye-catching appeals to the imagination. Cozy cashmere coordinates are just a shade away from shirts, suits or formal sportswear, all impeccably designed. Socks and ties round off a panoply of understated accessories on display in the somewhat lusterless salons. The extremely courteous sales staff will help you order those made-to-measure shirts or cashmere scarves you've been dreaming of. You may also happen upon such necessities as the oil-cloth hunting jacket or the famed four-button, straight-necked velvet jacket. If the prices are out of your reach, wait for sales days—but only if you're a fashion wizard. The white elephants foisted on customers can be laughable.

Pierre Balmain Homme
8th arr. - 44, rue François-Ier - 47 20 35 34
Open 10 a.m.-7 p.m. (Sat. 11 a.m.-1 p.m. & 2
p.m.-7 p.m.). Closed Sun. Parking: François-
Ier. Cards: V, AE, DC.

In this vast marbled space, the Patrick Aubert collections show their full glory. Aubert produces suits and jackets with an emphasis on the weave, in which Intarsia motifs create a play of subtle contrasts in such noble materials as alpaca, heavy silk, purest wool or fleecy leather. There is a theatrical, baroque element at work here. You can pick up a pair of flannel trousers for less than 1,000 francs. A shirt runs about 500 francs, while knitwear edges over the 1,000-franc mark. Expect poised fashion and good service.

Barbara Bui
2nd arr. - 13, rue de Turbigo - 42 36 44 34
Open 10:30 a.m.-7 p.m. Closed Sun. Parking:
Forum des Halles. Cards: V, AE, DC.

The Kabuki label earned Barbara Bui a name in the early '80s. She continues today with an elaborate collection of men's shirts, pants and jackets in select fabrics: cool wools, heavy cottons and linens. Bui swims against the dandy-look tide by creating carefully finished, clean lines. The result: seductively bold designs. Also available are socks, ties and coordinated footwear. The values are good, as is the warm welcome that awaits you.

Jean-Charles de Castelbajac Hommes
1st arr. - 5, rue des Petits-Champs
42 60 37 33
Open 10 a.m.-7 p.m. Closed Sun. No cards.

The little world of Don Castelbajac has finally thrown open its doors to men with a collection of basics, including Ko and Co Intégral plaid coats. The so-called Gypsy Celtic style, with its basic colors—so dear to the designer—that splash across jackets, shirts and sweaters, predominates. Knitwear, enlivened with rustic themes, has reached its zenith. The refreshing window displays and decor transform this shop into a charming gallery of crockery, linen and quilts.

Christian Dior Boutique Monsieur

8th arr. - 13, rue François-Ier - 40 73 54 44
Open 9:30 a.m.-6:30 p.m. (Mon. & Sat. 10 a.m.-1 p.m. & 2:30 p.m.-6:30 p.m.). Closed Sun. Cards: V, AE, DC.

Dominique Morlotti is now in charge of the men's ready-to-wear section at the prestigious house of Dior. Everything you need for an elegant, perfectly balanced wardrobe awaits, and you no longer get the impression that you're girding yourself in a suit of armor. The moment you step into the Boutique Monsieur, you are surrounded by traditional Dior good taste: double-breasted suits in striped fabrics, glen plaid wool, cashmere and linen; shirts in cotton poplin with stripes in every color of the (fashionable) rainbow. And, of course, the Dior accessories are always a good value, as they kill two birds with one stone: they are both chic and functional. The Boutique Monsieur targets the man who takes life seriously but refuses to wear boring clothes. The extensive range of sweaters, casual jackets, parkas and sports pants represents the preferred gear of the younger generation that patronizes this honorable establishment.

Jorge Johnson

3rd arr. - 4, rue Bernard-de-Clairvaux
48 04 05 73
Open 10 a.m.-8 p.m. Closed Sun. Parking: Beaubourg. Cards: V, DC.

A recent convert from the world of women's fashion, this Colombian designer displays his wares in a hip boutique crisscrossed by charcoal-black walkways. Jorge Johnson uses natural fibers (cotton, wool, silk) sometimes blended with synthetics to create coats, trench coats, shirts, pants and jackets that you can coordinate to your heart's content. Another novelty is Jorge Johnson's collection of undergarments, including athletic and full-body undershirts. Bloomingdale's in New York is already showing Jorge Johnson. And while prices are indeed high (about 5,000 francs for

a suit), the service (and the consultancy!) is delightfully attentive.

Guy Laroche Homme

16th arr. - 7, av. Victor-Hugo - 45 00 08 48
Open 10 a.m.-6:45 p.m. Closed Sun. Parking: Foch. Cards: V, AE, DC.

Finally a bit of bound and dash! Guy Laroche's new menswear store features Anglo-Latin quality clothes—madras, chevrons and houndstooth are juxtaposed with lively colors. We welcome Laroche's bounce back from the banal. You will be pleased to discover affordable prices (900 francs for a pair of whipcord pants) and an energetic welcome.

Marcel Lassance

6th arr. - 17, rue du Vieux-Colombier
45 48 29 28
Open 10 a.m.-7 p.m. Closed Sun. Parking: Saint-Sulpice. Cards: V, AE, DC.

For over a decade now the Left Bank's upper crust has been donning Monsieur Lassance's infallibly fine clothes. He will perhaps go down in social history as the man who helped transform President Mitterand's sartorial habits. Here you will find attractive pants, jackets, suits, shirts and shoes at reasonable prices. Worthy of mention is the return of Smiths trousers, work pants whose star rose in distant 1978. As always, there is an array of extra-large sizes for the big and tall.

Matsuda

7th arr. - 26, bd Raspail - 45 49 12 03
Open 10:30 a.m.-7:30 p.m. Closed Sun. Parking: Bon Marché–Velpeau. Cards: V, AE, DC.

Mitsuhiro Matsuda's menswear collection, which playfully employs natural fibers, thus flying in the face of so many other Japanese designers' synthetic *créations*, goes by the name of Monsieur Nicole. Matsuda's style is unquestionably revivalist: soft colors, blended materials and baroque detailing. A touch of refinement: each shirt or polo knit is rolled in tissue paper and packaged in a rough cardboard box. Ready-to-wear fashions are often beyond the reach of mere mortal pocketbooks, but accessories are affordable (for example, a pair of pants sells for 2,600 francs; a pair of socks, 150 francs). Alas, the warm marble-and-stone boutique decor does not make up for the wishy-washy welcome.

Issey Miyaké
6th arr. - 33, bd Raspail - 45 49 24 14
Open 10 a.m.-12:45 p.m. & 1:45 p.m.-7 p.m. Closed Sun. Parking: Bon Marché–Velpeau. Cards: V, AE, DC.

Quiet and elegant, the menswear collection of Issey Miyaké is an excellent example of carefully conceived, classic clothing. Less laudable are the stiff service and heart-stopping prices (500 francs for a printed T-shirt, about 2,000 francs for jogging-style pants made of heavy sailcloth).

Motton's
6th arr. - 39, rue du Cherche-Midi
42 22 29 97
Open 10:30 a.m.-7:30 p.m. (Mon. 2 p.m.-7:30 p.m.). Closed Sun. Parking: Bon Marché–Velpeau. Cards: V, AE.

Toss into a tumbler a handful of talented British designers, Jérôme and Eric Motton, plus a pinch of Stephen King, a sprig of Ally Capellino and a drop of Noreen Conwell. Add a shot of Chris Parry and shake it all up. You will have created the Motton's crazy-clothing cocktail. King's fine tweeds are cut wide like zoot suits. Capellino's supple knits and Parry's shirts are live wires with a dandy look. Conwell's hand-decorated silk-undergarment collection slips on nicely. All in all, it's a lively, accessibly priced ensemble. And it's so nice to feel wanted: the Motton brothers welcome you with open arms, and many a word of sound advice. A rare discovery!

Saint Laurent Rive Gauche
6th arr. - 12, pl. Saint-Sulpice - 43 26 84 40
Open 10 a.m.-7 p.m. Closed Sun. Parking: Saint-Sulpice. Cards: V, AE, DC.

This former sanctum of the saint of French fashion seems to have slipped into provincial torpor. But lift your gaze beyond the indifferent sales staff to the dizzy decor of mirrors and the maze of dressing rooms . . . there are the suits, the jackets, the sportswear, the bathing suits—all graced by the master's touch. Sumptuous materials come in a regal rainbow of colors: turquoise, saffron, pink, Naples yellow

on a black background. Some prices: 1,250 francs for a cotton sweater, 3,500 francs for a classic jacket.

Angelo Tarlazzi
6th arr. - 20, rue du Cherche-Midi
45 49 31 39
Open 10:30 a.m.-7 p.m. Closed Sun. & Mon. Parking: Bon Marché–Velpeau. Cards: V, AE.

This enfant terrible of fashion has finally opened a boutique for his menswear collections. The shimmering decor does not detract from the inviting ambience. On display are high-waisted pants, floppy-knit jogging suits that pass for formalwear, and creative jackets and coats. The cloth is superb, the finishing impeccable, and the prices affordable. All things considered, the result may be brash and glib but never insolent.

Yohji Yamamoto
6th arr. - 69, rue des Saints-Pères
45 48 22 56
Open 11 a.m.-7 p.m. Closed Sun. Parking: Saint-Germain. Cards: V, AE, DC.

Huge, stark and ruinously upscale, this new double boutique is an impressive showcase for Yamamoto's one-in-a-million creations. Suits sell for the trifling sum of 8,000 francs. But it's worth a visit simply to look while waiting for the sales season to start.

Ermenegildo Zegna
2nd arr. - 10, rue de la Paix - 42 61 67 61
Open 10 a.m.-7 p.m. Closed Sun. Parking: Opéra. Cards: V, AE, DC.

Renowned the world over, Ermenegildo Zegna is one of the giants of Italian fashion. He invented the pure-wool, no-wrinkle "high-performance" fabric that he uses so skillfully in his custom or ready-to-wear suits. Zegna's progressive approach to classic clothes includes lively new colors and an extended range of accessories. As you might imagine, the prices are stiff (shirts start at 600 francs), but the pure pleasure of the Zegna touch has enticed many to leap over monetary obstacles. A sophisticated and charming welcome awaits you in this must-browse shop, a showcase for both the far-flung and the Parisian fashion plate.

MORE TOP DESIGNERS

Agnès B. Homme
1st arr. - 3, rue du Jour - 42 33 04 13
Open 10:30 a.m.-7 p.m. Closed Sun. Parking: Saint-Eustache. Cards: V, AE.

Torrente
8th arr. - 9, rue du Faubourg-Saint-Honoré
42 66 14 14
Open 10 a.m.-7 p.m. Closed Sun. Parking: Concorde. Cards: V, AE, DC.

Ungaro
8th arr. - 2, av. Montaigne - 47 23 61 94
Open 9:30 a.m.-7 p.m. (Sat. until 6:30 p.m.). Closed Sun. Parking: François-Ier. Cards: V, AE, DC, MC.

Verri Uomo
6th arr. - 68, rue Bonaparte - 43 26 30 81
Open 10:30 a.m.-7:30 p.m. Closed Sun. Parking: Saint-Sulpice, Saint-Germain. Cards: V, AE, DC.

HATS

Gélot
8th arr. - 15, rue du Faubourg-Saint-Honoré - 42 65 14 40
Open 9:30 a.m.-6:30 p.m. (Mon. & Sat. 10 a.m.-1 p.m. & 2 p.m.-6:30 p.m.). Closed Sun. No cards.

Hats off to Gélot, the master headwear maker ennobled by Edward VII! Gélot has been working here, at the Lanvin Tailleur shop, since 1968. Gélot's made-to-measure hats start at 1,400 francs.

Motsch
8th arr. - 42, av. George-V - 47 23 79 22
Open 9:30 a.m.-1 p.m. & 2 p.m.-6:45 p.m. Closed Sun., Mon. & Aug. No cards.

Mad about hats? Motsch has been making and repairing headgear for over a century.

READY-TO-WEAR

Mason and Hedge
7th arr. - 200, bd Saint-Germain
45 49 10 73
Open 10 a.m.-7 p.m. Closed Sun. Parking: Saint-Germain, Montalembert. Cards: V, AE, DC.

This establishment's motto could well be "It is not the cowl that makes the monk." Indeed, Mason and Hedge make clothes that help men fashion their image. Whether you're a French fashion fiend or allergic to alpaca suits, your freedom of choice is fully respected. The attentive, friendly staff will help you choose the jacket or pants you want (and not the other way around). Pants come in myriad timeless hues in select fabrics, such as Zegna or Loro Piana brand fine Italian wool. The made-to-measure department is located in the basement and houses a vast array of colors and designs, including Prince of Wales check and chevron. The fine selection of poplins and cottons makes made-to-measure shirts a good investment (490 francs and a one-month wait). Also available are Hugo Boss jackets and Henry Cottons weekendwear.

Pierre Samary
6th arr. - 9, rue des Quatre-Vents
46 33 59 99
Open 10:30 a.m.-2 p.m. & 3 p.m.-7:30 p.m. (Mon. 3 p.m.-7:30 p.m.). Closed Sun. Parking: Saint-Sulpice. Cards: V, AE, DC.

A gray flannel jewel case, antique furnishings and an affable welcome are just the start of what you can expect to encounter at this neighborhood designer shop. Pierre Samary himself designs the shirts, pants and jackets after selecting the best Egyptian cotton, English poplin, Swiss linen and cashmere. The Samary collection is sober and pure, particularly popular with the understated elegant set. Brooks Brothers–style button-downs hug the neck well, while the polo shirts (direct from Brooks Brothers) have the discreet virtue of bearing no breast label. And they come in 30 colors—a bargain at 280 francs!

SHIRTS

Equipment

2nd arr. - 46, rue Etienne-Marcel
40 26 17 84
Open 10:30 a.m.-7:30 p.m. Closed Sun. Parking: Saint-Eustache. Cards: V, AE.

Basic whites with trompe l'oeil buttons, China-blue embroidered shirts, denims with folksy scenes stitched on, ruffled-front specials and so forth—Equipment wreaks havoc on the classics. Things change rather drastically from season to season in this tiny boutique's menswear department, whose stock ranges from sophisticated simplicity to butcher's-apron madness. Equipment's shirts are exotic but comfortable. Prices can run quite high (they start at 500 francs). But the shop's decor is sunny, and the service accommodating.

Alain Figaret

1st arr. - 21, rue de la Paix - 42 65 04 99
Open 10 a.m.-7 p.m. Closed Sun. Parking: Opéra. Cards: V, AE. Other branch: 99, rue de Longchamp - 16th arr. - 7 27 66 81.

Six collar styles, three sleeve sizes, short-sleeved models, several cuff styles, hundreds of colors for thousands of shirts in 600 types of fabric . . . you will find—not lose—your shirt at Alain Figaret's shop (prices start at 290 francs). There's always a crowd, so don't bother to wait around for things to slow down. A word of warning: Buy your shirts a size longer in the sleeve (they shrink after the first washing). Button-down collars are often too narrow to cover a tie properly, and anyone with big biceps will probably find their sleeves tight. While Figaret may not be the king of Paris shirtmakers, he's certainly a prince. Expect a warm welcome at either charming shop.

Hilditch & Key

1st arr. - 252, rue de Rivoli - 42 60 36 09
Open 9:15 a.m.-6:30 p.m. (Sat. until 7 p.m.). Closed Sun. Parking: Madeleine, Concorde. Cards: V, AE, DC.

Hilditch & Key shirtmakers, established nearly a century ago, is the last bastion of menswear shops in which refinement borders on the sublime. British poplins and fine cottons from France are among the 500 select fabrics to choose from. Cuffs and collars are made to a golden measure, with extraordinary accuracy. You can expect to pay about 1,600 francs for a custom shirt. Other ready-to-wear shirts are also available. And it's impossible not to mention the celebrated Hilditch & Key sweaters and gowns. Bertoni, the friendly CEO of Hilditch & Key, will gladly show you an exquisite "ancient-silk" dressing gown (7,950 francs), hand-printed somewhere in the depths of England, or a gorgeous double-ply V-neck cashmere sweater (they come in 35 colors and cost 2,950 francs). There is also a marvelous selection of camel-hair pullovers, cardigans and sleeveless sweaters.

Rhodes & Brousse

1st arr. - 14, rue de Castiglione
42 60 86 27
Open 9 a.m.-1 p.m. & 2 p.m.-6:30 p.m. Closed Sun. Parking: Opéra, Madeleine. Cards: V, AE, DC.

Since 1923 Brousse and fils have been selecting poplins finer than silk and turning them into magnificent shirts in four to five weeks (including fittings). The period-piece sculpted-wood shop is chockablock with the models and measurements, patterns and samples of Brousse customers' shirts. A remake of your favorite shirt will set you back about 1,050 francs. First-time customers must place a minimum order of three shirts (1,100 francs each). Ready-to-wear models can be had for 730 francs.

A. Sulka & Company

1st arr. - 2, rue de Castiglione - 42 60 38 08
Open 9:30 a.m.-6:30 p.m. (Mon. & Sat. 10 a.m.-6:30 p.m.). Closed Sun. Parking: Opéra, Madeleine. Cards: V, AE, DC.

Sulka is the paragon of refinement, a name with a slighly prewar ring to it. The discriminating clientele arrives from far-flung nations and provinces to order made-to-measure shirts in sailcloth, poplin, silk, flannel or wool. Timeless classics, these impeccable-quality items are handled by a courteous, deferential staff. First-time orders of custom shirts must be for six or more (at 1,500 francs each). Before filling the order, a pilot shirt is made, which you take home, wear, wash and then bring it back for Sulka to check for faults. Also available are double-ply cashmere V-necks and cardigans, five-ply cashmere jackets, polo shirts, scarves, ties, umbrellas, socks and a small selection of casualwear.

SHOES

Aubercy

2nd arr. - 34, rue Vivienne - 42 33 93 61
Open 10 a.m.-6:30 p.m. (Mon. 11:30 a.m.-6:30 p.m.). Closed Sun. Parking: Bourse. Cards: V, AE.

Aubercy shoes has ridden out the swells of style since 1935, all the while producing excellent-quality, traditional footwear for discerning customers. Sportswear and casual shoes, such as the Richelieu buckle loafer, are making headway among other offerings, which cater primarily to businessmen and traditionalists. Prices start at 1,200 francs.

Roberto Botticelli

6th arr. - 1, rue de Tournon - 43 54 14 54
Open 10 a.m.-7 p.m. (Mon. 2 p.m.-7 p.m.). Closed Sun & Mon. in Aug. Parking: Marché Saint-Germain. Cards: V, AE, DC.

Roberto Botticelli's Italian shoes demonstrate this designer's inventiveness. They are made of materials such as rubber, woven fabrics or blends of canvas and leather—the antithesis of the classic British style. Since 1988 the shop has also carried angular Akira Tamaoki shoes. Expect a reserved reception and somewhat cold decor but fair prices (all shoes cost under 650 francs). There is another Botticelli shop at the Forum des Halles (42 33 01 78).

Carvil

8th arr. - 67, rue Pierre Charron
42 25 54 38
Open 10 a.m.-7 p.m. (Mon. 2 p.m.-7 p.m.). Closed Mon. in Aug. & Sun. Cards: V, AE, DC, MC. Other branch: 4, rue Tronchet - 8th arr. - 42 66 21 58, open Mon. 11 a.m.-7 p.m., closed Sun., no cards.

At Carvil, the only place the shoe pinches is the pocketbook. It's known as the playboys' favorite, and it's a good thing that most playboys have large bankrolls. But you do get what you pay for: excellent quality and styles ranging from the conservative to the outrageous.

Church

6th arr. - 4, rue du Dragon - 45 44 50 47
Open 10:30 a.m.-7 p.m. Closed Sun. Parking: Saint-Germain. Cards: V, AE, DC.

These famous and indestructible shoes finally have a shop window all their own. From size 39 to 45 in a broad range of widths, Church shoes come in black, bordeaux, cognac, gold and other colors. With the incomparable finishing of Becket, Grafton and Burwood, they are perennial favorites.

Michel Delauney

1st arr. - 6, rue de l'Oratoire - 42 60 20 85
Open 10 a.m.-noon & 2 p.m.-6:30 p.m. Closed Sun. & Mon. Parking: Palais-Royal, Forum des Halles. Cards: V, AE.

Welcome to the world of marvelously comfortable, solidly built shoes at reasonable prices. Models run from mocassins to riding boots. Michel Delauney's walking shoes are elegant and long-lived. He will find the right shoe for you according to width, arch and instep—not just try to sell you the most expensive model. Sale shoes are often an excellent deal. This is definitely an address to discover!

Drake

16th arr. - 6, rue Franklin - 45 27 51 58
*Open 10:30 a.m.-1 p.m. & 2 p.m.-7:30 p.m.
(Mon. 2 p.m.-7 p.m.). Closed Sun. Parking:
Trocadéro. Cards: V,AE, DC.*

The sales policy at Drake is to offer name
brands such as Saxone, Bass and Paraboot at
10 to 30 percent discounts. Good-quality footwear and friendly service are the name of the
game.

Fratelli Rossetti

8th arr. - 54, rue du Faubourg-Saint-
Honoré - 42 65 26 60
*Open 10 a.m.-6:50 p.m. Closed Sun. Parking:
Madeleine. Cards: V, AE, DC.*

In the beginning there were sportswear
shoes. . . . The Rossetti family then launched
into the mocassin and pump market. Success
was close at heel. Nowadays the Fratelli
Rossetti line boasts several audacious designs,
including white or two-tone Derbys in textured pigskin, rough-cut boat shoe–style loafers or riding boots in kangaroo, zebu or
calfskin. They are light on the foot, the summa
of casual elegance (for about 1,000 francs).

Jan Jansen

7th arr. - 62, rue des Saints-Pères
42 22 32 34
*Open 10:30 a.m.-7 p.m. Closed Sun. Parking:
Bon Marché–Velpeau. Cards: V, AE.*

Jan Jansen is a Dutch designer who set up
shop in Paris in 1988, a challenger in the
Italian-dominated market. Jansen's boutique
is wonderfully comfortable and welcoming, a
fine showcase for this tireless inventor's wares.
Featured are shoes in original materials, such
as ostrich and nubuk, or calfskin with humorous impressed patterns that poke fun at the
grand classics of British shoes. Shapes run the
gamut, from square toes to Turkish slippers or
clogs revisited.

Stéphane Kélian

7th arr. - 13 bis, rue de Grenelle
42 22 93 03
*Open 10:30 a.m.-7 p.m. Closed Sun. & holidays.
Parking: Bon Marché–Velpeau. Cards: V, AE.*

This sumptuous marble-designed boutique
purveys Claude Montana and Jean-Paul Gaultier models made for Stéphane Kélian, master
of the braided-leather shoe. The smaller, pricey
boutique at 6, place des Victoires additionally
features seductive Italian shoes by Cesare
Paciotti (42 61 60 74).

John Lobb chez Hermès

8th arr. - 24, rue du Faubourg-Saint-
Honoré - 42 65 21 60
*Open 9:30 a.m.-6:30 p.m. Closed Sun. Parking:
Madeleine. Cards: V, AE, DC.*

Sublimely comfortable, perfectly proportioned shoes finished to fit the most exigent of
feet. Such are the masterpieces John Lobb
cobbles together for customers *chez* Hermès.
You will be greeted on the first floor by Quentin Dickenson, the man in charge of the John
Lobb line. He can help you order hand-decorated, custom-made house slippers or classic
models, crafted following traditional methods
and commonly requiring a wait of over six
months. Prices start at 12,000 francs per pair.
Ready-to-wear shoes include the popular
Fould and Bergen models.

Messageries

1st arr. - 6, pl. Sainte-Opportune
42 33 80 44
*Open 11 a.m.-7:30 p.m. Closed Sun. Parking:
Forum des Halles. Cards: V.*

Ten years ago Jean-Bernard Cardon earned
himself a place among the avant-garde by
launching the Cole Haan line, Derby shoes
with uppers in brown, white or two-tone suede
and red-rubber soles. The time has come to
rediscover this shop, a veritable institution,
where you will find English handmade shoes
by Tricker and American handmade loafers and
country shoes by Allen Edmonds.

---

*Remember that if you spend
1,200 francs or more in a store, you
are entitled to a full refund of
the value-added tax (VAT).
See "Basics" for details.*

François Villon

6th arr. - 58, rue Bonaparte - 43 25 98 36
Open 10 a.m.-1 p.m. & 2 p.m.-7 p.m. Closed Sun. No cards.

Renowned for shoeing women with wondrous creations, François Villon has turned his masterful hand to men's sportswear shoes. Featured are the perennially popular topsiders and a line of "all-weather" shoes that are billed as 100 percent leather but in fact have rubber soles. Footing the bill is not as blistering an experience as you might expect, since prices start in the neighborhood of 900 francs.

Weston

17th arr. - 98, bd de Courcelles
47 63 18 13
Open 9 a.m.-7 p.m. (Mon. 2 p.m.-7 p.m.). Closed Sun. Parking: Ternes. Cards: V. 3 other branches.

Once upon a time, young men lay awake at night and dreamt of handsome, solid, superbly finished Weston shoes (which were, in fact, the finest in ready-to-wear shoes). But Weston's reputation has tarnished of late. The average life of the celebrated "180" moccasin has dropped from eight to two years. Repairs are sometimes shoddy and reports have it that the soles sometimes leak! Faithful customers have turned to the Norwegian Hunter's shoe. A curious note: If you arrive wearing anything but Weston shoes you might receive a stiff welcome. And sale shoes are white elephants made especially for the cut-price selling season. At least the prices haven't gone up (but they start at 1,200 francs).

TAILORS

André Bardot

17th arr. - 19, av. de la Grande-Armée
45 00 25 02
Open 9:30 a.m.-8 p.m. Closed Sun. Parking: Foch. Cards: V, AE.

Imagine boasting about workmanship that smacks of the Middle Ages! Such is the proud claim of the president of the Paris Union of Master Tailors, André Bardot. His suits are all handmade and last, he claims, at least ten years. Well, at 10,000 francs a suit, that's the least one can expect! Also available are fine English fabrics and a substantial range of cashmeres, the house specialty. You can also order shirts made to measure.

Marcel Bur

8th arr. - 138, rue du Faubourg-Saint-Honoré - 43 59 45 68
Open 9 a.m.-12:30 p.m. & 2 p.m.-7 p.m. (Mon. 2 p.m.-7 p.m.). Closed Sun. & Aug. 15-30. Parking: rue Rabelais. Cards: V, AE, DC.

Marcel Bur's suits are the stuff dreams are made of. Bur's Saxbury "miracle fabric," made of combed, carded, blended, 100 percent pure wool, is guaranteed uncreasable. We are pleased to note that Bur's formerly conservative colors have been brightened up a bit. A custom two-piece suit runs upward of 9,900 francs, but semicustom models go for half the price. The ground floor boasts several beautiful cashmere items, as well as the equally fine house eau de toilet, Marcel Bur pour Homme.

Cambourakis

6th arr. - 97, bd Raspail - 45 48 22 23
Open 9 a.m.-noon & 2 p.m.-6:30 p.m. (Mon. 2 p.m.-6:30 p.m.). Closed Sun. & Aug. Parking: Rue de Rennes. No cards.

In this 1930s setting, complete with shaded lamps, you will find not the latest revival chic restaurant but Cambourakis, the king of cheviot fabrics. Also available are tweed and cashmere jackets. The cuts are classic, and the prices reasonable (about 8,000 francs for a suit).

Cifonelli

8th arr. - 31, rue Marbeuf - 42 25 38 84,
47 23 38 66
Open 9:30 a.m.-12:30 p.m. & 2 p.m.-7 p.m. (Sat. 2 p.m.-7 p.m.). Closed Sun. & Aug. Parking: François-Ier. Cards: V, AE, DC.

When Cifonelli opened for business in the '30s, he effectively introduced a light, timeless style that immediately won over worldly travelers. The elder Cifonelli's son, Adriano, has perfected his father's design. The shoulder, back and sleeve fittings are all impeccably precise. So providing the 14,000-franc tab is appropriate for your pocketbook, you, too, can have people ask for the address of your tailor. Indeed, these are noble threads.

Creed

8th arr. - 38, av. Pierre-Ier-de-Serbie
47 20 58 02
Open 9 a.m.-7 p.m. Closed Sun., Mon. & Aug. Cards: V, AE, MC.

Creed has been around for longer than we care to remember. It is the closest thing in Paris to a Jermyn Street shirtmaker. You may choose from among several models of striped custom shirts fashioned from fabulous, exclusive and *extremely* British fabrics. The formidable ready-to-wear selection should not be overlooked (900 francs; custom suits cost about 15,000 francs). Creed also has its own line of men's colognes and fragrances made from natural substances, which come in bottles that are sure to become collector's items in twenty years.

Lanvin Homme

8th arr. - 15, rue du Faubourg-Saint-Honoré - 42 65 14 40
Open 9:45 a.m.-6:30 p.m. (Mon. 12:45 p.m.-2 p.m.). Closed Sun. Parking: Madeleine. Cards: V, AE, DC.

The venerable Lanvin label has tailor-made itself a place at the forefront of the French menswear world. This shop, which appears on the registry of historical monuments, is a charming product of the Roaring Twenties. A ride in the marvelous elevator alone is worth a visit. Behind the array of suits, shirts and accessories stands a small army of craftsmen who draw on 50 years of Lanvin experience. Dozens of hours of work are dedicated to each suit. Flawless quality is the key here. Preferred fabrics include wool, silk, alpaca, cashmere and poplin cotton. The Lanvin ready-to-wear line bears the Patrick Lavoix label and is sold at 2, rue Cambon.

Claude Rousseau

8th arr. - 279, rue Saint-Honoré
42 60 16 13
Open 9 a.m.-noon & 2 p.m.-6:30 p.m. Closed Sat., Sun., Aug. & 1 wk. at Christmas. Parking: Madeleine. No cards.

Thanks to his claim that he is able to fill even the most eccentric orders, Claude Rousseau has become the standard-bearer of Parisian style. "Ours is a style, not a fashion," says Rousseau. He combines beauty and truth to create impeccable suits whose masterful finishing hides a thousand and one ingenious inventions tailor-made to please true connoisseurs.

Francesco Smalto

8th arr. - 44, rue François-Ier - 47 20 70 63
Open 10 a.m.-7 p.m. Closed Sun. Parking: François-Ier. Cards: V, AE, DC.

Francesco Smalto, king of the extravagant fabric, was trained at the renowned Ecole Camps. He continues to uphold his well-earned title of master tailor and serve a clientele that includes celebrities and millionaires. Smalto has even perfected a type of cashmere in which the tennis stripes spell out the name of the customer! His styles appear effortless. No wonder his custom suits start at 15,000 francs. But take heart: flawless ready-to-wear pieces are also available.

UNDERWEAR

Contre-Courant

1st arr. - 40, rue Saint-Honoré
42 33 47 06
Open 9:30 a.m.-7 p.m. Closed Sun. Parking: Forum des Halles. Cards: V. Other branch: 4, rue des Ecoles - 5th arr. - 43 54 95 49.

To find colorful, upbeat undergarments, shorts, pajamas, dressing gowns and robes in comfortable cotton designed by Zofia Rostad, we come here. Prices start at 150 francs. The friendly service at both shops is a bonus.

Soie et Lui

6th arr. - 7, rue des Canettes - 46 33 80 08
Open 11 a.m.-7:30 p.m. (Mon. 1:30 p.m.-7:30 p.m.). Closed Sun. Parking: Saint-Sulpice. Cards: V, AE, DC.

The men's undergarment collections on sale here are designed to make you "intimately handsome." In other words: an invitation to undress and show off at all hours. You will find such renowned brands as Hom, Dior, La Perla and Homme Invisible (for bathing suits), plus neo-Greek slips by Nikos and kangaroos by Calvin Klein. The courteous sales staff will assist you in your selection of anything from boxers to bathing gowns (primarily in cotton or silk). While the prices are moderate to high, they are justified.

Chantal Thomass

6th arr. - 11, rue Madame - 45 44 60 11
Open 10:30 a.m.-7 p.m. Closed Sun. Parking: Saint-Sulpice. Cards: V, AE, DC.

A few seasons ago Chantal Thomass, renowned for her lady's lingerie, came up with the idea of launching a men's undergarment collection inspired by the Hercules look by Nikos. Now that the brawny-boy look is a thing of the past, you will find several attractive lines for men in white cotton, grey chiné, houndstooth, pure black and other colors and fabrics (styles and finishing change with hue and type of material). Chantal Thomass's men's undergarments are well made, comfortable and versatile. The only drawback is the price: 250 francs for a slip, 950 francs for a T-shirt and 1,200 francs for a bathing suit.

WOMENSWEAR

DESIGNERS

Azzedine Alaïa
3rd arr. - 17, rue du Parc-Royal
42 72 19 19
Open 10 a.m.-7 p.m. Closed Sun. Cards: V,AE, DC.

More women dream of pouring themselves into an Azzedine Alaïa creation than can actually—decently—do so. The tiny Tunisian's artful cutting, stretch fabrics and suggestive seaming do wonders for svelte silhouettes. What they do to less-than-heavenly bodies we will leave to your imagination. Still, if Tina Turner dares to wear Alaïa, why shouldn't we? Well, the prices, for one thing—they're terribly high. What's more, Azzedine may just be running out of inspiration: his recent collections look awfully repetitive. The most original thing about the Alaïa phenomenon nowadays may just be his spectacular glass-and-steel headquarters (boutique, studio and offices) located in a former department store warehouse.

Chloé
8th arr. - 60, rue du Faubourg-Saint-Honoré - 42 66 01 39
Open 10 a.m.-6:30 p.m. Closed Sun. Parking: Madeleine. Cards: AE, V, DC. Other branch: 3, rue de Gribeauval - 7th arr. - 45 44 02 04.

Martine Sitbon's girlish designs have garnered mixed reviews from Chloé's traditional customers. When they shell out the considerable sums that the firm's creations command, they want something classic, wearable and flattering. Ever since designer Karl Lagerfeld and his successors, Guy Paulin and Philippe Guibourgé, turned in their scissors, Chloé has

had a hard time maintaining its image of luxury and elegance. Sales staff is unbearably stiff and sniffy.

Comme des Garçons
2nd arr. - 40, rue Etienne-Marcel
42 36 91 54
Open 11 a.m.-7 p.m. Closed Sun. Parking: Saint-Eustache. Cards: V, AE, DC.

The *vendeurs* size you up as you walk in, and if they don't like your "look," you can expect a pretty frosty reception. Indeed, the store itself exudes precious little warmth. As for the clothes (which, incidentally, the sales clerks just hate to see the customers touch), well . . . the polo shirts (obscenely expensive: 2,000 francs) are anemic; the knits are droopy and unattractive; the colors are depressing. Designer Rei Kawakubo's most recent models are reportedly fresher and more light-hearted, but we'll reserve judgment until we see them in the stores. In the meantime, if you want to take the measure of this reputedly gifted designer's talent, visit her furniture showroom (at the Marché Saint-Honoré, first arrondissement) instead.

Songeur Daiya
1st arr. - 245, rue Saint-Honoré
42 60 97 35
Open 10:30 a.m.-7:30 p.m. Closed Sun. Parking: Madeleine. Cards: V, AE, DC.

The Daiya group (a Japanese concern), recently opened this spectacular shop to showcase talented designers like Nikita Godart, Brigitte Masson, Laura Caponi and Brazilian stylist, Cristal. An international clientele comes here to look for chic, unusual (and expensive) ensembles for day and evening.

Paco Funada
4th arr. - 17, pl. des Vosges - 40 27 94 29
Open 11 a.m.-7 p.m. Closed Sun. Cards: V.

Paco Funada has abandoned menswear (he used to design for Cacharel and Marcel Lassance) for a new career in women's fashion. His is a dramatic, minimalist style which employs a narrow palette of muted colors, comfortable fabrics, superb craftsmanship and detailing. The collection is on view in an attractive shop under the arcades of the place des Vosges.

Irié

6th arr. - 8, rue du Pré-aux-Clercs
42 61 18 28
Open 10 a.m.-7 p.m. Closed Sun. Parking: Saint-Germain. Cards: V.

Irié has created a sober yet surrealistic black-and-white setting to show off his collection of hip, sophisticated clothes. Silk, angora, wool gabardine and mousseline are the major components of this designer's ultra-feminine, close-to-the-body creations. Irié is currently one of the darlings of the Left Bank set, who adore his boutique's courteous staff ("Madame, may I say that I think you've made an excellent choice . . .") and the reasonable prices: Outfits may be had for a hair under 1,000 francs; handsome winter jackets are priced at 3,000 francs.

Hiroko Koshino

8th arr. - 43, rue du Faubourg-Saint-Honoré - 42 65 83 15
Open 10 a.m.-7 p.m. (Sat. 11 a.m.-7 p.m.). Closed Sun. Cards: V, AE, DC, MC.

This Japanese newcomer to the Paris fashion scene creates appealing designs that make his customers feel oh-so-pretty.

Karl Lagerfeld Boutique

8th arr. - 19, rue du Faubourg-Saint-Honoré - 42 66 64 64
Open 10 a.m.-7 p.m. Closed Sun. Parking: Bristol, Madeleine. Cards: V, AE, DC.

Versatile, prolific Karl Lagerfeld, who has infused brilliant new life into the house of Chanel, continues to designs clothes and accessories for his personal label. Modern forms and strong colors characterize these witty, irreverent (and extremely expensive) fashions, displayed in the rather monumental premises Lagerfeld shares with Révillon on the Faubourg-Saint-Honoré.

Lolita Lempicka

4th arr. - 13 bis, rue Pavée - 42 74 50 48
Open 10:30 a.m.-1 p.m. & 2 p.m.-7 p.m. Closed Sun. & Mon. Parking: Saint-Paul. Cards: V, AE.

Let's be frank, shall we? For our money, designer Lolita Lempicka is more than just a little overrated. Her fussy, pretentious clothes (stiff suits, "Dynasty"-style evening gowns) are presented in a decor that (we suppose) is inspired by some Vincente Minnelli musical. Be warned that the sales staff becomes very cross if a customer interrupts their phone conversations with a question or a request for help.

Issey Miyake

7th arr. - 201, bd Saint-Germain
45 48 10 44
Open 10 a.m.-12:30 p.m. & 1:30 p.m.-7 p.m. Closed Sun. Parking: Montalembert, Saint-Germain. Cards: V, AE, DC.

In the deliberately theatrical setting of this Left Bank boutique, Issey Miyake's extravagant, extraordinary designs seem even more dramatic. While they look rather disconcertingly like rags on their hangers, when worn these soft, draped, cleverly knotted clothes prove to be impressive, even stately: Miyake's long duster coat, for example, makes even an unassuming individual look like a high priest! The prices these pieces command is terrifying—the merest T-shirt costs about 800 francs.

Popy Moreni

4th arr. - 13, pl. des Vosges - 42 77 09 96
Open 10:30 a.m.-7 p.m. (Mon. 11 a.m.-7 p.m.) Closed Sun. Cards: V, AE, DC.

Popy Moreni is one of the "grandes dames" of fashion design; her multi-faceted talent extends to clothes, accessories, furniture and housewares. This versatile Italian often looks to the Commedia dell'Arte for inspiration: note the oversized Pierrot collars on dresses and blouses. Her spacious, white boutique is rather badly organized, but among the piles of bright T-shirts, splashy espadrilles, chain belts, see-through plastic jackets and racks of clothes, one is sure to find something to covet. Those who wish to purchase, however, should come with lots of money, for the prices are excessively high.

Guy Paulin

2nd arr. - 1, rue du Mail - 42 61 32 61
Open 10 a.m.-2 p.m. & 7 p.m. Closed Sun. Parking: Saint-Eustache, Bourse. Cards: V, AE. Other branch: 26, rue Cambon - 1st arr.

Guy Paulin has finally received the recognition he deserves for his sane, sleek yet decidedly feminine fashions. Fetching lines and a judicious mix of natural and synthetic fibers characterize the designs that fill this tiny, cheerful, refreshingly low-key boutique. Suits (in muted colors, usually sporting a wealth of clever details) are a Paulin specialty.

Elisabeth de Senneville
1st arr. - 3, rue de Turbigo - 42 33 90 83
Open 11 a.m.-7 p.m. Closed Sun. Parking: Saint-Eustache. Cards: V.

Elisabeth de Senneville designs easy-to-wear fashions in wonderful fabrics. Her "city sportswear" is particularly inventive and flattering, with jackets, blazers and blousons that fit close to the body paired up with wide, flowing trousers. Ecru denim is a big Senneville favorite, shown plain, printed, lined and quilted. The stores also carry an amusing selection of witty and colorful children's clothes.

Georges Rech
16th arr. - 23, av. Victor-Hugo
45 00 83 19
Open 10 a.m. (1 p.m. Mon.)-7 p.m. Closed Sun. Parking: Foch. Cards: V, AE, DC, MC.

Rech makes clothes for active women with lots of personality, as vivacious as they are beautiful. The only fault to be found in his designs (and, we admit, this may be mere nitpicking), is that the garments are are so discreet as to virtually disappear behind the person wearing them. The detailing on every item is impeccable, and the Rech sales staff is very nearly perfect, too.

Téhen
4th arr. - 5 bis, rue des Rosiers
40 27 97 37
Open 11 a.m.-7 p.m. Closed Sun. Cards: V, AE.

Designer Iréna Grégori gets top billing in the Téhen shops with her fresh, vivid and uncomplicated styles. Prices are attractive, winter and summer, but at sale time they are downright irresistible.

Yuki Torii
2nd arr. - 38-40, gal. Vivienne
42 66 64 66
Open 10 a.m.-7 p.m. Closed Sun. Parking: Bourse. Cards: V, AE, DC.

Don't be misled by the austerity of his boutique; unlike his designing compatriots, this Japanese stylist does not go in for dramatic, ascetic "draperies." Yuki Torii likes bright colors and exuberant prints. A black wool jersey is strewn with silver stars; jungle flowers bloom on shirts and skirts; jacquards juxtapose all the hues of the rainbow, and then some. The clothes are supple, wearable and highly original. Pricey, too, of course. The sales staff is bashful but nice.

HAUTE COUTURE

In order to be a member of the most exclusive haute-couture "club," a couturier must host two press shows a year. These include a spring-summer collection and an autumn-winter collection of at least 75 designs worn by no fewer than three fashion models. Each collection must be shown at least 45 times to clients in salons reserved specifically for this purpose. The clientele numbers about 3,000 people worldwide. But these days, habits are changing. Video is everywhere and often cassettes are sent to special clients. The top models are interchangeable and make the round of the couturiers— Inès de la Fressange (Chanel) and Marie Seznek (Lacroix) are the exceptions to the rule. Despite its prestige, life in a haute-couture house is not as easy as it once was, despite the breath of fresh air brought to the profession by such personages as Christian Lacroix. Happily, many accessories—from perfumes, shoes and jewelry to the ready-to-wear lines— are keeping them alive.

EVENINGWEAR

Loris Azzaro

8th arr. - 65, rue du Faubourg-Saint-
Honoré - 42 66 92 06
Open 10 a.m.-7 p.m. Closed Sun. Parking: Madeleine. Cards: V, AE, DC.

The ground floor of the shop does nothing to prepare customers for the luxury that awaits them in the gray-marble showroom upstairs. There the imperturbable Loris supervises, while his sumptuous gowns are fitted on the fair figures of jet-set celebrities. Though he may be scoffed at by more classic *couturiers*, his customers adore the way Azzaro plunges a neckline, molds a silhouette. Predictably, his prices are far from negligible.

Narakas

16th arr. - 148, rue de Longchamp
47 27 23 20
Open 10 a.m.-6 p.m. Closed Sat. & Sun. Parking: Victor-Hugo.

Whether you need a "little" cocktail dress or a gown for a gala dinner, Alexandre Narakas will provide you with a design that won't go unnoticed. In his gilded atelier, aided by Yolande de Gourcuff, he fashions yards of silk, taffeta and satin for spectacular, one-of-a-kind creations priced from 2,000 francs.

Claude Pétin

8th arr. - 74, rue du Faubourg-Saint-
Honoré - 47 42 10 20
Open 9 a.m.-6 p.m. Closed Sun. & Aug. 1-20. Parking: Madeleine. Cards: V, DC. Other branch: 40, rue François-Ier - 8th arr. - 40 70 91 58.

Claude Pétin's evening wear is sometimes inspired by Hollywood vamps, sometimes by Victorian belles, but it's always exciting and glamorous. Some models may strike one as a bit "too-too," yet many are boldly inventive, with sculpted lines and daring proportions. Grace Jones wore Pétin's gowns for most of her stage shows. . . .

Yvan et Marzia

1st arr. - 4, pl. Saint-Honoré - 42 33 00 56
Open 11 a.m.-7 p.m. Closed Sun. & Mon. Parking: Marché Saint-Honoré. Cards: V.

If your figure is flawless, you're likely to love Yvan and Marzia's luscious gowns. The lumpy

and bumpy among us, however, would do well to look elsewhere. Prices start at about 2,000 francs.

FURS

Révillon

6th arr. - 44, rue du Dragon - 42 22 38 91
Open 10 a.m.-6:30 p.m. Closed Sun. Parking: Saint-Germain. Cards: V, AE, DC. 2 other branches.

Révillon has been the very symbol of furs since 1723. And they are still the most beautiful in the world. Here style goes hand in hand with quality. Karl Lagerfield designed the collection on the first floor at the top of the imposing pink-stone staircase. Of the fur-lined coats, muskrat suits, reversible jackets in blue mink or astrakhan, none is priced lower than 50,000 francs—in fact, they're generally four times that if you're into sable or chinchilla. Prices on the ground floor are somewhat lower. A men's department with coats and short jackets designed by Jean-Paul Avizou is housed on the basement floor.

Riccardo Rozzi

17th arr. - 13, rue de l'Etoile
47 66 37 37, 42 67 68 69
Open 10 a.m.-7 p.m. Closed Sun., Mon. & Aug. Cards: V, AE, DC.

Furs (including reversible models) in offbeat styles with wonderful, unique sleeves and enameled with colored copper make Riccardo Rozzi a designer for the young.

Robert Sack

8th arr. - 22, rue Royale
42 60 21 37, 42 60 40 91
Open 10 a.m.-6:30 p.m. Closed Sat. (except Sept. 15-Feb. 15), Sun. & Aug. Parking: Concorde, Madeleine. Cards: V, AE, DC.

Mink is Robert Sack's specialty. And the recent star of his show is a cashmere coat lined in mink, nutria (the durable, usually light-brown fur of the South American aquatic rodent) or beaver. It's styled loose or as a frock coat. Astrakhan is also making a comeback here in the style of a widely cut, belted jacket. Do not miss the May and January sales that offer 30 to 50 percent reductions.

HATS

Jean Barthet
8th arr. - 13, rue Tronchet - 42 65 35 87
Open 10 a.m.-1 p.m. & 2 p.m.-6 p.m. Closed Sun. Parking: Madeleine. No cards.

Most of the planet's celebrities have stuck their heads through the door of this institution—and with good reason. Jean Barthet makes hats that are refined and spectacular in their elegance. This is high fashion at over-the-top-hat prices! Along with Madame Josette, he is the last of the greats and deserves every possible prize.

Tête à Tête
8th arr. - 183, rue du Faubourg-Saint-Honoré - 43 59 39 89
Open 10 a.m.-7 p.m. Closed Sat. & Sun. Or by appt. Parking: Hoche. Cards: V, AE, DC.

Voluble, peremptory Madame Josette was for years a top designer at Paulette's (a well-known Parisian milliner). Now she crowns the world's aristocracy with her high-fashion hats and designs hats for great couturiers, such as Balmain. A quick call from New York, some sleight of hand and she'll produce the required creation. Everything is hand-sewn and costs between 1,800 and 2,000 francs. By appointment only.

Pierre Balmain
8th arr. - 44, rue François-Ier - 47 20 35 34
Open 10 a.m.-7 p.m. (Sat. 11 a.m.-1 p.m. & 2 p.m.-7 p.m.). Closed Sun. & 1 wk. in mid-Aug. Parking: François-Ier. Cards: V, AE, DC.

Erik Mostensen took over from Balmain in 1982 after a 30-year collaboration. Sales are held at the end of the season and by invitation only. The ready-to-wear lines, Ivoire and Diffusion, are designed by Patrick Aubert.

Carven
8th arr. - 6, Rond-Point des Champs-Elysées - 43 59 17 52
Open 9:15 a.m.-6:15 p.m. (Friday until 5:15 p.m). Closed Sat., Sun. & Aug. Parking: Matignon. Cards: V, AE, DC.

Madame Carven has a penchant for bright green and white. Her designs are shown in the salons Tuesday and Thursday at 3 p.m. from February 1 to May 15 and from September 10 to November 25. At the time of this writing, the launching of a menswear boutique was in the planning stages.

Chanel
1st arr. - 31, rue Cambon - 42 61 54 55
Open 9:30 a.m.-6:30 p.m. Closed Sun. Parking: Madeleine, Vendôme. Cards: V, AE, DC.

The fame and fortunes of the house of Chanel are known throughout the world. Foundress Coco Chanel died in 1971, and in 1981 designer Karl Lagerfield brought this great temple of haute couture out of the doldrums. Private shows are held fifteen times a season, on Tuesday and Thursday at 3:30 p.m. in the first-floor salons.

Christian Dior
8th arr. - 30, av. Montaigne - 40 73 54 44
Open 9:30 a.m.-6:30 p.m. (Sat. & Mon. 10 a.m.-1 p.m. & 2:30 p.m.-6:30 p.m.). Closed Sun. Parking: François-Ier. Cards: V, AE, DC.

Dior's "New Look" is making headlines

CHIFFON CHIC

For the kinds of fabrics used by the great couture houses, head for Max, 70, av. des Champs-Elysées, 8th arr., 45 62 10 70 or Rodin, 36, av. des Champs-Elysées, 8th arr., 43 59 58 82. Less expensive but with a huge stock and a vast range of prices is Tissus Reine, 3-5, place du Marché Saint-Pierre, 18th arr., 46 06 02 31.

---

again, but this time it isn't a revolutionary silhouette; it's a palace revolution that has the fashion mavens buzzing! Veteran designer Marc Bohan was unceremoniously ousted by Dior's hard-charging young management team. His replacement is Italian design whiz Gianfranco Ferré. Can this quintessentially French fashion house survive in the hands of an "outsider"? Time, and Ferré's first collection, will tell. Sales are held at the end of May and the beginning of December.

Louis Féraud

8th arr. - 88, rue du Faubourg-Saint-Honoré - 47 42 18 12
Open 10 a.m.-7 p.m. (Sat. 10:30 a.m.-7 p.m.). Closed Sun. Parking: Bristol. Cards: V, AE, DC, MC.

Arab princesses and Texas heiresses rub shoulders in these salons during the season. Louis Féraud started in Cannes, in the south of France, in the '50s and dressed such stars as Brigitte Bardot, Kim Novak and Liz Taylor. Today he is the dressmaker of France's first lady, Danielle Mittérand. His creations are feminine and expressive, denoting a man who loves women. . . .

Givenchy

8th arr. - 3, av. Georges-V - 47 23 81 36
Open 9 a.m.-6:30 p.m. Closed Sun. Parking: Georges-V. Cards: V, AE, DC.

Any fan of Audrey Hepburn is a fan of Givenchy. This lovely star has long represented the Givenchy haute-couture look: inaccessible, regal and ethereal. Shows are generally held on Thursdays at the Grand Hotel. Givenchy, who started his career alongside Balenciaga, also produces Life, a ready-to-wear collection at fairly reasonable prices for us mere mortals.

Christian Lacroix

8th arr. - 73, rue du Faubourg-Saint-Honoré - 42 65 79 08
Open 9 a.m.-7 p.m. Closed Sat. & Sun. Parking: Madeleine. Cards: V, AE, DC.

Christian Lacroix started his career at Hermès, and in 1981 became chief designer at Patou. Nowadays he heads his own haute-couture empire, and his scintillating creations are causing women's heads to spin—fast and hard. He marries folklore with fantasy; overall, his style is bathed in theatricality. He shows on Thursdays at the Galliera museum or the Hotel Inter-Continental. His *prêt-à-porter* line was launched in 1988.

Lanvin

8th arr. - 22, rue du Faubourg-Saint-Honoré - 42 65 14 40
Open 9:30 a.m.-6:30 p.m. (Mon. 9:30 a.m.-1 p.m. & 2 p.m.-6:30 p.m.). Closed Sun. Parking: Madeleine. Cards: V, AE, DC.

Meryll Lanvin is now running the haute-couture department and slowly but surely imposing her style on it.

Ted Lapidus

8th arr. - 35, rue François-Ier - 47 20 56 14
Open 10 a.m.-6:45 p.m. Closed Sun. Parking: François-Ier. Cards: V, AE, DC. Other branch: 52, rue Bonaparte - 6th arr. - 43 26 87 84.

Ted Lapidus promotes unisex fashion and remains faithful to his democratic principles. He shows on Tuesday at the Inter-Continental. Ready-to-wear for him and her are on sale at his Left Bank boutique, rue Bonaparte.

Guy Laroche

8th arr. - 29, av. Montaigne - 47 23 78 88
Open 9:30 a.m.-6 p.m. Closed Sun. Parking: François-Ier. Cards: V, AE, DC. 4 other branches.

Guy Laroche goes in for the sometimes flamboyant and often "suggestive" feminine styles. His creations are paraded on Tuesday and Thursday at 3 o'clock for clients. The press gets a look on Wednesday.

Lecoanet Hemant

8th arr. - 5, rue Lammenais - 42 25 24 24
Open 9 a.m.-6 p.m. (& by appt.). Closed Sat., Sun. & 3 wks. in Aug. Parking: Madeleine. Cards: V, AE, DC.

Didier Lecoanet and Hemant Sagar's creations received the haute-couture classification in 1984. The two give shows in unusual venues, and their lucky number is thirteen, the day they open their salons.

Hanae Mori

8th arr. - 62, rue du Faubourg-Saint-Honoré - 47 42 78 78
Open Mon.-Fri. 10 a.m.-7 p.m. by appt. & Sat. 1 p.m.-2:30 p.m. Closed Sun. Parking: Bristol, Madeleine. Cards: V, AE, DC.

Hanae Mori takes her inspiration from Japanese Kabuki theater, then translates her designs into a refined and international expression of haute couture.

Paco Rabanne

6th arr. - 7, rue du Cherche-Midi
42 22 87 80
Open Tues.-Fri. 10 a.m.-noon & 2 p.m.-6 p.m. Closed Aug. Parking: Bon Marché–Velpeau. No cards.

Paco Rabanne likes to defy convention. Remember his metal dresses, his use of plastic, the paper dresses? Well, these days he may be a bit more classical and a tad more practical, but he still has VIPs lining up to be avant-garde dress-ers. He also has a ready-to-wear collection for both men and women.

Nina Ricci
8th arr. - 39, av. Montaigne - 47 23 78 88
Open 10 a.m.-6:30 p.m. Closed Sun. Parking: François-Ier. Cards: V, AE, DC.

Nina Ricci symbolizes l'Air du Temps, the perfume for which the name is famous. Nowadays, Gérard Pipart continues to promote a style of delicate, classical femininity. His shows take place at the Musée des Arts Décoratifs in summer and winter. And there are sales in the basement of the boutique year-round.

Yves Saint-Laurent
8th arr. - 5, av. Marceau - 47 23 72 71
Open 9:30 a.m.-6 p.m. Closed Sun. Cards: V, AE. Other branches.

By now, Saint-Laurent is the password for French fashion. For 30 years, Dior's successor has been imposing his rigorous and luxurious style on the fashion world. Wednesday is press day at YSL, followed by six weeks of private by-appointment-only showings. No sales; you'll find those at the ready-to-wear boutiques, which need no introduction.

Jean-Louis Scherrer
8th arr. - 51, av. Montaigne - 43 59 55 39
Open 9:30 a.m.-6:30 p.m. Closed Sun. Parking: François-Ier. Cards: V, AE, MC.

Influenced by Yves Saint-Laurent, Jean-Louis Scherrer goes in for a classically elegant style. His customers include French television personalities and the Kennedys. He hosts shows for three days before releasing his creations to the press. There are few sales, and then only for faithful clients. His ready-to-wear line is ravishing and on sale at his boutique on the rue du Faubourg-Saint-Honoré.

Per Spook
8th arr. - 18, av. Georges-V - 47 23 00 19
Open 10 a.m.-7 p.m. Closed Sun. Parking: Georges-V. Cards: V, AE, DC.

Norwegian born Per Spook spent fifteen years with Louis Féraud before opening his own shop on the Left Bank. His creations are predictable, aimed at women who like to dress safely. He gets a large turnout for his shows.

Torrente
8th arr. - 9, rue du Faubourg-Saint-Honoré 42 66 14 14
Open 10 a.m.-7 p.m. Closed Sun. & Aug. Parking: Concorde. Cards: V, AE, DC.

Rosette Mett is the sister of Ted Lapidus. She shows at the Pavillon Gabriel on Sunday.

Emmanuel Ungaro
8th arr. - 25, rue du Faubourg-Saint-Honoré - 42 66 45 70
Open 10 a.m.-7 p.m. Closed Sun. Parking: Madeleine. Cards: V, AE, DC.

Emmanuel Ungaro doesn't go in for fashion trends so much as he aims to create torrid "climates." Three days after his press show, clients get a peek. There are no sales. Ungaro also designs a ready-to-wear line on sale at the same address.

Philippe Venet
8th arr. - 62, rue François-Ier - 42 23 33 63
Open 9 a.m.-12:30 p.m. & 2 p.m.-6 p.m. Closed Sun. Parking: François-Ier. Cards: V, AE, DC.

Philippe Venet trained with Givenchy before launching himself into the grand couture adventure. His clients now include Leslie Caron and Jackie Onassis. He shows at the Hôtel Meurice and favors black and white.

KNITS

Wolf Albrecht
2nd arr. - 4, rue du Mail - 45 08 57 11
Open 10:30 a.m.-7 p.m. Closed Sun. Parking: Bourse. Cards: V, AE, DC, MC.

A hop and a skip from the place des Victoires, German stylist Wolf Albrecht creates sweaters that are works of art. All his collections are made of jersey or 100 percent wool fibers. Summer designs include body-clinging dresses, low cut over bare shoulders; bright-colored skirts are either full or straight. In winter, Albrecht is really in his element. He mixes sober colors with monochrome pastels to create jacquard and other designs. He has set aside mohair and cashmere in order to keep his prices reasonable: sweaters are 900 francs and skirts begin at 600 francs.

Benetton

16th arr. - 82, av. Victor-Hugo
47 27 73 73
Open 10 a.m.-7 p.m. Closed Sun. Parking: Victor-Hugo. Cards: V, AE, DC, MC. 7 other branches.

Let's face it, who'd leave home without a Benetton sweater slung over his/her shoulders? Grown far beyond their just-sweater beginnings, United Colors of Benetton is a worldwide success, which, alas, appears to be neglecting quality in favor of a lot of high-profile advertising. Great colors and coordinates unfortunately do not always pass the first test wash. Well, for the price (and the colorful look), it's worth putting up with. Roll necks start at 195 francs.

Chandail

1st arr. - 65, rue Saint-Honoré
42 96 32 72
Open noon-7:30 p.m. Closed Sun. Parking: Les Halles. Cards: V.

The sweaters, exotic and eccentric, come from Peru, Norway and Austria and are decorated with dolls from the Andes or strange beasts. Comfort and folksiness is the order of the day. A more run-of-the-mill Italian knitwear collection caps the cozy ambience of this store, where prices run from 400 to 2,000 francs.

Crimson

8th arr. - 8, rue Marbeuf - 47 20 44 24
Open 10 a.m.-7 p.m. (Mon. noon-7 p.m.). Closed Sun. Parking: Georges-V. Cards: V, AE.

Men and women will find a rainbow selection of colors in lamb's wool, with twin sets selling for 700 to 1,400 francs, and long cardigans for 1,370 francs. There are also sweaters as soft as cashmere made from wool from the first sheering of a lamb's underside (610 francs). Roll necks, V-necks and Irish knitwear in unusual colors are also stocked here at prices from 1,280 to 1,520 francs.

Fac-Bazaar

6th arr. - 38, rue des Saints-Pères
45 48 46 15
Open 11 a.m.-7 p.m. Closed Mon, Sun. & 3 wks. in Aug. Cards: V.

Fac-Bazaar offers creative designs and seductive pullovers.

Christa Fieldler

6th arr. - 28, rue du Cherche-Midi
45 48 51 58
Open 11 a.m.-7 p.m. (Mon. 2 p.m.-7 p.m.). Closed Sun. Parking: Saint-Sulpice, Bon Marché. Cards: V, AE, DC.

Onetime model turned knitwear designer, Christa Fieldler marries comfort and elegance in her upbeat, refined collections. She uses strong reds, blues and blacks for winter months; soft pastel colors for summer. And she stocks plenty of accessories: turbans, scarves and gloves. Skirts start at 800 francs.

Richard Grand

1st arr. - 299, rue Saint-Honoré
42 60 58 73
Open 10 a.m.-7 p.m. Closed Sun. Cards: V, AE, DC.

This Paris-famed cashmere specialist has been in business now for over a quarter of a century. Nobody matches its spectacular range of 75 colors in over 50 styles for ladies and men. Richard Grand also manufactures cashmere-and-silk sweaters as light as feathers in a magnificient array of colors. Because the shop controls its own manufacturing, it can offer top-of-the-line chic at astoundingly (at least, sometimes) reasonable prices. A must for sweater fanciers in Paris.

Aux Laines Ecossaises

7th arr. - 181, bd Saint-Germain
45 48 53 41
Open 10 a.m.-7 p.m. Closed Sun. Parking: Saint-Germain. Cards: V.

Tradition reigns, as it always has, in this family-run establishment that was started at the end of the last century. Current owner Paul-Emile Clarisse greets his customers warmly and guides them around the shop "to feel the wares." On sale are top-quality lambswool pullovers (500 to 600 francs), Shetland sweaters (400 to 500 francs) and some double-ply cashmere (1,950 francs). Colors are conservative; classic brands include Ballantyne and Gladstone, and there are also Austrian jackets made by Astrifa (1,300 francs) and plaid dressing gowns (1,100 francs.)

Matière

4th arr. - 20, rue des Ecouffes - 42 78 47 72
Open 11 a.m.-2 p.m. & 3 p.m.-7 p.m. Closed Mon. Cards: V, AE.

You'll find a subtle mix of chenille, angora, lurex, pearls, ribbons and even cloth additions to designer-like sweaters and cardigans. The hand-dyed wool is also hand-woven. You can pick the color you want.

LINGERIE

Berlé

1st arr. - 332, rue Saint-Honoré
42 60 42 87
Open 9 a.m.-noon & 1 p.m.-5 p.m. Closed Sat., Sun. & Aug. Parking: Saint-Honoré. No cards.

For 70 years now, this noble house has manufactured and sold a single style of brassiere, which varies in the material used and how it is adorned. It gives contour to a generous bosom and emphasizes small breasts. Britain's Queen Mother and Princess Margaret are just two of Berlé's loyal clientele.

La Boîte à Bas

16th arr. - 77, rue de Longchamp
47 55 11 55
Open 10 a.m.-7 p.m. (Mon. 2 p.m.-7 p.m.). Closed Sun. Parking: Victor-Hugo. Cards: V.

It's all stockings and tights here, and all the major brands are represented: Cerutti, Dior, La Perla, Osé (the up-and-comer), Tiberghen and so forth. There are at least 8,000 pairs in stock and range from the coolest to the warmest (prices range from 20 to 400 francs).

Les Folies d'Elodie

16th arr. - 56, av. Paul-Doumer
45 04 93 57
Open 10 a.m.-7 p.m. Closed Sun. & Mon. Parking: Passy. Cards: V, AE, DC. Other branch.

Two sisters, Catherine and Nanou, reign over the two Folies boutiques. Their collections are aimed at millionairesses who will settle for nothing less than silk and lace dressing gowns and underwear. Bed linen, wedding dresses and their celebrated blouse with a ribbed yoke are also available.

Impulsifs

6th arr. - 182, bd Saint-Germain
45 48 30 13
Open 10 a.m.-7 p.m. (Mon. 12:30 p.m.-7 p.m.). Closed Sun. Parking: Saint-Germain. Cards: V, AE, DC.

Liliane Seigel is a former yoga professor who now specializes in luxury lingerie for people with difficult size requirements. Big or little, do not tarry. This uniquely gifted "yogi" will be able to reshape your figure to your liking!

Masson et Caille

6th arr. - 22, rue Saint-Placide
43 26 51 92
Open Mon.-Thurs. 9 a.m.-5:45 p.m. & Fri. 9 a.m.-noon & 1:30 p.m.-5:45 p.m. Closed Sat., Sun. & 2 wks in Aug. No cards.

Are you in the habit of judging by appearances? Well, if so, please don't be put off by this shop's (false?) claim to fame. It supplies the clergy in the Paris region, so it stands to reason that it will know all about thermal underclothes. Fancy a Carmelite's underwear? Well, why not? Amiable saleswomen also offer chic and fashionable silk blouses, cotton garter belts and stockings.

Les Nuits d'Elodie

17th arr. - 1 bis, av. Mac-Mahon
42 67 68 95
Open 10 a.m.-7 p.m. Closed Sun. & Mon. Parking: Etoile. Cards: V, AE, DC.

See Les Folies d'Elodie preceding.

Anita Oggioni

8th arr. - 19, rue François-Ier - 47 20 74 76
Open 10:30 a.m.-6 p.m. Closed Sun. Parking: François-Ier. Cards: V, AE, DC. Other branch: 30, rue de Grenelle - 7th arr. - 45 49 27 61.

For the Oggionis, women's underwear is a family matter. When Anita left Florence, she paid her dues with a grand couturier; in 1982, she opened her first shop. Lost under a cascade of ribbons, her enticing outfits come in hand-rolled crêpe and satin silk. Night attire is fabulously expensive (a nightgown costs about 20,000 francs). The half-cup brassieres, little panties and bras certainly will turn a man's head. (Anita now designs men's underwear as well). She was elected 1988 Woman of the Year by the Calais lace makers for her spectacular, not to say torrid, strapless petticoat.

Sabbia Rosa
6th arr. - 71-73, rue des Saints-Pères 45 48 88 37
Open 10 a.m.-7 p.m. Closed Sun., Mon. morning & Aug. Parking: Bon Marché. Cards: V, AE, DC.

This boutique is happy to receive couples in search of a few grams of satin or an ounce of crêpe de chine with which to spice up an evening. . . .

Chantal Thomass
6th arr. - 11, rue Madame - 45 44 57 13
Open 10 a.m.-7 p.m. (Mon. noon-7 p.m.). Closed Sun. Parking: Saint-Sulpice. Cards: V, AE, DC.

This queen bee has put nobility back into women's lingerie. Her underwear is in a class of its own: garter belts, brassieres, panties and negligees are musts for collectors.

MATERNITY

Bonpoint
7th arr. - 67, rue de l'Université 45 51 53 18
Open 10 a.m.-7 p.m. Closed Sun. Cards: V, AE, DC.

The Goutal sisters (of perfume fame) have the run of this street. The shop, for expectant mothers who come in with blind faith and a desire to look stylish while they await the happy event, offers friendly service and nice, roomy changing rooms.

Véronique Delachaux
6th arr. - 55, bd Raspail - 42 22 53 30
Open 10:30 a.m.-7 p.m. (Mon. 2 p.m.-7 p.m.). Closed Sun. Cards: V.

The former Madame Balloon has designed a stylish new look for pregnant women, who can now become slaves to fashion in straight skirts, stretch slacks, three-quarter jackets in gabardine and crêpe, waisted at the back and knit dresses with rounded shoulders (from 195 francs). Summer designs come in cotton, linen or silk (700 francs for a linen suit). Nice, airy changing rooms.

SILK

Farman-Farman
8th arr. - 15, rue Royale - 47 42 48 21
Open 10:30 a.m.-1 p.m. & 2 p.m.-6:30 p.m. Closed Sat., Sun. & July 15-Aug. 15. Parking: Madeleine.

Farman-Farman has all of Paris clamoring for their luxurious silk shirts (1,400 to 1,600 francs), crafted in a fourth-floor showroom/atelier on the rue Royale. The small collection of available models changes every three months.

Les Trois Marches
6th arr. - 1, rue Guisarde - 43 54 74 18
Open 12:30 p.m.-7:30 p.m. Closed Sun. & Mon. Parking: Saint-Sulpice.

Cathy Lullier's pocket-size boutique overflows with vintage gowns and dresses in silk, crêpe de chine and silk mousseline. She personally tracks each treasure down, then proceeds to restore and update it by hand. Button-front flower-print dresses start at about 700 francs; silk or lace blouses range from 300 to 500 francs. There is also a delicious selection of frilly cotton and eyelet underthings. Isabelle Adjani and Catherine Deneuve have been spotted shopping here.

SHOES

Maud Frizon
6th arr. - 83, rue des Saints-Pères 42 22 06 93
Open 10 a.m.-7 p.m. Closed Sun. Cards: V, AE, DC.

Characters in Judith Krantz novels covet their Maud Frizons as much as they do their Cartier baubles. Styles are audacious and always feminine, with a subtle use of canvas and crocodile, suede and leather. There are heels for all seasons and heights, as well as a plethora of ballet slippers, beach and evening sandals, pumps and dream boots. Each piece has been hand turned. Prices, 1,100 to 1,900 francs.

Harel
8th arr. - 64, rue François-Ier - 47 20 75 00
Open 10:30 a.m.-7 p.m. (Mon. & Sat. 10:30 a.m.-12:30 p.m. & 2 p.m.-7 p.m.). Closed Sun. Parking: François-Ier. Cards: V, AE, DC.

If you pride yourself on your elegance, you can't afford to ignore Harel. In fact, you owe it to yourself to own at least one pair of his marvels—sheer, simple luxury: three different arches, three widths and three heel sizes. Pumps, sandals and walking shoes, in a choice of satin, lizard, crocodile, ostrich, snakeskin and kid, come in twenty colors. Prices run from 1,250 to 2,650 francs (11,200 francs for crocodile). A pair of Harel's lasts a lifetime; if it doesn't, they'll send it to the factory for repairs.

Jan Jansen
7th arr. - 62, rue des Saints-Pères
42 22 32 34
Open 10:30 a.m.-7 p.m. Closed Sun. Cards: V, AE.

Dutchman Jan Jansen sculpts bizarre shoes in fish skin with metallic clips and weird miscellaneous bits of strange *things*. These are one-of-a-kind shoes that you won't see anywhere else. Love 'em or hate 'em . . . loyalists adore 'em.

Charles Jourdan
8th arr. - 86, av. des Champs-Elysées
45 62 29 33
Open 9:30 a.m.-7 p.m. Closed Sun. Cards: V, AE, DC. 3 other branches.

There's something here for every taste, including the best. Affordable fine-quality shoes are available in over twenty colors. Figure on spending about 995 francs for a pair of pumps.

Stéphane Kélian
1st arr. - 6, pl. des Victoires - 42 61 60 74
Open 10 a.m.-7 p.m. Closed Sun. Cards: V, AE, DC. 5 other branches.

King of the braided-leather shoe, Stéphane Kélian has based his reputation on this technique. He also adds pizzazz to classic styles for Gaultier and Montana. Be duly forewarned, however: there are six Kélian boutiques in Paris, and the service in all of them is execrable. Prices range from 950 to 1,000 francs.

Tokio Kumagai
1st arr. - 52, rue Croix-des-Petits-Champs
42 36 08 01
Open 10 a.m.-7 p.m. Closed Sun. Parking: Saint-Eustache. Cards: V, AE, DC.

The austere decor is counterbalanced with the courteous welcome and service. The shoes of this Japanese shoe designer are flat-heeled, come in animal shapes (such as roosters or mice) or automobile shapes (complete with windshield). Or try the sublime evening shoes with spiked heels. The ready-to-wear clothing is conservative, almost monastic compared to his funky footwear. Don't miss the January and July sales.

Sidonie Larizzi
8th arr. - 8, rue de Marignan - 43 59 38 87
Open 10 a.m.-7 p.m. Closed Sun. Cards: V, AE, DC.

Sidonie Larizzi designs for coutouriers Laroche, Lacroix and Balmain. Boutique creations blend classicism with originality. These are dressy shoes with a choice of heel size. Special orders and shoe modifications are also available.

John Lobb
8th arr. - 24, rue du Faubourg-Saint-Honoré - 42 65 24 45
Open 10 a.m.-6:30 p.m. Closed Sat. Cards: V, AE, DC.

Outrageously expensive shoes for sports fans with money to spend. You must place your order ten months in advance for a pair of sumptuous, custom-made walking shoes, golf shoes or riding boots. Remarkable shoes from all points of view. Prices are staggering (12,600 francs).

René Mancini
16th arr. - 72, av. Victor-Hugo
45 00 48 81
Open 10 a.m.-7 p.m. Closed Sun. & Mon. Cards: V, AE, DC.

René Mancini first made the black-tip shoe for Chanel. In 1964 he introduced square toes. And his daughter Claire has carried on the family tradition. A portion of the collection is handmade, and it is possible to match your shoes to your dress for a mere 2,400 francs and a ten-day wait. Mancini's ready-to-wear shoes are made in Italy and are more affordable. Prices at the boutique on avenue Victor-Hugo run 500 to 1,000 francs and include an Italian collection.

Laurent Mercadal

8th arr. - 26, av. des Champs-Elysées
42 25 22 70
Open 10 a.m.-7 p.m. Closed Sun. Cards: V, AE, DC. 2 other branches.

Laurent Mercadal creates some dicey marriages: calf and velvet, snakeskin and cloth that don't always wear well with time. But in any case, these shoes are always fashionable and reasonably priced (from 650 francs).

Miss Maud

7th arr. - 21, rue de Grenelle - 45 48 64 44
Open 10 a.m.-7 p.m. Closed Sun. No cards.

Less pricey but with the same Frizon chic.

Andréa Pfister

1st arr. - 4, rue Cambon - 42 96 55 28
Open 10 a.m.-7 p.m. (Mon. 2 p.m.-7 p.m.). Closed Sun. Cards: V, AE, DC.

Pfister makes fine, delicate shoes to suit the comely foot and well-turned ankle. This is Parisian elegance *par excellence*. Embroidered or sequined evening shoes sell for between 1,600 and 1,800 francs. The price for a pair of elegant snakeskin shoes slithers up to 2,000 francs. You can have shoes made to measure in the style and leather of your choice. Allow seven weeks with fittings.

Walter Steiger

5th arr. - 5, rue de Tournon - 46 33 01 45
Open 10 a.m.-7 p.m. (Mon. 2 p.m.-7 p.m.). Closed Sun. Cards: V, AE, DC. Other branch.

More foreigners than Parisians grace the portals of Walter Steiger, who find his evening sandals, daytime pumps and weekend boots indispensable. Prices run from 900 francs to the more upscale crocodile at 7,000 francs. Steiger also carries large shoe sizes.

François Villon

8th arr. - 8, rue Royale - 42 60 58 23
Open 10 a.m.-1 p.m. & 2 p.m.-7 p.m. Closed Sun. & Aug. Cards: V, AE, DC. 2 other branches.

This sort of high quality goes beyond the bounds of fashion. The boots are incomparable. Villon carries pretty dress pumps and casual shoes with low heels and as always the

Brides Villon sandals with black tips. Of course, these shoes don't come cheap: between 1,400 and 2,400 francs per pair.

SWIMSUITS

A la Plage

7th arr. - 6, rue de Solférino - 47 05 18 94
Open 10 a.m.-7 p.m. (Sat. 10 a.m.-1 p.m. & 2 p.m.-7 p.m.). Closed Sun. & 1 wk. in Aug. Cards: V.

The most beautiful swimsuits are available year-round.

Erès

6th arr. - 4 bis, rue du Cherche-Midi
45 44 95 54
Open 9:30 a.m.-7 p.m. Closed Sun. Parking: Saint-Sulpice. Cards: V, AE, DC. Other branch: 2, rue Tronchet - 8th arr. - 47 42 24 55.

A specialist when it comes to swimsuits, Erès is now assaulting the Left Bank. Two-piece suits, which, gratefully, are sold separately, are stocked in an incredible choice of adjustable tops and bottoms to suit just about any figure. The Beachwear collection includes coordinates for before and after *la plage*. Upstairs: a lingerie section.

Réard

8th arr. - 109, rue du Faubourg-Saint-Honoré - 42 89 07 98
Open 10 a.m.-7 p.m. (Mon. 12:30 p.m.-7 p.m.). Closed Sun. Parking: Madeleine. Cards: V, AE, DC.

A luxurious swimwear boutique with couturier prices. Réard sells custom-tailored swimsuits in the fabric, style and color of your choice. You will need three fittings, and prices start at 4,200 francs; or you can choose a style from the collection in a different fabric, with some alterations to suit your requirements (from 3,500 francs). Ready-to-wear prices start at 800 francs for a one-piece suit, and 500 to 600 francs for a bikini. There is also a grand choice of skirts and shorts.

WEDDING GOWNS

Claudia L.
6th arr. - 35, rue du Dragon - 42 22 03 71
*Open 10 a.m.-6:30 p.m. Closed Sun. Cards: AE,
V, DC.*

So he swept you off your feet and you need
a wedding dress, fast? No problem, says Clau-
dia L. In a mere two weeks she can whip up a
romantic (or a sexy, or a contemporary) gown
in any color you choose. Or if you prefer, she'll
update Grandmother's gown for you. And
what's more, she'll fit you out with all those
indispensable bridal accessories: a train, a
beaded garter, gloves in silk, satin or eyelet,
flowered combs for your hair. . . . Figure on
spending about 2,000 francs for a gown.

Monique Germain
6th arr. - 59, bd Raspail - 45 48 22 63
*Open 12:30 p.m.-7 p.m. (1 p.m.-6 p.m. Sat.).
Closed Sun. & Mon. Cards: AE, V, DC.*

The display window is classic and conventional—anything but exciting. But inside—
surprise!—you'll see sculpted bustiers for bare-
shouldered brides, sheath dresses with tulle
overskirts, bubble skirts, gowns that can be
transformed into cocktail dresses after the big
day. Alongside is a wealth of stylish accessories,
including hats, garlands and other pretty headgear.

Sara Shelburne
1st arr. - 10, rue du Cygne - 42 33 74 40
*Open 10 a.m.-7 p.m. Closed Sun. & Aug. Cards:
V.*

Shelburne's collection of wedding gowns
comprises some fifteen distinctive models (the
"star," the "siren," the "innocent") which can
be made up in a variety of fabrics (organdy,
satin, moiré, crêpe de chine). If you have a clear
idea of exactly what you want, bring in the
sketch and Sara Shelburne will create the dress
of your dreams. Her gowns cost between
8,000 and 15,000 francs, and can be delivered
in a week to ten days (though in an emergency,
she will get you your gown in 48 hours).

DEPARTMENT STORES

MODERATE

Inno Passy
16th arr. - 18-22, rue de l'Annonciation -
45 24 52 32
*Open 9 a.m.-8 p.m. (Fri. until 9 p.m.). Closed
Sun. Cards: V. Other branches.*

Though the Inno stores are kissing cousins
of the more familiar Monoprix chain, Inno
merchandise tends to be a tad more upscale in
certain departments. Features and services:
Purchases totaling more than 500 francs will
be delivered for a small fee; Inno Card carriers
benefit from additional reductions on merchandise throughout the store; alterations and
shoe repairs are performed while you wait; an
interesting selection of wines is always available, and connoisseurs can special-order fine
bottles or imports. There's also an in-house
catering service that will organize your next
buffet—from start to finish—and the fish department offers superb seafood platters (they'll
even open the shellfish for you!).

Marks & Spencer
9th arr. - 35, bd Haussmann - 40 73 90 30
Open 9:30 a.m.-6:30 p.m. Closed Sun. Cards: V.

Ever faithful to its mission, this Paris branch
brings a little bit of cozy old England to the
hard-edged French capital. The store is always
busy, particularly at back-to-school time (the
children's clothing is sturdy and adorable;
older kids like the lambswool and cashmere
sweaters, the tartan kilts and Oxford shirts) and
at Christmas (for the traditional holiday foods,
decorations and gifts). Among the features and
services are all the fixings for an authentic
English tea: tea, of course (loose and in bags),
biscuits (cookies), marmalades, scones, crum-
pets, muffins and the rest. Delicious, reasonably priced smoked salmon is available whole,
in slices or marinated in dill. And don't miss
the selection of chutneys, bottled sauces and
other typically English condiments. The numerous choices of single-malt whiskies are
complemented by several types of sherry and
good English beer. The women's clothing is
solid and stolid (oh, that no-nonsense British
underwear!). Skirts are available in three differ-

ent lengths and in large sizes. The storewide sales in January, July and August offer some fine buys in sweaters and other knitwear.

Monoprix-Uniprix
15th arr. - 2, rue du Commerce
45 79 94 86
Open 9 a.m.-8 p.m. Closed Sun. 19 other branches (opening hours may vary).

"The basics are what we do best." That's the Monoprix motto. A big factor in the stores' success is their strategic locations in the capital's busiest neighborhoods. Monoprix has its own label of clothing and toiletries of good quality at rock-bottom prices. The supermarket selection is constantly growing, with ready-to-eat dishes, catering services (at some stores) and the excellent Monoprix Gourmet line, which includes coffee, pasta, vacuum-packed ready-cooked entrées, low-calorie products and a new line of quick-cooking dishes for hungry folks in a hurry.

Prisunic
18th arr. - 32, rue du Poteau - 42 62 22 01
Open 9 a.m.-7:15 p.m. Closed Sun. Cards: V. 8 other branches.

Never content to rest on its marketing laurels, Prisunic has practiced the art of creative retailing ever since it opened up for business some 50 years ago. The newly renovated branch on the Champs-Elysées is now open until 10 p.m. (midnight in summer). Every week, its inventive merchandising team comes up with a new theme or sales promotion to spark shoppers' enthusiasm. Features include: clever, colorful housewares at affordable prices—dishes, linens, lamps and gadgets; a grocery section that offers fresh, fine-quality produce every day (Forza is the house brand of canned and packaged goods); a vast array of makeup and toiletries, at excellent prices.

TOP OF THE LINE

BHV
4th arr. - 52-64, rue de Rivoli - 42 74 90 00
Open 9 a.m.-6:30 p.m. (Wed. until 10 p.m.). Closed Sun. Parking: rue Lobau. Cards: V, AE.

Sooner or later, every do-it-yourselfer in Paris winds up in the BHV basement, a treasure trove of tools, hardware and home-improvement items. Whether it's a brass washer or a gold-plated faucet you're tracking down, just

seek it here and you're sure to find. What's more, you can count on competent advice from the sales staff on how to use or install your purchases. Savvy artists and sculptors also appreciate the BHV's first floor, which is stocked with canvases, easels, brushes and clay at unbeatable prices. Features and services include: in-house specialists to install goods and materials, from wallpaper to floor tiles to convertible-car roofs and more; bridal registry with complimentary "house kit" and a 5 percent discount on anything the couple buys in the store during their first year of wedded bliss; an engraving service for adorning china and glass with initials or the family coat of arms; repairs of all sorts, done on the premises (you can have your pearls restrung or your fishing reel adjusted) purchases totaling over 1,000 francs delivered free of charge; major appliances installed at no cost, with guaranteed follow-up service; made-to-order comforters, bedspreads and curtains. The BHV-Cofinoga credit card (30 francs per month) not only makes shopping easier, it entitles holders to special rates on insurance, credit, travel and other services.

Le Bon Marché
7th arr. - 38, rue de Sèvres - 42 60 33 45
Open 9:30 a.m.-6:30 p.m. (grocery store 8:30 a.m.-8:30 p.m.). Closed Sun. Parking: Bon Marché–Velpeau. Cards: V, AE, DC.

The good old Bon Marché has a chic new look and a sharp new logo. This full-service department store has placed a stronger-than-ever accent on fashion (check out the new first-floor women's shop) and frequent sales that are not to be missed. Features and services include the largest gourmet grocery in Paris, which is open every day but Sunday until 8:30 p.m. In stock are 150 types of tea, 240 kinds of cheese and over 200 different products "imported" direct from Fauchon. Discover the "daily menu" service (they deliver) and tasty health foods from La Vie Claire. The grocery prices are competitive; in fact, Le Bon Marché pledges to reimburse the difference if you find a better deal in another Parisian supermarket. There's also a convenient in-house travel agency and a ticket agency and a bank. Other services include custom-tailored clothing for men; fur storage and restoration, and Oriental-rug restoration. And, of course, there's a bridal registry, as well as birth and baptism registries.

Les Galeries Lafayette

9th arr. - 40, bd Haussmann - 42 82 34 56
*Open 9:30 a.m.-6:30 p.m. Closed Sun. Cards: V,
AE, DC, MC.*

"We are definitely the leader when it comes
to women's fashion," declares Jean-Michel
Girardin, one of the dynamic directors of Les
Galeries Lafayette. On the average, 100,000
women between the ages of 20 and 40 stroll
through Les Galeries each day. What draws
them is an enormous selection of clothing and
accessories, ranging from such avant-garde designers as Jean-Paul Gaultier, Yohji Yamamoto
and Azzedine Alaïa, to the classics, Cacharel,
Dior and Guy Laroche. All the stylists who
count are represented, and the store label ("Lafayette Collection") represents high fashion at
attractive prices. There are three entire floors
devoted to clothing and fashion accessories
from a vast range of manufacturers. Mode Plus
offers free fashion counseling on putting together a look that fits a woman's personality
and lifestyle. There's also a dazzling table and
kitchenware department that recently opened
on the basement level—a paradise for anyone
who loves to cook or entertain. Les Galeries
Lafayette has no fewer than three restaurants
for a wide selection of refreshments for weary
shoppers; a delivery service, so that altered
garments can be whizzed to one's home (in
Paris or nearby suburbs) in just two hours
(there is a charge); a beauty salon; and an
excellent fur-storage service.

Madelios

1st arr. - 10, pl. de la Madeleine
42 60 39 30
*Open 9:45 a.m.-6:30 p.m. Closed Sun. Cards: V,
AE, DC, MC.*

Madelios is the men's annex of the Trois
Quartiers department store, but, with its quality goods and service, it has the feel of an
upscale specialty shop. Situated in the "Golden
Triangle" formed by the Madeleine, rue
Royale and the Faubourg-Saint-Honoré, the
store is frequented by a star-studded clientele.
Features and services: a knitwear department
that carries an unbeatable selection of sweaters
and socks, with a choice of fifteen colors in
cashmere, twenty in lambswool; no fewer than
9,000 ties (in silk, cashmere, wool, leather)
always in stock, which go on sale for attractive
prices twice a year; and semi-custom-made
jackets (three different lengths) and shirts (two

sleeve lengths, with regular or French cuffs), a
chic and relatively economical compromise between off-the-rack and custom-made garments. Madelios showcases all the best English
and Scottish labels: shoes by Church and Mc-
George, Pringle cashmeres, Burberry menswear, Derek Rose pajamas and umbrellas by
Crigg. You'll also find the most elegant men's
handkerchiefs, including rare Swiss weaves,
with hand-rolled hems and hand-embroidery.

Printemps

9th arr. - 64, bd Haussmann - 42 82 50 00
*Open 10 a.m.-7 p.m. Closed Sun. Cards: V, AE,
DC, MC. 6 other branches.*

Printemps cultivates an image of
quintessentially Parisian chic and elegance.
The store targets a slightly less youthful clientele than its neighbor, Les Galeries Lafayette.
The typical Printemps customer is a woman of
style and taste who appreciates refinement in
both her dress and her surroundings. Top-of-
the-line women's fashions are presented on the
fourth floor in the rue de la Mode shop; a wide
and appealing array of menswear is found in
the Brummel shop, a separate annex that carries everything from underwear to cashmere
top coats. Features and services: the Boutique
Blanche is the premier bridal registry in France;
Le Printemps de la Maison is actually an entire
store (eight floors) devoted to home decor and
housewares, its private "Primavera" collection
ranges from attractive handcrafted gift items to
furniture designed by the likes of Andrée Putman and Philippe Starck; and the Printemps
free fashion-consulting service shows
customers how to put together a stylish, indi-
vidualized wardrobe. Following a marathon
shopping session, it's a pleasure to relax in the
panoramic rooftop restaurant.

La Samaritaine

1st arr. - 19, rue de la Monnaie
45 08 33 33, 42 33 81 75
*Open 9:30 a.m.-7 p.m. (Tues. & Fri. until 8:30
p.m., Wed. until 10:30 p.m.). Closed Sun. Parking free at certain hours. Cards: V, AE, DC,
MC.*

There's a revolution going on at La
Samaritaine! Having cast off its image as a
jumble of miscellaneous merchandise, the
city's biggest bazaar, the "Samar" has entered
the era of specialization. Throughout the store,
every department has been overhauled, modernized and streamlined. To top it off, the

entire interior has been spruced up and polished to its original brilliance: the etched glass, steel beams, lacquered ceramic tile and exuberant floral motifs haven't looked so good since opening day. Among the store's features is one of the finest views of Paris, enjoyed (from April to October) from the Samaritaine's rooftop terrace and belvedere. The recently renovated restaurant and tea room now serve breakfast, lunch and brunch. Sporting goods, equipment and clothing now occupy an entire store. What's more, on the second floor you can practice your putt, scale a climbing wall, test a tennis racquet or play a little Ping-Pong. The pet shop, on the sixth floor, is a treat for children. On the fifth floor of the main store are the most complete sewing and notions departments in town. Just a few of the services available at La Samaritaine: golf lessons, courses in tailoring and bicycle-repair and maintenance, an in-house astrologer who'll tell you your horoscope and/or read your palm (for 450 francs; call two days ahead), lamp shades made to order, resilvering of flatware, and picture framing. Mothers shopping with young children can rediaper them and warm

their bottles in the store nursery. And nearly every item on sale at La Samaritaine can be ordered by mail or phone, with payment on delivery.

Aux Trois Quartiers
1st arr. - 17, bd de la Madeleine
42 60 39 30
Open 9:40 a.m.-6:30 p.m. Closed Sun. & Mon. in July & Aug. Cards: V, AE, DC.
French real estate mogul Francis Bouygues recently purchased the Trois Quartiers, and the store is currently undergoing intensive remodeling. A glassed-in escalator takes shoppers from the street level to the second floor, which will remain open for the duration of the overhaul. The store's small scale makes shopping here far more restful than in any of the other Parisian *grands magasins*. The accessory departments are gems, particularly the glove, luggage, handkerchief and hosiery counters. Tableware, too, is given big play here. The sales staff is knowledgeable and friendly—throughout the store. Purchases can be sent anywhere in the world, with a minimum of fuss. For the convenience of its foreign customers, the Trois Quartiers has a currency-exchange counter.

FLOWERS

FLOWER SHOPS

Bisson
6th arr. - 41, rue Dauphine - 46 33 84 08
Open 10 a.m.-7 p.m. Closed Sun. No cards.
Alain-Frédéric Bisson is a specialist in rare plants who, in the two shops at this address, stocks a large selection of bonsai, cacti and orchids. He also hosts exhibitions, has an interesting collection of horticultural books and designs terraces and winter gardens.

Eve
15th arr. - 13, quai de Grenelle
45 78 72 06
Open 10:30 a.m.-7:15 p.m. Closed Sun., Mon. & Aug. Parking: quai Branly, bd de Grenelle. Cards: V, AE.
This boutique/jungle is a branch of the nursery run by the well-known landscape designer Edouard Avdeew. The luxuriant tangle

of rare and tropical plants will enchant you, and the choice is astounding.

FLOWERS, FLOWERS EVERYWHERE
Some 1,800 varieties of flowers are raised in Paris's greenhouses, located in the Auteuil area, and from time to time marvelous flower exhibits are held. You can pick up exhibit schedules at the local city halls (each arrondissement has its own city hall), or contact the Direction des Parcs et Jardins de la Ville de Paris, 3, av. de la Porte d'Auteuil, 16th arr., 42 76 50 00.

Guillet

7th arr. - 99, av. La Bourdonnais
45 51 32 98
Open 9:30 a.m.-12:30 p.m. & 2 p.m.-6:30 p.m. Closed Sun. & Aug. Cards: V, AE, DC, MC.

This old establishment specializes in floral decorating schemes and, in its own workshop, creates silk flowers to order. Faithful clients include the Opéra and the Comédie-Française, as well as some of Paris's big department stores.

Un Jardin en Plus

7th arr. - 224, bd Saint-Germain
45 48 25 71
Open 10 a.m.-7 p.m. Closed Sun. & Mon. in July & Aug. Parking: Saint-Germain drugstore. Cards: V, AE, DC.

It's a floral, floral world. At least it is in this shop, where there are flowers everywhere: cut flowers, potted flowers, garlands, flowers on fabric, wallpaper, sheets, towels, dishes, furniture and more.

Lachaume

8th arr. - 10, rue Royale - 42 60 57 26
Open 8:30 a.m.-7:30 p.m. (Sat. until 6 p.m.). Closed Sun. & Aug. Parking: Concorde, Madeleine. Cards: V, AE.

This is probably the most famous florist in Paris, and it's been here for over a hundred years. Marcel Proust stopped by every day to pick out the orchid he wore in his lapel (you can get the same kind today for 120 francs). The quality of the flowers is perfection itself. Short of buying a bouquet, you can admire the 150 varieties of flowers arranged in enormous vases in the shop window. Full bouquets start at about 350 francs.

Christian Ninin-Barus

2nd arr. - 12, rue des Capucines
42 61 05 08
Open 9 a.m.-7:30 p.m. Closed Sun. Cards: V.

Located in a beautiful old shop of mosaic and stone, Christian Ninin-Barus is one of the most creative florists in Paris. Influenced by Oriental design, he builds rather than arranges his bouquets. He likes to mix plants and simple

flowers; the results are always poetic. Bouquets start at 100 francs.

Emilio Robba

2nd arr. - 29-33, rue Vivienne - 42 61 71 43
Open 10 a.m.-6 p.m. Closed Sat. & Sun. Cards: V, AE, DC.

Emilio Robba has some exquisite flowers,

FLOWER SUPERMARKETS

These establishments sell remarkably fresh flowers, and they'll deliver anywhere in Paris: Monceau Fleurs, 92, bd Malesherbes, 8th arr.; 11, bd Henri IV, 4th arr.; 60, av. Paul Doumer, 16th arr.; 84 bd Raspail, 6th arr. (delivery is 20 francs). A prosperous ambience can be found at La Grange, 7, rue de Buci, 6th arr.; delivery is 35 francs, even in an emergency, and credit cards are accepted. Other addresses: Lamartine Fleurs, 188, av. Victor Hugo, 16th arr.; and Nice Fleurs, 19-21, rue de Lourmel, 15th arr., 128, bd Haussmann, 8th arr. and 5, rue de Rigny, 8th arr.

---

but it's really his vases that will knock you out, including cloth-draped ones that can double as lamps. He also sells room scents.

Christian Tortu

6th arr. - 6, carrefour de l'Odéon
43 26 02 56
Open 9 a.m.-8 p.m. Closed Sun. Cards: V.

The young florist took over the old establishment near Odeon a few years ago and has quickly made it into one of the better shops of its kind around. He blends, with happy results, rare and delicate flowers with simple greenery or tropical plants. His bouquets are perfect and quite natural looking, yet they're also sophisticated and wild at the same time. Full bouquets start at 200 francs.

René Veyrat

8th arr. - 168, bd Haussmann - 45 62 37 86
Open 8:30 a.m.-7 p.m. Closed Sat. & Sun. Cards: V. Other branch: 1 av. de La Motte-Piquet - 7th arr. - 47 05 49 93, open until 7:30 p.m., closed Sun., Mon. & Aug.

You'll be captivated by the window displays of this corner shop on the boulevard Haussmann. The flowers and plants are of the highest quality, the service is charming, and delivery is free for purchases of 150 francs and up. The big bouquets sell for 350 francs.

FLOWER MARKETS

Marché aux Fleurs de l'Ile de la Cité

4th arr. - Pl. Louis-Lépine (quai de Corse)
Open 8 a.m.-7:30 p.m. Closed Sun. No cards.

Marché de la Madeleine

8th arr. - Pl. de la Madeleine (east side)
Open 8 a.m.-7:30 p.m. Closed Sat., Sun. & Mon. (except holidays). No cards.

Marché des Ternes

17th arr. - Pl. des Ternes
Open 8 a.m.-7:30 p.m. Closed Mon. No cards.

FOOD

A yen for the exotic and a return to French culinary roots are the two most prominent—and paradoxical—features of the current Paris food scene. Palates titillated by travels to far-off lands crave those same foreign flavors when they get back home: hence the proliferation of stores offering foodstuffs and prepared dishes from all over the world. It's an amazing development; less than a generation ago, the chauvinistic French were particularly insular in their eating habits. But their current flirtation with foreign cuisines doesn't mean they've forsaken their native gastronomy. *Au contraire*, demand is increasing for fine aged cheeses and bread with old-fashioned flavor. And sales of sweets—pastry, ice cream, chocolate—are booming: People are ready to lay out lots and lots of francs to buy the very best.

BAKERIES

Au Bon Pain d'Autrefois

11th arr. - 45, rue Popincourt - 43 55 04 48
Open 6 a.m.-8 p.m. Closed Sun.

The delicious scent of sourdough wafts forth from this pretty bakery (designated an artistic landmark), which features superb pain de campagne (the classic country loaf), rustic rye loaves and delicious brioches.

Boulangerie de l'Ancienne Comédie

6th arr. - 10, rue de l'Ancienne-Comédie - 43 26 89 72
Open 24 hours (Sun. 6:30 a.m.-9 p.m.). Closed Aug.

Inveterate night owls with a yen for croissants at 4 in the morning can find them here, warm and comforting, along with good whole-wheat bread and a tasty house-specialty country-style loaf that combines rye with white dough.

Le Fournil de Pierre
15th arr. - 3, rue du Commerce
45 75 16 48
Open 8:30 a.m.-7:30 p.m. (Mon. 11:30 a.m.-7:30 p.m. & Sun. until 1 p.m.). Other branches.

The chain's 25 shops in the greater Paris area sell home-style breads whose sole flaw is that they are not always as oven-fresh as we might wish. But the variety of loaves is astonishing (there are over twenty), and we like the buns, cookies and pastries for their simple home-made goodness.

Ganachaud
20th arr. - 150-154, rue de Ménilmontant
46 36 13 82
Open 7:30 a.m.-8 p.m. (Tues. 2:30 p.m.-8 p.m. & Sun. until 1:30 p.m.). Closed Mon. & Aug.

If we could list only one baker in Paris, it would have to be Bernard Ganachaud. Although his shop is situated in the Parisian hinterlands, it attracts bread lovers from all over the city, loyal fans who are perfectly willing to brave traffic jams for just one bite of a loaf from Ganachaud's wood-fired ovens. The nut breads sold here contain real—fresh!—walnuts; the raisin breads are loaded with fruit. The traditional country loaf turned out fifteen to twenty times daily by this "Meilleur Ouvrier de France" is crusty perfection.

Haupois
4th arr. - 35, rue des Deux-Ponts
43 54 57 59
Open 6:45 a.m.-1:30 p.m. & 3:20 p.m.-8:15 p.m. Closed Thurs., Fri. & Aug.

Out of this small old-fashioned bakery emerges wonderful hand-formed loaves that rank among the finest in all of Paris. The country-style bread merits particular mention, as do the rye and other whole-grain specialties.

Poilâne
15th arr. - 49, bd de Grenelle - 45 79 11 49
Open 7:15 a.m.-8:15 p.m. Closed Mon.

Lionel Poilâne is indubitably the planet's best-known baker; he can be found hawking his famous sourdough bread in magazines and on television screens throughout the world. And even though his products are sold all over Paris in charcuteries and cheese shops, goodly numbers of Poilâne fans think nothing of crossing town and standing in line to *personally*

buy their favorite bread still warm from his ovens. Poilâne's walnut bread is, in a simple word, delicious, and we are also particularly fond of the shortbread cookies (sablés) and the rustic apple turnover (which makes a delicious and inexpensive dessert, accompanied by a bowl of thick crème fraîche). Lines tend to be shorter at this boulevard de Grenelle shop.

Max Poilâne
15th arr. - 87, rue Brancion - 48 28 45 90
Open 7:15 a.m.-8 p.m. (Sat. until 1 p.m.). Closed Sun.

Unlike his cousin Lionel, Max Poilâne is not a media animal. He sticks pretty close to his attractive bakery, located across from the old Vaugirard slaughterhouse, which was recently transformed into a lush park. His bread follows the family tradition fairly closely, though we find it less sour and perhaps more pleasant than the more famous loaf baked on the rue du Cherche-Midi. Max also turns out a fine walnut bread, and his croissants, brioches and chaussons (turnovers) are huge hits with neighborhood gourmands.

Poujauran
7th arr. - 20, rue Jean-Nicot - 47 05 80 88
Open 8:30 a.m.-8:30 p.m. Closed Sun.

He's a real darling, that Jean-Luc Poujauran! His bakery may be in a ritzy neighborhood, but he hasn't gone high-hat; food writers may regularly wax lyrical over his talent, but his head hasn't swelled an inch. And though he bakes a wonderful loaf with organically grown flour, he's not the type to think he's the greatest thing since sliced bread. Let's just hope he never changes. And let's hope that we will never have to give up his delicious little rolls, his old-fashioned pound cake (quatre-quarts), his buttery fruitcakes and those terrific frangipane-stuffed galettes that he bakes for the Epiphany (Three Kings' Day, January 6).

René Saint-Ouen
8th arr. - 111, bd Haussmann - 42 65 06 25
Open 8 a.m.-7 p.m. Closed Sun.

René Saint-Ouen has two passions in life: bread and sculpture. He brings the two together in his bakery on boulevard Haussmann, where he makes and sells golden loaves of bread (sourdough, raisin-nut and bacon, among others) fashioned into classic and fabulous shapes. Special orders are welcome. The bakery also serves light lunches and tea.

CATERERS

François Clerc
16th arr. - 63, bd Beauséjour - 45 20 80 10
Open 9 a.m.-7 p.m. Closed Sun.

Backed up by a team of more than 100 professionals, François Clerc and Yves Henrot have moved quickly into the top rung of French caterers. Clerc, a skilled and innovative chef, is passionate about food and cooking. Among his most recent creations, we highly recommend the magnificent pike "Harlequin" served with a subtle shellfish coulis, his unusual casserole of turbot with sea urchins and, among the sweets, Clerc's peerless coffee macaroons.

Dalloyau
15th arr. - 16 & 36, rue Linois
45 75 59 92
Open 9 a.m.-7 p.m. Closed Sun.

Dalloyau is indubitably one of the best catering firms in the capital. The dishes on its appetizing menu are fit for a king (in case one is coming to your party). Choose from oysters gently stewed in Champagne, Bresse chicken with prawns, stuffed suckling pig and a thrilling selection of desserts (the famous Dalloyau chocolate macaroons are our favorite!).

Potel et Chabot
16th arr. - 3, rue de Chaillot - 47 20 22 00
Open 8 a.m.-7 p.m. Closed Sun.

Potel et Chabot is the dean of Parisian caterers—and perhaps the most successful. It handles cocktail parties, receptions and other soigné soirees for the Opéra, the prime minister's office and for the president himself! The food runs to well-wrought classic dishes (stuffed saddle of lamb, chicken stuffed with foie gras and truffles), but of late, we've noticed some innovative specialties on the menu: tagliatelle with sea scallops, shellfish terrine served with a smooth lobster coulis, and a delicate, delicious blanquette of turbot and cucumbers.

CHARCUTERIE

Baumann
17th arr. - 64, av. des Ternes - 45 74 16 66
Open daily 7 a.m.-1 a.m. Other branch: 9, rue Coquillère - 1st arr.

This well-known brasserie sells tasty platters of choucroute (sauerkraut) to go: try the paysanne variety, which features fresh and smoked pork (52 francs per person), or the kind garnished with jambonneau (pigs' knuckle, at 55 francs), or with preserved duck (65 francs). If you place your order between noon and 7 p.m., the choucroute will be kept piping hot for you.

Charcuterie Charles
6th arr. - 10, rue Dauphine - 47 05 53 66
Open 8 a.m.-2 p.m. & 3:30 p.m.-8 p.m. Closed Sat. & Sun.

This prize-winning charcuterie, one of the finest in Paris, is the all-city champ when it comes to boudin blanc (white sausage). During the Christmas season, when boudin blanc is a traditional component of holiday meals, Charles displays some twenty varieties, all with different flavorings (truffles, prunes, pistachios and such). Andouillette (chitterling sausage) is another specialty, and we are great fans of Charles's sumptuous terrines (sweetbreads, duck breast and foie gras, herbed ham), his tarts and delicious hams.

Chedeville
1st arr. - 12, rue du Marché-Saint-Honoré
42 61 11 11
Open 7 a.m.-1:30 p.m. & 4 p.m.-7 p.m. Closed Sun. & Mon.

Chedeville knows pigs. From ears to tail, there's no part of the porker that this charcuterie's butchers don't prepare in the most appetizing fashion. You'll find meaty spareribs, expertly trimmed jambonneaux (pigs' knuckles) and fresh or salted shoulder of pork. Other savory specialties include fresh sausage and a full range of terrines (rabbit, duck, country pâté, chicken and foie gras), succulent stuffed pigs' trotters and juicy ham. And Chedeville's quality products are for the most part reasonably priced.

Au Cochon d'Auvergne
5th arr. - 48, rue Monge - 43 26 36 21
Open 9 a.m.-1 p.m. & 4 p.m.-8 p.m. (Sun. 9 a.m.-1 p.m.). Closed Mon.

Monsieur Léon really knows how to cook a juicy ham—his is certainly one of the most toothsome in town. Equal praise is warranted for his head cheese, and for the rich rillettes and confits he fashions from southwestern geese sent to Paris just for him. Do make a point of sampling his excellent sugar-free compotes, made from prime, organically grown fruits.

Gargantua
1st arr. - 284, rue Saint-Honoré
42 60 63 38
Open 8:30 a.m.-7:30 p.m. Closed Sun.

The opulent window displays of this well-known charcuterie could satisfy even the gigantic robust appetite of its Rabelaisian namesake. There are cured meats, foie gras and terrines, of course, but Gargantua also stocks an abundance of prepared dishes, breads, wines, pastries and ice cream. It's a fine place to go to put together a picnic.

Little Pig
8th arr. - 73, av. Franklin-Roosevelt
43 59 22 12
Open 8 a.m.-7:30 p.m. (Sat. 10 a.m.-6 p.m.). Closed Sun.

As you might guess from the name, Little Pig is a good place to go to stock up on hams of every description: boiled, baked, smoked, air-dried, Parma and more. You're certain to be pleased with the succulent terrines, galantines (generally boned poultry stuffed, rolled or shaped, and poached in gelatin stock), smoked salmon, as well as with the attractively priced prepared dishes that have become the house specialties.

Pou
17th arr. - 16, av. des Ternes - 43 80 19 24
Open 9:30 a.m.-1:15 p.m. & 3:30 p.m.-7:15 p.m. Closed Sun. & Mon.

Pou is divine, an excellent charcuterie whose sober decor and rich displays resemble nothing so much as a palace of earthly delights. A look in the window is an enticing, irresistible invitation to buy: black and white boudin sausages, duck pâté en croûte, glittering galantines, cervelas sausage studded with pale-green pistachios and now, sumptuous pastries, too. Since everything really is as good as it looks, making a choice is quite a task. And given the prices, paying isn't so easy, either.

Schmid
18th arr. - 199, rue Championnet
46 27 68 24
Open 8 a.m.-7 p.m. Closed Sun. 2 other branches.

Naturally, with a name like Schmid, you would expect this shop to specialize in sauerkraut. And you wouldn't be wrong. It is excellent—fine, crisp and tart. But don't overlook the aged Muenster, the light and airy Kugelhopf (a yeast cake sometimes made from brioche) and other Alsatian treats.

Vigneau-Desmaret
6th arr. - 105-107, rue de Sèvres
45 48 04 73
Open 9:30 a.m.-1 p.m. & 4 p.m.-7:30 p.m. Closed Sun.

If ever you should lose your appetite, come over to this old-fashioned charcuterie . . . we guarantee you'll find it. Who wouldn't salivate at the sight of succulent ham wrapped in a linen cloth and poached in aromatic broth? Who wouldn't long for a bite of perfectly aged saucisson? On hand, too, are light vegetable or fish terrines and an entire list of groceries, vegetables, cheeses and fruits.

Vignon
8th arr. - 14, rue Marbeuf - 47 20 24 26
Open 8:30 a.m.-7:30 p.m. Closed Sun. & Mon.

A rather grand marble facade sets the luxurious tone for this respected Parisian charcuterie. Monsieur Vignon, president of the professional association, turns out a superb terrine of foie gras, remarkable galantines of chicken and duck studded with truffles or pistachios, game pâtés and delicious, old-fashioned head cheese. Parma ham fanciers should note that Vignon stocks the excellent La Slega brand from Langhirano.

CHEESE

Androuët
8th arr. - 41, rue d'Amsterdam
48 74 26 90
Open 9:50 a.m.-7 p.m. Closed Sun.

Pierre Androuet, that most renowned *fromager*, retired and sold his medieval-looking cheese shop near the Saint-Lazare station. But the tradition continues, with messieurs Guérin and Blat-Viel supervising the aging of nearly 200 different types of cheese in the maze of cellars under the shop. A visit to Androuet is not only a pleasure for the eye and the palate, it is instructive as well. Each cheese bears a label with its name and origin, and competent sales clerks offer advice on how to compose an appetizing, varied cheese tray. Note that delivery is free of charge in the greater Paris area for purchases over 300 francs.

Marie-Anne Cantin
7th arr. - 12, rue du Champ-de-Mars
45 50 43 94
Open 8:30 a.m.-1 p.m. & 4 p.m.-7:30 p.m. (Sun. 8:30 a.m.-1 p.m.). Closed Mon.

Like father, like daughter: Marie-Anne Cantin is a worthy successor to the late Christian Cantin. Her customers and her cheeses benefit from large doses of tender loving care. She is an ardent defender of real (read: unpasteurized) cheeses and one of the few merchants in Paris to sell Saint-Marcellins as they are preferred on their home turf—in their creamy prime, not in their chalky youth. And so it is with the other cheeses she sells, all of which retain the authentic flavors of their country origins.

Créplet-Brussol
8th arr. - 17, pl. de la Madeleine
42 65 34 32
Open 9 a.m.-7 p.m. Closed Sun., Mon. & 1st 3 wks. of Aug.

Former supplier of Mimolette (a firm, nutty-flavored Dutch cheese) to General de Gaulle, Créplet-Brussol still boasts a large population of celebrities among its clientele (Sylvie Vartan, Catherine Deneuve, Carole Bouquet, among them). But what really counts here is the cheese: perfectly aged Camembert, creamy Brillat-Savarin, farmhouse Reblochon and tangy faisselle (fresh cream cheese) made right in the shop. The butter, cream and crème fraîche are divine.

Alain Dubois
17th arr. - 80, rue de Tocqueville
42 27 11 38, 46 22 92 43
Open 7:30 a.m.-1 p.m. & 4 p.m.-7:30 p.m. (Sun. 7:30 a.m.-1 p.m.). Closed Mon.

Alain Dubois's Gruyère, aged for at least two years in his cellars, is a royal treat. And there's more: Dubois offers farmhouse goat cheeses, unpasteurized Camembert and authentic Epoisses (which he rinses religiously with marc de Bourgogne). The problem is, now that his shop has expanded, this expert cheese merchant has filled it with so many enticements that we don't know which way to turn. You will not be astonished to learn that Dubois supplies premium cheeses to such great restaurants as Lucas-Carton, Guy Savoy, Michel Rostang, Laurent and more.

Ferme Poitevine
18th arr. - 64, rue Lamarck - 46 06 54 40
Open 8 a.m.-1 p.m. & 4 p.m.-8 p.m. (Sun. 8 a.m.-1 p.m.). Closed Mon. & Aug.

Monsieur Jack, the cheese man, is a Montmartre personality. He serves all his clients with the same warmth, whether they're famous or not. His many perfectly matured cheeses come from all over the French countryside. We particularly enjoy the flavorful Muensters, the rich Camemberts and the tender little goat cheeses marinated in herbed olive oil.

La Ferme Saint-Hubert
8th arr. - 21, rue Vignon - 47 42 79 20
Open 8:30 a.m.-7:15 p.m. Closed Sun.

Cheese seller Henry Voy is so passionate about his vocation that he has no time for anything else. Morning and night you can find him tending to his Beauforts (aged over two years), his farmhouse goat cheeses or his exclusive Saint-Hubert. He travels all over France, seeking out the best farmhouse cheeses. For true aficionados, Voy unearths such rarities as unpasteurized butter churned with spring water, and delicate goat's-milk butter.

La Fromagerie Boursault

14th arr. - 71, av. du Général-Leclerc
43 27 93 30
Open 8 a.m.-12:30 p.m. & 4 p.m.-7:15 p.m. (Sun. 8 a.m.-12:30 p.m.). Closed Mon.

It was here that Pierre Boursault created the famous cheese that bears his name. And it is here, naturally enough, that you will find Boursault at its creamy, golden best. Current owner Jacques Vernier has made the shop one of the most pleasant in Paris, a showcase for the rare specimens that he seeks out himself in the French hinterlands. Like the incomparable Beauforts aged under his supervision in their native Alpine air; the farmhouse goat cheeses (ah, those Picodons!); the handcrafted Saint-Nectaire from Auvergne, which has nothing in common with the industrially produced variety; and the flawless Camemberts. This is one of the few places on the planet where one may buy Bleu de Termignon, a blue-veined summer cheese from Savoie.

Lecomte

4th arr. - 76, rue Saint-Louis-en-l'Ile
43 54 74 54
Open 8 a.m.-1 p.m. & 4 p.m.-8 p.m. (Sun. 8 a.m.-1 p.m.). Closed Mon.

The best cheeses on the Ile-Saint-Louis are available at Lecomte: Pavés d'Auge from Normandy, Epoisses rinsed in marc de Bourgogne, handcrafted Cantal from Auvergne and robust Reblochon, all expertly aged. The fresh cream cheeses, made in the shop, are a delight, as are the goat cheeses from Périgord and the Aveyron region.

Georges Seigneur

12th arr. - Marché d'Aligre - 43 43 31 99
Open 8 a.m.-1 p.m. & 4 p.m.-7:30 p.m. Closed Mon. & Tues. morning.

One of the best and deservedly best-known merchants in the lively Marché d'Aligre, Georges Seigneur has an artistic approach to cheese. His cellar is filled with marvelous cheeses that he guides with tenderness toward maturity. Seigneur specializes in white-wine-washed cheeses (try his wonderful Langres), well-aged Tommes and Saint-Marcellin.

Spécialités Fromagères

7th arr. - 51, rue de Grenelle - 45 48 56 75
Open 8:30 a.m.-1 p.m. & 4 p.m.-7:30 p.m. Closed Sun. & Mon.

Roland Barthélémy reigns over the treasure trove of cheeses that he selects from farms all over the French countryside, then brings to perfect ripeness in his cellars. He is also the creator of several marvelous specialties that have the Who's Who of French officialdom beating a path to his door (he supplies the Elysée Palace, no less). The Boulamour (fresh cream cheese enriched with crème fraîche, currants, raisins and Kirsch) was Barthélémy's invention, as was a delicious Camembert laced with Calvados. We also enjoy the amusing Brie Surprise. But not to worry, tradition is never neglected here, witness the rich-tasting Alpine Beaufort, French Vacherin and the creamy Fontainebleau (the latter is made on the premises).

CHOCOLATE & CANDY

Bonbonnière de la Trinité

9th arr. - 4, pl. d'Estienne-d'Orves
48 74 23 38
Open 9 a.m.-7 p.m. Closed Sun. 2 other branches.

This charming little store dates from 1925. A real sweetshop, it stocks some 60 kinds of jam, 25 types of honey, 60 varieties of tea and countless candies. The chocolate truffles are quite good, but for us, the irresistible attraction here is the range of bitter and super-bitter chocolates sold in great, thick slabs, that are perfect for cooking or guilty nibbling.

Au Chocolat de Puyricard

7th arr. - 27, av. Rapp - 47 05 59 47
Open 9:30 a.m.-1 p.m. & 2 p.m.-7 p.m. Closed Sun. & Aug.

This shop is the exclusive Parisian source of the sweet (some might say, too sweet) chocolate truffles produced by the Provençal firm,

Puyricard. Like the chocolates, the delicious calissons d'Aix (almond candies) are made by hand in small quantities.

Comptoir du Chocolat et des Alcools (CCA)

92800 La Défense - Centre Commercial Quatre-Temps
Open 9:30 a.m.-2 p.m. & 3:30 p.m.-7 p.m. Closed Sun., Mon. & Aug. 6 other branches.

If you're planning to spend more than 150 francs, CCA offers attractive discounts on name-brand chocolates.

Confiserie de Saint-Pierre

16th arr. - 33, rue de Chaillot - 47 20 39 28
Open 9:30 a.m.-7 p.m. Closed Sat. & Sun.

In addition to a sparkling display of jams and jellies, this traditional candy store offers a representative assortment of sweets from the French provinces: bergamotes de Nancy, forestines de Bourges, pralines de Montargis, calissons d'Aix and more. And we find the decor to be as appealing as the merchandise.

Christian Constant

7th arr. - 26, rue du Bac - 42 96 53 53
Open daily 8 a.m.-8 p.m. Other branch: 37, rue d'Assas - 6th arr.

Christian Constant is mad for chocolate; in fact, he recently wrote a definitive book on the subject. His latest innovation is a chocolate bar with an 80 percent cocoa content, and he has also come up with some divine ganache fillings for his chocolate candies: ginger, cinnamon, tea, raspberry . . . yum!

Debauve et Gallais

7th arr. - 30, rue des Saints-Pères
45 48 54 67
Open 10 a.m.-1 p.m. & 2 p.m.-7 p.m. (Sat. until 6 p.m.). Closed Sun. & Mon.

With its picturesque shopfront designed by renowned nineteenth-century architects Percier and Fontaine (classified as a landmark by the Beaux-Arts) and its interior decorated with painted pillars, orange-wedge mirrors and antique lamps, Debauve et Gallais has loads of charm. The firm's filled chocolates, soft caramels, hazelnut pralines and chocolate truffles,

all prettily displayed in glass jars, are perhaps a bit overrated (we could not deem them "sublime"), but they are of perfectly respectable quality, and the shop itself is a treat to visit.

Duc de Praslin

8th arr. - 44, av. Montaigne - 47 20 99 63
Open 10 a.m.-7 p.m. Closed Sat. & Sun.

Named for a seventeenth-century aristocrat whose cook invented the confection known as the praline, the Duc de Praslin specializes in crunchy caramel-coated almonds. You'll also want to sample some of the delicious variations on that basic theme: amandas (almonds, nougatine and cocoa), mirabos (nougatine and orange, covered with milk chocolate) and passions (chocolate-coated caramelized almonds).

Godiva

17th arr. - 107, rue Jouffroy - 47 63 15 15
Hours vary from store to store. 7 other branches.

These renowned chocolates are superbly packaged, 'tis true, but we still find them (Lord knows, we've tried, and tried not to) far too sugary-sweet. The sales staffs in all the Godiva shops are uniformly courteous and friendly.

Jadis et Gourmande

8th arr. - 49 bis, av. Franklin-Roosevelt
45 25 06 04
Open 9:30 a.m.-7 p.m. Closed Sat., Sun. & Mon. morning. 2 other branches.

It is delightful indeed to browse around this sugarplum palace, where one is tempted in turn by delicious bonbons, hard candies, caramels and chocolate in myriad forms. The thick slabs of cooking chocolate make one want to rush to the kitchen and whip up a rich devil's food cake.

Lenôtre

16th arr. - 44, rue d'Auteuil - 45 24 52 52
Open 9:15 a.m.-7:15 p.m. Other branches.

Gaston Lenôtre's range of chocolates includes classic, intensely flavored truffles and remarkable palets d'or filled with rich, subtle buttercream. Brisk turnover ensures the freshness of all these marvelous confections. In addition to chocolates, Lenôtre produces creamy caramels, nougatines and, around Christmas, delicious candied chestnuts.

La Maison du Chocolat
8th arr. - 52, rue François-Ier - 47 23 38 25
Open 9:30 a.m.-7 p.m. Closed Sun. Other branch: 225, rue du Faubourg-Saint-Honoré - 8th arr.

There's something of the alchemist about Robert Linxe: never satisfied, he is ever experimenting, innovating, transforming mere cocoa beans into something very precious. His chocolates are among the finest in Paris, maybe even in the world. His renowned buttercream fillings—lemon, caramel, tea, raspberry and rum—will carry you away to gourmet heaven.

Peltier
7th arr. - 66, rue de Sèvres - 47 34 06 62, 47 83 66 12
Open 9:30 a.m.-7 p.m. (Sun. 8:30 a.m.-7 p.m.). Closed Mon.

Peltier's palets d'or (dark chocolates filled with chocolate buttercream and topped with a daub of real gold leaf) are among the capital's finest: light, suave and balanced. The legion of other varieties are equally luscious.

Richard
7th arr. - 258, bd Saint-Germain
45 55 66 00
Open 10 a.m.-7 p.m. Closed Sun. & Mon. morning.

A very good *chocolatier* from Lyons has established a Parisian outpost near the Chambre des Députés. The elegant emporium houses superbly presented chocolates with smooth, scrumptious buttercream fillings.

Tanrade
9th arr. - 18, rue Vignon - 47 42 26 99
Open 9:15 a.m.-noon & 1:30 p.m.-6:30 p.m. Closed Sun., Mon. & Aug.

It has been said that Tanrade's candied chestnuts are the finest the world has ever known. When chestnuts are out of season, one can always fall back on bright-tasting fruit leather (fruit rolls), delicate honey bonbons and hand-dipped chocolates, all crafted by expert artisans.

Tholoniat
10th arr. - 47, rue du Château-d'Eau
46 07 74 58
Open 8 a.m.-7:30 p.m. Closed Wed. & 1 month in summer.

Within these walls, a master pastry chef spins, sculpts, blows and shapes sugar and chocolate into tiny people, landscapes, fruit, flowers and even wee houses (with furniture!). Incredibly enough, his creations taste as good as they look. Special applause goes to Tholoniat's delicious and unusual pear- and orange-flavored chocolates.

COFFEE & TEA

Betjeman and Barton
8th arr. - 23, bd Malesherbes - 42 65 35 94
Open 9:30 a.m.-7 p.m. Closed Sun.

The name on the sign and the shop's decor are veddy, veddy British, but the firm itself is 100 percent French! The range of teas on offer is quite extensive, comprising over 150 natural and flavored varieties. Prices start at about 40 francs per 3.5 ounces, and go as high as 250 francs for an incomparable Darjeeling. Indeed, B and B's teas are of such high quality that Harrod's of London (no less) deigns to market them. To help you choose your blend, the staff will offer you a cup of tea—a comforting and highly civilized custom.

Brûlerie des Ternes
17th arr. - 10, rue Poncelet - 46 22 52 79
Open 9 a.m.-2 p.m. & 3:30 p.m.-7:30 p.m. Closed Mon.

Coffees from all over the globe are roasted and ground to perfection in this commendable shop, which draws a clientele made up, in part, of the chic and famous. Featured is the fabled Blue Mountain coffee from Jamaica, a rare and costly treat (380 francs per kilo). Each customer's individual blend is automatically recorded on a computer, so the recipe need never be lost or forgotten.

Couleur Café

8th arr. - 34, rue Ponthieu - 42 56 00 15
Open 10 a.m.-7 p.m. Closed Sat. & Sun.

The Braley family is dedicated to importing, roasting and blending the world's finest coffees. While it produces some fine house mixtures, pure Colombian, Ethiopian Moka and rare beans from Papua are also sold. You will be interested to learn that this is where the Brazilian embassy buys its coffee. In stock as well is a choice selection of tea, honey, jam and chocolates.

L'Espace Café

11th arr. - 89, bd de Charonne
43 70 28 92

Open 9 a.m.-7 p.m. Closed Sun. & Mon. in Aug.

Michel and François Toutain have a futuristic outlook on coffee. The shop's computer produces a sensorial analysis that allegedly matches the customer's personality with a particular bean or blend. But, of course, one may simply go in and ask for one's preferred brew: Javanese, Moka, Negus, Mexican or any one of a number of house specialties. All beans sold are carefully selected and roasted each day.

Mariage Frères

4th arr. - 30-32, rue du Bourg-Tibourg
42 72 28 11

Open 11 a.m.-7:30 p.m. Closed Mon.

Founded by a family of explorers, one of whose ancestors participated in a delegation sent by Louis XIV to sign a trade agreement with the Shah of Persia, Mariage imports no fewer than 350 varieties of tea from 30 countries. This comprehensive selection includes the exquisite Bloomfield Darjeeling, a splendid golden-tipped Grand Yunnan and other rarities that may be sampled in the shop's tea room, accompanied by pastries or light snacks.

Torréfaction Valade

12th arr. - 21, bd de Reuilly
43 43 39 27

Open 8:45 a.m.-1 p.m. & 4 p.m.-7:30 p.m. Closed Sun., Mon. & Aug.

In his modern, clean-lined shop, Pascal Guiraud celebrates his passion for coffee, a passion that he shares with his equally enthu-siastic customers. Beans from Cuba, Brazil, Kenya, Costa Rica, Haiti and elsewhere set free an irresistible aroma as they roast (and they are prepared only as needed, so the coffee is absolutely fresh). The house blends are marvelous as well: we like the Italian Roast (84 francs per kilo), which is one of the house's most popular, the Turkish Special and the spicy Orient Express. Don't overlook the shop's prestigious selection of jams, honey and condiments.

Twinings

8th arr. - 76, bd Haussmann - 43 87 39 84
Open 10 a.m.-7 p.m. Closed Mon. & Aug.

Twinings's utterly English boutique is, so they claim, the only place to procure genuine Earl Grey tea, the kind still drunk in quantity by the Grey family (11 francs per 3.5 ounces). Another exceedingly rare variety, Darjeeling Ringtong, is also available, for the rather more hefty sum of 70 francs. Regular customers have their names and favorite blends recorded in a large, bound ledger (oh, so chic). Tea fanciers will be glad to learn that Twinings also sells tea in bricks, just as it was sold back in the fourteenth century.

Verlet

1st arr. - 256, rue Saint-Honoré
42 60 67 39

Open 9 a.m.-7 p.m. Closed Sun., Mon. & Aug.

The Verlet family has been roasting and selling coffee beans in their delightful turn-of-the-century shop since 1880. Pierre Verlet imports the finest coffees from Papua, Costa Rica, Colombia, Jamaica, Malabar, Ethiopia and Brazil, and he also produces several subtle and delicious house blends. He will even create one specially for you, for he is a master at balancing different aromas, different degrees of acidity and bitterness to suit personal taste. If you prefer to taste before you buy, take a seat at one of the little tables and try, perhaps, the Petit Cheval blend, a marvelously balanced and smooth Moka. Verlet also stocks a selection of teas from all over the world and an appetizing array of dried fruits. At lunchtime, crowds pour in to enjoy the excellent croque monsieurs or a slice of cake and a cup of fragrant coffee.

ETHNIC FOOD

Afrique-Brésil
14th arr. - 9, rue Léopold-Robert
43 22 04 63
Open 9:30 a.m.-1 p.m. & 4 p.m.-8 p.m. (Mon. 4 p.m.-8 p.m.). Closed Sun. & Aug. 15-Sept. 15.

"We stock lots of Brazilian foods, some African items, a few things from the West Indies and a full line of Greek and Lebanese foodstuffs," the owner told us. As a result of this internationalist policy, you'll find black beans and carnececa for feijoada—the Brazilian national dish, a robust dish halfway between a soup and a stew—alongside the tabouli, hummus and eggplant spread for a Levantine feast, as well as an assortment of rums, Greek wines and tequilas.

Baucia
7th arr. - 76, rue du Bac - 45 48 85 68
Open 8:30 a.m.-1 p.m. & 4 p.m.-7:30 p.m. (Sat. 8:30 a.m.-1 p.m.). Closed Sun. & Aug.

The owner's rolled *R* and sunny accent betray his Italian origins. His insistence on selling only the finest hams from Parma and San Daniele, the most savory Cremona salami and the meatiest Piedmontese coppa is also typically Italian. Don't miss the appetizing selection of fresh and aged cheeses from the Boot on display in this simpatico shop.

Aux Cinq Continents
11th arr. - 75, rue de la Roquette
43 79 75 51
Open 9:30 a.m.-1:30 p.m. & 3:30 p.m.-10 p.m. Closed Sat., Sun. & Aug. Mon. mornings.

The Abramoff brothers reign over one of the city's most comprehensive sources of grains, cereals and imported delicacies. No fewer than fifteen kinds of rice are on stock here, along with ten varieties of dried beans (the black beans are wonderful with any kind of smoked meat) and various grades of semolina. Exotica includes a delicious dried mullet roe (called "poutargue"), Iranian pistachios, pastrami, corned beef, chewy Central European breads and flavored vodkas. The store also stocks a good supply of arcane kitchen utensils. Aux Cinq Continents is worth a visit for its nose-tickling scents alone.

Davoli
16th arr. - 61, rue de Passy - 42 88 20 30
Open 9:15 a.m.-1 p.m. & 3:30 p.m.-7:15 p.m. Closed Sun., Mon. & Aug. Other branch: 34, rue Cler - 7th arr.

Fresh stuffed pasta headlines the offerings: cappelletti filled with meat, tortellini filled with spinach, to name but two exemplary offerings. The Parma ham is excellent, and the rosy, unctuous mortadella hails straight from Bologna. A selection of fine Italian wines (as well as liqueurs and aperitivi) lets you wash all the good stuff down in the proper style.

Dolowski
4th arr. - 16, rue Charlemagne
42 72 14 16
Open 7 a.m.-8 p.m. Closed Sun., school holiday in Feb. & Aug. 15-31.

The romantic spirit of Poland pervades this venerable grocery and bar, where nostalgia flows as freely as the Polish vodka (Zytnia, Wyborowa, Zubrowka flavored with buffalo grass, and other varieties infused with cherries, plums or pepper). You'll also find dark, chewy rye bread, Warsaw-style pickles, sausages and sweet little poppyseed cakes.

Finkelsztajn
4th arr. - 22, rue des Rosiers - 42 72 78 91
Open 9:30 a.m.-1:30 p.m. & 3 p.m.-7:30 p.m. Closed Mon. & Tues.

In this pretty shop, the hospitable Sacha proposes several robust and savory Yiddish specialties. Among our favorites: the stuffed carp, chopped liver and delicious little piroshki (small turnovers or dumplings filled with a savory or sweet stuffing). For dessert, try the authentic vatrouchka (Russian cheesecake) or the poppyseed cakes.

The General Store
7th arr. - 82, rue de Grenelle - 45 48 63 16
Open 10 a.m.-7 p.m. Closed Sun.

Tacos, tortillas and all the other traditional fixings for a Tex-Mex feast may be found in this spic-and-span little shop. But the inventory doesn't stop there: You'll find buttermilk-pancake mix, a selection of California wines (not just Paul Masson), familiar American packaged foods (Karo syrup, cream cheese, canned pumpkin, chocolate chips, Hellmann's mayo) and even fresh cranberries at holiday time. If you crave a sweet snack, look for the yummy pecan squares and cookies whipped up fresh every day. As you would expect, English is spoken, and you can count on a warm welcome from the friendly owners (neither of whom, curiously, is American).

Jo Goldenberg

4th arr. - 7, rue des Rosiers - 48 87 20 16
Open daily 9 a.m.-midnight.

For over 60 years, this far-famed little grocery-cum-restaurant has supplied the Ashkenazi community of Paris with stuffed carp, zesty herring with a procession of sauces, smoked salmon, corned beef, smoked tongue and even caviar (kept under lock and key in its own special case).

Goldenberg

17th arr. - 69, av. de Wagram - 42 27 41 85
Open daily 8:30 a.m.-midnight. Other branch: 25, rue de Taitbout - 9th arr. - 47 70 89 96.

Familiar deli fare, made measurably more exotic by the fact that it's served within sight of the Arc de Triomphe. There's herring, there's corned beef, there's stuffed carp, there's pastrami and that well-known Yiddish dessert, the brownie.

Heratchian

9th arr. - 6, rue Lamartine - 48 78 43 19
Open 8:30 a.m.-7:30 p.m. (Mon. 8:30 a.m.-2 p.m.). Closed Sun.

All the mellifluous idioms of the Near East and the Balkans are spoken (and understood) at this fascinating, fragrant bazaar. The friendly sales staff will help you to fat, purple Kalamata olives, golden thyme-blossom honey, genuine sheep's-milk feta, Salonikan yogurt (made from a mix of cow's and sheep's milk) and savory kibbeh (bulghur and ground lamb, onions and pine nuts deep-fried or served raw).

ITS

15th arr. - 366 ter, rue de Vaugirard
40 60 04 09
Open 9 a.m.-7 p.m. Closed Sat.

Home to the finest vanilla from Madagascar and the Reunion Islands, as well as rum punches, tropical-fruit jams and that perennial island favorite, the sea turtle, available in the form of a soup or a savory stew.

Izraël (Le Monde des Epices)

4th arr. - 30, rue François-Miron
42 72 66 23
Open 9:30 a.m.-1 p.m. & 2:30 p.m.-7 p.m. Closed Sun., Mon. & Aug.

Solski and Françoise Izraël are the masters of this colorful, richly scented realm of spices, herbs, exotic foods and condiments. Burlap sacks overflow with basmati rice from Pakistan and Thailand; crates host fat dates and figs from Turkey; Greek olives soak in barrels of herbed, lemony marinades. Curries, chutneys and pink lentils have journeyed from India to this Paris spot; from Mexico, tacos and several types of fiery chiles. Argentinean empanadas, Louisiana pecans and Chinese candied ginger are just a few of the other international representatives found in this unique emporium.

Kioko

5th arr. - 176, rue Saint-Jacques
43 54 64 24
Open 10 a.m.-7 p.m. Closed Sun.

All the hard-to-find ingredients that go into Japanese cuisine can be purchased at this unprepossessing little Latin Quarter grocery. In addition to tofu, taro, Japanese-style rice and wheat noodles, Kioko stocks good native beers, like Kirin and Sapporo.

La Maison d'Allemagne

8th arr. - 45, rue Pierre-Charron
47 20 35 20
Open 9 a.m.-10 p.m. Closed Sun.

A representative sampling of *gemütlich* German foodstuffs is available at this attractive little shop. The hearty, appetizing enticements include Westphalian ham and real Frankfurt sausages, German-style herring, country breads, delicate Moselle wines and a mind-boggling collection of beers.

Maison de l'Ile de la Réunion

8th arr. - 1, rue Vignon - 42 68 07 88
Open 11 a.m.-7 p.m. Closed Sun. & Mon.

Creole cooking is a snap when you have all the right ingredients on hand. And here is the place to stock up on them: exotic foodstuffs are displayed over four floors of this grocery and take-out shop. Among the tropical delights on sale are (frozen) West Indian fish, fresh fruit and vegetables, powerfully hot peppers, ready-to-eat accras (salt-cod fritters), stuffed crab and colombo.

Marks & Spencer

9th arr. - 35, bd Haussmann - 47 42 42 91
Open 9 a.m.-6 p.m. Closed Sun.

The food section of this all-British emporium provides ample evidence that English gastronomy is not, as Parisians tend to think, a joking matter. The French, it seems, are genetically incapable, for example, of producing good bacon. Marks & Spencer's is wonderful: meaty, smoky, with no nasty bits of bone, no inedible rind. The cheese counter features Stilton, Cheddar, Leicester and other delicious English dairy products, and the grocery shelves are crowded with all sorts of piquant condiments and chutneys. Teas, biscuits, jams and marmalades are legion, of course, and a special refrigerated case offers fresh sandwiches for a quick lunch on the run.

Mourougane

10th arr. - 69 & 76, passage Brady
42 46 06 06
Open 9:30 a.m.-8:30 p.m. Closed Sun. & last wk. in Aug.

Over the past decade, Indo-Pakistani cooking has conquered Paris with its sunny, fragrant, spicy dishes. Mourougane, set in the quiet passage Brady, carries marvelous basmati rice, papadums, chutneys and all the colorful spices, chiles and curries one might need to whip up a full-course Indian or Pakistani feast.

Au Régal

16th arr. - 4, rue Nicolo - 42 88 49 15
Open 9:30 a.m.-10 p.m. (Sun. 3 p.m.-6 p.m.).

Delicacies from all the Russias are spotlighted here: caviar, vodkas of every description, coulibiac (salmon baked in a pastry crust) and pirozhki (more pastry-wrapped nibbles), marinated herring and blinis, vatrouchka (cheesecake) and walnut tart.

Raffi

16th arr. - 60, av. Paul-Doumer
45 03 10 90
Open 10 a.m.-1:30 p.m. & 3 p.m.-7:30 p.m. Closed Sun. & Mon.

This opulent food bazaar stocks all the specialties of the Mediterranean. Dried beans, semolina, a dozen varieties of olives, nuts and plump dried fruits, all of excellent quality, are staples. But the most interesting section of the shop for us is the take-out counter. Featured are juicy kibbeh (meatballs with pine nuts,

onions and spices), hummus, tabouli and creamy taramosalata.

Spécialités Antillaises

20th arr. - 16, bd de Belleville - 43 58 31 30
Open 10 a.m.-7:15 p.m. (Fri. & Sat. 9 a.m.-3:15 p.m.). Closed Sun. afternoon & Mon.

Here's a one-stop shop for Creole fixings and take-out foods. Among the latter, we recommend the scrumptious stuffed crabs, the crispy accras (salt-cod fritters), the Creole sausage and a spicy avocado dish called *féroce d'avocat*. The grocery section offers tropical fruits flown in fresh from the West Indies, as well as a selection of exotic frozen fish (shark, gilthead . . .) and an array of rums and punches.

La Table d'Italie

6th arr. - 69, rue de Seine - 43 54 34 69
Open 9 a.m.-7:30 p.m. Closed Sun., Mon. & Aug.

A lively, fun place to shop for Italian foods, the Table d'Italie offers superlative fresh pasta (ravioli, cannelloni, lasagne, fettuccine) and toothsome potato gnocchi, as well as some top-flight Italian charcuterie (we're thinking of the Parma ham and Neapolitan sausage in particular). The assortment of cheeses and wines are worth looking into as well. At lunchtime, join the friendly crush in sampling the specialties of the house at this very Parisian *tavola calda*.

Tang Frères

13th arr. - 48, av. d'Ivry - 45 70 80 00
Open 9 a.m.-7:30 p.m. Closed Mon.

Three times a week a cargo plane flies into Paris bearing a shipment earmarked for the Tang brothers. This gastronomic dynasty runs the biggest Asian supermarket in town, stocked with all manner of mysterious (to the uninitiated) roots, powders, dried mushrooms, canned bamboo shoots, rice and noodles, birds' nests, sharks' fins and so on . . . and on—there are literally thousands of items to choose from.

Than Binh

5th arr. - 18, rue Lagrange - 43 54 66 11
Open 9 a.m.-7:30 p.m. Closed Mon. & holidays. Other branch: 29, pl. Maubert - 5th arr. - 43 25 81 86.

From perfumed rice to instant soups, from fresh tropical fruit and vegetables to dried fish and sweet bean cakes, the Than Binh stores stock a staggering assortment of Oriental food products. Throngs of Asian shoppers come here regularly to purchase their culinary supplies, but the crowds don't seem to faze the calm and amiable staff.

GOURMET SPECIALTIES

Augé
8th arr. - 116, bd Haussmann - 45 22 16 97
Open 8:30 a.m.-12:30 p.m. & 2:30 p.m.-7:30 p.m. (Mon. 2:30 p.m.-7:30 p.m.). Closed Sun.

Augé was one of the first shops in town (maybe the only?) where eccentric gourmets could purchase such rare delicacies as bear steaks, reindeer roasts and elephant trunks. Nowadays this rather luxurious little shop specializes in fine wines and brandies. There is still a small grocery section, which includes excellent canned foods (always handy to have in the cupboard) and an enticing assortment of boxed cookies.

Paul Corcellet
2nd arr. - 46, rue des Petits-Champs
42 96 51 82
Open 9:30 a.m.-7 p.m. (Mon. 11 a.m.-7 p.m.). Closed Sun.

Paul and Bernard Corcellet want to put a little spice in your life. Or, more accurately, they want to spice up your ordinary mustards and vinegars with pink peppercorns or coriander, with tropical fruit or unusual herbs. The tangy chutneys and other exotic condiments that Corcellet has been cooking up since 1760 have no peer in Paris. The firm is known, too, for its canned foods that incorporates wild animals; though that particular line of products seems doomed, given the ever-more-stringent importation regulations. Lion, bear and termite fanciers may have to find new suppliers.

Detou
2nd arr. - 58, rue de Tiquetonne
42 36 54 67
Open 8:30 a.m.-6 p.m. (Sat. until noon). Closed Sun.

Home-bakers browse happily among the pastry supplies that comprise Detou's principal stock-in-trade: baking chocolate, powdered almonds, candied fruit and the like. But there are also rare and delicious jams here, as well as unusual cookies and savory canned goods (the mushrooms are particularly fine), Champagnes

and foie gras. Quality merchandise at surprisingly moderate prices.

Faguais
8th arr. - 30, rue La Trémoille
47 20 80 91
Open 9 a.m.-7:30 p.m. Closed Sun.

Yes, Grandmother would feel quite at home in this charming old grocery store. A dizzying variety of gourmet temptations is set out neatly on the shelves. Old-fashioned jams, oils, honeys, cookies, spices and condiments fairly cry out to be bought and sampled. As the shop's pervasive fragrance implies, fresh coffee beans are roasted on the premises daily.

Fauchon
8th arr. - 26, pl. de la Madeleine
47 42 60 11
Open 9:40 a.m.-7 p.m. Closed Sun.

In 1886, at the age of 30, Auguste Fauchon opened his *épicerie fine* on the place de la Madeleine, specializing in quality French foodstuffs. The rest is history. After more than a century, Fauchon is the uncontested paragon of what a gourmet grocery should be. The energetic and youthful president of Fauchon, Martine Premat, has brought a new luster and energy to the firm. All 300 employees are committed to the task of tasting, testing and selling the very finest, the rarest, the most unusual foods in the world. The number of spices alone—4,500—is enough to make your head spin. And you'll find such delicacies as black-fig or watermelon preserves, lavender or buckwheat honey, Mim tea from India or Keeyu tea from China, lavish displays of prime vegetables and fruits, and a world-renowned collection of vintage wines and brandies.

Fouquet
9th arr. - 36, rue Laffitte - 47 70 85 00
Open 9:30 a.m.-6:30 p.m. Closed Sat. & Sun.
Other branch: 22, rue François-Ier - 8th arr.

Christophe Fouquet is the most recent representative of the illustrious family of grocers who have been selling choice foodstuffs at this address since 1852. Fine chocolates are a longstanding specialty at this pretty, old-fashioned shop, but don't overlook the rare mustards (flavored with black currants, oranges or raspberries), appetizing bottled sauces, vinegars distilled according to a secret house recipe, liqueur-laced jams, fruity olive oils, imported cakes and cookies and excellent white brandies.

All the items are attractively packaged and make excellent gifts.

Hédiard

8th arr. - 21, pl. de la Madeleine
42 66 44 36

Hours vary from store to store. 5 other branches.

Only the finest, rarest foodstuffs are deemed worthy of entry into this shrine of epicureanism. Distinguished smoked salmon from the best "schools," sophisticated sugars and syrups, select vintage wines, ports and brandies, and over 4,500 carefully chosen grocery items attract virtually every cultivated palate in town. Even the ordinary is extraordinary here: mustard spiked with Cognac; vinegar flavored with seaweed; opulent fruits and vegetables, always prime, that hail from the ends of the Earth. Many of the items are as costly as they are exotic, but the wines consistently offer excellent value for the money.

Petit Quenault–Les Vieux Vins de France

1st arr. - 56, rue Jean-Jacques-Rousseau
42 33 46 85

Open 9 a.m.-12:30 p.m. & 2 p.m.-7 p.m. (Sat. 9 a.m.-noon & 3 p.m.-7 p.m.). Closed Sun. & Mon. morning.

Connoisseurs come here to store up on supplies of excellent canned and bottled vegetables, fruits, dried mushrooms (morels, girolles, cèpes) and other fine groceries. From ketchup to spices to baking needs (vanilla, chocolate, candied fruit), Petit Quenault has it, along with a fine range of quality kitchen staples, excellent Parma ham and, come Christmastime, smoked salmon. Prices tend to be well below standard retail; the wine department in particular offers some terrific bargains.

CAVIAR & SALMON

Caviar Kaspia

8th arr. - 17, pl. de la Madeleine
42 65 33 52

Open 9 a.m.-1 a.m. Closed Sun. Parking: Madeleine.

Caviar, it would seem, is best savored in a setting of serene austerity. Such is the impression made by the stark interior of Caviar Kaspia, where the choicest Russian and Iranian roes are sold (beluga for 6,900 francs per kilo), along with an assortment of superb smoked fish. The salmon is flawless, but we come for the fine smoked eel, trout or sturgeon, all of which are models of their kind. Should a hunger pang occur at the sight of these delights (how could it not?), just step upstairs to the first-floor restaurant, where all the house specialties may be ordered à la carte.

Le Coin du Caviar

4th arr. - 2, rue de la Bastille
48 04 82 93

Open 10 a.m.-midnight. Closed Sun. Parking: pl. de la Bastille.

No doubt about it, the neighborhood around the Bastille has become madly fashionable. The Coin du Caviar, right in the thick of things (across the street from the popular Bofinger brasserie), has made faithful customers out of the most finicky caviar and smoked-salmon fanciers. Prime Russian or Iranian caviars are featured (depending on the market); the pale, delicately smoky salmon hails from Denmark.

Comptoir du Saumon

15th arr. - 125, bd de Grenelle
40 56 97 96

Open 10:30 a.m.-1 p.m. & 3:30 p.m.-7:30 p.m. (Sun. 10:30 a.m.-1 p.m.). Closed Mon. & Aug. Parking: Métro La Motte-Picquet. Other branch: 60, rue François-Miron - 4th arr.

The French are crazy about smoked salmon. And it is this untempered enthusiasm that's behind the success of the Comptoir du Saumon, where Irish, Swedish, Norwegian and Scottish fish are sold at exceedingly attractive prices (from 350 to 450 francs for a one- to three-pound side). Also stocked are smoked or dill-marinated halibut, Dutch herring, Danish marinated herring and Iranian caviar.

Flora Danica

8th arr. - 142, av. des Champs-Elysées
43 59 20 41

Open 10 a.m.-10 p.m. (Sun. 11 a.m.-8 p.m.). Parking: Georges-V.

Does the phrase "Danish gastronomy" sound fishy to you? So it should, for salmon in myriad forms is its very foundation. Delicate pink specimens from the Baltic Sea are sold here, both smoked and marinated with dill. We suggest that you sample the delicious Danish herring—in fact, why not the entire array of sweet-and-sour sauces that go with it—then wash it all down with an icy, pale Carlsberg beer.

Dominique
6th arr. - 19, rue Bréa - 43 27 08 80
Open 9:30 a.m.-2:30 p.m. & 5:15 p.m.-10:30 p.m. Closed mid-July to mid-Aug.

Dominique has been a fixture on the Montparnasse circuit since time immemorial, and will probably remain so, despite occasional lapses in food and service. The take-out shop remains an excellent source of Iranian caviar, Danish smoked salmon and herring, as well as tender blinis (pancakes, often served with sour cream and caviar), zakuski (the traditional Russian hors d'oeuvres, starting with caviar and running the gamut) and the accompanying heady Russian vodka.

Maxoff
7th arr. - 44, rue de Verneuil - 42 60 60 43
Open 9:30 a.m.-3 p.m. & 3:30 p.m.-10:30 p.m. Closed Sun. & Mon.

Ossetra and sevruga caviars from Iran are featured in the take-out section of this pleasant little restaurant. Smaller spenders may prefer the pressed roe (it's considerably cheaper), or the good Danish smoked salmon, smoked eel, herring (there are ten types) or the assortment of Russian dishes like koulibiac (a pie filled with layers of salmon or fish, rice or kasha, herbs, mushrooms and onion), piroshki and cheesecake. Everything is fresh and of good quality.

Petrossian
7th arr. - 18, bd La Tour-Maubourg
45 51 38 74
Open 9 a.m.-1 p.m. & 2:30 p.m.-7 p.m. Closed Sun. & Mon. Parking: Invalides.

The Petrossian family introduced sturgeon eggs to France in the 1920s, a commercial coup that won them the undying gratitude of the Soviet Union. Today Christian Petrossian enjoys the rare privilege of choosing the very best roes on site at Caspian fishing ports. In addition to sublime ossetra, sevruga, beluga and pressed caviar, there are remarkably rich and unctuous Norwegian smoked salmon, smoked eel and sturgeon, Russian salmon roe and excellent Soviet vodkas.

A la Ville de Petrograd
8th arr. - 13, rue Daru - 42 27 96 55
Open 10 a.m.-10 p.m. Closed Mon. Parking: Wagram.

After inspecting the icons at the Russian Orthodox cathedral, we like to drop in at this charming restaurant-cum-grocery to indulge in caviar, Norwegian smoked salmon or a host of tempting Russian specialties.

ESCARGOTS

L'Escargot de la Butte
18th arr. - 48, rue Joseph-de-Maistre
46 27 38 27
Open 8:30 a.m.-7:30 p.m. (Sun. until 1 p.m.). Closed Mon.

"It's really a shame, but there are no more escargots de Bourgogne left in France," laments Monsieur Marchal. He imports them, therefore, from Germany. But his petits-gris come straight from the Provençal countryside, and arrive still frisky at his little shop located at the foot of the Butte Montmartre. He stuffs them with a deliciously fragrant blend of pure butter, garlic and parsley, and they are a remarkable treat!

La Maison de l'Escargot
15th arr. - 79, rue Fondary - 45 75 31 09
Open 8:30 a.m.-8 p.m. Closed Sun afternoon & Mon.

Snail fanciers from surrounding neighborhoods think nothing of making the trek to this commendable shop. Live petits-gris and escargots de Bourgogne of all sizes are prepared with a delicious snail butter—which is not too strong, not too bland—that is made according to the specifications of a secret recipe developed here in 1894.

FOIE GRAS

Les Choix de Sophie
15th arr. - 3, rue du Général-de-Castelnau
40 56 08 50
Open 9 a.m.-7 p.m. Closed Sat. & Sun.

The Sophie in question is Sophie Bardet, the vivacious spouse of master chef Jean Bardet of Tours. Her shop is a showcase for an entire range of foodstuffs prepared by noted cuisiniers, including some excellent foie gras de canard (whole fattened duck's liver). Mail orders accepted.

Comptoir Corrézien du Foie Gras et du Champignon

15th arr. - 8, rue des Volontaires
47 83 52 97
Open 9 a.m.-1:30 p.m. & 3 p.m.-8 p.m. Closed Sun.

Chantal Larnaudie is an energetic young woman who comes from a long line of foie-gras specialists. The specimens she offers in her shop, whole poached fattened goose liver, preserved in a terrine, are fine indeed, and attractively priced to boot.

Le Comptoir du Foie Gras (Bizac)

1st arr. - 6, rue des Prouvaires - 42 36 26 27
Open 7 a.m.-1 p.m. & 4 p.m.-7 p.m. Closed Sun. & Mon.

This shop is the Parisian outpost of Bizac, a renowned foie-gras processing firm from Brive, in southwestern France. Foie gras in cans and jars comes fully cooked or, if you prefer, lightly cooked (heated just to 90 degrees). If you wish to try your hand at preparing your own terrine de foie gras, raw fattened duck and goose livers are available.

Divay (Au Bon Porc)

17th arr. - 4, rue Bayen - 43 80 16 97
Open 7:30 a.m.-1 p.m. & 4 p.m.-7:30 p.m. (Sun. 7:30 a.m.-1 p.m.). Closed Mon. Other branch: 52, rue du Faubourg-Saint-Denis - 10th arr.

Priced at 580 francs per kilo, Divay sells the least expensive fattened goose liver to be found in the city. What's more, it's delicious.

Dubernet

7th arr. - 2, rue Augureau - 45 55 50 71
Open daily 9 a.m.-1:30 p.m. & 3:30 p.m.-7:30 p.m. Other branch: Forum des Halles, Porte Lescot, first floor - 1st arr.

These foies gras come from Saint-Sever, in the Landes region of southwestern France. Whole fattened goose and duck livers are sold fully cooked in cans or lightly cooked (just pasteurized) in jars. Prices are moderate: a whole fattened duck liver is 680 francs per kilo.

Aux Ducs de Gascogne

1st arr. - 4, rue du Marché-Saint-Honoré
42 60 45 31
Hours vary from store to store. 13 other branches.

This multistore chain specializes in canned and lightly cooked foie gras, sold at rather steep prices: 990 francs per kilo for the whole fattened duck liver; 1,050 francs per kilo for the whole fattened goose liver.

Foie Gras de Luxe

1st arr. - 26, rue Montmartre - 42 33 28 15
Open 6 a.m.-noon & 2:30 p.m.-5 p.m. (Mon. 8 a.m.-noon & 2:30 p.m.-5 p.m.). Closed Sat. & Sun.

This worthy establishment sells raw foie gras year-round, as well as lightly cooked fattened goose and duck livers, and marvelous cured hams from Parma, San Daniele and the Ardennes.

Les Produits Jean-Legrand

8th arr. - 58, rue des Mathurins
42 65 50 46
Open 10 a.m.-2 p.m. & 3 p.m.-6:30 p.m. Closed Sat., Sun. & Aug. Other branch: 18, rue Montmartre - 1st arr.

This processing concern turns out a fine terrine of fresh fattened goose liver (920 francs per kilo), an equally tasty poached version (850 francs per kilo), duck foie gras in a terrine (430 francs for 500 grams) and some interesting canned entrées: daube of boar with cranberries, beef goulash and lotte in mustard sauce.

OILS

A l'Olivier

4th arr. - 23, rue de Rivoli - 48 04 86 59
Open 9:30 a.m.-7 p.m. Closed Sun. & Mon.

After a four-year sojourn on the Ile-Saint-Louis, A l'Olivier has returned to its original site on the rue de Rivoli. Connoisseurs will find not only several fine varieties of olive oil but walnut oil, grilled-almond oil, pumpkin-seed oil, hazelnut oil and an incomparable top-secret blend of virgin olive oils as well. We applaud the shop's policy of selling exceptionally expensive and perishable oils in quarter-liter bottles.

Pierson

9th arr. - 82, rue de Clichy - 48 74 60 86
Open 9:30 a.m.-1:30 p.m. & 3 p.m.-8:30 p.m.
Closed Sun. & Aug.

Inside this adorable little shop is a veritable treasure trove of top-quality oils. First pressings of all sorts are featured—from peanut, sunflower and nettle to poppy, walnut and hazelnut. Fragrant, fruity olive oil from Tunisia comes highly recommended at 38.50 francs per liter. Conspicuous consumers may, however, prefer the horrendously expensive variety from Provence, priced at 119 francs per liter.

PASTA

Biletta

16th arr. - 35, rue d'Auteuil - 42 88 58 88
Open 8 a.m.-1 p.m. & 3:30 p.m.-7:45 p.m. (Sun. 8 a.m.-1 p.m.). Closed Mon. & Aug.

The selection is small—tagliatelle, ravioli, gnocchi, lasagne—but the pasta is golden and finely textured and wonderfully flavored.

Cipolli

13th arr. - 81, rue Bobillot - 45 88 26 06
Open 7 a.m.-1 p.m. & 3:30 p.m.-7:30 p.m. Closed Sun. & Aug.

Mr. Cipolli kneads and stretches his golden dough into an appetizing array of pasta specialties. The tagliatelle and ravioli have an authentic, old-fashioned flavor, while his lasagne is nothing short of sublime. The stuffed pastas (cappelletti filled with minced beef and ham, or mushrooms, or spinach and ricotta; "priests' hats" stuffed with salmon or ricotta and ham) are tender and savory.

TRUFFLES

Maison de la Drôme

9th arr. - 14, bd Haussmann - 42 46 66 67
Open 9 a.m.-7 p.m. (July & Aug. 11 a.m.-7 p.m.). Closed Sun.

The tourist office of the Drôme (a *département* in southeastern France) sells fresh truffles direct from the region—but only for a short period each year, beginning in November. Call for seasonal information.

Maison de la Truffe

8th arr. - 19, pl. de la Madeleine
42 65 53 22
Open 9 a.m.-8 p.m. Closed Sun.

Alongside extraordinary charcuterie, foie gras, good salmon and prepared foods, this luxurious food emporium offers truffles (both freshly dug and sterilized and bottled) at prices that are emphatically not of the bargain-basement variety.

HONEY, JAM & SYRUP

Daire–Aux Miels de France

8th arr. - 71, rue du Rocher - 45 22 23 13
Open 9:30 a.m.-2 p.m. & 2:30 p.m.-7 p.m. (Sat. 9:30 a.m.-1 p.m. & 3 p.m.-6:30 p.m.). Closed Sun., Mon. morning & Aug.

Renée Daire stocks a staggering selection of honeys: pine, oak, chestnut, heather, lavender, rosemary, thyme, acacia and more. Pollen and royal jelly are also on sale, as well as a richly honey-flavored gingerbread studded with walnuts and filberts. The delicious homemade jams that glitter enticingly on the shelves are prepared by none other than Madame Daire herself.

Maison du Miel

8th arr. - 24, rue Vignon - 47 42 26 70
Open 9:30 a.m.-7 p.m. Closed Sun.

Make a beeline to this "House of Honey" to try varieties from the various regions of France. There's Corsican honey, luscious pine honey from the Vosges mountains (which comes highly recommended for bronchial irritations), Provençal lavender honey, as well as choice varieties from the Alps and Auvergne, all rigorously tested by a busy hive of honey tasters. In addition, you'll find honey "by-products," such as beeswax, pollen and royal jelly, as well as a wide range of honey-based cosmetics.

A la Mère de Famille

9th arr. - 35, rue du Faubourg-Montmartre
47 70 83 69
Open 7:30 a.m.-1:30 p.m. & 3 p.m.-7 p.m. Closed Sun., Mon. & Aug.

Founded in 1761, this adorable emporium is the dean of Paris sweetshops. Today it is still a showcase for the very best sugarplums that the French provinces produce. You'll find specialties from every region: cakes, glazed chestnuts, hard candies, exquisite jams and honeys and delicious dried fruits. Excellent prices.

ICE CREAM & SORBET

Le Bac à Glaces
7th arr. - 109, rue du Bac - 45 48 87 65
Open 11 a.m.-7:30 p.m. Closed Sun., Jan. & Feb.

These guaranteed-handmade ice creams and sorbets are crafted of top-quality ingredients, with no artificial additives. Doubting Thomases are encouraged to watch the *glaciers* busily at work in their glassed-in kitchen. Alongside the standards, you'll find some delicious liqueur-flavored ices and other uncommon concoctions, like Camembert ice cream and carrot and tomato sorbets. We always find it difficult to decide between the scrumptious nougat ice cream and the honey-and-pine-nut combo. All these icy delights may be taken home in cartons or enjoyed on the spot in the pretty, old-fashioned ice cream parlor.

Baggi
9th arr. - 38, rue d'Amsterdam
48 74 01 39
Open 8 a.m.-7:15 p.m. (Sat. 10:30 a.m.-7 p.m.). Closed Sun.

The Baggis are not newcomers to the ice cream trade. Since 1850 their shop has been a mecca for lovers of frozen desserts. Today, many aficionados consider Guy Baggi, the firm's current creative force, to be the ice prince of Paris! Guy is forever dreaming up new flavor combinations—and winning prizes for them. Who wouldn't want to pin an award on the Princesse (wild strawberry and chocolate ice creams, pear sorbet and a touch of caramel) or on the Chocolatine (a symphony in chocolate, orange and caramel), or the justly celebrated Biscuit Rothschild. The flavors and dessert creations on hand on any given day vary in accordance with the seasons and Baggi's mood. Prices run from about 66 to 95 francs per liter.

Baskin-Robbins
6th arr. - 1, rue du Four - 43 25 10 63
Open noon-8 p.m. (Fri. & Sat noon-midnight). Closed Sun.

The French tend to find Baskin-Robbins ice creams too sugary-sweet and unnecessarily rich; but they are genuinely intrigued by the flavors: maple-walnut, banana-chocolate swirl, peanut-butter and chocolate (57 francs per liter). . . . But on summer nights, French ice cream fans come out of the woodwork to join the tourists of every other nationality to sip good ol' American milkshakes, a Baskin-Robbins specialty.

Berthillon
4th arr. - 31, rue Saint-Louis-en-l'Ile
43 54 31 61
Open 10 a.m.-8 p.m. Closed Mon. & Tues.

Berthillon is the most famous name in French ice cream. The firm's many faithful fans think nothing of waiting in line for *hours* just to treat their taste buds to a cone or dish of chocolate-nougat or glazed-chestnut ice cream. Berthillon's sorbets are our particular weakness: pink grapefruit, fig, wild strawberry. . . . The entire repertoire comes to some 70 flavors, including many seasonal specialties, all reasonably priced at 58 to 62 francs per liter.

Glacier Calabrese
14th arr. - 15, rue d'Odessa - 43 20 31 63
Open noon-11:30 p.m. Closed Aug.

The owner's lilting Calabrese accent and welcoming warmth are reason enough to visit this little ice cream parlor. But don't neglect to taste his delicious creations. In addition to an assortment of classic ice creams and tropical sorbets, he makes wonderful Italian-style ices: Amaretto, Croccantino (nutty and divine), mint-flavored Straciatella and Strega (for a cone with a kick!). The prices aren't half-bad either: from 5 francs for a single dip to 34 francs for a half-liter carton.

Le Sorbet de Paris
19th arr. - 33-43, rue des Alouettes
42 09 99 25
Open 9 a.m.-7 p.m. Closed Sun.

This fine *glacier* occupies an enviable site at the foot of the verdant Buttes-Chaumont park. Flavors tend to be classic rather than trendy, and vary with the seasons. Among our favorites are the smooth honey-walnut, vanilla and rich candied-chestnut ice creams, but we also like the bright-tasting fruit sorbets, which are especially refreshing in the summertime.

La Sorbetière
92200 Neuilly-sur-Seine - 26, rue Madeleine Michelis - 47 22 40 33
Open 10 a.m.-1 p.m. & 3:30 p.m.-7:30 p.m. (Sun. 10 a.m.-1 p.m.). Closed Mon.

Attention: artist at work! His chosen medium is ice cream, and his productions include pyramids, clowns, candy boxes, painters' palettes and any number of other amusing and original creations sculpted from a choice of over 50 flavors of ice cream and sorbet.

Gilles Vilfeu
1st arr. - 3, rue de la Cossonnerie
40 26 36 40
Open daily 10 a.m.-midnight.

Now Parisians wrap their taste buds around the unctuous ice creams and sorbets of Gilles Vilfeu, once exclusively enjoyed by the citizens of Cannes. Vilfeu's imaginative productions include surprising and sophisticated novelty flavors—tea, lavender and foie-gras sorbets—an ice based on Beaujolais nouveau, and ice creams flavored with licorice, cinnamon and ginger. We strongly encourage you to also sample the sumptuous frozen desserts, notably a molded cream-cheese sorbet served with a vivid raspberry coulis.

MEAT, GAME & FOWL

Boucherie Lamartine
16th arr. - 172, av. Victor-Hugo
47 27 82 29
Open 7 a.m.-7:30 p.m. (Sat. 1 p.m.-7:30 p.m.). Closed Sun.

Some of the best meat in France is sold in this pretty, old-fashioned butcher shop. It's not cheap, mind you, but then you can't put a price on perfection, can you? The expertly aged beef is sublime. And the milky-pink veal always cooks up to juicy perfection, unlike the more commonly available varieties, which have an annoying tendency to shrink in the pan.

Boucherie Marbeuf
8th arr. - 36, rue Marbeuf - 42 25 36 55
Open 7:30 a.m.-2:15 p.m. (Fri. until 3:45 p.m. & Sat. until 1 p.m.). Closed Sun.

This wonderful butcher shop has a secure place in the annals of Parisian gastronomy. Countless top-rated restaurants rely on the Boucherie Marbeuf's peerless professionals to supply them with superb beef (cuts from several elite breeds, including the rare and costly Simmenthal, said to be one of the world's finest), as well as veal from the Corrèze region, farm-raised pork from Auvergne and genuine Sisteron lamb.

Boucheries Bernard
20th arr. - 322, rue des Pyrénées
43 58 01 49
Hours vary from store to store. Other branches.

Over twenty years ago the Boucheries Bernard came up with a highly successful system for selling good-quality, custom-cut meat at unbeatable prices. The chain now has stores all over Paris and the suburbs, stores that offer excellent pork and lamb. The veal isn't always as appealing, and to spot bargains in the beef section, one needs a discerning eye. But the innards-and-offal counter is admirably stocked, and the poultry selection impressive.

Boucheries Roger
17th arr. - 83, av. de Saint-Ouen
46 27 63 77
Hours vary from store to store. 5 other branches.

Like Bernard, Roger specializes in meat of respectable quality, sold at the lowest possible price and cut to the customer's specifications. How do the two compare? Well, Roger might just have the edge when it comes to beef, which seems to us to be of generally higher quality.

Le Coq Saint-Honoré (André-Marie Josse)
1st arr. - 3, rue Gomboust - 42 61 52 04
Open 8 a.m.-1:30 p.m. & 4:30 p.m.-7 p.m. Closed Sun. & Mon.

We might as well make it clear right away: For our money, André-Marie Josse is one of Paris's top poulterers. It's no coincidence that his list of customers boasts such culinary notables as Robuchon, Savoy, Senderens and Terrail of La Tour d'Argent. Josse shrugs modestly when queried about the high standards he applies in choosing his fine-feathered specimens. "I'm not really all that finicky," he says,

"I just insist on the best." His refrigerated cases display choice Bresse chickens and guinea hens (fast becoming prohibitively expensive), as well as laudable Loué pullets, Challans ducks and plump rabbits from the Gâtinais region south of Paris. In season, Josse carries a fine selection of game, including authentic Scottish grouse—a rare and wonderful treat.

Maison Queulevée
15th arr. - 90, rue Cambronne
47 34 36 55
Open 8:30 a.m.-12:30 p.m. & 4 p.m.-7:30 p.m. (Sun. 8:30 a.m.-12:30 p.m.). Closed Mon.

What are the hallmarks of premium fowl? Freshness, first and foremost, because the fresher the chicken, the better it tastes. But lineage counts as well, and the birds here are pedigreed—from Loué, Périgord and other noted regions—along with ducks from Challans and, in season, one of the city's finest selections of feathered game.

Au Poulet de Bresse
16th arr. - 30, rue des Belles-Feuilles
47 27 88 31
Open 7 a.m.-1 p.m. & 4 p.m.-7:30 p.m. (Sun. 7 a.m.-1 p.m.). Closed Mon.

Whether you prefer it feathered or furred, if you like game, this shop is an excellent source. Pierre Desjardin is a specialist who travels down to the best hunting grounds of Sologne to select partridges, hares, venison and boar. Joël Louis, who oversees the domestic-fowl department, can supply magnificent Bresse chickens, delicious little hybrid ducks, broad-breasted capons and fine, fat hens. Raw foie gras is sold year-round, and fresh truffles are available in the winter months.

Tattevin
7th arr. - 15, rue du Champ-de-Mars
47 05 07 02
Open 6 a.m.-1 p.m. & 3:30 p.m.-8 p.m. (Sun. 6 a.m.-1 p.m.). Closed Mon.

No mere butcher, Tattevin. No, he is a knife-and twine-wielding artist who trusses up an original and delectable roast—we salivate at the thought of his loin of veal studded with nuggets of Parma ham, and the boned leg of lamb stuffed with kidneys. It goes without saying that Tattevin's raw materials are of the finest quality.

PASTRY

Bourdaloue
9th arr. - 7, rue Bourdaloue - 48 78 32 35
Open 8 a.m.-7:30 p.m. Closed Sun. afternoon in summer.

L'amour, toujours l'amour is what we feel for Bourdaloue's Puits d'Amour (translation: "wells of love"), a jam-and-puff-pastry concoction that was created here in the 1800s. We also have a lasting, strong affection for the excellent apple turnovers (among the best we've ever tasted in Paris), the hazelnut delights and Bourdaloue's own ice creams and delectable chocolates.

Cador
1st arr. - 2, rue de l'Amiral-de-Coligny
45 08 19 18
Open 10 a.m.-7:15 p.m. Closed Mon. & Aug. 10-Sept. 10.

Quite worthy of its prestigious setting just across from the Louvre, Cador is a regal little pastry shop with a regal interior decor. Seated at pink-and-taupe-marble tea tables, tourists and locals alike love to snack on the dainty cakes that make such a mouth-watering window display. The Petits Cadors (chocolate and orange peel on a short-pastry base) and mousselines, a recent creation that is accompanied by a luscious Grand Marnier custard sauce, attract their fair share of customers.

Clichy
4th arr. - 5, bd Beaumarchais - 48 87 89 88
Open 8 a.m.-7:30 p.m. (Sun. 8 a.m.-7 p.m.). Closed Mon.

Paul Bugeat is a passionate aesthete who composes sweet pastry, chocolate, sugar and cream into exquisite gâteaux. The specialties of the house are delicious, jewel-like petits fours, along with the Clichy (chocolate buttercream and mocha cream on an almond-sponge base), the Pavé de Bourgogne (almond sponge cake and black-currant mousse). When he isn't busy creating these delights in his kitchen lab, Bugeat teaches classes in the art of French pastry at Yale University.

Christian Constant

7th arr. - 37, rue d'Assas - 47 03 30 00
Open daily 8 a.m.-9 p.m. Other branch: 26, rue du Bac - 7th arr.

After a stroll in the Luxembourg Gardens, why not indulge in a treat from Christian Constant's new shop on the rue d'Assas? And one needn't feel too guilt-ridden, because these cakes are low in sugar, additive-free, all-natural and incredibly light. Try a millefeuille, or Constant's famed chocolate-and-banana tart (we agree with Sonia Rykiel that it is a minor masterpiece), or the intensely chocolate macaroons.

Coquelin Aîné

16th arr. - 1, pl. de Passy - 42 88 21 74, 45 24 44 00
Open 9 a.m.-7:30 p.m. (Sun. 9 a.m.-1 p.m.). Closed Mon.

Coquelin enjoys a solidly established reputation with its solidly establishment clientele. Joining the traditional pastries created for holidays (the King's Cake for the feast of the Epiphany is a neighborhood favorite) are the shop's occasionally produced, tempting, original desserts, such as the Hérisson d'Automne ("autumn hedgehog"), a frozen coffee- and chestnut-flavored sweet.

Couderc

11th arr. - 6, bd Voltaire - 47 00 58 20
Open 8:30 a.m.-8 p.m. Closed Mon., Tues. & Aug.

Couderc takes pride in its toothsome candies, pastries, ice creams and chocolates, all on display in this picturesque shop just off the lively place de la République. We suggest that you at least sample the rustic "peasant" and apricot tarts, and the more sophisticated Turquois (macaroons with chocolate mousse), or even the Délice (sponge cake, caramelized almonds and whipped cream with vanilla and chocolate).

Dalloyau

15th arr. - Centre Beaugrenelle - 36, rue Linois - 45 75 59 92
Open 9:45 a.m.-7:45 p.m. Closed Sun. 3 other branches.

Deservedly famous, Dalloyau is a temple of *gourmandise* revered by every discerning sweet tooth in town. Among the most renowned specialties are the memorably good macaroons, the chocolate-and-mocha Opéra cake (created in 1955 and still a bestseller) and the Mogador (chocolate sponge cake and mousse napped in raspberry sauce). Christmas brings succulent glazed chestnuts and gluttonously rich Yule logs; Easter calls for chocolate hens and bunnies romping among praline eggs and bells in the adorable window displays.

Gallet

16th arr. - 10, rue Mignard - 45 04 21 71
Open 7 a.m.-1 p.m. & 3 p.m.-8 p.m. Closed Sun., Mon. & Aug.

A reliable source of English treats for both the breakfast and the tea tables: buns, muffins, scones and pancakes, always fresh and always delicious. Special orders are gladly accepted for holiday cakes and pies.

Gérard Hée

17th arr. - 18, rue de l'Etoile - 43 80 60 08
Open 8 a.m.-8 p.m. Closed Sun.

Covered with awards and glory, Gérard Hée is a master of blown-sugar decorations. His delicate creations can turn any cake into a festive centerpiece. Hée is also an innovative pastry chef; his best-selling desserts include the exotic Cocos-Nuciféra (chocolate sponge cake, caramel and coconut mousse), the Tilsitt (chocolate mousse studded with diced apricots) and an addictive range of chocolate bonbons (bet you can't eat just one!).

Jean Le Bras

8th arr. - 16, galerie des Marchands, Gare Saint-Lazare
Open 7:30 a.m.-7 p.m. Closed Sat., Sun. & Aug.

In business at the foot of the grand staircase in the teeming Saint-Lazare train station since 1933, Jean Le Bras provides sweet comforts for weary travelers. The traditional pastries are handcrafted: cherry clafoutis, lemon and apricot tarts, buttery Breton galettes studded with candied fruit.

Lecoq

15th arr. - 120, rue Saint-Charles - 45 78 22 15
Open 8:15 a.m.-7:45 p.m. Closed Mon. & Aug.

Dainty, ethereal and lavished with mousse, Lecoq's cakes sport exotic names: Bacumba (a pairing of milk- and bitter-chocolate mousses), Venise (pistachio and coconut mousses laced with bits of candied pineapple), Pommela (raspberry and grapefruit mousses with caramelized apples) and Piémontais (Cointreau mousse on a layer of hazelnut sponge cake, garnished with bitter chocolate).

Lefèvre
12th arr. - 31, rue de Wattignies
43 07 36 69
Open 8 a.m.-8 p.m. Closed Tues. & Aug.

Of all the myriad goodies turned out by this all-purpose sweet shop (pastries, ice cream, chocolates, prepared foods), the cakes, in our opinion, take the cake. We adore the mocha Caraque, the orange Vénitien, the frozen Dame Blanche dessert (pear sorbet and hazelnut parfait) and the sponge cakes, with their feather-light buttercream fillings. We also have a soft spot for the meltingly tender almond tuile cookies, made without a trace of flour.

Lenôtre
16th arr. - 49, av. Victor-Hugo
45 01 71 71
Hours vary from store to store. 9 other branches.

Normandy native Gaston Lenôtre opened his first shop in Paris in 1957. His pastries and elaborate desserts are now internationally recognized as classics: the Opéra, the Plaisir, the Carousel . . . his latest creation is the Fantasme, a voluptuous fantasy in chocolate (chocolate sponge cake and bitter-chocolate mousse).

Mauduit
10th arr. - 54, rue du Faubourg-Saint-Denis - 42 46 43 64
Open 7:15 a.m.-7:30 p.m. (Sun. 7:15 a.m.-1:30 p.m.). Closed Mon. & Aug. Other branch: 12, bd de Denain - 10th arr.

Mauduit's windows, with their glittering displays of flawless little cakes and confections, attract quite an audience. In summer, fruit mousses garnished with fresh fruit or fruit purées sparkle invitingly, while winter brings the delicious Cointreau-flavored Tambourin; the refreshing Pacifique dessert (raspberry and lime bavarian creams) is available year-round.

Millet
7th arr. - 103, rue Saint-Dominique
45 51 49 80
Open 9 a.m.-7 p.m. (Sun. 8 a.m.-1 p.m.). Closed Mon. & Aug.

Jean Millet, whose shop is virtually an institution in the chic area ranks among the foremost practitioners of the art of French pastry. With his executive chef, Denis Ruffel, he turns out superb cakes and desserts that often give starring roles to seasonal fruit. Among Millet's best-sellers are his exceptional pear charlotte, his bitter-chocolate Guanaja and the silken almond-milk Royal with raspberries, pears, oranges and a fresh-tasting raspberry purée.

Le Moule à Gâteaux
94300 Vincennes - 22, rue du Midi
43 28 09 71
Open 9 a.m.-12:30 p.m. & 4 p.m.-7:15 p.m. (Sun. 9 a.m.-noon). Closed Mon. 10 other branches.

This prospering chain specializes in traditional, home-style cakes fashioned by young pastry cooks who care about their craft. They use time-tested recipes that we wish we still had the leisure (and know-how) to prepare in our own kitchens. We love the apricot feuilleté covered with a golden short crust; the Mamita, a poem in chocolate and crème fraîche; and the Carotin: almonds, filberts and carrots.

OYSTERS

Most large Parisian brasseries and many seafood houses have outdoor oyster bars for take-out service. Talented *écaillers* open the oysters (or clams or sea urchins) for you, and many will prepare stunning seafood platters with prawns, 'winkles, shrimp and crab as well. Unless the trays used are of the disposable variety, expect to pay a refundable deposit. (See the "French - Seafood" section of The World's Cuisine in Restaurants.)

Peltier
7th arr. - 66, rue de Sèvres - 47 34 06 62
Open 9:30 a.m.-8 p.m. Closed Mon.

Lucien Peltier's fame as a master pastry chef is well-earned. His most noteworthy achievements include the Ambre (almond sponge cake, praline-chocolate mousse with caramelized walnuts), the Riviera (almond sponge, lime and raspberry mousses) and a textbook example of Black Forest cake, made with real morello cherries.

Stohrer

2nd arr. - 51, rue Montorgueil
42 33 38 20
Open daily 7:30 a.m.-8 p.m.

The rosy corpulent allegories of Fame depicted in Paul Baudry's 1860 murals (he also decorated the Paris Opéra) are pleasant to contemplate while scarfing down a few of Stohrer's divine pastries.

REGIONAL FRENCH SPECIALTIES

Besnier

18th arr. - 28, av. de Saint-Ouen
43 87 65 63
Open 9 a.m.-1 p.m. & 4 p.m.-8 p.m. Closed Sun. & Aug.

Guy Besnier is a hard man to please, and only foods that win his full approval find their way into his shop, a showcase for gourmet specialties from Auvergne, Brittany and Corsica. Among them are tangy dried sausages from Chassagnard à Egletons, Corsican coppa and figatelli (garlicky liver sausage) and a superb assortment of cheeses, featuring tasty farmhouse chèvres.

Aux Bons Produits de France

13th arr. - 107, rue de la Glacière
45 89 44 00
Open 8:30 a.m.-1 p.m. & 4 p.m.-7:30 p.m. (Sat. 8 a.m.-1 p.m. & 4 p.m.-7:30 p.m.). Closed Sun., Mon. & July 14-Aug. 31.

An appetizing array of delicacies from virtually every region of France is on display here: excellent Alsatian ham (by advance order only), pungent Lyonnais sausage wrapped in golden brioche, pâtés en croûte, juniper-smoked ham from Savoie and genuine native quiches Lorraines. The cheese counter holds choice offerings from all over the French countryside.

La Campagne

15th arr. - 111, bd de Grenelle
47 34 77 05
Open 8:30 a.m.-1 p.m. & 3:30 p.m.-8 p.m. (Sun. 8:30 a.m.-1 p.m.). Closed Mon. & Aug.

Michel Christy harbors a special fondness for southwestern France, particularly for the Basque country. All of that region's succulent specialties may be purchased in his shop: pre-served duck and goose, homemade cassoulet with five kinds of meat (56 francs per portion) and authentic Basque pipérade (tomatoes cooked in olive oil with green bell peppers and onions, with lightly beaten eggs and sometimes ham or bacon added) with Bayonne ham (48 francs per portion). That same ham is available spiced up with hot Espelette peppers, and there are also such characteristic charcuteries as blood sausage, ventrêche and old-fashioned terrines (rabbit, duck and country pâté). Although it's unconscionably rich (not to say fattening), we love Christy's version of pork rillettes made with duck fat.

La Cigogne

8th arr. - 61, rue de l'Arcade - 43 87 39 16
Open 8 a.m.-7 p.m. (Sat. 8:30 a.m.-7 p.m.). Closed Sun. & Aug.

This firm turns out innovative food products rooted in the culinary traditions of Alsace: sweet pretzels, slices of Kugelhopf (a yeast cake) thickly dusted with cinnamon, and an unctuous cream-cheese tart. The region's classic dishes are not neglected, however—witness La Cigogne's wonderful strudel, quiche Lorraine, cherry, blueberry and damson-plum tarts and, in the savory category, cervelas (sausages), Weisswurst, Beerwurst and Bratwurst.

Comtesse du Barry

17th arr. - 23, av. de Wagram - 46 22 17 38
Open 10 a.m.-8 p.m. Closed Sun. 3 other branches.

From the Gers in southwestern France comes an extensive line of regional food products: preserved duck and goose, foie gras, fattened duck breasts (available fresh, vacuum-packed), as well as galantines, rillettes, pâtés, prepared foods (in tins or jars) and frozen entrées. Prices are not high, but the quality is uneven.

La Galoche d'Aurillac

11th arr. - 41, rue de Lappe - 47 00 77 15
Open 10 a.m.-midnight. Closed Sun., Mon. & Aug.

Robust fare from Auvergne may be sampled on the spot or taken home from this colorful shop on the rue de Lappe. We highly recommend the pounti (a savory loaf of pork and Swiss chard), the saucisse d'Auvergne, the regional pot-au-feu, the tangy little cabécous goat cheeses and, for dessert, the apple tart flambéed with Calvados. Wash these specialties down with sturdy local wines like Marcillac and Saint-Pourçain. The small selection of rustic brandies includes a Lou Rouergat flavored with walnuts or peaches (70 francs).

Jean-Claude et Nanou

17th arr. - 46, rue Legendre - 42 27 15 08
Open 9 a.m.-1 p.m. & 4 p.m.-8 p.m. Closed Mon.

Here's the sort of country food we can never get enough of. Jean-Claude and Nanou sell flavorful sausages dried under the ashes of a smoldering fire, aromatic mountain sausage and fresh Tomme (an unmatured cheese with a distinctive "barnyard" taste).

Produits d'Auvergne

1st arr. - 102, rue Saint-Honoré
42 36 02 00
Open 7:30 a.m.-1 p.m. & 4 p.m.-8 p.m. Closed Sun., Mon. & July 14-Aug. 31.

You can count on finding excellent traditional charcuterie from the Aveyron region at this appealing shop. Specialties include fricandeaux (fresh pork sausage wrapped in caul fat), fritons (minced pork meat and innards mixed with pork fat) and rich pork-liver confit. Typical regional cheeses are also on hand: Cantal, Laguiole, Roquefort. And to slice into all these savory goodies, buy yourself a trusty Laguiole pocket knife, manufactured in that part of south-central France.

Aux Produits de Bretagne et des Pyrénées

5th arr. - 42, bd Saint-Germain
43 54 72 96
Open 9 a.m.-10 p.m. Closed June 1-Oct. 15.

How is it that foods from two such far-flung regions share shelf space in a single shop? Simply because François Miras hails from the Pyrénées, while Madame Miras is a native of Brittany. So alongside the superb mountain-cured bacon, sheep's-milk cheese, Tarbais beans and delicious southwestern confits, you'll find jars of cèpes preserved in oil, hearty rural breads, sausages and other fine produce from Brittany.

Chez Teil

11th arr. - 6, rue de Lappe - 47 00 41 28
Open 9 a.m.-1 p.m. & 3:30 p.m.-7:30 p.m. (Sun. 9 a.m.-1 p.m.). Closed Mon. & Aug.

The turn-of-the-century-decorated shop is home to a mouth-watering selection of authentic Auvergnat charcuterie, processed by Patrick Teil himself at his family's meat-curing plant in Cayrols. By eliminating the middle man, Teil can market his hams, sausages, spreads, pigs' trotters and pâtés at attractive prices. Try his cheeses too, along with the fine crusty flat bread (fouace) and countrified sweets on display.

Terrier

9th arr. - 58, rue des Martyrs - 48 78 96 45
Open 8:15 a.m.-1 p.m. & 4 p.m.-7:30 p.m. (Sun. 8:15 a.m.-noon & 4 p.m.-7:30 p.m.). Closed Mon. & Aug.

For generous Lyonnais charcuterie, Terrier is *the* outpost in Paris. Among the typical treats on hand are sausage studded with truffles and pistachios, golden-brown pâtés en croûte, pike and salmon quenelles, Burgundy ham, head cheese and genuine rosette sausage, the pride of Lyons.

A la Ville de Rodez

4th arr. - 22, rue Vieille-du-Temple
48 87 79 36
Open 8 a.m.-1 p.m. & 3 p.m.-7:30 p.m. Closed Sun. & Mon.

Monsieur Batut has represented the earthy tradition of Auvergnat charcuterie in Paris for many years. His citron-studded fouace (flat bread) is ambrosial, his terrines are legendary, and his zesty dried sausage is among the most flavorful we've had the pleasure to taste—anywhere. Ville de Rodez is the place to find all the classic cuts of pork that go into a classic potée (mixed boiled pork and vegetables).

SEAFOOD

Le Bar à Huîtres

14th arr. - 112, bd Montparnasse
43 20 71 01
Open 10 a.m.-midnight (July & Aug. 10 a.m.-2:30 p.m & 6 p.m.-midnight). Parking: Montparnasse.

At the outdoor oyster bar, you can purchase dozens of succulent oysters, opened for you by the nimble-fingered *écaillers* and neatly arranged on disposable trays (no deposit, no return). A refreshing treat, this!

La Langouste
2nd arr. - 8, pl. des Victoires - 42 60 96 53
Open daily 10 a.m.-11:30 a.m. Orders accepted day before purchase.

The last gastronomic bastion remaining on the place des Victoires continues to resist the onslaught of the ever-more-numerous fashion boutiques. Live crustaceans (fished from basement tanks) may be acquired here, on condition that you place your order 24 hours in advance. Specialties include rock lobsters from Brittany, from the Canary Islands and from South Africa and Mauretania, as well as lobsters from North American waters.

Poissonnerie du Dôme
14th arr. - 4, rue Delambre - 43 35 23 95
Open 7 a.m.-1 p.m. & 4 p.m.-7:30 p.m. (Sun. 7 a.m.-1 p.m.). Closed Mon. & Wed.

The lucky residents of Montparnasse can satisfy their urge for seafood at this marvelous fish store, one of the very best in Paris. Manager Jean-Pierre Lopez admits only "noble" fish (sole, turbot, lotte, sea bass and the like) to his classy emporium (decorated by Slavik, no less). The merchandise, from French (particularly Breton) and foreign waters, is snapped up by such eminent restaurants as L'Ambroisie, Duquesnoy, L'Apicius and Gérard et Nicole. Need we mention that these rare and succulent denizens of the deep command regally high prices?

WINE & SPIRITS

L'Arbre à Vin
12th arr. - 2-4, rue du Rendez-Vous
43 46 81 10, 43 43 40 06
Open 8:30 a.m.-12:30 p.m. & 4 p.m.-8 p.m. (Sun. 8:30 a.m.-12:30 p.m.). Closed Mon.

This fascinating wine shop dates back to 1893. Present owner Jean-Michel Rotrou is a wine fanatic; he tirelessly tours the vineyards of France to discover the best regional bottlings. His superb vaulted cellars, decorated with an interesting collection of old farming tools, house Bordeaux both great and modest (Fourcas-Dupré '85 sells for 74 francs; Fort-de-Latour '79 goes for 195 francs) and a comprehensive array of Burgundies. Rounding out the selection are good country wines and some Italian and Spanish bottles (Coronas '82 from

Torres). We also like to check out the assortment of Corcellet gourmet groceries upstairs.

Jean-Baptiste Besse
5th arr. - 48, rue de la Montagne-Sainte-Geneviève - 43 25 35 80
Open 10:30 a.m.-1:30 p.m. & 4:30 p.m.-8:30 p.m. (Sun. 11 a.m.-1:30 p.m.). Closed Mon. & Aug. Parking: pl. Maubert.

Now well into his 80s, Jean-Baptiste Besse must be credited with having converted many a Parisian to the cult of Bacchus. Though the shop where he has spent some 50 years may look like a colossal shambles, Besse will infallibly have just the bottle you desire, from a modest red Cheverny to a majestic Château Cheval-Blanc. His choice of dessert wines (Sauternes, Banyuls, Beaumes-de-Venises) always flabbergasts us, as does his judicious selection of Cognacs and ports.

Cave J.-Ch. Estève
4th arr. - 10, rue de la Cerisaie
42 72 33 05
Open 9:30 a.m.-12:30 p.m. & 2:30 p.m.-7:30 p.m. Closed Sun. & Mon. Parking: pl. de la Bastille. Other branch: 292, rue Saint-Jacques - 5th arr. - 46 34 69 78, closed Sun. & Mon. (except in Dec.).

For Jean-Christophe Estève, wine isn't just a business; it's more like a sacred vocation. Endowed with a formidable palate, this Gascon native declares that every region of France produces good wines—it's just a question of tracking them down. Given his pedagogic bent (he used to be a Spanish teacher), he'll be happy to give you a lesson in comparing the relative merits of a jaunty Côtes-de-Duras, a superb Château Villars '83 from Fronsac, a Domaine de Pibarnon (Bandol) and an aristocratic Domaine de Chevalier.

La Cave aux Champagnes
6th arr. - 15, rue des Grands-Augustins
46 33 01 54
Open 11:30 a.m.-8 p.m. (Fri. until 10 p.m.). Closed Sun. & 3 wks. in Aug. Parking: Mazarine.

Unreconstructed Champagne buffs rejoice! Here's a place where you can indulge your passion for blanc de blancs and blanc de noirs; where bottles, magnums and jeroboams contain nothing but premium French bubbly. Three dozen of the best Champagne firms are represented. With luck, you may even happen upon such rarities as the Clos du Mesnil from Krug, or Bollinger "RD" (*récemment dégorgé*).

Cave de Gambrinus

4th arr. - 13-15, rue des Blancs-Manteaux
48 87 81 92
Open 11 a.m.-1:30 p.m. & 3 p.m.-8 p.m. (Sun. & Mon. 11 a.m.-3 p.m.). Parking: Cave de Gambrinus, BHV.

Owner Mike Courvoisier has two complementary enthusiasms: whisky and beer. Ever on the trail of the best scotch whisky, he has acquired some 200 brands, including an extremely rare Speyside malt (21 years old) that sells for the tidy sum of 1,385 francs (it comes in a crystal decanter). And then there are the 400-odd beers of which Courvoisier is justifiably proud. Among the French labels are northern brews (Jenlain, Enfants de Gayant), Alsatian beers and imports from Belgium, Germany, England and elsewhere. A small but choice selection of tequila, mescal and aquavit round out the intoxicating array.

La Cave de Georges Duboeuf

8th arr. - 9, rue Marbeuf - 47 20 71 23
Open 9 a.m.-1 p.m. & 3 p.m.-7:30 p.m. Closed Sun., Mon. & Aug.

What Lionel Poilâne is to bread, Georges Duboeuf is to Beaujolais: an assurance of quality. His Paris shop stocks excellent representative from all the villages of Beaujolais, but Duboeuf is not parochial by any means. His numerous wine-making chums all over France supply him with (for example) fine Burgundies from de Montille, de Vogüé, Rousseau and Trapet, Métaireau's Muscadets, Guigal's Côtes-du-Rhône and Alsatian vintages from Trimbach. Store manager Alain Bosser is a reliable source of sound advice.

Caves Pétrissans

17th arr. - 30 bis, av. Niel - 42 27 83 84
Open 9:30 a.m.-1:30 p.m. & 3 p.m.-8 p.m. (Sat. 9:30 a.m.-1:30 p.m.). Closed Sun., Aug. & 1 wk. in Feb.

For many a year this renowned Parisian *cave* has been a magnet for local oenophiles, owing to its extensive selection of fine wines. On a given day, a browser might come across an uncommon red wine from Corsica, the appealing Roussette de Seyssel from Savoie, Clos du Marquis ("second" wine of Saint-Julien's Château Léoville-las-Cases), Jaboulet's Saint-Joseph and tasty first-growth Champagne from Chigny-les-Roses. Sharing shelf space with the wines are some highly reputed Cognacs and fruit brandies, Armagnacs (vintages on hand include 1893, 1900, 1912 . . .) and rare whiskies, like the elegant Auchentoshan from the Scottish Lowlands and the peaty, invigorating Bowmore from the Isle of Islay.

Caves de la Madeleine

8th arr. - Cité Berryer, 25, rue Royale
42 65 92 40
Open 9 a.m.-7 p.m. (Sat. 10 a.m.-2 p.m.). Closed Sun. Parking: Madeleine, Concorde.

French winegrowers ought to erect a statue in honor of British wine merchant Steven Spurrier. A score of years ago, when wine was not the height of fashion, Spurrier traveled unflaggingly through French vineyards, going down into the cellars with the *vignerons*, sampling, judging, buying. He opened the first wine-tasting school in Paris (L'Académie du Vin), and helped make celebrities of then-unknown growers. With Spurrier's help, oenophiles discovered Guigal's Côte-Rôtie, Auguste Clape's Cornas and the premium Châteauneuf-du-Pape from Château de Beaucastel and Vieux-Télégraphe. Even now, every wine displayed on the shelves of his tiny shop near the Madeleine is personally tasted, retasted and selected by Spurrier himself. Rule Britannia!

Les Caves du Savour Club

14th arr. - 120-139, bd Montparnasse
43 27 12 06
Open 10 a.m.-8 p.m. (Sun. until 12:30 p.m.). Closed Mon. Parking: Raspail-Montparnasse, Savour.

The Savour Club is a wine warehouse that has managed to rise above the grayness of its underground premises (a parking garage) with a bright, light decor. Inside, you'll find bottlings appropriate for every occasion, each with a card bearing an informative description and comments. There are wines for everyday drinking (country wines at 10 or 12 francs), as well as special treats for connoisseurs (Château Haut-Brion '82 for 600 francs, Richebourg '84 priced at 250 francs).

Jean Danflou

1st arr. - 36, rue de Mont-Thabor
42 61 51 09
Open 8 a.m.-1 p.m. & 2 p.m.-6 p.m. Closed Sat., Sun. & Aug. 1-15. Parking: Vendôme.

Jean Danflou sells absolutely exquisite, fragrant, heady eaux-de-vie (clear fruit brandies) distilled especially for him in Alsace. You must sample his extraordinary aged Kirsch, his Poire Williams, his perfumed Framboise. A line of elegant Cognacs, Armagnacs and Calvados is also proposed, along with a small selection of wines from Burgundy and Bordeaux.

Grands Millésimes

8th arr. - 8, rue de l'Arcade - 42 66 98 39
Open 10 a.m.-8 p.m. Closed Sun. Parking: Madeleine.

In business since Christmas 1987, this smallish wine shop near the Madeleine, housed in the cellars of a former Ursuline convent, stocks more than 400 different French and foreign wines. An appreciable selection of older Bordeaux vintages is available, and prices are often quite interesting. Your choice will be expertly guided by owner de la Roche or his associate, Christian Pechoutre, elected Best Young Sommelier of 1988.

King Henry

5th arr. - 44, rue des Boulangers
43 54 54 37
Open 11 a.m.-10 p.m. Closed Sun. & Mon.

King Henry invites all the world's best beers to take their places on his shelves: Irish stout stands next to English ale, German lager next to Belgian Trappist and Gueuze brews. Here is your chance to discover rarities like Orval and Duvel d'outre Quiévrain, or the remarkable Paulaner Weissbier, brewed from wheat. As if that weren't enough, King Henry also offers an extraordinary range of whiskies—over 200 labels are on hand to fascinate connoisseurs.

Legrand Filles et Fils

2nd arr. - 12, galerie Vivienne - 42 60 07 12
Open 8:30 a.m.-7 p.m. (Sat. 8:30 a.m.-1 p.m. & 3 p.m.-7 p.m.). Closed Sun., Mon. & 15 days in Aug.

Even if his wines were not half as interesting as they are, Lucien Legrand's wine shop would be worth a visit for its old-fashioned charm and warm atmosphere. Daughter Francine offers a wide selection of carefully chosen, inexpensive country wines from up-and-coming growers in the South and the Val de Loire, along with a sampling of prestigious Burgundies and Bordeaux (wines from average years, affordably priced). Also, a few uncommon bottlings: luscious Muscat de Beaumes-de-Venise, Vin de Paille du Jura and some excellent vintage ports.

Nicolas

4th arr. - 35, rue Rambuteau - 48 87 97 49
Open 9 a.m.-midnight. Closed Sun. & Mon. Parking: Georges-Pompidou. 2 other branches: 13, rue de Buci - 6th arr. - 46 33 13 35; 8, av. de Wagram - 8th arr. - 42 27 22 07.

Looking sprucer than ever with its new gold-and-bordeaux decor, the familiar Nicolas stores continue to present a diverse and appealing range of wines for every budget. The monthly promotions are definitely worth following. They often feature unfamiliar French wines, imports (Spanish, Italian, even Australian bottlings) and novelties at attractive prices. The three (of over 400) shops we've listed above are open until midnight.

Peuchet

16th arr. - 95, av. Victor-Hugo
45 53 83 23
Open 9 a.m.-12:30 p.m. & 2 p.m.-7 p.m. Closed Sat., Sun. & Aug. Parking: Victor-Hugo.

This rather austere shopfront may not appear conducive to Bacchic abandon, but then Peuchet does not take the business of wine lightly. For a century now it has supplied the sixteenth arrondissement with house-bottled wines for everyday tippling, and with grand bottles for Sunday lunch and sundry family feasts. Jacques Peuchet favors the Burgundies of Louis Latour, fine Bordeaux (Cheval-Blanc '81), and he boasts a sublime collection of eaux-de-vie (clear fruit brandies) and Cognacs.

Michel Renaud

12th arr. - 12, pl. de la Nation
43 07 98 93
Open 9:30 a.m.-1:30 p.m. & 3 p.m.-8:45 p.m. (Sun. 3 p.m.-8:45 p.m. & Mon. 9:30 a.m.-1:30 p.m.).

Michel Renaud owns an estate in the Gers region of southwestern France, where he distills his own tasty Armagnacs from Folle Blanche grapes. His preference in wines runs to the earthy and authentic: frisky *vins de table* from the South sold by the liter; an '86 Bordeaux with not a trace of added sugar; Vigneau's traditional dark and tannic Madiran; La Ina sherry. Renaud's collecitons of Bordeaux and Burgundies are quite worthy.

Le Repaire de Bacchus

17th arr. - 39, rue des Acacias - 43 80 09 68
Open 10:30 a.m.-1:30 p.m. & 3:30 p.m.-8 p.m. Closed Sun. morning & Mon. Parking: pl. de l'Etoile.

Wine maven Steven Spurrier is now associated with this growing chain of wine shops. Splendid Burgundies and fine vintage Bordeaux are featured, of course, but you will be impressed with the wide assortment of Côtes-du-Rhône and Provençal offerings, from "village" wines to sumptuous Hermitages.

Les Toques Gourmandes

17th arr. - 1, rue d'Armaillé - 47 66 19 04
Open 11 a.m.-1 p.m. & 2 p.m.-9 p.m. Closed Sun. & Mon. Parking: rue des Acacias.

Like Alexandre Dumas's, these Three Musketeers are really four: Dutournier, Faugeron, Fournier and Morot-Gaudry. These noted chefs have banded together and launched a wine shop, with the help and invaluable advice of Jean-Claude Jambon, crowned *Meilleur Sommelier du Monde*. The inventory features gems from the finest growers in France: Dauvissat's Chablis, Auriot's Morey-Saint-Denis and an enticing range of Bordeaux.

Au Verger de la Madeleine

8th arr. - 4, bd Malesherbes - 42 65 51 99
Open 10 a.m.-1:30 p.m. & 3 p.m.-8 p.m. Closed Sun. Parking: Madeleine, Malesherbes.

Jean-Pierre Legras's staggering collection encompasses such unique and extravagant bottles as a Cognac Impérial Tiffon 1810, a Porto Barros dated 1833 (once the property of the French ambassador to Lisbon), a Solera Sercial Madeira from 1835 and a Clos-Peyraguey 1893. Such treasures are not for everyday drinking, but they make impressive, indeed unforgettable, gifts. All the first growths of Bordeaux (Cheval-Blanc, Pétrus . . .) are on hand as well, along with superb Burgundies from Montrachet and Meursault, and hard-to-find wines like Château-Grillet and Jasnières. And inexpensive offerings from the Côtes-d'Auvergne, Saint-Pourçain and Saumur.

Vins Rares et de Collection–Thustrup

17th arr. - 3, rue Laugier - 47 66 58 15
Open 10 a.m.-12:30 p.m. & 1:30 p.m.-7 p.m. Closed Sun. & Aug. 1-15.

Peter Thustrup's unquenchable passion for old, rare vintages leads him to auction rooms all over the world, in search of such finds as antique Yquem, ancient Pétrus and Mouton-Rothschild from another age (which sell, incidentally, for about 18,000 francs—just to give you an idea). Bordeaux, obviously, is well represented, but Thustrup can also show you some exceptional Vendanges Tardives from Alsace, mature Burgundies and collectible Côtes-du-Rhône.

GIFTS

Affaire d'Homme

6th arr. - 15, rue Bréa - 46 34 69 33
Open 10:30 a.m.-7:30 p.m. (Mon. 2 p.m.-7:30 p.m.). Closed Sun. & 1 wk. in Aug. Parking: bd Montparnasse. Cards: V, AE, DC, MC.

For that confirmed, set-in-his-ways bachelor who can't stand any colors other than gray, black and red, here is a collection of sleek, useful and handsome gadgets: foldable binoculars (910 francs), or a wood-and-resin valet that will press his trousers (just plug it in) while it simultaneously serves as a suit hanger and a

catchall for loose change and such. There are also gag gifts, like a lighter in the form of a fist (165 francs), brightly colored pens that grow longer when you take off the cap (get it?) and—are you ready?—hand-painted ties.

Affinités

8th arr. - 17, rue de Miromesnil
47 42 00 21
Open 10 a.m.-7 p.m. Closed Sun. & Aug. Parking: Hôtel Bristol. Cards: V.

Gray walls and gray carpet form a showcase for contemporary "masculine" knickknacks for the office and the home designed by the likes of Christian Duc (a hammered-metal dish), Hervé Houplain (cast-aluminum desk accessories) and Garouste et Bonnetti (sculpture lamps). We also found some handsome bibelots by Alessi and an amusing collection of ballpoint pens (100 francs), note pads and cigarette boxes by Spalding and Bros.

DESIGNERS' SHOWCASE

Ettore Sottsass, a brilliant exponent of Italian design, dreamed up this striking gallery, where the works of today's hottest designers are exhibited twice a year: Yves Gastou, 12, rue Bonaparte, 6th arr., 46 34 72 17.

Allure

6th arr. - 17, rue de Tournon - 43 54 86 00
Open 10:30 a.m.-7 p.m. (Mon. 1:30 p.m.-7 p.m.). Closed Sun. & first 2 wks. in Aug. Parking: Saint-Sulpice. No cards.

A native of Casablanca, Michel Taurel has a deep-rooted love for the simplicity, purity and allure of the color white. In the shop he owns with Laurence Aboucaya, the hand-picked objects range in tone from iceberg to pearl to eggshell to ivory. Some of the gift ideas are luxurious (hand-embroidered table linens edged in snowy lace), others are useful (a sleek fruit bowl designed by Enzo Mari, for 368 francs, or stainless-steel cutlery with pearly handles, 48 francs), and still others are inexpensive and amusing (pure-white pencils, just 6 francs each).

Atelier Jacques Leguennec

6th arr. - 14, rue de Seine - 43 26 28 24
Open 10 a.m.-6 p.m. Closed Sun., Mon. & Aug. Parking: Mazarine. No cards.

From Jacques Leguennec's lathe emerge handsomely crafted wooden furniture and decorative objects. Inspired by North American traditions, he recently created two lines of furniture, one in stained wood and the other in brushed iron, with a neoclassic look. In his Left Bank shop you'll also find Oriental crafts: blue Chinese porcelain, cherrywood trays and

baskets of all descriptions. Collagist Pascale Laurent, whose work is on display in the shop, puts together personalized "pell-mells" using materials provided by the customer (a framed "pell-mell" sells for about 4,500 francs).

Axis

11th arr. - 13, rue de Charonne
48 06 79 10
Open 10:30 a.m.-1 p.m. & 2 p.m.-7:30 p.m. Closed Sun. Parking: Ledru-Rollin. Cards: V.

Witty, imaginative and amusing gift ideas are the Axis trademark. But this policy does not exclude the useful: the Alessi coffeepot and the Dualite toaster are trendy as all get-out, but they also help you get breakfast on the table efficiently! Axis now produces its own collection of vases, picture frames, tableware and rugs, all sporting highly unusual designs.

RENT-A-DECOR

If you're setting up house in Paris for a limited time, you may wish to consult Soubrier, a company that rents furniture, appliances, curtains, rugs . . . everything to make your temporary home cozy and comfortable. For an estimate, contact Soubrier, 14, rue de Reuilly, 12th arr., 43 72 93 71.

Au Chat Dormant

6th arr. - 13, rue du Cherche-Midi
45 49 48 63
Open 11 a.m.-7 p.m. (Mon. 2 p.m.-7p.m.). Closed Sun. Parking: Saint-Sulpice, Bon Marché. Cards: V.

Within these walls the cat is king. Felines are featured on postcards (4.50 francs) and paintings (a special room serves as a gallery), and they come in bronze (antiques, about 2,500 francs), ceramic and linen and are embroidered on cushions (460 francs) and printed on umbrellas. Run by warm-hearted cat fanciers, the shop also serves as a clearinghouse for (real) kittens; if you wish to adopt one, just post an ad on the bulletin board.

Chaumette

7th arr. - 45, av. Duquesne - 42 73 18 54
Open 10 a.m.-6:30 p.m. Closed Sat., Sun. &
Aug. Cards: V.

Gérard Chaumette is no ordinary dealer in knickknacks and bibelots. He has a genuine passion for faïence (earthenware decorated with opaque colored glazes) and glass objects that reproduce and reinterpret nature. On our last visit to his enchanting shop, we found an extraordinary lamp base with mauve-tinged irises; glazed ceramic cachepots displaying bunches of grapes or vegetable still lifes; and stunning reproductions of ancient Roman glass. Prices for these small marvels range from 150 francs to the 6,000-franc neighborhood.

L'Entrepôt

16th arr. - 50, rue de Passy - 45 25 64 17
Open 10:30 a.m.-7 p.m. (Fri. & Sat. until 7:30
p.m.). Closed Sun. Cards: V, AE, MC.

Here's a treasure trove of clever gift items and household gadgets that will charm even the most blasé shopper. We saw a funny little alarm clock disguised as a deep-sea diver (550 francs), a miniature tool chest hidden inside a model car (355 francs) and an impressively diverse array of stationery, tableware, clothing—even jams and jellies! A delightful bazaar, improbably located in the classy Passy neighborhood.

Forestier

16th arr. - 35, rue Duret - 45 00 08 61
Open 10:30 a.m.-7:30 p.m. (Mon. noon-7:30
p.m.). Closed Sun. Parking: Maillot. Cards: V.

In the 1930s, it was a cheese and dairy shop, but an ex–landscape gardener has transformed the place into an original boutique that follows the rhythms of the seasons and holidays. Forestier carries all the tableware and decorative touches one would need to create a festive atmosphere for Halloween, Christmas, Valentine's Day, April Fool's and so on, as well as an attractive selection of handcrafted pottery and garden accessories for year-round use.

Homme Sweet Homme

4th arr. - 45, rue Vieille-du-Temple
48 04 94 99
Open 10:30 a.m.-8 p.m. Closed Sun. Parking:
rue Vieille-du-Temple. Cards: V.

Despite the cutesy-pie name, this shop stocks an interesting variety of (primarily masculine) gifts in a grand range of prices (15 to 2,000 francs). Wallets in all sizes, attractive fountain pens, geometric photo holders from the 1940s (300 francs) and tiny tools (130 to 250 francs) are just a few of the clever and useful items on sale. For the man who has everything (including a sense of humor), there's even a little fan in the form of a robot (just 530 francs).

Anna Joliet

1st arr. - 9, rue de Beaujolais - 42 96 55 13
Open 10 a.m.-7 p.m. (Mon. 2 p.m.-7 p.m.).
Closed Sun. & Aug. Parking: Bourse. Cards: V,
AE.

Anna Joliet sells music boxes in a delicious little shop under the Palais-Royal arcades. The mechanisms are Swiss, dependable and made to last, while the boxes themselves have a pleasingly old-fashioned look. Prices vary according to the complexity of the design and the number of tunes and notes the box plays. The simplest, an ideal gift for a newborn (whose name and birthdate can be engraved on the box), costs about 140 francs. The finest music box in the store, made of rare wood with a sophisticated mechanism that plays four tunes and well over a hundred notes, will set you back the tidy sum of 30,000 francs.

Rita Kim

10th arr. - 79, quai de Valmy - 46 07 50 88
Open 12:30 p.m.-7 p.m. Closed Sun., Mon. &
Aug. No cards.

We love Rita's collection of plastic stuff from the '60s: There's tableware, campy knickknacks to accent your "day-core" and irresistibly kitsch costume jewelry—don't miss the "Jesus" watch with the name of an apostle at each hour; it's the height of taste, and a steal at just 420 francs.

Shizuka

2nd arr. - 49, av. de l'Opéra - 42 61 54 61
Open 10 a.m.-7:30 p.m. Closed Sun. Parking: Saint-Honoré, Vendôme. Cards: V, AE, DC.

For years the avenue de l'Opéra has been a mecca for Japanese tourists. But of late they've been joined by Parisians who want to get a look at the best in contemporary Japanese design—and that's at Shizuka, a new, sleek, upscale shop. On the ground floor, clean-lined desk accessories and stationery are featured, along with robots and mechanical toys. A downstairs gallery showcases recent creations by Japanese designers, while the top floor is devoted to elegant tableware and cutlery, toilet articles and linens. It's hard to leave empty-handed, especially since prices start at the reasonable sum of 20 francs.

Tant qu'il y aura des Hommes

6th arr. - 23, rue du Cherche-Midi
45 48 48 17
Open 10:30 a.m.-7 p.m. (Mon. noon-7 p.m.). Closed Sun. & Aug. Cards: V.

Among the handsome and practical gifts for men on sale here, we particularly liked the silk boxer shorts (320 francs), the luggage (with lots of detachable pockets) and leather goods that look as if they could withstand hard wear, a classic Irish crewneck sweater (490 francs) and a good-looking leather-trimmed jacket for rough-and-tumble types (an excellent buy at 690 francs).

Territoire

8th arr. - 30, rue Boissy-d'Anglas
42 66 22 13
Open 10:30 a.m.-7 p.m. Closed Sun. & 2 wks. in Aug. Parking: Madeleine. Cards: V, AE.

What was once a hardware store is now a bright and spacious shop brimming with ideas for leisure activities. The stock changes with the seasons; in spring, the gardening section burgeons with Wilkinson tools and terracotta pots. In summer, sporting goods take over a greater share of shelf space (we saw an impressive foldable black canvas boat for 4,500 francs), and in winter, fireside games feature

more prominently. There are plenty of amusing gifts for children, including reproductions of old-fashioned board games and some spectacular kites. Prices range from about 50 to 5,000 francs.

H. et G. Thomas

5th arr. - 36, bd Saint-Germain
46 33 57 50
Open 11 a.m.-1 p.m. & 2 p.m.-8 p.m. Closed Sun. & Mon. Cards: V, AE.

This was one of the first men's gift stores to appear on the scene; it has since been copied many times over. No useless gadgets encumber these shelves, just useful, well-designed gifts and accessories for the refined, thinking man. The adjustable halogen microlamp (560 francs) is a good example of the sort of merchandise the management favors, as is the money converter (120 francs) for the astute traveler. Men and women alike appreciate Thomas's sturdy, attractive line of luggage.

Topka

4th arr. - 5, rue d'Arcole - 43 54 73 27
Open 10 a.m.-7 p.m. Closed Sun. & Mon. (except in summer). Parking: Notre-Dame. Cards: V.

A charming little emporium just steps away from Notre-Dame, for twenty years Topka has specialized in tableware and kitchenware, including baskets, pretty printed linens and droll gift items. The selection is renewed regularly, so there are always surprises in store: On a recent visit we found a ball-shaped alarm clock (220 francs) that turns off when it's thrown on the floor.

La Tuile à Loup

5th arr. - 35, rue Daubenton - 47 07 28 90
Open 10:30 a.m.-1 p.m. & 3 p.m.-7:30 p.m. (Sun. 11 a.m.-7 p.m.). Closed Mon. Parking: Patriarches. Cards: V, AE, DC.

As peaceful as a village square, this exceptional shop carries traditional handcrafts from all over France. You'll find beautiful glazed pottery from Savoie, Provence, Burgundy and Alsace, and stoneware from Puisaye and Le

Maine. There are handmade wooden objects, rustic tableware, wrought-iron weather vanes and decorative tiles for the kitchen, bath or

fireplace. Fascinating, too, are the many books documenting popular art forms and regional history.

HOME

BATH & KITCHENWARE

BATH

Bath Shop
16th arr. - 3, rue Gros - 45 20 10 60
Open 10 a.m.-12:30 p.m. & 2 p.m.-7 p.m. (Sun. & Mon. 2 p.m.-7 p.m.). Cards: V, AE.
Everything for the bathroom is on sale here—from sinks to denture glasses. Prices vary widely; the sink will set you back 6,230 francs, while the glass (real glass—it's even etched) costs just 35 francs. And there are lots of accessories: thick towels, terry robes, scented bubble bath and chic shower curtains.

A l'Epi d'Or
5th arr. - 17, rue des Bernardins
46 33 08 47
Open 11 a.m.-7 p.m. Closed Sun., Mon. & Aug. Parking: Saint-Germain. Cards: V.
After nearly a quarter century on the rue Saint-Jacques, this highly reputed bath shop has transferred its stock to more spacious quarters, under a vast skylight. Lovely antique and reproduction bathroom sinks are the main attraction, along with period and a few contemporary accessories. A genuine 1930s sink commands a minimum tariff of 7,000 francs, while a reproduction goes for 3,000 francs. An antique soap dish, however, will cost only about 600 francs.

CUTLERY

Isler
1st arr. - 44, rue Coquillière - 42 33 20 92
Open 9 a.m.-noon & 2 p.m.-6 p.m. Closed Sat., Sun. & Aug. No cards.
Not a single element of the shop's decor has changed in 50 years, but then neither has the excellent quality of the Swiss knives (including the world-famous Tour Eiffel brand), for

which Isler is known. All the great French chefs select their kitchen knives from among the 100 models in stock; and there are 40 types of pocketknives to pick from as well. The firm's latest success is a survival pocketknife with (at least) 29 functions (multiuse pliers, ballpoint pen, miniscrewdriver, you get the idea) that comes in a leather carrying case equipped with a compass, sharpening stone, mirror. . . . Alas, now the regular old penknife seems awfully ordinary in comparison.

Kindal
2nd arr. - 33, av. de l'Opéra - 42 61 70 78
Open 10 a.m.-6:30 p.m. (Sat. 11 a.m.-6 p.m.). Closed Sun. Cards: V, AE, DC, MC.
Faithful to its long family tradition, Kindal has carefully preserved its handsome mahogany paneling that dates back to the shop's grand opening in 1905. Knives of every sort are on view: table, hunting and pocket representatives with wooden or precious horn handles. Prices start at about 30 francs and rise to 12,000 francs for certain collectors' items. Knives are also repaired and sharpened on the premises.

KITCHENWARE

La Carpe
8th arr. - 14, rue Tronchet - 47 42 73 25
Open 9:30 a.m.-6:45 p.m. (Mon. 1:30 p.m.-6:45 p.m.). Closed Sun. & Aug. Parking: pl. de la Madeleine. No cards.
For nearly 70 years the Loiseau family has furnished chefs and knowledgeable home cooks with utensils at the cutting edge of kitchen technology. All the wares are intelligently displayed by type, so that you can find what you want quickly. The sales staff is friendly and generous with its good advice. Another store in the neighborhood, A la Petite Carpe (13, rue Vignon), carries a selection of gadgets and gizmos for the table.

Culinarion

17th arr. - 83 bis, rue de Courcelles
42 27 63 32
*Open 10 a.m.-7 p.m. (Mon. 2 p.m.-7 p.m.).
Closed Sun. & Aug. Cards: V.*

Culinarion is a dependable source of kitchen classics (cast-iron pots, charlotte molds, tart pans) at reasonable prices. But adventurous cooks will love the selection of arcana and novelties, like the combination mills that let you salt and pepper with one hand (99 francs) or the shopping bag specially designed for frozen foods (300 francs). We're also quite fond of the shop's handsome selection of barware and tableware.

Dehillerin

1st arr. - 18-20, rue Coquillière
42 36 53 13
Open 8 a.m.-12:30 p.m. & 2 p.m.-6 p.m. Closed Sun. Parking: Forum des Halles. Cards: V, MC.

Since 1820, the cream of the French food establishment have purchased their *batterie de cuisine* at Dehillerin. More recently, they have been joined by large numbers of American and Japanese culinary enthusiasts. Dehillerin stocks a truly amazing range of covetable cookware, superb knives and copper pots (a series of five

---

HANDCRAFTED POTTERY

The following shops are sources of exquisite hand-thrown pottery from the famed ateliers of Biot, Anduze, Castelnaudary and Tuscany. Custom orders are accepted, but expect to wait six months for delivery. Le Cèdre Rouge, 22, ave. Victoria, 1st arr., 42 33 71 05; Forestier, 35, rue Duret, 16th arr., 45 00 08 61; Jardins Imaginaires, 9 bis, rue d'Assas, 6th arr., 42 22 90 03; Terra Cotta, 7, rue du Pont-aux-Choux, 3rd arr., 40 27 05 93; La Tuile à Loup, 35, rue Daubenton, 5th arr., 47 07 28 90.

---

sells for about 960 francs—but that's without the lids). We suggest you come early in the day to shop here, don't expect much help from the staff and, above all, don't be in a hurry.

Kitchen Bazaar

17th arr. - 142, rue de Courcelles
43 80 77 37
*Open 10 a.m.-7 p.m. (Mon. 2 p.m.-7 p.m.).
Closed Sun. & 1 wk. in mid-Aug. Cards: V.*

Kitchenware from Kitchen Bazaar is always both high-style and high-performance. Lately, the house favorites have been high-tech as well: thick, matte-black plastic storage units, black melamine salad bowls (228 francs) and lacquered-chrome wire baskets (45 francs). The latest small appliances are always available here, with a preference for those with the sleekest designs. There's an interesting selection of cookbooks, too.

Geneviève Lethu

1st arr. - Forum des Halles, 2nd level
42 97 55 94
*Open 9:15 a.m.-7 p.m. (Mon. 2 p.m.-7 p.m.).
Closed Sun. Parking: Forum des Halles. Cards: V.*

There are at least 70 Geneviève Lethu shops, with their vast selections of bright, practical, cheerful kitchen furniture, utensils, tableware and linen, scattered all over France. The ever-growing collections of affordably priced dishes in lots of pretty colors and patterns are coordinated with fabric or wipe-clean tablecloths. We also particularly like the attractive, inexpensive glassware in myriad shapes and sizes (for example, the 28-franc lovely Champagne flute).

Mora

1st arr. - 13, rue Montmartre - 45 08 19 24
Open 8:30 a.m.-5:30 p.m. (Sat. noon-5:30 p.m.). Closed Sun. Parking: Les Halles. Cards: V.

The shopfront is brand-new, but Mora is an old established firm dating back to 1814. The most esoteric items of culinary equipment join the astonishing collection of knives and pots and pans in stainless steel, cast iron or copper, and the very best cake and tart pans coated with new-age anti-adhesives. Lay folks benefit from the same low prices as restaurant and catering pros, and they are greeted with the same amiability. The cookbook section boasts over 200 titles; if you think a picture is worth a thousand words, inquire about the cooking-demonstration videos.

Plastiques

8th arr. - 5, rue de Miromesnil
47 42 06 35
Open 10 a.m.-7 p.m. Closed Sun. & Aug. No cards.

Everything here is made of transparent or opaque, rigid or supple plastic. And useful stuff it is. We were truly impressed by the range of tablecloths, place mats, cutlery and dishes in cheerful and unusual colors. Look for the knives with Teflon blades in the same shade as the handle (pink, yellow, green, blue, for 120 francs each).

A. Simon

2nd arr. - 48, rue Montmartre - 42 33 71 65
Open 8:30 a.m.-6:30 p.m. Closed Sun. Parking: Forum des Halles. Cards: V.

This long-established family firm supplies kitchen and tableware to the likes of the Hôtel Méridien, the Café de la Paix and the Ecole de Cuisine in Osaka, Japan. But it also sells its vast range of dishes, glasses and utensils at the same prices to any customer who walks in off the street. For typically French dishes (like the ones you see in traditional brasseries), the prices can't be beat: flameproof porcelain plates for just 13 francs. You'll also find wine pitchers, carafes and ice cream *coupes* that will add an agreeable Gallic touch to your table. The rue Montmartre store specializes in kitchen supplies, while the store around the corner on rue Etienne-Marcel (same phone) deals chiefly in tableware.

Taïr Mercier

5th arr. - 7, bd Saint-Germain - 43 54 19 97
Open 10 a.m.-1 p.m. & 2:30 p.m.-7 p.m. Closed Sat., Sun. & Aug. Cards: V.

Place mats in appealing shapes (fruits, animals, city skylines) cut out of brightly colored pieces of plastic are big sellers here (20 francs each). But we also discovered attractive two-tone plastic shopping bags, melamine fish platters (195 francs for three), clear plastic knife rests and absolutely stainproof plastic-coated aprons, all of which convinced us that plastique, c'est chic!

FURNISHINGS

CONTEMPORARY FURNITURE

Academy

6th arr. - 5, pl. de l'Odéon - 43 29 07 18
Open 9:30 a.m.-12:30 p.m. & 2 p.m.-7 p.m. Closed Sun. & Aug. No cards.

Jean-Michel Wilmotte was the designer selected to decorate the space beneath the Louvre's glass pyramid, and to create the furnishings to be placed throughout the Grand Louvre. The shop that showcases his collection is austere, like the materials Wilmotte prefers: perforated sheet metal, glass slabs, chipboard. Prices for these singular pieces vary widely: A chair designed for the Palais-Royal, for example, sells for 1,450 francs, while the "Attila" sofa—a waxed rusted-metal frame with flannel seating—carries a 31,500-franc price tag.

Arredamento

4th arr. - 18, quai des Célestins
42 74 33 14
Open 10 a.m.-12:30 p.m. & 2 p.m.-7 p.m. (Sun. & Mon. 2 p.m.-7 p.m.). Cards: V, AE.

In a spacious and handsome two-level shop, Valentine Boitel and Bernard Renaudin present a wide-ranging selection of top Italian furniture and lighting designs. Connoisseurs with a taste for contemporary Italian design (and well-lined wallets) will applaud the modular storage units by Capellini, the sofas by Zanotta (from 20,000 francs), the coffee tables from Fontana Arte and the lamps by Flos. Fine French design is represented as well, though on a smaller scale—there are some marvelous lamps by Gilles Derain.

Avant-Scène

6th arr. - 4, pl. de l'Odéon - 46 33 12 40
Open 10 a.m.-7 p.m. (Mon. 2 p.m.-7 p.m.). Closed Sun. & Aug. 13-23. Cards: V.

An eclectic choice of furniture and objets d'art by young designers is on display at this beautiful shop on the place de l'Odéon. Elisabeth Delacarte and Anne-Marie Dalbarade present unusual sanded-glass candle holders and light fixtures by sculptor Marco de Gueltz, as well as furniture by Véronique Malcourant and Jean-Michel Cornu (who work with wood and print fabric) and Thierry Peltraut (new-age materials, classic workmanship). Prices start at less than 100 francs (for a small gilt dish) and soar up to 45,000 francs and beyond for, say, a table by Dubreuil.

Cohérence
7th arr. - 31, bd Raspail - 42 22 15 83
Open 10 a.m.-7 p.m. Closed Sun. Parking: Bon Marché. Cards: V.

Contemporary-furniture maven Margarita Corréa (owner of the two successful Ready Made shops) presents the masters of twentieth-century design (Breuer, Mackintosh, and others) in her new Left Bank shop. Reproductions of famous pieces are sold at interesting prices (the famous Mackintosh "high chair" sells for 3,450 francs), but she also presents a few more recent designs, notably some comfortable sofas.

DCA
1st arr. - 56, rue Jean-Jacques-Rousseau
42 33 37 27
Open 10 a.m.-1 p.m. & 2 p.m.-7 p.m. Closed Sun. & Aug. Parking: Les Halles. Cards: V.

All the creations—sofas, chests, coffee tables, rugs, chairs, dishes, lamps—of prolific designer Christian Duc are gathered together at DCA. His latest collections highlight wood and chipboard pieces. The African Queen chair, in beech and leather, has a price tag of 2,600 francs; the Norma Jean, a chest of drawers in chipboard, goes for 9,700 francs. On sale here, too, are the decorative accessories designed by Josef Hoffmann in 1902: vases, bowls and umbrella stands in white or black lacquered metal.

Ecart International
4th arr. - 111, rue Saint-Antoine
42 78 79 11
Open 9:30 a.m.-6:30 p.m. (Sat. 11 a.m.-6:30 p.m.). Closed Sun. No cards.

The headquarters of Ecart International occupies a town house near the Saint-Paul church in the Marais. The bright, spacious, strikingly beautiful showroom presents reissues of pieces by the great designers of the early twentieth century, including Mallet-Stevens, Eileen Gray, Pierre Chareau and Michel Dufet. Ecart also displays work by talented young French creators (Sacha Ketoff, Sylvain Dubuisson, Patrick Naggar, Olivier Gagnère), as well as designs by its own star, Andrée Putman. Prices start at about 1,000 francs and shoot up fast to over 25,000 francs.

GLAMOUR
Antiques and reissues of luxurious toilet and beauty accessories, towels, scents and other voluptuous personal indulgences can be found at Beauté Divine, 40, rue Saint-Sulpice, 6th arr., 43 26 25 31.

Edifice
7th arr. - 27 bis, bd Raspail - 45 48 53 60
Open 10 a.m.-7:15 p.m. Closed Sun. Parking: Raspail. Cards: V.

Each month, Edifice dreams up a splendid setting to highlight a piece or ensemble of pieces by a favorite designer. Owner Sarah Nathan is keen on avant-garde furniture, like Mario Botta's armchair, Guillaume Saalburg's screen, Ingo Maurer's splendid lamp. . . . The store presents almost all of Philippe Starck's creations for the home (his Costes chair, 3,112 francs, and the self-supporting bookcase, 2,945 francs, among them).

Etat de Siège
8th arr. - 21, av. de Friedland - 45 62 31 02
Open 11 a.m.-7 p.m. (Mon. 2 p.m.-7 p.m.). Closed Sun. No cards. Other branch: 1, quai de Conti - 6th arr. - 43 29 31 60.

You are certain to find a seat that suits you among the astonishing assortment stocked here. From Louis XIII *fauteuils* (easy chairs) to the most avant-garde chair/sculpture, Etat de Siège displays some 150 different designs, many of which are available in a variety of colors and finishes. Prices vary according to the quality of the wood or metal in question, the workmanship (hand- or factory-finished) and the style (side chairs range in price from 600 to 4,000 francs; armchairs, from 3,000 to 5,500 francs).

Galerie Neotu
4th arr. - 25, rue du Renard - 42 78 96 97
Open 10 a.m.-1 p.m. & 2 p.m.-7 p.m. Closed Sun. No cards.

Furniture collectors with a taste for the "neo" find this multifaceted gallery a sure source of aesthetic thrills. Some say the furniture and objects displayed here are the rare and precious antiques of the future. Whether or not that will prove to be the case, owners Gérard Dalmon and Pierre Staudenmeyer spotlight works by young artists, painters, sculptors and architects, particularly those pieces that border the realms of art and design. Most are unique or limited editions, and are thus quite expensive; but the gallery also exhibits some reasonably priced objets d'art.

Meubles et Fonction

6th arr. - 135, bd Raspail - 45 48 55 74
Open 9:30 a.m.-12:30 p.m. & 2 p.m.-7 p.m. (Sat. 10 a.m.-noon & 2 p.m.-7 p.m.). Closed Sun. & Aug. No cards. 2 other branches: see text below.

For almost 30 years, Pierre and Alice Perrigault have been admirers of and dealers in technically sophisticated contemporary furniture. Their stock is international, with pieces from B and B Italia and Rosenthal and Artifort, among others. A favorite piece is the Ant chair by the Danish designer Jacobsen (honored by a 1987 exhibit at the Museum of Decorative Arts), and Mario Botta's work is available here as well. The Perrigaults host frequent thematic exhibits at their three stores, and invite budding designers not yet out of art school to show their work. The branches in the eighth (139, rue du Faubourg-Saint-Honoré, 45 61 01 57) and the thirteenth (55, rue de la Glacière, 43 36 26 20) arrondissements specialize in office furniture.

Modernismes

16th arr. - 16, rue Franklin - 46 47 86 56
Open 10 a.m.-1 p.m. & 2 p.m.-7 p.m. (Sat. 11 a.m.-7 p.m.). Closed Sun. & Aug. Cards: V.

In this stunning commercial space designed by Gilles Derain, pieces by early-twentieth-century masters (Eileen Gray, Le Corbusier and others) stand side-by-side with the work of Mariscal or Boris Sipek, of the current generation. The furniture is quite austere, but the atmosphere in the shop is warm and cordial, thanks in part to a decor that features art by young painters, Eileen Gray rugs and attractive hand-thrown pottery. Naturally enough, Derain's superb lamps and decorative pieces are given top billing. A lounge chair in leather, wood and fabric, designed by Sipek for Driade, costs 18,200 francs, but you can walk away with a handsome Derain ashtray for 400 francs.

Perkal

3rd arr. - 8, rue des Quatre-Fils
42 77 46 80
Open 11 a.m.-7 p.m. (Mon. 2 p.m.-7 p.m.). Closed Sun. & Aug. Cards: V, AE, DC, MC.

Spaniard Nestor Perkal, interior architect and designer, has a thing for bright, primary colors. So for his marvelous shop, Perkal has selected pieces from Memphis, that wild and crazy bunch of designing Italians, and from the Spanish firm Ediciones. He recently marketed a collection of silver-plated objects ("Algorithms") designed by international names like George Sowden and Nathalie du Pasquier.

Protis

16th arr. - 24, av. Raymond-Poincaré
47 04 60 40
Open 9 a.m.-7 p.m. Closed Sun. Cards: V. Other branch: 153, rue de Faubourg-Saint-Honoré - 1st arr. - 45 62 22 40.

White walls and a gray-tile floor set the glass-and-steel furniture off to advantage. Protis, newly enlarged and remodeled, presents its own designs (coffee tables in glass and black lacquered metal), Italian pieces by Cattelan, Bieffeplast, Tonon and Technolinea (with a beautiful line of office furniture in walnut or rosewood) and a host of creations by noted architects. A leather-covered high-back chair by Cattelan sells for 2,400 francs or so.

OUTDOOR FURNITURE

Le Cèdre Rouge

1st arr. - 22, av. Victoria - 42 33 71 05
Open 9 a.m.-7 p.m. Closed Sun. & 2 wks. in Aug. Parking: Pont-Neuf. Cards: V, AE, DC.

Furniture for the patio and garden, in Burmese teak or colonial-style wicker, is the specialty of Le Cèdre Rouge. But you will also find handsome little lava tables in a score of colors, and copies of eighteenth-century furniture executed in steel and canvas. We could browse for hours among the many elegant pieces of handcrafted pottery (there are over 2,000 pieces in stock) from Biot, Aubagne and Tuscany. A section devoted to decorative objects for indoors includes lamps, Florentine ceramics and lovely rustic baskets.

Jardins Imaginaires

6th arr. - 9 bis, rue d'Assas - 42 22 90 03
Open 10:30 a.m.-7:30 p.m. (Mon. 2:30 p.m.-7:30 p.m.). Closed Sun. & Aug. Parking: rue d'Assas. Cards: V, AE.

A medley of handsome antique furnishings full of grace and wit; a selection of modern furniture and objets d'art for sophisticated gardens and conservatories; an original selection of statuary, pottery, urns and basins . . . the "imaginary gardens" evoked in this wonderful shop are brimming with charm, humor and taste. It's one of our very favorite shops in Paris.

SOFAS & CHAIRS

Jacques Bergaud

1st arr. - 62, rue Jean-Jacques-Rousseau
42 33 96 76
Open 10 a.m.-7 p.m. Closed Sun. No cards.

In spacious, airy premises, Jacques Bergaud exhibits furniture crafted of leather and rare woods, inspired by pieces from the 1930s (classic armchairs in leather or flannel with solid mahogany trim that incorporates a slide-out drawer or ashtray, 32,500 francs). Also on view are some superb architect's lamps in brass, copper and brushed steel, and lamps designed by Gilles Derain.

Cour Intérieure

3rd arr. - 109, bd Beaumarchais
42 77 33 10
Open 9:30 a.m.-1 p.m. & 2 p.m.-7 p.m. (Sun. & Mon. 2 p.m.-7 p.m.). No cards.

We started thinking we were in a comfortable country house: curtains on the windows, pictures on the walls and cozy stoves radiating warmth in every room. In this homey setting Gérard Saint-Fort-Paillard presents his collection of wood-and-marquetry furniture (a console runs about 20,000 francs). Pieces by other designers are on hand as well, and there are fabrics by Bisson Bruneel and lamps by François Privat mixed in with antique pictures and bibelots.

Fenêtre sur Cour

6th arr. - 27, rue Saint-Sulpice
43 26 45 85, 43 29 43 36
Open 9:30 a.m.-7 p.m. Closed Sun. Cards: V.

Don't hesitate to walk through the porte-cochère (carriage entrance) of 27, rue Saint-Sulpice. At the other end of the courtyard, in a small eighteenth-century pavilion, you will discover a marvelous collection of furniture assembled by Marianne and Jean-Claude Maugirard himself and Serge Kirszbaum. Most of the pieces are reproductions of early-twentieth-century masterworks by Otto Wagner, Adolf Loos and by American designers of the 1930s (Kaase Klint's leather-and-wood safari chair, or Mogens Kock's "Folding Chair"), but there are also creations by Jean-Claude Maugirard (including his "Intérieur Nuit" sofa, priced at 12,700 francs) and by other up-and-coming young designers.

HARDWARE

Garnier

12th arr. - 30 bis, bd de la Bastille
43 43 84 85
Open 8:30 a.m.-noon & 1:30 p.m.-6 p.m. Closed Sat., Sun. & Aug. Parking: 16, rue Saint-Antoine. No cards.

Established in 1832, Garnier is a specialist in ornamental hardware and locks. Reproductions of Louis XV, Louis XVI, Directoire, Empire and English locks and plaques are still manufactured and displayed—though not sold—here. A friendly and informative staff can provide a list of dealers who handle any model you might be interested in acquiring.

A la Providence (Leclercq)

11th arr. - 151, rue du Faubourg-Saint-Antoine - 43 43 06 41
Open 8:30 a.m.-6 p.m. Closed Sun. Cards: V, AE.

This is undoubtedly the most delightful hardware store on the Faubourg-Saint-Antoine (the cabinetmaker and woodworker quarter). Arlette, one of France's few female locksmiths, welcomes you into her domain, where she and her colleagues fashion handmade copies of locks and other hardware, working from antique originals. Some of the hard-to-find items available here are hand-cut crystal knobs for banisters (1,500 to 2,500 francs) and brass plaques for 1930s armoires (350 francs per pair).

INTERIOR DECORATION

INTERIOR DECOR

Arcasa
1st arr. - 219, rue Saint-Honoré
42 60 46 60
Open 10 a.m.-7 p.m. Closed Sun. Parking: Saint-Honoré. Cards: V, AE, DC.

Everything you'd need to furnish or accessorize a home is available at Arcasa. Patrick Dollfus presents an eclectic selection that ranges from traditional to contemporary. The ground floor is devoted to tableware, crystal and a multitude of small gift items, many from the Porsche Design collection (pipes, lighters, pens and leather goods). Furniture is displayed upstairs, and includes a fine group of Italian pieces, like Zanotta's marvelous Milan sofa, or Franco Raggi's solid-wood bookcase with glass shelving, alongside beautiful lamps from Flos and Porsche Design. A selection of tables, consoles, desks and other pieces can be made in any size you desire.

Christian Benais
16th arr. - 18, rue Cortambert
45 03 15 55
Open 10 a.m.-1 p.m. & 2 p.m.-7 p.m. Closed Sun. No cards.

Christian Benais's shop looks like the home of a private collector, where Napoléon III furniture cohabits comfortably with art deco bibelots and objets d'art. Benais adores antique linens, and he has amassed a considerable selection of turn-of-the-century embroidered tablecloths, as well as some fine contemporary pieces in embroidered linen and Egyptian cotton. He also works as a textile designer for Chotard-Brochier, creating marvelous fabrics (lots of swatches are on view). A set of bed linens trimmed with Valenciennes lace is priced here at 3,240 francs.

Isabelle de Borchgrave
7th arr. - 30, rue des Saints-Pères
45 44 76 35
Open 10:30 a.m.-6 p.m. (Sat. 2 p.m.-6 p.m.). Closed Sun. No cards.

Nestled at the far end of a lovely seventeenth-century courtyard, this lovely shop has the feel of an elegant living room. On display are varied creations by this talented artist and designer: hand-painted fabrics (350 francs per meter), painted panels (by special order only), cushions, linens, a few furniture pieces, some curious antique objects and some signed Isabelle de Borchgrave works.

Etamine
6th arr. - 49, quai des Grands-Augustins
46 34 01 74
Open 9:30 a.m.-6:30 p.m. Closed Sun. & 2 wks. in Aug. Cards: V, MC.

Etamine is without doubt the trendiest home-decor boutique in Paris. Françoise Dorget and Marilyn Gaucher have rounded up a superb collection of fabrics from all over the globe: neoclassic prints and cut velvets from Timney and Fowler, a horsehair look-alike made with a vegetable fiber from the Philippines and a plethora of designs from bright young members of the new generation. There is an ample selection of sofas, halogen lamps by Jean-Charles Detalante, objets d'art, Chinese armchairs and a few antiques. Fabric prices range from 98 francs per meter for good, solid

VINTAGE LINENS

Delicate hand-embroidered linens, decorated tablecloths and pillowcases; sheets trimmed in lace . . . these marvels and much more are obtainable at (relatively) reasonable prices from Christian Benais, 18, rue Cortambert, 16th arr., 45 03 15 55; Au Bain Marie, 10, rue Boissy-d'Anglas, 8th arr., 42 66 59 74; L'Ibis Rouge, 35, boulevard Raspail, 7th arr., 45 48 98 21; Dentelle et Noblesse, 26, avenue Bosquet, 7th arr., 45 51 02 98; Les Muses d'Europe, 64, rue de Seine, 6th arr., 43 26 89 63; Le Temps Retrouvé, 6, rue Vauvilliers, 1st arr., 42 33 66 17; Nostalgie, 23, rue Descombes, 17th arr., 42 67 07 66; Peau d'Ange, 1, rue Mesnil, 16th arr., 45 53 78 11.

canvas to 900 francs per meter for some custom-made lengths.

Galerie du Bac

7th arr. - 116, rue du Bac - 40 49 00 95
Open 10 a.m.-1 p.m. & 2 p.m.-6:30 p.m. Closed Sun. & Aug. No cards.

Galerie du Bac is a handsome, spacious showcase for the latest creations by Kostka—lamps, vases, bowls and small furniture pieces. Fabrics are by Métaphores (Fortuny pleats, moirés and unusual fibers), while Missoni supplies additional fabrics, rugs, linens and sofas.

David Hicks France

6th arr. - 12, rue de Tournon - 43 26 00 67
Open 10 a.m.-7 p.m. Closed Sat. in July & Aug. & Sun. Parking: Saint-Sulpice. Cards: V.

A warm, urbane atmosphere reigns in this pretty shop, a showcase for a marvelous collection of fabrics and rugs. The rugs—dhurries, English carpets in 70 different patterns (700 francs per linear meter) and tinted palm-fiber matting (300 francs per square meter)—can be made up in the colors of your choice. Christian Badin's most recent collection of fabrics is inspired by eighteenth-century designs; the patterns come in bright, slightly acidic colors printed on cotton or silk. Badin's furniture is crafted in natural beech (for example the 20,000-franc leather-topped desk) or in sycamore (a bedside table with several shelves, 3,600 francs). The splendid decorative objects are not the sort one sees everywhere; we were enchanted by some etched Austrian wine glasses, copied from an eighteenth-century model (230 francs). Decorating service available.

Juste Mauve

16th arr. - 29, rue Greuze - 47 27 82 31
Open 10 a.m.-7 p.m. (Mon. 2 p.m.-7 p.m.). Closed Sat., Sun. & Aug. Parking: Av. Georges-Mandel. Cards: V.

Anne-Marie de Ganay's shop has all the charm of a cozy English home, with its mix of mahogany (coffee tables from 5,000 francs) and flowered chintz, low stools and Chinese cachepots (700 francs), picture frames in burled elm and marquetry (500 francs). Piles of lacy cushions and a selection of ravishing lingerie lend a frothy, feminine note.

Nicole H.

6th arr. - 28, rue Bonaparte - 43 25 43 60
Open 10 a.m.-6:30 p.m. Closed Sun. & Aug. Parking: Saint-Germain. Cards: V.

Nicole Hannezo designs delightful furniture with a 1930s feel: writing desks, bars, dining room tables and coffee tables, in wood washed with ceruse (a white pigment), then lacquered or given a sharkskin finish. All the pieces are made to order, and prices are really unbeatable, considering their beauty and exquisite workmanship. An exceptional selection of fabrics from the best manufacturers is available here, as well as a decorating service.

Les Olivades

16th arr. - 25, rue de l'Annonciation 45 27 07 76
Open 10 a.m.-1 p.m. & 2:30 p.m.-6:30 p.m. (Mon. 10 a.m.- 1 p.m. & 4 p.m.-6 p.m.). Closed Sun. & Aug. Cards: V, AE.

Mary de Sacy has infused the wonderful warmth and charm of Provence into her tiny shop tucked away behind the rue de Passy. Redolent of olive oil and lavender, bright with the colors of the Midi, Les Olivades displays, among other treasures, traditional Provençal print fabrics. The shades are predominantly pastel and the prices are incredibly low (110 francs per meter). All can be quilted on request (220 francs per meter). If you're not handy with a needle, there are many small items already made up: bags, eyeglass cases, makeup cases, skirts and shawls. Also carries some attractive bracelets and earrings.

Souleiado

16th arr. - 83-85, av. Paul-Doumer 42 24 99 34
Open 10 a.m.-7 p.m. Closed Sun. Cards: V, AE, DC. Other branch: 78, rue de Seine - 6th arr. - 43 54 15 13.

Thanks to Charles Demery, Provençal fabrics are known and sought after the world over. Souleiado's original designs, many dating from the eighteenth century, are available in a riot of cheerful colors. Coordinated wallpaper and oilcloth (30 patterns) are on hand too, and the home-decor department also offers quilted bedspreads (2,950 francs) with matching sheets, tablecloths, fabric-covered boxes, shopping bags, picture frames and—the firm's best-seller—place mat and napkin sets (85 francs). The space devoted to fashion continues to grow: wool shawls sell for 945 francs, and there is now a line of men's shirts as well.

Valdrome

7th arr. - 42, av. de La Bourdonnais
47 53 88 10

Open 11 a.m.-1 p.m. & 2 p.m.-7 p.m. Closed Sun., Mon. & Aug. No cards.

Valdrome, a cloth manufacturer based in Provence, remains faithful to its long tradition: hand-printing fabrics with Indian and Persian motifs, which was initially introduced to France in the seventeenth and eighteenth centuries. All the creations (shawls, tablecloths, bedspreads) are blocked by hand on Egyptian cotton, mohair, wool or silk. The beautiful cotton paisley tablecloths are priced at 429 francs. Cotton cloth sells for 149 to 159 francs per meter, and quilted bedspreads command 2,000 francs.

Ville et Villégiature

15th arr. - 32, bd Montparnasse
45 49 32 41

Open 9:30 a.m.-12:30 p.m. & 2 p.m.-7:30 p.m. Closed Sun., Mon. & Aug. No cards.

If at times you yearn for a picturesque landscape to brighten up a dark corner of your apartment; if you long for the grandeur of elaborate moldings and cornices; if you dream of transforming your beat-up old furniture with trompe l'oeil marbled paint, this is the store that can make your wishes can come true. Panoramic murals cost about 1,500 francs per square meter (on average, a painter completes about one square meter per day). The shop also sells antique furniture and decorative objects from the turn of the century through the 1950s.

Laure Welfing

6th arr. - 30, rue Jacob - 43 25 17 03

Open noon-7 p.m. (Mon. 2:30 p.m.-7 p.m.). Closed Sun. & Aug. Parking: Saint-Germain. Cards: V, AE.

Faux bronze, *faux* marble, *faux* malachite, *faux* stone: Laure Welfing is the queen of the counterfeiters. Her charming realm is filled with decorative objects and furniture all meant to fool the eye, like the coffee tables that imitate bronze (2,500 francs), or the phony Etruscan vases (1,200 francs). Furniture may be made to order, with designs of your choosing; a large marquetry piece could run as high as 25,000 francs, but Welfing's shop (the

"stone" walls, incidentally, are her own work) also presents small objects—ashtrays, glasses and the like—at affordable prices.

MISCELLANY

Au Chêne-Liège

14th arr. - 74, bd du Montparnasse
43 22 02 15

Open 9:30 a.m.-6:30 p.m. Closed Sun., Mon. & Aug. Parking: Montparnasse tower. No cards.

A *chêne-liège* is a cork-oak, and cork is the specialty of this well-known Montparnasse emporium. And we've seen the most astonishing range of articles, all in cork—accessories for the wine cellar, for the desk and office, luggage and handbags and even women's clothing (believe us, nothing could be less kinky).

Marin et Tullet

8th arr. - 7, rue de Monceau - 42 25 09 10

Open 8 a.m.-noon & 2 p.m.-6 p.m. Closed Sat., Sun. & Aug. No cards.

Every high-class decorator in town knows about these specialists in silk braid and fringe (to trim curtains, chairs and lamp shades, for example), who will design to the customer's specifications. Marin et Tullet also manufactures reproductions of period curtain rods.

La Passementerie Nouvelle

1st arr. - 15, rue Etienne-Marcel
42 36 30 01

Open 9 a.m.-6 p.m. Closed Sat., Sun. & Aug. No cards.

When France needs new trimmings for the draperies at Versailles or Fontainebleau, it calls on La Passementerie Nouvelle. In addition to reproductions of historic pieces, the company works with period-style braids, trims and fringe specially adapted for contemporary fabrics.

SMH

10th arr. - 34, rue René-Boulanger
42 06 11 53

Open 9 a.m.-12:45 p.m. & 2 p.m.-6 p.m. Closed Sun. Cards: V. Other branch: 76, bd Richard-Lenoir - 11th arr.

Single- and double-curved moldings, cornices, carved door frames, baseboards and rosettes (in pine, oak, tropical wood, polyurethane or even Styrofoam) will dress up even the plainest prefab bungalow. SMH will cut all these elements to measure, then you take them home, paint them, put them up . . .

and presto! Hello Versailles! SMH also sells all sorts of supplies for do-it-yourself picture-framers.

RUGS & TAPESTRIES

L'Atelier d'Anaïs
6th arr. - 23, rue Jacob - 43 26 68 00
Open 10 a.m.-1 p.m. & 2 p.m.-6 p.m. (Mon. 2 p.m.-5:30 p.m. & Sat. 2 p.m.-6 p.m.). Closed Sat. in Aug. & Sun. Parking: Saint-Sulpice. No cards.

Practitioners of the art of petit point will think they've died and gone to heaven. L'Atelier d'Anaïs stocks a fabulous selection of hand-painted canvases. An alphabet sampler costs about 850 francs, wool included. Small squares, which can be sewn together to make rugs, are priced at 390 francs; or they can be made to order in any size or style.

Casa Lopez
6th arr. - 27, bd Raspail - 45 44 42 11
Open 10 a.m.-1 p.m. & 2 p.m.-6:30 p.m. Closed Sun. & 2 wks. in Aug. Parking: Raspail. Cards: V, AE.

Casa Lopez proposes covetable jacquard rugs in geometric patterns, many of which are reversible. Most designs are available in ten different sizes, in a range of 90 colors, for the reasonable price of 3,600 to 6,300 francs. Palm-fiber rugs in checkerboard, herringbone or houndstooth patterns have loads of casual charm, and we love the wool carpets with raised lozenge (diamond) or diagonal or ribbon motifs. Certain designs are also available on canvas, to make coordinating petit-point chair backs and seats.

Kell's Corner
7th arr. - 94, rue de Grenelle - 45 44 64 26
Open 10:30 a.m.-1:30 p.m. & 3 p.m.-7 p.m. Closed Sun., Mon. & 3 wks. in Aug. Parking: rue du Bac. No cards.

Kell's Corner's Madame Deschenes, an expert needlepointress, has, as they say in France, "the fingers of a fairy." She hand-paints all the canvases on display in her charming boutique, and designs samplers and tapestries as well (150 to 550 francs). Neophytes can be initiated into the mysteries of smocking, embroidery and needlepoint for the moderate sum of 95 francs per hour-long lesson (reduced rates for groups are available).

Tapisserie au Point
1st arr. - 128, galerie de Valois
42 61 44 41
Open 1 p.m.-6 p.m. Closed Sat., Sun. & Aug. Parking: Louvre. No cards.

Claudine Brunet designs needlepoint canvases that closely follow period models. For 2,500 to 3,000 francs, for example, you can make both the canvas and the wool for refurbishing a Louis XV armchair yourself.

WALLPAPER & FABRICS

Besson
6th arr. - 18, rue du Vieux-Colombier
45 48 87 62
Open 9:30 a.m.-6:30 p.m. Closed Sun., Mon. & 3 wks. in Aug. No cards.

The choicest English and French decorator fabrics and wallpapers have been featured at Besson for 30 years. The range of nostalgic, romantic, exotic and rustic patterns is considerable, and the sales staff, bursting with good advice, is also gratifyingly generous with samples.

Manuel Canovas
6th arr. - 7, rue de Furstenberg
43 25 75 98
Open 9 a.m.-7 p.m. (Mon. 9:30 a.m.-7 p.m. & Sat. 9:30 a.m.-1 p.m. & 2 p.m.-7 p.m.). Closed Sun. & 1 wk. in Aug. No cards.

Textile designer and manufacturer Manuel Canovas came up with a style that revolutionized interior decorating in the 1960s. This master colorist drew his inspiration from extensive travels in India, Japan and California, as well as from imagined botanical gardens. Canovas's extraordinary chintzes are done in slightly acid tones, while muted shades are preferred on such sophisticated fabrics as moiré. Coordinated wall coverings are available as well, and in the shop next door, fashion and home accessories are made up in Canovas fabrics.

Casal
7th arr. - 40, rue des Saints-Pères
45 44 78 70
Open 9:30 a.m.-6 p.m. Closed Sun. & Aug. No cards.

Casal's signature jacquard prints, inspired by traditional paisley patterns and kilim (a pileless tapestry-woven carpet, mat or spread) designs, look terrific on sofas. But in this spacious, skylit showroom (formerly an artist's studio) you will also find fabrics by Brunswick, David Hicks and Jean-Michel Wilmotte.

PARADISE

Rue de Paradis, 10th arr., is heaven for people who love to set a handsome table with fine china, silver and crystal. At number 12, Limoges Unic showcases delicate wares from the china capital of France (47 70 54 49). At number 30, Saint Louis displays its sparkling collections of crystal tableware and objets d'art (47 70 25 70). Baccarat (30 bis) presents unusual and historic pieces from its crystal collection in an upstairs museum; antique and modern pieces are sold downstairs (47 70 64 30). Also, at number 30, the Centre International des Arts de la Table hosts 140 French and foreign manufacturers' exhibits of their product lines for professional buyers or those with an introduction (42 46 50 50). One of the prettiest shops is Madronet, at 34 (47 70 34 59).

Etamine
6th arr. - 49, quai des Grands-Augustins
46 34 01 74
Open 9:30 a.m.-6:30 p.m. Closed Sun., Mon. & 3 wks. in Aug. No cards.

This ever-growing enterprise is the exclusive French showroom for several English decorating firms—Osborne, Colefax and Fowler, Collier and Campbell, among others. But the house collection is worthy of note as well, with attractive contemporary designs in fabric and wall coverings.

Pierre Frey
1st arr. - 47, rue des Petits-Champs
42 97 44 00
Open 10:30 a.m.-1 p.m. & 2 p.m.-6:30 p.m. Closed Sun. & Aug. Cards: V.

This firm is a family affair with an international reputation. Although the designers draw a good deal of their inspiration from traditional eighteenth- and nineteenth-century French patterns, Pierre Frey is also known for its vast—and ever-growing—line of contemporary fabrics and wall coverings. In the *Patrick* Frey home-decor shops, you'll find a selection of handsome bed linens, cushions, fabric-covered boxes and laminated trays, all in the Frey signature prints.

Mauny
16th arr. - 25 bis, rue Franklin
45 53 85 20
Open 10 a.m.-6:30 p.m. (Mon. 2 p.m.-6:30 p.m.). Closed Sun. & Aug. No cards.

Mauny prints wallpaper today just as it was done in the eighteenth century. The magnificent murals, panoramas and paper frescoes are manufactured by special order only, in the colors specified by the customer. Prices per roll start in the neighborhood of 450 francs. In stock is a fine collection of wallpaper friezes and borders.

Nobilis Fontan
6th arr. - 40, rue Bonaparte - 43 29 21 50
Open 9:30 a.m.-1 p.m. & 2 p.m.-6:30 p.m. Closed Sun. & 1 wk. in Aug. No cards.

Since it opened in 1928, this decorating firm has enjoyed a reputation for the high quality and refined taste of its design. Refined, but not conservative, Nobilis Fontan has always managed to evolve intelligently, keeping pace with contemporary designers. The wallpapers on display here are relatively expensive, but they are beautifully made. The fabric patterns are inspired by classic English, Japanese and Chinese models, and coordinate perfectly with the wall coverings. All merchandise can be delivered in 48 hours, which, at least in Paris, must be some sort of record.

Romanex de Boussac
2nd arr. - 27, rue du Mail - 42 33 46 88
Open 9 a.m.-5:30 p.m. Closed Sat. & Sun. No cards.

Romanex presents a superb collection of printed fabrics manufactured in the old Wesserling royal cloth factories near Mulhouse in Alsace. Considering its fine design (Andrée Putman and Jacques Grange have created lines for Romanex) and high quality, these fabrics are terrific values.

Zuber
6th arr. - 55, quai des Grands-Augustins
43 29 77 84
Open 10 a.m.-12:30 p.m. & 1:30 p.m.-6 p.m. Closed Sun. & 1 wk. in mid-Aug. Parking: Odéon, Saint-Germain. No cards.

A dynamic new owner has revitalized the venerable firm of Zuber, boosting its level of creativity to new heights. Using time-honored printing methods and working from a library of more than 100,000 antique patterns, Zuber's is an eye-popping collection of wallpapers: trompe l'oeil, panoramas, marbled and damask papers, as well as sublime friezes, cornices and borders of roses and other flowers in the subtlest of tints. The papers sell for 300 to 3,000 francs per roll; three- by four-meter panoramas cost 5,000 to 20,000 francs. Orders (excluding special orders) can be filled in 48 hours.

LIGHTING

Antica
7th arr. - 38, rue de Verneuil - 42 61 28 86
Open 10 a.m.-12:30 p.m. & 1:30 p.m.-6:30 p.m. Closed Sun., Mon. & Aug. No cards.

Madame Clérin can whip up a lamp shade from one of the rich and refined fabrics she has in stock in about ten days, or she'll sell you a ready-made shade (for about 30 percent less than the price of a custom-made shade). If you find yourself in a decorating quandary, she will come to your home to provide sage counsel and advice.

Artémide
8th arr. - 157-159, rue du Faubourg-Saint-Honoré - 42 89 15 15
Open 9 a.m.-12:30 p.m. & 1:30 p.m.-6 p.m. Closed Sat. & Sun. Cards: V.

If you are curious to see what sort of lamps and light fixtures the best European designers have come up with lately, come to Artémide. Mario Botta, Vico Magistretti, Ettore Sottsass and Richard Sapper are just some of the famous names represented in this huge two-level showroom.

Capeline
16th arr. - 144, av. de Versailles
45 20 22 65
Open 10 a.m.-7 p.m. Closed Sun., Mon. & Aug. No cards.

In this vast workshop, known to all the best Parisian decorators, craftspeople still turn out pleated, gathered and skirted lamp shades just like in the good old days.

Ready Made
6th arr. - 38-40, rue Jacob - 42 60 28 01
Open 10 a.m.-7 p.m. Closed Sun. Parking: Saint-Germain. Cards: V, MC.

Italian halogens are the specialty of this sleek and trendy shop near Saint-Germain. Flos, Artémide and Arteluce are a few of the manufacturers on hand, with lamps priced from about 1,800 francs. The furniture store next door, also owned by Margarita Corréa, exhibits its merchandise that is equally select, with outstanding designs by Gae Aulenti and Mario Botta.

LINENS

Boutique Descamps
6th arr. - 38, rue du Four - 45 44 22 87
Open 10 a.m.-7 p.m. Closed Sun. Cards: V.

The capital's newest Descamps boutique (there are 30 in the Greater Paris area) is located near Saint-Germain-des-Prés. The two levels house an encyclopedic collection of Primrose Bordier's creations for bed and bath. The prices are reasonable (a set of sheets, 320 francs; a large round tablecloth, 360 francs). Terrycloth towels come in 35 hues.The shop will make towels or other linens to measure.

Boutique Yves Delorme
1st arr. - 153, rue Saint-Honoré
42 97 00 46
Open 10:30 a.m.-7 p.m. Closed Sun., Mon. & Aug. 1-15. Cards: V, AE, DC.

In this healthy-size shop near the Louvre des Antiquaires, you will find linens for bed and bath signed Kenzo, Cerruti, Jourdan, Givenchy and Lanvin. There are also thick towels embroidered with a lyre motif designed specially for the "Opéra de Paris" (170 francs for a hand towel), as well as printed sheets in a choice of elegant pastel shades (375 francs for a sheet and two pillowcases). Children will be delighted by the towels and bathrobes printed with Babar and his friends.

Brod'Line
15th arr. - 8, rue Gramme - 48 56 00 61
Open 10 a.m.-7 p.m. Closed Sun. & Aug. Cards: V.

Hand-embroidered Italian linens are featured at this precious boutique; you can also have names and borders hand-embroidered on your own pieces in just three days (60 francs for a name, 90 francs for a name and a border).

Chambres Imaginaires
1st arr. - 7, rue de Castiglione - 42 96 33 81
Open 10 a.m.-7 p.m. Closed Sun. & Mon. Cards: V, AE, DC.

As a companion piece to her shop on the rue Bonaparte, Nicole Hannezo has opened a store exclusively for the bedroom. Among the refined offerings on hand are quilted bedspreads coordinated with embroidered sheets, eiderdown comforters and lacy pillowcases. Bedspreads can be specially ordered for 2,000 francs plus the price of the fabric.

Agnès Comar
8th arr. - 7, av. Georges-V - 47 23 33 85
Open 10 a.m.-7 p.m. (Mon. 2 p.m.-7 p.m.). Closed Sun. & 10 days in Aug. Cards: V, AE, DC.

Always bubbling with fresh, elegant ideas for the home, Agnès Comar now has a solution for your dingy living room sofa and chairs:

loose, flowing slipcovers in a linen-and-cotton blend that adapt to any shape, virtually any size, and are machine washable (for 2,500 francs). She also makes table skirts to measure, with luxurious quilted borders (from 4,800 francs), and felt bedspreads with adorable appliqués that coordinate with curtains and cushions. Sheets come in white or ecru, embroidered or edged with pleats or lace (matched with travel and makeup kits).

Olivier Desforges
6th arr. - 26, bd Raspail - 45 49 19 37
Open 10 a.m.-7 p.m. Closed Mon. & 3 wks. in Aug. Cards: V, AE.

Large and airy, gray and white, Olivier Desforges's shop gives his customers plenty of space in which to examine the lovely bed linens designed by Laurence Laffont. Patterns include a youthful tartan, pastel designs inspired by faraway lands, and wonderful white sheets paired with white ruffled pillowcases. Sheet fabric is available by the meter (for 97 francs per meter), and there's an embroidery service as well.

Maison Rêve
8th arr. - 29, rue Marbeuf - 43 59 02 46
Open 10 a.m.-7 p.m. (Sat. 10 a.m.-1 p.m. & 2 p.m.-7 p.m.). Closed Sun. Cards: V, AE, DC.

This "Dream House" sells stylish, cozy bed linens signed Dior, Givenchy, Yves Saint Laurent, Martine Nourissat and Daniel Hechter. Downstairs, a children's department carries robes, pajamas and colorful sweatsuits to make little ones' nights soft and comfy. Prices vary widely: a terry bath sheet costs 180 francs, but bedspreads (for example) can run up to several thousand francs.

Noël
8th arr. - 49, av. Montaigne - 40 70 02 41
Open 10 a.m.-6:30 p.m. Closed Sun. Cards: V, AE, DC.

After a twelve-year hiatus, Noël has re-opened its doors on the sleek avenue Montaigne. The new shop is a spacious, two-level affair where faithful customers from the old days are enchanted to find the sumptuous organdy and embroidered muslin tablecloths that made Noël's reputation (there are some 13,000 designs in the firm's archives). Danie Postel-Vinay, the creative director, also offers a line of contemporary embroideries and appliqués in a collection of sheets and tablecloths of cotton satin with organdy trim, an homage to the Vienna School. Such luxury doesn't come cheap, though: sheet sets start at 3,000 francs, embroidered tablecloths at 5,000 francs. Terrycloth hand towels, however, are a steal at just 150 francs.

Phédra
8th arr. - 1, rue Royale - 42 66 97 41
Open 10 a.m.-7 p.m. Closed Sun. Cards: V, AE, DC.

Next door to Maxim's, in the building where Benjamin Franklin signed the Franco-American alliance treaty in 1778, is a boutique, done up in neoclassic style, of refined, expensive household linens. Synthetic materials are banished from this shop: everything here is made of cotton, linen or silk. Patterns are inspired by classical mythology, and many are hand-embroidered. Four colors—gray, salmon, yellow and white—dominate. A rectangular tablecloth (six places) is priced at about 2,500 francs.

Porthault
8th arr. - 18, av. Montaigne - 47 20 75 25
Open 9:30 a.m.-6:30 p.m. (Sat. & Mon. 9:30 a.m.-1 p.m. & 2 p.m.-6 p.m.). Closed Sat. in Aug. & Sun. Cards: V, AE, DC.

Everyone who loves luxurious linens knows Porthault. Even if you can't afford these signature prints and exquisite embroideries (they are, of course, direly expensive—a tablecloth can cost up to 50,000 francs), you can browse, finger (discreetly!) and admire them in this tony shop on the avenue Montaigne. A lower-priced line, Porthault Studio, was recently introduced—but even lower-than-regular prices here isn't cheap. A pair of sheets and two pillowcases in embroidered cotton run to about 2,800 francs; a pretty white bedspread sells for 1,980 francs.

TABLEWARE

CANDLES

Cir-Roussel
6th arr. - 22, rue Saint-Sulpice
43 26 46 50
Open 10 a.m.-7 p.m. Closed Sun., Mon. & Aug. Cards: V, AE, DC.

In the wax-processing business since 1643, Cir-Roussel offers a considerable choice of candles in a variety of classic and imaginative shapes. Current bestsellers are "cake," "caviar" and "sandwich" candles. These, like any candle in the shop, may be personalized with your name or initials (or special message?) for the modest fee of 5 francs per candle.

Point à la Ligne
7th arr. - 177, bd Saint-Germain
42 22 17 72
Open 10 a.m.-7 p.m. Closed Sun. Cards: V, AE, DC.

You are certain to find candles to match your centerpiece or tablecloth (or your eyes, for that matter) in this pretty boutique near Saint-Germain-des-Prés. There are 36 shades available, each one coordinated with paper napkins, plates and tablecloths. Candle holders are available as well, in white or colored glass, along with hurricane lamps and a line of candles in imaginative shapes. If you wish, Point à la Ligne will custom-illuminate your house or garden for a special party.

TABLEWARE

Au Bain Marie
8th arr. - 10, rue Boissy-d'Anglas
42 66 59 74
Open 9 a.m.-7 p.m. Closed Sun. Parking: Concorde. Cards: V, AE.

In a setting that recalls the lobby of a palatial hotel, Aude Clément presents a vast assortment of tableware, kitchenware and accessories. Even the items that aren't expensive antiques look as if they ought to be: embroidered table linens, genuine crystal or just-glass glasses (initialed or not, as you wish), real and fake pearl-handled cutlery. . . . Pieces by the Memphis group and a collection of tableware by American architects are exhibited alongside witty, inexpensive treasures for the table. Don't miss the huge accumulation of cookbooks and magazines on food and wine.

Dîners en Ville
7th arr. - 27, rue de Varenne
42 22 78 33
Open 11 a.m.-7 p.m. Closed Sun., Mon. & 2 wks. in Aug. Parking: Bon Marché. Cards: V.

It's hard not to notice this shop, with its multiple display windows that wrap around the corner of the rue du Bac and the rue de Varenne. It's even harder not to stop and gape at the lavish tables draped in old-fashioned paisley tablecloths (700 to 1,000 francs) and set with turn-of-the-century French or English dishes, crystal and table decorations. Inside, there are glasses in an enchanting array of colors and, on the upper floor, a section devoted to the ritual of tea, with teapots, tea services, antique cookie jars and silver accessories.

Daum

2nd arr. - 4, rue de la Paix - 42 61 25 25
Open 9:30 a.m.-1 p.m. & 2 p.m.-6:30 p.m. Closed Sun. Parking: Vendôme. Cards: V, AE, DC.

Daum's elegant dual-level showrooms are situated in premises formerly occupied by the great couturier, Worth. Slate-gray walls and green-glazed bronze furniture form an ideal setting for the firm's latest creations. On the ground floor are the limited-edition (200 or 300 copies) glass pieces, in luminous colors: Fassianos's cobalt-blue head, carafes with cactus stoppers by Hilton McConnico, and the latter's sumptuous red vase. The lower level is devoted to Daum's lovely crystal table services.

Devine Qui Vient Dîner

15th arr. - 83, av. Emile-Zola - 40 59 41 14
Open 10:30 a.m.-7:30 p.m. Closed Sun. Cards: V.

This red-and-gray shop is known for its noteworthy assortment of late-nineteenth- and early-twentieth-century tableware, along with many finely crafted reproductions. Prices are amazingly reasonable, witness a set of engraved red whisky glasses (67 francs each) with matching carafe (357 francs) and an antique silver-plated bread basket (600 francs).

Doria

6th arr. - 4, rue Bourbon-le-Château
40 46 00 00
Open 10 a.m.-1 p.m. & 2 p.m.-7 p.m. Closed Sun., Mon. & Aug. Parking: Saint-Germain. No cards.

Florence Doria, mad for art deco, is extremely selective about the objects she offers for sale. You'll find only original crystal stemware and vases by René Lalique and Baccarat,

and silver by Puiforcat and Christofle here. The pieces tend to be rare, and therefore expensive: a sterling-silver service by Puiforcat could run to 140,000 francs; on the other hand, one can find silver-plated serving platters for the more moderate sum of 1,500 francs.

La Faïence Anglaise

6th arr. - 11, rue du Dragon - 42 22 42 72
Open 11 a.m.-7 p.m. Closed Sun. & 2 wks. in Aug. Parking: Saint-Germain. Cards: V, AE.

Anglophiles and other tea fanciers will love the selection of small Victorian antiques, figurines and 1930s lamps available here. But dishes and table and tea accessories are the principal specialty of the house. Teapots, cake plates and tea caddies range in price from about 270 to 400 francs.

Gien

1st arr. - 39, rue des Petits-Champs
47 03 49 92
Open 10:30 a.m.-2:30 p.m. & 3 p.m.-7 p.m. (Sat. & Mon. hours vary). Closed Sun. & Aug. 1-22. Cards: V.

The Gien faïence (earthenware/pottery) factory, founded in 1821, has been granted a new lease on life. Noted designers have been commissioned to create new patterns that are now on view in Gien's Paris showroom: Paco Rabanne came up with a service of square plates with delicate ridges, while Jean-Pierre Caillères designed triangular plates edged with black speckles. In a more traditional vein, Dominique Lalande painted his plates with fruit motifs and added a black-and-white border. People who prefer the Gien services that their grandmothers bought will be happy to see that they are still available.

Impression De

1st arr. - 54, rue de Richelieu - 42 96 39 13
Open 10:30 a.m.-6:30 p.m. (Sat. 2 p.m.-6 p.m.). Closed Sun. Parking: Pyramides, Palais-Royal. Cards: V.

Philippe Deshoulières now shows his pretty china—some of it designed by such fashionable names as Patrick Frey, Primrose Bordier (of Descamps) and Daniel Hechter—in this spanking-new shop. Hechter's square Squadra plates (which sell for less than 100 francs) are a current hit. Deshoulières cleverly decided to offer cookware in the same patterns as his china collections. So the dishes that go into the microwave, freezer or under the broiler can rest on the table and feel right at home.

Lalique

8th arr. - 11, rue Royale - 42 65 33 70
Open 9:30 a.m.-noon & 2 p.m.-6 p.m. Closed Sun. Parking: Concorde. Cards: V.

Three generations of creative Laliques have earned an international following with their enchanting crystal designs. Marie-Claude Lalique, who succeeded her father, Marc, at the head of the company in 1977, creates marvelous contemporary pieces in the true Lalique spirit—like her Atossa vase, decorated with a circlet of amber crystal-and-opaline flowers. In the courtyard of the rue Royale shop, Lalique has opened another boutique, devoted to "the art of the table." Alongside the Lalique productions are linens, silver and china by prestigious manufacturers.

La Maison du Week-End

6th arr. - 26, rue Vavin - 43 54 15 52
Open 10:30 a.m.-7 p.m. Closed Sun. & Mon. Parking: Montparnasse. Cards: V.

If your idea of a weekend treat is a shopping spree for linens and dishes to fill up your cupboards, we've got just the shop for you. Old-fashioned damask tablecloths, in a range of seven pastel shades, are made to order here (from about 300 francs); damask towels sell for 278 francs with fringe, 178 francs without. You'll also find table services in faïence (earthenware) or china; the most recent addition to the line is a china tea service decorated with tiny old-fashioned blossoms (teapot, 378 francs; teacup, 135 francs). Do you feel that what is lacking in your life is a gilded garden chair? Look no further.

Manufacture Nationale de Sèvres

1st arr. - 4, pl. André-Malraux - 47 03 40 20
Open 11:30 a.m.-6:30 p.m. Closed Sun. & Mon. Parking: Pyramides. No cards.

In an ultra-contemporary setting, with glass-and-brushed-steel shelves, La Manufacture Nationale de Sèvres presents its superb hand-painted, gold-trimmed china. Every piece is a work of art; some pieces are designed by top artists—Lalanne, Mathieu, Van Lith and Coloretti, among them. Also on display are reproductions of such extraordinary objets d'art as the dancers sculpted by Léonard and Carpeaux. Prices for plates range from 1,000 to 10,000 francs, and the most expensive vase commands 200,000 francs. Special orders take one to three months.

Odiot

8th arr. - 7, pl. de la Madeleine
42 65 00 95, 42 65 76 58
Open 9:30 a.m.-6:30 p.m. (Sat. 10 a.m.-6:30 p.m.). Closed Sun. Parking: Madeleine. Cards: V, AE.

Silversmiths in Paris since 1690, this illustrious firm maintains its traditions by continuing to reissue its eighteenth- and nineteenth-century pieces. Odiot will also execute silver or vermeil pieces as requested by a customer (a Napoléon-era desk lamp in gilded silver, priced at 267,000 francs, is the most expensive object in the shop). For shoppers of more modest means, there are some fine items in silver-plate, china and crystal. Appealing little brooches in the form of a bee cost 290 francs.

Pavillon Christofle

6th arr. - 17, rue de Sèvres - 45 48 16 17
Open 9:30 a.m.-6:30 p.m. (Mon. & Sat. 9:30 a.m.-1 p.m. & 2 p.m.-6:30 p.m.). Closed Sun. Parking: Sèvres-Babylone. Cards: V, AE, DC. Other branches.

Christofle was born in 1830, and began to produce the plated silverware that was to make it its fortune. Since then, Christofle has become the world's premier exporter of table silver. The current bestseller is the clean-lined, contemporary Aria setting (168 francs for a fork or tablespoon, 222 francs for a knife). A recent creation, the Talisman line of Chinese-lacquered settings, owes its beauty and durability to a jealously guarded secret process (fork or spoon, 298 francs; knife, 398 francs). Christofle has also enjoyed notable success with reproductions of its designs from the 1920s (like the coveted tea service in silver plate with briarwood handles), and a handsome line of classic china. (All settings are machine washable.)

Peter
8th arr. - 191, rue du Faubourg-Saint-Honoré - 45 63 88 00
Open 10 a.m.-1 p.m. & 1:30 p.m.-7 p.m. Closed Sun., Mon. & 1st 3 wks. in Aug. Parking: Foch. Cards: V.

For a couple of centuries, Peter's exclusive silverware patterns have adorned the dinner tables of the rich and refined (the Aga Khan and Giovanni Agnelli appear on the clients list, just to give you an idea). The most sumptuous setting in the shop, fashioned of lapis lazuli and vermeil, sells for 14,152 francs. But Peter accommodates less opulent tastes as well, with beautifully designed contemporary silver, china services, crystal and small gifts (an elegant nail clipper is priced at just 80 francs).

Puiforcat
8th arr. - 22, rue François-Ier - 47 20 74 27
Open 9:30 a.m.-6:30 p.m. Closed Sun. & Mon. Parking: François-Ier. Cards: V, AE, DC.

A few years ago, this world-renowned silversmithing firm had the bright idea to reissue Jean Puiforcat's stunning 1930s designs (like the table settings for the oceanliner the *Normandie*). More recently Puiforcat added a gift and jewelry department that stocks merchandise for nearly every budget. A silver-plated centerpiece sells for 1,100 francs; but a pretty silver chain bracelet sells for only 120 francs. Puiforcat continues to commission pieces from well-known designers such as Andrée Putman and Manuel Canovas.

Quartz Diffusion
6th arr. - 12, rue des Quatre-Vents
43 54 03 00
Open 10:30 a.m.-7 p.m. (Mon. 2 p.m.-7 p.m.). Closed Sun. Parking: Ecole de Médecine. Cards: V, MC.

There's lots of space in this shop, all of it devoted to the delicate art of the glassmaker.

The objects on display are signed by such talented artists as Baldwin, Guggisberg, Bouchard, Hinz, Gilbert and others who research the possibilities of glass for the Musée des Arts Décoratifs. Not everything is terrifyingly fragile or expensive, witness the "laboratory" glass carafe and salad bowl (125 francs and 130 francs, respectively). Glass tabletops, screens and shelves are available as well, and Quartz is also the exclusive source of a layered colored glass called Décor A IV.

Quatre Saisons
15th arr. - 20, bd de Grenelle - 45 77 46 39
Open 10:30 a.m.-7 p.m. (Mon. noon-7 p.m.). Closed Sun. Cards: V.

Here's a terrific collection of high-quality wooden table and kitchenware: carving boards, salad bowls, cheese boards (from 75 francs) and more. Pretty, inexpensive glassware (8 to 80 francs) is also on hand, along with rustic baskets and an assortment of fabric and plastic tablecloths in appealing colors.

Rosenthal
2nd arr. - 37, rue des Capucines
42 61 58 21
Open 10 a.m.-7 p.m. Closed Sun. Parking: Vendôme, Madeleine. Cards: V, AE, DC.

The German firm Rosenthal, known throughout the world, has finally opened a branch in Paris, where a comprehensive sampling of its designs is on view. Great artists and designers have created many unusual, imaginative pieces for Rosenthal. Currently, black-and-white motifs are the trend in china: Mario Bellini designed a service called Weiss, which combines black and white plates; Dorothy Hafner came up with a handsome service in the same colors. At the firm's request, 21 artists contributed their own distinct variations on the theme of a teacup. Some are sculptures, others paintings, and their incredible forms make them ideal collectors' items. Fine crystal is a specialty, too. (Bellini's glass for the Weiss collection costs 86 francs; a teapot designed by Gropius sells for 1,533 francs.)

IMAGE & SOUND

PHOTOGRAPHY

Fnac
1st arr. - Forum des Halles, level 2
40 26 81 18
Open 10 a.m.-7:30 p.m. (Mon. 1 p.m.-7:30 p.m.). Closed Sun. Parking: Forum des Halles. Cards: V. Other branches: Fnac Etoile - 26, av. de Wagram - 8th arr. - 47 66 52 50; Fnac Montparnasse - 136, rue de Rennes - 6th arr. - 45 44 39 12.

You'll find a large selection of top brands at interesting prices at Fnac stores, plus all kind of equipment for developing and printing film. The customer service is excellent. There are over 28 Fnac outlets dotted around Paris, where you can buy rolls of film, spools of super-8 film and blank video cassettes, as well as have your holidays snaps developed.

La Maison du Leica
11th arr. - 53, bd Beaumarchais
48 05 77 67
Open 9:30 a.m.-1 p.m. & 2 p.m.-7 p.m. Closed Sun., Mon. & Aug. Parking: pl. de la Bastille. Cards: V.

For all the lovers of this manufacturer, the Maison du Leica sells new and used equipment and repairs all Leicas. The prices are competitive with those of the big discount store, Fnac, and the service is perfect.

Nicablad
15th arr. - 8, bd Pasteur - 43 06 61 56
Open 10 a.m.-12:30 p.m. & 2 p.m.-7 p.m. Closed Sun., Mon. & Aug. Parking: Garibaldi. Cards: V.

This store undertakes to sell the very best equipment (Hasselblad, Contax, Leica, Nikon) at attractive prices. The personnel are highly qualified advisors, and recently some used equipment has been offered at prices that make it an excellent deal.

Verdeau Photo
9th arr. - 14, passage Verdeau - 47 70 51 91
Open 9 a.m.-1 p.m. & 2 p.m.-7 p.m. Closed Sat., Sun., Mon. & Aug.

Located between a stamp dealer and a bookseller in one of the prettiest passageways in Paris, this store buys, sells and exchanges used cameras, including movie cameras. Recommended for collectors and the nostalgic also.

RECORDED MUSIC & STEREO GEAR

Crocodisc
5th arr. - 42, rue des Ecoles - 43 54 47 95
Open 11 a.m.-7 p.m. Closed Sun. & Mon. Parking: Maubert.

In this discount record paradise, you can find reasonably priced imports, used records and compact discs and cassettes. Every genre is represented: rock, reggae, funk, blues, country, film scores, etc. In addition, you can listen to the records, and you can set them aside and pay several days later.

Crocojazz
5th arr. - 64, rue de la Montagne-Sainte-Geneviève - 46 34 78 38
Open 11 a.m.-1 p.m. & 2 p.m.-7 p.m. Closed Sun. & Mon. Parking: Maubert. Cards: V.

This is an arm of nearby Crocodisc, and it specializes in jazz. Crocojazz is run on the same principles.

Oldies but Goodies
4th arr. - 16, rue du Bourg-Tibourg
48 87 14 37
Open 12:30 p.m.-7:30 p.m. Closed Sun. Parking: Hôtel de Ville. Cards: V, AE, MC.

This shop specializes in used records, including jazz, blues, and rock and roll in French and

American versions. There are all sorts of goodies, old or rare or cheap. The store boasts a clientele that includes collectors and celebrities (Eddie Mitchell, Bernadette Lafont). Recently they added compact discs, and U.S. imports are making more frequent appearances.

Pan
6th arr. - 176, bd Saint-Germain
45 44 43 95
Open 10:15 a.m.-7:30 p.m. (Mon. until 2 p.m.). Closed Sun. Parking: Saint-Germain. Cards: V.
Guy Millètre opened this store in 1953 on the rue Jacob and has since moved to this address. He is a Conservatory-trained musicologist who is one of the top specialists in classical music. His infallible memory and unflagging kindness have helped many a collector in their search for the unfindable. Meanwhile the store is growing; his son has opened up a top-end TV and hi-fi department and his wife is expanding the record department, including a rock category now that is as seriously done as the rest. Prices are high but the service and the goods are the best.

Papageno
2nd arr. - 1, rue Marivaux - 42 96 56 54
Open 11:30 a.m.-7 p.m. Closed Mon. & Aug. Parking: Bourse. Cards: V.
This shop offers rare and imported records from everywhere, private editions, repressings of old 78s, compact discs and discount records. And they have just added a selection of operas on video, especially rare performances, that ought to thrill the hearts of opera buffs.

Parallèles
1st arr. - 47, rue Saint-Honoré
42 33 62 70
Open 10 a.m.-7 p.m. Closed Sun. Parking: Forum des Halles. Cards: V, MC.
This is mostly used records in rock, country, blues, reggae, etc. There are some interesting finds to be had, and you can buy music magazines unavailable elsewhere.

Paris-Musique
6th arr. - 10, bd Saint-Michel - 43 26 96 41
Open 9:30 a.m.-8 p.m. (Sat. until midnight, Sun. until 2 p.m.). Parking: Ecole de Médecine. Cards: V, MC.
This is one of the least expensive stores in the Latin Quarter. It features just about every style of music, with particularly strong points in rock and jazz. Discounts and sales are offered all the time, and you'll find lots of imports and compact discs.

VIDEO

Playtime
7th arr. - 44, av. Bosquet - 45 55 43 36
Open noon-8 p.m. Closed Sun. Cards: V. Other branch: 36, av. d'Eylau - 16th arr. - 47 27 56 22.
This is the place for movie buffs, where they can rent video cassettes from the collection of more than 3,000 titles. A nice plus for after shopping: customers can stop for a cup of tea in the adjoining tea room and bar. The help is very friendly, and cassette tapes are also available.

Victor Vidéo Vision
8th arr. - 40, rue du Colisée - 42 25 30 03
Open 10 a.m.-7 p.m. (Sat. 11 a.m.-7 p.m.). Closed Sun. & Mon. Parking: Rond-Point des Champs-Elysées. Cards: V.
This establishment is the former Video Club of France, with a new emphasis on sales, although it still offers some rental. You can buy video cassettes from a catalog of 6,000 titles.

Remember that if you spend 1,200 francs or more in a store, you are entitled to a full refund of the value-added tax (VAT). See "Basics" for details.

JEWELRY

ANTIQUE JEWELRY

C. Gustave
8th arr. - 416, rue Saint-Honoré
42 60 14 38
Open 10 a.m.-6:30 p.m. Closed Sat. (except Nov. & Dec.), Sun. & Aug. Cards: V, AE, DC.

This is the oldest boutique in the neighborhood; it is also the first in Europe to import cultured pearls. On the fringes of the international chic zone, Faubourg-Saint-Honoré, it has some lovely old bargains, stones of a quality you do not see anymore and pieces signed by Van Cleef and Boucheron.

Oxeda
1st arr. - 390, rue Saint-Honoré
42 60 27 57
Open 10:15 a.m.-6:15 p.m. Closed Sun. Cards: V, AE, DC.

Here you'll find previously owned jewelry, of both antique and recent vintage, including some with lofty pedigrees (Van Cleef, Cartier, Boucheron and others). There's always the possibility of finding some interesting deals. If you bring in jewelry to sell, be sure to know its worth beforehand; Oxeda does not appraise items, and your price likely could be different than theirs.

BEST OF THE BEST

Alexandre Reza
1st arr.- 23, pl. Vendôme - 42 96 64 00
Open 10 a.m.-1 p.m. & 2 p.m.-6:30 p.m. Closed Sun. Cards: V, AE.

Alexandre Reza, of Russian descent, is a major dealer in precious stones and always seems to have the most beautiful stones around his shop. An expert collector, he has transformed his basement level into a gallery exhibiting reproductions fashioned according to traditional techniques. Take a look, for example, at the necklace of pear diamonds, all in gems by Fowliss, a stunning and priceless piece. Next to such striking beauty, the Petit Coeur ring for 2,900 francs seems rather plain.

Boucheron
1st arr. - 26, pl. Vendôme - 42 61 58 16
Open 10 a.m.-1 p.m. & 2 p.m.-6:30 p.m. Closed Sun. Cards: V, AE.

Alain Boucheron, current bearer of the Boucheron family torch and president of the French Haute Joaillerie, is carrying the tradition of this house into new areas. In fact, with his Pluriels line of jewelry, he is expanding and developing the notion of what fine jewelry is: settings in gold for alternating rings or links of acacia, diamonds, coral and so on (a Pluriel piece therefore runs 6,000 francs or so). Beautiful pieces on plush trays, in a wood-paneled environment with, as always, the characteristic oval-pattern frieze above . . . that's when you'll know you are in chez Boucheron.

Bulgari
8th arr. - 27, av. Montaigne - 47 23 89 89
Open 10 a.m.-1 p.m. & 2:30 p.m.-7 p.m. Closed Sun. Parking: Rond-Point des Champs-Elysées. Cards: V, AE, DC.

The house of Bulgari got its start in Rome in 1881 when Sotirio Bulgari began selling the jewelry that he made at night from a pushcart in the streets. Today Bulgari jewels pay the price of success: they are among the most copied pieces in the world. The Bulgari style is marked by piles of precious stones built up on gold mountings, frequently invoking a mocking, overdone realism as in engraved gold Marlboro boxes or maps of the world in lapis lazuli and rubies or silver postcards. (Prices begin at about 60,000 francs.)

Cartier

1st arr. - 7, pl. Vendôme - 42 61 55 55
Open 10 a.m.-7 p.m. (until 6:30 p.m. in winter;
Mon. & Sat. 10:30 a.m.-7 p.m.). Closed Sun.
Parking: Vendôme. Cards: V, AE, DC, MC.

"It is better to have authentic junk than fake Cartier," exclaims Dominique Perrin, chief executive of Cartier, the most copied name in the world. The watches can be found all over the globe, as can the wine-red leather goods (from keyholders to eyeglass cases). Besides all the *must* Cartier goods, there remains the fine jewelry that made this establishment the most famous house in the world. Traditional jeweler services combined with inventiveness and know-how have conquered the world. In its Paris shops, Cartier will make up from simple sketches engagement rings or wedding bands, or they will wonderfully rejuvenate old or poorly cut stones.

Chaumet

1st arr. - 12, pl. Vendôme - 42 60 32 82
Open 9:30 a.m.-1 p.m. & 2:30 p.m.-6:30 p.m.
Closed Sun. Parking: Vendôme. No cards.

Following some wandering in the fiscal desert, Chaumet was picked up by the major holding group that owned Tiffany. Nevertheless, Chaumet continues to make up rare gems and precious metals into rings, necklaces and bracelets (prices begin at 50,000 francs). Next to the fine jewelry, the Temporel line and the Bréguet watches are sold. And the house has announced a new line of jewelry at more modest prices (remember, everything is relative) that may be distributed more widely than just from within the hallowed walls here on the place Vendôme.

Mauboussin

1st arr. - 20, pl. Vendôme - 42 60 32 54
Open 10 a.m.-1 p.m. & 2 p.m.-6:30 p.m. Closed
Sun. Parking: Vendôme. Cards: V, AE, DC.

Established in 1827, the house of Mauboussin gives off that impression of security and comfort one associates with old families, for whom the purchase of fine jewelry is the natural way to celebrate life's big moments. One is warmly welcomed into the discreet little offices where business is conducted. The house specializes in engagement rings, especially in colored stones (emeralds, rubies, sapphires) set off by diamonds. They are also the creators of the famous Nadia rings in carved mother-of-pearl and gold set with a diamond or a colored gem. Patrick and Alain Mauboussin have brought new life to the family tradition by offering a bicentennial collection of red, white and blue jewelry (sapphire, diamond and ruby). Prices here run 8,000 to 100,000 francs.

Mellerio dits Meller

1st arr. - 9, rue de la Paix - 42 61 57 53
Open 9:30 a.m.-1 p.m. & 2:30 p.m.-6:30 p.m.
Closed Sun., Sat. in July, Aug. & Sept. Cards:
V, AE, DC.

Marie de Medicis had no idea, of course, that she was founding a dynasty of jewelers when she granted her loyal Lombard chimney sweeps (who, from the other side of the flue, had overheard and reported a noble plot) licences first as peddlers, then street vendors and finally jewelers. Now, fourteen generations later, the great house of Mellerio is by no means resting on its ancient laurels. The oldest of all the fine jewelers of France, the Mellerio family comb the worldwide gem trade for those outstanding stones, regardless of size, that measure up to their noble tradition. Constituting one of the centers of the haut monde of fine jewelry, Mellerio exports half its trade to the far corners of the globe.

Poiray

8th arr. - 8, rue de la Paix - 42 61 70 58
Open 10 a.m.-1 p.m. & 2 p.m.-6 p.m. Closed
Sat. & Sun. Parking: Vendôme. Cards: V, AE,
DC. Other branch: Carré d'Or - 46 av. Georges-
V - 8th arr. - 47 23 07 41.

The house of Poiray is the youngest of the great jewelers. If a fine jewel can be said to have a soul, Poiray endows it with a spirit of youth. The multitinted style of its famous three-gold Tresse ring (12,500 francs), already seen on some very famous fingers around town, is henceforth available in necklaces and bracelets. There are lots of new items, such as the Three-Gold Heart and the Octogo line of gold-plated pieces, as well as the reknowned Poiray watches, which come in round, rectangular or square shapes in gold, steel, gold and steel, or dressed up in precious stones. As for fine jewels, Poiray has the Cascade collection, including a bracelet of gold bangles trimmed in diamonds, rubies and sapphires for 300,000 francs and up. But there are some lovely rings at much more affordable prices.

Van Cleef et Arpels
1st arr. - 22, pl. Vendôme - 42 61 58 58
Open 10 a.m.-1 p.m. & 2:30 p.m.-6:30 p.m. Closed Sun. Parking: Vendôme. No cards.

The most innovative of the jewelers of the place Vendôme, and originators of the "mere trifle" in gold and precious gems, this house boasts a unique technique for mounting stones that is virtually invisible. Everything is designed to emphasize the gem. The prices reflect the highest level of workmanship and creativity, but even modest budgets have access to the Van Cleef Boutique where rings, earrings and butterfly pendants, starting at about 3,700 francs, can be found.

Harry Winston
8th arr. - 29, av. Montaigne - 47 20 03 09
Open 9 a.m.-1 p.m. & 2 p.m.-6 p.m. by appt. Closed Sat. & Sun. No cards.

American jeweler Harry Winston is one of the most prestigious diamond dealers in the world. He sells uncut diamonds from his own mines to other dealers, to retailers and in his own showrooms. Many of the world's best-known diamonds have come from Winston, including five that belong to Queen Elizabeth II and one that graced the hand of Elizabeth Taylor-Burton. Even Marilyn, for whom diamonds were a best friend, liked to talk to about Harry Winston. The entrance to the establishment is discreet and perhaps overly guarded; you must have an appointment and be ready to virtually be frisked. In the two second-floor rooms, left in period style, the built-in showcases display diamond jewels, ornaments, earrings and other marvelous creations in a traditional but not ornate style. How much, you ask? In the millions of dollars, and for an international clientele or French customers seeking a solid investment.

COSTUME JEWELRY

Eric Ange Pena
2nd arr. - 3, rue d'Aboukir - 42 33 20 05
Open 10:30 a.m.-7 p.m. Closed Sun. Parking: Saint-Eustache. Cards: V, AE.

This is crowded quarters for Pena, a Mediterranean designer who fashions jewelry out of hardened, ebony-colored linen fabric! Do not delay in discovering this marvel. (Prices from 300 francs.)

L'Avant Musée
4th arr. - 2, rue Brisemiche - 48 87 45 81
Open 1 p.m.-7 p.m. Closed Sun. Parking: Beaubourg, Hôtel de Ville. Cards: V.

There are 24 artisans represented here, including Di Rosa (whose badges are creating a sensation), Grosso Modo, Virginia Campion and Happy Fingers. Elbow-to-elbow in the alleyways surrounding the Pompidou Center, rings, clips, bands, necklaces and bracelets in resin, metal and other materials are sold at moderate prices. It may not be all classic, but collectors already are snatching up the telephone-charge-card facsimiles designed by Toffe. And Richard Texier has been chosen as the tapestry artist for the bicentennial. Prices start at 50 francs.

Simon Azoulay
3rd arr. - 13, rue de Thorigny - 48 04 92 66
Open 10 a.m.-6:30 p.m. Closed Sun. Cards: V, MC.

Simon Azoulay's handcrafted jewelry sparkles with wit and originality. A wire muzzle from a Champagne bottle, dipped in gold, becomes an unusual brooch. Draped metal or bits of metal screen immersed in molten brass or bronze make clever, exclusive ornaments. Prices start at 250 francs.

Lei
1st arr. - 15, rue des Petits-Champs
42 86 00 16
Open 11 a.m.-7 p.m. (Sat. 2:30 p.m.-7 p.m.). Closed Sun. Parking: Saint-Eustache, Pyramides. Cards: V, AE.

Antonella Grammatico has a knack for choosing custom jewelry from yesteryear to suit contemporary tastes. Her collection includes huge "cocktail" rings from the '40s, Second-Empire pendants and other baubles and bangles in silver or gold. Interesting prices, from about 450 francs.

Othello
6th arr. - 21, rue des Saints-Pères
42 60 26 24
Open 11 a.m.-7:30 p.m. Closed Sun. Parking: Saint-Germain. Cards: V, AE.

Sheherazade would have loved the jewelry on display at Othello. Terracotta, pink ivory-wood, coral, jade beads and even yew-tree roots are used in the creation of these exotic ornaments straight out of a fairy tale. Prices begin at 250 francs.

Yamada

2nd arr. - 30, rue Danielle-Casanova
42 86 94 81
Open 10:30 a.m.-7 p.m. Closed Sun. Parking: Pyramides. Cards: V.

From classic pieces in ivory and to hard-lined "design" ornaments in ebony or malachite, this Japanese firm comes up with jewelry for every taste. Prices start at 380F.

QUALITY

A & A Turner

8th arr. - 16, av. Georges-V - 47 23 88 28
Open 10:30 a.m.-6:30 p.m. Closed Sun. & 2 wks. in Aug. Parking: Georges-V. Cards: V, AE, DC.

Françoise Turner is one of the younger names among French jewelers. Decorated with carved wood and old red floor tiles, her gallery is nothing but luxurious. Big rings, some hand-carved (from 5,000 francs), complement the necklaces of lapis lazuli (85,000 francs) or of rock crystal tipped in gold (from 40,000 francs). On our last visit there, we also found large beads in malachite, marble and slate or horn, gold and cut stones that can be worn with a pearl necklace, a large chain or simply strung on a leather thong (from 25,000 francs). More affordable is Turner's new line of solid-gold jewelry, with prices ranging around the 5,000-franc mark.

Arthus Bertrand

6th arr. - 6, pl. Saint-Germain-des-Prés
42 22 19 20
Open 10 a.m.-6:15 p.m. (Sat., Sun. & Mon. 10 a.m.- 12:30 p.m. & 2 p.m.-6:15 p.m.). Parking: Saints-Pères. Cards: V, AE.

Facing the church of Saint-Germain-des-Prés, next door to the famous Café Aux Deux Magots, is the establishment of Arthus Bertrand, sole remaining maker of medals and supplier of academic swords. The big bourgeois families come here for engagement rings done in an utterly classic style. Nobody comes to Arthus Bertrand for the warm welcome, which is about as friendly as a court martial. Specializing in reproductions of antique jewelry that's sold at the Louvre, Bertrand recently

began offering the exclusive Zolotas Prestige collection featuring a historical motif. You'll find 22-carat-gold jewelry, as well as silver and two-headed rings (lion, ram and so forth), and small refined pieces starting at 600 francs.

Cotailys

3rd arr. - 6, rue Réaumur - 42 72 23 79
Open 9 a.m.-6 p.m. Closed Sat. (except in Dec.) & Sun. No cards.

Aided by the expert advice of the friendly owner, you can select from a variety of necklaces, bracelets, rings and earrings that combine contemporary taste with timeless classicism. Diamonds, emeralds, sapphires and rubies in myriad sizes are set principally in yellow gold. The shop also takes care of repairs, will make new pieces from your old jewelry, and gladly executes special orders and designs. Wholesale prices.

Ebel

1st arr. - 2, pl. Vendôme - 42 60 82 08
Open 10 a.m.-6:30 p.m. Closed Sun. Parking: Vendôme. Cards: V, AE.

Since 1911 these "architects of time" have been seeking to make the perfect watch. They have succeeded, and you can find it at their gallery on the place Vendôme (with its decor by Andrée Putman): splendid, accurate watches dressed in cut diamonds and sapphires. The house also offers a designer line of jewelry by Italian Alexandra Gradi, featuring her necklaces and rings fashioned from rounded, tightly linked gold chain, delightful rings composed of colored gems encircled by large gold bands (ring prices range from 6,000 to 12,000 francs; bracelets, 38,000 francs; necklaces, 77,000 francs). The prices of the watches (from 56,000 francs) are justified by the precious materials and the custom fabrication used. An impeccably courteous reception is the house rule.

Fred Joaillier

8th arr. - 6, rue Royale - 42 60 30 65
Open 9 a.m.-6:30 p.m. (Mon & Sat. 9 a.m.- 12:30 p.m. & 2 p.m.-6:30 p.m.). Closed Sun. Parking: Madeleine. Cards: V, AE, DC, MC.

This is resolutely sports jewelry, featuring the Force 10 and Tennis lines. Gold and steel are set with diamonds, flexible bracelets of gold decorate the active life. There are some watches in a combination of steel and leather (4,000 francs), and fine jewelry featuring evening bags in mother-of-pearl and precious gems in exotic shapes, butterflies or scarabs. Figure a tidy million francs for the latter. Fred Joaillier also has boutiques in the Galerie du Claridge (a shopping arcade off the Champs-Elysées), the Méridien hotel and in Orly airport.

Ilias Lalaounis

1st arr. - 364, rue Saint-Honoré
42 61 55 65
Open 10 a.m.-6:30 p.m. Closed Sun. & Aug. Parking: Vendôme. Cards: V, AE, DC.

Here you will find braided gold, gold lions' heads, jewelry inspired by that of ancient Greece, and other creations that are much more contemporary but scarcely more affordable.

Jare

1st arr. - Cour Vendôme
42 96 33 66
Open by appt. only. Parking: Vendôme. No cards.

Overrun with business, this jeweler prefers to maintain a peerless standard of quality by limiting orders. Specializing in resetting the jewels that you already own, the magic worked by Jare turns your old, tired baubles into contemporary gems.

Jean Dinh Van

2nd arr. - 7, rue de la Paix - 42 61 74 49
Open 9:30 a.m.-6:30 p.m. (Mon. 10:30 a.m.-6:30 p.m.). Closed Sat. & Sun. Parking: Opéra. Cards: V, AE, DC.

Jean Dinh Van was discovered twenty years ago when the fashion world made his square-link chain a must. Since then he has become the recognized leader in modern jewelry for everyday wear. His is a sober style, often featuring square shapes with rounded corners. In the same vein are his heavy square bracelets, his link chains and his famous handcuff clasps (from 2,000 francs) for rejuvenating pearl necklaces. His earrings of two large bands in

gold or silver (from 2,300 francs) are graceful and lovely. And he offers some very pretty necklaces in black pearls, or in steel, gold or semiprecious stones (from 10,500 francs).

La Perle

16th arr. - 85, av. Raymond-Poincaré
45 53 07 62
Open 10 a.m.-6:30 p.m. Closed Sat. (except in Nov. & Dec.), Sun. & Aug. Cards: V. Other branch: Bijouterie Droz - 16, rue Halévy - 9th arr. - 47 70 85 74.

If you care to present your daughter with her first string of pearls or have your old string reset with precious stones, La Perle offers a variety of cultured pearls custom-strung to your liking as bracelets (5,500 francs and up), earrings, ropes or single strands. As well as transforming your old jewelry, the firm designs its own.

Phedra

8th arr. - 1, rue Royale - 42 66 97 41
Open 10 a.m.-7 p.m. Closed Sun. Parking: Concorde. Cards: V, AE, DC.

Some magnificent Italian jewels: gold rings covered in cut stones, necklaces of pearls set in rough gold and rectangular watches bordered with stones cut in a diamond shape. The collection here includes some rare and one-of-a-kind objects.

Pomellato

8th arr. - 66, rue du Faubourg-Saint-Honoré - 42 65 62 07
Open 10 a.m.-7 p.m. Closed Sun. & Mon. Parking: Concorde. Cards: V, AE, DC.

The Italian jeweler Pomellato just opened a new shop done in gray marble and featuring large display windows, in which he presents new pieces every week. His collection features gold jewelry set off with stones or silver. Necklaces, bracelets and rings come in all different versions of fine links or the richer braided gold, always involving an invisible clasp as part of the piece. The Pomellato offering includes flat, flexible chain bracelets decorated with cut stones (25,000 to 80,000 francs), rings (6,000 to 40,000 francs) and, at the lowest end of the price range, silver brooches (1,700 francs).

LEATHER & LUGGAGE

DISCOUNT LUGGAGE

Didier Ludot

1st arr. - 23-24 galerie Montpensier
42 96 06 56

Open 11 a.m.-2 p.m. & 3 p.m.-7 p.m. (Sat. 11 a.m.-1 p.m. & 2 p.m.-7 p.m.). Closed Sun. & 3 wks. in Aug. Cards: V, AE.

Didier Ludot's shop is located under the arcades of the Palais-Royal, which, in and of itself, is a good enough reason to come and see how he lovingly reconditions secondhand bags from Morabito and Hermès. He also carries a line of "surgical" bags used by doctors at the turn of the century and some superb 1920s-to-'30s suitcases lined with suede in vellum or crocodile.

La Maroquinerie Parisienne

9th arr. - 30, rue Tronchet - 47 42 83 40

Open 9:30 a.m.-7 p.m. (Mon. 1 p.m.-7 p.m.). Closed Sun. & 1 wk. in mid-Aug. Cards: V.

A huge shop filled with an enormous selection of cut-price leather goods, year-round: coin purses, suitcases (Delsey, Samsonite, Longchamp), canvas bags and crocodile handbags. Belts, gloves and umbrellas are also featured, and there is a 15 percent reduction on the marked price. Sale time is mid-January to mid-February.

FINE LUGGAGE

Bottega Veneta

16th arr. - 48, av. Victor-Hugo
45 01 70 58

Open 10 a.m.-7 p.m. (Mon. 2 p.m.-7 p.m.). Closed Sun. Parking: Victor-Hugo. Cards: V, AE.

Expect a grand reception befitting this high-quality Venetian leather-goods establishment. The braided lambskin bags lined in leather are unparalleled. And there are at least 40 models of classic, all-purpose handbags in eleven colors, including bright red and green. The lizard pocketbooks are expensive but always in fashion. To the right of the shop there's a handsome line of leather and vinyl luggage, including soft and hard suitcases. An urbane

staff proffers advice on how to clean or repair old leather.

Emilie

7th arr. - 9, rue de Grenelle - 42 22 37 67

Open 10:15 a.m.-7:15 p.m. Closed Sun. Parking: Bon Marché. Cards: V, AE, DC.

Fashion handbags, inspired by the '50s in half-moon shapes, nose-bag style and small squares. Some good classic styles as well.

Gucci

8th arr. - 2, rue du Faubourg-Saint-Honoré
42 96 83 27

Open 9:30 a.m.-6:30 p.m. (Wed. 10:30 a.m.-6:30 p.m.). Closed Sun. Parking: Madeleine. Cards: V, AE, DC. Other branch: 350, rue Saint-Honoré - 1st arr. - 42 96 83 27.

Located on the corner of the rue Royale and rue du Faubourg-Saint-Honoré is the larger of these two beautiful shops. Hiding behind the historic front are seemingly acres of showrooms sumptuously and soberly decorated in light marble and lemon wood. The leather goods on display are manufactured in Florence by the third generation of the Gucci family. The classic Gucci handbag for day or eveningwear in box calf is priced at 700 to 4,500 francs, crocodile at 6,000 to 25,000 francs. The bag also comes in ostrich and wild boar. The leather and vinyl luggage is marked discreetly with the Gucci logo, or in canvas with the distinctive red and green stripes. There's also a fine selection of leather accessories, with numerous gift possibilities, silver, gold, costume jewelry and shoes. The store at 27, rue du Faubourg-Saint-Honoré is reserved exclusively for ready-to-wear fashions, such as a classic blazer, straight skirts, silk blouses and lots of leather jackets and pants.

Hermès

8th arr. - 24, rue du Faubourg-Saint-Honoré - 42 65 21 60

Open 10 a.m.-6:30 p.m. (Sat. & Mon. 10 a.m.-1 p.m. & 2:15 p.m.-6:30 p.m.). Closed Sun. Cards: V, AE, DC.

Hermès needs little introduction. Its worldwide reputation, amply deserved, precedes it. It has been the purveyors of fine leather goods long enough to reign supreme as the undisputed leader of the pack. The very name is synonymous with leather-scented saddles, handbags, luggage and all the accompanying accoutrements of fine living and traveling. But what about the prices? Are they reasonable or completely beyond reality? The answer is both. Check the finish on the leather goods; think of the meticulous hand-work that went into the cutting, sewing and adjusting of these bags and luggage. You still shrug your shoulders? Then go and visit the workshop in the Hermès museum on the fourth floor (by appointment only). That settled, let's move on to the handbags. Will you be tempted by the Kelly design (1949) or the Constance (1969), the red Hermès, the grained leather, the linen-and-leather or the crocodile and ostrich, which are the pride of the house? You really can't go wrong with any of these classically chic styles. The average prices for the box calfs are 10,000 francs, 30,000 francs for crocodile. There is a prestigious line of handmade luggage in box calf with reinforced corners (28,000 francs for an eighteen-inch suitcase). There are cheaper models and, of course, more expensive ones. If you want something special, such as a leather covering for your bicycle seat or the cockpit of your private jet, the house will gladly oblige.

Lancel
9th arr. - 8, pl. de l'Opéra - 47 42 37 29
Open 9:30 a.m.-7 p.m. Closed Sun. Cards: V, AE, DC. 5 other branches.

These are fairly conventional leather goods branded with the *L* of the logo. However, the choice is huge and the quality unquestionably good. prices vary depending on whether leather or canvas is used (from 380 to 3,000 francs). There are also lots of small articles, such as wallets, pocketbooks and classically styled handbags for sale. Among the future bestsellers is the wonderfully supple "Nelac" line made from a rubber or leather base in practical and often geometric forms.

Morabito
1st arr. - 1, pl. Vendôme - 42 60 30 76
Open 9:30 a.m.-6:30 p.m. Closed Sun. Parking: Vendôme. Cards: V, AE, DC.

The automatic door is a bit brutal, but the reception is perfect. Once in, you'll find yourself swamped in a luxurious and stylized world of travel. (For years now, Morabito has had a

predilection for crocodile.) There is a choice of some 60 styles in audacious colors: turquoise, almond green, cobalt blue. A small pocketbook will cost you 6,950 francs; a medium-size sells for 15,000 francs and upward. For small budgets, there is the junior collection called Swing (890 to 2,950 francs).

Renaud Pellegrino
1st arr. - 10, rue Saint-Roch - 42 60 69 36
Open 10:30 a.m.-1 p.m. & 1:30 p.m.-7:30 p.m. Closed Sun. Cards: V, AE, DC. Other branch: 15, rue du Cherche-Midi - 6th arr. 45 44 56 37.

Despite his name, Renaud Pellegrino is not Italian, he's from Cannes and is a passionate devotee of leather. For a while, he worked for Carita before opening his own stores, one on each bank of the Seine. He has embraced the new fashion for miniature box-shaped bags with fine handles and carries them in five sizes (from 1,300 to 2,200 francs) in satin, as well as made-to-measure in ostrich or lizard (5,000 francs).

Schilz
9th arr. - 30, rue Caumartin - 42 66 46 48
Open 9 a.m.-6:45 p.m. (Mon. 2 p.m.-6:45 p.m.). Cards: V, AE, DC. Other branches.

Schilz opened for business in the French capital in 1815 and thenceforth became a supplier to the court and the aristocracy. Napoléon III's orders are now on exhibit at the Musée des Invalides. Leather goods in this shop are of top quality and are designed and made by hand on the premises. You can buy a saddle and bridle for your horse as well as kit yourself out with boots and gloves. A woman's shoulder bag costs between 2,000 and 2,700 francs. For men there are briefcases or portfolios from 300 to 5,400 francs. There are also ostrich goods, silk scarves and silver jewelry. Schilz guarantees repairs, and its prices are perfectly reasonable given the high quality.

Louis Vuitton
8th arr. - 97, av. Montaigne - 47 20 47 00
Open 9:30 a.m.-6:30 p.m. Closed Sun. Cards: V, AE, DC. Other branch: 78 bis, av. Marceau - 8th arr.

Vuitton lovers, here's a test. Put your bag down at the airline counter of an airport. Watch it disappear into a crowd of other

Vuittons . . . now try and identify it! If you haven't marked it somehow, you might be unlucky. The Vuitton madness has taken over the world. For many, the Vuitton bag has become a cult object. It consists of printed linen coated with vinyl, reinforced with lozine (which looks like leather; Vuitton jealously guards the formula) ribs, untreated leather for handles and straps, copper for rivets and hard corners. It may be top-notch quality, but you certainly pay the price. Tourists with strong currencies, such as the Japanese and the Americans, have long besieged this store, but with the opening of overseas branches, calm has returned to the mother house. Now's the time to go and admire the famous made-to-measure wardrobe trunks and the sumptuous suitcases. If a purchase doesn't work with your budget, console yourself with a card holder or racquet cover or even a key ring.

LEATHER

Barnabooth & Compagnie

7th arr. - 18, rue de Monttessuy
47 53 79 16
Open 11 a.m.-7:30 p.m. Closed Sun. Cards: V.

Barnabooth has bags and luggage in every possible material—from quilted cloth to fake fur, velvet to canvas, but also seersucker, loden and houndstooth. Lots of shapes, too: shoulder bags, square pocketbooks, makeup bags, toilet and lingerie bags and vanity cases, which come in three sizes (from 150 to 700 francs).

Daim-Style

2nd arr. - 8, pl. des Victoires - 42 60 95 13
Open 9 a.m.-6 p.m. Closed Sun. Parking: Bourse. Cards: V.

All the custom-made pieces in this classic shop are for sale at ready-to-wear prices. Lambswool miniskirts are manufactured in 50 colors (price: 1,000 francs; pigskin models start at 600 francs). Then there's shearling and Tuscan kid. Manager Bekier is in sole charge and will happily repare or make alterations,

even on items bought elsewhere. An important address to remember.

Jean-Claude Jitrois

8th arr. - 25, rue du Faubourg-Saint-Honoré - 42 65 27 32
Open 10 a.m.-7 p.m. Parking: Madeleine. Cards: V, AE, DC. Other branch: 44, av. Montaigne - 8th arr. - 47 20 23 04.

Jean-Claude Jitrois has become the couturier of leatherwear, thanks to his spectacular creations worn by Liz Taylor, Ursula Andress and Brigitte Nielsen. He produces a few "bare" basics but also some richly embroidered and studded dresses in a choice of eye-catching colors (from 3,900 francs to 12,800 francs). The new menswear collection hints at a junior line, of which sportswear rules. In short, we find these rowdy, vulgar styles destined for rich Texans straight out of *Dallas.*

Mac Douglas

8th arr. - 155, rue du Faubourg-Saint-Honoré - 45 61 19 71
Open 10 a.m.-7 p.m. Closed Sun. Parking: 1, rue Rabelais. Cards: V, AE, DC. 3 other branches.

Are you a leather lover? If the answer is yes, then you'll want to head straight for Mac and its infinite variety: glossy or dyed lambskin, goatskin, calfskin and suede. There are well-cut jackets in crinkled sheepskin and calfskin and dyed lambskin skirts. Prices are on the high side, but the designs are consistent in quality, well made and available in lots of colors. Good sales in January and July.

Ville et Campagne

6th arr. - 19, rue Guisarde - 43 29 63 03
Open 9 a.m.-7 p.m. Closed Sun. Parking: Saint-Sulpice. Cards: V, AE.

A buddy of Stephanie of Monaco, Jean-Jack Richard produces soft and comfortable leatherwear. His star attraction is a honey-colored suede-like pigskin shirt (950 francs) to wear over jeans. He also makes sporty motorcycle jackets bedecked with zippers (5,900 francs) and skirt and jacket coordinates in lambswool, suede-like pigskin and even stylish jackets for kids.

OPEN LATE

BAKERIES

Boulangerie de l'Ancienne-Comédie
6th arr. - 10, rue de l'Ancienne-Comédie
43 26 89 72
Open 24 hours (Sun. 6 a.m.-8 p.m.). Closed Aug. No cards.
This narrow little shop is located on the same street as the venerable Procope restaurant. The prices of the breads, pastries and croissants change from day to evening to midnight.

Feri's
8th arr. - 8, rue de Ponthieu - 42 56 10 56
Open 11 a.m.-6 a.m. (Sat. & Sun. until 8 p.m.). Cards: V, AE, DC. Other branch: 76, rue Mazarine - 6th arr.
You can get bread here at 5 in the morning—also croissants, brioches, sandwiches and drinks. In short, there's a bit of everything, though it's all standard, run-of-the-mill stuff.

BOOKSTORES

Shakespeare and Company
5th arr. - 37, rue de la Bûcherie - No phone
Open daily noon-midnight. No cards.
This American bookstore stocks its sidewalk stands full of secondhand books, but we like it almost as much for its incomparable view of Notre-Dame and the Seine. Don't confuse it with the legendary Shakespeare and Company of Sylvia Beach, though owner George Whitman claims that he is carrying on the tradition, albeit in different premises. Shelves are filled to the bursting point in this modern Prospero's cell, with books new and old covering every subject imaginable. Poetry meetings take place every Monday evening at 8, and Whitman hosts tea parties upstairs for selected guests on Sunday afternoons. There's always room for overflow in the rare-book room next door, and hidden away on the upper floors is also a free library where future Hemingways and Prousts can nurse their insomnia in old leather armchairs.

DRUGSTORES

Drugstore des Champs-Elysées
8th arr. - 133, av. des Champs-Elysées
47 23 54 34, 47 20 94 40
Open 9 a.m.-2 a.m. (Sun. 10 a.m.-2 a.m.). Parking: Georges V. Cards: V, AE, DC. 3 other branches: Drugstore Matignon, 1, av. Matignon - 8th arr. - 43 59 38 70, parking, Rond-Point des Champs-Elysées; Drugstore Saint-Germain, 146, bd Saint-Germain - 6th arr. - 42 22 92 50, open at 10 a.m.; Multistore Opéra, 6, bd des Capucines - 9th arr. - 42 65 89 43, open daily 11:15 a.m.-midnight, parking, Capucines.
Be it premium bubbly or Alka-Seltzer, a little night music or earplugs for a noiseless morning after . . . they've got it all here!

GROCERIES

Alsace
8th arr. - 39, av. des Champs-Elysées
43 59 44 24
Open daily 24 hours. Cards: V, AE, DC.
Beyond the main restaurant is a catering service–cum-boutique where you can purchase essentially Alsatian specialties: sauerkraut, cured meats and foie gras, as well as sandwiches and other fine foods. There is a take-out service should you be tempted to take home a dish for a midnight snack.

L'An 2000
17th arr. - 82, bd des Batignolles
43 87 24 67
Open 5 p.m.-1 a.m. (Sun. 11 a.m.-1 a.m.). Closed Aug. Cards: V.

After an evening at the Théâtre des Arts-Hébertot, you can put together a nice after-theater supper with provisions from L'An 2000. All sorts of appetizing dishes are on display at this spacious emporium, and though prices are a bit higher than those across the street (Drug Night), we feel they are justified. From caviar to charcuterie, from bread and fresh-vegetable terrines to cheese and fresh fruit, you'll find all the makings of a charming midnight feast.

Bruneau
1st arr. - 1, rue Montmartre - 42 36 40 97
Open 4:30 a.m.-7 p.m. (Sat. until 6 p.m. & Sun. until 11 a.m. or 11 a.m.-7 p.m.). Closed Mon. No cards.

If you crave a nice juicy steak or a thick slice of pâté at 3 in the morning, here's where to find it.

Chez Georges
1st arr. - 11, rue des Canettes - 43 26 79 15
Open noon-2 a.m. Closed Sun., Mon. & July 14-Aug. 15. Parking: Saint-Sulpice. No cards.

You can obtain wine and spirits here. The establishment accepts cash only.

Le Cochon Rose
18th arr. - 44, bd de Clichy - 46 06 86 25
Open 6 p.m.-5 a.m. Closed Thurs. & Aug. No cards.

After getting a taste of the thrills and chills of "Pigalle by Night," you can shop until the break of dawn at this well-known take-out and grocery store. The good charcuteries and other prepared foods, fruit, wine and spirits are joined by a wide variety of tasty sandwiches (the bread is made fresh on the premises). Note, however, that the management accepts cold cash only: no checks, no credit cards.

Drug Night
8th arr. - 55, bd des Batignolles
42 93 47 49
Open 6 p.m.-3 a.m. (Sat. until 5 a.m.). Cards: V, AE, DC.

Veteran nighthawks drop in to Drug Night for fresh, fragrant Mediterranean dishes to go (Greek and Armenian foods are house specialties), as well as the accompanying wines, Champagnes and spirits.

Flo Prestige
16th arr. - 42, pl. du Marché Saint-Honoré
42 61 45 46
Open daily 8 a.m.-midnight. Cards: V, AE, DC, MC. Other branches.

Flo boutiques are cropping up all over town. The latest is in the fifteenth arrondissement and is a perfect place for late-night food shopping. Temptations include foie gras from Strasbourg, Norwegian smoked salmon and sauerkraut washed down with bison grass vodka. A terrific formula.

Les Frères Layrac
6th arr. - 29, rue de Buci - 43 25 17 72
Open daily 9 a.m.-3 a.m. Cards: V, AE, DC.

There is a wide selection of precooked dishes, but the pride of Les Frères Layrac is its seafood platter. A well-lit, spacious delicatessen with everything neatly displayed, it adjoins two late-night restaurants, Le Petit Zinc and Le Muniche, and is open until 3 a.m.

Libre-Service
9th arr. - 33, bd de Clichy - 42 85 16 38
Open noon-midnight. Closed Wed. & Jan. No cards.

Grocery goods, fruits and vegetables.

La Tonnelle
18th arr. - 2, rue Houdon - 42 51 35 24
Open 6 p.m.-5 a.m. Closed Tues. No cards.

Grocery store.

PHARMACIES

Pharmacie Azoulay
9th arr. - 5, pl. Pigalle - 48 78 38 12
Open 9 a.m.-1 a.m. (Sun. 5 p.m.-1 a.m.). Parking: Pigalle. Cards: V.

Pharmacie Derhy
8th arr. - 84, av. des Champs-Elysées
45 62 02 41
Open daily 24 hours. Cards: V.
  Note the convenient, *all-day-all-night* hours of this drugstore.

Pharmacie Lagarce
11th arr. - 13, pl. de la Nation
43 73 24 03
Open 8:30 a.m.-midnight (Sun. 8 p.m.-midnight). Closed Mon. morning. Cards: V.

POST OFFICES

Poste Centrale
1st arr. - 52, rue du Louvre - 42 33 71 60
Open daily 24 hours. No cards.
  The central post office is open 24 hours a day. Long-distance telephone calls can be made from the first floor, ordinary postal transactions on the ground floor. Don't be surprised to find a few homeless tramps enjoying some late-night Muzak in the post office's warm recesses.

RECORD STORES

Champs-Musique
8th arr. - 84, av. des Champs-Elysées
45 62 65 46
Open 9:30 a.m.-1 a.m. (Sun. until 8 p.m.). Cards: V, AE, DC.
  Let there be music! Here in this shop on the world's most beautiful avenue is a fine selection of popular and classical music.

Lido-Musique
8th arr. - 68, av. des Champs-Elysées
45 62 30 86
Open 10 a.m.-1:30 a.m. (Sun. 1:30 p.m.-8:30 p.m.). Cards: V, AE, DC.
  Jazz, classical, pop and rock. Records, compact discs and cassettes available.

SPORTING GOODS

CLOTHING & EQUIPMENT (GENERAL)

Alésia Sport
14th arr. - 74, rue d'Alésia - 45 42 40 49
Open 9:45 a.m.-7 p.m. (Mon. 2 p.m.-7 p.m., except July & Aug.). Closed Sun. Cards: V, AE, DC.
  This Left Bank store carries the largest selection of sporting goods in Paris.

Go Sport
15th arr. - 16, rue Linois - Centre Beaugrenelle - 45 75 70 82
Open 10 a.m.-7:30 p.m. Closed Sun. Parking: Monoprix. Cards: V, AE, DC, MC. 5 other branches: 2, pl. de la Porte-Maillot - 17th arr., 46 40 22 46, parking, Palais des Congrès; 110, bd Diderot - 12th arr. - 43 47 31 17, parking, Reuilly, cards, V, MC; 30, av. d'Italie - 13th arr. - 45 80 30 05, parking, Galaxie, cards, V, AE, DC; 68, av. du Maine - 14th arr. - 43 27 50 50, cards, V; Pte. Pierre-Lescot, Forum des Halles level 3 - 1st arr. - 45 08 92 96, parking, Forum des Halles, cards, V.
  The stores in this fast-growing international chain vary drastically in size and style from one to another, but all conduct business using the same successful formula: friendly help, professional advice and quality equipment. Some of the stores specialize in equestrian equipage (the Les Halles and Montparnasse branches). Tennis and fitness equipment are featured at every branch.

Au Petit Matelot

16th arr. - 27, av. de la Grande-Armée
45 00 15 51
Open 10 a.m.-7 p.m. (Mon. 2 p.m.-7 p.m.).
Closed Sun. Cards: V, AE, DC.

About to celebrate its 200th birthday, Au Petit Matelot is aging quite nicely. The striped sailor shirts are less in evidence than they once were, but the foul-weather gear is as good as ever, as are the pea coats. Ladies and gentlemen come here to dress for the hunt, the saddle or the tiller. Be advised that only sporting *clothes* are found here—you'll need to go elsewhere for your windsurfer.

Sportscenter

8th arr. - 162, rue du Faubourg-Saint-Honoré - 42 25 84 34
Open 10 a.m.-6:45 p.m. Closed Sun. Cards: V, AE, DC.

Every manner of sporting look—from the reliable classics to the extremes of taste—is assembled here.

Tunmer

8th arr. - 5, pl. Saint-Augustin
45 22 75 80
Open 10 a.m.-6:45 p.m. (Mon. 2 p.m.-6:45 p.m.). Closed Sun. Parking: Bergson.
Cards: V, AE, DC.

Since sports clothes have invaded the world of fashion, it has been difficult to say whether this is principally a store for sport or style. Well, no matter, this venerable establishment stocks the very best for outfitting and decking out alike: Lacoste polos in twenty colors, a tantalizing array of golf shoes and so forth. The ski suits are beautiful. In fact, all the sports equipment is lovely, but clearly it's the clothes that

---

To discover Paris's best annual sporting events, from the Tour de France to horse shows, see "Goings-On" in the Basics chapter.

---

take the prize. What to wear to the French Open? You'll find it here.

DANCE

Repetto

1st arr. - 22, rue de la Paix - 47 42 47 88
Open 10 a.m.-7 p.m. Closed Sun. No cards.

This is the preferred spot of Sylvie Guilhem, the newest star of the Paris opera scene and a former gymnast.

FISHING

Au Martin-Pêcheur

1st arr. - 24, quai du Louvre - 42 36 25 63
Open 9:30 a.m.-7 p.m. Closed Sun. & Mon. Cards: V, AE, DC.

This old establishment really hasn't changed much—it is still one of the prettiest shops in Paris. In addition to all the fishing equipment, there's a section for diving accessories, including an underwater-photography department. The fishing equipment features unusual finds from the United States. A must stop for devotees.

Motillon

15th arr. - 83 bis, rue de l'Abbé-Groult
48 28 58 94
Open 9 a.m.-12:30 p.m. & 2 p.m.-7 p.m. Closed Sun. & Mon. Cards: V.

This venerable institution sells the necessities, the accessories, and the luxuries for every sort of fishing. Everything can be mail-ordered from its wonderful catalog.

GOLF

9/18

17th arr. - 87, av. Niel - 42 67 44 81
Open 10 a.m.-7 p.m. Closed Sun. Parking: Ternes. Cards: V, AE, DC.

Just recently opened, this shop aspires to be the niftiest collection of golf clothes and equipment around, with fashions from Italy, England and the United States. And it also provides a unique service: a travel agency that specializes in golf holidays in dreamy, faraway places.

Comptoir du Golf

17th arr. - 22, av. de la Grande-Armée
43 80 15 00
Open 10 a.m.-7 p.m. (Mon. 2 p.m.-7 p.m.). Closed Sun. Parking: Batignolles. Cards: V, AE.
A very British place, right down to the cool reception. Shoes, clubs, polo shirts and carts abound, as well as its own line of golf clothes in addition to the well-known makers'. It's worth the detour, even if you aren't a golfer, for the colorful piles of all sorts of items.

Golf-Plus

17th arr. - 212, bd Pereire - 45 74 08 17
Open 10 a.m.-7 p.m. (Mon. 2 p.m.-7 p.m., Thurs. 10 a.m.-9 p.m.). Closed Sun. Parking: Wagram. Cards: V.
The crowded little shop on the rue Dulong has given way to these new and much lovelier quarters, but the attractions of the original establishment remain. The owner, Laurence Schmidlin, several times the French champion, offers friendly assistance to his customers. Good-quality clothes and equipment are sold at likable prices. If you find what you bought here elsewhere for a lower price, you can come back and receive a credit, plus 10 percent. A branch of the operation offers equipment rentals and repairs, and plans for a Cannes branch are underway. The Schmidlin family's success has not affected the attentive, personal service they lavish on their customers.

La Main Qui Passe

17th arr. - 26, rue Pierre-Demours
42 27 76 59
Open 10:30 a.m.-7:30 p.m. Closed Sun., Mon. Parking: Ternes. Cards: V.
Practice cages, carts, made-to-measure clubs and, in particular, top-of-the-line used clubs at good prices.

HUNTING & SHOOTING

Alex

8th arr. - 63, bd de Courcelles
42 27 66 39
Open 9 a.m.-12:30 p.m. & 2 p.m.-7 p.m. (Mon. until 6 p.m.). Closed Sun. Cards: V.
Traditionally a firearms dealer, Alex has taken over the shop next door and devoted it to clothing, and he has his eye on the bakery next to that. He features the finest brands of rifles, as well as good selections of optical equipment, knives and cartridges. As for hunting-related clothing, you won't find a collection like this anywhere else: wool socks, elegant and practical storm coats and, of course, Paraboots. There is also an interesting hunting-themed gift department, which includes clever little knives in the form of ducks and cuckoos. An excellent store.

Fauré Le Page

1st arr. - 8, rue de Richelieu - 42 96 07 78
Open 9:30 a.m.-7 p.m. (Wed. until 10 p.m.). Closed Sun. Parking: Pyramides. Cards: V.
A specialist in rifles since 1716, this establishment still sells its own make of double-barrel rifles (nine- to twelve-month wait and 14,500 to 25,000 francs for made-to-orders). Also found here are handguns, artisanal quality knives, carbines for target shooting and competition, sights and other such accessories. For collectors, there's an array of sword-canes and rifle-canes, and, for quieter hunting, there's always the Barnett Commando crossbow for 2,960 francs.

Gastinne Renette

8th arr. - 39, av. Franklin-Roosevelt
42 25 74 17
Open 9:15 a.m.-6:30 p.m. Closed Sun. & Mon. Parking: Champs-Elysées. Cards: V.
This famous establishment sells its own brand of rifles. And it doesn't give them away: prices start at 19,000 francs. But there are also used guns at attractive prices. An added feature is the shooting range in the basement, which

permits customers to test the merchandise. Extremely diversified, the shop also stocks books, archery equipment and security systems, along with a selection of classic clothing, but not at competitive prices. And the gift department is, of course, consistent with the hunting theme.

Tir 1000

13th arr. - 90, rue Jeanne-d'Arc
45 83 34 41
Open 10 a.m.-7 p.m. (Thurs. until 10 p.m.). Closed Sun. & Mon. Parking: Casino. Cards: V.

Tir 1000 stocks a good selection of arms, knives, sights and repair services. Meanwhile, on the basement level, there's a shooting range for handguns, which is available to subscribers (1,100 francs for an annual subscription). The range also offers handgun rental and introductory instruction.

RIDING

Duprey

17th arr. - 5, rue Troyon - 43 80 29 37
Open 9:45 a.m.-12:30 p.m. & 1:30 p.m.-6 p.m. Closed Sun. Parking: Etoile. Cards: V, AE.

This venerable shop has been hidden away on a little street near the Arc de Triomphe since 1902. Marked by tradition, it is a family affair upheld by three generations. They make all their riding equipment themselves and are well known in the highest horsey circles. Their excellent and comfortable saddles, virtually custom-made, are well appreciated (from 7,000 francs). Stirrups, bridles, girths . . . this is the kingdom of ready-to-wear for horses. There is no apparel for the rider, but everything in leather for your mount, and a special old-fashioned preparation for caring for its hide.

Hermès

8th arr. - 24, rue du Faubourg-Saint-Honoré - 42 65 21 60
Open 10 a.m.-6:30 p.m. (Mon. & Sat. 10 a.m.-1 p.m. & 2:15 p.m.-6:30 p.m.). Closed Sun. Cards: V, AE, DC.

Housed in the tasteful luxury of this celebrated store is a complete range of equipment for horse and rider. Hermès turns out roughly 60 saddles a month, all handmade in the firm's workshops. The store will also custom-make and sew saddles made to measure in whatever leather you wish (one well-heeled customer even had a saddle made in crocodile). Should you decide to organize your own racing team, you can have Hermès fit out your jockeys in its famous uniforms.

Padd

15th arr. - 14, rue de la Cavalerie
43 06 56 50
Open 10 a.m.-7 p.m. (Sat. until 6 p.m.). Closed Sun. & Mon. Cards: V, AE.

In this functional environment, you'll find every kind of saddle at every sort of price. They come from everywhere: Spain, England, the United States. The clothing department is well stocked, and you'll surely find what you're looking for—except any element of charm. It's Duprey or Equitable for that.

SKIING

La Cordée

8th arr. - 60, rue de Rome - 43 87 45 10
Open 10 a.m.-7 p.m. Closed Sun. & Mon. Parking: Saint-Lazare. Cards: V.

The chalet decor houses a complete professional range of equipment. Excellent ski boots and repair services are available. One of the most reliable stores in Paris.

La Haute Route

4th arr. - 33, bd Henri-IV - 42 72 38 43
Open 9:30 a.m.-7 p.m. (Mon. 2 p.m.-7 p.m.). Closed Sun. Parking: Bastille. Cards: V, AE.

You can rent everything here but the mountain: complete ski equipment in the winter, rock-climbing gear in the summer. This specialized store is an excellent resource that really ought to be better known.

Passe Montagne

14th arr. - 102, av. Denfert-Rochereau
43 22 24 24
Open 11 a.m.-7 p.m. (Wed. until 9 p.m., Sat. 10 a.m.-7 p.m.). Closed Sun. & Mon. Cards: V. Other branch: 39, rue du Chemin-Vert - 11th arr. - 43 57 08 47.

Climbing, hiking, alpine skiing, cross-country—this place appears to have it all. Both stores are open Wednesday until 9 p.m. Equipment rental is available at the Chemin-Vert store only.

Le Vieux Campeur
5th arr. - 48-50, rue des Ecoles
43 29 12 32
Open 10 a.m.-8 p.m. (Mon. 2 p.m.-8 p.m.). Closed Sun. Parking: Maubert. Cards: V, AE.

Actually housed in nine shops spread around the neighborhood, the Vieux Campeur is still the place to go for all manner of sporting equipment. The latest innovations and variations on a theme arrive here first. Climbing and mountaineering remain the specialty of the house, but the reputation for quality includes everything from running shoes to tennis racquets, sold with professional advice. We suggest that you avoid a Saturday visit, as the crowds are horrendous. A climbing wall is set up to be used for trying out shoes before you buy them.

WINDSURFING

Crit
17th arr. - 2, rue Toulouse-Lautrec
40 11 98 40
Open 10 a.m.-1 p.m. & 2 p.m.-7 p.m. Closed Sun. & Mon. Parking: Porte de Saint-Ouen. Cards: V, AE.

Good-quality one-piece suits can be found here, but it's the Crit brand windsurfers that the place is known for.

Hawaii-Surf
94200 Ivry-sur-Seine - 69, rue Danielle-Casanova - 46 72 07 10
Open 10 a.m.-1 p.m. & 2 p.m.-7 p.m. Closed Sun. & Mon. Cards: V.

Surfboard and skiboard city! You'll think you're in Hawaii. Hawaii-Surf carries the latest equipment from the States, and the young owner is a surfing fanatic. A prevacation stop here, and you'll really wow your friends.

Mistral Shop
16th arr. - 24, rue Mirabeau - 45 24 38 55
Open 10 a.m.-1 p.m. & 2 p.m.-7 p.m. Closed Sun. & Mon. Parking: Porte d'Auteuil. Cards: V.

This windsurfing shop reflects the polish of its tony neighborhood: the boards are the finest made, the swimsuits are *très chic*, and the staff consists primarily of handsome beach boys. A number of designs are available but only one choice of quality—the best. These are serious boards for the committed windsurfer.

Nautistore
17th arr. - 40, av. de la Grande-Armée
42 67 61 55
Open 10 a.m.-6:30 p.m. Closed Sun. & Mon. Parking: Etoile. No cards.

This shop has been discounting new and old windsurfing boards for about fifteen years.

TOBACCONISTS

ACCESSORIES

Au Caïd
6th arr. - 24, bd Saint-Michel - 43 26 04 01
Open 10 a.m.-7 p.m. Closed Sun. Parking: Ecole de Médecine, Odéon. Cards: V, AE, DC, MC.

The charming *mesdames* Schmitt still reign over this pipe-smokers' paradise. Featured is an excellent selection of pipes in clay, porcelain, cherry and briar. Accessories include tobacco pouches and cigar cases, cigar holders and pipe racks. Join the ranks of such satisfied former customers as the Duke of Windsor and Jean-Paul Sartre. The service is renowned.

Alfred Dunhill
2nd arr. - 15, rue de la Paix - 42 61 57 58
Open 9:30 a.m.-6:30 p.m. (Mon. 10:30 a.m.-6:30 p.m.). Closed Sun. Parking: Vendôme. Cards: V, AE, DC, MC.

The Alfred Dunhill shop remains the domain of men—and women—who have about them the expensive aroma of Havana cigars and fine leather. Foremost among the luxurious items featured around the mahogany-paneled, turn-of-the-century shop are, of course, the famed Dunhill pipes, some of the world's best (prices range from 760 to 16,000 francs). Collectors will not want to miss the minimuseum of clay, briar and meerschaum pipes. Dunhill is also a gift shop, with a large selection of sunglasses, necktie pins, wristwatches and pens (after all, Dunhill owns Mont-Blanc), fine leather goods and hundreds of other gift ideas at reasonable prices. But the lion's share of the shop is given over to smokers' accessories: lighters (priced from 1,200 to 46,500 francs), cigarette holders, cigar boxes and humidors in rare woods. Dunhill also makes classic menswear and men's personal-care products.

Guyot
17th arr. - 7, av. de Clichy - 43 87 70 88
Open 10 a.m.-7 p.m. Closed Sun., Mon. & Aug. Parking: Escoffier, Hôtel Ibis. Cards: V.

Gilbert Guyot is one of the three remaining master pipe makers in France. When we visit his shop, we generally find Guyot (and his son) crafting, repairing, restoring or smoking a pipe and sizing up their customers. Before selling a customer his wares, Guyot peaonally interviews him, because, as Guyot puts it, "The pipe is the man." All kinds of pipes in every imaginable material and in a wide range of prices are sold in an atmosphere of quality and time-honored tradition.

Aux Mines d'Ecume
3rd arr. - 3, bd Saint-Martin - 42 72 69 19
Open 9 a.m.-7 p.m. Closed Sun., 10 days in July & 10 days in Aug. Parking: rue Saint-Martin. No cards.

Master pipe maker Cardon is one of France's top specialists in briar and meerschaum pipes. He guarantees that the products from his fam-

THE BEST SMOKES IN TOWN
France's hit parade of cigars has been considerably upgraded in the last year by new imports. Finds include Lusitanias, 8/9/8 and Partagas Number 1 by Partagas; the Epicure Number 2 by Hoyo de Monterrey; and the Punch Punch by Punch. The smallest of all Havanas—the Puritos by Quintero—costs 5 francs.

ily-run establishment, which was founded in 1865, are of the finest quality, and his advice, faultless. Pipe tobacco is not on sale here, but a selection of lighters and accessories is available. Doubles as a repair workshop.

Sommer
2nd arr. - 11, passage des Princes
42 96 99 10
Open 9:30 a.m.-6 p.m. Closed Sat., Sun. & 2 wks. in Aug. Parking: Drouot. Cards: V, AE, DC.

This ancient establishment boasts hundreds of boxwood, briar and meerschaum pipes, as well as every brand of tobacco available in France. At once luxurious and somber—decorated with dark, antique carved wood—Sommer attracts celebrities and discerning smokers alike. A special service: custom-sculpted pipes.

CIGARS & TOBACCO

NO BARGAINS HERE

As you will note, cigars cost an arm and a leg here. Why? The state considers them a "drug" and taxes them at four times their value. But take heart: At the shops we have listed in this section you are sure to find a fresh, high-quality cigar and not, as too often happens, a once-cherished cheroot that has turned into a roll of stale, bitter-tasting compost.

Boutique 22
16th arr. - 22, av. Victor-Hugo
45 01 81 41
Open 10 a.m.-7 p.m. (Mon. 2 p.m.-7 p.m.). Closed Sun. Parking: Foch. Cards: V, AE, DC, MC.

Cigar lovers consider Boutique 22 the mecca of Davidoffs (even though it is no longer owned by Zino Davidoff). You will find not only Davidoff's "1000" but every other brand of Havana cigar imported in France, including slim Joyitas and thick Hoyo des Dieux and Carousoas. Boutique 22 is big on lesser-knowns as well and has the exclusive distributorship for the Compagnie des Caraïbes. You will discover such Caribbean delights as sweet and aromatic Cerdeaus, robust Juan Clementes and claro claro/50 Don Miguels, from Cabo Verde. Also featured are 100 models of off-the-shelf humidors and vaults, plus refurbished antique models. For the made-to-measure crowd, you may order haute-couture custom vaults, monogrammed by request (they come equipped with a patented climate-control system that guarantees your cigars' freshness for one month). The accessories department groans with deluxe lighters and fountain pens (Dupont, Cartier, Dunhill, Mont-Blanc), plus crystal wares by Lalique, Daum and Baccarat.

La Cave à Cigares

10th arr. - 4, bd de Denain - 42 81 05 51
Open 7:30 a.m.-7 p.m. Closed Sat., Sun., Feb. 1-15 & Aug. Parking: Gare du Nord. No cards.

Owner Gérard Courtail is the inventor of the much-imitated vertical humidifier/display case. Although he is by profession a master pipe maker, member of the *confrérie des maîtres pipiers* (brotherhood of master pipe makers), he is nevertheless a cigar connoisseur and an excellent source of information and advice. Do not miss his collection of pipes, including such brands as Chacom, Dunhill and Butz-Chuquin. Also, a wide range of smoking accessories, for experts and novices.

THE ART OF THE CIGAR

Before you give someone a cigar, ponder this: A cigar is more than just a compact roll of tobacco leaves often tapered at the ends. A core of whole and half leaves is tucked into a whole-leaf sub and outer skin. This causes the layers to burn faster from the outside in. The way the skin is stretched determines the final shape of the cigar. Craftsmanship, leaf quality and freshness are key. Thickness, too, determines taste, since a slower burn means more flavor. The ideal storage temperature *chez* the tobacconist's is 60 to 65 degrees Farenheit at 70 to 80 percent humidity, with cigars preferably packed in a rare-wood case—cedar, for instance.

A la Civette

1st arr. - 157, rue Saint-Honoré
42 96 04 99
Open 8:30 a.m.-7 p.m. Closed Sun. Cards: V, MC.

Habitués lovingly refer to this venerable establishment as the Civette du Palais-Royal. Founded in 1763, it is Paris's first tobacconist and was for many years *the* place of pilgrimage for cigar and tobacco lovers. Although it is no longer the city's foremost, it remains among its highest ranks. Tobacco goods featured run the gamut from everyday chewing weed to the very best Havanas, including the Hoyo de Monterrey, imported directly from Cuba. La Civette was the first shop in Paris to install climate-controlled vaults for its cigars. It was also the first to import Monte-Cristos. Also available is a wide range of accessories: deluxe lighters and pipes (Chacom, Butz-Choquin, Dunhill), humidors in all shapes and sizes, pens, leather goods.

Drugstores Publicis

8th arr. - 1, av. Matignon - 43 59 38 70
Open daily 9 a.m.-2 a.m. (Sun. 10 a.m.-2 a.m.). Parking: Rond-Point des Champs-Elysées. Cards: V. 2 other branches: 149, bd Saint-Germain - 6th arr. - 42 22 92 50, parking, Saint-Germain; 133, av. des Champs-Elysées - 8th arr. 47 23 54 34, parking, Georges-V.

A large selection of good-quality humidified cigars is available at each of the three Drugstore Publicis year-round and late into the night.

Lemaire

16th arr. - 59, av. Victor-Hugo
45 00 75 63
Open 8:15 a.m.-7:30 p.m. (Sat. 9 a.m.-7:30 p.m.). Closed Sun. & holidays. Cards: V.

This century-old institution is one of France's most prestigious tobacconists. Of course you will find the cigar of your dreams perfectly preserved and presented with rare flair. Havanas and San Domingos—Zinos, Don Miguels and Juan Clementes—top the list. Lecroq's astonishing vaults accommodate thousands of cases of cigars in ideal temperature and humidity conditions. Cigar boxes and humidors, humble or extravagant, are guaranteed for workmanship and reliability (the gamut runs from a solid cedarwood three-cigar pocket humidor to a vault the size of a writing desk, for a mere 32,000 francs). Pipe smokers will discover the entire range of tobaccos available in France, plus a large selection of pipes (all major brands, with a particularly good collection of meerschaum). Lemaire's vast array of accessories includes all major brands of lighters, cases, pouches, plus 1,100 fountain, ballpoint and felt-tip pens.

SIGHTS

AMUSEMENTS

CLASSES & HOBBIES

ADVENTURE GAMES

Les Compagnons du Crépuscule
94370 Sucy-en-Brie - 1, allée des Noyers
45 90 18 95
Open 2 weekends a month from late April to mid-Oct. Closed Sun. & Mon. Costumes required. Price: 250-300F per evening.

This group organizes Dungeon and Dragon role games of a bizarre sort. The players meet at 4 p.m.; the adventure begins at sundown and continues all night. The course to be followed is extremely physical, including walks in the woods, battles and so forth, and is full of surprises, in natural and urban settings. Monsters, ambushes, thrills and chills; cardiac cases are not encouraged to join in the fun.

Les Grandes Compagnies de l'Est Parisien
12th arr. - 79, av. de Saint-Mandé
46 27 91 87
Open Fri. 7 p.m.-midnight. Price: 240F per year.

This organization makes history live again through games of strategy played with elaborate assemblies of hundreds of painted lead figurines. To play, you will do research in the costumes, armies and history of a specific epoch. Players normally are collectors of figurines and toy soldiers who possess large inventories. To get you going, you'll be lent the necessary equipment, and then be expected to build your own army. The games are set in antiquity, the Napoleonic era, the Renaissance, World Wars I and II and fantasy periods.

BILLIARDS

Académie de Paris
17th arr. - 47, av. de Wagram - 43 80 35 60
Open 12:30 p.m.-midnight (Sat., Sun. & holidays 1:30 p.m.-midnight). Price: 34.50F per hour.

A dozen French and American billiard tables are arranged in two rooms, one of which is reserved for club members.

Café Terminus
9th arr. - Hôtel Concorde, 108, rue Saint-Lazare - 42 94 22 22
Open 10:30 a.m.-1 a.m. Price: 38F per hour.

This remarkable setting—there are ten French billiards tables—has become a popular spot after 6 p.m.

COOKING

Bibiane Deschamps
7th arr. - 17, rue de Grenelle - 45 48 72 35
Open 7 p.m.-10 p.m. Closed Sun. & summer. Price: 130F per course.

Each course of this traditional homestyle-French-cooking school involves the completion of a first course, main dish and a dessert. Five people per course.

Le Cordon Bleu
7th arr. - 8, rue Léon-Delhomme
48 56 06 06, 48 56 03 96
Open 9 a.m.-7 p.m. Closed Sat. & Sun. Price: classes 2,900F per wk., demonstrations 110F.

You can attend the daily demonstrations from 9:30 a.m. to 11:30 a.m., 1:30 p.m. to 4 p.m. or 4 p.m. to 6:30 p.m. Traditional French cooking and pastry making.

Marie-Blanche de Broglie
7th arr. - 18, av. La Motte-Picquet
45 51 36 34
Open 10:30 a.m.-5 p.m. Closed Sat. & Sun. Price: classes 4,000F per wk., regional cuisine lessons 420F.

Regional cooking, market cooking, cuisine nouvelle and, as of this year, low-calorie cooking and the art of hospitality are the curricula here. Courses are also taught in English and Spanish. From August 1 to September 11, week-long courses are offered at Limesy in Normandy.

Ecole de Gastronomie Française Ritz-Escoffier
1st arr. - 15, pl. Vendôme - 42 60 38 30
Open 9 p.m.-6 p.m. Closed Sat. & Sun. Price: 3,500F per wk., demonstrations 180F.

You can learn it all here—baking, pastry making and the confectioner's art. There are also special Christmas courses available from

December 18 to 23 and 26 to 30 that teach traditional cooking (6,500 francs for the week). Courses are also offered in languages.

DANCE

Centre de Danse du Marais
4th arr. - 41, rue du Temple
42 72 15 42, 42 77 58 19
Open daily 9 a.m.-10 p.m. Price: 60F per course; per-class price is reduced with each additional class taken.

Everything is taught here—from the Argentinean tango and contemporary Japanese *buto* dancing to primitive African dance, flamenco or Brazilian and Oriental dance. There are 35 disciplines in all, taught in somewhat tumble-down surroundings but in a friendly, non-threatening atmosphere.

Roger et Michèle Dolléance
1st arr. - 40, rue Quincampoix
48 83 36 79, 42 74 55 96
Closed July 15-Sept. 1. Intensive classes during school holidays. Price: private lessons 150F per half hour; per-class price is reduced with each additional class taken.

We suggest that you select the individual instruction; the group courses are over-crowded. Students are primarily on the young side. There is perhaps a bit more ambience than technique here.

Andres Serrita
9th arr. - 25, rue de Bruxelles - 42 80 40 25
Telephone information available mornings. Price: 600F for 4 lessons.

This is a friendly place where you can act, sing and dance. Courses: theater, voice and flamenco, Oriental and Renaissance dance. There are also yoga courses for pregnant women, along with flamenco guitar.

FLOWER ARRANGING

Centre d'Art Floral Ikebana
17th arr. - 26, rue d'Armaillé - 45 74 21 28
Open 2 p.m.-6 p.m. Closed Sat. & Sun.

The tradition of Japanese flower arranging was originally a religious practice developed by Buddhist monks. There are several different schools of Ikebana in Japan. At this address you will be taught the pure and simple style of Ohara.

Ecole d'Horticulture du Luxembourg
6th arr. - 64, bd Saint-Michel - 45 48 55 55
Open 8 a.m.-noon & 2 p.m.-6 p.m. Closed Sun.

From October to December, a theoretical course is hosted on Thursday and Saturday morning, and from January through May, the practical courses run. Year-round registration.

Société Nationale d'Horticulture de France
7th arr. - 84, rue de Grenelle - 45 48 81 00
Open 9 a.m.-5:30 p.m. Closed Sat. & Sun. Price: 25F per lesson.

This is the place if you want to know how to graft trees or put your balcony in flowers.

MUSIC

Conservatoire Rachmaninov
16th arr. - 26, av. de New-York
47 23 51 44
Open 10 a.m.-1 p.m. & 2 p.m.-7 p.m. Closed Sun. & Aug. Price: 580F per month (private lessons).

This conservatory has a flexible enrollment policy for its solfège, harmony and music-history courses. This is the only conservatory that we will mention, because the others normally do not cater to adult education. You're better off with the various associations or private lessons.

Le Projet Musical
10th arr. - 23, rue du Faubourg-Saint-Denis - 42 46 27 26
Open 1 p.m.-8 p.m. Closed Sat. & Sun. Apprenticeships offered July 1-25. Price: 4,600F per year (2 hours' instruction per wk.).

Instruments are taught in individual lessons, and solfège in small groups. Instruction in all instruments, in classical or jazz, as well as in voice.

NEEDLEPOINT & EMBROIDERY

L'Atelier de la Dentellière
13th arr. - 9, rue de Patay - 45 86 14 78
Open Thurs. 9 a.m.-noon, Fri. 9:30 a.m.-8 p.m., Sat. 2 p.m.-5:30 p.m. Closed Sun. (Initiation: 10 courses minimum.) Price: 1,400F per trimester (1 course per wk.).

Under the tutelage of Lysiane Brulet, professor of lacemaking, you'll learn how to use linen, cotton or silk thread with finesse to make lace trim for curtains, blouses and napkins. This painstaking work teaches the lovely rewards of patience.

R. Malbranche
9th arr. - 17, rue Drouot - 47 70 03 77
Open 9 a.m.-noon & 2 p.m.-8 p.m. Closed Sat., Sun. & Aug.

For sale here are linen sheets, cotton mousseline napkins, linen handkerchiefs, and cambric placemats all delicately embroidered by hand—in short, it's the household linen of your dreams. And at prices that leave you still dreaming: 1,000 to 3,000 francs per place mat, 1,115 francs for a pillow slip. More affordable are the ladies' handkerchiefs at 200 francs. The workmanship and the exquisite materials justify the prices. You can learn how to make these masterpieces of patience yourself. Courses are taught by a Best French Worker award winner on Thursday afternoons and evenings (eight two-hour classes cost 560 francs). You'll be taught all the basic stitches plus some of the more complicated ones that require real address. This is the real, old-fashioned embroidery.

PAINTING & DESIGN

Ateliers des Beaux-Arts de Paris
1st arr. - 15, rue Jean-Lantier - 42 36 06 68
Open 9 a.m.-12:30 p.m. & 2 p.m.-6 p.m. Closed Sun. Price: 160-400F per year (material furnished).

Drawing, painting, sculpture, engraving, ceramics, photography, art history, musical training and choral singing . . . all are taught here. The introduction to the plastic arts is open to anyone—beginners, experienced amateurs, or students preparing for entry to the School of Fine Arts. Courses are taught by professional artists. Enrolee spots are limited, and registration takes place before September 1. Courses are three hours, twice a week.

Ecole du Louvre
1st arr. - Palais du Louvre - 42 60 39 26
Open 9:45 a.m.-5:45 p.m. Closed Tues.

Evening art-history courses are offered free of charge. Summer courses (300 francs) include theory, museum visits and seminars.

PARLOR GAMES

L'As Vegas
16th arr. - Palais des Congrès, level 1, Porte Maillot - 47 58 21 15
Open 10:30 a.m.-7:30 p.m. Closed Sun.

This shop has a little of everything but specializes in casino games (roulette wheels from 300 to 12,000 francs) and chess and backgammon sets.

Le Baguenaudier
6th arr. - rue Saint-Sulpice - 43 26 45 83
Open 10:30 a.m.-12:30 p.m. & 1:30 p.m.-6:30 p.m. Closed Sun.

There isn't a new game that can't be found here, from board games to card games, including some lovely reproductions of old versions of the latter.

Games
92800 Puteaux - La Défense, Les Quatre Temps, level 2 - 47 73 65 92
Open 10 a.m.-7:30 p.m. Closed Sun. Other branch: Forum des Halles, level 2 - 1st arr. - 42 97 42 31.

This is a grownup's game shop featuring chess sets carved in precious woods or onyx, electronic games, brain-teaser puzzles, billiards, roulette wheels, slot machines and more. Also, role games complete with books and figurines.

Stratejeux
14th arr. - 13, rue Poirier-de-Narçay
45 45 45 87
Open 10:30 a.m.-1:30 p.m. & 2 p.m.-7 p.m. Closed Sun. & Mon.

Every Wednesday and Saturday afternoon, Stratejeux hosts demonstrations of strategy games. All the necessities for strategy games and role games are sold on the premises.

Le Train Bleu
16th arr. - 2-6, av. Mozart - 42 88 34 70
Open 10 a.m.-7 p.m. Closed Sun. Other branch: 55, rue Saint-Placide - 6th arr. - 45 48 33 70.

This is a sort of luxury supermarket of games. The basement level is reserved for adults, at least until they rediscover their childhood and go rushing up to the other three floors, specializing in fun stuff for young tousled heads.

SELF-DISCOVERY

Association Zen Internationale
13th arr. - 17, rue des Cinq-Diamants
45 80 10 00
*Open 9:30 a.m.-12:30 p.m. & 2 p.m.-7 p.m.
(Sat. 10:30 a.m.-1 p.m. & 3 p.m.-7 p.m.).
Closed Sun. morning & Mon. Price: 230F per
year (students 180F).*

The meditation and Zen instruction here is
translated into English, German and Spanish.
There is also a boutique that stocks kimonos,
cushions and other vital paraphernalia, as well
as incense, pottery, flower holders, calligraphic
brushes and the like.

La Maison de l'Astronomie
4th arr. - 33, rue de Rivoli - 42 77 99 55
Open 9:45 a.m.-6:45 p.m. Closed Mon.

This bookstore specializes in books, posters
and sky maps pertaining to astronomy, as well
as equipment for searching the heavens: tele-
scopes, photo equipment, binoculars. There
are introductory courses of five one-and-a-
half-hour sessions for 400 francs. There is also
a course in astronomic photography, and there
are three-day courses offered at the Chateau
Bierville south of Paris.

Société Française de Graphologie
7th arr. - 5, rue Las-Cases - 45 55 46 94
*Open 9 a.m.-noon (1 course per wk. 6 p.m.-7:45
p.m.). Closed Aug. Price: 50F per 1-year membership, 1,500F per 28-course cycle (3 cycles in
program).*

This association for handwriting analysis
puts out a quarterly publication containing the
latest research in the field and, although it is
not a school, offers courses in the subject from
October to May. Each class is part lecture
presentation, part practical work. Written
homework assignments are corrected
individually.

SPORTS

The below-mentioned list includes the
names of associations and clubs that can provide detailed information on how and where
you can practice your favorite sports.

ATHLETICS

Fédération Française d'Athlétisme
10th arr. - 10, rue du Faubourg-
Poissonnière - 47 47 90 61

CYCLING

Bicy-Club de France
17th arr. - 8, pl. de la Porte-Champerret
47 66 55 92

Fédération Française de Cyclisme
10th arr. - 43, rue de Dunkerque
42 85 41 20

Fédération Française de Cyclotourisme
13th arr. - 8, rue Jean-Marie-Jégo
45 80 30 21

DANCE

Janine Stanlowa
8th arr. - 250, rue du Faubourg-Saint-
Honoré - 45 63 20 96
Open by appt. only.

FENCING

Fédération Française d'Escrime
9th arr. - 45, rue de Liège - 42 94 91 38

FLYING

Fédération Nationale Aéronautique
8th arr. - 52, rue de Galilée - 47 20 39 75

GOLF

Chévry 2
91109 Gif-sur-Yvette - RN 306
60 12 40 33

Golf de Villennes
78670 Villennes-sur-Seine - Rte. d'Orgeval
39 75 30 00

Haras Lupin
92420 Vaucresson - 131, av. de la Celle-
Saint-Cloud - 47 01 15 04

Parc-étang de Saint-Quentin-en-Yvelynes
78190 Trappes - RN 12 - 30 50 86 40

Saint-Aubin
91190 Saint-Aubin - Rte. du Golf, RN 306
69 41 25 19

GOLF PRACTICE

Club de l'Etoile
17th arr. - 10, av. de la Grande-Armée
43 80 30 79

Hôtel Concorde–La Fayette
17th arr. - 3, pl. du Maréchal-Koening
47 58 12 84

Rennes-Raspail
6th arr. - 149, rue de Rennes - 45 44 24 35

HEALTH CLUBS

Club Jean de Beauvais
5th arr. - 5, rue Jean-de-Beauvais
46 33 16 80
*Open 7 a.m.-10 p.m. (Sat. 8:30 a.m.-7 p.m.,
Sun. 9:30 a.m.-5 p.m.). Parking: Maubert-
Saint-Germain. Other branch: 14, rue Jaucourt
12th arr. - 46 28 60 40; parking: Nation.*

A doctor watches over your progress, a chi-
ropractor advises you, a gym instructor personally takes charge of your training, and a
nutritionist supervises your ingestion. For
those who have decided, finally, to take themselves in hand, it's a complete overhaul. The
new location, housed in a fifteenth-century

convent on the rue Jaucourt, is less spectacular
but more spacious and slick than its former
home. For already-sporting types just looking
for a tune-up, there's ski readiness in the fall
and windsurfing prep in the spring.

Garden Gym Elysées
8th arr. - 65, av. des Champs-Elysées
42 25 87 20
*Open 9 a.m.-10 p.m. (Sat. 10 a.m.-5 p.m.).
Closed Sun. Parking: Rond-Point des Champs-
Elysées.*

This is a friendly little upstairs private gym,
with the added feature of Amadeo, an extraordinary dancer.

Thermes Monceau
8th arr. - 39, av. Hoche - 42 25 06 66
*Open 9 a.m.-11 p.m. (Sun. 10 a.m.-8 p.m.).
Parking: Royal-Monceau.*

Sporting-type nymphs lounge by the pool,
millionaires pedal away in a supremely outfitted, rarely crowded workout room. The personnel is discreetly attentive—from the gym
instructor to the masseuse, the makeup artist
to the beautician. A classical air is lent to the
proceedings by the Doric cloumns, the oval
pool under a Roman-style glass roof, lots of
green plants, soft sofas and luxurious Turkish
baths. The emphasis here is more on relaxation
than on hard-core waistline maintenance.

Vitatop
17th arr. - 58, bd Gouvion-Saint-Cyr
47 58 12 34
*Open 9 a.m.-9 p.m. (Wed. & Fri. until 10 p.m.,
Sat. until 7 p.m., Sun. until 3 p.m.). 2 other
branches: 118, rue de Vaugirard - 6th arr. - 45
44 38 01; 8, rue Louis-Armand - 15th arr. - 45
54 79 00.*

This chain remains the leader of Paris health
clubs, thanks to its longevity and its Swiss
origins. The three locations have nearly iden-
tical facilities: pool, Jacuzzi, comfortable dressing rooms and showers, sauna and so forth.
Courses are offered all day long in fitness and
related disciplines (yoga, jogging, personal
health/nutrition supervision) for no extra

charge. Each site has a highlight: Maillot, a climbing wall and the Bois de Boulogne to run in; Vaugirard, natural light and a youthful ambience; Sofitel, a fine view of Paris and a topless sunbathing deck. Membership is good for use at all three clubs. The sporting bourgeois are in their element here.

HIKING

Office National des Forêts
12th arr. - 2, av. de Saint-Mandé
40 19 58 00

Randonneurs d'Ile-de-France
14th arr. - 66, rue de Gergovie
45 24 24 72

HORSE RACING

The major racetracks are located at Auteuil (Hippodrome d'Auteuil, bois de Boulogne, sixteenth arrondissement, 45 27 12 25), Enghien (Hippodrome d'Enghien, place André Foulon, 95160 Soisy-sous-Montmorency, 39 89 00 12), Longchamp (Hippodrome de Longchamp, bois de Boulogne, sixteenth arrondissement, 42 24 13 29), Saint-Cloud (Hippodrome de Saint-Cloud, 1 rue du Camp Canadien, 92210 Saint-Cloud, 47 71 69 26) and Vincennes (Hippodrome de Vincennes, bois de Vincennes, 2, route de la Ferme, twelfth arrondissement, 43 68 35 39).

ICE SKATING

Centre Sportif Pierre-de-Coubertin
92600 Asnières - bd de Coubertin
47 66 96 06

Patinoire
94220 Charenton - av. Jean-Jaurès
43 68 59 18

Patinoire des Buttes-Chaumont
19th arr. - 30, rue Edouard Pailleron
46 07 59 08
Hours vary.

MOTORCYCLING

Fédération Française de Motocyclisme
11th arr. - 74, av. Parmentier - 47 00 94 40

RIDING

Club Hippique de Meudon-la-Fôret
92190 Meudon - rue Henri Etlin
46 30 35 02

Club Hippique de la Villette
19th arr. - 211, av. Jean-Jaurès
42 06 42 10
Open 2 p.m.-9 p.m. (Sat. & Sun. 9 a.m.-9 p.m.).

Délégation Nationale aux Sports Equestres
8th arr. - 164, rue du Faubourg-Saint-Honoré - 42 25 11 22

Le Manège de Neuilly
92200 Neuilly - 19 bis, rue d'Orléans
46 24 06 41
Open 7 a.m.-9 p.m. Closed Sun. afternoon.

RUGBY

Comité de l'Ile-de-France de Rugby
10th arr. - 43, rue d'Enghien - 42 46 68 66

SHOOTING

Ligue Régionale de Tir de l'Ile de France
15th arr. - 9, villa Thoréton - 45 57 34 20

SKIING

Fédération Française de Ski
17th arr. - 81, av. des Ternes - 45 72 64 40

SQUASH

Squash Front de Seine
15th arr. - 21, rue Gaston-de-Caivallet
45 75 35 37

Squash Montparnasse
14th arr. - Tour Maine-Montparnasse, 37,
av. du Maine - 45 38 66 20

Stade Français
16th arr. - 2, rue du Commandant-
Guilbaud - 46 51 66 53

SWIMMING

Our selection listed below includes public
(P), semiprivate (SP) and hotel pools (H),
arranged according to arrondissement. There
is a free-of-charge leaflet (*Les Piscines*) available
from attendants at any of the 26 public pools,
which includes addresses, open hours and pool
dimensions. Regular swimmers (in public
pools) can purchase a three-month pass (130
francs). The other pools are slightly more expensive but do not generally require membership. Exceptions are the hotel pools, which, in
addition to being very pricey, expect you to
become a member.

Saint Merri (P)
4th arr. - 18, rue du Renard - 42 72 29 45

Jean-Tharis (P)
5th arr. - 16, rue Thouin - 43 25 54 03

Marché Saint Germain (P)
6th arr. - rue Clément - 43 29 08 15

Deligny (SP)
7th arr. - quai Anatole-France
45 51 72 15

Valeyre (P)
9th arr. - 22, rue de Rochechouart
42 85 27 61

Keller (SP)
15th arr. - 8, rue de l'Ingénieur-Robert-
Keller - 45 77 12 12

Armand Massard (P)
15th arr. - 66, bd du Montparnasse
45 38 65 19

Hôtel Nikko (H)
15th arr. - 61, quai de Grenelle
45 75 25 45

Hôtel Sofitel Paris (H)
15th arr. - 8, rue Louis Armand
40 60 30 30

Henri de Montherlant (P)
16th arr. - 32, bd Lannes - 45 03 03 28

Molitor (SP)
16th arr. - 2-8, av. de la Porte-Molitor
46 51 10 62

TENNIS

For detailed information regarding clubs
and courts, contact the Ligue de Paris de
Tennis, 74, rue de Rome, eighth arrondissement, 45 22 22 08. International tennis championships are held every year, for two weeks, at
the Stade Roland Garros, near the Porte
d'Auteuil, in Paris (sixteenth arrondissement),
from the end of May to the beginning of June.

Stade Henri de Montherlant
16th arr. - 48, bd Lannes - 45 03 03 64

Tennis de Longchamp
92100 Boulogne - 19, bd Anatole-France
46 03 84 49

Vitis
92800 Puteaux - 159, rue de la République
47 73 04 01

ARTS

GALLERIES

GEOGRAPHY

A gallery's address is a fairly reliable indicator of its artistic allegiance. The Right Bank, from avenue Matignon to avenue de Messine, is the place to view established contemporary artists; the Left Bank, from rue Guénégaud to rue des Beaux-Arts, is home to slightly more "advanced" art. The turf of the real avant-garde extends from Beaubourg and Les Halles to the Bastille.

FINE ART

L'Aire du Verseau
4th arr. - 119, rue Vieille-du-Temple
48 04 86 40
Open 1 p.m.-7 p.m. (Sat. 10 a.m.-7 p.m.). Closed Sun., Mon. & Aug. Cards: V, MC.
Nathalie and Nicky Verfaille devote two floors to often-unknown avant-garde artists, including Alsterlind, Bourdette, Donzelli, Gilli, Kissel, Perrone, Potage and Vila. The Verfailles have also created a service for leasing contemporary works of art.

Arnoux
6th arr. - 27, rue Guénégaud - 46 33 04 66
Open 11 a.m.-1 p.m. & 2 p.m.-7 p.m. Closed Sun., Mon. & Aug. Parking: Mazarine. Cards: V, MC.
An ex–advertising executive with a passion for abstract art from the period 1910–1960 runs this new gallery. His is an impressive collection of works by both well-known and less-well-known painters: Charchoune, Dmitrienko, Estève, Jenkins, Larionov, Noël, Poliakoff and Zack.

Artcurial
8th arr. - 9, av. Matignon - 42 99 16 16
Open 10:30 a.m.-7:15 p.m. Closed Sun., Mon. & Aug. 1-22. Parking: Rond-Point des Champs-Elysées. Cards: V, AE, DC, MC.
This artistic offshoot of the l'Oréal group is the largest gallery in Paris. It offers great variety and is home to one of the finest art libraries in all of Europe, collections of contemporary furniture, carpets, ceramics, lithographs and jewelry on show. The artists it exhibits include Chirico, Sonia Delauney, Etienne-Martin, Laurens, Masson, Miró and Zadkine.

Jacques Barbier–Caroline Beltz
6th arr. - 9, rue Mazarine - 43 54 10 97
Open 2:30 p.m.-7 p.m. Closed Mon., Tues. & Aug. Parking: Mazarine. No cards.
A discreet, efficient gallery run by a man who has never hesitated to pursue such "difficult" artists as Barré, Dufour, Kallos, Messagier and Pincemin.

Berggruen
7th arr. - 70, rue de l'Université
42 22 02 12
Open 10 a.m.-1 p.m. & 2 p.m.-7 p.m. Closed Sun. & Mon. Parking: Montalembert. Cards: V, MC.
H. Berggruen retired and handed over the reins of this traditional gallery to Antoine Mendihara. The solid array of paintings by Arroyo, Dali, Klee, Mason, Matisse, Miró, Picasso and Zao Wouki are complemented by the drawings of contemporaries Beringer, Hartmann, Janssen and Paguignon. The sublime little catalogs are works of art.

Claude Bernard
6th arr. - 9, rue des Beaux-Arts
43 26 97 07
Open 10 a.m.-12:30 p.m. & 2:30 p.m.-6:30 p.m. Closed Sun., Mon. & Aug. No cards.
Claude Bernard is one of the most famous gallery owners of the postwar period, who sells everything he exhibits: works by Bacon, Balthus, Botero, Giacometti, Hockney, Ipousteguy, Nevelson and Szafran.

Francka Berndt
11th arr. - 4, rue Saint-Sabin - 43 55 34 07
Open 2 p.m.-7 p.m. Closed Sun., Mon. morning & Aug. No cards.
Francka Berndt's second gallery is more avant-garde than the one in the sixth arron-

dissement and includes such artists as Leppie, Bédard, Bert, Colone, Floris, Massart, Porte and Gunagawa. Exhibits may be so new and unique as to throw you off balance, but they are always worth seeing.

Bernheim Jeune
8th arr. - 83, rue du Faubourg-Saint-Honoré - 42 66 60 31, 42 66 65 33
Open 10:30 a.m.-12:30 p.m. & 2:30 p.m.-6:30 p.m. Closed Sun., Mon. & Aug. 1-Sept. 6. Parking: Champs-Elysées, Bristol. No cards. Another entrance at 27, av. Matignon.

Michel Dauberville follows the period from Impressionists to present day. There are paintings and sculpture by Monet, Pissaro, Belloni, Fulerand, Morgan-Snell, Pédonssaut, Selinger and Stacey.

Alain Blondel
4th arr. - 50, rue du Temple - 42 71 85 86
Open 11 a.m.-7 p.m. Closed Sun., Mon. & Aug. Parking: Beaubourg. No cards. Other branch: 4, rue Aubry-le-Boucher - 4th arr. - 42 78 66 67; parking: Beaubourg.

This is the gallery of the king of trompe l'oeil who goes in for resolutely figurative works. Realism and hyperrealism abound in the works of Lauge, Mazo, Pomeyrol, Renonciat, Van Hove and Yvel.

Boulakia
6th arr. - 20, rue Bonaparte - 43 26 56 79
Open 10 a.m.-noon & 2 p.m.-7 p.m. Closed Sun., Mon. morning & Aug. Parking: Saint-Germain. Cards: V, AE, MC.

Two sons have successfully taken over where their parents left off. The important collection built up over the last twenty years has been supplemented with auction buys and exhibitions of contemporary art by Baselitz, Basquiat, Blais, Debré and Degremont.

Isy Brachot
6th arr. - 35, rue Guénégaud - 43 54 22 40
Open 11 a.m.-12:30 p.m. & 2 p.m.-7 p.m. Closed Sun., Mon. & July 8-Sept. 14. Parking: Mazarine. No cards.

Surrealism and fantastic realism are the hallmarks of this originally Belgian gallery. Some of the biggies are here: Delvaux, Ensor, Labisse, Magritte. Also present are De Andrea, Dado and Roland Cat.

Claudine Breguet
11th arr. - 10, passage Turquetil
46 34 66 28
Open 3 p.m.-8 p.m. Closed Sun. & Mon. No cards.

In her new premises near the place de la Nation, Claudine Breguet exhibits works by Arman, Blanchard, de Bouchony, Ceccobelli, Dessi, Frize, Gallo, Merz, Thaden, Vallet and many others.

Jeanne Bucher
6th arr. - 53, rue de Seine - 43 26 22 32
Open 9 a.m.-1 p.m. & 2 p.m.-7 p.m. Closed Sun., Mon. morning & July 16-Sept. 1. Parking: Mazarine. No cards.

Yet another traditional gallery of the Rive Gauche with, as always, Dubuffet, Bissière, De Stael, Veira Da Silva and Jean-Pierre Raynaud.

Claire Burrus
11th arr. - 30-32, rue de Lappe
43 55 36 90
Open 10:30 a.m.-7 p.m. Closed Sun., Mon. & Aug. No cards.

Now in a new location, Claire Burrus is going in for such new artists as Bourget, Thomas, Nils-Udo and Varini. A few of the old-guard from the old gallery, Le Dessin, are also present in the form of Agid, Baruchello, Degottex and Voss.

Farideh Cadot
3rd arr. - 77, rue des Archives - 42 78 08 36
Open 10 a.m.-1 p.m. & 2 p.m.-7 p.m. Closed Sun. No cards.

Farideh Cadot is one of the most "in" of the avant-garde galleries. Its outlook is international, and it is always on the prowl for new talent. Artists include Boisrond, Favier, Laget, Oppenheim, Raetz, Rousse and Tremblay.

Carlhian
11th arr. - 35, rue de Charonne
47 00 79 28
Open 2:30 p.m.-7:30 p.m. Closed Sun., Mon. & July 15-Sept. 6. Parking: Pl. de la Bastille. No cards.

Constructive abstractivism and the primacy of matter—such is the stuff of this gallery. There's also plenty of sculpture on show. Artists include Cantépacos, Di Téana, Licata, Novoa, Tomasello. . . .

Louis Carré
8th arr. - 10, av. de Messine - 45 62 57 07
Open 10 a.m.-6 p.m. Closed Sat., Sun. & Aug. Parking: Bergson. No cards.

Patrick Bongers, Louis Carré's grandson, carries on the tradition by keeping alive the great names of this gallery's past: Delaunay, Dufy, Hartung, Léger, Poliakoff and Soulages. He also exhibits artists like Bitran and even had Di Rosa paint his car.

Charles Cartwright
4th arr. - 6, rue de Braque - 48 04 86 86
Open 2 p.m.-7 p.m. Closed Sun., Mon. & Aug. 1-Sept. 10. Parking: Sainte-Croix-de-la-Bretonnerie. No cards.

Cartwright has a most personal outlook, still resolutely avant-garde. This very young gallery owner currently exhibits Armleder, Bowes, Condo, Joubert, Levine, Van Sampel and Troeckel.

Jeanne Castel
8th arr. - 3, rue du Cirque - 43 59 71 24
Open 10 a.m.-12:30 p.m. & 2:30 p.m.-6:30 p.m. Closed Sat. & Sun. Parking: Matignon. No cards.

Marie-José Lefort is doing a good job of keeping Jeanne Castel's memory alive, as well as preparing a descriptive catalog on Fautrier, the gallery's artistic luminary. Other artists represented include Borès, Hartung, Hélion, Le Corbusier and more recent artists, Mathieu, Matta, Tapies, Toubeau, Vilato and Warren.

Clivages
7th arr. - 46, rue de l'Université
42 96 69 57
Open 2:30 p.m.-7 p.m. (Sat. 10:30 a.m.-7 p.m.). Closed Sun., Mon. & July 23-Sept. 10. Parking: Montalembert. No cards.

This discreet gallery, with very safe taste, also publishes books. On our last visit there were works on display by Brunschwig, Dilasser, Imhoff, Marfaing and Talcoat.

Caroline Corre
6th arr. - 14, rue Guénégaud - 43 54 57 67
Open 10 a.m.-7 p.m. Closed Sun., Mon. & July. Parking: Mazarine. Cards: V, AE, DC, MC.

This very contemporary gallery has moved from Montmartre to the heart of the Left Bank. Caroline Corre likes to back the as-yet unknowns: Baume, Bédarride, Bettencourt and Judlin. Her exhibitions of "artists' books" travel all over the world.

Lucien Durand
6th arr. - 19, rue Mazarine - 43 26 25 35
Open 10:30 a.m.-12:30 p.m. & 2:30 p.m.-7 p.m. Closed Sun., Mon., July & Aug. Parking: Mazarine. Cards: V, MC.

For 30 years, Lucien Durand has been discovering young artists and organizing first exhibitions. Thanks to this sensitive, eagle-eyed picture dealer we have César and Dmitrienko. Durand's current group of artists include Braconnier, Canteloup, Frize, Lechner, Nadaud and Vanarsky.

Durand-Dessert
3rd arr. - 3, rue des Haudriettes
42 77 63 60
Open 2 p.m.-7 p.m. Closed Sun., Mon. & July 23-Sept. 10. Parking: Beaubourg. No cards.

Durand-Dessert displays European avant-garde at its loftiest level, where you'll find such international high-flyers as Richter, Beuys, Merz, Kounelis, Morellet, Garouste, Lavier and Tosani.

Jacqueline Felman
11th arr. - 8, rue Popincourt - 47 00 87 71
Open 2:30 p.m.-7 p.m. Closed Sun., Mon., July & Aug. Cards: V, MC.

This new gallery is making a valiant effort to rehabilitate figurative painting—as long as it is based on a well-mastered technique. Some of the meticulous and highly talented artists represented are Buffoli, César, Cussinet, Haijima, Martelet, Sélim, and Wong Moo Chew.

Mathias Fels
8th arr. - 138, bd Haussmann - 45 62 21 34
Open 10 a.m.-12:30 p.m. & 2:30 p.m.-6 p.m. Closed Sat. morning, Sun. & Aug. Parking: Haussmann. No cards.

We owe Mathias Fels a great deal for having promoted the painting of such artists as Arman, Fontana, Hains and Klasen in the '60s. Recently he has rejuvenated his stable with works by James Brown, Combas, Dietman, Di Rosa, Haring, alongside those of Erro, Rancillac, Télémaque and Villeglé.

Jean Fournier
4th arr. - 44, rue Quincampoix
42 77 32 31
Open 10 a.m.-12:30 p.m. & 2 p.m.-7 p.m. Closed Sun., Mon. & 2 wks. in Aug. Parking: Beaubourg. No cards.

Jean Fournier has been in his vast book-lined premises for 30 years, remaining faithful to the new abstraction movement of the postwar period: Buraglio, Sam Francis, Hantai, Joan Mitchell and Viallat.

Galerie 1900–2000
6th arr. - 8, rue Bonaparte - 43 25 84 20
Open 10 a.m.-12:30 p.m. & 2 p.m.-7 p.m. Closed Sun., Mon. morning & Aug. Parking: Mazarine, Saint-Germain. Cards: V, AE, MC.

This gallery organizes good, varied exhibitions on such themes as hyperrealism, pop art and fringe artists. Represented are Max Ernst, Hérold, Marcel Jean, Matta, Picabia, Man Ray, Gaston Louis Roux, Takis and Warhol.

Galerie Beaubourg
4th arr. - 23, rue du Renard - 42 71 20 50
Open 10:30 a.m.-1 p.m. & 2:30 p.m.-7 p.m. Closed Sun., Mon. & Aug. Parking: Beaubourg. No cards.

Here, at one of the most important galleries in the Beaubourg area, Pierre and Marianne Mahon favor artists of the '50s, new realists and other contemporaries. Works are sold worldwide, including to museums. We can happily recommend the Mahons for some sure values: Arman and César, as well as Baselitz, Basquiat, Beuys, Boisrond, Cane, Combas, Dado, Garouste, Klossowski, Monory, Paladino, Raysse, Villeglé, Warhol and Wols.

Galerie de France
4th arr. - 50, rue de la Verrerie
42 74 38 00
Open noon-7 p.m. Closed Sun., Mon. & Aug. Parking: Hôtel de Ville. No cards.

Its museum-like space spanning three floors makes Galerie de France ideal for sculpture exhibits. (It also hosts a number of international art festivals.) Artists include Aillaud, Antoniucci, Brancusi, Degottex, Gonzales, Kantor, Manessier, Matta, Pincemin, Raynaud, Soulages, Zao Wou-Ki. The excellent photography exhibitions comprise works by Alice Springs, Domela and Gisèle Freund. Galerie de France also has been responsible for promoting contemporary Soviet artists.

Galerie la Hune
6th arr. - 14, rue de l'Abbaye - 43 25 54 06
Open 10 a.m.-1 p.m. & 2 p.m.-7 p.m. Closed Sun., Mon. morning & Aug. Parking: Saint-Germain. Cards: AE.

M. Gherbrant specializes in contemporary graphic arts as well as in books illustrated by such painters as Alechinsky, Arroyo, Bellmer, Dado, Hayter, Titus-Carmel, Velickovic and Philippe Favier.

Galerie Jacob
6th arr. - 28, rue Jacob - 46 33 90 66
Open 10:30 a.m.-12:30 p.m. & 2:30 p.m.-7 p.m. Closed Sun., Mon. & Aug. No cards.

Denise Renard has been at the helm of this gallery, which is known for its discretion and good taste. Early days included the likes of Szenes, Vieira Da Silva and Olivier Debré. Today's luminaries are Khoa Pham, Lovay, Nikodemou, Segeral and Michel Duport.

Galerie Lelong
8th arr. - 13, rue de Téhéran - 45 63 13 19
Open 9:30 a.m.-1 p.m. & 2:30 p.m.-6 p.m. Closed Sun. & Aug. Parking: Téhéran. No cards.

Known as the "spiritual son" of Maeght, Daniel Lelong's internationally known gallery is one of the most important in Paris. In addition to Lelong's branches in Zurich and New York, he has a sideline publishing venture. He exhibits great contemporary artists: Bacon, Calder, Chagall, Lindner, Moore, Bram Van Velde, as well as Adami, James Brown, Garcia Sevilla, Kienholz, Tàpies and Titus-Carmel.

Galerie Loft
6th arr. - 3 bis, rue des Beaux-Arts
46 33 18 90
Open 10 a.m.-1 p.m. & 2 p.m.-7 p.m. Closed Sun., Mon. & Aug. Parking: Mazarine. No cards.

Young Jean-François Roudillon has plenty of talent and get-up-and-go. On show are works by Beau Geste, Mesnager, Mosner, Quentin, Roncillac and more.

Maurice Garnier

8th arr. - 6, av. Matignon - 42 25 61 65
Open 10 a.m.-1 p.m. & 2:30 p.m.-7 p.m. Closed Sun., Mon., July & Aug. Parking: Time-Life, Rond-Point. No cards.

Since 1978 Maurice Garnier has represented a single painter: Bernard Buffet, whom Picasso believed was the most talented painter of his generation. Each year, in February and March, Garnier puts on a thematic exhibition of Buffet's work.

Daniel Gervis

7th arr. - 14, rue de Grenelle - 45 44 41 90
Open 10 a.m.-12:30 p.m. & 2:30 p.m.-6:30 p.m. (other than exhibitions, by appt.). Closed Sun., Mon. & Aug. Parking: Saint-Germain, Bon Marché. No cards.

Daniel Gervis, coproducer of the FIAC, Paris's annual International Fair of Contemporary Art, also sponsors original engravings and lithographs. His taste runs toward the abstract: Benrath, Olivier Debré, Dubuffet, Hartung and Malaval.

Katia Granoff

8th arr. - 92, rue du Faubourg-Saint-Honoré - 42 65 24 41
Open 10 a.m.-1 p.m. & 3 p.m.-7 p.m. Closed Mon. & July 15-Sept. 10. Parking: Hôtel Bristol. Cards: V, MC.

You'll find works from the Impressionists to the current school—from Monet, Marquet, Chagall and Zadkine to Laprade, the Rouen school and on to the more contemporary Pagès-Berard.

Gutharc-Ballin

11th arr. - 47, rue de Lappe - 47 00 32 10
Open 10 a.m.-7 p.m. Closed Sun., Mon. & Aug. Parking: Pl. de la Bastille. No cards.

A small space for a young dynamic duo. Artists include Michèle Blondel, Dufour, Klemensiewicz, Quesniaux. . . .

Samy Kinge

7th arr. - 54, rue de Verneuil - 42 61 19 07
Open 10:30 a.m.-1 p.m. & 2:30 p.m.-7 p.m. Closed Sun., Mon. & July 9-Sept. 6. Parking: Bac. No cards.

This fairly recent gallery may be difficult to typecast, but it often plays host to the works of such excellent artists as Brauner, Malaval, Raynaud, Raysse, de Saint-Phalle and Tinguely.

Laage-Salomon

4th arr. - 57, rue du Temple - 42 78 11 71
Open 10:30 a.m.-12:30 p.m. & 2:30 p.m.-7 p.m. Closed Sun., Mon. & Aug. Parking: Forum des Halles, Beaubourg. No cards.

Gabrielle Salomon's outlook is clearly an international one. The gallery goes in for German artists (Baselitz, Luperts, A. R. Penck and Immendorf) as well as exhibits works by the American sculptor Chamberlain, the English artist Ackling and French artists Cogné, Mercier, Messager and Di Rosa.

Yvon Lambert

3rd arr. - 108, rue Vieille-du-Temple
42 71 09 33
Open 10 a.m.-12:30 p.m. & 2:30 p.m.-7 p.m. Closed Sun., Mon. & Aug. No cards. Other branch: 5, rue du Grenier-Saint-Lazare - 3rd arr. - 42 71 04 25; parking: Horloge, As-Eco supermarché.

The reserved Yvon Lambert is an institution of the avant-garde. A onetime aficionado of minimalist and conceptual art, Lambert now aims in another direction: Lewitt, Oppenheim, Tuttle and Twombly, as well as Christo, Blais, Barcelo and Combas.

Laourière Frélaut

4th arr. - 23, rue Sainte-Croix-de-la-Bretonnerie - 42 74 02 30
Open 11 a.m.-7 p.m. Closed Sun. & Mon. No cards.

Initially famous for its engraver's studio in Montmartre, where some of the century's greatest painters came to work, Laourière Frélaut these days exhibits works of old friends as well as some new ones: Cane, Dado, Delaunay, Hérold, Karilovsky, Lardera, Singier Condé, Suzzoni and Zao Wou-Ki.

Baudoin Lebon

4th arr. - 34, rue des Archives - 42 72 09 10
Open 10 a.m.-7 p.m. Closed Sun., Mon. & Aug. Parking: Lobau. Cards: V, MC.

Allow us to forewarn you: this gallery is a little offbeat. Expect, for example, to see an exhibition of aboriginal art and works by Ben, Bissier, Dado, Dine, Michaux, Pagès,

Rauschenberg, Titus-Carmel and Viallat. There's some publishing activity as well.

Louise Leiris

8th arr. - 47, rue de Monceau - 45 63 28 85
Open 10 a.m.-noon & 2:30 p.m.-6 p.m. Closed Sun. & Mon. No cards.

Founded by D. H. Kahnweiler, this "picture dealer of the century" (Picasso, Léger, Gris, Braque and others) is indeed a venerable and historically important gallery that should not be missed. Its collections of paintings rank among the highest imaginable—Masson, Laurens, Beaudin and, more recently, Elie Lascaux.

Levignes-Bastille

11th arr. - 27, rue de Charonne
47 00 88 18
Open 11 a.m.-7 p.m. Closed Sun., Mon. & July 25-Sept. 1. Cards: V, AE, MC.

Since 1985 this gallery has devoted four floors to contemporary artistic expression: Fraser, Grataloup, Hahn, Lukaschewsky, Rotella, Sandorfi and occasionally Warhol.

Albert Loeb

6th arr. - 12, rue des Beaux-Arts
43 26 45 62, 46 33 06 87
Open 10 a.m.-1 p.m. & 2 p.m.-7 p.m. Closed Sun., Mon. & Aug. Parking: Mazarine. No cards.

Albert Loeb runs one of the most famous galleries on the Left Bank, inherited from his father Pierre Loeb, one of the great pre–World War II dealers. Among the many sculptors showing their works here are Bérard, Cassel, Gamarra, Gillioli, Jeanclos, Lam and Messagier.

Adrien Maeght

7th arr. - 42-46, rue du Bac - 45 48 45 15
Open 9:30 a.m.-1 p.m. & 2 p.m.-7 p.m. Closed Sun. & Mon. Parking: rue du Bac. Cards: V, AE, DC.

Adrien Maeght (the son of Aimé Maeght), along with Kahnweiler, is one of the best-known picture dealers around. His stock of paintings, housed in several galleries throughout Europe, is tremendous. He and his two daughters also publish fine books and promote

young artists from the Maeght "stable": Broto, Bury, Delpart, Grau, Klasen, Kuroda and Solana.

Daniel Malingue

8th arr. - 26, av. Matignon - 42 66 60 33
Open 10:30 a.m.-12:30 p.m. & 2:30 p.m.-6:30 p.m. Closed Sun., Mon. morning & Aug. Parking: Matignon, Champs-Elysées. No cards.

Twice a year, Daniel Malingue sets up prestigious exhibitions of such major twentieth-century artists as Dufy, Léger, Matisse and Vlaminck, as well as César, Lobo, Matta and Moore.

Niki Diana Marquardt

11th arr. - 9, pl. des Vosges - 42 78 21 00
Open 10 a.m.-7 p.m. Closed Sun., Mon. & Aug. Parking: Hôtel de Ville. No cards.

This gallery, which may be one of Paris's finest, is set in an old lamp workshop. Niki Marquardt is of American origin and claims that "one doesn't need direction, just vision, to know something about the plastic arts." Certainly the works of Bader, Bourgeaud, Dunoyer, Flavin, Kumrov and Vlugt have a life of their own.

Marwan Hoss

1st arr. - 12, rue d'Alger - 42 96 37 96
Open 10 a.m.-12:30 p.m. & 2:30 p.m.-7 p.m. Closed Sat., Sun. & Aug. Parking: Vendôme. No cards.

Apart from a few great classics, such as Matisse, Bonnard and Calder, this gallery pipes a contemporary tune from Giacometti to Garcia with some stopovers for Chillida, Brown, Music, Millares and Soulages.

Montenay

6th arr. - 31, rue Mazarine - 43 54 85 30
Open 11 a.m.-1 p.m. & 2:30 p.m.-7 p.m. Closed Sun., Mon. & Aug. Parking: Mazarine. No cards.

Marie-Hélène Montenay's has one of the most beautiful spaces in her part of town. And this new gallery owner is going full guns. Her artists are as varied as they are contemporary: Allington, Autard, Dalbis, Deacon, Laget, Martin and Skoda.

Françoise Palluel
3rd arr. - 91, rue Quincampoix
42 71 84 15
Open 2:30 p.m.-7:30 p.m. Closed Sun., Mon. &
July 9-Sept. 10. Parking: Beaubourg. Cards:
DC.

The space may not be great, but Françoise
Palluel works untiringly to discover and promote young artists. Her discoveries include
nonrepresentational artists Guérin, Godefroy,
Pandini and Soulié.

Proscenium
6th arr. - 35, rue de Seine - 43 54 92 01
Open 10:30 a.m.-12:30 p.m. & 2 p.m.-7 p.m.
Closed Sun., Mon. & July 20-Aug. 31. Parking:
Mazarine, Saint-Sulpice. No cards.

This very pretty gallery often hosts exhibitions of theater decor and costumes (it displays
few contemporary artists' works). Bakst,
Bérard, Cocteau, Dupont, J. Hugo and
Wakevitch are the primary artists, though Erté
and Pizzi are also represented.

Denise René
7th arr. - 196, bd Saint-Germain
42 22 77 57
Open 10 a.m.-1 p.m. & 2:30 p.m.-7 p.m. Closed
Sun., Mon. & Aug. Parking: Saint-Germain.
No cards.

In 1945 Denise René's pioneering gallery
became the rallying center for geometrical abstraction. Since then she has sung its praises the
world over and adopted the offshoots of con-
structivism—Agam, Albers, Claisse, Dewasne,
Herbin, Naraha, Soto and Vasarely.

Charles Sablon
15th arr. - 21, rue du Maine - 45 48 10 48
Open 2 p.m.-7 p.m. Closed Sun., Mon., July &
Aug. Parking: Montparnasse. No cards.

A beautiful spot at the end of a flowered
path, this gallery expands every time a next-
door neighbor moves out. Pictorial and photographic works predominate, though there
are also a number of drawings on exhibition.
Artists include Albert, Bott, Casadeus,
Lagoutte, Sebes, Willis and Anne Garde.

Stadler
6th arr. - 51, rue de Seine - 43 26 91 10
Open 10:30 a.m.-12:30 p.m. & 2:30 p.m.-7 p.m.
Closed Sun., Mon. & July 10-Sept. 10. Parking:
Mazarine. Cards: V, MC.

Since its opening in 1955 Rodolphe
Stadler's gallery has become a Left Bank institution. Some of its regular contributing artists
include: Delay, Huftier, Luthi, Mahdavi,
Mathieu, Rainer, Saura, Serpan, Tapies and
two newcomers, Ruhle and Thupinier.

Leif Stahle
11th arr. - 37, rue de Charonne
48 07 24 78
Open 11 a.m.-7:30 p.m. Closed Sun., Mon. &
Aug. Parking: Ledru-Rollin. Cards: AE.

Leif Stahle, organizer of the Stockholm Fes-
tival, came to live in Paris in 1986. His beautiful, well-lit gallery is devoted to
contemporary abstract art and, according to
Stahle, "not just to lyrical abstraction." Artists
Choi, Debré, Englund, Gandin, Kallos,
Kinahara, Limérat, Rosenthal and Weil have
found a home here.

Nane Stern
11th arr. - 26, rue de Charonne
48 06 78 64
Open 3 p.m.-7:30 p.m. Closed Sun. & Mon.
Parking: Ledru-Rollin. Cards: V, AE, DC.
Other branch: 25, av. de Tourville - 7th arr. -
47 05 08 46, closed Sun., Mon. & July 1-Sept. 1.

Nane Stern, impassioned by painting, is an
ex-crony of Pierre Loeb. She rushes to the
defense of abstraction because she believes
figurative painters are wallowing in the decorative, that sworn enemy of what she calls
"painting-painting." Her painters include
Guiot, Kallos, Koch, Lafoucrière, Péron,
Pfnür, Violet and Terziev.

Daniel Templon
3rd arr. - 30, rue Beaubourg & 1, imp.
Beaubourg - 42 72 14 10
Open 10 a.m.-7 p.m. Closed Sun., Mon. & Aug.
Parking: Beaubourg. No cards.

This was the first gallery to open (March
1972) near the Pompidou Center. From the

start it emulated New York's SoHo galleries and has since become the leading champion of American art in Paris. Works of De Kooning, Warhol, Lichtenstein, Stella and Serra are on display here, as are pieces by some of the younger transatlantic members of the avant-garde, such as Clemente, Chia and Cucchi. French artists are represented by the likes of Debré, Appel, Alberola, Giorda and Rouan.

Patrice Trigano

6th arr. - 4 bis, rue des Beaux-Arts
46 34 15 01
Open 10 a.m.-1 p.m. & 2:30 p.m.-6:30 p.m. Closed Sun., Mon. & Aug. Parking: Mazarine. No cards.

After a spell on rue Beaubourg, Patrice Trigano has set up shop on the Left Bank where he specializes in art of the '50s. He exhibits César and Harman (he started out with them) but also Atlan, Hérold, Lanskoy, Lapicque, Masson, Riopelle, Schneider, Soulages, Talcoat, Bram, Ger Van Velde and Jenkins.

POSTERS & PRINTS

Ariel

8th arr. - 140, bd Haussmann - 45 62 13 09
Open 10:30 a.m.-1 p.m. & 2:30 p.m.-6:30 p.m. Closed Sat., Sun. & July 14-Sept. 5. Parking: Haussmann-Berry. No cards.

For 30 years, Jean Pollak has represented top artists of his generation—the Cobra Alechinsky group, Appel, Doucet and Jorn, as well as Bitran, Debré, Dubuffet, Hartung, Lindstrom, Messagier, Poliakoff and Saura. He also displays sculpture by Anthoons, Reinhard and Subira-Puig.

Ciné-Images

7th arr. - 68, rue de Babylone - 45 51 27 50
Open noon-7 p.m. (Sat. 2 p.m.-7 p.m.). Closed Sun., Mon. & Aug. 13-Sept. 6. No cards.

Ciné-Images is dedicated to film. According to the pros, this is an absolute "must" visit for serious movie-poster collectors. All the greats are represented.

Documents

6th arr. - 53, rue de Seine - 43 54 50 68
Open 10 a.m.-12:30 p.m. & 2:30 p.m.-7 p.m. Closed Sun., Mon. & Aug. Parking: Saint-Germain, Odéon. Cards: V, MC.

In 1953 Michel Romand put together a collection of posters amassed by Sagot, his great-grandfather. His stock of superb original posters dating from 1875 to 1930, for sale to the public, has been responsible for his meteoric rise to success. He still has works by Toulouse-Lautrec, Mucha, Chéret, Capiello and Steinlen, among others.

Galerie Jacques Fivel

6th arr. - 20, rue Serpente - 43 25 96 34
Open 3 p.m.-7 p.m. Closed Sun. Parking: Ecole de Médecine. Cards: AE.

The large selection of French and foreign posters for amateur and professional collectors alike includes such subjects as sports, travel, "1900," art deco and decorative panels.

Galerie Jean-Louis Fivel

6th arr. - 20, rue Serpente - 46 33 64 21
Open 2 p.m.-7 p.m. Closed Sun. & Aug. Parking: Ecole de Médecine. No cards.

Jacques and his brother, Jean-Louis, have successfully coexisted as next-door neighbors. Jean-Louis, who has a penchant for theatrical and circus posters, is a specialist and sells to museums and collectors.

Galerie Princesse, Comptoir de l'Affiche

6th arr. - 18, rue Princesse - 43 25 25 18
Open 10 a.m.-7:30 p.m. Closed Sun. Parking: Saint-Sulpice. Cards: V, MC.

Hand over a color slide and 130 francs, allow eight days, and you, too, can be a pinup (about 15 by 20 inches). Framing is also available here, and there are reproductions—primarily of movie posters—for sale. This setup is duplicated at 58, rue d'Auteuil in the sixteenth arrondissement.

A l'Imagerie
5th arr. - 9, rue Dante - 43 25 18 66
Open 10 a.m.-1 p.m. & 2 p.m.-7 p.m. Closed Sun. & Mon. mornings. Parking: Lagrange. Cards: V, AE, MC.

The selection of old French and foreign advertising posters (selling for 500 to 1,000 francs and up) here is grand. There's also Belle Epoque lithographs, some 1925 stencils and Japanese prints. Exhibitions are held frequently.

Nouvelles Images
5th arr. - 6, rue Dante - 43 25 62 43
Open 11 a.m.-7 p.m. Closed Sat., Sun. & Aug. Parking: Lagrange. Cards: V, MC.

Among this grand choice of posters, there are pieces to suit everyone. In addition, you will find postcards as well lots of works on painting, architecture and contemporary photography. Posters from the national museums as well as those issued by major galleries are for sale.

Odermatt et Cazeau
8th arr. - 85, rue du Faubourg-Saint-Honoré - 42 66 92 58
Open 10 a.m.-6:30 p.m. Closed Sun. & Aug. Parking: rue Rabelais. No cards.

This gallery specializes in works by nineteenth- and twentieth-century masters, Impressionists and post-Impressionists and has fine sculpture displays (Germaine Richier, Gonzales, Zadkine). A few contemporary artists—Yuri Kuper, Paul Manés and John Alexander, among them—also show their work here.

MUSEUMS

MAJOR MUSEUMS

Cité des Sciences et de l'Industrie
19th arr. - 30, av. Corentin-Cariou
46 42 13 13
Open 10 a.m.-6 p.m. (Wed. noon-9 p.m., Sat., Sun. & holidays noon-8 p.m.). Closed Mon. Parking: under the Cité (direct access). Cafeterias. Access for the handicapped. Admission: 30F, reduced rate 23F & children under 7 free.

A *cité* indeed—or maybe a citadel of knowledge. This gigantic steel, glass and concrete former meat-packing plant casts a formidable shadow across the wacky Parc de la Villette, with its geodome and moats set in an enormous green swath along the Ourcq Canal in northeast Paris. It is the world's largest science and industry museum, conceived for the 21st century. In the outsized 120-foot-high entrance hall hangs a scale model of a space station with astronauts at work. Yet once you get over that initial dizzy spell, you'll find that the Cité is, paradoxically, made to the measure of man. Floors are divided into modular cells, which are shuffled around to create scenic effects. Visitors are challenged to penetrate the mysteries of science. And we've found that it is best to be curious—and daring. Get the most out of the Cité by examining and playing with exhibits. Then sit back and contemplate. Scores of computer terminals beckon, ready to measure your knowledge, to lead you through experiments of weightlessness or the speed of sound, to activate robots, take you on a trip through outer space, heighten your senses, put you in touch with experts in various fields of knowledge. . . .

The permanent exhibitions, known collectively as Explora, occupy the upper three floors of the Cité. The focus of all of them is man— From Earth to Universe, The Adventure of Life, Matter and the Work of Man, Languages and Communication. The Green Bridge is a futuristic greenhouse hanging garden featuring in vitro specimens. Temporary exhibits range from The Age of Plastics to Television's 50th Birthday and last from three to five months.

Marie Curie, Claude Bernard and Diderot areas can be found on Levels 1 and 2. The Planetarium houses a dome-screen equipped with an "astronomical simulator," a multimedia complex and a 3-D sound system. There are special shows for children ages 5 to 10. (Hours: Tuesday, 11:45 a.m. to 5 p.m.; Wednesday, 11:30 a.m. to 7 p.m.; Thursday and Friday, 10:30 a.m. to 5 p.m.; weekends, 1:15 p.m. to 5 p.m. Tickets: 15 francs, free for children under 7.)

The Inventorium, on Level 3, for children ages 3 through 12, has exhibits designed to make the discovery of science an informal, fascinating experience. (Hours: Tuesday, Thursday and Friday, 10 a.m. to 5 p.m.; Wednesday and weekends, 12:30 p.m. to 6:30 p.m. Tickets: 15 francs.)

The Multimedia Library, on Level 1, is one of the world's best-stocked science-documentation centers (and is open daily noon to 8 p.m., Wednesday until 9 p.m.). The Children's Multimedia Library, for 3- to 14-year-olds, is open Wednesday and weekends, from 2 p.m. to 6:30 p.m.

The Louis Lumière Cinema presents science films, documentaries, cartoons and science-fiction films, and is open to the general public on the ground level. The Experimental Gallery, of particular interest to contemporary artists, filmmakers, writers and musicians, houses works representing the relationship between art, technology and science. The Science Newsroom showcases companies' most recent achievements and developments, with science writers providing running commentary.

In front of the Cité, the Géode, an imposing sphere of polished stainless steel houses an ultra-modern movie theater, with its Omnimax motion picture system (enhanced by lasers and holograms). Shows are presented on the hour, Tuesday and Thursday, 10 a.m. to 6 p.m.; Wednesday, Friday and weekends, 10 a.m. to 9 p.m. (call 40 05 06 07 for additional information and schedules; reservations via Minitel, 3615 code Villette.

Information booths are located throughout the museum.

Musée d'Art Moderne de la Ville de Paris

16th arr. - 11, av. du Président-Wilson
47 23 61 27
Open 10 a.m.-5:30 p.m. (Wed. until 8:30 p.m.). Closed Mon. Parking: av. du Président-Wilson. Temporary exhibitions. Access for the handicapped. Admission: 13.50F, reduced rate 7F.

The MAM—as this museum is called—has always been a whirlwind of change. But while collections may waltz in and out, the various "isms" of modern art are always represented: from Fauvism (Vlaminck and Derain) to cubism (Picasso and Braque) to cinetism (Vasarely, Agam). It is your opportunity to view a remarkable series of paintings by Rouault and Gromaire, compositions by Robert and Sonia Delaunay, works by Léger, Soutine, Chagall, Pascin and others. And, of course, still on view is the celebrated *Electricity Fairy* by Raoul Dufy and Matisse's terrific triptych *Dance*. The fourth-level ARC (*Animation, Recherche, Confrontation*) is the liveliest section of the museum, used primarily to showcase contemporary art forms (plastic arts, photography, poetry, contemporary music and jazz). Often, several shows and events run simultaneously, with an accent on new talent. The children's museum is designed to acquaint youngsters (and their parents) with modern art (enter at 14, avenue de New-York).

Musée des Arts Décoratifs

1st arr. - 107, rue de Rivoli - 42 60 32 14
Open 12:30 p.m.-6 p.m. (Sun. 11 a.m.-6 p.m.). Closed Mon. & Tues. Parking: Pyramides. Temporary exhibitions. Access for the handicapped. Admission: 20F.

The French lifestyle and love of life are displayed in this jewel of the Paris museum world. A five-year facelift has rejuvenated its more than 100 rooms and galleries that trace the history of French homes from the Middle Ages to the present. One-of-a-kind and mass-produced tapestries, ceramics, tableware and furniture demonstrate how taste, form and style have evolved. The exquisite suite of 1920s art deco rooms was crafted for fashion designer

MUSEUM PASS

The Carte Musée, available at museums, travel agencies and many Métro stations, allows you to wander at will through every museum in Paris and the greater metropolitan area. A single-day pass sells for 50 francs, and three- and five-day passes are available as well, for 100 francs.

Leanne Lanvin. Avant-garde designs by Breuer, Perriand and others flank creations by Eames, Tallon and Paulin in a sweeping panorama of the last 50 years of French and international design. Recent additions: the delightful eighteenth- and twentieth-century toy collection, plus a handsome gift—paintings and sculptures (1942–1966) by Jean Dubuffet. Extensive reference sections cover wallpapers (open Thursday, 2 p.m. to 6 p.m. and by appointment), textiles and patterns (by appointment). And workshops buzz with activity: plastic arts for children and adults; art deco for youngsters, stylism, engraving, guided tours and so on (call 42 60 32 14 for information). The library, a treasure trove of documentation on arts and crafts (109, rue de Rivoli), is open from 10 a.m. to 5:30 p.m. (with the exceptions of Sunday and Monday mornings). Excellent museum book and design shop. A neighbor worthy of note is the Musée des Arts de la Mode (109, rue de Rivoli).

Musée du Grand Louvre

1st arr. - Cour Napoléon - 42 60 39 26
Open 9:45 a.m.-5 p.m. (6:30 p.m. central section). Closed Tues. & holidays.

The Musée du Louvre, traditionally France's greatest museum, has become the Grand Louvre, reborn with a sparkling glass pyramid de-signed by Chinese-American architect I. M. Pei. The 200-plus halls and Grande Galerie, the miles of wall space, are currently being remodeled and reorganized. Even the once-confusing signs indicating the direction to the *Mona Lisa*, the *Venus de Milo* or, for that matter, the rest rooms, have been rethought. Why? The Louvre's three million or so annual visitors (60 percent to 80 percent of which are foreigners) were dropping from exhaustion and losing their way among the museum's 400,000-plus cataloged works of art. The prestige of the museum had been in steady decline, hardly surprising since this former palace of kings had remained static for nearly 200 years (it opened August 10, 1793, as the Muséum Central des Arts). How to remedy the situation? And in keeping with maintaining the architectural integrity of the buildings (even after all the storming, burning, enlarging and remodeling they had gone through over the last five centuries)? Pei's answer was a huge underground complex with reception and ticket areas, restoration labs, gift shops and parking facilities. In addition, the office of the Minister of Finance was transferred from the Rivoli Wing of the palace to a new site at Bercy on the Seine. (Restoration of the Rivoli Wing and its courtyards will continue for another five years or so.)

Now that all the hubbub has died down, people are noticing that Pei's controversial glass pyramid rises a mere 67 feet above the Cour Napoléon. Flanked by three smaller pyramids and several reflecting pools, it is in essence a high-tech skylight and entrance. In the vast void beneath, a futuristic helicoidal staircase-cum-elevator, plus a bank of double escalators, should help control traffic flow. From inside the pyramid, the view of Lefuel's 1853 facades is marvelous. An unexpected bonus: archeological excavations uncovered the foundations of the ancient Louvre palace (along with some 25,000 objects from the Middle Ages). The admirably restored crypt, which soon will open to the public, features an imposing section of wall from 1660, the Saint-Louis hall from the thirteenth ceuntry and the Philippe-Auguste tower. Three giant temporary exhibit halls and an auditorium round out the Cour Napoléon complex. Of course, space limitations here do not allow us to do justice to the Grand Louvre; we urge you to consult specialized books for further details.

Musée de l'Homme

16th arr. - Palais de Chaillot, pl. du
Trocadéro - 45 53 70 60
Open 9:45 a.m.-5:15 p.m. Closed Tues. & holidays. Restaurant le Totem. Admission: 16F, reduced rate for students & children.

The marvels of mankind stored in this exotic museum are being dusted off and reshuffled in a festive frenzy of 50th-anniversary-plus (the museum actually began life in 1938) celebrations. No longer a daunting jumble amassed over the years, the renovated entrance hall—with its design showcases—as well as the anthropology and Africa sections, are a sparkling success. Descriptions and displays are now easy for the layman to understand. But that's just the tip of the iceberg: the Arctic room is enjoying a warm renaissance, with superb collections unfrozen from the warehouse. The heavenly planetarium whisks visitors across five continents to follow man and his evolution, his arts and crafts, rites and religions. Don't miss the Chinese theater costumes, African masks, Indian jewelry, Eskimo sculptures and other oddities from distant lands. Alas, when will the amazing Aztec skull in polished quartz escape from its safe-deposit box? The museum offers countless activities in anthropology, prehistory and ethnology for children, teenagers and adults, as well as lecture tours, exhibits, films and concerts. Information is available from the cultural activities service: 47 27 18 17.

Musée de la Marine

16th arr. - Palais de Chaillot, pl. du
Trocadéro - 45 53 31 70
Open 10 a.m.-6 p.m. Closed Tues. & holiays.. Guided tours, conferences, temporary exhibitions. Access for the handicapped. Admission: 16F.

Ships ahoy! The world's largest maritime collection is solidly moored at Trocadéro, where waves of enthusiastic youngsters regularly innundate the Musée de la Marine. They may sail right by the magnificent Joseph Vernet paintings, but they always go overboard for the antique and modern navigational instruments, the sidearms and cannons, the old charts and the countless scale-model ships, which cover five centuries of maritime history: caravels (small fifteenth- and sixteenth-century sailing ships), galleys, royal vessels, yachts, frigates, trawlers, war ships and atomic submarines. A favorite is Napoléon's golden-winged long-

boat. Likewise, the gut-wrenching wreckage of the *Juste*, which went down in 1725 with over 500 men on board and was discovered in 1968. Deep-sea divers in a grotto, diving suits and the first sailboard to cross the North Atlantic (1985) are among the museum's fascinating flotsam. The library and photo archives are awash with documents. Before setting sail, we like to stop for a view of the Trocadéro gardens or drop anchor at Le Totem bar/restaurant (with terrace), which is open from 10 a.m. to midnight.

Musée Marmottan

16th arr. - 2, rue Louis-Boilly - 42 24 07 02
Open 10 a.m.-5:30 p.m. Closed Mon. & holidays. Admission: 18F.

This Sleeping Beauty's Castle–style museum (First Empire furniture, objects and paintings, admirable tapestries from Louis XII's reign) awoke one day in 1970 in an explosion of color and light when the works of Claude Monet and fellow Impressionists burst onto the scene. More than 165 oils, sketches and watercolors by Monet were donated, a stunning complement to the Donop de Monchy gift. This is the home of Monet's *Waterlilies*, plus major works by Pierre-Auguste Renoir, Camille Pissarro, Alfred Sisley . . . a premier Impressionism showcase. In 1987 a new Impressionist collection, the Duhem, was installed on the first floor in newly refurbished rooms. We were as thunderstruck by Paul Gauguin's *Bouquet de Fleurs* as we were disheartened by the loss of Monet's *Impression, Soleil Levant*, which was stolen in 1985. Don't miss the extraordinary Wildenstein collection of miniatures from the thirteenth through the sixteenth century.

Musée National d'Art Moderne (Centre Georges Pompidou)

4th arr. - 120, rue Saint-Martin
42 77 12 33, 42 77 11 12
Open noon-10 p.m. (Sat. & Sun. 10 a.m.-10 p.m.). Closed Tues. Parking: Saint-Martin. Restaurant, bar, cafeteria. Access for the handicapped. Admission: 22F, reduced rate 16F, free on Sun. & holidays until 2 p.m. & for children under 18.

When it opened on January 31, 1977, the Centre Georges-Pompidou was called a hideous oil refinery, destined to rust away before the very eyes of a disgusted public. Twelve years later, some 90 million visitors had passed through its modern art galleries, museum, cinemas, concert hall, vast library (with many books in English), exhibition spaces, industrial creation center, periodicals room and record archives (with extensive listening facilities). The language lab is a veritable babel, with over 95 tongues, from Bambara to Tibetan. Since space is limited, the Centre is constantly being remodeled and enlarged. The latest metamorphosis of note: the permanent collection rooms on the third and fourth floors, which have been "rebuilt" by Italian architect Gae Aulenti (also responsible for the interior of the Musée d'Orsay). The result is a sorely needed reshuffle of the museum's 17,000 works (shows revolve several times a year). The permanent collection traces the history of modern art from 1914 on. In extent, it is rivaled only by the Museum of Modern Art in New York. One of the two screening rooms of the Cinémathèque (National Film Archives) is located in the building. And the sloping plaza in front teems with jugglers, mimes, palm readers, portrait artists, musicians, fire-eaters and other exotic specimens of humanity. Then, there's always the astonishing view of Paris rooftops from the top-floor restaurant—the twin towers of Notre-Dame to the pearly domes of Sacré Coeur. The decor here may not be the snazziest (it never was), but the food (fixed-price menus range in price from 50 to 120 francs) is much improved of late (excellent pastries).

Workshops: training for future Picassos Wednesday and Saturday, 2 p.m. to 3:30 p.m. and 3:45 p.m. to 5 p.m. (ages 6 to 14). Summer workshops: June 23 to October 1. Bookshop: One of Paris's best-stocked art book stores carries deluxe editions published by the Centre (architecture, film, music and so forth), plus temporary-exhibit catalogs, many of which have become collector's items. (Annual-membership card is 130 francs and offers priority access to all shows, invitations to expo openings, and discounts on admission to shows, concerts and films, and on books, postcards and posters, as well as meals at the restaurant.)

Musée d'Orsay
7th arr. - 1, rue de Bellechasse
45 49 11 11
Open 10 a.m.-6 p.m. (Thurs. until 9:45 p.m. & Sun. 9 a.m.-6 p.m.). Closed Mon. Parking: Deligny, Invalides, Montalembert. Daily guided tours: 11 a.m. & 1 p.m. (Tues. 7 p.m.). Admission: 23F, reduced rate 12F, children under 18 free.

Tempest in a teacup department: In a league with the Eiffel Tower, the Pompidou Center and the Louvre pyramid, the Musée d'Orsay was buffeted by a wild storm on the Seine. And now, a mere three years after President Mitterand snipped the ribbon, there is little or no sign of the appalling verbal squall that surrounded the opening of the museum. The Musée d'Orsay is a resounding success. To think that this former train station was slated for demolition, judged a prime example of horrid fin de siècle taste (it was designed in 1900 by architect Victor Laloux). . . . The derelict station's exterior and frame were restored and strengthened—a careful work of preservation and enhancement. Italian architect Gae Aulenti worked her peculiar magic on the vast interior. The result is impressive. Now the Grand Central Terminal of nineteenth-century art, the Musée d'Orsay's collections trace the jagged path of painting, sculpture, photography, decorative and industrial art from 1848 to 1914. Thanks largely to generous donations from intrepid patrons of the arts, the work of greats formerly outside the mainstream, from Gustave Courbet to Edouard Manet and the Impressionists, now have a stunning home in the Orsay. Among the Orsay's finest: Honoré Daumier's classic 36-bust series *Les Parlementaires* (1832); Claude Monet's *Rue Montorgueil* (1878), bursting with noisy life; Georges Seurat's pointillistic *Poseuse de Dos*, seemingly composed of little more than air and light; and Giovanni Boldini's Proustian *Portrait de Madame Max* (1896). Several of the museum's halls are filled with temporary exhibits (a theme, a work, a school). Films, concerts and conferences are scheduled for the auditorium, and there are workshops for children ages 5 to 15.

Shows scheduled for 1989–1992: The Centennial of the Eiffel Tower; Guimard and Art Nouveau; Museums in the 19th Century; Masterpieces of Impressionism from the Annebert Collection; Munch and France; the Nadar Museum; Georges Seurat.

The terrace of the Café des Hauteurs (upper floor) affords a superb panorama of Paris. At the old station restaurant, now the museum restaurant, pastries, as delicious as they are lovely to look upon, are served. The restaurant's decor is 1900-rococo; open for lunch and dinner (after museum hours, enter at 62 bis, rue de Lille). The museum bookshop is large and well stocked; there's also a museum boutique/gift shop that's accessible from inside the museum or from the street.

Musée du Petit Palais
8th arr. - av. Winston-Churchill
42 65 12 73
Open 10 a.m.-5:40 p.m. Closed Mon. Parking: François-Ier. Admission: 7F.

Beyond the hugely popular temporary exhibits, all is quiet at the Petit Palais. Built in 1900 for the Exposition Universelle, the Petit Palais is marked by its stone-and-iron frame, and its rococo galleries decorated with allegories and ornate cupolas are excellent examples of the architecture of the time. Its rather eccentric permanent collection is largely neglected, which means you'll be able to enjoy an unobscured view of the exquisite Dutuit donation (works from antiquity to the seventeenth century), featuring rare examples of Egyptian and Greek art, and the sumptuous Rembrandt self-portrait in Oriental garb. The Tuck Collection, comprising furniture, tapestries and other eighteenth-century items, is also housed here. The municipal collections boast several nineteenth-century gems: magnificent paintings by Gustave Courbet, Eugène Delacroix, Pierre Bonnard, Edouard Vuillard and Paul Cézanne, plus Impressionist works that have escaped the Musée d'Orsay dragnet. An entire hall is given over to a sublime series by Odilon Redon. Elsewhere you'll find sculptures by Auguste Rodin. The inner garden is a delightfully cool refuge during the dog days of summer.

Musée Picasso
3rd arr. - Hôtel Salé, 5, rue de Thorigny
42 71 25 21
Open 10 a.m.-5:15 p.m. (Wed. until 10 p.m.). Closed Tues. Tea room, restaurant. Admission: 21F, children under 18 free.

This is indeed art in an artful architectural frame. The magnificent seventeenth-century Hôtel Salé, one of Paris's most spectacular Marais town houses, was painstakingly restored to house the paintings and artworks of Pablo Picasso (donated to the state in lieu of inheritance taxes). Here we've rediscovered one of this century's greatest artists through a complete panorama of his favorite works— "Picasso's Picassos" (he selected five of his own paintings each year plus a copy of each lithograph; the sculptures never left his studio). The treasure trove totals 200 paintings, 149 sculptures, 16 collages, 29 montages, 86 ceramics, over 3,000 drawings and engravings, illustrated books and manuscripts, sketchbooks and original drawings. There's even proof of Picasso's precocity: several astonishingly polished paintings done when the artist was 14 years old—*La Petite Fille aux Pieds Nus, L'Homme à la Casquette*, among them.

Muséum d'Histoire Naturelle
5th arr. - Jardin des Plantes, 57, rue Cuvier
43 36 14 41
Open 1:30 p.m.-5 p.m. Closed Tues. & holidays. Parking: Gare d'Austerlitz. Admission: 11F, temporary exhibitions 25F.

Taken bit by bit, this magical, many-faceted museum-cum-garden is a marvel. The lovely Jardin des Plantes that surrounds the natural history museum is a leafy oasis in summer, a riot of color and fragrance in spring. Its sycamore-lined gravel lanes link carefully planted and labeled flowerbeds and botanical gardens, a small zoo and a wildly exotic tropical greenhouse. The museum's galleries tell the tale of the earth—of life and its history. The anatomy and paleontology hall is a huge, surreal world filled with skeletons and prehistoric monsters. The paleobotany hall is even odder, with plant specimens from two billion to 250 million years ago. In the cavernous mineralogy hall there are thousands of meteorites, extraordinary crystals, cut gems, precious stones (the Salle du Trésor reveals an astounding wealth of emeralds, sapphires, rubies, turquoise, platinum and gold nuggets from the Bank of France's safes). A flight of fancy awaits lepidopterists (and all butterfly catchers/fanciers) in the entomology hall's collections (45, rue Buffon). In case you're wondering: the museum was originally the modest medicinal plant garden of Louis XIII, later the royal garden. It flowered from 1739 to 1788 under the scientific guidance of Buffon, then became a natural history museum in 1789 by decree of convention. The dilapidated main gallery (built in 1889) was closed nearly 30 years ago. Only five enormous, immovable whale skeletons remained in the darkened building. In the last five years, the state has begun renovations (the interior is soon to become an evolution museum). Beasts are back in business, with the recent remodeling of the zoology hall and zoo. There are learning labs on birds, animal languages, minerals and more, as well as a museum bookshop. The museum hosts guided tours Wednesday at 2:30 p.m. for parents with children aged 7 and older (43 36 54 26).

Palais de la Découverte
8th arr. - av. Franklin-Roosevelt
43 59 16 65, 43 59 18 21
Open 10 a.m.-6 p.m. Closed Mon. Parking: Rond-Point des Champs-Elysées. Cafeteria. Access for the handicapped. Admission: 15F, planetarium 11F.

The futuristic Cité at La Villette has nearly knocked the wind out of this exploratorium. Indeed, the palatial aspect of the Palais de la Découverte has lost lots of luster. The floor is shedding mosaics while the carpets curl and the *Sciences* and *Techniques* statues collect dust. Still, enthusiastic toddlers, eager adolescents and bemused tourists discover science in the electricity, solar system, nuclear physics and chemistry-and-biology-in-the-service-of-man galleries. We guess it's just too bad when the computers refuse to play games as programmed or when the knobs and buttons of the touch-me experiential devices come off in your hand.... But the planetarium still features

star-studded astrological projections. And outer space fans can admire the teeny French flag planted on the moon by the Apollo XVII crew. The Jean Perrin astronomy club caters to curious kids aged 14 to 18 (43 59 16 65).

UNUSUAL FINDS
Historial de Montmartre
18th arr. - 11, rue Poulbot - 46 06 78 92
Open daily 10:30 a.m.-6:30 p.m. Admission: 20F, reduced rate 10F.

We could write a book about the beauty of this museum's location, with its panoramic view across Paris. The amusing historical wax works evoke vivid images of yesteryear at Montmartre and of famous people and places. A must for Musée Grévin fans.

Maison de Balzac
16th arr. - 47, rue Raynouard - 42 24 56 38
Open 10 a.m.-5:40 p.m. Closed Mon. & holidays. Temporary exhibitions. Admission: 10F.

The rustic charm of Honoré de Balzac's pavilion and verdant garden—*la cabane de Passy,* where he lived from 1840 to 1847—was only one reason the penurious novelist holed up here. The other is a discreet back entrance and escape route down the rue Berton. Because when Balzac wasn't penning immortal prose like *The Human Comedy,* he was keeping his eye out for debt collectors. The flavor of his checkered life comes through in his austere study, which, entirely intact, is stuffed with letters, documents and everyday objects—an inkwell shaped like a padlock and primed for sixteen hours of work—and decorated with portraits of the women he loved and admired. Armchairs and tables entice visitors to sit down and have a good read. The documentation center on the rue Berton is open to the general public.

Maison de Victor Hugo
4th arr. - 6, pl. des Vosges - 42 72 16 65
Open 10 a.m.-5:40 p.m. Closed Mon. & holidays. Admission: 10F.

Victor Hugo lived from 1832 to 1848 in this seventeenth-century house on the place des Vosges. He wrote several chapters of *Les Misérables* and scores of other plays and poems here in these seven rooms, which effectively re-create the atmosphere of the *salon rouge,* the Guernesey dining room and the death chamber of the avenue d'Eylau. Family portraits, yellowed souvenirs and piously preserved memorabilia in glass cases rather blandly trace Hugo's tormented life. But the rooms do provide an excellent idea of how Hugo amused himself when he was not writing: a series of somber pen and ink drawings executed in a state of "almost unconscious reverie" or the eccentric wooden cabinets he cobbled together. The haunting initials V. H. seem to appear everywhere.

Manufacture des Gobelins
13th arr. - 42, av. des Gobelins
45 70 12 60
Open Tues.-Thurs. (last tour's departure 2 p.m.-3:15 p.m.). Parking: Pte. d'Italie. Guided tour. Admission: 18F.

Nestled among ancient, charmingly provincial homes, the Gobelins (Beauvais and Savonnerie) national manufactures is not a museum but a busy tapestry and carpet-weavers school and workshop. Visitors stroll through the imposing 1912 edifice as looms spin out tomorrow's masterworks.

Musée Adam Mickiewicz
6th arr. - 6, quai d'Orléans - 43 54 35 61
Open Thurs. 3 p.m.-6 p.m. (or by appt.). Admission: free.

This little musuem, which highlights the life, times and friends of Poland's greatest poet, Adam Mickiewicz (1798–1835), is growing more and more popular.

Musée de l'Air et de l'Espace
93350 Le Bourget - Aéroport du Bourget
48 35 92 49
Open 10 a.m.-6 p.m. Closed Mon. Admission: 10F.

The sky's the limit in this megamuseum of flying machines. From the first balloons to the *Kitty Hawk* to today's spaceships, we found here everything we ever wanted to know about the history of man and the sky.

Musée des Antiquités Nationales
78103 Saint-Germain-en-Laye - pl. du Général-de-Gaulle - 34 51 53 65
Open 9:45 a.m.-noon & 1:30 p.m.-5:15 p.m. Closed Tues. & holidays. Parking: by the church. Admission: 15F, 60 years and over 8F, under 18 free.

This marvelous antiquities museum was created by Emperor Napoléon III. Beautifully laid out in a nineteenth-century Renaissance-style château, it contains the world's richest collection of archeology pertaining to prehistory—from the rock paintings at Lascaux (scale reconstruction of the Bull Chamber) to the first bone and flint tools, through the Bronze and the Iron Ages, the Gallo-Roman and Merovingian periods. Sculptures, glassware, pottery, weapons and precious gold jewelery.

Musée de l'Arc de Triomphe
8th arr. - pl. Charles-de-Gaulle
43 80 31 31
Open 10 a.m.-5 p.m. Parking: Georges-V. Admission: 22F, reduced rate 12F.

This high-rise museum's displays are pretty paltry fare: a collection of documents, including pictures and engravings, plus photos showing the arch's construction and the burial of the Unknown Soldier in 1921, and a short video on the history of the monument. But if you climb to the terrace 160 feet above the Champs-Elysées, you will discover before you a breathtaking vista, one of the best views of Paris the city has to offer.

Musée de l'Armée
7th arr. - Hôtel des Invalides - 45 51 92 84
Open 10 a.m.-5 p.m. (April 1-Sept. 30 until 6 p.m.). Parking: Promenade des Invalides. Concerts, Saint-Louis des Invalides church, cafeteria. Admission: 21F, children under 18 free.

Arm yourself for the onslaught of countless weapons and machines of war designed to slash, club, explode, flatten, puncture and otherwise exterminate your neighbor. Every imaginable type of weaponry is on display in this extremely popular museum (right up there with the Eiffel Tower and the Château de Versailles in terms of tourist visits). Louis XIV had the Invalides built by architects Libéral Bruant and Jules Hardouin as a veterans' hospital. Mansart erected the towering Dôme church, which is visible from all over Paris. The Invalides is still considered one of the city's most handsome architectural ensembles. True to character, Emperor Napoléon appropriated the church as a monument to his own glory, and he is entombed in the elaborate carved-porphyry Emperor's Tomb under the cupola. However, we found the astounding engraved sword by Benvenuto Cellini, the gigantic François-Ier on horseback, the 1914–1918 section, with its moving displays, and the 1939–1945 galleries, with their superb model of the Normandy landings, far more interesting. For Napoléon-trivia fans, there's the bizarre stuffed white charger he rode on Saint-

Hélène and the dog that kept him company during his exile on the island of Elba. Be forewarned: you will never be able to see it all in one go.

COLLECTOR'S ITEMS

A collector's consuming passion knows no bounds—but space may become a problem. Some solve it by converting their collection into a "museum" and allowing the public to share their enthusiasm. Curious, droll, interesting, entertaining—here is a sampling of *petits musées* worth exploring: Musée des Lunettes et Lorgnettes (eyeglasses and opera glasses), 2, avenue Mozart, 16th arrondissement, 45 27 21 05; Musée de la Seita (tobacco), 12, rue Surcouf, 7th arrondissement, 45 56 60 17; Musée de la Musique Mécanique (music boxes, nickelodeons, player pianos, etc.), impasse Bertaud, 3rd arrondissement, 42 71 99 54; Musée du Vin (wine), 5, square Charles-Dickens, 16th arrondissement, 45 25 63 26; Musée de la Parfumerie (fragrance in all its forms), 9, rue Scribe, 9th arrondissement, 47 42 93 40; Musée Bouilhet-Christofle (silver), 12, rue Royale, 8th arrondissement, 42 60 34 07); Musée de l'Holographie (holographic images), Forum des Halles, 1st arrondissement, 42 96 96 83; Musée du Baccarat (crystal), 30 bis, rue de Paradis, 10th arrondissement, 47 70 64 30; Musée de la Coiffure (hairdressing and related accoutrements), 28, rue Vivienne, 2nd arrondissement, 42 33 21 12; Musée Piaf (memorabilia of singer Edith Piaf), 5, rue Crespin-du-Gast, 11th arrondissement, 43 55 52 72.

Musée d'Art et d'Histoire de Meudon
92190 Meudon - 11, rue des Pierres
45 34 75 19
Open 2 p.m.-6 p.m. Closed Mon., Tues., holidays & Aug. Admission: free.

This lovely seventeenth-century house, once owned by Molière, hosts a hodgepodge collection of fine works, documents and memorabilia united by a single theme: they all pertain to artists, musicians and personalities who lived in or around Meudon. Highlights: two busts by Rodin, sculptures by Arp and paintings by Schuffenecker, Magnelli, Dunoyer de Segonzac, Stalhy and memorabilia related to Ronsard, Céline, Mme. de la Pompadour and Wagner, who composed most of *The Flying Dutchman* here.

Musée de l'Assistance Publique
5th arr. - 47, quai de la Tournelle
46 33 01 43
Open 10 a.m.-5 p.m. Closed Mon. & Tues. Admission: 10F.

Fear not, hospital haters, this museum of public health care, from the Middle Ages to the present, is captivating. The museum is housed in the handsome and newly renovated sixteenth- and seventeenth-century Hôtel Miramion, across the Seine from Notre-Dame. There's an interesting collection of paintings, drawings and engravings, among them a series of moving etchings showing the agonies of war, by Jacques Callot. Medical instruments on display include Dr. Dupuytren's surgical gear, and there's also a fine collection of porcelain apothecaries' jars. Don't miss the 3 o'clock Sunday-afternoon concerts (from October to May), held in the music room.

Musée d'Art et d'Histoire de Saint-Denis
93200 Saint-Denis - 22 bis, rue Gabriel-Péri
42 43 05 10
Open 10 a.m.-5:30 p.m. (Sun. 2 p.m.-6 p.m.). Closed Tues. Admission: 9F, reduced rate 6F, exhibitions 12F (reduced rate 8F).

Winner of the coveted Prix Européen du Musée, this marvelous former Carmelite convent (seventeenth and eighteenth centuries), superbly restored in 1981, makes the trip to dingy Saint-Denis worthwhile. On display is a fine collection of religious art and archeological finds pertaining to the city and the Carmelite order. Easy to reach (the RER express subway takes you there from central Paris in just a few minutes), it is located next door to the phenomenal Cathedral of Saint-Denis, resting place of the French kings.

Musée d'Art Juif

18th arr. - 42, rue des Saules - 42 57 84 14
Open 3 p.m.-6 p.m. Closed Fri. & Sat. Admission: 15F.

Objects used at temple services, popular art, scale models of synagogues from the thirteenth through the nineteenth century, rare books, contemporary paintings and drawings (Marc Chagall, among them) are on display at this fascinating museum housed in the Montmartre Jewish Center. (There are temporary shows, too.)

Musée d'Art Naïf Max Fourny–Musée en Herbe

18th arr. - Halle Saint-Pierre, 2, rue Ronsard - 42 58 74 12
Open 10 a.m.-6 p.m. Parking: under the square d'Anvers. Tea room. Admission: 15F.

This two-in-one museum, housed in the sunny nineteenth-century Saint-Pierre Halle, is one of Paris's most entertaining and refreshing. A vast second-floor loggia houses Max Fourny's renowned collection of naïf art. The ground floor, called the Musée en Herbe, features thematic exhibits that last from eight to ten months and cover an almost infinite range of subjects. The museum also hosts a number of workshops for children, as well as cultural and art activities for both kids and adults, spin-offs of the temporary shows.

Musée des Arts Africains et Océaniens

12th arr. - 293, av. Daumesnil
43 43 14 54
Open daily 9:45 a.m.-noon & 1:30 p.m.-5:15 p.m. Access for the handicapped. Admission: 20F, children under 18 free.

Kids love this place, with its alligator pits and an immense aquarium swimming with piranhas. On the edge of the Bois de Vincennes at the Porte Dorée, the massive 1931 former Musée des Colonies is a remarkable example of the architecture of its age. Outside is an outsized bas-relief of some riotously rich colonial kingdom of flora and fauna. Inside is the marvelous collections of masks, statues in wood and bronze, jewelry and finery. The museum hosts mask-making workshops for 4- to 18-year-olds and music classes for kids aged 14 and up. (For information, call 43 43 14 54.)

Musée des Arts de la Mode

1st arr. - 107, rue de Rivoli - 42 60 32 14
Open 12:30 p.m.-6 p.m. (Sun. 11 a.m.-6 p.m.). Closed Mon. & Tues. Parking: Pyramides. Admission: 25F, reduced rate 18F.

This lovingly restored museum of fashion arts at the Pavillon de Marsan comprises five floors of linen, accessories, shoes, bags and hats (eighteenth- to twentieth-century collections from the Arts Décoratifs and the Union Français des Arts du Costume)—in all, about 32,000 pieces of clothing. Exhibits change regularly. Don't miss the haute-couture collections by Doucet, Poiret, Chanel and Dior. Researchers may view videos of some 24,000 patterns (at a cost of 70 francs per hour). On sale in the museum store are reproductions of hard-to-find clothing items and accessories (from 75 to 2,000 francs). Long-running temporary shows are a highlighted staple. In 1990: the history of men's fashion from the eighteenth century to the present.

Musée des Arts et Traditions Populaires

16th arr. - 6, av. du Mahatma-Gandhi
47 47 69 80
Open 9:45 a.m.-5:15 p.m. Closed Tues. Access for the handicapped. Admission: 15F.

Another favorite among the young, this is the sort of museum that captivates some and loses others right off. Collections of objects from popular traditions trace the development of rural civilization in France. Arranged with startling precision and displayed in huge Plexiglas cases are a blacksmith's forge, a cooper's shop, the interior of a Breton peasant's house, a wheelwright's and carpenter's workshop, a trawler with sail spread and numerous other life-size models and various regional costumes, implements and decorative items. Impressive temporary exhibits, archives, library and other research facilities are available to researchers.

Musée Bourdelle

15th arr. - 16, rue Antoine-Bourdelle
45 48 67 27
Open 10 a.m.-5:40 p.m. Closed Mon. & holidays. Access for the handicapped. Admission: 10F, 15F.

Riotous green gardens strewn with Antoine Bourdelle's bronzes are hidden in the heart of old Montparnasse. We like to visit in the spring when the trees are bursting with blossoms. This house/museum has been suspended in time since the sculptor's death in 1929. The collection of hundreds of sculptures, original plasters, terracottas, wax masks, paintings and watercolors is surrounded by family portraits, furniture built by Bourdelle's father, as well as miscellaneous memorabilia. You can rummage among the master's tools and teaching tables in the cluttered studios and workshops. Bourdelle's brawny art represents a powerful reaction to the sculpture of its time (he was, when young, Rodin's assistant). Giant original plasters are featured in the exhibit hall: *Le Centaur Mort, L'Epopée Polonaise* and the equestrian statue of Alvéar. The Beethoven series of bronze heads overflows with pathos. Don't miss Bourdelle's bas-reliefs (1912–1913, restored in 1987) on the facade of the Champs-Elysées theater.

Musée Bricard (de la Serrurerie)

3rd arr. - 1, rue de la Perle - 42 77 79 62
Open 10 a.m.-noon & 2 p.m.-5 p.m. Closed Sun., Mon., Aug. & last wk. in Dec. Admission: 5F, 10F.

This unusual museum holds the key to the locksmith's ancient art. On display are locks from early Christian times, door handles and knobs, ornamental lock casings, bolts, keys, door knockers and all such devices designed to lock, enclose, seal, protect and hide. Banal? You may be surprised to find yourself getting all keyed up over these odd objects: the first rudimentary key from Gallo-Roman times, a massive medieval lock, glittering goldsmithery, seventeenth-century twelve-tooth keys, Napoléon's imperial door bolt, the Marquis de Sade's safe. . . . The museum is in an exquisite seventeenth-century Marais town house (designed by Libéral Bruant, architect of the Invalides) just down the street from the Picasso museum. It was restored by Bricard, the 150-year-old French lock manufacturer, to house its immense collections.

Musée du Cabinet des Médailles et Antiques

2nd arr. - 58, rue de Richelieu
42 61 82 83
Open 1 p.m.-5 p.m. Closed on holidays. Parking: Bourse. Admission: 10F.

Even hard-core numismatists are floored by this awesome collection of 400,000 coins and medals (the world's largest collection of cameos and intaglios), precious works from antiquity (including a remarkable Hellenistic torso of Aphrodite), the Middle Ages and the Renaissance, plus Persian silverwork and paintings by Boucher and Van Loo. Housed in the Bibliothèque Nationale building, it is one of the most venerable Paris museums, dating to the 1500s.

Musée Carnavalet

3rd arr. - 23-29, rue de Sévigné
42 72 21 13
Open 10 a.m.-5:40 p.m. Closed Mon. & holidays. Admission: 13F, reduced rate for students.

The Hôtel Carnavalet recently swallowed up its next-door neighbor, the Hôtel Le Peletier de Saint-Fargeau. Five years of restoration and remodeling have produced a museum worthy of the history of Paris—from its ancient origins to the present day. The sound and fury of years gone by, the restitching of the urban fabric, the beautification and destruction of the metropolis are captured in topographical models of neighborhoods, scale models of monuments and paintings and prints. Other collections feature carved wood paneling, period furniture, historical documents and miscellaneous curios. The town house itself is a prime exhibit: begun in the 1500s by Pierre Lescot, floors were added by François Mansart in the seventeenth century, and further additions made in the nineteenth century. Yet it is one of the most harmonious architectural ensembles in the Marais, with a lovely inner-court garden graced by sculpted shrubs, flower beds and fountains. From 1777 to 1796 the mansion was inhabited by Madame de Sévigné, famed in French letters for her epistolary excellence. French Revolution devotees will not want to miss the blood-stained letter Robespierre was writing when the Terror turned upon him. The Révolution and the nineteenth- and twentieth-century collections, as well as the print collection (300,000 items), are housed here. The museum's new gift shop (which opened in July

1989) went all-out celebrating the bicentennial—originals and reproductions, jewelry, foulards, stationery, games, porcelain, scale models—and there are probably still some left-overs.

Musée de Céramique de Sèvres
92310 Sèvres - pl. de la Manufacture
45 34 99 05
Open 10 a.m.-noon & 1:30 p.m.-5:15 p.m. Closed Tues. & holidays. Parking: in front of the museum. Admission: 15F, reduced rate 12F, children under 18 free.

Countless plates, platters, dishes, vases and cups arrayed in flawless order fill cases and walls. Islamic flower and bird designs, mythological scenes on Urbino majolica, Chinese-inspired Delftware . . . Sèvres ceramics lovers will swoon. Empress Catherine II's table service, as well as those of Mme. Du Barry and Talleyrand are displayed in a handsome Louis XV decor. It is a truly monumental collection. The Manufacture de Sèvres is open to visitors from 1:15 p.m. to 3:30 p.m. the first and third Thursdays of the month (except July and August). And, of course, ceramics are sold in the showroom sales area.

Musée Cernuschi
8th arr. - 7, av. Velasquez - 45 63 50 75
Open 10 a.m.-5:40 p.m. Closed Mon. & holidays. Parking: Malesherbes, Anjou. Admission: 10F.

An astonishingly fine collection of Chinese and Japanese art is displayed in this austere, chillingly charmless museum (chem-lab-green walls, cut-rate showcases, poor lighting). It features many rare pieces from prehistoric times to the Sung Dynasty (thirteenth century). Exquisite ceramics, antique jades and bronzes reveal the greatness of these civilizations. An astonishing series of terracotta funeral statuettes from the Han, Wei and T'ang Dynasties (from the third century B.C. to the eighth century A.D.) depict ladies of the court, dancers and musicians, soldiers and a host of imaginary men and beasts. A recent acquisition is a Han funeral vase decorated with acrobats. Formerly of the private collection of Henri Cernuschi, which he assembled during a prolonged stay in Asia, it was given to the city of Paris in 1896. On Saturday Korean expert Ung no Lee gives painting and calligraphy classes for adults and children (3 p.m. to 5 p.m.).

Musée de la Chasse et de la Nature
3rd arr. - 60, rue des Archives - 42 72 86 43
Open 10 a.m.-12:30 p.m. & 1:30 p.m.-5:30 p.m. Closed Tues. & holidays. Access for the handicapped. Admission: 10F.

"Nature at the service of hunters" would be an accurate way to describe this museum. Featured is the history of how the chase changed from a necessity to a sport. Antihunters needn't be put off; for them, there's the magnificent 1654 Marais town house built by François Mansart. Always a hit with youngsters of all ages are the fine collections of weapons—from flint arrowheads to precision firearms, carved powder horns, gold-encrusted carbines, ancient elephant guns. . . . Impressive trophies from three continents and a superb collection of paintings about the hunt by Rembrandt, Desportes and Monet, among others, make this a museum to be sure and visit.

Musée du Cinéma
16th arr. - Palais de Chaillot, pl. du Trocadéro - 45 53 74 39
Open 10 a.m.-4 p.m. Closed Tues. Parking: across av. du Président-Wilson. Guided tours. Admission: 20F.

This is heaven for motion picture devotees and a must for anyone interested in the history of cinema. Its collections range from magic lanterns, Robertson's photographic plates and Lumière's 1895 movie camera to present-day films. A fine collection of documents pertaining to Charlie Chaplin, plus scripts, short and feature-length films, movie sets, photos and memorabilia are also on display. For those still starving for a screening, the Cinémathèque Française is right next door.

Musée des Collections Historiques de la Préfecture de Police
5th arr. - 1 bis, rue des Carmes
43 29 21 57
Open 9 a.m.-5 p.m. (Fri. until 4:30 p.m.). Closed Sat. & Sun.

Armed policemen in bullet-proof booths, heels clicking in corridors, suspicious eyes staring through metal wickets . . . such is the setting of this museum of Paris police lore. Featured are interesting documents from the sixteenth century to the present, plus uniforms, royal warrants of arrest, weaponry (from kitchen knives to Molotov cocktails) and often intriguing reports of legendary crimes and criminals.

Musée de la Contrefaçon

16th arr. - 16, rue de la Faisanderie
45 01 51 11
Open Mon. & Wed. 2 p.m.-4:30 p.m., Fri. 9:30 a.m.-noon. Admission: free.

A curious, somber little museum, the Musée de la Contrefaçon features famous counterfeits and fakes, from chocolate (*Meinier* instead of Menier) to perfume (*Chinarl* instead of Chanel). Wines, liquors, jewelry, clothing, luggage and so forth—every imaginable item and its dubious double.

Musée d'Ennery

16th arr. - 59, av. Foch - 45 53 57 96
Open Thurs. & Sun. 2 p.m.-5 p.m. Closed Aug. Parking: Foch-Etoile. Admission: free.

This is one extraordinary Oriental bazaar of a museum, boasting some 7,000 art objects from Japan and China assembled last century by Clémence d'Ennery, wife of the wealthy dramatist Alphonse d'Ennery. Tang pottery, Nam Ban lacquered bangle boxes, bone, ivory and porcelain buttons and an impressive menagerie of mother-of-pearl cases swarm in the dizzying decor of this nineteenth-century town house.

Musée Ernest Hé

6th arr. - 85, rue du Cherche-Midi
42 22 23 82
Open 2 p.m.-5:45 p.m. Closed Tues. Admission: 10F, reduced rate 5F, free for students.

Onward, the intrepid! This is the unjustly unknown museum of forgotten painter Ernest Hébert (1817–1908), the rage of his day. Here, we rediscovered the pricey painter of the princesses of the imperial court, winner of the Prix de Rome and countless accolades, the worldly portraitist of the Comtesse Greffulhe, immortalized by Marcel Proust. . . . Well, if Hébert's old-fashioned art leaves you cold, at least come and see the admirable eighteenth-century mansion furnished with Princess Mathilde's Louis XVI best.

Musée Eugène Delacroix

6th arr. - 6, rue de Furstenberg
43 54 04 87
Open 10 a.m.-5:15 p.m. Closed Tues. Parking: Saint-Germain. Admission: 10F, reduced rate 5F.

Anyone with a 100-franc bill already owns a valuable Delacroix (1798–1863). In a secret garden off the place Furstenberg, romantic as can be, the Eugène Delacroix home/museum (the painter's apartment and sunny studio are linked by a curious footbridge) is one of Paris's great little-knowns. There are no masterworks here but rather a fine series of drawings, watercolors and pastels (plus studies for such famous paintings as *The Death of Sardanapalus*), an astonishing self-portrait, the palette and easel this Romantic artist used to paint his early works, pages from his journal and various other oddities of the artist. We like to follow up with a visit to the nearby church of Saint-Sulpice, where Delacroix, advanced in years, decorated the Saints-Anges chapel.

Musée de la Femme

92200 Neuilly - 12, rue du Centre
47 45 29 40
Open 2:30 p.m.-5 p.m. Closed Tues., July & Aug. Admission: 10F, reduced rate 5F.

Here you will find rather capricious and comical collections of "women and their objects," not "women as objects." Marie Antoinette's corset and a room full of home appliances are part of this ecclectic ensemble of sculptures, paintings, clothing, photos and mementos of queens, famous actresses and other such illustrious women of intrigue.

Musée Français de la Photographie

91570 Bièvres - 78, rue de Paris
Open 9 a.m.-12:30 p.m. & 1:30 p.m.-6 p.m. Admission: 10F.

Confusion reigns in this fascinating museum. Wonderful one-of-a-kind collections of photographic and moving-picture equipment from pioneer days (Niepce, Daguerre, Nadar) to mass-market items (Kodaks from 1888 to the present) are, alas, tastelessly displayed and poorly documented.

Musée du Grand Orient de France et de la Franc-Maçonnerie

9th arr. - 16, rue Cadet - 45 23 20 90
Open 2 p.m.-6 p.m. Closed Sun., holidays, &
Sept. Parking: Montholon. Admission: free.

This is no ill-lit hideaway for regicides (king killers) and fearful freethinkers, but a modern, rather stark museum of French Freemasonry. Displayed in glass cases in a somber hall are paintings, sculptures, engravings and medals, pertaining primarily to political figures, intellectuals and military leaders. You will discover scores of illustrious names on the roster: Philippe Egalité (a supporter of the French Revolution who was guillotined during the Reign of Terror), Voltaire, Montesquieu, Marshal Joffre, the Comte de Bourbon-Condé and, surprise, even a Roosevelt.

Musée Grévin

9th arr. - 10, bd Montmartre - 47 70 85 05
Open 1 p.m.-7 p.m. Admission: 38F, reduced
rate for children under 14.

You and the other 650,000 annual visitors to the Musée Grévin will either chuckle at or pale among the petrified personages assembled here. The delirious decor of this monumental waxworks (the fourth most frequently visited museum in Paris) ranges from the Cabinet Fantastique, a charming little theater done up by Bourdelle and Chéret, to a madcap mob that includes Leonid Brezhnev and Presidents Reagan and Mitterand all dressed as astronauts with the ever-haggard Woody Allen as space cadet floating above. The ground floor features current celebrities. The basement galleries groan with scenes from France's long and eventful history.

Musée Grévin

1st arr. - Forum des Halles, level 1
40 26 28 50
Open 10:30 a.m.-6:45 p.m. (Sun. 1 p.m.-7:15
p.m.). Parking: Les Halles. Admission: 34F, stu-
dents 30F, children 7-15 22F.

The Forum des Halles branch features Paris in the Belle Epoque, a series of animated tableaux and Reynaud's Optical Theater—the praxinoscope, the predecessor of the Lumière brothers' cinematograph—which he operated at Montmartre from 1892 to 1900.

Musée Guimet

16th arr. - 6, pl. d'Iéna - 47 23 61 65
Open 9:45 a.m.-5:15 p.m. Closed Tues. Audio-
visual & conference rooms. Admission: 15F.

Ten years of remodeling and enlarging have transformed this venerable temple of Asian art from a jumbled bazaar into a shining showcase. Unique treasures have finally been retrieved from the warehouse and put on display. You will be whisked across the vast territory of Oriental art: Khmer statues from ninth-through eleventh-century Cambodia; smiling gods and eyeless kings that well up in a halo of light. There is also a huge collection of Buddha paintings (from Nepal and Tibet), a cubist-like head of Kasyapa sculpted in gray chalkstone (sixth-century China) and, from the monasteries of Hadda in Afghanistan, delicate, fragile stucco and dried-earth figurines. Chinese ceramics and porcelain fill several halls.

Musée Gustave Moreau

9th arr. - 14, rue La Rochefoucauld
48 74 38 50
Open 10 a.m.-12:45 p.m. & 2 p.m.-5:15 p.m.
Closed Tues. Admission: 15F, reduced rate 8F.

"If you want to get a job done right, do it yourself," thought symbolist painter Gustave Moreau (1826–1898). So he erected this Renaissance Revival building in the lovely place Saint-Georges, a temple to his own posterity. It is worth a visit just to see the spectacularly baroque spiral staircase that links the third and fourth floors, where an enormous workshop and grand gallery house Moreau's works. (Surrealist writer André Breton was for decades the sole defender of Moreau's prodigious talents.) Admittedly, the 850 or so mostly unfinished giant paintings that hang from floor to ceiling are, to say the least, a dizzying spectacle. We've spent hours rummaging through the nearly 5,000 drawings, studies and watercolors that verify Moreau's fertile creativity.

Musée Henri Bouchard

16th arr. - 25, rue de l'Yvette - 46 47 63 46
*Open Wed. & Sat. 2 p.m.-7 p.m. Closed last 2
wks. of each season. Access for the handicapped.
Admission: 15F.*

Chisels and chips of stone, sketches and
photos thumbtacked to the wall in delightful
disarray—the liveliest sculptor's studio in town
is the Musée Henri Bouchard (1875–1960).
The masterful academic's work leave some
cool, but the guided tours (Wednesday at 7
p.m., limited to twenty participants; cost is 35
francs) and lectures on the sculptor's trade,
won't.

Musée de l'Histoire de France
(Archives Nationales)

3rd arr. - 60, rue des Francs-Bourgeois
42 77 11 30
*Open 2 p.m.-5 p.m. Closed Tues. & holidays.
Admission: 8F, 12F.*

What could be more precious than the history of a nation? Which explains the choice for
the National Archives: the magnificent Hôtel
de Soubise, considered by many to be the finest
eighteenth-century town house in Paris. In
these exquisite apartments, decorated by some
of the most illustrious artists of the time—
Boucher, Restout, Natoire and Van Loo,
Lemoyne and Adam—are cases containing
medieval manuscripts covering the period
from the Merovingians (the dynasty of Frankish kings that flourished from the fifth century
to 751) to the Hundred Years War, as well as
an impressive collection of documents pertaining to the French Revolution (the *Declaration
of the Rights of Man*). Long-running exhibits
generally feature some sort of written document, so a working knowledge of French is
helpful. Regardless of language, a stroll
through the town house and inner gardens are
worth the visit. Recently enlarged, the reading
rooms are now housed at 11, rue des Quatre-
Fils (around the corner) in a new wing.

Musée de l'Ile-de-France

92330 Sceaux - Château de Sceaux
46 61 06 71
*Open 10 a.m.-noon & 2 p.m.-6 p.m. (summer
until 7 p.m., winter until 5 p.m.). Closed Mon.
morning & Tues. Parking: Château de Sceaux.
Admission: 8F, children 4F, students free.*

We recommend this rich museum to untir-
ing walkers and unblinking gazers. Seven de-

partments overflow with paintings, sculpture,
furniture, costumes, ceramics and miscellaneous objects pertaining to the château and the
Paris region. A sweeping park designed by Le
Nôtre and a superb orangerie by Mansart (used
for temporary exhibits and concerts), plus a
pavilion by Claude Perrault (cupola decorations by Le Brun), round out the attractions.
For the hardy, there is a lovely forest walk that
starts at the museum (path GR 11) and continues for 36 miles!

Musée Jacquemart-André

8th arr. - 158, bd Haussmann - 45 62 39 94
*Open 1 p.m.-6 p.m. Closed Tues. & Aug. Park-
ing: Haussmann-Berri. Admission: 15F, temporary exhibitions 25F.*

Rent-a-museum? Lamentably, there were
too few visitors to the Jacquemart-André, so
this huge nineteenth-century town house has
become a showcase for temporary exhibits
from abroad. There is no guarantee that you
will be able to view the masterworks by Paolo
Uccello, Andrea Mantegna, Sandro Botticelli,
Luca della Robbia, Peter Paul Rubens and
others. What wasn't nailed down or painted on
the walls may be locked away, so phone ahead
and ask. Definitely worth a neckache are the
marvelous ceiling frescoes by Giambattista
Tiepolo and Tintoretto, which were recently
restored.

Musée Jean-Jacques Henner

17th arr. - 43, av. de Villiers - 47 63 42 73
*Open 2 p.m.-5 p.m. Closed Mon. Admission:
12F.*

This sleepy town house/museum dedicated
to the once-renowned painter Jean-Jacques
Henner (1829–1905) is awash with hundreds
of oils: somber or smiling portraits, red-haired
naiads and blushing bathing beauties. Three
floors' worth of paintings, drawings and fine
sketches culminate in a charming studio. An
Arabian prince's loggia, hidden by a screen,
imparts a pinch of exoticism to the ambience.

Musée Jean-Jacques Rousseau

95160 Montmorency - 5, rue Jean-Jacques
Rousseau - 39 64 80 13
*Open 2 p.m.-6 p.m. Closed Mon. Admission:
10F.*

The wandering philosopher and scribe Jean-
Jacques Rousseau settled down from 1757 to
1772 in this modest abode and compiled *La
Nouvelle Héloïse*, *L'Emile* and the *Lettre à*

d'Alembert. Rousseau's furniture, various letters and manuscripts are among the memorabilia. The charming garden's path of ancient lime trees—tradition has it that Rousseau planted two of them—leads to a tiny pavilion that houses the philosopher's workroom.

Musée du Jouet
78300 Poissy - 2, enclosure of l'Abbaye
39 65 06 06
Open 9:30 a.m.-12:30 p.m. & 2 p.m.-5:30 p.m. Closed Mon., Tues. & holidays. Admission: 10F, children 3-10 5F.

This museum is nothing to toy with—you can look but not touch! Overflowing with thousands of exquisite but fragile toys—from porcelain dolls to lead soldiers and mechanical merry-go-rounds from the nineteenth century. It is housed in an attractive former priory in suburban Poissy.

Musée Kwok On
4th arr. - 41, rue des Francs-Bourgeois
42 72 99 42
Open 10 a.m.-5:30 p.m. Closed Sat. & Sun. Access for the handicapped. Admission: 5F, 10F.

An uncertain future awaits this astonishing collection of objects pertaining to the theatrical traditions of Asia. Kwok On is the name of the Hong Kong collector and Chinese opera buff who assembled these countless theater costumes, actors' masks, string-rod-and-shadow puppets, musical instruments, rare recordings and porcelain figurines and then donated to Paris. There is a reference center, where video films (Cantonese opera, Japanese Kabuki or No theater) are shown on request, and a Chinese weaving, lacquer-making and painting workshop. Kathakali dance classes are taught by an Indian dancer (8:30 a.m. weekdays). No time to lose: The museum's grant runs out in 1990 and the collection will be at the mercy of City of Paris underwriters.

Musée Lambinet
78000 Versailles - 54, bd de la Reine
39 50 30 32
Open 2 p.m.-6 p.m. Closed Mon., Fri. & holidays. Admission: free.

No pomp and circumstance, as in the neighboring Château de Versailles. Here you will find a delightful eighteenth-century town house lost in a restful green garden, collections of Sèvres and Saint-Cloud ceramics, Houdon sculptures, eighteenth-century paintings, period furniture plus nineteenth-century statuettes and works by painters Dunoyer de Segonzac and André Suréda, all pleasantly displayed.

Musée de la Légion d'Honneur
7th arr. - Hôtel de Salm, 2, rue de Bellechasse - 45 55 95 16
Open 2 p.m.-5 p.m. Closed Mon. Parking: Solférino. Projection & conference rooms. Admission: 10F.

Military decorations galore from French and foreign orders: the Toison d'or, the Ancien Régime, the Légion of Honor, featuring a necklace once worn by Napoléon (who created the Legion in 1802 as a reward for civil and military service), plus a staggering display of crosses, insignia, medals, grand collar chains and more. The museum is housed in the elegant Prince Salm-Kyrbourg 1787 town house on the banks of the Seine opposite the Tuileries. Lectures and guided tours organized by the museum are available.

Musée de Minéralogie de l'Ecole des Mines
6th arr. - 60, bd Saint-Michel - 42 34 91 39
Open Tues. & Sat. 10 a.m.-12:30 p.m. & 2 p.m.-5 p.m. (Wed.-Fri. 2 p.m.-5 p.m. only). Closed Sun. & Mon. Parking: Soufflot. Admission: free.

Rock around the block . . . this is one of the world's foremost mineral museums, displaying some 85,000 samples from 600 types of crystals, meteorites, precious stones, rocks and minerals. The backdrop—the austere eighteenth-century Hôtel de Vendôme—isn't bad, either.

Musée de la Mode et du Costume
16th arr. - Palais Galliera, 10, av. Pierre-Ier-de-Serbie - 47 20 85 23
Open 10 a.m.-5:40 p.m. Closed Mon. Parking: across av. du Président-Wilson. Temporary exhibitions. Access for the handicapped. Admission: 22F.

Housed here is one of the world's richest wardrobes: 5,000 costumes in a 50,000-piece collection of fashions for men, women and children of all social classes—from the eighteenth century to the present. Interested in the remarkable wardrobes that once belonged to the Countess of Greffulhe (Marcel Proust's muse) and the Countess of Castellane? The museum's collections are brought out for rotating exhibits, each with a different theme. Most models of clothing shown are accompanied by several fashion drawings or engravings.

Musée de la Monnaie

6th arr. - 11, quai de Conti - 43 29 12 48
Open 11 a.m.-5 p.m. Closed Sat. & Sun. Parking: pl. de l'Institut. Visits by workshop staff Mon. & Wed. 2 p.m. & 3 p.m. Admission: free.

The end of the rainbow for numismatists: a staggering array of precious coins and medals housed in the gorgeous Hôtel des Monnaies. A mere 200 years or so after its creation (1768 by Louis XV), the museum has been reborn. On display are coins from ancient times to the present, paintings of coin presses, plus scales, tools and books pertaining to minting techniques. Just the town house's court of honor and the many superb salons are worth the visit.

Musée de Montmartre

18th arr. - 12, rue Cortot - 46 06 61 11
Open 2:30 p.m.-6 p.m. (Sun. 11 a.m.-6 p.m.). Temporary exhibitions. Admission: 15F, reduced rate 8F.

Relive the notorious Montmartre Bohemia of politicians and artists (which include the likes of Picasso, Utrillo and Renoir) in this sunny, charming museum, formerly the home of actor Claude la Roze de Rosimond.

Musée des Monuments Français

16th arr. - Pl. du Trocadéro, Palais de Chaillot - 42 27 35 74
Open 9:45 a.m.-12:30 p.m. & 2 p.m.-5:15 p.m. Closed Tues. & holidays. Temporary exhibitions. Access for the handicapped. Admission: 15F.

This cathedral-size museum is chockablock with monumental yet scrupulously accurate phonies—reproductions of France's sculptural monuments from pre-Roman times to the nineteenth century.

Musée Mémorial Ivan Tourgueniev

78380 Bougival - 16, rue Ivan-Tourgueniev 39 69 20 00
Hours and admission prices vary.

This delightful *dacha* was the great Russian writer's slice of home (so what if it looks more like a Swiss chalet!). He lived here happily, near friends Louis and Pauline Viardot (his pavilion is actually located in their garden; pretty Pauline was his secret lover). A pleasant pilgrimage for Turgenev devotees.

Musée National de l'Amitié Franco-Américaine de Blérancourt

02300 Blérancourt - (16) 23 39 60 16
Open 10 a.m.-12 p.m. & 2 p.m.-5 p.m. Closed Tues. Parking: available. Restaurant. Admission: 10F, 5F on Sunday, free for children under 18, ages 18-21 and over 60 5F.

This museum of Franco-American friendship, located in the lovely Château de Blérancourt, belongs to the French National Museums group. The seventeenth-century château was designed by Salomon de Brosse, architect of the Luxembourg Palace in Paris. Although it has undergone many changes over the centuries, Brosse's ornamented portals, pavilions and portions of the *corps de logis* (the main part of the building) have survived. In 1915 Ann Morgan, daughter of American financier J. P. Morgan, set up a Red Cross infirmary in the château. After World War I she began the painstaking restorations that have only recently been completed. Blérancourt's permanent collection comprises some 50 paintings from the United States and France, formerly displayed at the Musée d'Orsay and the Pompidou Center, plus a sculpture garden and landscaped grounds. Situated minutes from the forest of Compeigne, where the Armistice was signed, and Viollet le Duc's spectacular Pierrefonds Château, Blérancourt is also a charming Picardy village. Trains from the Gare du Nord stop at Noyon; a taxi will transport you the rest of the way.

Musée National de la Batellerie

78700 Conflans-Sainte-Honorine - Château du Prieuré, 3, pl. Jules-Gévelot 39 72 58 05
Open 3 p.m.-6 p.m. Closed Tues. Admission: free.

From the museum's terrace, the view of the valley and the Seine and the countless canal boats and barges is of rare beauty. Inside, the 100 or so scale models provide a sweeping panorama of the evolution of canal boats. Anchors, propellers, prows and poop decks are piled in an inner courtyard. We like the bizarre touch of the ancient orange grove in the park, which is inhabited by monkeys.

Musée Nissim de Camondo

8th arr. - 63, rue de Monceau - 45 63 26 32
Open 10 a.m.-noon & 2 p.m.-5 p.m. Closed
Mon., Tues. & holidays. Admission: 15F.

This grand 1914 town house is a nearly exact replica of the Petit Trianon at Versailles. Count Moïse de Camondo built it on the edge of the Parc Monceau and filled it with his priceless collection of eighteenth-century furniture (designed by such master craftsmen as the Jacob brothers, Riesener and Leleu), paintings (by Vigée-Lebrun and Hubert Robert) and sculptures (by Houdon and Pigalle). Sèvres porcelains, Beauvais tapestries and rare Savonnerie carpets round out the exquisitely harmonious ensemble, perfectly restored and presented as the count knew it. A true labor of love. The only drawback is that you're almost forced to purchase a catalog (50 francs) in order to follow the exhibits, which lack adequate description.

Musée de l'Opéra

1st arr. - Pl. de l'Opéra, near rue Auber
47 42 07 02
Open 10 a.m.-5 p.m. (theater 11 a.m.-5 p.m.).
Closed Sun. Parking: Pyramides. Admission:
10F.

In the wings of the sumptuous Palais-Garnier, to the left of the enormous library rotunda, you'll find this tiny museum for ballet and bel canto lovers. Musical scores and costume designs, Debussy's writing desk, Njinski's sandals and various scale models of sets from the nineteenth century are some of the highlights. On sale in the museum shop (in the Grand Hall) is an original designer line of bags, foulards, sweatshirts and so forth.

Musée de l'Orangerie

1st arr. - Terrace des Tuileries, pl. de la Concorde - 42 97 48 16
Open 9:45 a.m.-5 p.m. Closed Tues. Parking:
Pyramides. Admission: 15F, reduced rate 8F.

Claude Monet's dazzling *Waterlilies*, painted in Giverny between 1890 and his death in 1926, hang here in the two oval basement rooms, custom-designed according to the wishes of the artist. Upstairs, the Walter-Guillaume collection contains just one Monet but several undisputed masterpieces from the end of the nineteenth and the beginning of the twentieth century (by Amedeo Modigliani, Auguste Renoir, Paul Cézanne, Henri Matisse, Pablo Picasso). For a Monet pilgrimage, 70 kilometers (about 45 miles) west of Paris at Giverny is the artist's home and garden, restored to its original splendor (32 51 28 21).

Musée du Pain

94220 Charenton-le-Pont - 25 bis, rue Victor-Hugo - 43 86 43 60
Open Tues. & Thurs. 2 p.m.-4:30 p.m. Closed
July 14-Sept. 1. Admission: free.

This delightful little museum kneads you in all the right places as it recounts the history of bread as art. Installed in the granary of a flour mill, the only thing missing is the smell of baking bread. It's up to you to add that pinch of imagination.

Musée Pasteur

15th arr. - 25, rue du Docteur-Roux
45 68 82 82
Open 2 p.m.-5:10 p.m. Closed Sat., Sun. &
holidays. Admission: 10F.

The apartment where the great scientist and inventor Louis Pasteur lived is movingly simple, quite a contrast to the Byzantine chapel in which he is buried. The room that displays the souvenirs of science is wonderfully nostalgic.

Musée Paul Landowski

92100 Boulogne-Billancourt - 14, av. Max-Blondat - 46 05 82 69
Open 10 a.m.-noon & 2 p.m.-5 p.m. Closed
Wed., Sat. & Aug. Admission: free.

An intriguing if disorganized arrangement of sculptor Paul Landowski's (1900–1961) work is on display here in his former studio. Monumental sculptures in the garden and a large underground hall featuring sketches, plaster casts, scale models, watercolors and so forth provide an overview of this master of academism's work. You can also see Landowski in the streets of Paris: the gigantic *Sainte Geneviève* on the Tournelle bridge and the statue of Montaigne at the Sorbonne.

Musée de la Poste

15th arr. - 35, bd de Vaugirard
43 20 15 30
Open 10 a.m.-5 p.m. Closed Sun. & holidays. Parking: Gare Montparnasse. Admission: 10F.

A first-class museum for philatelists and anyone interested in the history of the postal service. Displays range from Roman wax tablets to featherweight airmail paper, from mailboxes to high-tech video encoders. On our last visit, our favorite piece was a rural mailman's bicycle from the nineteenth century. A word to the wise: bring a magnifying glass to properly view the stamp collections.

Musée du Prieuré–Maurice Denis

78100 Saint-Germain-en-Laye - 2 bis, rue Maurice-Denis - 39 73 77 87
Open 10:30 a.m.-5:30 p.m. Closed Mon., Tues. & holidays. Admission: 20F, reduced rate 10F.

This exceptionally fine museum is housed in a seventeenth-century priory, which is surrounded by a lovely terraced park punctuated by Bourdelle statues. The home of Nabis-influenced symbolist painter Maurice Denis (1870–1943), it was the preferred haunt of many an artist of Denis's school. Its collection includes works of Sérusier, Vallotton, Bonnard, Vuillard, Roussel and Piot—and the recent acquisition of a portrait by Paul Gauguin.

Musée de la Préhistoire de l'Ile-de-France

77140 Nemours - Av. de Stalingrad
64 28 40 37
Open 10 a.m.-noon & 2 p.m.-5:30 p.m. Closed Wed. Parking: at the museum. Admission: 8F, reduced rate 4F.

The setting alone is worth the trip. This ultra-modern museum, which was designed by the architect of the Musée Picasso, is located smack in the center of the beautiful Fontainebleau forest. Instructive, attractive displays of archeological digs, pleasant patios filled with the fauna of prehistoric epochs, make this a lovely and lively showcase.

Musée de la Publicité

10th arr. - 18, rue de Paradis - 42 46 13 09
Open noon-6 p.m. Closed Tues. Parking: Gare de l'Est. Admission: 18F, reduced rate 10F.

Tiled friezes and murals in the turn-of-the-century neo-Renaissance style decorate the facade of this superb museum of advertising.

Some 40,000 posters dating from 1750 to the present are displayed in temporary public exhibits (researchers cannot handle the fragile paper posters but are provided the opportunity to view slides). A recent addition: TV and movie-theater commercials, plus a collection of press, radio, TV and movie documents and items used as advertisements.

Musée de Radio-France

16th arr. - 116, av. du Président-Kennedy
42 30 21 80
Open 10 a.m.-noon & 2 p.m.-5 p.m. Closed Mon. & May 1. Parking: av. du Président-Kennedy. Guided tours on the half hour. Admission: 8F, students 4F.

"Message received despite the fog." It all began on a November day in 1898, when Eugène Ducretet established the first radio contact between the Eiffel Tower and the Panthéon. This amusing museum of the history of communications starts with Roman fire beacons and winds up with today's color TV studios. Included are Italian physicist and inventor Guglielmo Marconi's devices and a vast collection of equipment and documents.

Musée Renan-Scheffer

9th arr. - 16, rue Chaptal - 48 74 95 38
Open 10 a.m.-5:40 p.m. Closed Mon. Temporary exhibitions. Admission: 10F, reduced rate 5F.

Ary Scheffer (1795–1858) was Louis-Philippe's court painter. Ernest Renan (1823–1892), the renowned writer, was Scheffer's nephew. But, surprise, this museum is given over to yet a third celebrity: George Sand. There are a few Scheffer paintings, nothing at all by Renan and an interesting collection of Sand memorabilia that includes furniture, carpets, family portraits, plus a plaster cast of Sand's and Chopin's hands. The real attraction is the house—a handsome two-story Restoration-period town house surrounded by a lovely garden at the end of an ivy-draped lane—where time stands still.

Musée Rodin

7th arr. - Hôtel Biron, 77, rue de Varenne
47 05 01 34
Open 10 a.m.-5 p.m. (summer until 6 p.m.). Closed Tues. Parking: Pl. Joffre. Cafeteria in the park. Admission: 16F.

Come when the roses in the courtyard bloom around Auguste Rodin's *The Thinker*, then wander through the eighteenth-century garden. Along the lanes stand the sculptor's monumental bronzes *The Burghers of Calais*, *The Hell Gate* and the imposing *Balzac*, to name just a few. The 1728 rococo town house belonged to the Duchess du Maine and the Maréchal de Biron before it was divided into apartments where the likes of Matisse, Cocteau and Rilke spent time. Rodin moved in at the peak of his career, and his presence saved the town house from demolition. Also on display is an impressive array of sketches and studies. Don't miss the excellent jade carving *Les Bavardes*, by Rodin's student and lover, Camille Claudel. (See the following entry for the Rodin museum annex.)

Musée Rodin

92190 Meudon - 19, av. Auguste-Rodin
45 34 13 09
Open 1 p.m.-6 p.m. Closed Sat., Sun., Mon. & Oct. 1-April 1. Admission: 8F.

This is the must-see Rodin annex, housed in the red-brick Louis XIII Villa des Brillants. The pastoral setting on a hill is one of the loveliest locations in the Paris area. Studies for Rodin's masterworks are displayed here.

Musée de la Sculpture en Plein Air

5th arr. - Jardin et quai Saint-Bernard
Open year-round. Admission: free.

This monumental sculpture garden covers a half-mile stretch of the Seine between the Pont d'Austerlitz and Pont de Sully, featuring works donated or loaned by artists Gilioli, César,

Ipoustéguy, Arman and Etienne-Martin. A breath of fresh air in a lovely green setting.

Musée des Thermes et de l'Hôtel de Cluny

5th arr. - 6, pl. Paul-Painlevé - 43 25 62 00
Open 9:45 a.m.-12:30 p.m. & 2 p.m.-5:15 p.m. Closed Tues. & holidays. Admission: 8F, 15F.

A marvelous miscellanea of thousands of medieval art and handcraft items, on display in the superb fifteenth-century Hôtel des Abbés de Cluny. Collections include ivory works, wood sculptures, paintings, stained-glass windows, furniture, jewelry, ironwork, tapestries and such. In the Gallo-Roman baths next door are the barrel-vaulted frigidarium ("cold bath") and other impressive halls (filled with statuary and masterpieces of goldsmithery) restored with rare flair. Do not miss the famed series of fifteenth-century unicorn tapestries, *La Dame à la Licorne*.

Musée Zadkine

6th arr. - 100 bis, rue d'Assas - 43 26 91 90
Open 10 a.m.-5:40 p.m. Closed Mon. & holidays. Admission: 10F.

The Russian sculptor Zadkine (1911–1967), creator of the celebrated *La Femme à l'Eventail*, lived and worked here most of his life. Today, a forest of sculptures stands in the tiny garden, an idyllic enclave on the edge of Montparnasse. We like it best in the spring when the daffodils are in bloom.

BOAT RIDES

Les Bateaux-Mouches

8th arr. - Embarcadère de l'Alma - Port de la Conférence - 42 25 96 10
Open daily 10 a.m.-noon, 1 p.m.-7 p.m. & 8 p.m.-11 p.m. Admission: daytime 20F, evenings 25F, children 10F, 15F.

These whales of river cruisers go nosing down the Seine packed with thousands of tourists, often eliciting a sarcastic smirk from Parisians. But the laugh is on the cynics. These fast, smooth boats provide one of the few ways to see Paris from a new angle. Take an early-morning or dusk cruise, when the light is at its loveliest. On night cruises, the Bateaux-

Mouches' floodlights unveil a phantasmagoric cityscape that fascinates tourists and seen-it-all Parisians alike. Lunch, tea and formal dinners (no children or dogs allowed) are available on board at reasonable prices, considering the incomparable view that accompanies your meal.

Canauxrama

19th arr. - 13, quai de la Loire
46 07 13 13
Open 9 a.m.-7 p.m. Closed Dec.-March. Admission: 70-170F, reduced rate for children.

Did you know that the Saint-Martin and the Ourcq Canals flow from the Seine in central

Paris as far (upstream) as Meaux? Well, now you do. So why go by bus or subway when you can take a boat back from La Villette's Cité des Sciences? Canauxrama's cruises are one of the city's most pleasant, unhurried, uncrowded excursions. The view of Paris and the Ile-de-France from a comfortable canal boat (sunroof, on-board bar, guided tours) has a special softness. Canauxrama offers a day-long trip on the Canal de l'Ourcq through the charming countryside between Paris and Meaux, with a stopover at Claye-Souilly for a picnic or bistro lunch. Also featured is a tour of the exciting La Villette neighborhood, which includes passage through the deepest lock in the Paris region. Departures take place at the pier opposite 5 bis, quai de la Loire (nineteenth arrondissement) and from the Paris-Arsenal canal port opposite 50, boulevard de la Bastille (twelfth arrondissement), just down from the new opera house.

Paris-Canal-Quiztour
9th arr. - 19, rue d'Athènes - 48 74 75 30
Open 9 a.m.-6:30 p.m. (Sat. 10:30 a.m.-4 p.m.). Closed Sun. Admission: 90-180F, reduced rate for children.

Quiztour offers Canal Saint-Martin and Seine cruises from April 1 to November 13 on board the *Patache* and the *Canotier*, two comfortable river boats that carry between 50 and 100 passengers. The ambience is particularly fine in the off-season. Boats are also available for receptions or private cruises, and there are houseboats and canal boat/hotels as well.

Les Vedettes de Paris-Ile-de-France
15th arr. - Port de Suffren - 47 05 71 29
Open daily 10 a.m.-11 p.m. Admission: 30F.

A summery dance-hall atmosphere reigns on these tea-dance cruises with such themes as historic Paris or the Val-de-Marne.

Les Vedettes du Pont-Neuf
1st arr. - Square du Vert-Galant
46 33 98 38
Open daily 10 a.m.-11 p.m. Admission: 25F, children 12F.

For anyone who knows Paris well, the tour commentary (in several languages) is somewhat bewildering. Les Vedettes du Pont-Neuf runs medium-size boats and is centrally located. Its one-hour pleasure cruises and run up and down the Seine. Departures take place every 30 minutes from 10 a.m. to noon and from 1:30 p.m. to 6:30 p.m. From May through October there are illuminated tours from 9 p.m. to 10:30 p.m. (departures every half hour).

FOR CHILDREN

ACTIVITIES

Centre Georges-Pompidou
4th arr. - 120, rue Saint-Martin
42 77 12 33
Open noon-10 p.m. (Sat. & Sun. 10 a.m.-10 p.m.). Closed Tues.

Gael Bernard runs this children's workshop on the ground floor of the center. Children are familiarized with the diversity of creative contemporary-artistic output. Workshops are free on Wednesday and Saturday.

Centre d'Animation Les Halles–Le Marais
1st arr. - 6-8, pl. Carrée, point Saint-Eustache - 40 26 87 88, 40 26 46 82
Open 10 a.m.-8:30 p.m. (Sat. 2 p.m.-6 p.m.). Closed Sun. & Aug. Parking: Saint-Eustache. Subscription: 100F per year (60F for children). Lessons: 400F per quarter (360F for children).

Situated in the heart of Les Halles, this center offers a plethora of activities for 4- to 14-year-olds. The only inconvenience is that everything takes place underground. There is musical appreciation for the youngest, checkers, chess, pâtisserie, computer training and video filming for the older children. During school holidays activities go on all day.

MUSEUMS

The following is a list of museums of special interest to children.

Centre Georges-Pompidou
4th arr. - 120, rue Saint-Martin
42 77 12 23
Open noon-10 p.m. (Sat. & Sun. 10 a.m.-10 p.m.). Closed Tues.

This Parisian cultural center hosts a children's workshop with facilities for theater, dance, video and film shows. Children are generally delighted by several pop art structures outside the Georges-Pompidou.

Cité des Sciences et de l'Industrie
19th arr. - 30, av. Corentin-Cariou
40 05 70 00, 46 42 13 13
Open 10 a.m.-6 p.m. (Wed. noon-6 p.m. & Sat., Sun. & holidays noon-8 p.m.). Closed Mon. Parking: Cité des Sciences. Admission: 30F, reduced rate 23F & children under 7 free.

The Cité des Sciences may make your head spin, but, curiously, we don't notice this happening with children. They delight in the "Géode," a kind of geodesic dome that houses a huge panoramic cinema screen, and the Planetarium and the Inventorium. There are also any number of video games for hands-on play. It's a user-friendly spot where a child would be hard-put to get bored. Outside, the funny-looking red houses built by Bernard Tschumi house various workshops—one of which, devoted to video, allows children to become television producers for a day.

Egouts de Paris
7th arr. - 93, quai d'Orsay - 43 20 14 40
Open Mon., Wed., & last Sat. of the month 2 p.m.-5 p.m. Closed holidays and day after. Admission: 8F, group rate 4F.

This long guided tour is done on foot, so wear good shoes! Visits are cancelled if it's raining too hard or if the river is high.

Musée de l'Armée
7th arr. - Hôtel des Invalides - 45 55 30 11
Open 10 a.m.-6 p.m. (Oct. 1-March 31 until 5 p.m.). Admission: 21F, children under 18 free.

This military museum exhibits arms, uniforms and scale models of famous battle scenes, and screens films of World Wars I and II.

Musée des Arts Africains et Océaniens
12th arr. - 293, av. Daumesnil
43 43 14 54
Open 10 a.m.-noon & 1:30 p.m.-5:30 p.m. (Sat. & Sun. until 6 p.m.). Closed Tues. Admission: 20F, children under 18 free.

This museum located on the edge of the Bois de Vincennes features the largest aquarium in Paris. Children adore the alligator pit.

Musée Carnavalet
4th arr. - 23, rue de Sévigné - 42 72 21 13
Open 10 a.m.-5:40 p.m. Closed Mon. & holidays. Admission: 13F, reduced rate for students.

This town house exhibits French history from the Renaissance to the French Revolution (including a scale model of a guillotine).

Musée de la Chasse et de la Nature
3rd arr. - 60, rue des Archives - 42 72 86 43
Open 10 a.m.-12:30 p.m. & 1:30 p.m.-5:30 p.m. Closed Tues. & holidays. Admission: 10F.

Paintings, sculptures, ceramics, tapestries and wildlife exhibits are found in this museum devoted exclusively to hunting.

Musée du Conservatoire des Arts et Métiers
3rd arr. - 270, rue Saint-Martin
40 27 22 20
Open 10 a.m.-5:30 p.m. Closed Mon. & holidays.

You'll find historical objects on display here, as well as exibits of modern-day technology.

Musée Grévin
9th arr. - 10, bd du Montparnasse
47 70 06 53
Open daily 1 p.m.-7 p.m. Admission: 38F, reduced rate for children under 14.

Founded in 1882, this wax museum features historical figures and distorting mirrors to amuse those of all ages.

Musée de l'Homme

16th arr. - Palais de Chaillot, pl. du
Trocadéro - 45 53 70 60
Open 9:45 p.m.-5:15 p.m. Closed Tues. & holidays. Admission: 16F, reduced rate for students & children.

This is an excellent museum to visit with children not only for its history-of-mankind exhibits but also for the excellent Le Totem restaurant (47 27 74 11), a great place to take the kids. There are fixed-price menus (from 75 to 145 francs) and a terrific salad bar; you don't have to pay a museum entrance fee to eat in the restaurant.

Musée de la Marine

16th arr. - Palais de Chaillot - pl. du
Trocadéro - 45 53 31 70
Open 10 a.m.-6 p.m. Closed Tues. & holidays. Admission: 16F

Exhibits and scale models on naval history and marine archeology are favorites with young visitors to the Musée de la Marine. The museum also displays maritime art, as well as artifacts of the technical, historical and scientific evolution of navigation.

Palais de la Découverte

8th arr. - av. Franklin Roosevelt
40 74 80 00
Open 10 a.m.-6 p.m. Closed Mon. & holidays. Parking: Rond-Point des Champs-Elysées. Restaurant. Admission: 15F, planetarium 11F.

This museum is an excellent place for children interested in science. Experiments are conducted by staff members every afternoon for the public. A list of daily activities is posted to the left of the museum's entrance.

Muséum d'Histoire Naturelle

5th arr. - 57, rue Cuvier - 40 79 30 00
Open 10:30 a.m.-5 p.m. Closed Tues. & holidays. Admission: 11F, temporary exhibitions 25F.

Located within the Jardin des Plantes, this museum houses fascinating exhibits on paleontology, paleobotany and mineralogy. Of greater interest to older children.

PARKS & GARDENS

Bois de Boulogne

16th arr.

Entrances are located at the Porte Maillot, Porte Dauphine and Les Sablons. This enormous wooded park, which covers part of the sixteenth arrondissement, and the suburb of Neuilly, features a lake, horseback-riding clubs, a lovely children's park (Jardin d'Acclimatation), a marvelous floral garden (Parc de Bagatelle) and numerous paths that wind through trees and lawns. Bicycles for adults and children are available for rental. There is a wonderful restaurant, La Ferme, in the Jardin d'Acclimatation, where live animals roam among the tables.

Le Champ de Mars

7th arr.

Located under the Eiffel Tower, this park extends to the Ecole Militaire. Near the avenue de Suffren side there's a toddler's park with sandboxes and a small jungle gym.

Jardin des Plantes

5th arr. - 57, rue Cuvier or rue Buffon
43 36 14 41
Open 7 a.m.-5 p.m. (summer until 6 p.m.).

The Botanical Gardens (Jardin des Plantes) contain more than 10,000 classified plants. There is also a Winter Garden (Jardin d'Hiver), with many tropical plants, and the Alpin Garden (Jardin Alpin), which includes mountain- and polar-region plants. The open-air zoo is a big hit with youngsters.

Jardin du Luxembourg

5th arr.

Within these attractive gardens, situated between Saint-Michel and Montparnasse, there are pony rides, tennis courts, a marionette theater, sandboxes, jungle gyms and a small children's park for toddlers up to 5 years old.

Palais-Royal

2nd arr.

In the courtyard of this historic edifice, which dates back to 1632, is a stately park that attracts healthy numbers of local children who come to sail their boats in the central fountain or play in the sandboxes.

POOLS

Piscine Armand-Massard

17th arr. - 66, bd du Montparnasse
45 38 65 19
Hours vary. Closed Mon.

This pool park has something for children of all ages. There is a small wading pool for toddlers, and the large adult-size pool is shallow enough at one end to be safe for children just learning to swim.

Piscine Jean-Tharis

5th arr. - 16, rue Thouin - 43 25 54 03
Hours vary. Closed Mon.

One of the nicest pools in Paris is located near the Panthéon. It features a shallow pool for learners, as well as access for the handicapped. The big bay windows look out over a delightful private garden.

Piscine des Halles

3rd arr. - Pl. de la Rotonde - 42 36 98 44
Hours vary.

Though it's certainly a spectacular Olympic-size swimming pool worth visiting with your children, it may not be the ideal place to take your younger children (under 7), as the pool is deep at both ends. There is, however, a small toddler's pool.

PARKS & GARDENS

Le Jardin Shakespeare

16th arr. - Bois de Boulogne - Pré Catelan
Open year-round.

This delightful little 300-seat theater is hidden among the greenery of the Bois de Boulogne. Plays by Shakespeare and others are performed regularly. The stage is surrounded by landscape plantings that depict scenes from *Macbeth*, *Hamlet* or *The Tempest*.

Jardin d'Acclimatation

16th arr. - Bois de Boulogne, Porte des Sablons - 40 67 90 80
Open daily 10 a.m.-6 p.m. Admission: 3 and up 6.50F, school groups of more than 10 children 3.30F.

A favorite among lovers and children, this formal French garden of the Hôtel Biron (built in 1728 by Jacques Gabriel) bristles with rose bushes and monumental sculptures, among them Rodin's *The Thinker*.

Jardin des Plantes

5th arr. - 57, rue Cuvier - 43 36 14 41
Open 10 a.m.-5 p.m. Closed Tues. Admission: 11-25F, children 6-15F, school groups 2.50-10F.

This most French of Paris parks started out as the Sun King's botanical garden. Parisians promenade en masse among the charming shaded walks of the labyrinth that encircles the Belvedere, the park's sole surviving metal structure from before the French Revolution. You will discover rare species of trees, flowering shrubs and countless other plants from cold climes (in the Jardin d'Hiver, or Winter Garden) or warm (in the huge greenhouse, a jungle of tropical flora and cacti). Reptiles, deer, bears, apes and birds of prey are housed in quaint Second Empire buildings, which have been recently renovated. (See *Museums, Muséum d'Histoire Naturelle.*)

Jardin du Rodin

7th arr. - 77, rue de Varenne - 47 05 01 34
Open 10 a.m.-5:15 p.m. Closed Tues. Admission: 16F, 18-25 years 8F, children under 18 free.

The formal French garden of the Hôtel Biron is known for its rosebushes and monumental sculptures, among them Rodin's *The Thinker.*

NATURE WALKS

Paris isn't made only of asphalt and stone; nature thrives in parks, squares and odd corners of each arrondissement. For guides to the city's flora and fauna, and some suggested itineraries that will allow you to discover them, pick up a *Sentiers Nature* guide at the local *mairie* (town hall).

Jardins Albert-Kahn

92100 Boulogne - 5, quai du 4-Septembre
46 03 31 83
Open daily 9:30 a.m.-12:30 p.m. & 2 p.m.-7 p.m.

One of Paris's prettiest parks, this landscape garden on the banks of the Seine was created in the early twentieth century by wealthy diamond merchant Albert Kahn, who dreamed of bringing together all his favorite scenes of nature in a single park. You may wander through a freshly renovated Japanese garden, a Vosges forest, a formal French garden, a placid lake bordered by trees, a Romantic English garden and a coniferous and a deciduous wood. We particularly like to visit here from March to June, when the daffodils, hyacinths, azaleas, rhododendrons and roses are in bloom.

Mirapolis

95000 Cergy-Pontoise - Rte. de Courdimanche
34 43 20 00, 34 22 11 11
Open 10 a.m.-7 p.m. (Sat. until 9 p.m.). Closed Oct 17-May 7. Access from autoroute A15, Cergy-Pontoise direction. Admission: 75F (Sun. 90F) children under 4 free.

Mirapolis has been the French answer to Disneyland, a huge theme park dedicated to Gargantua, the fictional giant from Renaissance writer François Rabelais's classic work. There are 36 attractions, from the Château des Sortilèges (Magic Castle) to the Manège Quick-up (a riding school) to the Village Impressionniste, plus three daily parades (in the morning, at noon and at closing time). Good fun, but you pay for it. To get your money's worth, arrive early and spend the whole day. Mirapolis is only a few years old and does not yet compare to Disneyland in terms of quality or organization.

Parc Floral de Paris

12th arr. - Bois de Vincennes - 43 43 92 95
Open daily 9:30 a.m.; closing hours vary. Admission: 3.90F, children 6-10 2F.

This extraordinary flower park features a rich variety of flora, including medicinal plants. Some of the park's 56 acres are filled with an impressive array of rhododendrons and azaleas (which bloom in May and June). Scattered around the leafy aisles are sculptures by Calder, Agam, Penalba and Stahly. And there is a children's area fitted out with a locomotive from 1900, slides to play on, pedal cars, a Formula 1 go-carting loop and more. The Maison de la Nature, three pavilions housing exhibits on Paris's underlying rock formations and surrounding nature, opens soon.

Parc Zoologique de Paris

12th arr. - Bois de Vincennes - entrance av. Daumesnil
Open daily 9 a.m.-6 p.m. (5:30 p.m. in winter).

This world-class zoo is set in the lovely Bois de Vincennes just beyond the Daumesnil lake. You can spot its imitation-Andes concrete mountain from afar. Some 1,100 animals—

pandas, Andean flamingos, penguins, deer, furry okapi (an African mammal closely related to the giraffe but with a relatively short neck), among them—are lovingly cared for by busy zookeepers bent on keeping this vintage-1934 operation comfortable, clean and pleasant.

Parc de Bagatelle

16th arr. - Bois de Boulogne - 46 24 67 00
Open daily 8:30 a.m.-8 p.m.

Spring, fall, or winter, in the early morning or near dusk, you can wander around this elegant park in the sole company of peacocks, ducks and squirrels. During peak hours you will not be alone: over 500,000 visitors flock to the Bagatelle annually, and with good reason. This incomparable 48-acre landscaped garden was created in 1778 by the celebrated English designer Blackie at the request of the Count d'Artois, the future Charles X. It explodes with nearly 10,000 rosebushes (over 850 species of rose), tulips, narcissi and hyacinths, which bloom in spring, and enchanting clematis, water lilies and iris. The small eighteenth-century château is closed to the public, but the trianon and orangery feature painting and photography exhibits. The open-air tea house and restaurant are located in one of the loveliest garden settings in Paris. The main gate to the Bagatelle park is located near the intersection of the allée de Longchamp and the allée de la Reine Marguerite; there's a smaller entrance off the route de Sèvres in Neuilly.

Le Parc de Belleville

20th arr. - Rue des Couronnes & rue Julien-Lacroix
Open year-round.

This new park in far-flung Belleville boasts an impressive pergola, an orangery, an open-air theater and hills landscaped with waterfalls. Topping it all is a panoramic point—the highest in Paris—with a sweeping view of the city.

Parc des Buttes-Chaumont

19th arr. - 5, rue Botzaris
Open year-round.

This wildly romantic park at hilly Buttes-Chaumont is crosscut by creeks and roaring waterfalls fed by the nearby Ourcq Canal. A tiny Greek Revival temple perches on a peak in the middle of a swan-filled lake. The temple and panoramic point is reached from below, via a suspension bridge, or from above, by crossing a narrow walkway 100 feet above the lake. The park's main cascade tumbles into a stylized grotto, newly renovated and open to the public for the first time since 1945. This former quarry and dump was, in the late nineteenth century, one of Paris's most fashionable public gardens. The mark of the park's designer, Baron Haussmann, is evident in the cast-concrete railings and benches made to look like tree branches. Over $1 million have been spent to restore the Buttes-Chaumont to its original splendor. A job well done!

TOURS

Cityrama

1st arr. - 4, pl. des Pyramides - 42 60 30 14
Open daily 6:30 a.m.-10 p.m.

Cityrama's double-decker, ultra-comfortable tour buses whisk all around Paris morning, noon and night (call for schedules and fares). A recorded commentary describes the scenery and comes in the language of your choice. For the courageous, there is a simply superb crack-of-dawn tour in spring and summer.

Panam' 2002

8th arr. - 5, rue Lincoln - 42 25 64 39
Open daily 9 a.m.-7 p.m. Admission: 196F.

While others lunch or dine on bateaux-mouches (excursion boats), you can be chugging around Paris on the blacktop in this wagon train–style bus/restaurant. From the place de la Concorde via the Opéra, the Eiffel Tower, the Champs-Elysées and onward, you will enjoy glorified microwaved TV dinners with airline-hostess-style commentary on the cityscape. All for a mere 196 francs.

Paris et son Histoire
9th arr. - 82, rue Taitbout - 45 26 26 77
Open 10 a.m.-noon & 2 p.m.-6:30 p.m. Closed Sun. Admission: 250F, 350F per couple.

As the name indicates, this association specializes in the history of Paris (and the surrounding Ile-de-France region). Members attend lecture tours throughout the year; and from March to October, bus trips are organized to points of interest in the Paris area. Annual membership fees are 250 francs (350 francs for couples) and include a monthly bulletin of events. Meeting times and other information are provided by phone, or at tourist offices and libraries affiliated with the Association des Amis du Louvre.

Paris Passion
8th arr. - 45, rue de Lisbonne - 42 89 17 30
Open 9 a.m.-6 p.m. Closed Sun. Prices vary.

If you like the idea of an informed guided tour but don't want to be herded about on an impersonal bus, give Emanuelle Daras a call. This smart young woman has created a series of small, first-class, personalized tours. In a luxurious minivan (stocked with Champagne, no less), no more than five people at a time are taken to such places as artists' ateliers, foie-gras makers, the Cartier workshops and much more.

Paris Secret
2nd arr. - 12, rue Chabanais - 42 61 81 03
Open daily 9 a.m.-5 p.m. Admission: 50-180F.

These walking and bus tours initiate interested parties in the hidden Paris of secret gardens, untraveled alleys and ancient byways that Balzac might have described. Tours last from three hours to a full day and cost 50 to 180 francs, including transportation and refreshments.

Paris-Vision
1st arr. - 214, rue de Rivoli - 42 60 31 25
Open daily 8 a.m.-10 p.m.

Cityrama's main competitor, Paris-Vision hosts bus tours in seemingly every imaginable language.

RATP
8th arr. - Pl. de la Madeleine (behind the flower market) - 40 06 71 45
Open 7:30 a.m.-7 p.m. (Sat. & Sun. in summer 6 a.m.-6 p.m.).

Bus tours in every imaginable language.

UNDERGROUND

Catacombes de Paris
14th arr. - 1, pl. Denfert-Rochereau
43 22 47 63
Open 9 a.m.-noon & 2 p.m.-4 p.m Closed Mon. Guided tours. Admission: 13.50F, 20F.

The museum of Paris's catacombs is located in the former Montrouge quarry, which once beyond the city walls is now on the place Denfert-Rochereau. To improve sanitary conditions in the capital, about six million skeletons were brought here in 1786 from the cemeteries and charnel houses of central Paris. Open for visiting is about a one-mile, well-lit section of this immense catacomb. The entrance is in the center of the place Denfert-Rochereau.

Le Cellier des Bernardins
5th arr. - Caserne de Poissy, 24, rue de Poissy
Open daily.

The Poissy firehouse was once the refectory of the Collège des Bernardins, whose fourteenth-century vaulted cellar is one of the largest and finest in the Paris area. To visit, simply request permission at the firemen's guardhouse.

La Chapelle Saint-Denis
5th arr. - 14 bis, rue Pierre-Nicole
Open year-round. Inquire upon visit.

An impressive example of ancient Romanesque architecture, the Saint-Denis chapel is buried under a parking lot near the Luxembourg gardens. Popular tradition has it that Saint-Denis himself said mass here as long ago as the third century. The chapel once served as the crypt of the Notre-Dame-des-Champs monastery (which is no longer standing). Here you will find several plaques with mysterious inscriptions, plus the tomb of Renaud (Régnaux), laid to rest in a side chapel in 1220.

Le Réservoir de Montsouris
14th arr. - 113, rue de la Tombe-Issoire
Open year-round. Inquire upon visit.

This immense subterranean reservoir provides half of Paris with drinking water. Once the pride of France, it was the largest of its kind in Europe. Built in the last century, the impressive structure rests on 1,800 columns supporting a seemingly endless series of vaults. Visitors learn how water is channeled, purified and pumped to users. We also were fascinated by the curious acquariums teeming with trout and the gigantic caverns of still, pure water with an eerie, tropical-lagoon-like tint.

OUT OF PARIS

INTRODUCTION

T hose lucky Parisians. Not only do they have the rare good fortune to live in a glorious city; that city is ringed with equally glorious forests and accessible countryside. The following constitutes ten excursions in the Ile-de-France region, calculated to combine fresh air and greenery with visits to places of notable historic and/or cultural interest. And naturally Gault Millau wouldn't take you anywhere without scouting out the best places to dine and spend the night!

The French people's passion for hunting goes back as far as the days when they were still the Franks. Hugues Capet, founder of the Capetian line and ancestor of the Valois and Bourbon monarchs, was elected king in 987 at Senlis, a royal estate north of Paris known for its excellent hunting. Indeed, that election took place only because Capet's predecessor, Louis V (the last of the Carolingians), fell off his horse while chasing a stag, and died.

The neighboring domain of Chantilly, for centuries home to some of France's most powerful lords—the Bouteillers, the Montmorencys, the Condés—was also celebrated for its densely wooded forests, alive with game. The châteaux at Fontainebleau, Rambouillet (where Renaissance monarch François I departed this world with his hunting boots on) and Saint-Germain-en-Laye were all particularly beloved by their royal proprietors for the sport they enjoyed there. Even Versailles, that epitome of regal grandeur, was, before the Sun King transformed it, the preferred (and rather swampy) hunting ground of his father, Louis XIII.

It is thanks to this kingly obsession and to the personal interest French monarchs took in their *chasses royales* (private hunting grounds) that the forests of the Ile-de-France, with their ancient stands of oak, beech and hornbeam, have been responsibly managed over the centuries and preserved.

So, like the generations of royalty before them who could just pop off to their country castles whenever struck by that atavistic urge to bag a boar or down a deer (or when things got too hot for them in Paris—and we don't just mean the weather), present-day Parisians can hop on a train and, after a mere hour-or-so journey, alight near one of a half dozen splendid forests, complete with magnificent châteaux.

But even if they don't fancy the forest primeval, nature lovers will find lots to like in the environs of Paris. Admirable parks like those at Ecouen and Rambouillet and elegant gardens like Le Nôtre's seventeenth-century *jardins à la françaises* at Saint-Germain-en-Laye, Vaux-le-Vicomte, Chantilly and Versailles will please those who prefer more manicured landscapes.

Travelers in search of a rural antidote to city stress can head for the farmlands of the Beauce region, southwest of the capital. The soothing sameness of these wheat-bearing plains is broken only by grain-gorged silos (this is the bread basket of France) and by the dramatic spires of the Chartres cathedral. Northwest of Paris, along the meanders of the Seine, where the Ile-de-France meets Normandy, is a region of farmlands and river valleys overflowing with bucolic charm. Known as the Vexin, it is loved for its picturesque stone houses and a plethora of Romanesque churches. It was in Vexin that Claude Monet spent the last years of his life, painting in his garden at Giverny.

So, by venturing just 20, 30 or 50 miles beyond the Paris city limits and the bleaker *banlieues* (suburbs), you can discover a bounty of gently beautiful scenery, bathed in the unique light that inspired not only Monet and the Impressionists, but Corot, the Barbizon painters, Derain and the Fauvists. Set down in these luminous landscapes are a wealth of historic monuments and landmarks, as well as masterpieces of religious, civil and domestic architecture—and all fine for fair-weather-promenading destinations.

CHANTILLY

Reflected in the shimmering blue waters of its moat, the Château de Chantilly looks like a fairytale castle, almost too perfect to be true. And in a way, it is: The Renaissance-style Grand Château isn't much more than 100 years old (though the adjoining Petit Château dates from the sixteenth century). The castle that previously stood on this site was razed during the Revolution by angry citizens for whom Chantilly (about 50 kilometers north of Paris by Autoroute du Nord A1), fief of two ancient warrior families, the Montmorencys and the Condés, symbolized aristocratic privilege and military might.

The Grand Château houses the Musée Condé and its gem of a collection that ranges from the curious—a wax head of King Henri IV, the pink Condé diamond—to the sublime—Piero di Cosimo's *Portrait of Simonetta Vespucci*, Raphael's *Virgin of Loreto*, works by Botticelli, several pictures by Poussin, two masterpieces by Watteau, a splendid series of Renaissance portraits by the Clouet brothers (including the famous *Catherine de Medici* and *Henri III*) and an admirable collection of illuminated manuscripts. Arranged just as the Duc d'Aumale, the last owner of Chantilly, left it (with orders that it never be changed), the museum has the personal and agreeably eccentric style of a private collection.

Connoisseurs of fine horseflesh also know Chantilly as the site of a famous racetrack and thoroughbred training center. The fascinating Living Horse Museum occupies the colossal eighteenth-century stables, the Grandes Ecuries, which are more imposing, from an architectural perspective, than the château itself (not so surprising if you consider that the Prince of Condé, who built them, was convinced that he would be reincarnated as a horse).

The Château de Chantilly's park, complete with a canal, gardens and pools planned by seventeenth-century landscape artist André Le Nôtre, is crisscrossed by shady walks and velvety lawns. But the immense (nearly 16,000-acre) Chantilly forest, with its hiking paths and ponds (the étangs de Commelles), is by far the best choice for a long ramble. Take care, however, between 9 a.m. and noon—3,000 Thoroughbreds work out there every morning.

Château de Chantilly is open daily, except Tuesday, from April through September, 10 a.m. to 6 p.m.; from October through March, 10:30 a.m. to 5 p.m. The Musée Vivant du Cheval is open daily, except Tuesday, from 10:30 a.m. to 5:30 p.m. (2 p.m. to 4:30 p.m. on winter weekdays). Call (16) 44 57 03 62 for information, (16) 44 57 08 00 for reservations.

RESTAURANTS & HOTELS

 Campanile
Rte. de Creil (3 km N on N 16), Gouvieux - (16) 44 57 39 24
Open year-round. 47 rms 210F-230F. Half-board 182F-202F. TV in 31 rms. Pets allowed. Parking. Telex 140065. Cards: V.
At the edge of the Chantilly forest, the Campanile is quiet, modern and well maintained. Restaurant.

Hostellerie du Lys 🌳🍽
63, 7e av., Lys-Chantilly, Rond-Point de la Reine, Lamorlaye
(16) 44 21 26 19
Closed Dec. 21-Feb. 5. 35 rms 155-415F. Half-board 310-530F. TV. Pets allowed. Parking. Telex 150298. Cards: V, AE, DC, MC.
A beautiful, cozy weekend inn with comfortable rooms and a nice, quiet ambience. Tennis, golf and swimming are nearby. Restaurant.

⑭ **Le Relais Condé**
42, av. du Maréchal-Joffre
(16) 44 57 05 75
M. Rios. Open until 9:30 p.m. Closed Sun. dinner & Mon. Terrace dining. Pets allowed. Cards: V, AE, DC.
The nicest and classiest restaurant in Chantilly is located near the racetrack, under the frame of a nineteenth-century Anglican chapel. Young Patrice Lebeau creates a thoughtful, unpretentious, simple and consistently good cuisine: délice du Périgord (warm foie gras baked with a sauce made from eggs and fresh cream), lotte brochette with red bell pepper, perfect veal kidneys in mustard sauce and a beautiful three-chocolate cake with crème anglaise. Nothing spectacular, just fine work and generosity—particularly on the two fixed-price menus. One of the nicest wine cellars in the region.
A la carte: 300F and up. Menus: 105F, 150F.

⑬ **Relais du Coq Chantant**
21, rte. de Creil - (16) 44 57 01 28
M. Dautry. Open daily until 9:45 p.m. Pets allowed. Parking. Cards: V, AE, DC, MC.
This white cottage along the road lives up to its looks: a comfortable place for the "beau monde" of golfers and horse riders who frequent the region. The à la carte prices confirm the opulent tone, as does the decor—a mélange of pinks and flowered tapestries. Try the scorpionfish with a delicious saffron aspic, the grilled turbot and the raspberry gratin, which is nice despite a slightly oversweet crème anglaise. Fixed-price menus, good service.
A la carte: 350F. Menus: 89F and 159F (weekdays only), 148F and 287F (weekends and holidays only).

COMPIEGNE

Château de Bellinglise 🌳🍽
Elincourt-Ste-Marguerite
(16) 44 76 04 76
Open year-round. 5 stes 820-870F. 42 rms 385-680F. Half-board 565F. TV. Tennis. Parking. Telex 155048. Cards: V, AE, DC, MC.
This immense Louis XIII-era castle on a 600-acre estate has been remarkably preserved and restored; guests can stay in one of the attractive rooms in the hunting lodge. Pond, tennis, conference facilities. Fine wood-paneled restaurant with a disciple of Robuchon and Fréon in the kitchen.

12/20 **Hostellerie du Royal-Lieu**
9, rue de Senlis - (16) 44 20 10 24
M. Bonechi. Open daily until 9:30 p.m. Garden dining. Pets allowed. Hotel: 3 stes 400F; 15 rms 300F. Parking. Cards: V, DC.
This lovely, luxurious weekend inn has a pleasant terrace off the dining room that overlooks the forest. The traditional but lightened cuisine is skillfully prepared by the owner: anise-seasoned escargots, tagliatelle with turbot and a lobster coulis, young pork filet mignon with tarragon.
A la carte: 350F. Menus: 180F, 250F.

See also "Senlis," below.

CHARTRES

Long before the Cathedral of Notre-Dame dominated the horizon, before Christianity had penetrated the Ile-de-France, before Caesar had marched into Gaul—even then, Chartres was a holy place. Legend has it that Celtic druids assembled in Chartres (90 kilometers southwest of Paris by Autoroute A10) every year to celebrate their mysteries around a wellspring now enclosed in the cathedral crypt.

What is certain is that from the fourth century on, a sanctuary consecrated to the Virgin Mary began to attract the faithful to Chartres. When, in 876, Charles the Bald endowed the church with a precious relic (said to be the Virgin's tunic or veil), it gained even greater importance as a shrine, drawing pilgrims from all over Christendom in a steady stream that neither invasions, fires nor revolutions have been able to completely stanch. Even today, students organize a pilgrimage to Chartres each May in honor of the Virgin.

The ancestor of the current cathedral, a Romanesque structure built in the eleventh and twelfth centuries, was ravaged by fire in 1194, sparing only the crypt, two towers and the lower portion of the western facade, with its majestic Portail Royal (royal entrance). Very quickly, the people of Chartres set about rebuilding their cathedral, with such a collective mighty will—and generous contributions from rich lords and wealthy townspeople—that it was completed in an impressively short span of time: 30 years. It is to the builders' speed that the cathedral owes its unusual stylistic unity. And it is to their skill in applying new architectural advances—notably the flying buttress—that Chartres owes its immense height and rare luminosity: The buttresses shouldered weight that would otherwise have fallen on the walls, making it possible to build them higher, with taller windows.

It would be impossible to do justice here to the aesthetic and spiritual riches of Chartres. A visitor with plenty of time, patience, curiosity and an observant eye will find innumerable sources of pleasure and interest. Here are a couple of points worth noting, one outside and one inside the cathedral.

The Portail Royal, unscathed by the fire of 1194, represents one of the oldest examples of Gothic sculpture in existence. While the emphasis of the ensemble is on the figure of Christ, depicted in infancy and in majesty above each of the three doors, viewers often feel irresistibly drawn to the nineteen elongated figures, a combination of statue and column, lined up on either side of the doors. Interestingly, these Old Testament figures belong to two different eras, the Romanesque and the Gothic; they are the survivors of the old cathedral and, at the same time, heralds of the new sculptural style that first emerged at Chartres. In their extraordinarily sensitive faces, in the contrast between their expressive features and rigid, stylized bodies, a visitor can trace the mysterious passage from one age—one way of viewing and representing human reality—to another.

Inside the cathedral, among the ravishing, jewel-like shadows and colors of stained glass, there are three windows and a portion of another that, like the Portail Royal, escaped the fire of 1194. They are the windows inserted in the western facade that depict the genealogy, life and resurrection of Christ, and, to the left, the fragment known as Notre Dame de la Belle Verrière (*The Madonna of the Window*), one of Chartres's most venerated images. They merit your special attention because they are the sole remaining examples of the miraculous *bleu de Chartres*, a blue tint rich (as we now know) in cobalt and copper, but which for centuries no one could manage to reproduce.

In medieval times, Chartres was a flourishing town, its wealth based on cloth and farming. It was also a renowned intellectual center, with its own philosophy school. Investigating the many ancient houses and churches in the Old Quarter (the fifteenth-century Maison Saumon and the Hôtel de la Caige; the medieval church of Saint-Pierre, with its striking stained glass) can be an extremely rewarding way to spend an afternoon.

Thanks to farming, the region still thrives, and the prosperous Beaucerons are fond of the table: Between a tour of the cathedral and a stroll through the town, hungry visitors can find any number of excellent places to relax and restore themselves.

The cathedral is open from 7:30 a.m. to 7:30 p.m. For additional information, contact the Office du Tourisme, place de la Cathédrale (16-37 21 54 03).

RESTAURANTS & HOTELS

12/20 La Blanquette

45, rue des Changes - (16) 37 21 99 36
M. Lavenir. Open daily until 10 p.m. Pets allowed. Cards: V.

This charming little find was recently opened by Bernard Roger as an annex of La Vieille Maison. We like to go there for good local wines by the glass and a generous bistro cuisine: beef-cheek confiture, veal or fish blanquettes, clafoutis.

A la carte: 230F. Menus: 230F (wine incl.), 65F, 110F.

Le Grand Monarque

22, pl. des Epars - (16) 37 21 00 72
M. Jallerat. Open daily until 9:30 p.m. Terrace dining. Pets allowed. Parking. Telex 760777. Cards: V, AE, DC, MC.

Behind the eighteenth-century facade is a newly renovated dining room with a nice beige-tone decor, flowers, elegant tables and a peaceful winter garden. Georges and Geneviève Jallerat are still the perfect hosts, as they have been for some twenty years. The cuisine (prepared by the well-qualified Bruno Letartre) is based on simplicity and the season. The à la carte list is short but ever-changing. Only the hors d'oeuvres seemed a bit overdone (a too-creamy sauce on the sweetbreads salad). Try the émincé of pigeon with fresh pasta, turbot grilled over a charcoal fire, young Challans duck with turnips and the famous pots de crème with chocolate or coffee. The wine cellar is thick with Loire and Bordeaux vintages. The à la carte prices are steep but worth it, and the fixed-price menus are quite attractive.

A la carte: 350F. Menus: 180F, 269F.

Le Grand Monarque

(See restaurant above.)
Open year-round. 3 stes 565-875F. 54 rms 247-410F. TV. Pets allowed.

The best hotel in Chartres has charming new rooms in two turn-of-the-century buildings surrounding a garden. Nice modern suites. Interior patio for breakfast.

Henri IV

31-33, rue du Soleil-d'Or
(16) 37 36 01 55
Mme. Cazalis. Open until 8:45 p.m. Closed Mon. dinner, Tues. & Feb. Pets allowed. Cards: AE, DC.

The old and famous Maurice Cazalis is gone, but he has left the kitchen in good hands—with his trainee for some twenty years. Jacques Corbonnois perpetuates Cazalis's tradition of rich haute cuisine that is old-fashioned but rigorously executed, even when excessive. In reality, Corbonnois has been cooking alone for some time, and other than a reduction in cooking time, little has changed from the good old days. From the large dining room's windows, one views the famous Chartres cathedral's spire. The widow Cazalis is still a charming hostess, and her staff serves with a flair her delicious Chartres terrine of partridge and pistachios, a well-seasoned Henri IV salad (vegetables and shellfish), a remarkable lotte pot-au-feu (in fact, a sort of bouillabaisse) served with rouille (a garlicky, spicy mayonnaise), a blanquette of sweetbreads with creamed foie gras and such fine, old-fashioned desserts as Triomphe soufflé (à la liqueur) or bombe (pudding) with glazed chestnuts. The wonderful wine cellar is rich and varied.

A la carte: 300-350F. Menus: 165F (weekdays only, wine incl.), 220F, 275F.

11/20 Le Manoir du Palomino

Saint-Prest - (16) 37 22 27 27
M. Ribieras. Open until 9:30 p.m. Closed Sun. dinner, Mon. & Jan. 15-Feb. 15. Garden dining. Pets allowed. Parking. Cards: V.

This old manor house in the delightful Eure Valley woods has been sumptuously restored. The scenery is magnificent, the dining room has exposed beams, and the owner displays charm and a desire to please. The cuisine started out cautiously and rather plainly: salmon boudin with sorrel, generous duck confit. Intelligent wine list. We'll have to wait and see.

A la carte: 230-250F. Menus: 100F, 195F.

🏠 Le Manoir du Palomino 🌲

(See restaurant above.)

Closed Jan. 15-Feb. 15. 1 ste 500F. 12 rms 150-400F. Half-board 300-600F. TV. Pets allowed. Tennis. Golf.

A fine weekend escape from Paris, for relaxing or for conferences. The 40-acre estate provides golf and tennis facilities, and the spacious, quiet, luxuriously decorated rooms have charm, flowers, beams and fine views of the landscape.

⑬ La Sellerie

48, rue Nationale, Thivars
(16) 37 26 41 59

M. Heitz. Open until 9 p.m. Closed Sun. dinner (off-seas.), Mon. dinner, Tues., Jan. 9-24 & July 31-Aug. 22. Terrace dining. Pets allowed. Parking. Cards: V.

The dining room may look like an antiques dealer's shop, but the interior garden is pleasant, with plenty of flowers. Equally pleasant is the well-executed cuisine: tête de veau beauceronne, sole with a fennel-cream sauce, sweetbreads and eggplant in a millefeuille. The fine wine list includes excellent Bordeaux. Service seems a bit stiff but is in general amicable.

A la carte: 300F and up. Menus: 115F, 260F.

⑮ La Vieille Maison

5, rue au Lait - (16) 37 34 10 67

M. Roger. Open until 9:15 p.m. Closed Sun. dinner & Mon. Pets allowed. Cards: V, AE, DC, MC.

This is an antique restaurant with a young cuisine. Bernard Roger is a radiant, self-assured cuisinier who loves fine, strong flavors and creates dishes that are wonderfully rich (and costly). His à la carte menu is short but ever-changing, inspired by the trends of the market. You'll find new asparagus accompanied by large, juicy langoustines, spring vegetables next to tender tournedos sauté, coquilles St-Jacques pan-fried in a foie gras coulis, an extraordinary Beauceron chicken stuffed with truffles under the skin and roasted with fresh lasagne au foie gras, pigs' feet stuffed with truffles, and desserts that are less imaginative but elaborate and well prepared. Prices are a

bit steep (except for the first fixed-price menu), but we can't call them unjustified; everything is generous, successfully executed and served in a charming ambience of little nooks dispersed throughout the dining room and the flowery patio.

A la carte: 350-400F. Menus: 160F (weekday lunch only, wine incl.), 160F (dinner only), 220F, 300F.

ST-SYMPORIEN-LE-CHATEAU

⑯ Château d'Esclimont

(16) 37 31 15 15

M. Spitz. Open daily until 9:30 p.m. No pets. Parking. Telex 780560. Cards: V.

René Traversac, who collects châteaux throughout France (Artigny, Isenbourg, Divonne and so on), does a better job selecting his managers and his cooks than his decorators. He buys up these sumptuous mansions and attempts to get them back into shape without skimping, but there is always something not quite right, perhaps machine-made tapestries or candy-pink silk. One day, we hope, he will stop buying his family as decorators and go to a professional. Only then will the "château life" promised at each of his establishments be truly that, rather than just an approximation.

But enough criticism. This astonishing man—who would eat lion meat until his dying day—knew how to make this Renaissance château of the La Rochefoucaulds, vigorously revamped in the nineteenth century, an outstanding weekend-getaway spot (it's just 45 minutes from Paris). There are lavish grounds, a pond, a river, tennis courts, a pool . . . in brief, heaven. And let's not forget the musical evenings in the former seventeenth-century stables, which have been transformed into "trophy rooms."

The other attraction, which isn't negligible, is that the cuisine improves with each new chef. Far from causing us to miss his former excellent master, Patrick Guerry, who has just been promoted up from Jean-Michel Diot's number-two to his successor, beguiles us in his own way. With his evident talent and what he has learned from his predecessors, Guerry is a real find for the manager of the château, Raymond

Spitz. In fact, if we knew for sure that he would be here a year from now, that he would rewrite the menu with fewer frills, and that he would be a little more careful with his presentations, we would grant a third toque right away. For that's what several of the dishes we tried recently deserved—namely the incredibly light lobster lasagne with a truffle sauce, the roasted truffled local pigeon served with delicious braised cabbage, the wonderful fricassée of lotte with lentils and the dish of pears with cacao sorbet. The wine cellar is excellent—with perhaps even too many Burgundies—the service is perfect, and the ambience is pleasant in spite of the business breakfasts, receptions and conferences that seem to always be going on.

A la carte: 400-500F. Menus: 250F, 430F.

Château d'Esclimont 🏕🌲

(See restaurant above.)
Open year-round. 6 stes 1,430-2,100F. 48 rms 520-1,210F. TV. Pets allowed. Heated pool.Tennis.

The 48 rooms and six suites of this château are classic, comfortable and well situated in the middle of a 150-acre expanse of completely walled-in grounds at the bottom of a valley, which is traversed by a river and situated near the road that connects Rambouillet and Chartres. Guests can play tennis, swim in the heated pool and attend wintertime musical evenings, for which weekend packages are proposed at quite reasonable prices (less than 2,000 francs per couple). Relais et Châteaux.

ECOUEN

There's no need to travel as far as the Loire Valley to visit a superb French Renaissance château. Just 25 or so kilometers north of Paris rests Ecouen, an admirably preserved castle built between 1538 and 1555 for François I's closest comrade-in-arms, Constable Anne de Montmorency (who also commissioned the first château at Chantilly).

As befitted a great feudal lord and powerful military chief, the constable made Ecouen a formidable fortress. Situated on a hill overlooking the wide plain below, and surrounded by moats and fortified by steeply sloping walls, Ecouen was designed to withstand even artillery fire—a wise precaution on the eve of the Wars of Religion, which ravaged the region in the later sixteenth century.

Yet the constable and his wife, Madeleine de Savoie, were also humanists and patrons of the arts, who engaged the best architects and sculptors of the day to embellish their home. Framed in the portico that leads to the grand courtyard, an equestrian statue of Anne de Montmorency in the garb of a Roman warrior proclaims the constable's taste for antiquity. That taste is also reflected in the château's architecture. Niches in the monumental colon-

nade of the southern (left) wing once housed Michelangelo's *Slaves* (now in the Louvre), which was a gift to the constable from King Henri II.

In 1632, the constable's grandson, Henri II de Montmorency, accused of conspiracy against Richelieu, was beheaded. Ecouen reverted to the Condé family, who spent little time there, preferring their estate at Chantilly. During the Revolution, the contents of the castle were confiscated by the state, and eventually dispersed.

Since 1962, Ecouen has housed the Musée de la Renaissance, a unique collection of period French, Italian and Flemish furniture and decorative arts. The most dazzling exhibit is surely the 246-foot-long tapestry displayed in the Galerie de Psyché. Woven in Brussels in the early sixteenth century, this masterpiece of silk, wool and silver thread relates the story of David and Bathsheba.

What makes all the objects on view particularly interesting is their setting in the château's authentic, beautifully restored Renaissance interior. Do take the time to examine and admire the immense fireplaces, decorated with biblical scenes, for which Ecouen was famous in its glory days. And nothing gives a better idea of the grandeur of a Renaissance lord's castle than the Grande Salle, where the Montmorencys received their vassals. A visitor cannot help but be impressed with the monumental fireplace of porphyry and polychrome marble; or with the magnificent gold-and-cerulean tile floor displaying the entwined arms of Anne de Montmorency and Madeleine de Savoie.

We like to wind up a tour of Ecouen with a stroll in the garden; the park affords an impressive, sweeping view of the plain below. Hardier souls might want to go exploring in the forest that borders the château.

The Musée de la Renaissance is open daily from 9:45 a.m. to 12:30 p.m. and 2 p.m. to 5:15 p.m., except Tuesday and holidays; call 39 90 04 04 for information.

FONTAINEBLEAU

Just as Versailles was created at the whim of young Louis XIV, Fontainebleau owes its splendor to the sudden caprice of Renaissance monarch François I. In 1528 he decided to transform a neglected royal manor near the forest of Bière into a personal residence fit for a king. After his humiliating two-year captivity in Madrid, the Roi Chevalier wanted to show Emperor Charles V and King Henry VIII of England (who were then erecting spectacular palaces at Grenada and Hampton Court, respectively) that he could equal, indeed surpass, them in magnificence.

Every aspect of the new château in Fontainebleau (65 kilometers south of Paris by Autoroute du Sud A6) was calculated to glorify France's first absolute ruler (the first to be addressed as "Majesty," a title previously reserved for the emperor), and François's spirit remains present at Fontainebleau today.

The actual architecture of the palace has undergone considerable remodeling over the centuries. The Galerie François I, the most celebrated decorative ensemble of the French Renaissance, was constructed between 1528 and 1530 and embellished with marvelous stuccowork and frescoes by Florentine artist Il Rosso, a pupil of Michelangelo. The recently restored frescoes illustrate a complicated and fairly obscure symbolic scheme. One remarkable figure is an elephant emblazoned with fleur-de-lis and sporting a salamander (François's emblem) on its forehead, which signifies the royal virtue of wisdom. Other scenes commemorate the king's Italian campaigns or his role as a patron of art and literature.

The Salle de Bal (ballroom) is another impressive Renaissance creation. Commissioned by François I, it was completed under the supervision of his son, Henri II, by architect Philibert Delorme (who also worked on the Louvre). The frescoes—superbly restored—were designed by Il Primatice and executed by Niccolo dell'Abbate, two of the foremost Italian artists of the first Fontainebleau school. The ballroom created such a sensation in its day that painters and engravers came from all over to record its sumptuous decoration. Even now, the room provides a fairly accurate idea of the opulence of the Valois court.

Though Fontainebleau was relatively neglected during the second half of the sixteenth century, it flourished once again under Henri IV. Dated from this era are the *Cabinet de Théagène* (marvelously preserved, it's the birthplace of Louis XIII) and the Chapelle de la Trinité, decorated with biblical frescoes by Mathieu Fréminet, a French master of the baroque.

The Bourbons made a habit of spending the autumn at Fontainebleau, and continued to embellish and enlarge the palace even after the court took up residence at Versailles. Marie-Antoinette, who loved the château, completely redecorated several rooms, including the Salon du Jeu ("Gaming Room") and the charming Boudoir de la Reine, which was designed by Mique, her favorite architect.

Napoléon, also quite fond of Fontainebleau, refurnished the palace entirely. Today it boasts Europe's finest collection of Empire furniture, as well as extensive holdings of Napoleonic relics and memorabilia culled from various national museums.

The palace is surrounded by what is surely one of the most beautiful forests in France. In autumn and winter, hunters still thunder through the russet groves of oak, riding to hounds just as French kings did centuries before them. Less bloodthirsty nature enthusiasts prefer to explore the innumerable bridle and hiking paths, or scramble around the spectacular rock formations, cliffs and gorges that make the Forêt de Fontainebleau an excellent and highly popular training ground for aspiring alpinists.

The Château de Fontainebleau is open daily (except Tuesday) from 9:30 a.m. to noon and 2 p.m. to 5 p.m.; the park and gardens are open from dawn to dusk; and the Musée Napoléonien is open from 10 a.m. to noon and 2 p.m. to 5 p.m. (closed Sunday, Monday, September and holidays). Call 64 22 34 39 for further information.

RESTAURANTS & HOTELS

⑭ L'Aigle Noir

27, pl. Napoléon-Bonaparte
64 22 32 65

M. Duvauchelle. Open daily until 10 p.m. Garden dining. Pets allowed. Parking. Telex 694080. Cards: V, AE, DC, MC.

Although finicky, the cardinal of Retz would look with satisfaction upon the innumerable improvements that Pierre Duvauchelle has brought over the last few years to his old palace, whose windows open onto the gardens of Diana. Most recently, the Empire room underwent a facelift that restored the tapestries and fabrics to their original splendor. But it is in the lovely garden, calm in the refreshing shade of green-and-beige parasols, that you can most enjoyably savor the lamb salad with thyme and the strawberry soup with mint. Chef Daniel Dumesnil's work is simple but perfectly executed and graciously served.

A la carte: 400F. Menus: 200F, 280F.

L'Aigle Noir

(See restaurant above.)
Open year-round. 6 stes 1,025-2,500F. 51 rms 620-980F. Half-board 995-1,250F. TV. Pets allowed. Heated pool.

Facing the garden or the château, the luxurious rooms, just recently renovated, are decorated in Louis XVI, Empire or Restoration style.

12/20 Chez Arrighi

53, rue de France - 64 22 29 43
Mme. Amprou. Open until 10 p.m. Closed Mon. & Feb. school vacation. Pets allowed. Cards: V, AE, DC, MC.

Corsican food in the emperor's old neighborhood? Why not. The "imperial" decor may be a bit faded, but not so the ravishing owner. Be sure to taste the migisca (a ragoût of lamb with red beans) and the sheep's cheese, accompanied by a powerful red wine from the region.

A la carte: 220F. Menus: 89F (weekdays only), 125F, 172F.

Hôtel Legris et Parc

36, rue du Parc - 64 22 24 24
Closed Dec. 20-Jan. 25. 3 stes 350F. 27 rms 210-350F. Half-board 325-465F oblig. in seas. TV. Pets allowed. Cards: V, MC.

This pleasantly renovated old building is well situated in front of the entrance to the château's grounds. The best of the extremely comfortable rooms look out on the flowers of an interior garden. Restaurant.

BARBIZON

⑯ Le Bas-Bréau

22, rue Grande - 60 66 40 05
M. Fava. Open until 9:30 p.m. Closed Jan. 2-Feb. 18. Garden dining. Pets allowed. Parking. Telex 690953. Cards: V, AE, MC.

A weekend in the most beautiful inn in the Fontainebleau forest will obviously cost you an arm and a leg, particularly if you ask Jean-Pierre Fava for the sumptuous villa-bungalow at the back of the vegetable garden—but you'll be rewarded with a veritable feast for the eyes. Another option is a stay in the charming historic inn where Robert Louis Stevenson wrote *Treasure Island* and where you can lunch in front of the fireplace, in the rustic dining room or in the lush interior courtyard. The food is pricey but savory: langoustines royales, lobster salad in hazelnut oil, fresh cod in truffle butter, aromatic braised turbot, spiced squab, remarkable veal cutlets with asparagus and, in season, sumptuous game (that doesn't taste like it's from the farmyard). The 280-franc fixed-price lunch menu includes wine and, for example, a delightful warm salad of red mullet and green beans, pan-fried brill, filet of Limousin beef with marrow in an exquisite bordelaise sauce, excellent cheeses (especially when Fava happens to find "coeur de Fontainebleau") and fine desserts. This place is practically an enchanted forest in itself.

A la carte: 600F and up. Menus: 260F and 300F (weekday lunch only, wine incl.).

Le Bas-Bréau

(See restaurant above.)
Closed Jan. 2-Feb. 18. 8 stes 1,520-2,380F. 12 rms 880-1,300F. TV. Pets allowed. Tennis.

On the edge of the forest, this Fontainebleau inn, one of the nicest and most refined in the Paris region, is surrounded by roses and century-old trees and has a simple, pleasant atmosphere. There's one deluxe, astonishingly comfortable bungalow at the back of the vegetable garden. And now, owner Jean-Pierre Fava plans to build a heated indoor-outdoor pool, a sauna, a Turkish bath and a solarium on a piece of land he's just purchased. Relais et Châteaux.

12/20 Les Pléiades

21, rue Grande - 60 66 40 25
M. Karampournis. Open daily until 9:30 p.m. Closed Sun. dinner (off-seas.) & Feb. 6-26. Garden dining. Pets allowed. Parking. Telex 692131. Cards: V, AE, DC, MC.

On a flower-laden terrace on the street or in a quiet garden out back, you'll enjoy a fine 135-franc fixed-price meal of haddock and grapefruit salad, lotte in beurre blanc, cheese and dessert. We'll move the ranking up another point.

A la carte: 300F. Menus: 135F (weekdays only), 190F, 350F.

Les Pléiades

(See restaurant above.)
Closed Feb. 6-26. 3 stes 370-520F. 20 rms 250-330F. Half-board 350-370F. TV. Pets allowed.

The former house of painter Daubigny was recently renovated from top to bottom. Most of the rooms are quite attractive, and the hotel boasts a beautiful, large flower garden on the edge of the Fontainebleau forest.

See also Melun in "Vaux-le-Vicomte" below.

GIVERNY

It isn't a palace or royal legend that brings travelers to this tiny village 75 kilometers west of Paris, on the border of the Ile-de-France and Normandy regions; what draws crowds to Giverny is the sovereign artistic talent of Claude Monet. From 1883 until his death in 1926, Monet lived and worked in these sublime surroundings, a setting he created largely by and for himself. Giverny provided the light, the multifaceted landscape and the meandering Seine that the painter so loved. But Monet himself provided the grand design, as well as 40 years of unrelenting efforts to make his ravishing garden a reality. It soon became the central motif of his pictures, and in the end was the only subject that Monet chose to paint.

Shortly before his death, assailed with doubts about the value of his work and despite public acclaim, Monet came to consider the garden as his ultimate creation. He kept six gardeners hard at work in it, full-time. The painter's garden had been left to itself for half a century when the American Versailles-Giverny Foundation undertook its, and the house and studio's, restoration in 1977. Well before Europe recognized his genius, America had embraced Monet at his first New York show in 1889. Now, owing in large part to American generosity, Monet's admirers may visit the house where he worked and entertained fellow artists Mary Cassatt, the poet Mallarmé and many more.

Nothing less resembles a formal French garden than this glorious, painterly composition of flowers, water and greenery. Ordinary fruit trees were banished from the orchard where the flower garden now blooms; Monet replaced them with exotic Japanese strains of ornamental cherry and apple. With the arrival of spring, perennial beds lose their disciplined, linear look under an exuberance of bright blossoms. Interestingly, except for the roses and peonies, all the flowers at Giverny are humble varieties: iris, foxglove, poppies and lupine. Yet they are planted so artfully and their colors, textures and shapes are accustomed to such advantage that an observer's eye roams over the banks and borders of the garden with as much pleasure as it does over Monet's *Waterlilies* in the Orangerie in Paris.

At the far end of the winding central path (take care not to trample the nasturtiums that grow pretty much wherever they please) is the famous pond that Monet always insisted on showing off to his guests after lunch (he had paid a not-so-small fortune to have it installed). In spring, a curtain of languid wisteria nearly hides the "Japanese bridge," which looks out over a hypnotizing profusion of water lilies. Massed on the surface of the pond, they seem to form a huge artist's palette of delicate tints: white, yellow, pink, blue and mauve.

The house and three studios at Giverny—including one Monet had built specially to paint *Les Nymphéas*—give the haunting impression that the people who live and work there have only just stepped out for you to see for a moment. Everything is exactly as it was on an ordinary day at the turn of the century, from the pots and pans set out in the kitchen (Monet loved rich, complicated cooking), to the master's fascinating collection of Japanese prints. To borrow a phrase from Marcel Proust, Monet's contemporary and admirer, the evocative atmosphere of Giverny rewards the pilgrims who journey there with a sense of time recaptured.

The Musée Claude Monet is open every day but Monday—the gardens are open from 10 a.m. to 6 p.m.; the museum is open from April 1 through October 31, 10 a.m. to noon and 2 p.m. to 6 p.m. Call (16) 32 51 28 21 for further information.

RESTAURANTS & HOTELS

PACY-SUR-EURE

⑬ Château de Brécourt
Douains - (16) 32 52 40 50
M. Savry. Open daily until 9:30 p.m. Pets allowed. Parking. Telex 172250. Cards: V, AE, DC, MC.

This lovely seventeenth-century château, here at the gateway to Normandy, has always

been one of the shining links in the Relais et Châteaux chain. We also used to be able to look forward to delicious, well-thought-out cooking served with the finest manners. This is not exactly—actually, not at all—true any longer; the sole pleasure left to us on recent visits has been the splendid dining room of old beams, polished brick-tile floor, beautiful table settings and a view of the Norman woods. Otherwise, we were offered a distracted reception, left to sloppy service amid a noisy crowd, and fed just barely adequate food: overjellied beef stew, rack of lamb without distinction, great cheeses and an acceptable hot tart. Attractive, reasonably priced wine list.

A la carte: 400F. Menus: 150F (weekday lunch only, wine incl.), 310F (Fri. dinner only), 205F, 315F.

Château de Brécourt 🌲
(See restaurant above.)
Open year-round. 4 stes 900-1,100F. 20 rms 375-800F. Half-board 645-845F. Pets allowed. Heated pool. Tennis.

Amenities include spacious, comfortable, stylishly furnished rooms (though the bathrooms are a bit small), new conference rooms and marvelous grounds. Relais et Châteaux.

12/20 L'Etape
(16) 32 36 12 77
Mme. Angot. Open daily until 9 p.m. Terrace dining. Pets allowed. Hotel: 1 ste 210-313F; 8 rms 69-189F; half-board 160-190F. Parking. Cards: V, MC.

Located on the banks of the Eure, this handsome house has a garden and lush greenery overhanging the river—not to mention a new chef who is committed to bringing a nice élan to cuisine such as sweetbreads with morels, bourride of lotte with cabbage and roast lamb sautéed in red wine.

A la carte: 220F. Menus: 81F (weekdays only), 132F, 185F.

VERNON

⑮ La Gueulardière
Lieu-dit Le Village, Port-Villez
34 76 22 12
M. Marguerite. Open until 9:30 p.m. Closed Sun. dinner & Mon. Terrace dining. Air cond. Pets allowed. Cards: V, DC.

Transplanted from his Relais du Pavé near Houdan, Claude Marguerite can now be found at a picturesque site on the Seine, just across from Monet's house and gardens at Giverny. This accomplished chef (late of Lasserre and the prestigious catering firm Potel et Chabot) has bloomed in these new surroundings; his dishes are lighter and more imaginative than ever. The menu is on the long side, but it encompasses such delights as homemade chicken terrine and duck sausage, a "maritime symphony" of firm, beautifully cooked ocean fish served with a delectable curry sauce, an admirable assortment of game preparations (in season, of course) and an array of desserts designed to please people who like to wind up a meal with elaborate, complicated sweets. A glassed-in terrace overlooking the Seine is a welcome addition to the somewhat cluttered, country-style dining room. The service, we are happy to note, is deft and efficient.

A la carte: 350F. Menu: 150F (weekdays only).

VETHEUIL

⑬ **Auberge Saint-Christophe**
1, Grande-Rue - (16) 34 78 11 50
M. Boizette. Open until 9:15 p.m. Closed Wed., Feb. school vacation & Aug. 16-Sept. 6. Pets allowed. Cards: V, AE, DC.

Just a stone's throw from the big church Monet painted, and on the way to the Monet museum in Giverny, Michel Boizette's restaurant keeps decidedly pleasant company. One dines here under the vaulted ceiling of a pretty room; even the food tries hard to leave behind its once-insipid guise and become more attractive. The à la carte menu may force your pocketbook to do something it had not intended, but both of the fixed-price menus are remarkable. Picture this meal: warm salad of fish and crustaceans, filet of beef with three peppers, green salad, cheese and a bavarois with raspberry coulis. Good little wines, priced from 35 francs, are available.

A la carte: 230F. Menus: 149F, 179F.

RAMBOUILLET

Now a peaceful summer refuge for the president of France, the château at Rambouillet has been the scene of some of the more dramatic moments in the nation's history. In 1547 François I, who enjoyed hunting in the nearby forest, died in a tower of the castle (which then belonged to the captain of his guards). Forty years later, Henri III, driven out of Paris by the League, took refuge at Rambouillet (located about 50 kilometers from Paris by Autoroute Chartres–Orléans A10). In 1815, before his departure for exile, Napoléon spent a last night of melancholy reflection at Rambouillet. It was there, too, that Charles X learned of the Revolution of 1830 and announced his abdication. And it was from Rambouillet, in August 1944, that General Charles de Gaulle gave the order for Leclerc's armored division to liberate Paris.

Yet Rambouillet has seen more tranquil times as well. Today, little remains of the sixteenth-century château, save the cool red-and-gray Salle des Marbres (marble room). The eighteenth century and Empire are the periods now best represented at Rambouillet. The Count of Toulouse, a legitimized son of Louis

XIV, purchased the château in 1705. He enlarged the existing structures and had the new west wing decorated with enchanting rococo woodwork. For the garden, he commissioned a system of canals and artificial islands on which magnificent fêtes were held throughout the century. The count's son, the Duke of Penthièvre, completed the canals and, in the English garden, had an incredibly kitsch cottage constructed of seashells and slivers of mother-of-pearl.

In 1783, Louis XVI purchased Rambouillet for the exceptional hunting the nearby forest afforded. Marie-Antoinette was less than enthusiastic: She called the place "the toad hole" and longed for her Trianon at Versailles. To appease her, in 1785 Louis had the neoclassic *laiterie* (dairy) constructed, where ladies of the aristocracy came to sip new milk and sample fresh cheese. Today the dairy is no longer in operation, but the *bergerie* (sheepfold), built the following year, is still home to some 800 sheep, including 120 merinos descended from the flock and presented to Louis XVI by the king of Spain (and they, naturally, will have nothing to do with the other 680).

Rambouillet was virtually abandoned during the Revolution, and its furniture removed and sold, but Napoléon decided to restore the château. Today, visitors may view the emperor's study, his private apartments ornamented with "Pompeiian" frescoes and the grand dining room—still used for state dinners—with its enormous, 550-pound bronze chandelier.

The densely treed forest of Rambouillet, a great favorite with hunters and mushroom gatherers, covers close to half a million acres and begins virtually at the door of the château.

The Château de Rambouillet is open daily, except on Tuesday and when the president is in residence, from 10 a.m. to noon and 2 p.m. to 6 p.m. (until 5 p.m. from Oct. 1 through March 31). La Laiterie de la Reine Marie-Antoinette is open daily, except Tuesday, March 15 through October 31, from 10 a.m. to noon and 2 p.m. to 6 p.m. Call 34 83 00 25 for further information.

RESTAURANTS & HOTELS

MONTFORT-L'AMAURY

Les Préjugés
18, pl. Robert-Brault - 34 86 92 65
M. Scoffier. Open until 9:30 p.m. (10:30 p.m. in summer). Closed Jan. 8-Feb. 2. Garden dining. Pets allowed. Cards: V, AE.

Jean-Pierre Scoffier, once a doctor in Cambodia, returned home with several adopted Cambodian children who help him run this lovely village restaurant. One of the children,

Henri, studied with the grand chefs and was so gifted that he has now taken over the ultra-functional kitchen. In a picturesque, cozy setting with a flower garden and fireplace, we found the most unexpected cuisine, original and subtle, with the taste of family-style cooking from both Asia and France: langoustines with watercress pulp, fresh salmon with oysters, veal filet mignon with ginger, bass in lettuce, spiced apple strudel. Good low-priced fixed menus.

A la carte: 350-500F. Menus: 200F (weekday lunch only), 195F, 290F, 420F.

La Toque Blanche
12, Grande-Rue, Mesnuls
34 86 05 55
M. Philippe. Open until 9:30 p.m. Closed July 23-Sept. 1 & Dec. 24-Jan. 3. Garden dining. Pets allowed. Cards: V, AE.

With a bit more creativity, Jean-Pierre Philippe, the burly chef with the booming voice, could be considered one of the best chefs in the western Paris region. Still, he is impressive not only for his bulk but for his rigorous classicism, his generosity and his mastery of seafood and organ meats. We can recommend his remarkable langoustines with artichokes and shellfish, "symphony" of duck (filets and tiny sweetbreads) in a perfect wine sauce, popular tête de veau (calf's head), pear bavarois with a nice minty flavor and tasty sorbets. Pleasant flowery decor in a village-square setting.

A la carte: 300F and up.

See also Saint-Symphorien-le-Château in "Chartres," above.

SAINT-GERMAIN-EN-LAYE

Emperor Napoléon III, an ardent archeology buff (his great boast was that he had discovered the site of the Battle of Alésia, where Caesar defeated Vercingetorix, leader of the Gauls, in 52 B.C.), established the Musée des Antiquités Nationales at Saint-Germain-en-Laye (about 20 kilometers west of Paris by Autoroute de Normandie A13) in 1862. The oldest artifacts found on French soil are housed

in this fascinating museum, which follows the course of history up to the time of the Merovingians (the first Frankish dynasty). Today, nothing could be simpler than to take this journey back in time (the RER links Saint-Germain to the center of Paris in a matter of minutes).

On the museum's vast mezzanine, the exhibits document the millennia that preceded

Rome's occupation of Gaul. It is strangely moving to contemplate these age-old traces of human artistry. Most of the pieces are quite small, like the *Dame de Brassempouy*, the oldest-known representation of a human face, which is thought to predate Christ's birth by about 20,000 years; or the famous *Bison Licking Its Fur* carved in bone, from Dordogne (16,000 B.C.); or the many images that remind us that it was in France that the buffalo roamed and the deer (and antelope) played—at least until the end of the Ice Age.

Even visitors who are not archeology buffs will be riveted by artifacts discovered in the tombs of Celtic princes of the first Iron Age (Hallstatt period), particularly the funeral chariots (that indicate that the entombed belonged to the aristocracy), the iron swords, daggers and personal ornaments. Other finds verify that Gaulish tribes traded with Greece and Etruria, thus invalidating the theory that Gaul lived in isolation before the Romans burst on the scene. The very existence of coins minted by the principal Gallic tribes, of amphoras and other luxury goods, bears witness to the wealth of Gaul's aristocracy, and to their links with the Mediterranean world.

Exhibits on the upper floor illustrate the period of Roman colonization and include a model of the Battle of Alésia, which marked the end of Gaul's independence. The number of statues representing Gaulish divinities underscores Rome's generally tolerant attitude toward foreign religions, while an abundance of manufactured goods—ceramics, glass objects—give us a picture of France's earliest industries. The barbarian invasions that followed this period of prosperity are evoked by jewels and impressively worked weapons unearthed at Frankish tomb sites.

Though Saint-Germain-en-Laye is now synonymous with prehistory, it holds a significant place in the history of France: A prestigious royal château, it was the birthplace of Henri II, Charles IX and Louis XIV (who preferred it over all other châteaux until he built Versailles). From the twelfth century through the nineteenth, substantial building and tearing down altered the château's appearance many times over. What the visitor sees today is the Vieux Château, rebuilt by François I (but heavily restored in the nineteenth century), the first important example of brick-and-stone architecture in the Ile-de-France.

The former splendor of Saint-Germain is perhaps best translated by Le Nôtre's magnificent gardens, and the Grande Terrasse bordered with linden trees. What's more, with its 8,500 acres of flat, sandy paths, picturesque hunting pavilions and majestic stands of oak, the Saint-Germain forest offers ideal hiking terrain within easy reach of Paris.

The Musée des Antiquités Nationales is open daily, except Tuesday and holidays, from 9:45 a.m. to noon and 1:30 p.m. to 5:15 p.m. Call 34 51 53 65 for further information.

See also "The Suburbs" in the Restaurants and Hotels chapters.

SENLIS

When you walk through the narrow medieval streets of Senlis (50 kilometers north of Paris by Autoroute du Nord A1), don't be surprised if you suddenly recognize the set from your favorite French costume drama. This compact, well-preserved town on the border of the Ile-de-France and Picardy offers a fascinating glimpse into the history of pre-Revolutionary France. Understandably, it is a popular location with film-production companies.

North of the town, the Jardin du Roy (king's garden) lies in what was once the moat surrounding a Gallo-Roman defensive wall. The garden affords a marvelous overall view of Senlis, and of one of the best-preserved Roman fortifications in France. About 13 feet thick and 23 feet high, the wall dates back to the barbarian invasions of the third century. It once linked together 28 watch towers, 16 of which have survived.

The nearby Château Royal, despite its grandiose name, is now nothing more than a park scattered with romantic ruins that date from antiquity to the Renaissance. Built on the site of a first-century Roman fortress, the château was a king's residence from the time of Clovis, in the fifth century, until the reign of Henri IV, early in the seventeenth century. It was there, in 987, that the Capetian line of monarchs was founded, with the election of Hugues Capet, Duke of the Franks, to the throne of France.

The remarkable Musée de la Vénerie (Hunting Museum) evokes the royal passion for the hunt, with paintings by Desportes and Oudry, mounted trophies of glaring boar and majestic stags, intricately carved daggers, huge horns and an impressive, colorful collection of elegant hunting gear.

If you cross the pretty square in front of the Cathedral of Notre-Dame, you can best admire the monumental portal with its celebrated Gothic sculpture. Begun in 1153, ten years before Notre-Dame de Paris, the cathedral at Senlis served as a model for those at Chartres, Amiens and Reims. Yet by the sixteenth century, recurrent fires had made it necessary to rebuild the northern and southern facades practically from scratch. The work was directed by Pierre Chambiges, who created one of the finest (and last) examples of flamboyant Gothic architecture. Crowning the northern portal are the initial and emblematic salamander of François I.

After visiting the cathedral, we always take the time to wander through the winding, ancient streets of Senlis: Rue de la Tonnellerie, rue du Châtel, rue de la Treille and rue de Beauvais all boast sixteenth-century houses and mansions with splendid carved entrances (many of which are open to visitors every two years, including 1989 and 1991, during the month of September for the Rendez-vous de Senlis). You'll end up at the thirteenth-century church of Saint Frambourg, restored through the efforts of pianist and composer George Cziffra, and now used as a concert hall.

If you have time and a car, drive a few kilometers north to the Italianate Château de Raray (seventeenth century), where Jean Cocteau filmed his magical *Beauty and the Beast.* Who knows? Perhaps, as you stand admiring the fantastic hunting scenes sculpted on Diana's Gate, your own Beauty—or Prince Charming—will suddenly appear!

Jardin du Roy, Château Royal and Musée de la Vénerie are open daily, except Tuesday and Wednesday morning, from 10 a.m. to noon and 2 p.m. to 6 p.m. (Monday until 5 p.m.). The cathedral is open from 7 a.m. to 7 p.m. Call (16) 44 53 00 80 for further information.

RESTAURANTS & HOTELS

⑬ **Les Gourmandins**
    3, pl. de la Halle - (16) 44 60 94 01
M. Knecht. Open until 10:30 p.m. Closed Mon. dinner & Tues. Pets allowed. Cards: V, MC.

Sylvain Knecht, who left Le Vert-Galant in Senlis, has moved to the center of town with his young wife, Marie-Christine, to open this two-level bistro inside the pale-yellow walls of a former boutique. To be fully prepared, he even took a brush-up course at Robuchon. And if everything still isn't perfect, it's getting there, as you will see from the warm duck salad with truffles and potatoes, the ragoût of sole with basil butter and the delicious gratin of red fruit. The wine cellar is quite impressive for such a new restaurant.

Menus: 95F (weekdays only), 165F, 285F.

See also Chantilly and Compiègne in "Chantilly," above.

VAUX-LE-VICOMTE

As we stand in the unfinished Grand Salon of Vaux-le-Vicomte, looking out over Le Nôtre's gardens, we can almost picture the scene: the dog days of August 1661 . . . Nicolas Fouquet, France's brilliant finance minister, is entertaining his young sovereign, Louis XIV, at an indescribably lavish reception. A thousand fountains play in the magnificent Jardins à la Française, while Molière's troupe performs

the comic ballet *Les Fâcheux.* Courtiers applaud the water jousts, the concerts, the fireworks. . . . At dinner—prepared by Vatel, the foremost chef of his day—the king and his table are served on solid-gold plates. Legend has it that the dinner stuck in Louis's throat. Historians claim that Colbert, Fouquet's rival for control of the royal treasury and subsequent successor, had calumniated Fouquet and set the king against him. Indeed, the king may have set up Fouquet himself, wangling an invitation to Vaux, virtually sure that his vainglorious minister would flaunt his riches, and thus be hoist by his own petard!

Whoever laid it, the trap was sprung that August day at Vaux-le-Vicomte (about 60 kilometers south of Paris by Autoroute de Sud A6). A few weeks later, Louis sent d'Artagnan, the captain of his musketeers, to arrest Fouquet at Nantes. He sent workmen to take the finest tapestries, furnishings and paintings from Vaux and carry them straight into the royal collection. Then he sent for Fouquet's architect, Le Vau, his decorator, Le Brun and his landscape designer, Le Nôtre, and set them all to work at Versailles.

After a trial that dragged out over three years, the courts recommended a sentence of banishment for Fouquet. Louis, implacable, overruled them, and condemned his former minister to life imprisonment. Fouquet was, in all probability, a rascal. Yet the story of his fall and miserable end (after nineteen years in prison) still colors our view of Vaux's splendors with a tinge of melancholy.

That we can still see the château and gardens much as they were on that fateful day in 1661 is largely thanks to Alfred Sommier, a sugar-refining magnate who purchased the dilapidated property in 1875. He spent prodigious amounts of money and energy rebuilding sagging roofs and walls, furnishing the nearly empty house with seventeenth-century antiques, and taking pains to restore the gardens to their former beauty. The last task alone took a good half century. Using Le Nôtre's plans and contemporary engravings, Sommier was able to reconstitute the terraces, the pools and the complicated system of pipes that feed the fountains. He planted acres of trees and bushes, and he bought antique statuary and commissioned pieces from modern sculptors to replace the statues confiscated by Louis XIV.

In addition to the gardens, three levels of the château are now open to the public. On the upper floor are the Fouquets' private living quarters—studies, boudoirs and bedrooms—handsomely fitted out with period furniture and hung with tapestries and reproductions of paintings from the minister's (confiscated) collection. Above the fireplace in Mme. Fouquet's study is Le Brun's famous smiling portrait of Nicolas Fouquet.

To us, the most appealing aspect of the reception rooms downstairs (the Grands Appartements) is Le Brun's decoration. Actually, *decoration* is not an adequate term to describe this virtuoso performance with paint, stucco, gilt and carving. The scores of rosy nymphs, cherubs, squirrels (Fouquet's emblem) and other allegorical figures that populate the ceilings and woodwork of the Salon des Muses and Cabinet des Jeux (Gaming Room) fill these formal rooms with a rapturous charm. Le Brun's stucco-and-fresco decor in the Chambre du Roi (Royal Chamber) is the model for what would become known throughout Europe as the "French style," which reached its apotheosis at Versailles.

Bare of its intended decoration, the Grand Salon demonstrates the measure of architect Le Vau's genius; the eye, unsolicited by bright allegories and visions, is naturally drawn outside, to the harmonious perspectives of Le Nôtre's gardens, his masterpiece. In their more modest way, the workrooms and staff quarters on the lower level are also quite interesting. The kitchens (in use until 1956) display a dazzling collection of copper pots and pans scoured to a high polish.

Those in search of rare sensations and exquisite atmospheres will surely want to visit Vaux-le-Vicomte by candlelight on a Saturday evening in summer. The scene is unforgettable—indeed, it is enough to rouse the envy of a king!

The Château de Vaux-le-Vicomte is open daily (except Christmas Day) April 1 through October 31, from 10 a.m. to 6 p.m.; November 1 through March 31, from 11 a.m.-5 p.m. Candlelight tours are held Saturday evenings from May through September (Sunday evenings in July and August), 8:30 p.m. to 11 p.m. Fountain displays occur the second and final Saturday of each month from April through October. Call 60 66 97 09 for further information.

RESTAURANTS & HOTELS

MELUN

⑬ **Grand Monarque**
Av. de Fontainebleau - 64 39 04 40
M. Colin. Open daily until 9:30 p.m. Garden dining. Pets allowed. Telex 690140. Cards: V, AE, DC.

In the middle of the forest stands this restaurant, with well-dressed tables, a cheery and comfortable modern decor and a terrace in the lovely foliage. Service is attentive (though a bit slow during conferences), and Jean-Luc Hentry's cuisine is worthy of its toque: fine pan-fried oysters and mushrooms, sweetbreads with warm fresh figs (original and well balanced), grilled John Dory à la tomate (natural, without sauce). Desserts are more modest, and the wine list could be more informative. Prices seem to be calming down.

A la carte: 280F. Menus: 90F (dinner only), 190F (weekends and holidays only), 160F.

Grand Monarque ♣♟
(See restaurant above.)
Open year-round. 5 stes 550-650F. 45 rms 320-450F. Half-board 325F. TV. Heated pool. Tennis.

The small but perfectly equipped rooms open onto the park. Conference facilities. Excellent service.

⑭ **Quai Voltaire**
249, quai Voltaire, Dammarie-Les-Lys
64 39 31 55
Open until 10 p.m. Closed Sun. dinner & Mon. Terrace dining. Pets allowed. Cards: V.

We first noticed Joël Leduc a dozen years ago near Caen. He was a promising talent then, and we were delighted to rediscover him here, where his talents have come into full bloom. The 32-year-old chef (who looks 25) has set himself up in this old refurbished house along the Seine, using modern-cuisine techniques and mixing flavors that are sometimes bold but always harmonious: remarkable foie gras with a perfectly seasoned salad, a surprising turbot filet, salmon steak with a vegetable médaillon in a light sauce with a fine fish taste, fruit gratin (which can often be dull but is exceptionally well made here). The wine list is limited but well chosen, and the waitresses sociable. Leduc will earn his second toque soon—we think. A timid sort of lawn is growing in the courtyard garden, where tables are set in nice weather.

A la carte: 250F. Menus: 89F, 119F.

See also Fontainebleau and Barbizon in "Fontainebleau," above.

VERSAILLES

Versailles, undoubtedly the world's most famous palace, has been a favorite destination for day-tripping Parisians since 1833, when King Louis-Philippe turned the abandoned (since 1789) château into a "museum of the glories of France." Today, Versailles (about 25 kilometers west of Paris by Autoroute de Normandie A13) offers pleasures with every season, in every kind of weather. Visitors can amble through parks dotted with romantic statuary, admire a wealth of art, furniture and architecture (comparing Louis this with Louis that) or simply spread out a blanket and picnic beside the Grand Canal.

It took Louis XIV just 40 years to build the palace and its park around a hunting lodge erected by his father, Louis XIII. And though his successors made many changes, Versailles still bears the unmistakable stamp of the Sun King, who, from 1682 on, made it the permanent residence of the court, the sole seat of royal power and the political capital of France. The court's permanent presence explains the colossal proportions of the palace, which housed the royal family, the princes of the blood, the courtiers, the king's councilors, everyone's servants . . . it's little wonder that the western facade of the palace stretches out nearly 2,000 feet.

Lodging his considerable household and entourage was not all that Louis had in mind when he built Versailles. He also saw the palace as a powerful propaganda tool, a monument to the glory of the French monarchy and a showcase for masterworks by French artists and craftsmen. Versailles was open to all. The most modest subjects of the realm could wander freely through the Grands Appartements to gape at the cream of the royal collections. Classical statues and busts stood in marble-lined halls; paintings from the French and Venetian schools hung on walls covered in velvet, damask and brocade. Today's tourists are the heirs of those visitors who, at the end of the seventeenth century, marveled at the dazzling Galerie des Glaces (Gallery of Mirrors) or the Salon d'Apollon before attending the king's supper or submitting a petition to Louis XIV as he made his way to mass at the royal chapel.

But we have the advantage over those tourists of long ago, for we can visit parts of Versailles that were then off-limits to the public, even to courtiers. Among the most beautiful of the private quarters is the Petit Appartement, fitted out for Louis XV just above his official suite, a place where he could relax alone—or with friends (like Madame du Barry, who had her own room there).

An intimate mood, and scale, are even more evident in the two Trianons, situated about half a mile from the main palace. The Grand Trianon was built for Louis XIV in 1687, and he spent many a quiet summer evening there surrounded by his family. Today it houses heads of state on official visits. The Petit Trianon is an exquisite neoclassic structure designed by Gabriel in 1764 for Louis XV, who wished to live closer to his beloved botanical garden. It was also the preferred residence of Marie-Antoinette, whose spirit pervades the place. There, on October 5, 1789, she learned of the Parisians' march on Versailles.

In fine weather, the gardens of Versailles are an irresistible invitation to wander. They cover over 200 acres with an enchanting variety of landscapes. The classical French *parterres* (flower beds), with their vast perspectives,

pools and lawns, were designed by Le Nôtre at the height of his powers; his is also the genius behind the marvelous *bosquets* (coppices) that combine thickly massed greenery and spectacular waterworks. Scattered throughout are hundreds of marble and bronze statues, many inspired by the myths of Apollo. If you happen to be in Versailles between May and September, make a point of touring the gardens when the Grandes Eaux are scheduled: all over the gardens, in every bed and *bosquet*, the fountains put on a magical display.

And in summer, it is well worth the effort to obtain tickets for a performance at the Opéra Royal, an architectural masterpiece by Gabriel, inaugurated in 1770 for the marriage of the future Louis XVI and the Archduchess Marie-Antoinette. The elegance of its proportions, its superb acoustics and the splendor of its decoration make it perhaps the most beautiful theater in the world.

The Château de Versailles is open daily, except Monday and holidays, from 9:45 a.m. to 5:30 p.m. The park and gardens are open daily from dawn to dusk. And the fountain displays occur two or three Sundays a month in May through September at 4 p.m. to 5 p.m. Call 30 84 74 00 for further information.

RESTAURANTS

See "The Suburbs" in the Restaurants and Hotels chapters.

SIGHTS

Following is a highly condensed list of Versailles's most noteworthy sights.

The Château de Versailles (a must!), with more than four million visitors per year (from May to September its parks host the Grandes Eaux and the Fêtes de Nuit); the Trianon Palaces; the Salle du Jeu de Paume (recently opened to the public); Notre-Dame church (designed by Hardouin-Mansart); the king's vegetable garden (school of horticulture); the Carrés Saint-Louis (modest lodgings during the time of the Old Régime); the antiques and secondhand market (passage de la Geôle, next to the colorful market at Notre-Dame); the

Hôtel des Ventes (former home of the Light Cavalry); the delightful Musée Lambinet (still under restoration, with beautiful eighteenth-century paintings); the Couvent des Récollets.

EATING ON THE RUN

Following are the best places in Versailles for a quick bite.

Le Boeuf à la Mode, 4, rue au Pain (open until midnight, seafood specialties); Alain Chaminade, 44, rue de la Paroisse (varieties of teas, ice cream and quick lunches, open on Sunday); A La Côte Bretonne, 12, rue des Deux-Portes (more than 200 crêpes and pancakes); L'Entrecôte, 18 bis, rue Neuve-Notre-Dame (grilled meats, open daily until 11 p.m.); Le Feuille Thé, 2, rue Royale (fast lunches in a quiet courtyard); L'Orangerie, 4 bis, rue de la Paroisse (wine bar and fixed-price lunch menu); La Palette, 6, rue des Deux-Portes (near the Versailles marketplace and the antiques shops, regulars from the quarter); Le Roi Gourmet, 21, rue des Réservoirs (smoked fish and specialties from the southwest of France are sold in the shop next door); Tarte Julie, 104, rue de la Paroisse (savory and sweet tarts); and L'Hôtel des Voyageurs, 12, rue Philippe-de-Daugeau (not too expensive, highly valued by the *tout* Versailles; pleasant terrace).

BARS & CAFES

Following are Versailles's best spots for a quick drink or refreshment.

La Civette, passage St-Pierre (a typical bar/tobacco shop with an old-fashioned decor); and La Civette du Parc, 17, rue des Réservoirs (nice, conservative bar frequented by young locals).

SHOPS

Following are the finest food and wine shops in town. Keep them in mind for a picnic meal, a gift or a treat.

Bakeries: Galupeau, 20, rue des Chantiers (the cakes are beautiful and delicious); Joseph, 21, rue Carnot (for its pain au raisin); and Didier Lhoste, 19, rue de Satory (for the paillasse, an excellent country bread). **Charcuteries:** Christophe, 62, rue de la Paroisse (*the* charcutier/caterer in Versailles); Gentelem, in the Versailles marketplace (game specialties); and Le Roi Gourmet, 21, rue des Réservoirs (see "Eating on the Run"). **Chocolates:** Aux Colonnes, 14, rue Hoche (such specialties as the "favorites du Roy" and the golden palets). **Gourmet foods:** Hédiard, 1, rue Ducis (near the Versailles marketplace, with the same products as those sold at Hédiard on pl. de la Madeleine). **Cheese:** Michel Beignon, 6, rue Royale (Brie, cheeses from Auvergne and goat cheeses). **Fruit and vegetables:** Castel, 49, rue Royale (there is permanent excitement around this "cours des halles," which sells beautiful fresh produce). **Pastries, confections:** Guinon, 60, rue de la Paroisse (a gourmet institution; try the délicieux and the picois); and Pellisson, 44, rue de la Paroisse (sample the pavé de Versailles and l'Adélaïde, a chocolate specialty). **Wine and spirits:** Les Caves du Château, 9, pl. Hoche (a tremendous collection of great vintages, as well as the well-informed advice of M. Jean); and Les Caves Royales, 6, rue Royale (good regional wines and some 50 kinds of Armagnacs).

BASICS

GETTING AROUND

Paris is a well-designed city divided into twenty *arrondissements*, or districts. Essential to getting around Paris is a knowledge of the excellent transportation system and a pocket-size street index called *Paris par Arrondissement*. Available in most bookstores and at major newspaper stands, it includes comprehensive maps of Paris and the subway system (Métro).

BUSES

Riding the bus is a great—and cheap—way to tour the city. The no. 24 bus, for example, passes by many historical monuments. Buses take you almost everywhere within the metropolitan area for just two tickets (one ticket is good for two zones). You can purchase tickets (5 francs) on the bus or a book (*carnet*) of ten tickets (31.20 francs) at Métro stations or in some tobacco shops, which is an economical investment. Special three- and five-day tourist passes (*Paris Visit*) allow unlimited travel on buses, the Métro and the RER express line and are sold at major Métro stations and at R.A.T.P. tourist offices. The major bus routes operate from 7 a.m. to 12:30 a.m. every day. The bus numbers are indicated by a black number inside a white disk at the bus stops. The less important routes, marked by a white number inside a black disk, do not run on Sundays or holidays, nor does the service go on much after 8 or 9 p.m. There is an excellent late-night service (*Noctambus*): Buses leave Châtelet every hour on the half hour. Every bus stop in Paris posts fares, times, routes and bus numbers. Listening to an irate Parisian bus driver caught in rush-hour traffic is also an excellent way to learn some interesting French words that you won't find in the dictionary!

METRO

Getting the knack of the Métro system is a cinch. You'll find a Métro map posted at each station, outside on the street and inside as well. Let's imagine you want to go from the Gare du Nord to Saint-Germain-des-Prés. Locate the two stations on your map and check whether they are on the the same line (each line is indicated in a different color). In this case, they are, so follow the line from your station of departure to your station of arrival, then note the name of the station at the end of the line (in this instance it's the Porte d'Orléans). That means that Porte d'Orléans is the name of the direction you will be taking. Inside the station, look for signs indicating "direction Porte d'Orléans," and when you reach the platform, check again on the sign located in the middle of the platform.

The middle car is for first-class ticket holders only. Tourist or not, you will have to pay an on-the-spot fine if you're caught in a first-class car with a second-class ticket (except before 9 a.m. and after 5 p.m.). A single ticket will take you anywhere on the Métro system and within zones 1 and 2 of the RER system (see RER, below). Don't forget to keep your ticket until you leave the Métro, for you may be asked to produce it by a Métro official.

By the way, do watch out for pickpockets on the Métro, especially Gypsy teenagers and children (easy to spot by their colorful Romany clothing); they are real professionals.

RER

The *Réseau Express Régional* is a network of fast commuter services linking the center of Paris to destinations all over the Greater Paris Region. Quite a number of interesting places to visit are accessible by RER, and you can pick up brochures listing these from any Métro information kiosk. There is also a very good bicycle-hire service (*Roue Libre*) run by the RER that allows you to explore some beautiful woodlands around Paris (like the Chevreuse Valley, the Forest of Saint-Germain-en-Laye and so forth). The flat-rate system on the regular Métro does not apply to the RER, so you must consult the diagrams on the automatic ticket machines to determine the cost of your ticket. It is possible to get round-trip tickets, and the machine will give change on any coins you care to use (though it doesn't take bills).

TAXIS

There are some 14,300 taxis available in Paris (until you really need one!). There are three ways of getting yourself a taxi: The first is simply to flag one down (it is available if its roof light is fully illuminated); the second is to go to a taxi stand (*Tête de Station*); the third is to call up a radio taxi that will arrive five to ten minutes later at your address (the meter will already be running, but don't get in if it's more than 30 francs). Refer to the Phone Directory leter in this chapter for radio-taxi numbers. Normally, you pay 9.50 francs to get in the cab and about 2.58 francs per kilometer. You'll be charged a supplement if the taxi leaves from a train station, airport terminal or racetrack, and for each item of baggage. Tip the driver 10 to 15 percent.

AT YOUR SERVICE

TOURIST INFORMATION

For all the brochures and other "literature" that the sage sightseer might need:

Bureau Gare d'Austerlitz
13th arr. - bd de l'Hôpital - 45 84 91 70
Open 8 a.m.-10 p.m. (off-seas. until 3 p.m.). Closed Sun.
Located at the international arrivals area.

Bureau Gare de l'Est
10th arr. - bd de Strasbourg - 46 07 17 73
Open 8 a.m.-10 p.m. (off-seas. 8 a.m.-1 p.m. & 5 p.m.-8 p.m.).
Located at the arrivals lobby.

Bureau Gare de Lyon
12th arr. - 20 bd Diderot - 43 43 33 24
Open 8 a.m.-10 p.m. (off-seas. 8 a.m.-1 p.m. & 5 p.m.-8 p.m.). Closed Sun.
Located at the exit of the international lines.

Bureau Gare du Nord
10th arr. - 18, rue de Dunkerque
45 26 94 82
Open 8 a.m.-10 p.m. (Sun. & off-seas. until 8 p.m.). Closed Sun. in off-seas.
Located at the international arrivals area.

Eiffel Tower Office
7th arr. - 45 51 22 15
Open 11 a.m.-6 p.m. Closed in off-seas.

Office de Tourisme de Paris
8th arr. - 127, av. des Champs-Elysées
47 23 61 72
Open 9 a.m.-9 p.m. (Sun. until 8 p.m. & Sun. in off-seas. until 6 p.m.).

24-Hour Information Line
47 20 88 98
In English, of course.

ORIENTATION

Here are a few facts of French life for foreign visitors:

Remember that in France, the ground floor (*rez-de-chaussée*) is what Americans call the first floor; the French first floor (*premier étage*) corresponds to the American second floor, and so on.

When dining out, the service charge (15 percent) is always included in the bill. An additional tip (a few francs) can be left if you are satisfied with the service. Hairdressers are generally given a 10 to 15 percent tip. Porters, doormen and room service are tipped small change. A hotel concierge makes all sorts of reservations for you (theater, restaurant, plane, train and so on) and can offer advice about getting around in Paris; don't forget to tip him afterward for his considerable services. Ushers at some movie houses, sporting events, ballets and concerts expect a tip, and can be vengeful if you fail to shell out two or three francs.

French and American voltages differ, so your electrical appliances (shavers, hairdryers) will require a transformer. You will doubtless also need an adapter for the round prongs of French plugs. These items can be obtained in the basement of the Samaritaine department store. (See "Department Stores" in the Shops chapter.)

Hallway lighting systems are often manually operated. Just to one side of the entrance, in a conspicuous place on each landing or near the elevator, you'll find a luminous switch that is automatically timed to give you one to three minutes of light. To enter many buildings, you must press a buzzer or a numerical code usually located at the side of the front door.

The French postal services (PTT) have created plastic telephone cards that may be used instead of coins in public phone booths. They sell for 96 francs or 40 francs and may be purchased at the post office, cafés and some bookstores. Their microchip technology gives you a certain number of units, which are gradually used up as you make your calls. Don't count too heavily on using telephones in cafés and restaurants unless you have a drink or meal there. Most modern pay phones have instructions in English printed on them. A local call costs 1 franc. You can phone abroad from most pay phones using either your plastic card or a large reserve of 5-franc coins. Collect calls can be made from pay phones by dialing 19, then 33 after the tone, and then the code for the country you want (Australia, 61; Britain, 44; Canada and the United States, 11). The Louvre post office (52, rue du Louvre, first arrondissement, 40 28 20 00) has a 24-hour international telephone/telegraph service. Also note that Paris telephone numbers have eight figures. If you should come upon a Parisian number with only seven figures you must dial 4 before the number.

USEFUL ADDRESSES

Here are some addresses and phone numbers of particular interest to English-speaking travelers:

CHURCHES

American Cathedral in Paris
8th arr. - 23, av. Georges-V - 47 20 17 92

American Church
7th arr. - 65, quai d'Orsay - 47 05 07 99

Christian Science
14th arr. - 36, bd Saint-Jacques
47 07 26 60

Church of Scotland
8th arr. - 17, rue Bayard - 47 20 90 49

Great Synagogue
9th arr. - 44, rue de la Victoire
45 26 95 36

Liberal Synagogue
16th arr. - 24, rue Copernic - 47 04 37 27

Society of Friends
6th arr. - 114, rue de Vaugirard
45 48 74 23

St. George's (Anglican)
16th arr. - 7, rue Auguste-Vacquerie
47 20 22 51

St. Joseph's (Catholic)
8th arr. - 50, av. Hoche - 42 27 28 56

St. Michael's English Church
8th arr. - 5, rue d'Aguesseau - 47 42 70 88

EMBASSIES

American Embassy
8th arr. - 2, av. Gabriel - 42 96 12 02

Australian Embassy
15th arr. - 4, rue Jean-Rey - 40 59 33 00

British Embassy
8th arr. - 35, rue du Faubourg-Saint-Honoré - 42 66 91 42

Canadian Embassy
8th arr. - 35, av. Montaigne - 47 23 01 01

New Zealand Embassy
16th arr. - 7 ter, rue Léonard-de-Vinci
45 00 24 11

ENGLISH-SPEAKING ORGANIZATIONS

American Chamber of Commerce
8th arr. - 21, av. Georges-V - 47 23 80 26
Open 9 a.m.-5 p.m. Closed Sat. & Sun.

American Express
1st arr. - 11, rue Scribe - 42 66 09 99
Hours vary for the different services.

Here you'll find traveler's checks and American Express card and travel services. You can also arrange to pick up mail and wire money or have money wired to you.

American Legion
8th arr. - 49, rue Pierre-Charron
42 25 41 93

The American Women's Group in Paris, the Association of American Wives of Europeans, the Council on International Educational Exchange, the USO and the University Club of Paris are some of the organizations headquartered at this address.

American Library
7th arr. - 10, rue Général-Camou
45 51 46 82
Open Tues., Thurs. & Fri. 2 p.m.-7 p.m., Wed. & Sat. 10 a.m.-7 p.m. Closed Sun., Mon., French & American holidays, and 1 wk. in Sept.

This library houses the largest English-language library on the continent. There is also a selection of records and cassettes. You must, however, be an official resident of France to take books out of the library. A membership fee is required.

British Council
7th arr. - 9, rue Constantine - 45 55 95 95
Open 9:30 a.m.-1 p.m. & 2:30 p.m.-6 p.m. Closed Sat. & Sun. Hours vary in different departments.

The council features a library of English books and records.

Canadian Cultural Center
8th arr. - 5, rue Constantine - 45 51 35 73
Open 10 a.m.-7 p.m. Closed Sun.

This Canadian cultural center offers dance, theater and musical performances, as well as a library, art gallery and a student-exchange-program office.

HOSPITALS (ENGLISH-SPEAKING)

Hôpital Américain (American Hospital)
92200 Neuilly sur Seine - 63, bd Victor-Hugo - 47 47 53 00

A consultation here is more expensive than at most hospitals in Paris. You can pay in dollars. Dental services are also provided, and there is a 24-hour English-speaking emergency service.

Hôpital Franco-Britannique (British Hospital)
92300 Levallois-Perret - 3 rue Barbès
47 58 13 12

This hospital provides complete services.

PHARMACIES

Swann Pharmacy
1st arr. - 6, rue Castiglione - 42 60 72 96
Open 9 a.m.-7:30 p.m. Closed Sun.
   This is the only pharmacy in Paris where your English prescription will be translated and an equivalent medicine made up by a pharmacist.

PHONE DIRECTORY

Police/Help
17

Fire Department
18

SAMU (Ambulance)
45 67 50 50

S.O.S. Médecins
43 37 77 77

S.O.S. Crisis Line (in English)
47 23 80 80
Open 2 p.m.-11 p.m.

Centre Anti-Poisons (Poison Control Center)
40 37 04 04

TAXIS

Les Taxis Bleus
42 02 42 02

G7 Taxis
47 39 33 33

Artaxi
42 41 50 50

DUTY-FREE SHOPPING

   The bad news is that just about everything in France is subject to Value Added Tax (VAT), ranging from 4 percent to 28 percent, depending on the item you're buying. The good news is that people living outside Europe can get a 100 percent VAT rebate on items they export from France. Luxury goods, such as jewelry, perfume, cameras, VCRs, TVs, cars and some furs, are all taxed at 25 percent; the 18.6 percent rate is applied to clothes, shoes, accessories, luggage, leather, suede and other such items. To qualify for a rebate, you must spend more than 1,200 francs in one shop.
   To get reimbursed, have the store fill in the Détaxe Légale form (make sure the shop carries it before you make the purchase). Bring your passport, because you'll be required to show it. Along with the form, the store will supply you with an envelope bearing its address.
   When you leave France, show the forms at the Bureau de Détaxe or at Customs and have the Customs officer stamp them. Then seal the forms in the envelope supplied by the shop and mail it back. Keep your receipt.
   The rebate can be credited directly to your account. Some stores charge a commission for this service, while others (especially the tax-free shops on the Champs-Elysées and the avenue de l'Opéra) charge no commission and even give a 40 percent discount on some items.

> *If you visit Paris in August, you can count on lots of peace, quiet and uncrowded streets. But don't count on many shops, restaurants and other businesses to be open.*

GOINGS-ON

As an international city, Paris is the site of many artistic festivals, trade fairs and sporting events. Exact dates vary from year to year, so we've simply listed the month in which they occur.

National holidays are January 1, May 1, May 8, July 14 and November 11; religious holidays fall on Easter, Easter Monday, Ascension Thursday, Pentecost Sunday and the following Monday, Assumption Day (August 15), All Saint's Day (November 1) and Christmas. A word of warning: Banks and some shops will close early the day before a public holiday, and often a three-day weekend will become a four-day weekend when holidays fall on a Tuesday or a Thursday.

FEBRUARY

Brocante de Paris
17th arr. - Porte de Champerret
Antiques and bric-a-brac.

Foire à la Ferraille de Paris
12th arr. - Parc Floral de Paris, Bois de Vincennes
An amusing collection of taste treats and cast-iron junk.

Salon Mondial du Tourisme et des Voyages
15th arr. - Parc des Expositions, Porte de Versailles
World tourism and travel.

MARCH

Jumping International de Paris
12th arr. - Palais Omnisports de Bercy, 8, bd de Bercy
International horse-jumping trials.

Salon International de l'Agriculture
15th arr. - Parc des Expositions, Porte de Versailles
International agricultural show.

APRIL

Expolangues
15th arr. - Parc des Expositions, Porte de Versailles
Everything connected with foreign languages.

Foire de Paris
15th arr. - Parc des Expositions, Porte de Versailles
Food, wine, household equipment and gadgetry.

Foire du Trône
12th arr. - Pelouse de Reuilly, Bois de Vincennes
All the fun of a fair.

SICOB
Parc d'Expositions, Paris-Nord - Villepinte
International office machinery, computers and supplies.

MAY

Championnats Internationaux de France de Tennis (French Open)
16th arr. - Stade Roland Garros - 2, av. Gordon-Bennett
Top international tennis championship.

Foire du Trône
12th arr. - Pelouse de Reuilly, Bois de Vincennes
See April.

Les Cinq Jours de l'Objet Extraordinaire (Carré des Antiquaires Rive Gauche)
7th arr. - rues du Bac, de Beaune, de Lille, des Saints-Pères, de l'Université, de Verneuil & quai Voltaire

Paris's top antiques shops hold open house: rare and unusual objects.

Marathon International de Paris
Departure pl. de la Concorde, 8th arr.
Arrival Hippodrome de Vincennes, 12th arr.

26 miles or 42 kilometers, it's all the same to the runners.

Salon du Livre
15th arr. - Parc d'Expositions, Porte de Versailles

A mammoth book fair.

JUNE

Course des Garçons de Café
1st arr. - Departure & arrival at L'Hôtel-de-Ville

Waiters race in the Paris streets holding a tray with a full bottle and a full glass of beer.

Fête de la Musique à Paris (June 21)
Streets of Paris

Anyone who wants to can blow his horn on Music Day.

Paris Villages
Various Paris neighborhoods

Local festivities with a working-class flavor: parades, drum majorettes, folk dancing, fun and games for all.

JULY

Arrivée du Tour de France Cycliste
8th arr. - av. des Champs-Elysées

The Tour de France cyclists triumphantly cross the finish line.

Bastille Day Eve (July 13)
Free public dancing in squares and neighborhood firehouses. Disco and accordion music.

Bastille Day (July 14)
National holiday celebrating the French Revolution of 1789. Military parade on the Champs-Elysées. Fireworks display in the evening.

Festival Estival de Paris
A celebration of cultural events in the nation's capital.

AUGUST

Virtually everything is closed in August, but true Paris lovers regard this as the best month of the year to be in their favorite city.

SEPTEMBER

Biennale Internationale des Antiquaires
8th arr. - Grand Palais, av. Winston Churchill

This major antiques fair takes place once every two years.

OCTOBER

La Biennale des Antiquaires
8th arr. - Grand Palais, av. Winston Churchill.

This major antiques show is held every two years, on even years—so look for it in 1990 and 1992.

Fête des Vendanges
18th arr. - Butte Montmartre, corner of rue des Saules & rue Saint-Vincent

A grape harvest at the only working vineyard within the city limits.

Foire Internationale d'Art Contemporain (F.I.A.C.)
8th arr. - Grand Palais, av. Winston Churchill
An international contemporary-art show.

Les 6 Heures Motonautiques de Paris
16th arr. - Pont de Iéna; 15th arr. - Pont Garigliano
Moorboat race on the Seine (lasts six hours).

Open de la Ville de Paris
12th arr. - Palais Omnisports de Bercy, 8, bd de Bercy
The City of Paris Open Tennis Championships.

Prix de l'Arc de Triomphe
16th arr. - Hippodrome de Longchamp
A day at the races and a chance to win a lot of money.

Salon International de l'Alimentation (S.I.A.)
Parc d'Expositions, Paris-Nord - Villepinte
An international food-products exhibit.

NOVEMBER

Grand Prix d'Automne
16th arr. - Hippodrome de Longchamp
Horse racing.

Salon du Motocycle
15th arr. - Parc des Expositions, Porte de Versailles
An international automobile and motorcycle show (held only in even-numbered years).

Salon d'Automne
8th arr. - Grand Palais, av. Winston Churchill
New artwork by budding talents.

Salon de la Gastronomie
CNIT - 92000 La Défense
Gastronomy, cooking and tableware.

DECEMBER

Salon du Cheval et du Poney
15th arr. - Parc des Expositions, Porte de Versailles
Horses and ponies galore, and all the accompanying trappings.

Salon Nautique International
15th arr. - Parc des Expositions, Porte de Versailles
International boat show.

MAPS

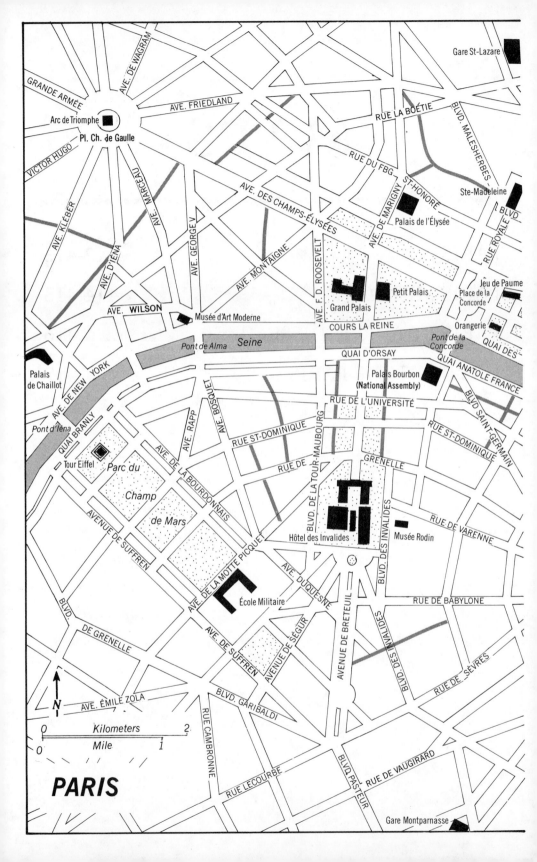

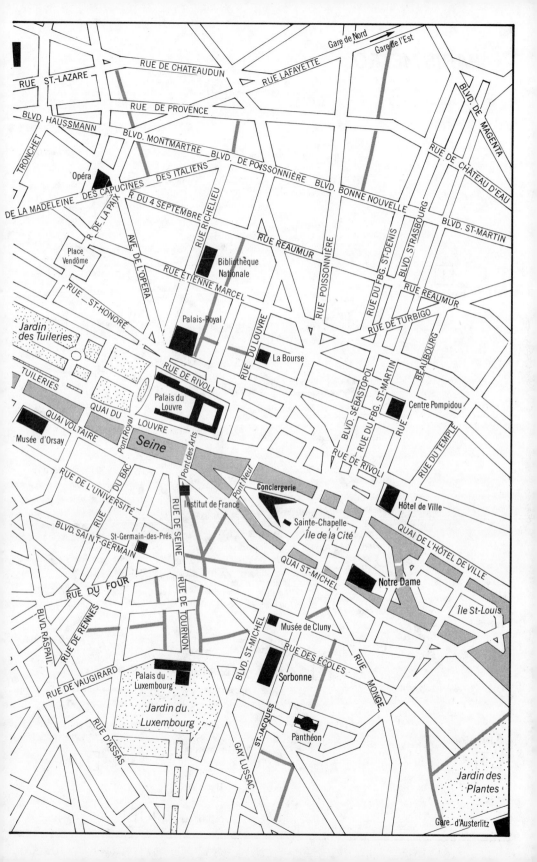

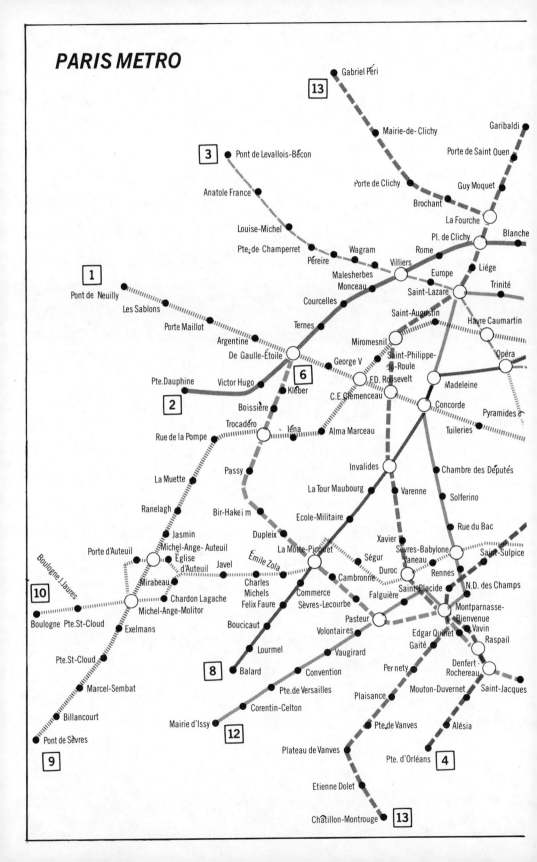

PARIS METRO

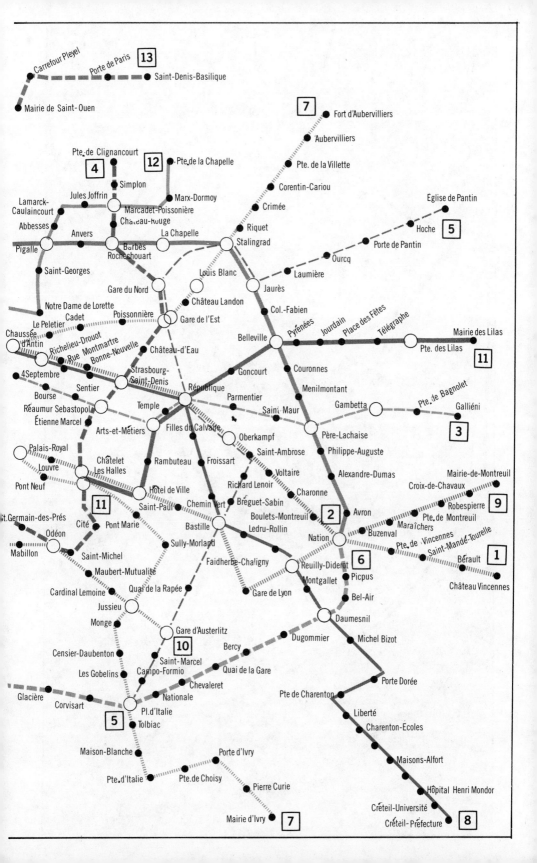

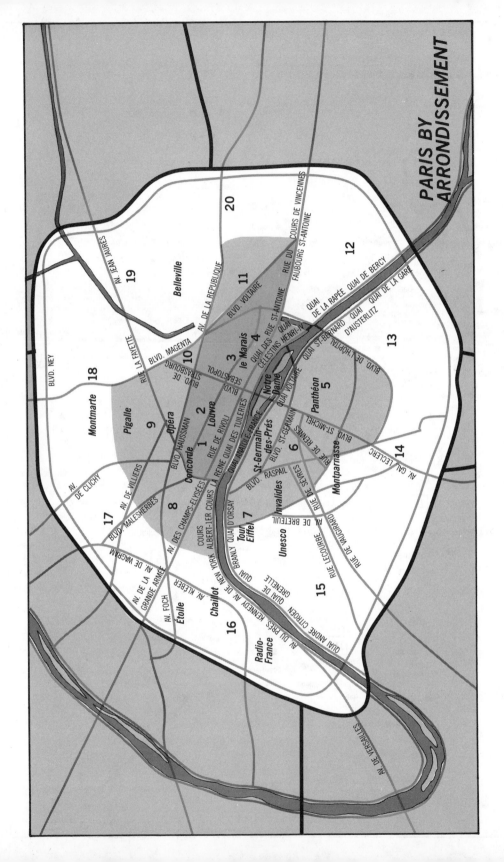

PARIS BY ARRONDISSEMENT

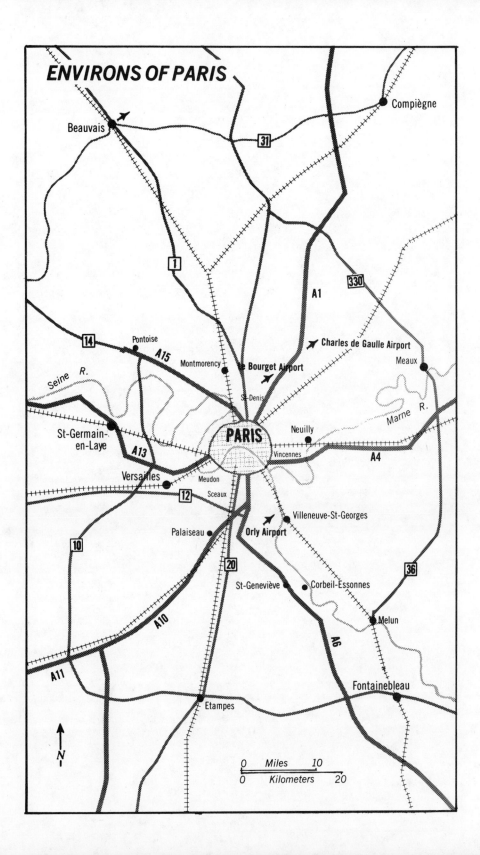

ENVIRONS OF PARIS

Beauvais

Compiègne

31

1

330

A1

14   Pontoise

A15

Charles de Gaulle Airport

Montmorency

Bourget Airport

Meaux

Seine   R.

St-Denis

Marne   R.

PARIS

Neuilly

St-Germain-
en-Laye

A13

Vincennes

A4

Versailles

Meudon

Sceaux

12

Villeneuve-St-Georges

10

Palaiseau

Orly Airport

36

St-Geneviève

Corbeil-Essonnes

20

A10

Melun

A6

A11

Fontainebleau

N

Etampes

0   Miles   10

0   Kilometers   20

INDEX

B

C

D

E

F

G

H

I

J

K

L

M

N

T

U

MORE GAULT MILLAU "BEST" GUIDES

Now the series known throughout Europe for its wit and savvy reveals the best of major U.S. and European areas—New York, Washington, D.C., Los Angeles, San Francisco, Chicago, New England, France and Italy. Following the guidelines established by the world-class French food critics Henri Gault and Christian Millau, local teams of writers directed by André Gayot, partner of Gault Millau, have gathered inside information about where to stay, what to do, where to shop, and where to dine or catch a quick bite in these key locales. Each volume sparkles with the wit, wisdom and panache that readers have come to expect from Gault Millau, whose distinctive style makes them favorites among travelers bored with the neutral, impersonal style of other guides. There are full details on the best of everything that makes these cities special places to visit, including restaurants, destinations, quick bites, nightlife, hotels, shops, the arts—all the unique sights and sounds of each city. These guides offer practical information on getting around and coping with each city. Filled with provocative, entertaining, and frank reviews, they are helpful as well as fun to read. Perfect for visitiors and residents alike.

Please send me the books checked below.

☐ The Best of Chicago $15.95
☐ The Best of Hong Kong $16.95
☐ The Best of Los Angeles $14.95
☐ The Best of New England $15.95
☐ The Best of New York $14.95
☐ The Best of San Francisco $14.95
☐ The Best of Washington, D. C. $14.95
☐ The Best of France $16.95
☐ The Best of Italy $16.95

PRENTICE HALL TRADE DIVISION
Order Department—Travel Books
200 Old Tappan Road
Old Tappan, New Jersey 07675

In U.S. include $2 shipping UPS for 1st book, $1 each additional book. Outside U.S., $3 and $1 respectively.

Enclosed is my check or money order for $ _____

NAME _____

ADDRESS _____

CITY_____STATE _____ ZIP_____